THE VALUATION OF REAL ESTATE

Fourth Edition

James H. Boykin, *Ph.D., MAI, SREA*

The Alfred L. Blake Chair Professor
of Real Estate
and
Director, Virginia Real Estate Research Center
Virginia Commonwealth University

Alfred A. Ring, *Ph.D., MAI, SRPA*

Professor Emeritus of Real Estate
and Urban Land Studies
University of Florida

Regents/Prentice Hall
Englewood Cliffs, New Jersey 07632

Library of Congress Cataloging-in-Publication Data

Boykin, James H.
   The valuation of real estate / James H. Boykin, Alfred A. Ring —
4th ed.
      p.   cm.
   Ring's name appears first on the previous ed.
   Includes bibliographical references and index.
   ISBN 0-13-948431-0
   1. Real property—Valuation.   I. Ring, Alfred A.   II. Title.
HD1387.R5   1993
333.33′2—dc20   92-12577
                                                                                 CIP

Acquisitions editor: Jim Boyd
Editorial/production supervision: Tally Morgan, WordCrafters Editorial Services, Inc.
Cover design: Marianne Frasco
Prepress buyer: Ilene Levy
Manufacturing buyer: Ed O'Dougherty

This book is dedicated to the multitude of real estate valuation instructors and practitioners who have added to and refined the body of knowledge central to informed real estate value decisions.

Printed in the United States of America
10 9 8 7 6 5 4 3 2 1

ISBN 0-13-948431-0

Prentice-Hall International (UK) Limited, *London*
Prentice-Hall of Australia Pty. Limited, *Sydney*
Prentice-Hall Canada Inc., *Toronto*
Prentice-Hall Hispanoamericana, S.A., *Mexico*
Prentice-Hall of India Private Limited, *New Delhi*
Prentice-Hall of Japan, Inc., *Tokyo*
Simon & Schuster Asia Pte. Ltd., *Singapore*
Editora Prentice-Hall do Brasil, Ltda., *Rio de Janeiro*

About the Authors

James H. Boykin is the Alfred L. Blake Professor of Real Estate and Director of the Virginia Real Estate Research Center in the School of Business, Virginia Commonwealth University. Prior to becoming an educator, Dr. Boykin served with the Federal Housing Administration in Detroit and in Richmond, Virginia. Later, he was with the Richmond-based firm of Rountrey and Associates. He has also served with the Urban Land Institute in Washington, DC. Additionally, he has had his own real estate appraising and consulting business. He has qualified as an expert witness in thirteen different courts of law and has lectured to mortgage lending and real estate valuation groups throughout the United States.

Dr. Boykin is a member of several professional real estate organizations and holds the SREA and MAI professional appraisal designations. He has held various positions in these organizations, including being a member of the governing council and vice president of the American Institute of Real Estate Appraisers, chairman of the Real Estate Research Center Directors and Chair Holders Association, and serving on the board of directors of the American Institute of Corporate Asset Management and the Virginia Real Estate Appraiser Board.

Dr. Boykin has been listed in numerous bibliographies, such as *Outstanding Educators of America* and *Who's Who in Finance and Industry*. He is also a member of Lambda Alpha honorary land economics fraternity, a fellow of the Homer Hoyt Advanced Studies Institute, and a faculty fellow of the School of Mortgage Banking. In addition to numerous professional journal articles, research monographs, and reports, he has written the following books: *Industrial Potential of the Central City* (Urban Land Institute), *Mortgage Loan Underwriting* (Mortgage Bankers Association of America), and *Financing Real Estate* (D. C. Heath). He is the coauthor of *Basic Income Property Appraisal* (Addison-Wesley) and *Valuation of Real Estate* (Prentice-Hall) as well as the editor-in-chief of *Real Estate Counseling* (Society of Industrial and Office Realtors) and coeditor of *The Real Estate Handbook* (Dow Jones-Irwin), and *Real Estate Analyses* (American Society of Real Estate Counselors).

Alfred A. Ring is a Professor Emeritus at the University of Florida in Gainesville, having served as professor and chairman of the real estate department from 1948 to 1970. He is a past president of the Appraisal Institute's Florida Chapter No. 2.

Active in civic affairs, Ring is a member of the American Economies Association, the Gainesville Board of Realtors, the Florida Association of Realtors, Beta Gamma Sigma Lamda Alpha, and the National Tax Institute.

A graduate of New York University, Ring earned his Ph.D. in philosophy majoring in public utilities and land economics. He resides in Gainesville.

Ring's contributions in other publications include: *Real Estate Principles and Practices, Questions and Problems in Real Estate Principles and Practices, The Valuation of Real Estate, Real Estate Encyclopedia Americana,* and the *Study Guide* for *Real Estate Principles.* He also co-authored *Real Estate Fundamentals,* and has published 35 articles in the following publications: *The Appraisal Journal, The Real Estate Appraiser, Appraisal Institute Magazine* (Canada), *The Florida Realtor, Economic Leaflets-University of Florida,* and *Public Utilities Fortnightly.*

Contents

Preface, xix

SECTION 1   Fundamentals of Value, 1

   1   NATURE AND IMPORTANCE OF VALUE, 1

      Learning Objectives, 1
      Individual Versus General Market Value, 1
      Market Conditions and Terms of Sale Influencing Value, 3
      What Makes Value?, 5
      Value Characteristics, 6
      Types of Value, 7
      The Meaning of Market Value, 9
      Value in Use, 13
      Organization of the Book, 13
      Summary, 14
      Review Questions, 15
      Reading and Study References, 15

   2   HISTORY AND IMPORTANCE OF VALUE THOUGHT, 17

      Learning Objectives, 17
      Mercantilism, 18
      The Physiocrats, 18
      Classical Economics, 19
      The Austrian School of Economics, 22
      The Neoclassical and Equilibrium School of Economics, 24
      Early Twentieth-Century Value Theory, 25
      Contributions of Valuators and Valuation Theorists, 27
      History of Appraisal Organizations, 35
      Influence of Value Theory upon Appraisal Practice, 36

v

Summary, 37
Review Questions, 38
Reading and Study References, 39

3   NATURE AND PRINCIPLES OF PROPERTY VALUATION, 40

Learning Objectives, 40
Wealth Versus Property, 41
The Legal Concept of Property, 41
The "Bundle of Rights," 42
Ownership Limitations, 43
Principles of Real Estate Valuation, 44
The Concept of Highest and Best Use, 44
Consistent Use, 51
Substitution, 52
Marginal Productivity, 52
Supply and Demand, 53
Balance in Land Use and Development, 54
Anticipation of Future Benefits, 55
Conformity, 55
Changes in Socioeconomic Patterns, 57
Summary, 57
Review Questions, 58
Reading and Study References, 58

SECTION 2   External Influences on Property Value, 60

4   IMPACT OF POLITICAL, SOCIAL, AND ECONOMIC FORCES, 60

Learning Objectives, 60
Political Forces Influencing Value, 61
Social Forces Influencing Value, 64
General Economic Forces Influencing Value, 68
State or Regional Forces Influencing Value, 72
Summary, 74
Review Questions, 74
Reading and Study References, 75

5   REGIONAL AND COMMUNITY ANALYSIS, 76

Learning Objectives, 76
The Real Estate Market, 77
Causes of Urbanization, 78
Regional Analysis, 86
Population Trends and Characteristics, 88

Economic Measures of Community Growth, 89
The Nature and Character of Cities, 91
The City's Plan and Land Use Pattern, 92
Summary, 94
Review Questions, 95
Reading and Study References, 95

6 NEIGHBORHOOD VALUE ANALYSIS, 97

Learning Objectives, 97
Neighborhood Defined, 97
The Neighborhood Age Cycle, 98
Neighborhood Characteristics, 100
Neighborhood Boundaries, 102
Location Characteristics, 102
Social Forces Influencing Neighborhood Values, 105
Neighborhood Economic Characteristics, 106
Neighborhood Analysis in Form Reports, 110
Neighborhood Attributes of Retail Districts, 112
Office Districts, 113
Industrial District Attributes, 114
Summary, 115
Review Questions, 116
Reading and Study References, 116

SECTION 3 Site Analysis and Valuation, 118

7 CONSIDERATIONS IN SITE ANALYSIS, 118

Learning Objectives, 118
Site Analysis Principles, 119
Nature of Terrain and Soil Characteristics, 130
Street Improvements and Availability of Essential Public Utilities, 136
Shape, Size, Depth, and Corner Location Influences, 136
Zoning and Contractual Limitations on Ownership, 141
Summary, 143
Review Questions, 144
Reading and Study References, 144

8 FUNDAMENTALS OF LAND VALUATION, 145

Learning Objectives, 145
Sales Comparison Approach, 146
Land Residual Earnings Approach, 155
Subdivision Development Method, 157

Site Value-to-Property Value Ratio (Allocation), 159
Land Value Extraction Method, 162
Summary, 162
Review Questions, 163
Reading and Study References, 164

SECTION 4   Sales Comparison and Depreciated Cost Approaches, 165

  9   SALES COMPARISON APPROACH TO VALUE, 165

Learning Objectives, 165
Verification of Sales, 166
Price Adjustments for Time and Transfer Terms, 167
Market Comparison Adjustment Techniques, 173
Detailed Property Analysis Technique, 174
Overall Property Rating Technique, 177
Percentage Adjustments: Their Use and Limitation, 179
Regression Analysis, 181
Sales Comparison Approach for Commercial and Industrial Properties, 184
Gross Income Multipliers as a Guide to Market Value, 186
Summary, 190
Review Questions, 191
Reading and Study References, 191

 10   BUILDING CONSTRUCTION AND PLAN READING, 193

Learning Objectives, 193
Building Components, 194
Plan Reading for Proposed Construction, 200
The Importance of Written Specifications, 202
Computing Building Measurements, 204
Basic Attributes of Good Floor Planning, 204
Importance of Construction Knowledge, 208
Building Inspection, 208
Summary, 209
Review Questions, 209
Reading and Study References, 210

 11   THE DEPRECIATED COST APPROACH: COST ESTIMATING, 211

Learning Objectives, 211
Steps in the Depreciated Cost Approach, 211
Pros and Cons of the Depreciated Cost Approach, 212
Cost Versus Value, 213
Direct and Indirect Costs, 214

Quantity Survey Method, 217
Unit-in-Place Construction Method, 217
The Comparative Unit Method, 219
Estimating the Standard or Base House, 223
Estimating Cost New of the Subject House, 227
Cost Indexing Method, 230
Commercial Cost Services, 231
Summary, 233
Review Questions, 234
Reading and Study References, 235

12   THE DEPRECIATED COST APPROACH: MEASURING ACCRUED
     DEPRECIATION, 236

Learning Objectives, 236
Depreciation Versus Amortization, 237
Depreciation Theory, 238
Economic Life Versus Physical Life, 239
Economic Age-Life Method, 241
The Breakdown, or Observed Condition, Method, 242
Market Extracted Depreciation, 248
Depreciation Estimates: Their Limits of Use, 250
Summary, 251
Review Questions, 252
Reading and Study References, 252

SECTION 5   Income-Expense Analysis and Capitalization, 253

13   INCOME FORECASTING AND ANALYSIS, 253

Learning Objectives, 253
Income as a Measure of Value, 254
Actual Versus Average Income, 255
Market Versus Contract Rents, 256
Importance of Typical Management, 257
Estimating the Quantity of Income Flow, 257
Quality and Duration of Income, 259
Rental Schedule Construction and Analysis, 263
Lease Analysis, 263
Owner's Income Statements and Adjustments, 270
Income Adjustment for Changes in the Purchasing Power of the Dollar, 271
Summary, 272
Review Questions, 273
Reading and Study References, 274

14 OPERATING EXPENSE FORECASTING AND ANALYSIS, 275

Learning Objectives, 275
Income Deductions Versus Operating Expenses, 276
Income Tax and Property Tax Considerations, 276
Classification of Operating Expenses, 277
Operating Expense Schedule Reconstruction, 280
Reserves for Replacements, 283
The Significance of Operating Expense Ratios, 285
Capital Expenditures, 287
Summary, 287
Review Questions, 289
Reading and Study References, 290
Listing of Published Income-Expense Sources, 290

15 DETERMINING THE RATE OF CAPITALIZATION, 292

Learning Objectives, 292
Types of Rates of Return, 295
Capitalization Rate Selection Methods, 299
Summary, 308
Review Questions, 309
Reading and Study References, 310

16 COMPOUND INTEREST AND DISCOUNTING, 312

Learning Objectives, 312
Compound Amount of 1, 314
Future Worth of 1 per Period, 315
Sinking Fund (Amortization) Factor, 320
Present Worth of 1, 321
Present Worth of 1 per Period, 323
Installment to Amortize 1, 325
The Importance of Logarithmic Functions, 328
Special Applications of Compounding and Discounting, 329
Special-Purpose Tables, 333
Summary, 335
Review Questions, 336
Reading and Study References, 337

17 INCOME CAPITALIZATION METHODS, 339

Learning Objectives, 339
Capitalization of Income Extending into Perpetuity, 340
Capitalization of Nonperpetuity Income, 341
Discounted Cash Flow, 349

Summary, 353
Review Questions, 355
Reading and Study References, 356

18 PHYSICAL RESIDUAL TECHNIQUES OF CAPITALIZATION, 357

Learning Objectives, 357
The Residual Character of Land, 359
Land Residual Technique, 360
Building Residual Technique, 364
Property Residual Technique, 368
Summary, 374
Review Questions, 375
Reading and Study References, 375

19 LEASEHOLD ESTATES AND LEASED FEE APPRAISING, 377

Learning Objectives, 377
Importance of Lease Provisions, 378
Component Interest Valuation, 379
Leased Fee Valuation, 380
Valuation of Leaseholds, 384
Sandwich Lease Valuation, 387
Summary, 389
Review Questions, 390
Reading and Study References, 392

20 MORTGAGE-EQUITY APPRAISING, 393

Learning Objectives, 393
Trading on the Equity, 393
Property Appraising Versus Equity Appraising, 396
Mortgage Loan Balance, 404
Ellwood's Tables for Capitalization, 406
Summary, 409
Review Questions, 410
Reading and Study References, 411

SECTION 6 Condemnation Appraisals and Professional Reporting, 412

21 CONDEMNATION APPRAISING PRACTICES AND PROCEDURES, 412

Learning Objectives, 412
Power of Eminent Domain, 413
Due Process of Law, 413

Just Compensation, 414
Meaning of Value, 415
Measures of Value, 415
Severance Damage, 418
Treatment of Benefits, 420
Consequential Damage, 421
Excess Condemnation, 421
The Expert Witness, 422
Pretrial Preparation, 423
Direct Examination, 425
Cross-Examination, 426
Summary, 428
Review Questions, 429
Reading and Study References, 429

22 APPRAISAL REPORT WRITING, 430

Learning Objectives, 430
Appraisal Process, 430
Value Reconciliation, 434
The Appraisal Report, 435
Professional Standards for Appraisal Reports, 435
Suggestions for Improved Report Writing, 440
The Demonstration Appraisal Report, 442
Narrative Appraisal Report, 443
Letter or Abbreviated Report, 444
Letter of Opinion, 444
Short-Form Appraisal Reporting, 444
Summary, 446
Review Questions, 448
Reading and Study References, 449

23 PROFESSIONAL APPRAISAL STANDARDS, 450

Learning Objectives, 450
Professional Standards and Responsibilities, 450
Importance of Professional Conduct, 451
Professional Qualifications, 452
Standards of Professional Conduct, 453
Appraiser's Rules of Conduct, 455
Uniform Standards of Professional Appraisal Practice, 457
Summary, 460
Review Questions, 461
Reading and Study References, 462

APPENDIX I   GLOSSARY, 463

APPENDIX II   MARKET VALUE APPRAISAL OF THE KEEGAN'S MILL
                 APARTMENTS, 471

APPENDIX III   CASE STUDIES, 573

                 Case Study 1: Land Development Approach to Value, 573
                 Case Study 2: Apartment House Property, 574
                 Case Study 3: Retail Store Property, 577
                 Case Study 4: Store and Office Building, 582
                 Case Study 1: Suggested Solution, 584
                 Case Study 1: Alternative Plan Suggested Solution, 584
                 Case Study 2: Suggested Solution, 585
                 Case Study 3: Suggested Solution, 588
                 Case Study 4: Suggested Solution, 590

APPENDIX IV   SUGGESTED SOLUTIONS TO CHAPTER REVIEW
                 QUESTIONS, 594

                 Chapter 1, 594
                 Chapter 2, 595
                 Chapter 3, 596
                 Chapter 4, 596
                 Chapter 5, 597
                 Chapter 6, 598
                 Chapter 7, 599
                 Chapter 8, 599
                 Chapter 9, 600
                 Chapter 10, 601
                 Chapter 11, 602
                 Chapter 12, 603
                 Chapter 13, 605
                 Chapter 14, 606
                 Chapter 15, 608
                 Chapter 16, 610
                 Chapter 17, 611
                 Chapter 18, 612
                 Chapter 19, 614
                 Chapter 20, 616
                 Chapter 21, 619
                 Chapter 22, 620
                 Chapter 23, 621

APPENDIX V   FINANCIAL TABLES, 623

APPENDIX VI   LAND MEASUREMENT TABLE, 632

APPENDIX VII   VALUATION SYMBOLS AND EQUATIONS, 634

INDEX, 637

Preface

Since the first edition of *The Valuation of Real Estate* was published in 1963, great strides have been made in perfecting the practice of property valuation and in elevating the status of appraising as a respected field of specialization. The role of the appraiser, too, as a professional practitioner in the broad area of real estate economics is increasing in importance. The bulk of national wealth, both public and private, is invested in real property, and no significant transfer of ownership of real property is likely to take place without professional assistance from experts in the field of valuation.

The current edition of this book is a distillation of the authors' many years of experience in teaching, research, and appraising. This popular book has been updated substantially, reorganized, and expanded to strengthen time-honored appraisal methodology by integrating contemporary valuation thinking and procedures. Each chapter contains review questions and selected readings so students can test their comprehension and expand their understanding of chapter material by reading other works. Completed form and narrative appraisals allow the reader to see how professional appraisal reports are prepared. An actual professionally prepared income property appraisal report is included (Appendix II). This illustrative report is enhanced with annotations and references to related sections of the book, and many questions are raised that should provoke valuable insights and classroom discussion. Other attractions of this book are its logical grouping of chapters, use of step-by-step problem solutions, case studies to reinforce the text, current standards of professional appraisal practice, standardized symbols used by the leading appraisal societies, a glossary, and the explanation of valuation problems by use of financial tables and calculators.

The ever-increasing importance of ownership of real property as an estate-building asset, as a hedge against inflation, as a tax shelter device, and as a permanent and secure investment has caused ownership of realty to become popular and widespread. This is evident from the increasing number of real estate transactions that are presented annually for public recording. To assure "arms-length" bargaining in these transactions at prices reflecting market supply and demand, an expert opinion concerning value is deemed essential.

This book is written essentially as a text for classroom use and study in schools of business and for persons who aspire to become licensed by states or designated by professional appraisal societies. Every effort was made to keep this writing and the applied theory and practice of property valuation technically current yet "down to earth." There is, however, no easy road to learning. A book, no matter how masterly written, can by self-study alone contribute little to an expansion of human wisdom or to the perfection of human judgment. These human attributes can best be obtained through the broad school of field experience and professional involvement. A well written book, nevertheless, can stimulate experience, challenge the reader to reach for perfection, and encourage him or her through interesting arrangements of facts and explanatory statements to seek mastery of the art of a chosen profession.

It is important to remember that *value* is the heart of economics. More important still is the indisputable fact that only *people* can make value. A sound theory of value, thus, must keep the human factor in focus and be attuned to practices that are the outgrowth of sociopolitical forces that operate within a capitalistic economy where dollar democracy expresses itself in free and open market operations.

The book is an outgrowth of over six decades of teaching appraising principles and practices at the college level and for real estate appraisal and other related professional groups throughout the United States. Added to this background is the over 65-year consulting and appraising background of the authors. Although the topical presentation of subject matter is traditional and follows procedure recommended for use by leading appraisal societies, new concepts of valuation theory and practice are introduced to stimulate classroom study and discussions and to aid in the modification of field practices where tested results warrant their application.

The authors want to acknowledge the special contributions made to this writing by their many students at the professional, graduate, and undergraduate level, whose questioning of valuation concepts and teaching methods have contributed greatly to this latest edition. Grateful acknowledgment is made for valuable assistance and continued encouragement and support over the years from a long-time friend and colleague Herbert B. Dorau (deceased), Professor of Economics Emeritus and formerly Chairman of the Department of Real Estate at New York University. For valuable suggestions offered during the manuscript stages of earlier versions and for constructive editorial comments, our thanks are expressed to Richard U. Ratcliff, MAI, University of Wisconsin; W. D. Davis, MAI; William N. Kinnard, Jr., MAI, SREA, University of Connecticut; H. Grady Stebbins, Jr., MAI, SREA; Ronald O. Boatright, Ph.D.; Terry V. Grissom, Ph.D., MAI, Texas A&M University; Joseph M. Davis, MAI, SRPA Arizona State University; James D. Vernor, Ph.D., MAI, Georgia State University; Wallace F. Smith, University of California-Berkeley; Kenneth M. Lusht, SRPA, Pennsylvania State University; Anthony B. Sanders, Ohio State University; and Scruggs Love, Jr., MAI, SREA, San Antonio, Texas. Debra C. Isley was invaluable in the typing of the manuscript.

Several people provided us with valuable suggestions in the writing of the present edition. These include: Linwood M. Aron, MAI, SREA, Linwood M. Aron, Inc., Richmond, VA; Douglas S. Bible, Ph.D., Louisiana State University—Shreveport; Byrl N. Boyce, SREA, CRE, Byrl N. Boyce and Associates, Mansfield Center, CT; Douglas C. Brown, MAI, Douglas C. Brown and Assoc., Inc., Columbia, SC; William L. Christensen, MAI, SRA, CRE, CPM, William L. Christensen and Assoc., Salt Lake City, UT; John R. Crunkleton, Ph.D., Old Dominion University, Norfolk, VA; Arthur J. Frahm, MAI, Des Moines, Iowa; James E. Gibbons, MAI, CRE, Sackman-Gibbons Associates, Garden City, NY; Donald J. Hartman, MAI, Dean Appraisal Company, Birmingham, MI; Nathaniel W. Hauser, MAI, Maryland National Bank, Baltimore, MD; Mary Alice Hines, Ph.D., Washburn University, Topeka, KS; Harvey P. Jeffers, MAI, SREA, CRE, Harvey P. Jeffers, Charleston, SC; John M. McCracken, MAI, John McCracken and Assoc., Inc., Greensboro, NC; Charles A. Moore, Jr., CRE, ASA, Republic Real Estate Appraisal Corp., Vienna, VA; Hugh Nourse, Ph.D., University of Georgia; Thomas M. Olinger, Architectural Intern, Richmond, VA; Joe R. Price, MAI, Callaway and Price, Inc., West Palm Beach, FL; J. Parks Rountrey, MAI, SRPA, Knight, Dorin, and Rountrey, Richmond, VA; Gerald B. Schulz, MAI, and Julie W. Ashby, Love and Dugger, Houston, TX; Gerald A. Teel, MAI, Gerald A. Teel Co., Inc., Houston, TX; and James D. Vernor, Ph.D., MAI, Georgia State University.

Not only are the authors grateful for the many ideas offered by contributors to the earlier and the current edition, but welcome your suggestions for improving this book.

James H. Boykin
Alfred A. Ring

1

Nature and Importance of Value

Learning Objectives

After reading this chapter, you should be able to:

- Understand the difference in value of a property to an individual and the value of the same property to the general public
- Appreciate how prices generally occur when the forces of supply and demand are in equilibrium
- Explain why there is more than one type of value
- Discuss the meaning of market value and the requisites for its existence
- Distinguish between value in use and market value
- Comprehend the characteristics required for a good or service to have value

Real estate valuation may rightfully be designated as the heart of all real estate activity. In fact, valuation is the heart of all *economic* activity. Everything we do as individuals or as groups of individuals in business or as members of society is influenced by the concept of value. A sound working knowledge of the principles and procedures of valuation is essential in all sorts of decisions relating to real estate buying, selling, financing, developing, managing, owning, leasing, trading, and in matters involving income tax considerations. Sound valuation is basic to zoning, ad valorem taxation, city planning, and to effective management of urban affairs in order to put land and its improvements to the highest, best, and hence most profitable use.

INDIVIDUAL VERSUS GENERAL MARKET VALUE

Although the importance of value as an economic measure is generally recognized, there is a wide variance of understanding as to the character, nature, and meaning of value, especially among the general public who comprise the broad market for real property. This wide variance, and the lack of understanding of the available means of measuring the magnitude of value, is explained by the failure

1

of most persons to recognize fully the difference between the value of a property to a particular individual and the value of that same property to the public in general.

In the final analysis all value, no matter how defined, has its origin in individual measures of worth. Everyone has a scale of preference for a particular real property. This preference between an individual and a given property is influenced continuously and in varying degrees by personal traits and by cultural, religious, and governmental forces that influence each person as a member of society. This subjective value can readily be demonstrated by a scatter diagram, wherein each circle represents the worth (or sacrifice a person would willingly make for it) of a given quantity of a good or service as measured in units of dollars. Each circle may stand for one or more individuals, or it may represent a second or third measure of worth by one or more individuals for additional units of the same type of property.

Thus someone may be willing to pay $160,000 for a home, offer no more than $150,000 (as an investment in a like residence), and express no desire (demand) for ownership of a third property. Another person may offer no more than $155,000 for the same property and express no interest in another even as a recommended investment on a reduced or discount basis. Each person thus expresses his or her preference (or estimate of subjective worth) for one or more units of a commodity (or property) by bidding along a scale as shown in Figure 1.1. The fitted curve may then appropriately be labeled as a composite diagram

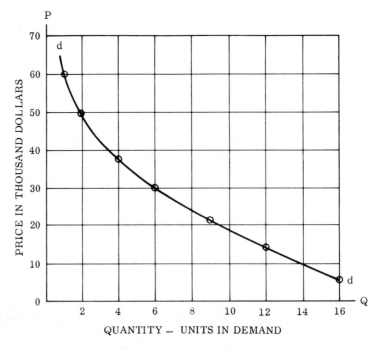

Figure 1.1 Demand Curve

that projects the relationship of offering prices for given properties to quantities of such real estate offered for sale at a given time and place in an open, free, and generally normal market.

Demand for real estate arises from necessity or from human desires which are backed by purchasing power, cash, or credit. As individual or group desires are molded by environmental influences, human behavior reacts accordingly and expresses itself in a changed pattern for the kinds of real estate sought after in the marketplace. To gain a better understanding of the ever-changing socioeconomic forces that underlie the concept of objective value, a study of the basic law of market supply and demand is therefore deemed essential.

An offer to exchange a quantity of dollars for a given real property does not, by itself, create a market. There must be owners who supply these properties and who are ready, willing, and able to meet the demand at the price offered. Each property must be *produced* or supplied at a certain sacrifice of the various factors of production involving land, labor, capital, and entrepreneurial effort. Some suppliers are more efficient than others; and as a result of volume of production, increased mechanization, or other factors that lower builders' costs, they are able to market their properties at lower prices.

In market areas where builders' earnings are relatively high, and where market demand is considered expandable, other suppliers of properties are competitively attracted. Ignoring for the moment the customers' ability or willingness to pay even the warranted cost of an efficient producer, a scale of increasing individual producer costs can be plotted as a scatter diagram, as illustrated in Figure 1.2. The most efficient producers are able to supply the desired product at the lowest possible cost; they are followed along the scale by producers of lower quantities and generally lower efficiency and higher per unit costs.

By superimposing the demand curve in Figure 1.1 on the cost of production curve in Figure 1.2, it is possible to measure the interaction of market supply and demand for given classes of real estate. As shown in Figure 1.3, where the supply and demand lines intersect at this point, the individual value forces of users and producers merge into a market-determined measure of value. The demand below the point of merger is classified as submarginal, or inadequate to meet the marginal costs of production. The supplier's costs above the point of merger are likewise submarginal—that is, above the highest bids offered at the time and place for the real estate in demand.

MARKET CONDITIONS AND TERMS OF SALE INFLUENCING VALUE

Where analysis of market data permits accurate presentation of the interacting economic forces that influence the shape of the supply and demand curves shown in Figure 1.3, the resulting findings offer conclusive evidence in support of the equilibrium price or market value as verified by actions in the open market. The market price thus obtained is in effect a synthesis or equilibrium of the interacting subjective values or forces that comprise a *market.* No informed person who

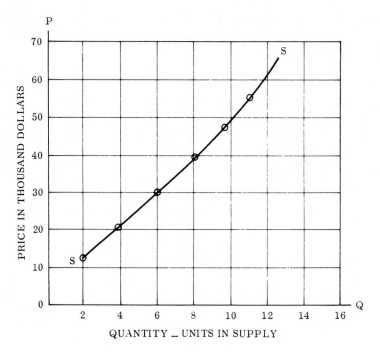

Figure 1.2   Cost of Production Curve

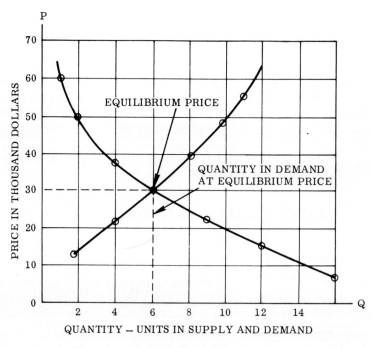

Figure 1.3   Market Supply and Demand Curve

buys with due care is warranted to pay more than the prevailing market price, and no equally informed seller will accept less. Attention is called to the fact that in all value discussions presented here it is assumed that the forces of supply and demand are in equilibrium for a given submarket (e.g., houses in the $250,000 to $400,000 range) and that no artificial or temporary barriers impede either supply or demand. Scarcity in supply as well as over- or underconsumption will temporarily influence the price of the product and cause payments of either premiums or discounts, depending on the nature of market conditions. Therefore, in solving a value problem it is essential to stipulate either whether or not market conditions are normal; or, if they are not, the dollar extent to which value adjustments must be made to reflect peculiarities of the market that favor either buyers or sellers.

To illustrate: In the late 1980s, many home builders realized that business executives were being transferred from expensive housing markets into their moderately priced markets, and began to build unprecedented numbers of homes in the $500,000 to $800,000 bracket. Later, as the economy softened in the expensive Northeast markets, transferrees were left with less money from the sale of their former homes, plus many of these lower-priced markets became overbuilt. The result was glutted upscale housing markets. Some builders were forced to sell their new homes for less than their construction cost; others filed for bankruptcy.

Another condition requisite in an estimate of market value is that the exchange of dollars for quantities of goods or services is in *present* dollars on a cash or cash-equivalent basis. Promises of future dollars create interest costs and hazards of collection which must be compensated for over and above the value imputed to a good or service on a *cash* or cash-equivalent basis.[1] Just as favorable terms of sale increase the price at which realty is exchanged in the open market, conversely restrictive terms, such as high mortgage interest rates, can decrease the price below the amount a property would command if available for transfer on typical—that is, conventional—terms of sale. Further consideration will be given in Chapter 9 to the impact of *terms* of sale on *prices* of real estate.

WHAT MAKES VALUE?

A frequently posed question is: What makes value? Is a property or a commodity valuable because it possesses *intrinsic* qualities such as are attributed, for instance, to gold or silver, or is value entirely *extrinsic* to the object and created wholly in the minds of people who seek to possess that object? Theoretically, support can be given to a contention that, to be valuable, a product must possess certain qualities that attract the buyer and user and thus create a desire for ownership. Such qualities, if indeed assignable to an inanimate object, are then classified as intrinsic and thus inherent in the product per se. Those subscribing to a humanistic philosophy of value hold that value is a product of the mind, and that in the final analysis *people* create value—not wood, steel, brick, or mortar.

---

[1]"Cash equivalent" as used here and in subsequent chapters refers to typical financing terms: equity down payment plus mortgage loan amounts which were available to a typical purchaser when a particular comparable sale property was conveyed.

Adherents to this school of thought hold that value is extrinsic in character, and that logically an object or service cannot possess intrinsic value. They illustrate this contention as follows. If gold or silver, for instance, should suddenly rain like manna from the heavens, its so-called intrinsic value would disappear; in fact, its superabundance might create a nuisance that would give it a negative rather than a positive value under the circumstances. Changes in modes and fashions, too, may cause an object (through no fault or diminution of its intrinsic qualities) to be classed as obsolete or relatively useless.

Progress in the arts and sciences, development of new and rapid modes of transportation, and changes due to computerized technology all give weight to the concept that to a large degree it is people who make value and that value, therefore, must be considered as basically being extrinsic in character. Nevertheless, at a given place and time, the object under value study must possess certain economic and legal characteristics in order to be wanted and thereby claim attributes of value.

VALUE CHARACTERISTICS

For a good or service to have value, it must possess certain economic and legal characteristics, specifically the following: (1) utility, (2) scarcity, (3) demand, and (4) transferability.

Utility may be defined as the power of a good to render a service or fill a need. Utility must be present for a good or service to be of value. However, utility is only one of the characteristics that make up value. Thus where utility is present but demand or scarcity is absent, market value will not exist. For instance, water and air possess utility—yes, total utility, for both are essential to life itself. The value of neither air nor water, however, is measurable in terms of dollars, for each is abundant and free to all. To have market value, therefore, a useful good or service must be scarce. The influence of utility on value, too, must be considered in relation to the size, shape, or form of the property, its geographic or spatial location, and its mobility and availability at given times. Variations in utility characteristics influence value; value differences, therefore, are caused by form, space, or time utility.

Scarcity is a relative term, and must be considered in relation to demand and supply and the alternate uses—present or prospective—to which the good or service may be put. Thus Christmas trees may be scarce the day before Christmas, and most abundant the week after. Value, too, will fluctuate accordingly. Gold and silver are relatively scarce, but their degree of scarcity, and hence value, can be affected by the discovery of new sources of supply or the introduction of a new metal offering equal or even greater utility. Everything else remaining equal, value differences will result with changes in the relative scarcity among market goods and services. Generally, the greater the *scarcity*, the more spirited becomes the competitive bidding for goods or services and the higher, as a rule, the transaction price or market value.

Demand is an economic concept that implies not only the presence of a "need" but also the existence of monetary power to fill that need. Wishful-buyer thinking or necessity alone, no matter how strong, does not constitute demand; to bring about the latter, purchasing power must be available to satisfy the perceived need. Builders, developers, and investors in particular should keep the purchasing-power aspects of demand in mind. For example, large-scale housing developments are often planned and carried out to fill a long-felt "need," only to end in financial grief because of failure to consider accurately the effective buying power of the prospective tenants. Hotels, amusement enterprises, and large commercial projects have also experienced a high rate of financial mortality chiefly because of failure to distinguish between need and demand, and because of an inability to measure accurately the effective purchasing power of their customers.

Transferability is a legal concept that must be considered in the estimation of property value. Even though the characteristics of utility, scarcity, and demand are present, if the property cannot be transferred in whole or in part, market value cannot exist. The moon, for instance, has utility; it is scarce (there is only one); and there might possibly be a demand for it if ownership and use of it could be controlled. The lack of transferability, however, keeps the moon a free good marketwise. Transferability does not necessarily mean physical mobility—it means rather the possession and control of all the rights that constitute ownership of property.

Assuming that other things remain relatively equal, a change in any one of the characteristics of a property—be it utility, scarcity, demand, or transferability—will inevitably be reflected in its value. Consequently, an increase in utility as evidenced by greater soil fertility will increase the net income of farmland and thus enhance its value. An increase in relative scarcity resulting from an increase in population generally will also be reflected in higher values for marketable properties. An increase in demand caused by a rising standard of living will increase competitive bidding for more and better home sites, increasing the values of the properties so affected. Transferability, too, has an important influence on value. Generally, the greater the liquidity of a commodity, the greater its value because of the greater opportunity and flexibility present to exchange one property for another or its price equivalent. The appraiser must therefore carefully consider possible changes in value characteristics, especially where forecasts need to be made for the economic life of properties extending over 30, 40, or more years into the future. The same concern pertains to nonresidential property where the holding period may be for 10 years or less. The nature, type, and impact of forces that influence value characteristics of real properties will be more fully discussed in Chapters 4 through 7.

TYPES OF VALUE

Although logic would dictate that only *one* type of value could possibly measure the economic significance that individuals attach to a good or service in a given market, the specialized needs of persons have introduced many types of value, a few of which are briefly defined as follows:

Appraised value. Value estimated by an appraiser.

Assessed value. Used for tax purposes and is based on fair market value estimated by assessors.

Book value. An accounting value; acquisition cost plus capital improvements less depreciation reserves.

Capital value. Value of fixed assets used in business.

Cash value. Value associated with an all-cash purchase.

Depreciated value. Value remaining after depreciation is deducted from original acquisition price.

Economic value. Value associated with a useful object that is scarce and capable of measurement.

Exchange value. Value expressed in terms of other goods offered in exchange, usually money.

Extrinsic value. Value determined by persons who wish to purchase a property.

Face value. Value set forth in a security, such as a bond, stock, or mortgage.

Fair value. A transaction price that is fair to all parties of the transfer.

Improved value. Value of a property after on-site construction is completed.

Insurable value. Actual cash value of improvements subject to damage from fire or other destructive hazards and excludes such items as site, excavation, pilings, and underground drains.

Intrinsic value. Value inherent in the object itself, such as a precious metal.

Investment value. Established by an individual investor, based on his or her particular criteria which may differ from those of the market in general.

Leasehold value. A tenant's value in a property as a result of favorable lease terms.

Liquidation value. Distress price received by owner without benefit of usual market exposure; sometimes called "forced sale value."

Mortgage loan value. Based on a percentage of market value or other mortgage underwriting standards.

Nuisance value. Price paid to gain relief from an objectionable situation, such as a derelict adjoining property.

Potential value. Based on occurrence of some future event such as a proposed plan for a future development.

Real value. In contrast to potential value; excludes value increment due to speculative future events.

Rental value. Value as a function of a property having been leased.

Replacement value. Sum of money necessary to rebuild a structure if destroyed by fire or earthquake.

Sales value. Based on the price that a property might bring upon being sold.

Salvage value. Price paid for a property or its improvements, taking into account cost of removal of the structure, including delays.

Speculative value. A hoped-for price that an investor expects based on an influential event such as rezoning or population or economic growth.

Stable value. Assumes unchanging market and property conditions.

Use value. Based on the profitability of a property's present and anticipated uses.

Warranted value. Equivalent to market value, but seldom used.

This listing by no means exhausts the many variations of the term *value* in use today. A complete enumeration would take many pages, especially if the variations of value related to political, social, and religious matters were added to those used to define the importance of business and economic operations. Is it any wonder that a learned U.S. Supreme Court Justice once said that "value is a word of many meanings"? Undoubtedly, the late Justice Brandeis had in mind the many uses of the term that prove puzzling to business managers even to this day.

The question may now be asked: Can there really be that many types of value? Is there one value for the buyer, another for the seller, a third for the lender, and so on? The answer is "yes" where the estimate of value is to serve a special or limited purpose. To illustrate, value for fire insurance purposes would differ in amount from value for mortgage loan purposes. In the former case, emphasis is placed on the replacement cost of improvements that are subject to fire hazards regardless of the marketability or income-producing capacity of the subject property. Where the value estimate is to serve as a basis for mortgage loan origination, principal reliance must be placed on the earnings capacity of the property and on its marketability in case of default in mortgage payment. This illustration points up the fact that a property can have different values for different persons where investment, commercial, or special-use purposes must be considered and given due weight in the value estimate.

To prevent misinterpretation and error in acting on the basis of a value estimate, it is most important that the purpose of the valuation assignment be clearly stated in the letter of transmittal as well as in the body of the appraisal report, and that a definition of value be fully expressed as a guide to action by the reader or client to whom the report is submitted.

Where the estimate of value is to establish the most probable price that a property can command if exposed for sale in a relatively free, open, and competitive market, and at a given time, place, and under specified market conditions, there can be only *one* value. This kind of value, which most frequently is the object of economic search and analysis, is created by the multitude of buyers and sellers who cause a synthesis or interaction of the forces of supply and demand for specific goods or things that are traded in an open market.

THE MEANING OF MARKET VALUE

Even if investment value and value in use are excluded, we still find divergence in professional judgment as how best to define the concept of market value. Therefore, to pinpoint the problem, it is necessary that a single clear-cut definition be formulated. The meaning of value can best be expressed in two closely related ways:

1. The power of a good or service to command other goods or services in exchange.
2. The present worth of *future* rights to income.

The first concept of value, generally known as the "barter" or purchasing power definition of value, is useful in measuring the worth of exchange of one commodity directly for another: in short, how much fish for how much game, or how much wheat for how much corn. Under this definition of value no money as a medium of exchange is necessary to measure the value of one good compared with another. If a standard dwelling of a given size and quality is worth the equivalent of five automobiles of a given make and model in a given year, and 10 years later the relationship of these commodities remains the same, then no change in value has taken place so far as autos and houses are concerned—no matter what happened to the value of money or to the level of prices. In a broader sense, we measure to a large extent the welfare of a group or a nation by the hours of labor (value) necessary to achieve a given standard of living or quantity of goods and services.

The second definition of value is more helpful and more readily applicable as a measure of value where *money* serves as a medium of exchange. Most goods and services are sold for specific purposes—generally to render buyer satisfaction (utility) for one or more years into the future. Thus a home is purchased for a sum of X thousand dollars to provide, throughout the remaining economic life of the dwelling, rental savings as well as psychic income (amenities) derived from the pleasure and prestige of home ownership. The *present value* of direct and/or indirect income from a property over future years can be translated into the present worth by *discounting* these future rights to income into a present sum. This process of discounting, better known as *capitalization*, will be explained more fully and demonstrated in Chapters 15 through 17.

With the introduction of money as a medium of exchange, the barter relationship of one commodity to another became more complex. In a dollar economy, prices essentially serve as a measure of the exchange power of goods for dollars and dollars for goods. This price relationship in a free market has caused acceptance of the meaning of value as being synonymous with the term *exchange* (or *market*) value. As used by real estate appraisers, and as sanctioned by court decisions, market value has been defined under the "willing buyer, willing seller" concept as follows:

> *Market value* is the highest price estimated in terms of money which a property will bring if exposed for sale in the open market allowing a reasonable time to find a purchaser who buys with knowledge of all the uses to which the property is adapted and for which it is capable of being used.[2]

[2]V. Viliborghi, Prescott School, District 55, Arizona 230, 100 Pac. (2nd ed., 1940), p. 178.

> Market value is the most probable price in cash, terms equivalent to cash, or in other precisely revealed terms, for which the appraised property will sell in a competitive market under all the conditions requisite to a fair sale, with the buyer and seller each acting prudently, knowledgeably, and for self-interest, and assuming that neither is under undue duress.[3]

The first definition, like many others that concern value, was judicially influenced and has been widely used by practicing appraisers everywhere. Nevertheless, the concept that market value is the *highest* price that a property will bring suggests to the lay reader of a valuation report that there also must be a *lowest* or at least a lower price that a purchaser should initially offer. Under the equilibrium market value theory, the price that a property commands in the open market is in fact neither the highest nor the lowest—as measured by individual worth—but rather one balanced or equated by all the prevailing forces of market supply and consumer demand. Thus it may be said that market value is that price that a property ordinarily would bring under usual market conditions. It then follows that the more recent concern with "probable price" is more realistic.

Market value, as usually defined, seems to suppose that ordinary buyers and sellers are bestowed with the patience, resources, and mental prowess to be fully cognizant of all conditions influencing the present and future uses of a property. These conditions seldom exist, however. Also, it is questionable whether an appraiser can actually ascertain whether a party to a sales transaction possesses such knowledge.

Although market value continues to be the basis for most appraisals, earlier definitions are cumbersome and smack of artificiality. It is like describing "economic man" rather than those persons generally dealing in the real estate market. Stated differently, it depicts what ought to be in an ideal sense rather than actual conditions that face market participants. It is questionable whether these buyers and sellers are ever fully informed of all the present and future uses of a property. One key group of participants, real estate brokers and sales agents, when listing a property, are concerned about the price that it will probably bring within a reasonable period, which is usually the 60- to 90-day listing period. Therefore, it is suggested that appraisers place greater emphasis on the price a property is likely to bring ("probable price") within a given time frame and the economic environment in which the sale is expected to occur than on such matters as expressed in an idealized market value definition. The give and take of prospective buyers and sellers is depicted in Figure 1.4.

To reinforce the understanding that an estimate of value is a studied and considered approximation of the most probable amount for which a property can be exchanged under cash or cash-equivalent terms of sale, the following more precise definition of market value for use in appraisal reporting has been agreed upon by federal financial institutions in the United States:

---

[3]See American Institute of Real Estate Appraisers, *The Dictionary of Real Estate Appraisers* (Chicago: AIREA, 1984), pp. 194–95.

Figure 1.4   Price Range Refined Through Negotiation to Reflect Market Value

The most probable price which a property should bring in a competitive and open market under all conditions requisite to a fair sale, the buyer and seller each acting prudently and knowledgeably, and assuming the price is not affected by undue stimulus. Implicit in this definition is the consummation of a sale as of a specified date and the passing of title from seller to buyer under conditions whereby:

1. buyer and seller are typically motivated;

2. both parties are well informed or well advised, and acting in what they consider their best interests;

3. a reasonable time is allowed for exposure in the open market;

4. payment is made in terms of cash in United States dollars or in terms of financial arrangements comparable thereto; and

    5. the price represents the normal consideration for the property sold unaffected by special or creative financing or sales concessions granted by anyone associated with the sale.[4]

As this definition suggests, the time of sale, the terms of sale, the relationship of the parties, knowledge concerning rights to be conveyed, present and possible potential uses to which the property may be put, time for the transaction to mature and close normally, and the immediate transferability of good and marketable title all influence the estimate of a warranted price. More detailed consideration of the impact of conditions and terms of sale will be given in succeeding chapters.

VALUE IN USE

Value in use is the value of a property for a specific use, which usually is its present use. There are two primary situations where this value concept applies. (1) A property may have been designed or altered for a particular use and currently is used for that purpose. Suppose, for example, an older multistoried loft property was designed for a gravity flow manufacturing process. If that use continues to function efficiently in the building, the property would retain a reasonable value. However, if the specialized building design severely restricts other potential users from profiting from using the building, then the property's exchange value (market value) in turn would be depressed. (2) Another example of value in use is where preferential tax treatment is given to a property because it is being put to a suboptimal use such as timber or cropland rather than a more intensive and valuable use. The trade-off for a jurisdiction accepting lower real estate tax revenue is that certain desired community objectives are achieved, such as the preservation of open space.

ORGANIZATION OF THE BOOK

This book contains six sections in addition to seven appendices. Section 1, "Fundamentals of Value," provides a foundation for the balance of the book through an exploration of various value concepts, history of valuation thought, and importantly—a discussion of principles of real property valuation. Section 2, "External Influences on Property Value," presents a sequentially refined examination of factors external to a property that affect its value. Initially, this section covers the value effects of political, social, and economic forces. Next considered are regional, community, and neighborhood value influences. Section 3, "Site Analysis and Valuation," contains two chapters. The first thoroughly covers elements of site analysis followed by a discussion of several proven site valuation

---

[4]*Uniform Standard of Professional Practice* (Washington, D.C.: Appraisal Standards Board of the Appraisal Foundation, April 20, 1990), p. I-7.

methods. Section 4, "Sales Comparison and Depreciated Cost Approaches," is divided into four chapters. The first chapter focuses on different ways in which comparable sales data can be used to estimate market value. The following chapter provides important information on building construction and plan reading. The final two chapters deal with the two phases of the depreciated cost approach: cost estimating and measuring accrued depreciation. Section 5, "Income-Expense Valuation and Capitalization," is the largest section in the book. Herein are covered such topics as income and expense analysis, different capitalization and discounting methods as well as physical residual techniques. Covered as well in this section are leasehold, leased fee, and equity appraising. The concluding Section 6, "Condemnation Appraisals and Professional Reporting," covers three topics. These are condemnation appraising, appraisal report writing, and the important subject of professional appraisal standards.

The final part of the book, containing seven appendices, includes a glossary of valuation terms, a narrative valuation report, four case studies, suggested solutions to chapter problems, financial tables, a land measurement table, and valuation symbols and equations.

SUMMARY

Valuation is the heart of all economic activity. In turn, a sound working knowledge of the principles and procedures of valuation is essential in all sorts of decisions relating to real estate.

Everyone has a scale of preference for a particular real property. This preference between an individual and a given property is influenced continuously and in varying degrees by personal traits and by cultural, religious, and governmental forces that influence each person as a member of society.

Scarcity in supply as well as over- and underconsumption will temporarily influence the price of real property. Therefore, in solving a value problem it is essential to stipulate either whether market conditions are normal, or, if they are not, the dollar extent to which value adjustments must be made to reflect peculiarities of the market that favor either buyers or sellers.

Some people hold that a commodity is valuable because it possesses *intrinsic* qualities, whereas others believe that value is entirely *extrinsic* to the object and is created wholly in the minds of people who seek to possess that object.

In order for a property to have value, it must possess the following qualities: (1) utility, (2) scarcity, (3) demand, and (4) transferability. *Utility* is the power of a good to render a service or fill a need. *Scarcity* is a relative term, and must be considered in relation to demand and supply and the alternate uses to which the good or service may be placed. Generally, the greater the scarcity, the higher the value of the object. *Demand* is an economic concept that implies not only the presence of a "need" but also the existence of monetary power to fill that need. *Transferability* is a legal concept which refers to the possession and control of all the rights that constitute ownership of property rather than physical mobility. Unless a property can be transferred in whole or in part, market value cannot exist.

There are many different types of value. Therefore, in order to prevent misinterpretation and error in acting on the basis of a value estimate, it is most important that the purpose of the valuation assignment be clearly stated in the letter of transmittal as well as in the body of the appraisal report, and that a definition of value be fully expressed as a guide to action by the reader or client to whom the report is submitted.

Two basic ways in which value can be expressed are:

1. The power of a good or service to command other goods or services in exchange.
2. The present worth of future rights to income.

Probable price is the price a property is likely to bring within a given time frame and the economic environment in which the sale is expected to occur.

Value in use is the value of a property for a specific use, which usually is its present use. Such use may be for a particular designed use for which the property is presently being used or for a suboptimal use which entitles the property for preferential tax treatment.

REVIEW QUESTIONS

1. Explain how a property can have one value for an individual but a different value for the public in general.
2. What does the term "equilibrium price" mean in the context of market-determined value?
3. Why is it necessary for the appraiser to understand fully and state clearly the specific value sought in an appraisal report?
4. List the key components of the market value definition used by financial institutions.
5. Discuss how a knowledge of value characteristics is useful in appraising real property.
6. Critique the market value concept, setting forth both its strengths and weaknesses.

READING AND STUDY REFERENCES

ENTREKEN, HENRY C. "Are We Really Seeking Market Value?" *The Appraisal Journal* 48, no. 3 (July 1980), pp. 428–431.

HARRIS, THOMAS B., JR. "What Is Market Value Today?" *The Real Estate Appraiser and Analyst* 51, no. 3 (Fall 1985), pp. 66–67.

HARRISON, HENRY S., and BARBARA J. KAYE. "A New Appraisal Dilemma: What Is Actual Cash Value?" *The Appraisal Journal* 52, no. 3 (July 1984), pp. 348–355.

KORPACZ, PETER F., and RICHARD MARCHITELLI. "Market Value: A Contemporary Perspective," *The Appraisal Journal* 52, no. 4 (October 1984), pp. 485–493.

PENNELL, CARROLL E., II. "The Role of the Professional Appraiser in the 1980's," *The Appraisal Journal* 49, no. 2 (April 1981), pp. 205–213.

RATCLIFF, RICHARD U. Chapters 3 and 4, "The Physical Foundations of Real Estate Value," and "The Locational Basis of Real Estate Value," *Real Estate Analysis*. New York: McGraw-Hill Book Company, 1961.

SACHS, DAVID. "The Insurance Appraisal," *The Appraisal Journal* 53, no. 3 (April 1985), pp. 244–248.

WENDT, PAUL F. Chapter 1, "What Is Value?" *Real Estate Appraisal: Review and Outlook*. Athens: University of Georgia Press, 1974.

WILLIAMS, THOMAS P., and ROLAND D. NELSON. "The Dilemma of Defining Liquidation Value," *The Appraisal Journal* 52, no. 1 (January 1984), pp. 132–135.

2
History and Importance of Value Thought

Learning Objectives

After reading this chapter, you should be able to:

- Trace the key contributions to value theory made by early value thinkers
- Relate the early theories of value to contemporary appraisal practice
- Appreciate the evolution of valuation theory and techniques advocated since the early part of this century
- Better appreciate the relative merits of present valuation procedures in view of the support and criticism each has received over the years

Development and progress in any art or science depends heavily on the knowledge that accumulates throughout history. In a way, we must stand on the shoulders of those leaders in a given field who have gone before us in order that we may raise our sights beyond the horizon of present-day knowledge and perfect the application of established principles and practices.

The field of valuation has a rich history. Much of the value thought that has developed over the past centuries is of significance today, and an understanding of the history of this thought is essential for those who seek professional status as real estate appraisers. It is the purpose of this chapter to trace the landmarks of value thought and to demonstrate their impact on prevailing methods and theories in the field of property valuation.

The concept of value as a ratio measuring the significance of goods or services demanded in exchange for other goods or services dates back to the Middle Ages. Religious beliefs, moral customs, and philosophical reasoning influenced the measures and standards by which people judged the fairness of servitude, trade, or barter as practiced among themselves. St. Thomas Aquinas, in his greatest work, *Summa Theologica* (1266–1273), as translated from Latin, speaks of true value and just price. To sell a thing for more than its worth he regarded as immoral. Economic motives were thus subjected to ethical scrutiny. To this day we find social, political, and other nonmarket measures influencing the thoughts of people, judges and jurors who are called on to rule what constitutes fair, true, real, sound, or just value, especially in the compulsory taking of property as in "eminent domain" proceedings or in instances where there is absence of unimpeded trade and exchange.

MERCANTILISM

The first organized theory of value is attributed to a group of thinkers and writers known as *mercantilists*. Under the theory of *mercantilism*—which held sway for nearly three centuries before the American Revolution in 1775—the power and well-being of a nation depended on ever-increasing stocks of gold and silver or bullion and the maintenance of a favorable balance of export-import trade. Manufacturing and employment of productive labor (for exportable goods) were encouraged in order to increase national wealth through international barter. The goal of mercantilists in guiding and shaping economic policy was to strengthen and increase the status of national and military power. By edict or decree, exports were encouraged and imports discouraged in order that a greater share of the world's stock of precious metals might be secured by the individual nation as a measure of national power and security.

During the sixteenth, seventeenth, and part of the eighteenth centuries (the mercantilistic period in the history of trade), a transition took place from religious, moral, and philosophical concepts of value to pseudo-economic concepts based on intrinsic and extrinsic values. The latter constituted *objective value* as molded by the forces of market supply and demand, whereas *intrinsic value* was a measure of the objects' inherent utility to render service or satisfaction in use. Development, too, of the natural sciences gave rise to a "natural" value based on competitive forces in place of "just" value that primarily rested on philosophical and moral supports. The mercantilists also emphasized production rather than distribution of wealth, and counted merchants among the best and most profitable members of the commonwealth.

Although mercantilism as an economic policy is long outdated, the theory underlying this nationalistic value and power concept is still very relevant. The relative international power status of a nation continues to be basic not only to the welfare of its individuals but also to the value of the goods and services it trades in the open market. Appraisers as well as economists should pay careful heed to data that measure national well-being and prestige in terms of the balance of international trade and the value of domestic currency. These and other economic measures such as employment, fiscal policy, and inflation should be carefully observed in order to be alert to changes that influence property value.

THE PHYSIOCRATS

A revolt against mercantilism, with its emphasis on balance of trade, wealth, power, and frequent national wars, took place in France. François Quesnay, a brilliant court physician to Louis XV, undertook at the monarch's request a study of the production and distribution of the national wealth. As a by-product of this study—and to support his findings—Quesnay conceived his famous *tableau economique*, in which the production, distribution, and circulation comprising the economic activity in France was diagrammatically demonstrated. Quesnay is recognized as the founder of the *physiocratic school*, which is credited with laying the groundwork for the study of economics as a science as well as for the related field of political economy.

The physiocrats effectively demonstrated that production rather than trade constituted the life of a nation and that trade in fact was a "sterile," derived, and secondary economic activity depending wholly on that nation's vigor, strength, and volume of production. In the eighteenth century this production was principally agricultural in character and later writers, beginning with Adam Smith, labeled the physiocratic theory as the "agricultural system."

It is interesting to note that the physiocrats did not regard value as intrinsic or inherent in things. Further, the concepts of price and value were accepted as interchangeable terms, both reflecting a market price that could far exceed the cost of production. Generally, the physiocratic theory may be viewed as a revolt against trade and the role attributed to nonproductive (money) wealth.

Study of physiocratic economic doctrine is rewarding to a student of appraising, since it reveals historical support for the productivity theory of value and the application of the capitalized net operating income approach as a measure of value.

CLASSICAL ECONOMICS

No attempt will be made here to discuss the writings of all those individuals in many nations who contributed to the science of economics as it developed after the publication of Adam Smith's *Wealth of Nations* in 1776. Emphasis will be placed rather on the individuals and the important theories that brought about the evolution of the concept of value specifically.

Classical economics and the development of early value theory were chiefly founded on the lectures and writings of Adam Smith, Thomas Malthus, and David Ricardo. In fact, Adam Smith is often called the founder of economics as a science. Although this is not strictly true, he was nevertheless the first to bring together in one comprehensive volume a logical and well-written treatise on the operation of those economic forces that create value and control the well-being of a nation. Smith effectively reasoned that labor constituted the foundation of national wealth, and that the *value* of any good or service is equal to the quantity of labor that it allows its owner to purchase or command. Smith's greatest contribution to economics as a science was his analytical study of the impact of the division of labor and his logical development of the price system in which exchange value was the center of economic life. Even though the importance of land and capital as factors of production was minimized by Smith, his *barter* definition of value ("the power of a good to command other goods or labor services in exchange") remains valid to this day.

Two other significant contributions to modern value theory were made by Adam Smith. First, he stressed the important distinction between "value in use" and "value in exchange." He logically demonstrated that it was only when the utility of a service or good was accompanied by conditions of scarcity and demand that exchange or market value could arise. His second important contribution to value thought was the noteworthy distinction between the concepts of "market value" and "market price." Market (or "natural") value undoubtedly referred to "normal" prices that covered long-term costs of wages, rent, and profit. Market prices—to the extent that such differed from natural prices—reflected short-run influences exerted by temporary forces of scarcity or monopoly. To Smith, value was basically a cost-of-production theory. Since technological changes were slow in developing during the eighteenth century, it was left to later thinkers to stress the importance of *replacement cost* rather than *reproduction cost* as a better and more reliable measure of value.

The optimistic outlook of Adam Smith—that the uncontrolled economic interests of the individual (the laissez-faire economy) will best tend to increase the wealth of nations—was given a pessimistic twist by his classical-theory successors. Malthus, for example, was to gain prominence with a startling theory—that the world's natural population growth would eventually outstrip the possible and effective growth of its food supply. The tendency for humanity to increase in number geometrically, as compared with the arithmetic increase in agricultural production capacity, forecast a dire economic state at low subsistence levels for society at large unless artificial measures could be taken to check the birthrate. Although technological developments in the century following Malthus' writing appear to have disproved his population theory, modern economists—in pointing to present-day population growth problems in China, India, and even in much of the Western world—find Malthus' scholarly analysis of population growth tendencies essential to a better understanding of current economic theory and practice.

In the development of value thought, Malthus was the first to work out a theory of underconsumption. He warned that production does not create its own demand (as held by Adam Smith and Ricardo) and that overproduction or underconsumption may in fact create market gluts. The economic experience during the deep business depressions of later years provided not only the validity of Malthus' early theory but also his deep understanding of economic phenomena. Malthus, too, made a noteworthy contribution to a better understanding of the role of *rent* as a price-determined (surplus) return to the landowner and not, as held by Adam Smith, a price-determining cost of production. This rent theory was enlarged upon and refined by his contemporary and friend David Ricardo.

The residual theory of land value as taught today had its beginning in David Ricardo's work, *Principles of Political Economy and Taxation*. Although Malthus in prior writings stressed the importance of soil quality as a rent-producing source of income, it was Ricardo who developed the theory that long-term prices (value) equaled the cost of production at the marginal point where the last and poorest land was brought into cultivation. On this marginal soil (no-rent land) the price of the product exactly equaled the cost of labor and the cost of capital. Thus the greater productivity possible where more fertile land was employed yielded a surplus, or land residual return—*rent*—which accrued to the landlord. With an ever-expanding population and the need to bring poorer and less desirable land into production, increased costs of production would cause prices to rise, thus yielding an ever-higher return to the better and relatively more fertile lands.

Rent as defined by Ricardo was the excess payment over the amount necessary to bring land into production and consisted of that portion of total income paid to the landlord for the original and indestructible powers of the soil. In analyzing this residual earning capacity of land, Ricardo developed the theory of the interacting margins of intensive and extensive development of land that is valid and important in land utilization studies to this day. Where (after "apparently" full capacity of land use) it was possible to make the land more productive by an expenditure of additional units of labor or capital, and by doing so produce an excess of income above that derived where like amounts of labor or capital were expended on adjacent land of like or inferior quality, then the more intensive or vertical use of land would produce a higher residual rent than could be realized by extensive or horizontal land utilization. This theory of the interactions of margins in the intensive and extensive utilization of land is of vital importance presently whenever appraisers are charged with the responsibility to ascertain the highest and best use of land, as will be more fully developed in the following chapter.

The rather cold and dismal picture of an "economic man" struggling for bare subsistence was disputed by later writers and critics of the classical school of economics. Two writers who took exception to the pessimism of Malthus and Ricardo were the French economist Frédéric Bastiat (1801–1850) and the American writer Henry Carey. Both were optimists who saw a great future, with humanity enjoying the wonders of bountiful nature. To Bastiat, value was measured not by the labor expended but rather by the labor *saved* through effective use of investment capital. The harmony he saw in the economic system was later attacked by socialistic writers such as Karl Marx as a theory of exploitation of the labor class and a means to perpetuate the class struggle.

Carey's optimism sprang from the seemingly limitless economic opportunities that were open to all in the new and virgin territory of America. He is best known for taking exception to Ricardo's theory of rent, which was based on the extensive utilization of successively poorer (marginal) land. Carey, on the contrary, held that the poorest land was generally cultivated first and that better and more fertile land was reached as population growth made clearing of forest lands and draining of river-bottom land a necessity. Carey's theory, overinfluenced by the special and short-run conditions peculiar to virgin territory, had no lasting impact or influence on the development of value thought.

An attempt to restate the classical school of economic thought and to humanize the theory of political economy was made by a brilliant and clear-thinking writer, John Stuart Mill. Mill agreed with Adam Smith to the "truck and barter" concept of the power of a good to command other goods in exchange.

In his book *Principles of Political Economy*, published in 1848, Mill differentiates between *normal* value and market price. The concept of value, he reasoned, is set and determined at the lowest point of profitable production cost, whereas market price may be higher because of temporary or disturbed market situations. Since a rise in price above normal value will increase the supply of goods, an equilibrium of price and value is bound to be established over the long run of economic activity.

Mill was also the first economist to use the term "unearned increment" as applied to rising land values. Ascribing this increment in value to social (increased population) causes rather than a landlord's capital improvements, he favored the taxing of such excess and unearned windfalls of value. This, at the time, appealing mechanism to establish a more equitable distribution of wealth was readily supported by other welfare economists, and sparked a political campaign for a single (land) tax and the ultimate public ownership of land. The implementation of such a tax was espoused dramatically as the true remedy of economic injustice by Henry George in his well-known book *Progress and Poverty—The Remedy*, published in 1879. The fallacy of a single tax as well as the error of the classical school to take a minimum market demand for granted was belabored by the later Austrian School of Economics.

A further significant contribution to the development of value thought was made by the German estate owner and economist Johann Heinrich von Thünen. In his book, published in 1826, entitled *Der Isolierte Staat* (The Isolated State), von Thünen improved on Ricardo's rent theory by introducing the effect of economic location. Although largely hypothetical, von Thünen's writings offered a valuable study of how the economy of a region is affected by its distance from the imaginary city and by changes in prices and taxes. Von Thünen was the first economist to treat clearly and systematically the influence of distance from the marketplace on the cost and production of agricultural economics. Stress was laid in his writings on the interacting forces of intensive and extensive land utilization. Von Thünen pointed out that as an intensive utilization of land near villages caused the cost of production to rise, extensive utilization of land at more distant places became profitable. The cost of transportation served as a balancing factor between the extensive and intensive margins of land use. Thus, even at equal fertility, rent as a measure of land value was imputed to location in reference to marketability for the products in demand. Von Thünen laid some of the groundwork on which the marginal utility economists in later years built their theory of value. He is also recognized as the founder of the economic theory of agriculture, which is based on land location and the market theory of supply and demand.

THE AUSTRIAN SCHOOL OF ECONOMICS

The classical economists conceived value to be influenced and determined by the cost of production. The nature of the economy prevailing at the close of the eighteenth century caused classical writers to take the demand for a product largely for granted. Evolution in production and the increasing importance of product utility gave rise to a new theory, and school, of economic psychology, founded in Austria by a trio of writers: Karl Menger (1840–1921), Friedrich von Wieser (1851–1926), and Eugene von Böhm-Bawerk (1851–1914). These writers developed the Austrian or *marginal utility* theory of economics which greatly influenced economic thought for nearly half a century.

The shortcomings of the classical school in overemphasizing one extreme of economic analysis—production—were overcompensated for by the Austrian-school adherents to the other extreme of economic analysis—demand. Menger, in fact, held that the value of any good or product was determined by the marginal utility of the last unit essential to meet demand irrespective of the cost necessary in its production. The principal weakness of the utility theory, when judged with hindsight, rested on its failure to distinguish the effects on value of both short-run and long-run economic tendencies and market forces as influenced by supply and demand. Considering short-run market conditions alone, however, the dominant role of utility as a concept of value unquestionably must be acknowledged.

Another important contribution to economic analysis made by the Austrian school was the theory of *imputation*. As logically presented by von Wieser, the value of the whole (product) in essence is derived or inferred from the value of the respective component parts. The theory of imputation served to explain the distribution of the value product—income—over the factors of production as measured by rent, wages, and profits. Von Böhm-Bawerk further refined the utility theory by developing a *market-merger* measurement (a market synthesis) of the individual scales of consumer preferences for market goods. *Market price* was held to be a compromise of marginal preferences supported by the subjective valuation of buyers and sellers. Von Böhm-Bawerk was also the first to develop a logical and practical theory of interest. He conceived *interest* to be a measure of time preference for the immediate use or consumption of capital, and *present value* as a discounted sum of future rights to capital income. This Austrian-school theory thus became the cornerstone of the present utility or income concept as a measure of economic value.

Since value from the individual point of view is largely subjective in character, it follows that utility in a sense "sanctions" sacrifice and thus the cost of production of a good or service. The weakness of this applied theory as espoused by the Austrian school rests chiefly in the concept that costs have no price-determining importance. The pendulum of economic theory marking the actions of the classical school had by the beginning of the twentieth century reached the extreme reaction where value was explained by a search for the greatest utility at the least possible sacrifice.

The important and lasting impact on value theory made by the Austrian or utility school of economics was principally the importance that it placed on the *human* or *demand* concept of value. People, it was argued, in the final analysis determine value—not objects or things. Since the wishes and economic needs of people are given expression on the demand side of the economic equation, the pendulum of value reasoning swung to the opposite extreme of that held by the adherents of the classical school of value thought.

THE NEOCLASSICAL AND EQUILIBRIUM SCHOOL
OF ECONOMICS

The need for a reappraisal of economic principles grew steadily greater in a world becoming increasingly mechanistic and industrial in character. Alfred Marshall (1842–1924), a brilliant, scholarly individual, trained for the ministry in his youth. Drawn into economic studies by the widespread existence of poverty and exploitation nurtured by monopolistic competition, he dedicated his life to economic teaching and writing and brought his influential concepts to the world's attention in his book *Principles of Economics*, first published in 1890. Alfred Marshall is best described as the father of modern economic thought and analysis.

Recognizing the importance and validity of the utilitarian concepts of value, Marshall reintroduced with diagrammatic skill the importance that production costs exert in affecting an equilibrium of market value in the interplay of the forces of supply and demand. Marshall expertly likened the underlying causes and value influences of cost versus marginal utility (or demand) to the functions served by the blades of a pair of scissors. Each blade, he reasoned, is important, but both are needed to effect smooth and efficient cutting. This balance or interplay of economic forces in the determination of value as seen by Marshall caused his teachings to be called the *equilibrium school*.

Another noteworthy contribution to economic analysis made by Marshall was the development of a *dynamic* as opposed to a *static* theory of value. He effectively demonstrated that the separation and study of any given economic force or cause under the doctrine "everything else remaining equal" was fraught with pitfalls and errors of logic. This he made clear by referring to the position and gravity force interplay of billiard balls in a glass bowl. The removal of any one of the balls in a bowl would bring about a realignment and repositioning of the remaining balls. Modern textbooks on appraising stress the Marshallian theory of value by emphasizing the importance of correlating the social, political, and commercial activities of individuals and society in the final determination of value. The impact of changes in the purchasing power of money, in economic potential and social prosperity, in population growth and composition, and finally, in fashions, tastes, and habits of society all influence the forces of supply and demand and the relative prices or values at which goods and services can be exchanged.

After its publication in 1890, Marshall's *Principles of Economics* served as the bible of economic theory in all of the leading universities for nearly a generation. It was left to later economists—identified with the neoclassical school—to build on the equilibrium theory in areas of applied economics related to business, industry, and commerce. Development of economic thought as deduced from the study and operation of the business cycle theory and the imperfect, or monopolistic, competition theory was a task left to later writers such as Joan Robinson, A. C. Pigou, Edward Chamberlain, Dennis H. Robertson, and John Maynard Keynes.

EARLY TWENTIETH-CENTURY VALUE THEORY

The periodic impact on employment, consumption, capital flow, interest, prices, and value caused by variations in the business cycle as measured by economic booms, recessions, and depressions logically led to a restudy of "traditional" economic theory in the light of social welfare and public policy. Paving the way for current value theory and practice was the scholarly contribution made by Wesley Clair Mitchell in the field of business cycles.[1] Based on extensive and analytical research into the causes and effects of cyclical business behavior, Mitchell drew the substantiated conclusion that cyclical business behavior was not due to accident or acts of God but rather to the inevitable results of the unrestricted workings of the economic system within the framework of capitalistic society. Mitchell's studies exploded the theory of an economic norm, or equilibrium, and strengthened the acceptance of an ever-changing norm in accordance with the economic principle of change and the resultant integration and disintegration of economic components—with the passage of time. To Mitchell, an equilibrium as conceived by the classical and Austrian schools of economics was nonexistent. He saw instead a continual cumulative change from one phase of a business cycle to another. Thus a boom contains seeds of recession that lead to a depression, and the latter contains seeds of prosperity that bring recovery and a recurring boom.

Another shock to traditional classical and neoclassical economics was administered by the influential writings and teachings of John Maynard Keynes. Keynes made far-reaching contributions to the theories of consumption, employment, savings, interest, and investment. Specifically, Keynes rejected the equilibrium concept as conceived by the classical and neoclassical schools even where applied to dynamic economic society. Keynes demonstrated that in a rising economy, the propensity to consume diminishes as individual incomes climb to higher brackets. Conversely, the propensity to save increases proportionately. Thus Keynes held that underconsumption rather than overproduction was the basic cause of lasting depressions. To prevent money hoarding by saving, he advocated a fiscal policy that would encourage investment and plant expansion to increase employment and consumption in times of economic stress. Conversely, at "full employment" the reverse fiscal policy is called for; savings are encouraged by rising interest rates (tight-money policy) to avoid or at least mitigate inflation. The Keynesian theory of full employment and deficit financing where necessary to maintain maximum productive capacity had significant influence on economic and political policies throughout the world.

After almost four decades of experimentation with fiscal and economic policies on a national level, Keynesian economic theory, designed to adjust the forces of supply and demand, became a firm and nationally accepted policy. The operations of the national economy, however, at least as far as total investment, employ-

[1] Mitchell's pioneer works were *Business Cycles* (Berkeley: University of California Press, 1913) and *Business Cycles, the Problem and Its Setting* (New York: National Bureau of Economic Research, Inc., 1927).

ment, and money-spending power are concerned, can no longer be left to an uncontrolled laissez-faire system. In fact, the latter system lacked a stabilizer or an economic thermostat designed to adjust planned savings and investment at a level to maintain "full employment." To achieve a feasible equilibrium level of income and production and to safeguard the purchasing power of the dollar, government fiscal and political policy until the early 1980s attempted to stabilize the national economy by

1. Changing tax rates with a rise or fall in national income.
2. Increasing or decreasing public expenditures to "heat" or "cool" the economy.
3. Priming the economic pump in times of recession through payments of unemployment compensation and increased welfare (social security) transfer.
4. Providing subsidies through farm-aid programs.
5. Establishing financial aids or interest rate control to encourage or discourage corporate and family savings.

A new generation of economists in the 1970s began to question the accuracy of Keynesian doctrine with regard to unemployment, fear of saving, and its unjustified faith in government intervention. Much of this doctrine has been replaced by what has come to be known as "supply-side" economics. These economists hold that Keynesian thinking has increased unemployment and depressed savings in part by relying too much on central government. Savings have been depressed to the lowest level among industrialized nations in recent years because of

1. Tax rules that penalize savings.
2. A social security program that makes saving virtually unnecessary for the majority of the population.
3. Credit market rules that encourage large mortgages and extensive consumer credit while limiting the rate of return available to the small saver.
4. Perennial government deficits that absorb private saving and thereby shrink the resources available for investment.[2]

Since a stabilized economy also promotes a stabilized value for real and personal property, the appraiser must know and study government socioeconomic activity, which now serves as the fifth and "steering" wheel that controls and directs the wheels of production—land, labor, capital, and entrepreneurial management—on which the capitalistic value system is dependent.

[2]Martin Feldstein, "The Retreat from Keynesian Economics," *The Public Interest* (Summer 1981); reprinted in *Annual Editions Economics 82/83*, Glen Besson and Reuben S. Slesinger, eds. (Guilford, Conn.: The Dushkin Publishing Group, Inc., 1982), p. 125.

CONTRIBUTIONS OF VALUATORS AND VALUATION THEORISTS

The term *theory* means "a belief," "an unproven assumption that nevertheless is plausible." Further, theories concerned with real estate value may be thought of as plausible and generally accepted principles that explain phenomena affecting the value of real estate. Although complex at times, the means used to predict or derive an estimate of value are better classified as procedures and processes—and not as valuation theories.

The time span for the development of real estate value theory is divided into three eras. The first period extends roughly from 1906 through 1944. The second period is the post–World War II era extending to the early 1960s. The final era extends to the present.

1906–1944

Pioneering work on the related topics of capital value and income capitalization was carried out by Irving Fisher shortly after the turn of the century. He clearly enunciated several key concepts in his book in 1906. He wrote "The rate of interest acts as a link between income-value and capital-value." He also stated that "value is simply the present worth of the future income from the specified capital."[3] He correctly observed that present worth still could be calculated even if the income was level, variable, or accrued continuously or intermittently.

Fisher also presented an early expression of highest and best use theory, which over the years has been a conceptual cornerstone of appraising. His early version made use of an agricultural model wherein the highest capitalized value was viewed as the optimum land use.

Frederick Babcock's initial book, *The Appraisal of Real Estate*, was published at this time (1927). Babcock observed that there is no absolute iron-clad method of computing real estate values.[4] Later with the founding of real estate appraisal societies, the admirable effort to elevate appraisal standards often froze both appraisal thinking and technique. The aversion to depart from accepted dogma also has stunted experimentation and the advance of individualized value problem solutions. Even in the 1920s Babcock advocated different processes for different classes of property; seldom were all three of the traditional approaches to value thought to be necessary.

During the 1920s and 1930s, there was a propensity to refer to appraising as a science. Depth and corner reference tables and curves were devised for assessment of lots. It was considered "another important fundamental principle of scientific appraising to separate land and building values."[5] State law required this

[3]Irving Fisher, *The Nature of Capital and Income* (New York: The Macmillan Company, 1906), p. 202.

[4]Frederick M. Babcock, *The Appraisal of Real Estate* (New York: The Macmillan Company, 1927), p. 2.

[5]W. L. Prouty, Clem W. Collins, and Frank H. Prouty, *Appraisers and Assessors Manual* (New York, 1930), p. 13.

separation in most states and it was held that common sense should require it elsewhere. Land values and building values were judged by Babcock to be subject to entirely different conditions and any composite appraisal method would be both illogical and inequitable. Not all appraisers agreed with this notion.

Despite having devoted considerable effort to present value theory, Frederick Babcock saluted the market comparison approach in at least two important ways:

1. Value is a market phenomenon and the market approach cannot be avoided; and it is necessary to translate future productivity into present value, by discovering how the typical and informed market translates such factors into present value.[6]
2. The presence of a quantity of conveyances does not necessarily connote fair market value. Thus Babcock held that the warranted price should dictate market value, not mere sales.[7]

Later in the 1960s, there was much debate about probable value, the avoidance of point value estimates, and the strong logic to expressing estimated value within a specified range. Babcock in his landmark book on measuring the accuracy of an appraisal held that the mathematics of probability should be used and the estimated value would be given along with upper and lower brackets within which the value was situated.[8]

Babcock, in estimating accrued depreciation, relied chiefly on accounting methods such as sum-of-years' digits, sinking fund, and Hoskold's formula.

The depreciated cost approach would continue to be under attack even to the present. Babcock, in his 1932 book, quoted the "Standards of Appraisal Practice" of the National Association of Real Estate Boards as follows: "It is unethical for an appraiser to issue an appraisal report on a property in which the total reported value is derived by adding together the market value of the land (or leasehold) as if unimproved, or the value of the land (or leasehold) as if improved to its highest and best use, and the reproduction cost of the improvements less accrued structural depreciation."[9] There nevertheless are two principal merits of gaining a knowledge of the actual cost of a new or proposed structure. These are to ascertain if (1) the required yield is achievable and (2) the investment exceeds the value as revealed by income and transfer data.

Later, Babcock voiced renewed criticism of the cost approach by saying that it was suspect. He further chastised appraisers for falling back on it when there

[6]F. M. Babcock, "Common Errors in Appraisal Method—An Analysis," *National Real Estate Journal* (November 24, 1930), p. 17.

[7]*Ibid.*, p. 15. An excellent source of information related to changes in the income approach used in this chapter and recommended to the reader is James H. Burton, *Evolution of the Income Approach* (Chicago: American Institute of Real Estate Appraisers, 1982).

[8]F. M. Babcock, *Valuation of Real Estate* (New York: McGraw-Hill Book Company, 1932), p. 532.

[9]*Ibid.*, pp. 178–79.

was an alleged lack of market data. He wrote: "If we find difficulty in applying a correct process, we cannot improve the valuation by using an incorrect one." He was also critical of the correlation phase of the appraisal process. Babcock went so far as to state that this practice was "dishonest and disgracefully misleading."[10]

Babcock stated that cost and value were distinct. Replacement cost was not, in itself, valuation and was considered an incorrect approach to value. Unlike later writers, who argued against the validity of depreciated cost as a measure of market value, he was against equating cost and value, but later would oppose the depreciated cost approach as well. During the early 1930s, many appraisers favored the depreciated cost approach due to the ease of estimating reproduction costs and the difficulty of making an accurate earnings forecast.

A fairly common practice during the late 1920s and 1930s was where one appraiser found the value of the site and another derived the value of the improvements, with the site value being estimated without any consideration of the improvements, and vice versa. This summation approach violates the principle of consistency as we know it today. During this era a distinction was made between normative, or market price, and "justified price." The latter price differed from the price that people in general were paying and was that price that was justified under the present conditions. Two of Philip W. Kniskern's observations in 1933 still have not been resolved well over a half century later. He argued against the division of either income or value between land and building. Any division between land and building was thought to be arbitrary. He also refuted the practice of valuing the fee estate by valuing the equity and adding that value to the unpaid face amount of the mortgage.[11]

An early contribution to appraisal education and theory was made by Thurston H. Ross, who developed the band-of-investment "theory." Ross first developed this procedure in 1925. Then in 1927, he applied it in an empirical study of properties sold two to five years prior to a consulting study he performed for a Los Angeles bond house. He found the expected mortgage terms and equity yields of recently conveyed real property. Significantly, he may have been the first to consider the effect of mortgage terms as well as equity return on capitalization rates. His formula made no provision for equity or debt recapture. Later, these two items would be included. Not until 1936 did this process have a name. Harry Grant Atkinson, with Ross's consent, labeled it the "band-of-investment theory."[12] Following Ross's 1937 article in *The Appraisal Journal*,[13] appraisers made widespread use of his procedure.

S. Edwin Kazdin in 1944 refined Thurston Ross's band-of-investment method for deriving capitalization rates. Instead of just using the weighted aver-

[10]F. M. Babcock, "The Three Approaches," *The Real Estate Appraiser* (July–August 1970), pp. 5–6.

[11]Philip W. Kniskern, *Real Estate Appraisal and Valuation* (New York: The Ronald Press Company, 1933), p. 476.

[12]Thurston H. Ross, correspondence with James H. Boykin, April 2, 1984.

[13]Thurston H. Ross, "Rate of Capitalization," *The Appraisal Journal* (July 1937), pp. 216–17.

age of mortgage interest rate times the loan-to-value ratio, he recommended use of the mortgage constant rate, which provided for loan interest and amortization.[14] Presumably, the equity yield rate similarly provided for a return of capital to the equity position. Thus a full accounting was made for return on and of capital in the capitalization rate so derived.

An improvement suggested in value theory at this time failed to have a great impact for a number of years. Arthur A. May criticized George L. Schmutz et al.'s built-up capitalization rate method. This rate commenced with a "safe rate" and was adjusted by allegedly recognizing influences on rates caused by management, risk, and illiquidity. May stated, "It is true that the rate reflects these elements, but it is not true that rates can be measured by weighing them."[15] Nevertheless, this discredited method continued in the appraisal literature until 1978.[16]

Post–World War II–1962

This period was a fertile era in refining valuation procedures. The term *most probable market price* was initiated during this period. This term was introduced in a 1953 book by the Italian economist Giuseppe Medici. He seemed to be concentrating on the most probable net income that would be capitalized into value.[17]

Three individuals were especially prominent in this period, and their contributions to value theory would continue for nearly two more decades. Their names were Paul F. Wendt, Leon W. Ellwood, and Richard U. Ratcliff.

Paul Wendt, in addition to offering new ideas on real estate appraising, questioned much of what had already been written. Wendt expressed concern over contemporary capitalization theory being "replete with highly technical mathematical symbolism which in many ways lacks a supporting body of theoretical rationalization." Wendt was a proponent of the gross income multiplier over the capitalized income method. The perceived advantages were: (1) data are usually available in the market; (2) for comparable properties, it removes some of the guesswork implicit in the capitalized income method; and (3) the GIM method is simpler and more easily understood than some variations of the capitalized income approach.[18]

Both he and Babcock agreed that it was an invalid notion that value indications produced by the market comparison, capitalized income, and depreciated

[14]S. Edwin Kazdin, "Capitalization under Present Market Conditions," *The Appraisal Journal* (October 1944), p. 314.

[15]Arthur A. May, *The Valuation of Residential Real Estate* (New York: Prentice-Hall, Inc., 1942), p. 180.

[16]See American Institute of Real Estate Appraisers, *The Appraisal of Real Estate*, 7th ed. (Chicago: AIREA, 1978), pp. 367–68.

[17]Giuseppe Meidici, *Principles of Appraisal* (Ames: The Iowa State College Press, 1953), pp. 29–30.

[18]Paul F. Wendt, *Real Estate Appraisal: A Critical Analysis of Theory and Practice* (New York: Henry Holt and Company, 1956), pp. 145–46.

cost approaches should be equivalent. In a later book Wendt held that such equivalence was ignored in security analysis.[19]

As early as 1950, Richard U. Ratcliff criticized use of the split capitalization rate. He argued that whatever the sources of income, the rate is undifferentiated. Consequently, it is improper to divide the income stream. Any risk affects equally each dollar in the net income prediction. Hence different rates, as applied to land and land improvements, are inappropriate.[20]

In his 1965 book, Ratcliff argued for using the concept of "most probable selling price"[21] (introduced by Giuseppe Medici over a decade earlier). He also suggested that the appraisal process should be a predictive model rather than a measurement process. The only two acceptable devices for predicting value were said to be statistical inference and simulation. He recognized that, ordinarily, insufficient data are available to use the former. Simulation, however, was important in that the appraiser should use the same assumptions and formulas as the investor.[22] The failure to do this caused him to criticize the depreciated cost approach, Inwood, Hoskold, and to a lesser degree, Ellwood's technique.

Several times in his writings, he derides the depreciated cost approach, especially its inability to predict value. Additionally, he saw no merit in either the land or the building residual techniques since they had little relation to investor practices and offered no improvement over the property residual method. On the other hand, investors are strongly inclined to the price/earnings ratio method (GIM).

Ratcliff, in 1964, pointed out that there had been few significant advances in appraisal theory and practice for over 40 years. He was apprehensive about the future professionalization of the real estate appraisal field in large part because due to his or her own efforts the appraiser is recognized as a journeyman capable of having only a single skill—the determination of value. Professionalization will not arrive until the appraiser is more knowledgeable and capable of solving a variety of complex problems on the basis of professional knowledge.[23]

Leon W. Ellwood's widely recognized tables for appraising and financing were first published in 1959. His mathematical procedure for deriving a capitalization rate abruptly departed from prevailing theory. It refuted such accepted techniques as direct capitalization with straight-line recapture, declining annuities, split rates, and much of the accepted thinking on the various forms of ac-

[19]Paul F. Wendt, *Real Estate Appraisal: Review and Outlook* (Athens: University of Georgia Press, 1974), p. 23.

[20]Richard U. Ratcliff, "Net Income Can't Be Split," *The Appraisal Journal* (April 1950), p. 172.

[21]Ratcliff, *Modern Real Estate Valuation: Theory and Application* (Madison, Wis.: Democrat Press, 1965), p. 5.

[22]*Ibid.*, p. 65. See also Ratcliff, "A Neoteric View of the Appraisal Function," *The Appraisal Journal* (April 1965), p. 174.

[23]Ratcliff, "A Restatement of Appraisal Theory," *The Appraisal Journal* (January 1964), p. 53. See also Ratcliff, "The Price and Rewards of Professionalization," *The Real Estate Appraiser* (August 1967), p. 4.

crued depreciation. A principal contribution by Ellwood was to substitute the forecast holding period of a property usually used by investors in place of the much longer and uncertain remaining economic life of the building since there was no need for the latter even if it could be computed.[24] Another break from the past was set forth in Ellwood's contention that property appreciated as well as depreciated. Such future increases in value could be accompanied in a capitalization rate. He also held that property seldom sold for all cash; therefore, the mortgage terms should be considered as well as the probable resale proceeds available to the buyer. This premise built on the previously mentioned work of Ross and Kazdin.

One of the most articulate practitioner-theorists has been James E. Gibbons. At least since 1962, he has stressed the interrelationship between money market behavior and capitalization rates for real estate. His logic has been sound, especially in view of the competition between the money and real estate markets for institutional investment funds. Additionally, Gibbons stressed the importance of appraisers comprehending after-tax equity yields. The validity of after-tax income analysis has been supported from counseling, appraising, and investment analysis perspectives. In 1980, Gibbons developed a methodology for deriving real estate investment equity yields from stock market data. He concluded that bond yields were excellent predictors of mortgage interest rates.[25]

1963–Present

The Wisconsin Colloquium on Appraisal Research convened in March 1963 for the purpose of providing an opportunity to raise fundamental questions, identify weaknesses, and point the way toward the refinement of appraisal theory and practice.

Some key observations brought out in this colloquium were as follows:

1. Human reactions and behavior in response to the value characteristics of real estate are the fundamental bases for the judgment of the appraiser.
2. In arguing for more widespread use of simulation models and multiple correlation analysis, it was stated that fact should be substituted for the fallible judgment of appraisers whenever possible.
3. To properly appraise investment real estate, the appraiser must first understand investor behavior and influences on their behavior, such as financing, tax considerations, and their own investment objectives.
4. Educators at universities had begun to redirect appraisal education to reflect the fact that appraisal is a form of research and thus an analytical func-

---

[24]Leon W. Ellwood, "Analysis and Reconstruction of Operating Statement of Walk-Up Apartments," *The Appraisal Journal* (October 1957), pp. 524–25.

[25]James H. Burton, *Evolution of the Income Approach* (Chicago: American Institute of Real Estate Appraisers, 1982), p. 191, citing James E. Gibbons, "Equity Yield," *The Appraisal Journal* (January 1980), p. 35.

tion. This education should convey an understanding of the business world and land economics.[26]

William Kinnard offered a companion theory to Medici's and Ratcliff's "most probable selling price" in 1966. This was the "most probable use." Kinnard's *most probable use* was defined as the use to which the land and building would most likely be put. It was a market-oriented notion rather than an idealized value maximization model or "abstracted set of conditions unlikely and probably impossible to be achieved."[27]

In his 1972 book, *Valuation for Real Estate Decisions*, Ratcliff contended that appraisal is a behavioral science and that "people establish prices."[28] He quarreled with use of the income approach as currently structured as a valid simulation model in part because

1. The predictions of productivity represent the judgment of expert appraisers and do not necessarily equate with the predictions in actual use by investors in the market.

2. Most of the conventional capitalization models are not actually in general use by investors for many types of income property.[29]

Beginning in the 1970s, greater emphasis was placed on the development of quantitative valuation techniques such as regression analysis. The general lack of observations (rentals and sales) has caused some lack of acceptance of this method for nonresidential appraising. Even for residential appraising, other than mass assessment work, there is some question of absolute reliance on this technique. For example, in 1975 an empirical study of four residential neighborhoods using multiple regression analysis led W. Porcher Miles to conclude that "the accuracy of this method is less than could be expected from a competent appraiser using conventional methods."[30]

With the introduction of sophisticated quantitative and statistical models came the question raised earlier by Ratcliff: Is the appraiser's role to measure or predict value? In either case, it seems necessary that appraisers must have a clear grasp of the intricate interworkings of the real estate markets, land economics, investor motivation, and primary criteria used in real estate decision making.

[26]Richard U. Ratcliff, ed., *The Wisconsin Colloquium on Appraisal Research: Papers and Proceedings* (Madison: Bureau of Business Research and Service, University of Wisconsin, August 1963), pp. 67, 68, 70, and 71.

[27]William N. Kinnard, Jr., "New Thinking in Appraisal Theory," *The Real Estate Appraiser* (August 1966), p. 8.

[28]Richard U. Ratcliff, *Valuation for Real Estate Decisions* (Santa Cruz, Calif.: Democrat Press, 1972), p. 66.

[29]*Ibid.*, pp. 246–47.

[30]W. Porcher Miles, "Applied Multiple Regression Analysis," *The Real Estate Appraiser* (September–October 1975), pp. 29–33.

A topic that received particular attention during the mid-1970s (and up to the present) was equity yields. Different approaches were used in considering this subject. One of the initial equations used excluded direct consideration of equity yields. This was the capitalization equation offered by Ronald E. Gettel: $R = M(f)/\text{DCR}$, where M is the loan-to-value ratio, f is the annual mortgage constant, and DCR is the debt coverage ratio.[31] Nevertheless, this model produced results reasonably close to computed overall capitalization rates. One article reported a difference of only 0.2 percent.[32] Critics faulted this theory because it failed to recognize equity yield. Kenneth M. Lusht and Robert H. Zerbst modified this equation to provide for the present worth of the equity return (based on the long-established property residual method) by taking into account the present worth of the cash flow instead of net operating income, plus the present worth of the equity reversion.[33] During this period, it became popular to extract equity rates from the market and to use the cash flow band-of-investment method to synthesize an overall rate for an appraised property.

Recent contributions have been made in the area of real estate investment analysis by refining discounted cash flow analysis, risk analysis, and by presenting a clearer understanding of internal rate of return. However, much of the theoretical modeling of recent years has lacked consideration of empirical studies, especially regarding investor practices, priorities, and methods used to reach investment decisions. For example, two empirical studies found that investors preferred cash flow as the key financial criterion in analyzing real estate investments.[34] For real estate valuation theorists or practitioners to ignore such findings results in a disservice to clients and reports of little practical value.

Recent breakthroughs in the area of computers have been astounding, especially with microcomputers. The reasonable prices of desktop and portable computers have allowed increasing numbers of appraisers to use this equipment. The power and variety of repetitive functions performed by computers is impressive. Microcomputers, now prevalent in appraisal offices, can perform calculations, store information, process data as directed by the appraiser, print the results in a variety of formats, and serve as word processors, as well as provide the basis for a bookkeeping system.

Microcomputers are used in each of the traditional approaches to value in increasingly sophisticated ways. Electronic spreadsheets can be used to prepare income-expense statements, comparable sales analyses, depreciated cost approach, and multiyear cash flow projections. The electronic worksheet is best applied to repetitious calculations. Other uses of the computer in appraising are

[31]Ronald E. Gettel, "Good Grief, Another Method of Selecting Capitalization Rates," *The Appraisal Journal* (January 1978), p. 90.

[32]James H. Boykin, "Creative Financing in Historical Perspective," *Property Tax Journal* (June 1983), p. 119.

[33]Kenneth M. Lusht, "Inflation and Real Estate Investment Value," *The Real Estate Appraiser and Analyst* (November–December 1979), p. 23.

[34]James H. Burton, *Evolution of the Income Approach,* citing research by Arnold H. Diamond and Robert J. Wiley in the 1970s; see p. 205.

regression analysis for a property having similar characteristics to a fairly large
number of other properties, and retrieval of replacement cost information via telephone services with such firms as Marshall Swift Publication Company and
Bockh Publications.

Unquestionably, the wide availability of microcomputers and software custom designed for real estate analyses will expand appraisal and consulting opportunities over the next decade. Judgment will still be needed by appraisers, but
they will have the potential of judging data superior to those used in the past.

A major change in the manner in which the real estate appraisal profession
was regulated occurred in mid-1991. Based on the failure of numerous savings
and loan associations and problems with faulty appraisals in the 1982–1985 period, Congressional hearings began late in 1985. These hearings produced a report that examined the impact of faulty and fraudulent appraisals on federally
insured financial institutions as well as government agencies.[35] It was found that
although several of the appraisal societies did a respectable job of educating and
policing their members, only a quarter of the nation's real estate appraisers were
affiliated with such professional organizations.

On August 9, 1989, President Bush signed "Title II—Real Estate Appraisal
Reform Amendments," which were intended to protect federal financial and public policy in real estate transactions by establishing specified appraisal standards
that would be subject to effective supervision. Thus, in 1991, there was a shift
away from self-regulation of the minority of appraisers by professional organizations to certification and licensing for all appraisers engaged in the valuation of
property loans insured by federal agencies. The actual regulation of appraisers
was handled by state appraisal boards based on regulations that were in compliance with federal law.

HISTORY OF APPRAISAL ORGANIZATIONS

During the boom years of the 1920s and early 1930s, real estate appraisals were
made on a part-time basis by real estate agents. The lack of expertise of these so-
called appraisers had contributed to a menacing problem of properties being purchased at prices and mortgaged for amounts bearing little relationship to value.
Even after the stock market crash of 1929 and the collapse of real estate values,
this appraisal situation still had not improved; persons appointed to appraise
properties that had gone into receivership lacked an operational knowledge of
value theory.

In an effort to devise national standards of performance and self-regulation
as well as development and application of sound appraisal theory, Henry A.
Babcock became the first chairman of the National Association of Real Estate

---

[35]*Impact of Faulty and Fraudulent Real Estate Appraisals on Federally Insured Financial Insti-
tutions and Related Agencies of The Federal Government.* Hearings Before a Subcommittee of the
Committee on Government Operations, 99th Congress, December 11 and 12, 1985 (Washington,
D.C.: U.S. Government Printing Office, 1986).

Boards Appraisal Division's Committee on Standards of Practice. In 1929, he published the "Standards of Appraisal Practice for Realtors, Appraisers and Appraisal Committees of Member Boards."[36] This division was chartered on July 1, 1932, as the American Institute of Real Estate Appraisers. Three years later, in 1935, the Society of Residential Appraisers (later renamed the Society of Real Estate Appraisers) was organized. Another three years passed and the Appraisal Institute of Canada was formed (1938).

At about the time Babcock was helping to organize the forerunner of the American Institute of Real Estate Appraisers (1929), the American Society of Farm Managers and Rural Appraisers was founded. Yet probably the first real estate appraisal organization to be created was the Royal Institution of Chartered Surveyors in England in 1863. Twenty years later, the New Zealand Institute of Surveyors was founded. During the 1960s and 1970s, several new appraisal groups were formed in this country. The National Association of Review Appraisers was created through a merger of two organizations in 1985. The most recent change in appraisal organizations was the creation of the Appraisal Institute. This 12,000-plus member body resulted from a January 1, 1991 merger of the American Institute of Real Estate Appraisers and the Society of Real Estate Appraisers.

INFLUENCE OF VALUE THEORY UPON APPRAISAL PRACTICE

As stated in the introductory paragraph of this chapter, today's appraiser depends heavily on the body of ideas and knowledge created by past thinkers in the fields of economics, value, and valuation. The value theories briefly outlined here have each contributed a link to the chain of value thought. Value theory and practice as taught by leading appraisal societies today are largely a synthesis of the important ideas and economic concepts developed by leaders of the classical, Austrian, neoclassical, and modern schools of value theory. The three approaches to value applied in current appraisal practice especially reflect the impact of value theory and processes as it has developed over the past two centuries. The depreciated cost approach to value largely follows the teachings of the classical school, with greater emphasis placed perhaps on replacement cost than on reproduction cost—as was the case at the time of Adam Smith. The capitalized income approach in effect is a utilitarian measure of value which yields the present worth of future rights to income without reference to the relevant cost of the agents of production. The market sales comparison approach places emphasis on the short-run market forces of supply and demand, and yields an index of prevailing prices at a given time and place which may or may not equal a measure of long-term, stabilized, or warranted value. These three approaches to value are really three different ways of measuring the same value and are useful as a check one upon the other in judging the accuracy of the end (value) results.

Many of the practices and procedures used today rest on the logical approaches to value problem solving that have been brought forward by practicing

[36]James H. Boykin, "Real Property Appraisal in the American Colonial Era," *The Appraisal Journal* (July 1976), pp. 362–63.

appraisers. Courts, clients, academicians, and appraisers continue to improve appraisal thought and practice by maintaining an inquiring attitude. To understand these value forces better, a firsthand study of the principal writings of the masters in economic and valuation literature, as referenced here, is a "must" for those appraisers seeking attainment of a truly professional status. The evolution of value theory, no doubt, will continue in the future as it has in the past. Alertness and awareness of ever-changing value trends must therefore be the watchwords of the appraisal profession.

SUMMARY

The concept of value as a ratio measuring the significance of goods or services demanded in exchange for other goods or services dates back to the Middle Ages. The first organized theory of value is attributed to a group known as the *mercantilists*, who developed such value theories as objective and intrinsic value; they also emphasized "natural" value in place of "just" value.

The French *physiocrats* effectively demonstrated that production rather than trade constituted the life of a nation and thus established historical support for the productivity theory of value and the application of the capitalized net operating income approach as a measure of value. This school also held that price and value were interchangeable terms.

The three most noted economists in the *classical school* were Adam Smith, Thomas Malthus, and David Ricardo. Smith asserted that the value of any good or service is equal to the quantity of labor that it allows its owner to purchase. He stressed the distinction between "value in use" and "value in exchange" as well as the difference between "market value" and "market price."

Malthus warned that production does not create its own demand and that overproduction or underconsumption may create market gluts. Also, he provided a better understanding of the role of rent as a price-determined return to the landowner.

Ricardo initiated the residual theory of land value. He held that rent was the excess payment over the amount necessary to bring land into production, and it was that portion of total income paid to the landlord for the indestructible powers of the soil.

The *Austrian school of economics* conceived value to be influenced largely by demand. People were thought to determine value, not objects or things. This school introduced the theory of imputation and utility which said that the value of the whole is derived from the value of the respective parts, such as rent, wages, and profits.

The *equilibrium school* was led by Alfred Marshall, who wrote that production costs were important in affecting an equilibrium of market value in the interplay of the forces of supply and demand. He also introduced the concept of dynamic value instead of static value which today takes into account the correlation of social, political, and commercial activities in determining value.

Two influential early twentieth-century economists were Wesley Clair Mitchell and John Maynard Keynes. The former refuted the earlier classical and

Austrian schools' concept of equilibrium. Instead, he saw a continual cumulative change from one phase of a business cycle to another. Keynes demonstrated that in a rising economy, the propensity to consume diminishes as individual incomes climb to higher brackets, and in turn the propensity to save increases proportionately. He held that underconsumption rather than overproduction was the basic cause of depressions.

Real estate valuators and valuation theorists have made significant contributions to the current practice of appraising. An early contributor was Irving Fisher, who introduced ideas on both present value and highest and best use theory. Frederick Babcock claimed that there was no absolute method of computing real estate values. He also held that the cost approach was suspect. Later, Philip Kniskern argued against the division of either income or value between land and building as well as refuted the practice of valuing the fee estate by valuing the equity and adding that value to the unpaid face amount of the mortgage.

Thurston Ross, in his band-of-investment procedure, was the first to consider the effect of mortgage terms as well as equity return on capitalization rates. Paul Wendt questioned contemporary capitalization theory as being overly complex, while supporting the gross income multiplier as an alternative. Another educator, Richard Ratcliff, criticized use of the split capitalization rate and use of the depreciated cost approach. He, along with Giuseppe Medici, used the idea of "most probable selling price" instead of market value. Ratcliff also advocated that the appraisal process should be predictive instead of a measurement process. In the 1950s, L. W. Ellwood refuted such accepted techniques as direct capitalization and many forms of accrued depreciation. Instead, he substituted a shorter investment holding period, recognized that property can appreciate as well as depreciate, and that both mortgage terms and the probable resale proceeds of a property should be considered.

William Kinnard introduced the idea of "most probable use," which is the use to which land and building would most likely be put.

Following the stock market crash and real estate market collapse in 1929, the American Institute of Real Estate Appraisers and the Society of Real Estate Appraisers were organized. During the 1960s and 1970s, several new appraisal organizations came into existence. Following the savings and loan crisis in the mid-1980s which was caused in part by lax appraisal practices, state and federal agencies and boards played a stronger role in the regulation of real estate appraisers.

REVIEW QUESTIONS

1. List and discuss the principal contributions to present-day appraisal practices of each of the early schools of economic thought.
2. Discuss the similarity between the terms "most probable selling price" and "most probable use."

3. Do you agree with the underlying logic of Thurston Ross's band-of-investment method of developing a capitalization rate? Explain your answer.

4. Discuss Frederick Babcock's criticism of the cost approach: "If we find difficulty in applying a correct process, we cannot improve the valuation by using an incorrect one."

5. Discuss the major departures from prevailing valuation procedure made by Ellwood.

6. List and briefly discuss at least five contributions made to the present practice of appraisal procedures in this century, being certain to identify each contributor.

READING AND STUDY REFERENCES

BABCOCK, FREDERICK M. *Valuation of Real Estate.* New York: McGraw-Hill Book Company, 1932.

BOYKIN, JAMES H. "Real Property Appraisal in the American Colonial Era," *The Appraisal Journal* 44, no. 3 (July 1976), pp. 361–374.

BURTON, JAMES H. *Evaluation of the Income Approach.* Chicago: American Institute of Real Estate Appraisers, 1982.

FELDSTEIN, MARTIN. "The Retreat from Keynesian Economics," *The Public Interest* (Summer 1981). Reprinted in *Annual Editions Economics 82/83*, Glen Beeson and Reuben E. Slesinger, eds. Guilford, Conn.: The Dushkin Publishing Group, Inc., 1982, pp. 121–127.

GREER, GAYLON E., and MICHAEL D. FARRELL. Chapter 21, "Contemporary Valuation Techniques," *Contemporary Real Estate: Theory and Practice.* Hinsdale, Ill.: The Dryden Press, 1983.

GRISSOM, TERRY V. "Value Definition: Its Place in the Appraisal Process," *The Appraisal Journal* (April 1985), pp. 217–225.

HURD, RICHARD M. *Principles of City Land Values,* 3rd ed. New York: The Record and Guide, 1911.

KINNARD, WILLIAM N., JR. (ed.) *1984 Real Estate Valuation Colloquium*: A Redefinition of Real Estate Appraisal Precepts and Processes. Boston: Oelgeschlager Gunn and Hain for Lincoln Institute of Land Policy, 1984.

PEARSON, THOMAS D. "Education for Professionalism: A Common Body of Knowledge for Appraisers, Part I: Background and Historical Trends," *The Appraisal Journal* (October 1988), pp. 435–450.

RATCLIFF, RICHARD U. "A Restatement of Appraisal Theory," *The Appraisal Journal* 32, no. 1 (January 1964), pp. 50–67.

WEIMER, ARTHUR M. "History of Value Theory for the Appraiser," *The Appraisal Journal* 28, no. 4 (October 1960), pp. 469–489.

WENDT, PAUL F. *Real Estate Appraisal: A Critical Analysis of Theory and Practice.* New York: Henry Holt and Company, 1956.

WENDT, PAUL F. Chapter 2, "The Development of Appraisal Theory," *Real Estate Appraisal: Review and Outlook.* Athens: University of Georgia Press, 1974.

3
Nature and Principles of Property Valuation

Learning Objectives

After reading this chapter, you should be able to:

- Appreciate the importance of the legal concept of property value
- Understand the principles of real estate valuation and how they are interrelated
- Understand how fee simple ownership of real property may be restricted by public and private limitations
- Discuss the nature and importance of highest and best use as a basis for real estate valuation

Although the history of value thought supports the contention that value is the heart of economics, and that all things of value created or wanted by human beings are objects with which economics as a science is concerned, there are nevertheless valid arguments that "property" valuation is greatly influenced by legal and institutional constraints. The basis for such arguments is the contention that real property and real estate—which are the subjects of valuation—are principally legal and not physical or economic in character. The terms *property* and *estate* denote measures of rights and ownership which are legally identified and constitutionally guaranteed to the true owner under the *allodial*[1] system of land ownership which prevails in the United States.

The legal concept of property value and ownership, as will be demonstrated, is very important. Without a thorough understanding of the nature and character of rights in real property as recognized and supported by law, appraising as a professional practice would not be feasible. In the final analysis, the appraiser is con-

[1]Private land ownership as a basic right is subject to broad governmental limitations, as opposed to ownership under a state-controlled (communistic) or feudal system, under which absolute ownership of land rests with the king or the sovereign government.

cerned not so much with the physical aspects of the property under value study but rather with the possible and legal uses to which the property may be put—under competent ownership and effective management.

WEALTH VERSUS PROPERTY

All tangible and useful things owned by human beings which have attributes of economic value are classified as "wealth." Thus wealth includes all material and physical things controlled and owned by persons to which an economic or monetary scale of value can be applied. *Property*, on the other hand, is an intangible concept, being the right to own or possess wealth and to put it to legal uses if one wishes. Property thus is a legal right that expresses the relationship between owners and their possessions. To illustrate: A 40-acre farm in North Carolina may possess certain given physical characteristics and measurable natural qualities of fertility. These physical facts are known, and the land can rightly be classified as wealth. The value of this farm, however, depends on the legal and permissible uses (property rights) to which this farm may be put. If only cotton can be grown commercially, one value will result; but under corn or truck farming, another and higher value will accrue to the land. If a government allotment makes possible the growing of leaf tobacco, a still higher—and perhaps maximum—farm use value will result. This illustration should make it clear that the appraiser is concerned only secondarily with the physical attributes of wealth. The appraiser's chief and prime interest must be the valuation of rights or property in land and its improvements.

The distinction between wealth and private property can further and more dramatically be illustrated by considering the impact that national decree can transfer (confiscate) the ownership of all land from the estates of individuals to the nation as a whole. Such a shift of ownership actually did occur in Cuba in 1960, and has been national policy in all communistic countries until 1990 when Eastern Europe governments began to loosen their hold on real property. Confiscation of wealth and the shifting of property rights which control this wealth from one person or persons to another or to the state as a whole does not alter the inventory or magnitude of total national wealth, but it does destroy the value of such property (rights) as were vested in the individual. To safeguard Americans from such governmental decrees, the Fifth and Fourteenth Amendments to the Constitution provide that no life, liberty, or property may be taken from anyone without due process of law and without just compensation where such taking is for public use and in the public interest.

THE LEGAL CONCEPT OF PROPERTY

Land is the original and basic factor of production. Without land human beings could not exist. No commodity can be produced and no improvement erected without using land. Land as nature provided it consists of the earth's crust, including the underlying soil which provides life-sustaining fertility and supporting power for structures and other artificial improvements. Legally, possession of a given part of this crust of land includes rights to the control of minerals, gas, and oil below the earth's surface as well as the air space above the ground. Thus the boundaries of any parcel of land extend in the shape of an inverted pyramid from the center of the earth upward to the limits of the atmosphere. Of course, there are certain physical and legal constraints imposed on these boundaries.

Land as originally provided by nature probably no longer exists anywhere on earth. All land has been directly or indirectly modified by human beings—directly by the construction of improvements on the site and indirectly by improvements related to the site, such as access roads, bridges, canals, and parks. Land, together with all improvements that are permanently affixed thereto, is known as *real estate*. Real estate is physical in nature and includes not only land and buildings, but also fixtures. A *fixture* is personal property that is attached or used in such a manner that it is considered to be part of the real estate. The courts generally use four tests in deciding whether an item is a fixture. These are: (1) intention of the parties, (2) express agreement, (3) mode of attachment, and (4) adaptation of item to real estate.

Intention of the parties means what a person exercising ordinary prudence and who is familiar with the subject business, local customs, and the circumstances of the transaction would be expected to believe the parties intended. Express agreement relates to the agreement that the involved parties had regarding the removal of personal property at the end of the agreement, such as a lease. Ordinarily, the item will be viewed as personal property unless its removal will injure the real estate. Mode of attachment holds that if an item is affixed in a manner that allows its removal without injury to the real estate, it probably will be considered as personal property. Although lighting fixtures and furnaces may be removed without injury to the real estate, these are viewed as being fixtures. Adaptation of item to real estate means that if the personal property is attached to improve and make the real estate more valuable, then it is judged to be a fixture. For example, factory machines are held to be fixtures.

Real property is defined as the rights, interests, and benefits associated with the ownership of real estate. Appraisers are responsible for estimating the value of property interests in real estate and not just the physical attributes of real estate. For instance, an assignment may involve estimating the present value of a life estate or an equity or a leasehold interest in real property.

THE "BUNDLE OF RIGHTS"

The largest possible estate in real property is known as *fee simple*. Where such ownership exists to the exclusion of all others, the possessor is said to have the complete *bundle of rights*. That is, the "bundle" contains all the individual interests essential to fee simple ownership, including the right to use or not to use the property, the right to lease all or parts of the property (air rights, surface rights, mineral rights, easements, and rights-of-way), the right to sell or not to sell, and the right to donate or grant the property to others as a gift. Care must be taken by the appraiser to ascertain whether the entire bundle of property rights is to be conveyed by sale or included in the valuation. Since property rights are both separable and divisible, it is likely that the bundle of rights is incomplete—whether by partial sale, lease, or by private or governmental limitation—in which case the value of the property is bound to be affected. The appraiser must determine which property rights have been conveyed for any comparable sale properties as well as those rights to be appraised for the appraised property.

OWNERSHIP LIMITATIONS

All land in the United States—whether owned in *fee simple, fee upon conditions, fee determinable*, or as a *life estate*—is subject to certain government limitations on ownership, imposed for the mutual welfare of all citizens. These limitations fall under[2]:

1. The police power of government.
2. The right of eminent domain.
3. The right of taxation.
4. Escheat to the state.

Police Power

The *police power* is a sovereign power inherent in state government and exercised or delegated by it to the village, city, county, or other governing agency to restrict the use of real property in order to protect the well-being of its citizens. Under police power the rights in property, its use, and occupation may be restricted—without any compensation whatever—when government deems such restrictions necessary in the interest of the welfare, morals, general health, or safety of its citizens. This power protects citizens with regard to city planning and zoning as well as for building and subdivision controls. Regulations of rent control authorities and building, fire, and health departments are exercises of the police power and are in fact limitations on the "use" of land.

Eminent Domain

The right of *eminent domain* is the power inherent in a governmental body to "take" an owner's land, or any part of it (air rights, road easements, etc.) by due process of law, when the necessity arises. Only two requirements must be met: The use must be public, and just compensation must be made to the owner. Whether or not the owner wants to surrender the land makes no difference—nor can the owner set his or her own price. The owner's desires are not considered, but a fair value, fixed, as a rule, by expert appraisers, is paid. Land is obtained for

[2]For a full discussion of real estate interests and ownership, see Chapter 5 of Alfred A. Ring and Jerome Dasso, *Real Estate Principles and Practices*, 10th ed. (Englewood Cliffs, N.J.: Prentice-Hall, Inc., 1985).

streets, parks, public buildings, and other public or social purposes through the exercise of this power.

Taxation

Under the right of taxation, the state levies taxes for its support and for the maintenance of all its varied branches that protect and benefit its citizens. It is fair that citizens should pay for the protection and benefit they receive. Land, because of its permanence and accessibility, is a convenient article to tax and is usually the basis for local taxation. If such taxes, when levied, are not paid in due course the owners may lose their land as the result of tax law enforcement. Taxes, too, are a cost of land use and operations. Where such taxes are excessive, the value of land and its improvements are adversely affected.

Escheat

Under the allodial system *escheat* does not limit land ownership but rather provides for the reversion or escheat of land to the state when an owner of land dies and leaves no heirs or fails to dispose of the land by will. This, however, seldom happens for generally—difficult as it may sometimes be—heirs can usually be found. Since it is not possible to conceive of land becoming "unowned," the law of escheat to the state provides a logical solution. The nonpayment of real estate taxes does not necessarily result in escheat, but is used as evidence of abandonment of property.

In addition to the governmental limitations, real property is often subject to private or contractual limitations on ownership. Such limitations are usually contained in deeds, easements, leases, and in mortgage instruments. Where the bundle of rights is limited, the appraiser must note such restrictions and estimate the effect on value as reflected by typical market operations.

PRINCIPLES OF REAL ESTATE VALUATION

Every field of study and vocation has its principles. These principles provide the underlying basis for endeavors within these fields. Real estate valuation is no different. There are certain principles or rudiments that provide the foundation for the application of knowledge and business experience to valuation situations. It is essential that appraisers master these principles and apply them in their analysis of real property. Although there may be some other influences on the valuation of real estate, the following principles are judged to be of greatest relevance and guidance in its proper valuation.

THE CONCEPT OF HIGHEST AND BEST USE

The principle of highest and best use might well be thought of as the premise or hypothesis upon which an appraisal is based. It is of extreme importance to the accurate valuation of real property. If the appraiser mistakenly judges a property's highest and best use, all subsequent work and analysis in arriving at the property's value is wasted. Suppose, for example, that an appraiser judges the highest and best use of a parcel to be for single-family detached homes when, in fact, it has a potential for garden apartments. Consequently, as a result of this initial error, the appraiser would obtain zoning, construction, rental income and expense, and sales information for single-family homes rather than for the more intensive and valuable use as garden apartments. Thus extreme care must be taken to truly analyze a property at its highest and best use rather than simply including a brief and incomplete statement concerning its optimum use.

Another important aspect of highest and best use is that it is the connecting tissue between external and internal influences on value. That is, in judging a property's highest and best use, it is necessary to consider all pertinent neighborhood and community influences along with the existing or proposed improvements for the site. After having considered these external and on-site influences, an appropriate highest and best use of the site can be reached.

Vacant Site Use

A logical approach to arriving at a site's highest and best use is to begin with the definition of such use. *Highest and best use is defined as that use or succession of available, legal, and physically permitted uses for which there is sufficient demand that produces the highest present site value.* Examining each key word in this definition provides a working guide for the appraiser in his or her property analysis. For example, *succession of uses* implies that there may be an interim or short-term use of the property until such time as market conditions improve sufficiently, possibly rezoning occurs, or public utilities are extended to the site. At this time, a higher and better use can be achieved. *Available uses* implies that the use is achievable rather than speculative or remote. Conceivably higher values may be achieved from given uses, but if it is not possible to achieve such uses in the foreseeable future, they should be excluded from consideration. *Legal uses* direct the appraiser to an examination of both public and private limitations on the use of a site. If there is demand for a use such as highway commercial use but the zoning ordinance prohibits such use and it is extremely unlikely that the necessary rezoning can be obtained, the potential highway commercial uses will not be realized. The same constraint applies to private deed restrictions that prohibit certain uses considered to be incompatible with the subdivided land. Also, a long-term lease may constrain a site from realizing its highest and best use. *Physically permitted uses* deal with the suitability of terrain and shape of the site, as well as its subsoil conditions. Thus it is compelling for the appraiser to consider such physical constraints in order to judge whether a prospective highest and best use would likely be achieved at the site in question. Increasingly, environmental restrictions such as wetlands and toxic-waste contamination must be considered in judging a property's highest and best use.

Sufficient demand is often the critical test for determining whether a site realizes its potential highest and best use. If there are no willing and able buyers, investors, or tenants, a proposed use fails the test of highest and best use. This factor must thoroughly be examined when dealing with proposed construction in overbuilt markets. It is important to consider all of these factors when judging a property's highest and best use.

Often it is desirable to consider several probable highest and best uses. Some of these uses, although initially seeming reasonable, may quickly be set aside due to obvious legal constraints or physical difficulties. Once having eliminated some of the more obvious unsuited uses, the appraiser may project income streams for two or more prospective uses for a given site. As will be considered later in Chapter 18, highest present income is not always the most reliable indication of a site's highest and best use. Different remaining economic lives of the buildings or different building or land capitalization rates can eventually cause a prospective use with a comparatively high gross income to have a lower residual income to the land and, when combined with the higher capitalization rate, also a lower site value.

Duration and Intensity of Site Uses

For any site analysis, it is critical that both the duration and intensity of uses be specified. Some critics might argue that it is difficult to forecast accurately either the holding period for the entire property or the remaining economic life of the site improvements. Although this point is not disputed, nevertheless, the duration of uses must be eventually addressed in an appraisal. There is no better time for this than in the highest and best use section. The necessity of specifying this time period is later considered in the various approaches to value. The intensity of site use simply means that a specific use rather than a generalized use should be specified. For example, rather than state that the highest and best use is residential, the appraiser needs to indicate whether the site has development potential for three dwelling units per acre or 14 units an acre.

It should be remembered that the largest, most expensive improvement is not necessarily the highest and best use of a site. Importantly, the relationship of community, neighborhood, site, and improvements must be considered in order to reach the optimum use and value combination. For example, if the improvements are excessive for the size or location of the site, the accompanying expenses may greatly erode the profitability and value of the underlying site.

Improved Site Use

Generally, highest and best use is thought to pertain to the site as if vacant. There will be instances where the client is interested in knowing the highest and best use of an improved property, which, of course, involves both the site and buildings or for other reasons the owner chooses to retain the present buildings. It may be that the present use cannot be altered due to deed or lease restrictions. Another very important reason for ascertaining the highest and best use of an already improved property is to consider several alternative uses of the property via adaptive use. In such cases, the appraiser will project alternative conversion expenses and then weigh the resulting income against such expenses in order to judge the highest and best use of the upgraded property.

Because labor, capital, and entrepreneurial compensations have priority claims on the income or products of land, only the balance remaining after the due shares to the mobile factors of production (labor, capital, and entrepreneurial compensations) are paid serves as a measure of the earning power of land. Because land receives what is *left* as a *residue* of the total income stream, land earnings are said to be *residual* in character.

The passive nature of land, which causes its income to be residual, makes it of prime importance that land be employed under its *highest and best possible use*. Only under such use can land attain its maximum return of income and hence its maximum value. It must be kept in mind that a given parcel of land may be available for alternative and competitive uses. Nevertheless, a site can have only *one*, or one combination of, highest and best use at a given time. The latter condition would apply to a mixed-use development where each part of the total site would be devoted to a particular use. Contrastingly, the highest and best use of an urban site may be to leave it vacant in order that it may "ripen" into an anticipated use that forms a higher present value than it would under the immediate and alternate uses to which the land might be put. This may be the case, for instance, where a tract of land can be developed for garden apartment purposes, but thorough study has disclosed that the site location will prove ideal as a neighborhood shopping center in three to five years. The proper choice in this instance should be supported by an appraisal study in which the value findings will serve as a guide to appropriate economic action. If the present worth of future rights to income will be higher under a commercial use, allowing for the property being idle during the years of ripening, then this use is found to be the property's highest and best use. Although a site is limited to one or one combination of land use activities at a given time, there may be a series of uses for a site over a specified period of time.

The determination of the highest and best use of a given parcel of land at a given time requires careful study and expert analysis of the social, political, and economic forces that influence land utilization and land income over the economic life of the improvements. Basically, the amount of net income that can accrue to a parcel of land is essentially limited by the *law of diminishing returns*. Under this law employment of additional units of production will yield an increasing residual (net) income to land until a maximum of income per unit of investment is reached, after which diminishing returns set in until a point is reached at which the last unit of input yields only an income great enough to cover its cost with no return to land. It is at this point that the aggregate income to land is highest. By analysis of the current and hypothetical uses to which a site can legally and physically be employed—now and in years to come—the appraiser is able to select that use which will yield to land its highest present value.

The ability of land to absorb additional units of labor and capital profitably is economically classified as land *capacity*. Capacity refers to the volume of labor and capital expenditures. Some sites have the capacity to absorb millions of dollars before the point of negative return to land is reached. Other sites reach maximum capacity on the expenditure of a few thousand dollars. In the illustration shown in Figure 3.1, the capacity of the site is reached on expenditure of labor

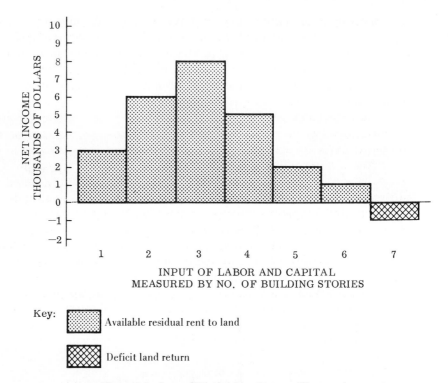

Key:

Available residual rent to land

Deficit land return

Figure 3.1 Law of Diminishing Returns Illustrated

and material sufficient to erect a six-story building. Significantly, however, construction of less than three stories in this instance would constitute an underimprovement, and construction of a higher structure an overimprovement. Either under- or overimprovement will reduce the value of this site.

The construction of a one-story building as shown in Figure 3.1 results in a net income sufficient to cover not only building operating expenditures, but also required earnings to meet interest payments on labor and capital investment plus an excess or residual return (rent) to land in the amount of $3,000. The erection of a second-story unit further increases excess rent income to $6,000. A three-story structure yields $8,000 as excess land income. At this point, and under this selected use, the efficiency of land per unit of labor and capital input is at its highest. Beyond this level, no further intensity of development is warranted. In fact, adding a seventh floor would result in a deficit land income, thus diminishing both land income and property value. The economic loss caused by an overimprovement of a subject property is chargeable, as will be demonstrated later, as external obsolescence to the building improvements and not to the value of the land. For the latter's value logically is established under the highest and most profitable use.

A study of land capacity for just one particular use, however, is insufficient in a determination of highest and best use. The appraiser also needs to consider the efficiency of land return in relation to land capacity under alternative types of uses. Two sites with equal capacity may differ in efficiency of land return and hence differ in value. Sites developed for apartment housing often have greater capacity (to absorb construction dollars profitably) than commercial sites in downtown areas. However, the greater efficiency of business property may more than offset the lack of land capacity. Whereas *capacity* refers to the ability of land to absorb capital outlays profitably, *efficiency* refers to a measure of profitability as represented by the ratio of dollar input (capital improvements) to dollar land output in terms of residual income.

The more efficient land use, as shown in Figure 3.2, is to improve the property with a three-story office building. Zoning permitting, the residual rent for an office building substantially exceeds that realized for an apartment development. The available residual rent under the apartment use is $8,000 as compared with $10,000 under the more efficient office use. Assuming the invested capital to construct both the apartment building and the office complex is $100,000, then the comparative returns are 8 percent ($8,000/$100,000) and 10 percent ($10,000/$100,000). The higher the ratio of output (return) in relation to input (invested capital), the greater the efficiency of land use. As demonstrated, the highest and

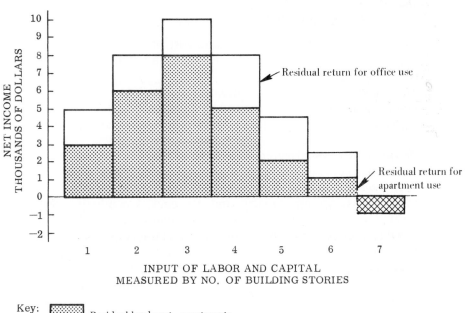

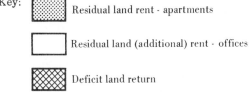

Figure 3.2 Residual Land Rent

best use of a site is not necessarily that use which permits development to the greatest capacity nor that use with the greatest efficiency. It is rather that use in which the composite results of capacity and efficiency of land use brings the greatest net return that forms a basis for the land's highest present value. Only by careful study and analysis of permissible and economically feasible alternative land uses can the appraiser accurately determine the highest present value of a site.

Once the highest and best use of a site has been determined, and the value under such use fixed, it stands to reason that the misuse of a site either through over- or underimprovement cannot subtract from this value. Human errors arising from improper land utilization must be charged against the value of the improvements as a form of functional or external obsolescence (depreciation). To illustrate: Assume that a two-story apartment building costing $600,000 is placed on a site worth $100,000. The total value of land and building upon completion proves to be only $650,000, then the value of the component parts is derived as follows:

Total value	$650,000
Value of land under highest and best use	100,000
Value of improvement	$550,000

The difference between the building cost of $600,000 and building value of $550,000 is a monetary loss (depreciation) in the amount of $50,000 due to an overimprovement.

To restate the land utilization principle: Land value is based on residual land income under the highest and best use of the land. Under any other use both income and value diminish and the value loss incurred constitutes "built-in" depreciation. *Only under the highest and best land use are costs of improvement equal to the market value of such improvements.*

The income that is ascribable to land under its highest and best use is known as *market rent*. It is that rent which the land is capable of producing when employed to its optimum capacity and efficiency. Any other income or rent agreed on between owner and tenant is known as *contract rent*. Where the contract rent is less than the economic rent, an owner in fact transfers a portion of the land value to the user. Where contract rent exceeds market rent, the owner realizes a bonus value which is computed by capitalization of these excess earnings at an appropriate risk rate (capitalization rate) as will be demonstrated in Chapter 19.

In addition to the concept of highest and best land use and the law of diminishing returns resulting from intensive land utilization, it is essential for the student of appraising to understand the operations of other principles and market rules of real estate market operations as follows:

1. Consistent use.
2. Substitution.
3. Marginal productivity.

4. Supply and demand.
5. Balance in land use and development.
6. Anticipation of future benefits.
7. Conformity.
8. Changes in socioeconomic patterns.

CONSISTENT USE

A corollary of the principle of highest and best use is *consistent use*. This principle holds that both the site and improvements must be valued for the same use. This principle is best applied in transitional neighborhoods, that is, neighborhoods that are changing from one set of land use activities to a set that generally would be of a higher order. A good example of this would be in a residential neighborhood that is traversed by a busy traffic artery. In such areas, the homes gradually are converted to interim uses. Later, the land becomes so valuable that the converted residences are demolished and more substantial improvements properly designed for such uses as retail or office space are constructed. The dilemma facing the appraiser in these changing neighborhoods is the tendency to appraise the land for the more valuable use and the improvements at their higher value (such as residential). Imagine, for example, that a property's total value is $500,000. Its component values under residential and neighborhood office uses are as follows:

	Residential use	Retail use
Site value	$ 80,000	$300,000
Building value	350,000	200,000
Total value	$430,000	$500,000

Assuming the highest and best use of the property currently is for neighborhood retail uses, the correct allocation of site and building values would be $300,000 and $200,000. Any other allocation, such as $300,000 (site value) and $350,000 (building value) for a total of $650,000 would be incorrect.

The consistent (or unitized) use principle is violated when the appraiser seeks to assign a value to the land based on one highest and best use and a value to the improvements based on a different highest and best use. Thus sound appraisal theory requires that the appraiser consider the property's single highest and best use on the basis of the transitional nature of the neighborhood. It is permissible to consider time-phased highest and best uses, which recognizes the interim and ultimate highest and best uses. This concept is fairly simply administered by discounting the income available to the property under each of the highest and best uses by time period. For example, the highest and best use may be for home-converted office space for the next five years, followed by a larger office building after this interim period.

SUBSTITUTION

All properties, no matter how diverse their physical attributes or how varied in geographic location, are substitutable economically in terms of service utility or in income productivity. The economic concept of *substitution* thus establishes an upper limit of value that is set by the cost of acquiring an equally desirable substitute property, provided such can be obtained without undue (costly) delay.

The principle of substitution is applicable not only to the replacement of a new property of reasonably equal service utility or earnings capacity but also to an existing old or equally depreciated replica. The theory of substitution provides the basis for using substitute (comparable) properties in the direct market, income, and cost comparison approaches to value, which will be demonstrated more fully in the following chapters. An appraiser therefore should focus on the similarity between comparable properties and an appraised property instead of sale prices.

MARGINAL PRODUCTIVITY

The principle of *marginal productivity* (often called the principle of contribution) is concerned with the value that the presence of a property component contributes to the overall value of that property. Conversely, it is the reduction in the overall property value caused by the absence of the component. This principle frequently is used in economic feasibility decisions, where an analyst discerns between (1) incremental cost and value or (2) expenses and income. For example, if the addition of a $10,000 air-conditioning system results in an increase in property value of $15,000, the expenditure would probably be judged feasible.

Another important application of this principle involves making adjustments in the market comparison approach. Two examples will illustrate this statement. Suppose that a sale property has a two-car garage and the appraised property has only a one-car garage. The question is not how much more the two-car garage costs but rather how much it contributes to the value of the sale property. This amount then provides the basis for the dollar adjustment to reveal the estimated value of the appraised property. Another example is shown in Figure 3.3.

The sale site shown in Figure 3.3 sold for $60,000, which in turn reflected its depth of 250 feet. The question now becomes how much the extra 50 feet of depth contributed to the value of the 250-foot-deep site. If, for instance, it was $5,000, the indicated value of the subject site would be $55,000.

An understanding of the principle of marginal productivity is also important in a determination of highest and best land use. A highest and best use study undertaken to test the economic advantages of alternate land uses requires a study of marginal productivity to determine the point where an intensive or vertical land use surpasses horizontal or extensive land utilization. When productivity under intensive or extensive land uses produce a higher value, the principle of marginal productivity is illustrated.

Figure 3.3 Application of Marginal Productivity

SUPPLY AND DEMAND

In applying the principle of marginal productivity, the practicing appraiser essentially makes a comparison between capital input and output under proposed or alternate improvement plans. Since the output of income from rentals or business operation is governed by the economic law of supply and demand, the value of a given improvement may or may not equal its capital cost, depending on the status of the market and the present and potential quantity of competition. Care must be taken to analyze thoroughly the market operation under *typical* conditions in order to avoid the pitfall of capitalizing excess income, which is temporary in nature and due to consumer time preference as to the moment of purchase, caused by scarcity or transitional monopoly. Like water seeking its natural level, so excess income (profit) will seek its natural level through competition from nearby competitive properties.

Where market forces are competitively free to operate, and where population is unrestricted in movement and migration from farm to urban and from urban to suburban areas, the shift in balance or changes in the interaction of supply and demand for housing causes prices to fluctuate from a high point at extreme scarcity to bargain prices below cost of replacement in a buyers' market and generally in areas where supply is superadequate. Economists characterize this trade imbalance by reference to long-range values and short-run prices. Since appraisals are made as of a given date or moment in the overall sequence of time, it is important that market forces which abnormally influence supply and demand for real property in a given community be carefully analyzed and their impact on present value noted and explained.

The *principle of supply and demand* holds that price tends to vary directly according to demand and inversely proportional to supply, that is, higher prices will be paid when there is strong demand for a good. Alternatively, when a market is oversupplied such as in many U.S. cities in the late 1980s and early 1990s, prices decline. The importance of this concept is twofold. (1) When analyzing prior market information such as rentals or sales, it is necessary to consider the state of the market before making adjustments to reveal the appraised property's value. For example, if there is a sellers' market (possibly resulting from strong demand and low supply) and the current market is not as favorable for sellers, the sales or rental data should be adjusted downward. Similarly, if the prior rentals or sales occurred in a buyers' market (some combination of low demand and high supply), an upward adjustment would need to be made to reflect such circumstances if a more positive market occurred today. (2) The other factor to consider would be the state of the current market. Is it depressed or is it a booming market but not likely to be sustained in future years? The appraiser must take this supply-demand situation into consideration when making his or her appraisal.

BALANCE IN LAND USE AND DEVELOPMENT

An understandable error which many appraisers are liable to make is evaluating property without due consideration of the *principle of balance*. According to this principle, value is created and maintained in proportion to the supply of and demand for a particular property type and in relation to consumer preferences for on-site amenities in relation to a property's function. If the price of a site under the World Trade Center or some other well-known skyscraper has been established, it does not necessarily mean that the site adjacent to it warrants either a similar structure or a like value. A market study may disclose that one skyscraper will amply serve the space needs of a community for many years, whereas the construction of another may spell economic loss if not disaster to the owners of both. The resulting loss in property value would be a direct measure of the degree to which the principle of balance had been violated. The presence of too many hotels, motels, restaurants, drugstores, or other building facilities brings about a "buyers' market" in which lowered values will reflect the degree of imbalance in relation to demand.

To accurately gauge property balance, an appraiser must know the community and be thoroughly conversant with effective land utilization, population and business growth trends as well as with community planning policies. This principle relates the neighborhood to the property, the site to the improvements, and each part of the building to the whole building. This will be discussed more fully in Chapter 6.

The principle of balance and its influence on value can also be effectively considered in judging interior design and the efficiency of a floor plan. Too many or inadequate bathrooms, bedrooms, or storage areas; wasted space in kitchens, halls, or living rooms; ceilings that are too high or too low; and over- or undersized heating, or plumbing—all are symptoms of interior imbalance that may be reflected in value losses. The computation procedure used to measure the amount of such losses will be more fully treated in Chapter 12.

ANTICIPATION OF FUTURE BENEFITS

This principle could just as well be referred to as the principle of futurity since the appraiser's responsibility is to interpret the attitudes of persons trading in the real estate market. Thus he or she is obligated to consider both the likelihood of future trends and the impact that such trends will have on the reactions of buyers, sellers, and tenants, as expressed in present market transactions. It might be argued that the depreciated cost approach (to be discussed in a later chapter) has its roots in the past. The direct market comparison approach, however, reflects the buyer's and seller's attitudes of the past and especially of future expectations for a property. Without question, futurity undergirds the income approach since a person leases a property for future benefit. Leases themselves often go several years beyond the present date. The appraiser must bring future income and expense expectations back to a present value.

It sometimes is said that a home buyer buys the largest home that he or she can currently afford. There is both truth and logic to this observation. A home buyer certainly would not go into debt for 15 to 25 years to acquire a property that served only his or her family's immediate needs. Hence the amenities acquired provide a future benefit.

Market value, although limited in amount by the operation of the forces of supply and demand, nevertheless provides the owner or user of real property a measure of anticipated property utility. Hence it may be defined as "the present worth of future benefits." It is the future and not the past with which the appraiser must be concerned. Thus the *principle of anticipation of future benefits* holds that the present value of a real property is based on users' and owners' perception of the nature, magnitude, and duration of its expected future benefits. The history of operation of the subject, or like properties in a market area, is important only in ascertaining a trend in anticipated earnings over the remaining economic life or holding period of the property under valuation. Past operations and other than "typical" management practices may hinder or in the case of accumulated good will accelerate (at least for a time) income production. Such assets or liabilities of a property must be considered in the measure of present value.

Changes in anticipated demand caused by such off-site improvements as highways, freeways, bridges, schools, and parkways have an important impact on value even though such improvements are in the planning stage and not visible at the time of the appraisal. The principle of anticipation thus points up the importance of being fully informed of community affairs and with economic changes anticipated in the market area in which the subject property is located.

CONFORMITY

The *principle of conformity* states that a property's value is maximized when it conforms to the surrounding properties, neighborhood, and tastes and desires of prospective users and purchasers. In a residential sense, conformity refers to compatible but not necessarily monotonous "look-alike" dwellings. Often this compatibility is regulated by subdivision restrictive covenants that specify the architectural design and exterior materials as well as the size of dwellings. The old adage of "birds of a feather tend to flock together" has merit in this case. Persons interested in purchasing a two-story, brick colonial design home are unlikely to look in a neighborhood characterized by modern, one-story frame dwellings, or vice versa. Nor will they be attracted to the colonial-designed home in the midst of a contemporary-designed neighborhood.

The same principle pertains to nonresidential structures as well. The nonconforming use generally is a departure from established styles and designs within a particular market. A departure from these architectural, size, or amenity norms often results in adverse market reaction to such properties. The final result is that such properties are not worth as much as surrounding properties.

Conformity is also related to *under-* and *overimprovement* of a site. There is a residential condominium development in one of the eastern states where the developer built the maximum number of housing units allowed by the local zoning ordinance. However, the development site was one with unfavorable terrain. When the project was completed, there were parking problems as well as severe street cuts and unusually high site-preparation expenses. The end result was a displeasing visual effect, market resistance, and considerable price discounts that were required to market the condominium units at all.

Another example of an overimprovement would be where a person builds a six-bedroom dwelling with a three-car garage and swimming pool in a neighborhood of three- and four-bedroom homes with one- and two-car garages and no swimming pools. In a six-bedroom, three-car-garage, swimming pool neighborhood, the owner would likely recoup all or most of his or her investment. However, this property is incompatible with its existing neighborhood, and consequently, the owner normally cannot expect to recover the full amount of his or her expenditure. Thus in this case the property value tends to seek (*regress toward*) the neighborhood value norm. The converse of this situation would be where a modest dwelling was built in a neighborhood of expensive homes. In this case, two things might happen. It may be so grossly underimproved there would be no market for the property, or the property value would be pulled up to (*progress toward*) the neighborhood value norm.

Still another example of nonconforming use is where a property fails to conform with the current zoning laws. Often a property may have been built prior to the present zoning ordinance being enacted. For example, a building may contain six apartment units in a zoning classification which currently allows only four dwelling units for a similar site. In this case, the nonconforming use results in the property being worth more than a four-unit site, but since it could not be restored to six units in case of fire, it is reasonable to expect that the property would not realize its full six-unit value as would similar properties that are legally permitted this number of units.

CHANGES IN SOCIOECONOMIC PATTERNS

To the student of appraising it must now be apparent that the principles of property valuation as outlined previously are interrelated and that all of them must be considered separately and as a whole if a reliable and accurate estimate of value is to be derived. Perhaps the single greatest error in value judgments is that of inexperienced appraisers taking the present status quo for granted. Next to death and taxes, nothing is as certain as the prospect of change. Change, of course, is a product of technological progress and the resulting shift in socioeconomic styles of living. One need only reflect on the causes that led to a decline in the value of horses and buggies, bicycles, passenger ships, and railroads. Even once-popular land use schemes, such as streetcar-dependent subdivisions, inefficient load-bearing walls of earlier office buildings, or strip retail centers have fallen into public disfavor to varying degrees. An appraiser must not only be conscious of the forces of change, but must also learn to evaluate their impact. This is essential in measuring the degree of anticipated changes causing functional and possible external obsolescence as well as the ever-present value losses caused by age, wear, tear, and actions of the elements.

SUMMARY

Land, together with all improvements that are permanently affixed thereto, is known as *real estate*. A *fixture* is personal property that is attached or used in such a manner that it is considered to be part of the real estate. *Real property* is defined as the rights, interests, and benefits associated with the ownership of real estate. Appraisers should be familiar with each of these distinctions.

The largest possible estate in real property is known as *fee simple*. This estate gives its owner a complete bundle of rights which is subject to four government limitations on ownership. These limitations fall under (1) police power of government, (2) right of eminent domain, (3) right of taxation, and (4) escheat to the state.

A keystone in the appraisal of real property is a proper highest and best use analysis. *Highest and best use* is defined as that use or succession of available, legal, and physically permitted uses for which there is sufficient demand that produces the highest present site value. This principle also applies to a property as currently improved. The latter may suggest that these improvements should either be retained, removed, or rehabilitated.

Other valuation principles that should be understood by professional appraisers include the principle of *consistent use*. This principle holds that both the site and improvements must be valued for the same use.

The principle of *substitution* establishes an upper limit of value that is set by the cost of acquiring an equally desirable substitute property, provided such can be obtained without undue or costly delay.

The principle of *marginal productivity* (principle of contribution) is concerned with the value that the presence of a property component contributes to the overall value of that property or the reduction in the overall property value caused by the absence of the component.

The principle of *supply and demand* holds that price tends to vary directly according to demand and inversely proportional to supply, that is, higher prices will be paid when there is strong demand for a good. This principle is important in comparing sales and rentals of comparable properties to determine the amount of adjustment required.

The principle of *balance* asserts that value is created and maintained in proportion to the supply and demand of a particular property type and in relation to consumer preference for on-site amenities in relation to a property's function.

The principle of *anticipation of future benefits* holds that the present value of a real property is based on users' and owners' perception of the nature, magnitude, and duration of its expected future benefits.

The principle of *conformity* states that a property's value is maximized when it conforms to the surrounding properties, neighborhood, and tastes and desires of prospective users and purchasers. Conformity is also expressed as *under-* and *overimprovement* of a site. The value of an overimproved property tends to regress toward the neighborhood value norm, whereas the value of an underimproved property generally progresses or rises toward the typically priced property.

REVIEW QUESTIONS

1. What, if any, relationship exists between real estate and fixtures?
2. Explain the terms "police power" and "eminent domain" and discuss how an affected property owner is compensated under each.
3. Discuss why an accurate highest and best use analysis is so important in the appraisal of real estate.
4. List and discuss the importance of the key terms in the concept of highest and best use.
5. How can the marginal productivity concept be applied to the sales comparison approach?
6. Distinguish wealth from property and state why the valuator is concerned with the appraisal of property rather than with the appraisal of wealth.
7. It is stated that "where the building codes or local conditions make construction more costly in one city than another, the general land values are lower." Is this statement true? Give your reason.

READING AND STUDY REFERENCES

ABSON, GARY K. "Highest and Best Use: Theory and Practice," *The Canadian Appraiser* (Spring 1989), pp. 26–35.

American Institute of Real Estate Appraisers. Chapter 3, "Foundations of Appraisal," *The Appraisal of Real Estate*. Chicago: AIREA, 1987.

BABCOCK, FREDERICK M. Chapter 13, "Axioms of Valuation," *The Valuation of Real Estate*. New York: McGraw-Hill Book Company, 1932.

CLARK, KIMBERLY K. "Acquiring and Financing Escheated Property," Real Estate Research Report 131 (April 1984). Richmond, Va.: Virginia Real Estate Research Center, Virginia Commonwealth University, 54 pp.

DERBES, MAX J., JR. "Highest and Best Use—What Is It?" *The Appraisal Journal* 49, no. 2 (April 1981), pp. 166–178.

FLOYD, CHARLES F. Chapter 6, "Private and Public Restrictions on Ownership," *Real Estate Principles*. Chicago: Longman Financial Services Publishing, 1990.

ORDWAY, NICHOLAS, and JACK HARRIS. "The Dynamic Nature of Highest and Best Use," *The Appraisal Journal* 49, no. 3 (July 1981), pp. 325–334.

RUGGLES, ROBERT K., and JAMES J. WALSH. "Supply, Demand and the Nature of Value," *The Appraisal Journal* 51, no. 2 (April 1983), pp. 190–201.

THAIR, STEVEN. "What's the Use?—Most Probable Use Versus Highest and Best Use." *The Appraisal Journal* (April 1988), pp. 190–199.

VANDELL, KERRY D. "Toward Analytically Precise Definitions of Market Value and Highest and Best Use," *The Appraisal Journal* 50, no. 2 (April 1982), pp. 253–268.

EXTERNAL INFLUENCES ON PROPERTY VALUE

4

Impact of Political, Social, and Economic Forces

Learning Objectives

After reading this chapter, you should be able to:

- Appreciate the influences on property value resulting from regional, national, and international political, social, and economic forces
- Realize how governmental intervention in the economy can both positively and negatively affect real estate markets
- Understand the demographic changes and population shifts that have occurred in the United States and their effect on real estate
- Discuss how the "political climate" of a state or region within a state can influence economic development

The value of every parcel of land located anywhere within the United States, no matter how small its dimensions, is subject to political, social, and economic forces. In fact, the general forces that influence property values on a local level increasingly come from beyond the borders of our country. Not only are these three forces important to real estate as viewed in the traditional local sense, but increasingly, national and international events have a strong influence on the demand for and value of real estate in local communities. Often it is difficult to distinguish between these forces. For example, a civil war in some foreign country may have an adverse economic impact in the United States. The same cause and effect relationship is true of international politics and economics.

Up until 1973, the United States maintained a very favorable trade balance with its trading partners. But in that year, the Organization of Petroleum Exporting Countries (OPEC) pushed the price of exported petroleum up to unprecedented levels. Massive trade deficits began. Real estate operating costs soared. The latter factor affected the income and value of oil-heated real estate. Oil prices moderated over the next 17 years until Saddam Hussein invaded Kuwait with his Iraqi troops in mid-July 1990. The price of crude oil stood at $20 a barrel, but soared to $40 by late September. Whereas there were long waiting lines at service stations in 1973, there were ample oil supplies in 1990. In both instances, some prospective home owners and investors hesitated in buying properties.

Breaking down racial and sex barriers has greatly broadened employment and housing opportunities for racial minorities and women. These changes have expanded the market for real estate and made it easier for both of these groups to purchase more expensive and presumably valuable housing. Another social change has been the growing mobility of our population and a resulting greater emphasis on maintenance-free housing. The advent of more two-spouse wage-earning households has further reinforced the market for convenience-designed, smaller homes (often apartments) as well as a stronger demand for recreational properties.

The savings and loan industry has undergone dramatic deregulation since the early 1980s. In the first phase (1980–1983), thrifts were faced with the high cost of capital and low investment yields. This mismatch was largely overcome over the balance of the 1980s by the introduction of certificates of deposit along with the elimination of deposit interest rate ceilings. In the latter 1980s, thrifts entered the second phase of deregulation by aggressively moving away from their traditional emphasis on home mortgages and into more profitable (and risky) development, construction, and commercial lending. By venturing into investments with which savings and loans had little experience, losses mounted sharply and many thrifts failed nationwide.

By mid-1989, President Bush signed into law a bill that greatly changed the thrift industry. The new regulations were intended to require thrifts to eliminate high-risk investments and return to residential lending. These regulatory changes surely will affect the nature of the real estate field and conduct of its business.

Of course, it is not primarily the appraiser's opinion that counts, but rather the actions of buyers and sellers as reflected by the opinion of political and economic experts who study market operations and who make it their business to publish the effects of world trends and shifts in international relations. A number of national services and others in related economic fields keep an ear to the international ground, warning their readers of probable coming events and their consequent effects on the value of real property. In every valuation it is the appraiser's duty to stipulate whether the value reported does or does not reflect possible and impending changes in international relations and, if so, to what degree and amount. The client or reader of the appraisal report is then in a position to make his or her own value adjustments based on personal observation of market operations and his or her investment risk position.

POLITICAL FORCES INFLUENCING VALUE

Under our allodial system of property ownership (as opposed to state or feudal control of land and land improvements), property values are derived from property rights. Although these private rights are constitutionally guaranteed to the fee owner, they are nevertheless subject to important modification by legislative, executive, and judicial action. Even the form of government and the underlying philosophy guiding political leadership can influence market operations and investment choices made by individuals or corporations. Earlier this century, in the USSR and the other communist-controlled nations of Europe and Asia, for example, ownership of land was seized in the name of the "people," and private rights and value in real estate for these nations were liquidated as a result of communist political policy. Some dramatic consequences followed the centralization of planning, ownership, and production in these countries. For example, the average Russian citizen was required to work three hours in 1927 to buy five pounds of beef, but by 1985 it took 22 hours of labor in order to purchase the same amount of beef. Another measure of the difference in quality of life is seen in the relative number of automobile registrations in Russia and the United States—12 per 1,000 persons versus 570. In 1987, West Germany in producing 4,430,000 motor vehicles had a sizeable trade surplus, whereas communist East Germany manufactured only 217,000 vehicles and had a trade deficit.

A remarkable change began in the Eastern block countries in 1990 with transfer of central government property and businesses to individual citizens. This remarkable change should foster a new class of professionals. Real estate appraisers will be needed to gauge the value of real estate under a market-based pricing system.

In the United States, Great Britain, and many western European nations, attempts have been made to transfer to the state or nation the value increments in land which—as claimed—unjustly accrue to private owners. The so-called unearned land value increment theory reached its popular peak with the effective writing of the American economist Henry George, who in his book *Progress and Poverty*, published in 1879, suggested the "single-tax" remedy whereby value increments in land created by community life and action could be returned to the "people," from whence it came. In the United States, adherents of the single-tax doctrine made a concerted and powerful effort to have this socialistic theory implemented by legislative action. Since the power to tax, in the hands of unwise or biased government, is tantamount to the power to destroy property values, special safeguards are provided in the U.S. Constitution (the Fifth and Fourteenth Amendments) and by statutory law in the various states to protect property owners.

The political attitude and national policy toward home ownership, urban revitalization, and public housing is also of interest to the appraiser, since changes in national policy as expressed in housing legislation have a direct and often significant effect on property values. To illustrate, passage of the Home Owners Loan Corporation Act as an emergency measure by Congress to prevent disastrous and large-scale mortgage foreclosures during the depression years of 1932–1935 stabilized the real estate market and prevented foreclosure action for about four out of five home borrowers who sought the corporation's aid. Enactment of rent control during World Wars I and II prevented runaway prices threatened by war-induced home scarcities and limitations on home construction. Retention of rent control, however, beyond the period of an emergency—for political rather than economic purposes—depresses the values of property so affected and discourages investment in rental real estate wherever such controls are still operative, as in New York City or overseas in France, Italy, and England to this day. The chronology of events typically associated with rent control has been: (1) the quality of housing suffers and the quantity is reduced; (2) the private ownership sector withdraws; and (3) the government (using tax dollars) attempts to provide replacement housing.

Urban renewal legislation provides a direct subsidy by the federal government to a given county or city government and indirectly contributes to the enhancement of the values of property located adjacent to or in the immediate vicinity of rehabilitated areas. A boon to private rehabilitation of older city properties came about in the mid-1970s when the federal income tax laws were changed. It became profitable to upgrade underutilized and vacant properties. In turn, investors returned to our cities in search of profitable ventures with whole districts often being rehabilitated. Often new uses were created for apparently obsolete structures.

In the 1980s, even after the 1986 Tax Reform, numerous certified historic properties were rehabilitated. The National Trust for Historic Preservation estimated that between 1982 and 1985, $8.8 billion in private capital was invested in nearly 12,000 historic properties. The investment tax credit caused many abandoned or underutilized properties to be rehabilitated. Former schools became apartments and condominiums. Factories were changed to functional offices. Warehouses became fashionable restaurants and retail establishments. These tax incentives, when applied to economically sound projects, proved to be of great benefit to municipalities.

The significant increase in home ownership and home construction everywhere in the United States is directly traceable, in a large measure, to federal financing aids and fiscal policy controls. The Federal Housing Administration and the Veterans Administration loan programs are largely responsible for the increase in home ownership and home construction during the two decades following World War II. Later, with the advent of the high-loan-to-value conventional loan made possible through the use of private mortgage insurance, the market share of these two federal agencies waned. These loan programs, too, have encouraged suburban land development and have thus brought about a shift of commercial land use activities traditionally associated with the central city to outlying residential areas. Government fiscal policies and their effect on money interest rates also must be watched closely by the real estate appraiser in order to measure the effect of rate changes on the value of income-producing real property. As a rule, changes in the rate of interest or interest rate structure have an inverse relationship to real property values. A rise in the rate of interest lowers property value, and a fall, for instance, in rates is reflected in higher value. This is due to the direct relationship that income bears to value, with the interest rate serving as leverage for conversion of income into value. For example, a $1,000 income in perpetuity at 10 percent interest is worth $10,000 ($1,000/10%); whereas a rate of 5 percent interest produces double the value, or $20,000 ($1,000/5%). Moreover, rising interest rates discourage the sale of residential property even with price concessions. Income property, with an increased mortgage debt burden, produces a lower income and in turn a lower value.

SOCIAL FORCES INFLUENCING VALUE

Since people create value it is important to keep abreast of changes in the number, age and income distribution, and household sizes of the total population. A vigorous growth and a positive trend in the national population may not necessarily be reflected in an equally beneficial population pattern on a state or local level. Nevertheless, the impact of local population forces cannot be effectively understood or interpreted unless the national pattern is used as a background for growth comparison. As shown by the chart in Figure 4.1, the total U.S. population

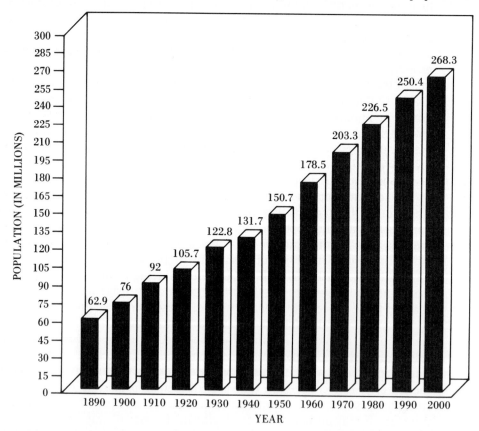

Figure 4.1   Population Growth in the United States
Source: *Statistical Abstract of the United States 1990*, U.S. Department of Commerce, Bureau of the Census, pp. 7 and 16.

steadily increased from approximately 62.9 million in 1890 to 245.8 million in 1988. The forecast for total population by the year 2000 is 268.3 million. This increase of nearly 183 million people during the past 98 years is also reflected in the increase in population per square mile of land from 21.2 persons in 1890, to 64.0 persons in 1980.

Even more important from a real estate valuation perspective is where this growth has occurred. In the past 48 years, for example, our nation's population has become more urbanized. Whereas 53 percent of the total U.S. population lived in metropolitan areas in 1940, by 1988 this share had risen to 77 percent. Moreover, during this same period, the share of land area more than doubled in these metropolises (going from 7 percent to 16.3 percent).[1] The remarkable fact revealed is that over three-quarters of the nation's population is housed on just 16 percent of our land. Another important point can be drawn from this trend—population growth creates demand for real estate, which in turn increases the value for vacant land and improved land alike.

Another important influence on real estate demand and its value is the differences in regional population growth patterns. In the last century, and even up through the 1940s, there were huge migrations of population from the rural South to northern and north-central cities. Generally, the motivating force was jobs in these highly industrialized regions. In the 1970s, this trend was sharply reversed, but moderated somewhat in the 1980s. As shown in Table 4.1, population shifts were from the Northeast and Midwest to the South and West. Losses from the Midwest slowed considerably by 1987–88, net migration continued to strengthen in the South but the customary gains in the West reversed by 1987–88 in part due to the high living expenses, especially housing in southern California. Moreover, the moves, in all regions except the West, have tended to be from cities to suburbs and nonmetropolitan areas. Although, as stated previously, a greater proportion of the nation's population now lives in metropolitan areas, an increasing proportion of that population lives in the suburbs instead of cities. Not only have there been these population shifts, but over the past 190 years, there has been a continual westward movement, as shown in Figure 4.2. In 1790, the center of U.S. population was 23 miles east of Baltimore, Maryland, but by 1980 it had shifted to one-quarter mile west of DeSoto in Jefferson County, Missouri.

TABLE 4.1 INTERREGIONAL NET MIGRATION (THOUSANDS)

	Region			
Date	Northeast	Midwest	South	West
1980–1981	−242	−406	+407	+161
1987–1988	−231	− 88	+418	− 98

Source: *Statistical Abstract of the United States 1990*, U.S. Department of Commerce, Bureau of the Census, Table 24, p. 19.

[1]U.S. Department of Commerce, Bureau of the Census, *Statistical Abstract of the United States 1982–83*, Table 15, p. 14, and Tables 32 and 35, pp. 27 and 28, in the 1990 edition.

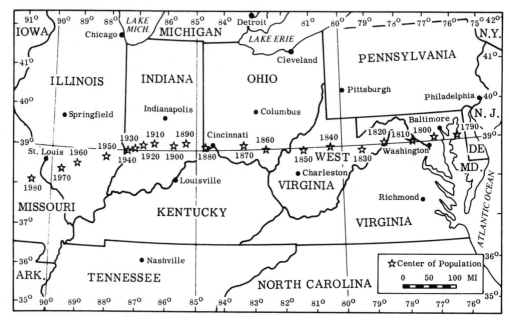

Figure 4.2 Population Shifts in the United States
For dates of admission of the states and changes in areal definition, see "State Origins and Boundaries," *United States Summary, U.S. Census of Population: 1960*, Vol. 1. For year of admission to state-
hood, see Table 338.
Source: *Census of Population: 1980*, U.S. Bureau of the Census, Vol. 1.

Although the concentration of people took place largely in metropolitan
areas, the overall increase in population is nevertheless remarkably related to an
increase in the value of all U.S. lands. Over the years, the net increase in U.S. land
values generally has been directly proportional to the rise in the overall population shown in Figure 4.1. The significance of population is thus of prime importance, and its impact must be considered carefully in appraising a given property.

Another significant trend which is important to the appraiser is the steadily
increasing demand for housing units per 1,000 population as shown in Table 4.2.
Dwelling units increased from 12.69 million in 1890, to 102.652 million in
1987—or by 809 percent—compared with an increase in population of 387 percent for the same period. This housing demand, brought about by increasing di-
vorces, delayed birth of children, more single-person households, and "un-
doubling" (where two or more persons were living together and at least one
moved out to create a new household) has reduced the average population—as
shown in Table 4.2—from 4.93 persons per dwelling unit in 1890, to 2.66 persons
per dwelling unit in 1987. In effect, this means that whereas 493 persons exerted a
demand for 100 dwelling units in 1890, the same number of persons demanded
and occupied 185 dwelling units in 1987. Even if no growth in population had
taken place during the past 98 years, housing on the basis of changes in family formation alone would have increased by over 85 percent. Replacement of an aging

TABLE 4.2   TOTAL HOUSING UNITS IN THE
UNITED STATES, 1890–1987

Year	Housing units (thousands)	Persons per housing unit
1890	12,690	4.93
1900	15,964	4.76
1910	20,256	4.54
1920	24,352	4.34
1930	29,905	4.11
1940	34,949	3.77
1950	42,857	3.37
1960	58,326	3.33
1970	68,672	3.14
1980	88,207	2.76
1987	102,652	2.66

Source: *Population Series Reports*, U.S. Department of Commerce, Bureau of the Census, 1960; *Current Population Reports*, Series P-20, No. 116, *American Housing Survey for the United States in 1987*, U.S. Department of Commerce and U.S. Department of Housing and Urban Development, and *Statistical Abstract of the United States 1989.*

housing stock stimulated additional demand. Since the trend toward smaller families is expected to continue, this factor must also be considered in the appraisal of real property, especially in areas where high standards of living prevail.

Another factor of increasing importance in the evaluation of the general forces that affect changes in property values is the changing age composition of the U.S. population. People not only live longer but, through pension, Medicare, and social security plans, are economically and medically better cared for. For the most part, these people are not poor. Persons who are over 50 years old control over 77 percent of all financial assets in this country. These aging citizens demand independent dwelling units in increasing numbers, most often seeking retirement opportunities in geographic areas where mild climate keeps housing and related costs at a minimum. As a result, Sunbelt states such as California, Arizona, New Mexico, and Florida have experienced greater than average population gains during recent years, which have been directly reflected in rapidly advancing market activity and prices of real property. Whereas 6.8 percent of the total U.S. population was 65 years old and over in 1940 (9.0 million persons), this percentage of senior citizens increased to 12.3 percent by the year 1988 (30.4 million). An even higher ratio of elderly were women in 1988 (14.3%).

These changing demographics through the 1990s will result in 1 of every 2 Americans being middle aged. The over-50 age group will grow by 18.5 percent, while the under-50 group will expand by only 3.5 percent.

Both housing and office demand will be reduced in the decade of the 1990s. Home ownership rates for households in the 25-to-29-year bracket fell from 43 percent in 1980 to 36 percent in 1988. This trend suggests a need for affordable housing along with a revived apartment market. With fewer households in the 25-to-35-year bracket, there will be less pressure on housing prices. Children born in the final stages of the post–World War II baby boom are now passing through the household formation stage which will end the housing boom of the 1980s. Additionally, fewer new office buildings will be needed. The office work force will grow only half as fast as in the 1980s.

GENERAL ECONOMIC FORCES INFLUENCING VALUE

Since real estate activity, property price levels, and real estate values are directly influenced by the general economic activity and economic well-being of the country as a whole, the appraiser must be seriously concerned with the general economic forces that influence value. Important indexes that should be observed as a barometer of general economic progress include the following:

> Gross national product.
> Per capita income and real wage levels.
> Unemployment as a measure of full employment.
> Personal savings and investments.
> General business and real estate activity.

Although all the preceding are related as measures of economic well-being, the year-to-year variations, or lag of one index as compared with another, may provide an important clue to anticipated changes in general economic activities which are bound to influence the value of real property. The measure most widely used as a yardstick for economic progress in the United States is the gross national product (GNP), which aggregates in dollars the annual value of all goods and services produced, consumed, saved, and invested by individuals, business corporations, and government operations. Using 1950 as a base, the GNP grew from 288.3 billion dollars in that year to 5,233.2 billion in 1989. The percentage growth in economic activity from year to year over the past 39 years may be observed by study of the chart in Figure 4.3. General economic activity prior to and during wars is accelerated, and readjustments following a war cause overall business operations and consumptions to decline. The rise in the GNP through 1989 also reflects rising prices caused by dollar inflation and a consequent loss in the purchasing power of the dollar during this time period as shown by the difference in the two trend lines (1982 and current dollars). The rate of economic progress in constant dollars has averaged 3.25 percent per year over the past 39 years, with the sharpest declines being in 1953–54, 1956, 1974, and 1980. Growth at this level over the coming decade depends largely upon the relationship of the political, social, and economic forces discussed earlier in this chapter.

Per capita income and the changing level of real wages provide another and more refined measure of economic well-being as seen from the consumer's point

SEASONALLY ADJUSTED ANNUAL RATES, QUARTERLY

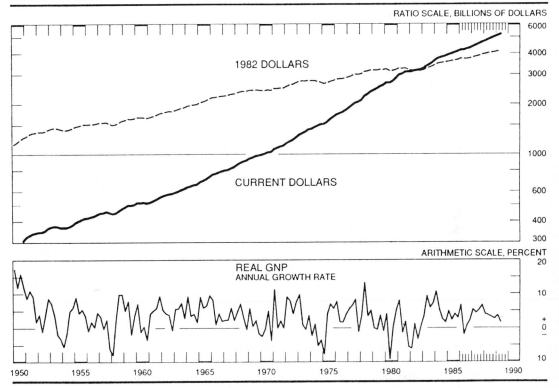

Figure 4.3 Gross National Product
Source: *1989 Historical Chart Book*, Board of Governors of the Federal Reserve System, Washington, D.C., p. 12.

of view. Although overall dollar productivity for the country as a whole is of prime importance, the appraiser must temper his or her value conclusions for given types of real property in accordance with the distribution of this total income flow to the factors of production, including tax payments to government. The steadily rising standard of living is a direct result of increasing productivity and wage increases. Disposable personal income (income after payment of state and federal taxes) has risen from 610 billion dollars in 1968, to 3,478 billion dollars in 1988. This constitutes an increase of 570 percent. In constant dollars, based on the purchasing power of the dollar in 1982, the increase is 80.1 percent. This was a strong rise in disposable personal income over this 20-year period. It is this continuing rise in the financial well-being of individuals that largely accounts for the significant increase in the number of home owners from 43.6 percent of all dwelling units in 1940, to 61.9 percent in 1960, to 64.4 percent in 1980 falling off to 63.5 percent in 1985 before rising to 64.0 percent in 1987. Some observers conjecture that in the future this level of home ownership is not likely to increase significantly, if at all.

Another and more sensitive measure of economic well-being that is important to property appraisers is the degree of unemployment in relation to the total available labor force. Accepting labor analysts' conclusions that labor turnover and willfully unemployed persons comprise a "normal" unemployment rate of approximately 2 percent of the total labor force, an increase in the percentage of idle workers above this rate—discounting seasonal unemployment—will adversely affect the value of real property. This is understandable, since expenditures for ownership of shelter are less important for subsistence than outlays for food and clothing. There is a direct correlation between unemployment, property foreclosures, and property tax delinquencies. When national unemployment reached the peak of 24.9 percent of the civilian labor force in 1933, property values also hit the century's lowest ebb; and, as pointed out, government emergency laws were passed to create a debt moratorium to halt the avalanche of foreclosures. In recent years, unemployment has fluctuated from a high of 9.7 percent in 1982 to a low of 5.3 percent in 1989. These changes in the level of unemployment are of national concern because they are accompanied by changes in the economic progress and international competitiveness of American goods and products and rates of increase in land values throughout the nation. Thus the appraiser should reflect in his or her value estimates the prospect for property demands as based on a forecast of the health of the labor-consumer market as a whole.

Investor confidence and national economic stability can also be judged by the amount of personal savings as related to total disposable personal income after all taxes. Patterns of expenditures change, as does consumer saving philosophy; hence the importance of time preference in consumption. The cause for a decreasing rate of personal savings should be carefully analyzed, for a continued downward trend in savings will decrease investment capital and hence the demand for and value of real property. The percentage relationship of personal savings to disposable personal income for selected years since 1940 is shown in Table 4.3.

Although no fixed percentage of savings to disposable income is recommended as an optimum guide to capital reinvestment, it is apparent that venture capital is dependent on this source for capital funds. A continued rate of savings below 5 percent may foreshadow insufficient capital formation to maintain modern industry, causing our nation to be noncompetitive in a worldwide economy with a resulting rising level of unemployment. An increase, however, in the annual rate of savings above 7 percent may prove equally disconcerting if the increased thrift reflects *underconsumption* or lack of investor confidence in the economic progress and stability of the United States. In any case, changes in this index as a barometer of economic climate call for analysis and value interpretation by professional real estate appraisers.

Savings in the United States, as a percentage of disposable personal income, have trended downward since 1971, reaching a low of 3.2 percent in 1987. This decline rests in part on federal tax law that encourages borrowing instead of sav-

TABLE 4.3 PERSONAL SAVINGS AS PERCENTAGE OF TOTAL DISPOSABLE INCOME, 1940–1988 (BILLIONS OF DOLLARS)

Year	Disposable personal income	Personal outlays	Personal savings	Savings as percentage of income
1940	75.7	71.8	3.9	5.1
1945	150.2	120.7	29.5	19.7
1950	206.9	193.9	13.0	6.3
1955	275.3	259.5	15.8	5.7
1960	352.0	332.3	19.7	5.6
1965	475.8	442.1	33.7	7.0
1970	715.6	657.9	57.7	8.1
1975	1,096.1	1,001.8	94.3	9.2
1980	1,918.0	1,781.1	136.9	7.1
1985	2,838.7	2,713.3	125.4	4.4
1988	3,477.8	3,333.1	144.7	4.2

Source: *Economic Report of the President, Transmitted to Congress*, Bureau of the Census, February 1968; U.S. Department of Commerce, *Statistical Abstract of the United States 1982–83*, 1982; and U.S. Department of Commerce, *Survey of Current Business* 64, no. 11 (November 1984), p. S-1, *Statistical Abstract of the United States 1990*, p. 432, Table 700, U.S. Department of Commerce, 1990, and *Business Statistics 1961–88*, U.S. Department of Commerce, Bureau of Economic Analysis, p. 2.

ing. Partially offsetting the decline in voluntary savings has been a greater dependence on involuntary savings through pension plans, health and disability insurance and social security programs. Nevertheless, savings in the United States were grossly inferior to savings in such leading industrial countries as West Germany (12.6%) and Japan (15.2%) in 1988.[2]

A composite of all the forces that motivate economic activity within a nation is reflected in the position of the business cycle that measures the intensity of general business operations. A historical study of business cycles in the United States discloses a rhythmic recurrence of business booms and depressions to such a degree that economic forecasts on the basis of past experience with a high degree of accuracy were deemed possible. Under normal unimpeded economic behavior in a capitalistic nation, business reflects consumer and investor cycles of optimism, overoptimism, caution, or pessimism. Cyclical business behavior, it seems, is attributable to violations of the economic laws of supply and demand and the lack of central business control. In studying past cyclical behavior of business activity to forecast future business operations, the appraiser must keep in mind that in recent years federal government controls have successfully counteracted adverse economic behavior and, with varying degrees of success, have revitalized business operations by means of pump-priming government expenditures in a vast variety of public construction projects and general improvements. The necessity for increased government action is a sign of maladjustment in the pri-

[2]"Saving: Not the American Way," *Newsweek* (January 8, 1990), pp. 44–45.

vate sector of the national economy, and requires careful attention by the real estate appraiser translating the impact of the general national economy, especially in times of extreme booms or depressions affecting real estate activity on a regional, state, and local level.

The combination of waste and overspending by the federal government has threatened the numerous economic advances made by investors, workers, and business owners in the United States. Much of the capital otherwise available for strengthening enterprises in the private sector is siphoned off by the federal government debt. This growing encumbrance is depicted in Figure 4.4.

STATE OR REGIONAL FORCES INFLUENCING VALUE

The same pattern of statistical analysis that guides the real estate appraiser in interpreting the value influence of general forces on a national level should be used in the analysis of state or regional forces that influence property values. Here again the nature, character, and comparative general quality of social, political, and economic forces must be carefully studied and interpreted as a basis for reaching a professionally sound and reliable value conclusion. This is not to suggest that the appraiser conduct a state or regional analysis for every appraisal re-

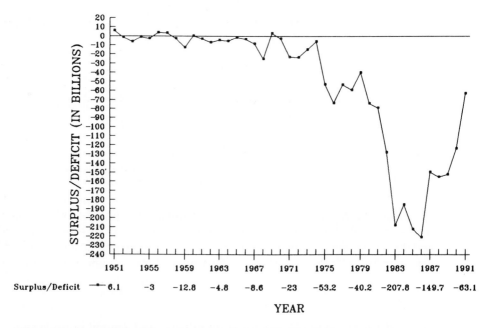

Figure 4.4   Annual Federal Surpluses and Deficits 1951–1991 (Billions of Dollars)
Note: 1990 and 1991 amounts are estimates.
Source: *Economic Report of the President, Transmitted to Congress* (February 1990), Table C-76, p. 383.

port. Instead, it implies that there should be a continual awareness of such value-influencing trends.

Unless the population within a state or region increases as favorably as that of the nation as a whole, local property values will reflect—on a broad level—the area's retarded growth. The center of population within the continental United States has steadily shifted west by southwest since the formation of this country. A continued rapid population increase in states such as California, Arizona, New Mexico, and Florida seems assured as long as people and industry, aided by advances in rapid transportation and electric power, seek milder climates and areas where natural resources can more advantageously be exploited. Accelerated growth in these states by necessity is accomplished at the expense of a decelerated growth—if not a decline—of population in other states and regions. Thus, though the nation as a whole may experience a favorable growth in total population, care must be taken to relate this growth to regional prospects and developments.

Although for the country as a whole total population was used as a measure of growth significance, the population analysis of a state or region must give greater emphasis to population quality and characteristics. With the aid of federal and state census data, appraisers should keep abreast of population changes and interpret for their clients the long-term effects of regional population trends on the value of real property. Several useful federal sources of population and other data are listed at the end of the chapter.

Equally important as a population factor affecting the value of real properties is the political climate in which people and industry find opportunities to prosper. Many states have passed legislation—often by constitutional referendum—to favor business, industry, or resident home owners in order to spur state economic growth. The relatively simple and economically favorable laws of incorporation in Delaware, the homestead exception tax law of Florida, and freedom from state income taxes in Maine and other states are instances where the law has been designed to foster state growth and development. In some states, however, what once was considered beneficial to a growing economy may prove in later years an investment handicap—even a financial burden—to a more mature economy. The rent control laws still in effect under state law in New York City and Chicago discouraged apartment developments for years until such laws—at least for new construction—were made inapplicable. The homestead tax exception law in Florida, too, has long since outlived its economic usefulness, and the revenue burden that this law places on populous counties often necessitates oppressive indirect and business taxation to offset this outdated legislation.

Since property values reflect the present worth of *future* rights to income, appraisers must not only analyze the nature and character of present state laws and the quality of government but they must interpret the trend of government and legislation for better or worse in the years to come. The stability and quality of government, as will be demonstrated in subsequent chapters, is directly reflected in the rate of interest at which capital for investment purposes becomes available. The higher this rate of interest, as a rule, the greater the risk of investment ownership and hence the lower the investment value for a given anticipated flow of income dollars.

The current economic status and prospects for anticipated economic development must also be given careful attention. To judge effectively the economic status of a given state or region, the appraiser must gather for ready reference and use in his or her office or appraisal library statistical data from which comparative value judgment conclusions can be drawn. The importance of the state or region to the economy of the nation as a whole should be ascertained. To what extent is dollar or resource competition threatened? Is the state economy sufficiently diversified to withstand rapid technological changes in production and marketing demands? The economic hardships of the "cotton" South, the "shipping" Northeast, the "corn-belt" Midwest, the "cattle" Southwest, and the coal mining and steel smelting regions of the country are still fresh enough in memory to serve as vivid reminders that the principle of change is ever active. No appraiser can hazard a judgment based on an extension of the status quo. Unless a state or region is strong enough to resist strains of powerful economic readjustments caused by changes in technology—as, for example, having the resources to adjust itself to new developments in atomic energy and space—the remaining economic life of property because of anticipated obsolescence is shortened. The possible loss of future productive income years is translated, of course, into lower property values by informed investment buyers.

It is the appraiser's responsibility to gather pertinent social, political, and economic data on a national, state, or regional level, and to interpret the meaning of such data in the light of action taken by *typical* buyers and sellers in the marketplace. Generally, the appraiser should decide whether the outlook for real estate investment over the years to come is good, bad, or uncertain. Data should then be supplied to support the appraiser's conclusions and to aid the reader of the valuation report in reaching his or her own value judgment where circumstances warrant subjective rather than objective considerations.

SUMMARY

The value of all land in the United States is subject to political, social, and economic forces. An example of political forces influencing property value includes the high ratio of U.S. citizens who own their own homes. This result is traceable largely to federal financing aids and fiscal policy controls.

Social forces impacting on real estate value are shifts in population, household size, home ownership rate, and changing age composition of the population.

Economic forces influencing real estate value include gross national product (GNP), per capita income and real wage levels, unemployment rates, personal savings and investments, and general business and real estate activity.

REVIEW QUESTIONS

1. How has the reduction of racial and sex discrimination barriers affected real estate demand and values?

2. Discuss the likely sequence of events of municipal rent control laws.

3. Briefly describe the changes that have occurred in household size in this country. How have these trends affected the demand for housing?

4. How can the rate of savings eventually influence the well-being of a nation?

5. What has been the result of savings and loan associations' aggressively moving away from their traditional emphasis on home mortgages?

6. List and discuss the implications of the apparent leveling off in the rate of home ownership, including those given in the chapter and any that you may think of.

7. Can zoning regulations prevent value decline in residential districts? Discuss.

READING AND STUDY REFERENCES

BAXTER, CHERYL. "The Impact of Government Policies and Programs on Land Values," *The Real Estate Appraiser and Analyst* 45, no. 3 (May–June 1979), pp. 42–45.

GREER, G. WILLIAM. "Tax Reform 1986: Impacts on Historic Rehabilitation," *Perspective.* Society of Industrial and Office Realtors (James H. Boykin, ed.), March/April 1987.

HARRIS, JACK C. *The Savings and Loan Crisis*, Technical Report. College Station, Texas: Real Estate Center, August 1990.

MILLS, EDWIN S. "Has the United States Overinvested in Housing?" *AREUEA Journal* 15, no. 1 (Spring 1987), pp. 601–616.

MURRAY, ALAN, and PAULETTE THOMAS. "The Bush Bailout Plan for Savings and Loans Could Spell Extinction," *Wall Street Journal* (February 7, 1989), p. A13.

PLATTNER, ROBERT H. "Regional Migration: Its Impact on Land Use," *The Real Estate Appraiser and Analyst* 49, no. 2 (Summer 1983), pp. 5–12.

RUDOLPH, PATRICIA M., and BASSUM HAMDEN. "An Analysis of Post-Deregulation Savings and Loan Failure," *AREUEA Journal* 16, no. 1 (Spring 1988), pp. 17–33.

SCHUSSHEIM, MORTON J. "The Impact of Demographic Change on Housing and Community Development," *The Appraisal Journal* 52, no. 3 (July 1984), pp. 375–381.

U.S. Bureau of the Census. *Census of Retail Trade* (every five years, by groups of counties). Washington, D.C.: U.S. Government Printing Office.

U.S. Bureau of the Census. *Characteristics of Population* (every 10 years, by counties). Washington, D.C.: U.S. Government Printing Office.

U.S. Bureau of the Census. *Housing Authorized by Building Permits and Public Contracts* (monthly, by individual places). Washington, D.C.: U.S. Government Printing Office.

U.S. Bureau of the Census. *Housing Characteristics for States, Cities and Counties* (every 10 years, by large areas and SMSAs). Washington, D.C.: U.S. Government Printing Office.

U.S. Department of Commerce. *Business Statistics*, Bureau of Economic Analysis. Washington, D.C.: U.S. Government Printing Office.

5
Regional and Community Analysis

Learning Objectives

After reading this chapter, you should be able to:

- Recognize the nature of the real estate market
- Appreciate the relationship of regional and community analysis in the valuation of real estate
- Understand the motivation for the settlement of villages and how many of these same forces influence urban spatial layout today
- Discuss the urban growth models and their relevance to anticipating future growth trends
- Explain the fundamental principles of the economic base theory
- Discuss the economic measures of community growth

There are several key factors that the appraiser must keep in mind when appraising real property. One is that all parts of the valuation analysis must lead toward a clear and convincing conclusion of (1) the highest and best use and (2) the value of the appraised property. As the regional and community analysis is undertaken, the appraiser needs to be a bit of a skeptic, continually raising the question "Does this information assist me in arriving at the highest and best use and value of the appraised property?" If not, then, however interesting the data may be, they should be discarded and the appraiser's efforts redirected to uncover information that will shed light on these two key issues. Another important concern is to ascertain the social, political, and economic implications of the region and community as related to the appraised property's market appeal and value. Too often there is a tendency to "plug in" irrelevant data simply because it permits the appraiser to quickly complete the regional analysis section. Again, if the information provides no insight as to a property's highest and best use and value, there is no reason for it to be included. It simply clutters the report, increases the cost of the appraisal service, and causes many clients to scoff at the inclusion of superfluous information that has no practical value for business decision making.

There is no set way of analyzing a region and community for all classes of property or for all valuation purposes. The nature of the property and assignment dictate the geographic breadth of regional analysis as well as the intensity with which such analysis is pursued. For example, the appraisal of a single-family residence does not involve consideration of the same regional forces as an appraisal of a factory. Residential value is governed strongly by community and neighborhood concerns. The industrial property value also may be influenced by neighborhood factors, but its value is tied to a larger extent to regional influences such as employment pools, education and training facilities, access to materials, transportation, and markets.

THE REAL ESTATE MARKET

To understand more fully the nature and predictability of property income, the appraiser must be aware of the peculiar characteristics of land and how these affect income and the market for real estate. Immobility, indestructibility, and non-homogeneity of land cause the market for real estate to be *local* in character. As a commodity, real estate cannot be moved from place to place. An oversupply of land in one community cannot be used to balance an undersupply in another. Real estate must be employed where it is, and, because of its fixity in geographic location, it is extremely vulnerable to economic effects caused by shifts in local demand.

Property dissimilarity further imposes special market conditions. Because of location, no two parcels of real estate are physically alike. Each parcel is geographically fixed and has distinct legal descriptions which as a rule are accurately set forth in public plat book records. Since no one parcel of land may be legally substituted for another without the purchaser's consent, value considerations must reflect this market immobility.

The durability of real estate, too, causes maladjustments in both supply and demand on a local market level. Thus, where demand for any reason suddenly falls, the inability to adjust supply quickly will cause real estate prices to fall as well. An oversupply of real estate creates a buyer's market, which in turn results in lower price offerings and hence lower market values. A sudden increase in demand also is difficult to meet. The resultant scarcity causes market prices of real estate to rise, creating an upward swing in the real estate cycle.

The appraiser must take great care to study objectively the underlying forces creating supply and demand for real property. Since value, by definition, is a measure of the present worth of future rights to income, temporary booms or depressions must be analyzed to determine their cause and to forecast their duration and effect on typical buyer-seller bargaining power. The real estate cycle, sometimes induced by land speculations, more often reflects the state of general business and housing or construction cycles. This cycle is influenced by demand factors, positively or negatively, through increased or decreased overall employment, wage levels, supply of mortgage funds, interest rates, and personal savings. The real estate cycle operates on the supply side as well, reacting to population changes, family formation, vacancy ratios, and cost of land and housing supply in relation to prevailing and anticipated income or rental levels.

Although physically abundant, land that is economically usable is often in short supply. Improvements, in the form of access roads, drainage facilities, water, and other community utilities, must be added to raw land before it ordinarily can be subdivided and offered for sale through marketing channels. Because such improvements are costly and can be successfully carried out only with community sanction and on a relatively large scale, there often is a shortage of land that economically warrants being used. This lack of building sites in turn causes upward pricing of real estate holdings to a point where community development and real estate market activities may be adversely affected. On the other hand, speculative optimism, unchecked by a concern for community planning and infrastructure and public service costs, may cause potentially valuable land to be developed in quantities too great to be absorbed by prevailing demand, thereby creating an oversupply which may depress the market for real estate for many months or even years.

There is a definite relationship between business booms and depressions on the one hand, and real estate market activity on the other. As a rule the downward swing of the real estate cycle precedes the downward swing of business activity caused by business recession, and lags long beyond the period of general business recovery. As economic adjustments or recessions cast their shadows, typical home and land buyers prefer to wait and to maintain a cash position during periods of adversity. In a like manner, when business recovery takes place, expenditures for fixed investments are undertaken only after all immediate needs for clothing, food, and other necessities are met. Thus the economic inflexibility of real estate as a commodity and its sensitivity to mortgage interest rates is directly accountable for the greater intensity of real estate booms and depressions and the longer life of the real estate cycle as compared with the normal upward and downward swing of general business activity. It is important, therefore, that the appraiser keep a finger on the pulse of business as well as on real estate market activities in order to forecast with reasonable accuracy shifts in market conditions and changes in the anticipated income flow that forms, for a given property and at a given time, the basis of real estate value. The impact of social, political, and economic forces on the market for real estate from a national, state, and community level has been discussed at length in the preceding chapters.

CAUSES OF URBANIZATION

If we are to consider the effects of regional forces on real estate values, we should understand why people have come together to form villages, towns, and cities over the years. We should also understand the spatial evolution and growth of cities. Initially, there was the *tribe*, which, in its earliest stages, was nomadic rather than agrarian. The size of an area controlled by a tribe was a function of its ability to defend it. Later, tribal communities were faced with three choices for survival:

1. Migrate to newer and better hunting grounds.
2. Split the tribe and part of the members move to another place (this same practice was later employed in the Roman city-states).
3. All remain in the same place—with agriculture then becoming the principal vocation rather than relying on hunting as previously.

Villages grew from the third option first. The key to growth of the village was the ability of those who tilled the soil to produce and store and trade the surplus. This specialization of labor freed others to pursue different trades. In fact, this period might be thought of as the beginning of job specialization. Even in these early days of settlement, villages were transitory due to soil and game depletion. Settlers moved every 20 years or so. The size of villages was largely determined by the distance that water could be carried. During this period, more productive plant cultivation and animal domestication occurred, allowing for more permanent settlements.

The next type of human settlement was the *preindustrial city*, where several different modes of development occurred. During this era, villages and then later medieval cities were created essentially for reasons of government, commerce, culture, religion, courts, and mutual protection.

During the Industrial Revolution (the steam age), greater specialization and subdivision of work occurred. Factories were developed with the wealthy living nearby, often a convenient carriage drive away. The poor lived farther away, sometimes beyond the safety of the walled city. Later, as transportation and communication facilities improved, the wealthy moved to outlying areas and the poor migrated to points within walking distance of the factories.

In ancient times the location of cities such as Rome on its seven hills and Paris on an island were chosen largely for defense. In this country examples of such defense settlements or fort communities were Fort Pitt (Pittsburgh), Nashborough (later named Nashville), and Savannah. Trade routes—the lines of least resistance between the sources of products and their final markets—in all ages have prompted commercial cities to be situated at places where a break in transportation occurred, such as on rivers and at harbors, gaps in mountain chains, and at the fall line of rivers. The confluence of rivers or the intersection of a river with a bay has also influenced the founding of cities. A favorable elevation has caused cities to be built. Memphis is such an example. The intersection of plains with mountains requires a change in modes of transportation. Cities such as Milan and Munich have developed at such places. Proximity to raw materials has prompted the settlement of many cities, such as Saginaw and Seattle, with proximity to forests, or Los Angeles and San Jose, near orchards. Water power, sufficient to generate electricity, has created many cities, such as Fall River and Lowell in New England. Political seats have created other cities, such as Washington, D.C. River cities tend to flourish where there is deep water sufficient for barge transportation.

Comparative Advantage

David Ricardo is credited with articulating the concept of *comparative advantage* or cost, which holds that a country should produce those goods in which it has the greatest comparative advantage and least comparative disadvantage with other countries. He argued that economic specialization between countries explained why some areas produced a limited number of goods and then imported other complementary goods. Although comparative advantage cannot always be isolated to a single factor, some of the initial reasons that villages and, later, cities were developed were based on their inhabitants' trying to gain an advantage or to make their lives more pleasant by taking advantage of natural resources, climate, and rivers as a source of transportation and power.

City Spatial Form and Growth

Several theories have been set forth over the years to explain the physical form of cities. The balance of this section will identify some of the key urban growth models. These growth theories, for the most part, are static in nature and do not fully explain all the variations of urban growth. Nevertheless, an understanding of these theories is helpful in gaining a better insight into why urban areas have developed as they have over the years. Also, it allows the appraiser to forecast more accurately the probable future nature, direction, and rate of urban development.

Concentric Ring Growth Theory

Ernest W. Burgess developed the concentric ring theory of growth in the 1920s.[1] This static model of urban growth can be challenged as to its inability to explain fully contemporary city growth. It is overly simplistic in its giving the appearance that there are distinct zones. Yet this spatial development model gives appraisers a systematic means for analyzing the growth patterns of a metropolis.

To some extent all cities have grown in a circular fashion except as inhibited by physical, social, or political forces. This circular growth is the result of the maximum land use activities being contained within a minimum surface area. Moreover, transportation routes can be minimized through this form of spatial development. Land use activities throughout a city generally follow some logical pattern. The appraiser should seek this pattern in anticipating the sustained productivity and value of properties throughout a metropolis.

Burgess divided his model city into fixed zones as shown in Figure 5.1. His model oversimplified actual growth patterns since the various zones would be irregular in shape. The center (or ring 1) is the financial and office district and the retail shopping zone. Generally, the central business district (CBD) forms the cen-

---

[1] See R. E. Park and E. W. Burgess, *The City* (Chicago: The University of Chicago Press, 1925), pp. 47–62.

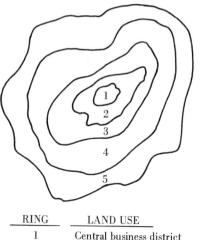

RING	LAND USE
1	Central business district
2	Transition zone
3	Low-income housing zone
4	Middle-to high income housing zone
5	Commuters' zone

Figure 5.1   Concentric Ring Growth Pattern

tral point of this inner zone. It is located at the point with convenient access to people from throughout the city. Burgess recognized the likelihood of satellite business centers, which developed independently of the central business district. These subcenters were generally located at or near subway railroad stations or intersecting points between principal highways.

The transition zone is the second ring, adjacent to the central business zone but usually not entirely encircling it. Scattered throughout this zone are old residential dwellings that form the residential section of an earlier and smaller city. This district provided housing for immigrants until they were financially able to move out to more desirable neighborhoods. This area contained the city's slums. At its outer perimeter were the wholesale and manufacturing activities.

The low-income housing zone (ring 3) was for "working men's" homes. These homes generally did not completely encircle the central part of the city, which might be viewed as a breakdown in the concentric circle theory. Many of these homes were substandard and previously had been large homes. Immigrants from ring 2 tended to move into this zone as they became financially able.

Ring 4 is the middle-to-high-income housing zone. The higher rent areas in the residential zone tend to radiate out from the city but do not generally completely enclose the city. More expensive apartments and single-family homes are located here.

The commuters' zone (ring 5) was found beyond the periphery of the city in the form of scattered, isolated communities having diverse values of homes. Lots in ring 5 tended to be comparatively large. This zone formed a buffer between the urban and rural areas. Today we would call this the suburbs.

Axial Growth Theory

Residential areas tend to develop along the fastest transportation routes, according to Richard M. Hurd.[2] These transportation routes frequently elongated the centrifugal development to form the spokes of the starlike urban pattern described in Figure 5.2. Other types of development, such as industrial activities, often developed in a lateral pattern along the shores of a river.

Hurd spoke of axial growth characterizing city growth, based on quick access to or from the business center by way of turnpikes.[3] Chicago is a prime example of a city developed in a spokelike fashion along the turnpikes and later, commuter railroad lines. He observed that there was "a continual contest between axial growth pushing out from the center along transportation lines and central growth, constantly following and obliterating it, while new projections are made further out the various axes."[4]

The normal result of axial and central growth is a star-shaped city. The growth extends first along the main thoroughfares radiating from the center, and later the parts lying between are filled in with land uses not so strongly dependent on immediate access to the main traffic arteries. Varying topography may alter this type of growth somewhat.

Sector Growth Theory

Beginning in 1934, Homer Hoyt compiled data on over 200 cities for the purpose of studying the internal structure and growth of American cities.[5] Nine major observations were drawn from this Federal Housing Administration residential study. This study was conducted to identify residential mortgage lending risks; therefore, it focused on residential neighborhoods. This theory provides one more perception of growth in American cities that should be appreciated by real estate appraisers. The sector theory as illustrated in Figure 5.3 holds that the direction and pattern of growth in cities tends to be governed by some combination of the following considerations:

1. High-grade residential growth trends to proceed from a given point of origin, along established lines of travel or toward another existing nucleus of buildings or trading centers.
2. The zone of high-rent areas tends to progress toward high ground, which is free from the risk of floods, and to spread along lake, bay, river, and ocean fronts, where such water fronts are not used for industry.
3. High-rent residential districts tend to grow toward the section of the city that has free, open country beyond the edges and away from "dead-end" sec-

[2]Richard M. Hurd, *Principles of City Land Values*, 3rd ed. (New York: The Record and Guide, 1911) (originally written in 1903).

[3]*Ibid.*, p. 41.

[4]*Ibid.*, p. 59.

[5]Homer Hoyt, *The Structure and Growth of Residential Neighborhoods in American Cities* (Washington, D.C.: Federal Housing Administration, 1939).

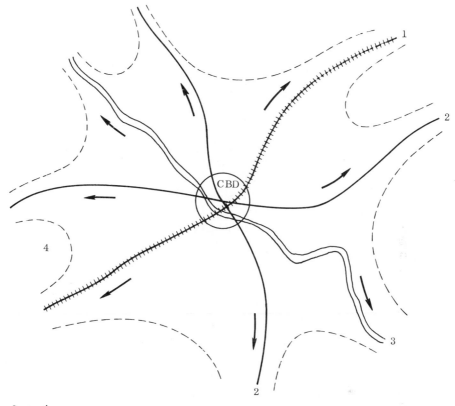

Legend:

CBD   Central Business District
  1   Railroad
  2   Expressways and Highways
  3   Navigable River
  4   Boundaries of Major Development
➤   Major Paths of Growth

Figure 5.2   Axial Growth Pattern

tions which are limited by natural or artificial barriers to expansion. It was found that open fields, golf courses, country clubs, and country estates act as a magnet to pull high-grade residential areas in their direction.

4. Higher priced residential neighborhoods tend to grow toward the homes of the leaders of the community.

5. Movement trends of office buildings, banks, and stores pull higher priced residential neighborhoods in the same general direction.

6. High-grade residential areas tend to develop along the fastest existing transportation lines.

7. Growth of high-rent neighborhoods continues in the same direction for a long period of time.

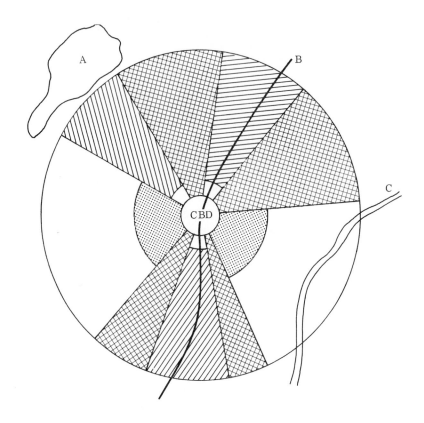

Legend

A   Scenic Lake
B   High Speed Traffic Artery
C   River – Subject to Flooding
CBD   Central Business District

High Grade Residential Neighborhood

Middle Income Residential Neighborhood

Low Income Residential Neighborhood

Industrial Activities

Figure 5.3 Sector Theory of Urban Growth

8. Deluxe high-rent apartment areas tend to be established near the business center in old residential areas.

9. Real estate promoters may bend the direction of high-grade residential growth. Such developments and communities as Miami Beach, Coral Gables, and Roland Park in Baltimore typically have quality amenities and strong architectural controls.[6]

[6]*Ibid.*, pp. 117–19.

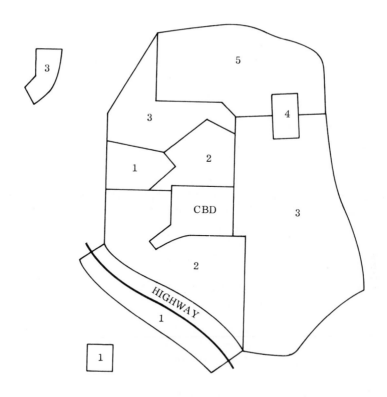

CBD	Central Business District
1	Industrial Cluster
2	Low-Income Residential
3	Middle-Income Residential
4	Business District
5	High-Income Residential

Figure 5.4 Multiple-Nuclei Growth Theory

Multiple-Nuclei Growth Theory

In 1945, Chauncey D. Harris and Edward L. Ullman observed clusters of fairly discreet forms of land use activities (see Figure 5.4). From these observations they developed the multiple-nuclei theory of urban growth. They found different nodes of development for retail, industrial, residential, and wholesale land use activities.[7] A major feature of this urban land development model was that the various nodes of development were caused by certain activities requiring specialized facilities. Certain similar activities group together because they benefit from close proximity. Certain unlike activities are repulsed by other unlike activities. Certain activities can afford occupancy only in various districts.

[7]Chauncey D. Harris and Edward L. Ullman, "The Nature of Cities," *The Annals of the American Academy of Political and Social Sciences* (November 1945).

None of these urban development models is universal or infallible. The appraiser, however, should be familiar with each theory to use the appropriate parts to recognize past growth patterns and project future land use development trends. Influences on the direction and intensity of urban growth should be tracked continually. These include the availability of developable tracts of land and public services as well as the nature and quality of supporting services such as schools, employment, and shopping centers.

REGIONAL ANALYSIS

This section presents a generalized approach to regional analysis and is concluded with a discussion of two methods of regional economic analysis. The first method is economic base analysis, and the second is input-output analysis. However, virtually all regional analyses begin with employment, which provides the basis for population projections.

General Concerns in Regional Analysis

Although the regional environment is too often neglected in favor of site and building inspection and analysis, it is critically important to the success of any land use activity. Sometimes it is easier to conclude on the structural and design adequacy of a building than the more subtle economic implications of external demographic trends. These trends may not be readily perceptible, but within any region, they are present and the appraiser should identify and convey to the client the implications of regional trends.

One dimension of the economic "health" of any region is its employment opportunities. This includes the diversity of employment as well as the unemployment rate and recent and probable future employment trends. Some of the extreme situations to be alerted to are those regions with few industries or different but closely related and interdependent industries. Such lack of diversity can cause economic turmoil and property value declines if those industries' products fall into disfavor. The same difficulty can exist in areas where the economy is largely dependent on a military base. If the base closes, a calamitous effect is felt throughout the region. Thus employment diversification is an important factor to consider especially for lenders who want to avoid making too many loans in areas lacking such diversification.

Other regional data of interest to the appraiser are the master plan for jurisdictions within the region. The proposed directions and nature of future growth, when considered along with established development patterns, zoning, and planned utility routes, can greatly assist in judging the probable growth areas for the future.

The comparative supply and demand for real estate is another key component of regional analysis. If, for example, the appraisal is of a residential rental project, it is important to have some idea of the demand for such rental space. This demand estimate will be based in large part on available and competing space, success of competing projects, availability of utilities, and adequacy of transportation and jobs throughout the region. Also, it is important to understand population trends. Is the population becoming older or younger? Are households growing or shrinking in size? Are there more two-household wage earners? Are there large percentages of teenagers in households? Are there strict environmental regulations that severely restrict future development? All this information is beneficial in trying to judge the probable success and value of projects or individual properties.[8]

Regional Analysis Techniques

Two types of regional analysis often used are economic base and input-output analysis. These techniques are too elaborate for most appraisal assignments. Nevertheless, the methodology and regional considerations embraced in each analytical technique are of value to the appraiser.

Economic Base Analysis

This technique was initially developed by Robert M. Haig and later refined by Homer Hoyt. This method focuses on how a community earns its living. The economic base of a community is broken down into two parts. These are basic (export) industries and nonbasic (service) industries. A ratio of the number of service jobs created by basic industry jobs sometimes can be developed for short periods of time, but this relationship does not uniformly hold up for all communities. Nevertheless, the important concern is that a community cannot grow by "taking in its own laundry" but must sell products or services to others beyond its region. A regional economic base study typically seeks to

1. Identify regional export activities.
2. Forecast the probable growth in these activities.
3. Evaluate the impact of export activity on nonbasic activities of the region.[9]

This analysis, which generally is undertaken by local government planning departments, provides a basis for appraisers to judge the nature and size of future population changes within the region.

This once-popular method has largely been replaced with available data from the U.S. Census Bureau so that the actual output performance of industries can be readily determined. A criticism of this approach is the use of fixed relationships between the basic and nonbasic industries and the assumption that industries in various categories of Standard Industrial Classifications (SIC) are either basic or nonbasic. This relationship is a function of the product produced

[8]A good reference on regional analysis is Lawrence A. Kell, Chapter 5, "Location Analysis," in *Real Estate Counseling*, James H. Boykin, ed. (Chicago: American Society of Real Estate Counselors, 1984).

[9]Edgar M. Hoover, *An Introduction to Regional Economics* (New York: Alfred A. Knopf, Inc., 1971), p. 222.

and the location of an establishment within a region. For example, a perishable product manufactured near the center of a region tends to be sold largely within the local region.

A variation of economic base analysis is location quotient. In using this method, regional employment by SIC is listed from published sources such as the U.S. Department of Labor. The percentage of each SIC category is computed and then compared to corresponding national figures. This ratio can be used to project employment for the region when only national employment projections are available. Errors may occur as economic and social shifts take place for the region in comparison to the nation as a whole.

Regional Input-Output Analysis

This technique is used largely by regional economists and planners in trying to trace the impact of demand on a region's income and employment. It sets up a series of "accounts" to describe the relationship of economic activities between the region and area beyond the region as well as among establishments within the region. The basis for input-output analysis is regional businesses, households, all levels of government within the region, the stock of capital in the region, and individual activities beyond the region.

The idea underlying regional input-output analysis is to trace industrial output and purchases from producer to consumer in order to show the effect of an increase of output by one industry on purchases by other sectors of the economy. This technique is not one ordinarily used by appraisers.

In using any studies or reports on a region, the appraiser should be concerned with the credibility of the forecast as well as the purpose of the study. Not all data obtained for use in regional analysis by the appraiser are necessarily unbiased. Hence, if the highest and best use, demand for property, or its value rests on such forecasts, care should be used in discerning the validity of such information. If valid, it can provide a means to study interregional relationships and the comparative economic soundness and functioning of different regions.

POPULATION TRENDS AND CHARACTERISTICS

Because of the direct correlation between the growth of population and rising values of real property, the real estate appraiser must be fully informed as to the history of population changes in his or her community, especially over the preceding decade. In addition, population shifts, deaths, births, and migratory patterns must be analyzed to forecast the population status over periods extending 20 or 30 years into the future—or, in any case, a period not shorter than the remaining economic life of the property under appraisal. The city's growth pattern, whether favorable or unfavorable, can best be ascertained by comparison with the rate of growth for the state and the nation. Where community population increases faster than that of the nation and the state, real estate values generally will also keep pace with the accelerated growth. A study of population trends should extend over several decades. A meaningful population study must also consider, among other things, the following:

1. *Age-group analysis.* It is important to know the number of persons aged under 20, 20 to 40, 40 to 60, and 60 and over. A favorable ratio of persons in the 20-to-60 age group provides the work force on which the community depends for economic support. Excessive ratios of young or dependent old people may pose community problems, the effects of which, if any, must be known and evaluated.

2. *Income bracketing.* To judge the demand for different price brackets of residences, it is beneficial to know the breakdown of the population by per capita or household income groupings. This information will reveal the probable demand for different-priced apartments and houses as well as for different goods and services.

ECONOMIC MEASURES OF COMMUNITY GROWTH

Although measures of economic growth may be equally applicable in small as in large communities, it must be kept in mind that the hazards of economic forecasting increase with a decrease in community size. An estimate of probable changes in economic standing for a city of 100,000-and-over population can be made with greater certainty than a similar estimate for a community of 25,000-and-under population. The loss of a dominant industry, for instance, due to plant relocation may prove economically disastrous in a small community. A similar loss in a metropolitan city, however, may go wholly unnoticed because of the constant readjustments that take place in the everyday economic life of a large city. For instance, thousands of businesses come and go each year in and around New York City and Chicago without creating a noticeable effect on the balance of these cities' overall economic growth and activity. Indicators of economic growth that warrant observation and provide a basis for judging the quality of investment prospects in a community include, among others, the following:

1. Number of banks, bank deposits, and savings.
2. Office space absorption and vacancy trends.
3. Construction and building permits (volume and dollar amounts).
4. Automobile and truck registration.
5. Railroad, airline, and bus passenger traffic.
6. Assessed value of real property.
7. Number of electric meters and telephone service connections.
8. Retail sales and buying income per household.
9. Number of gainfully employed by type of employment.
10. Real estate sales volume.

As a rule, the economic growth of a community is best judged by comparison with other communities of like size and character within the region or by a per capita or per family basis comparison with similar cities anywhere in the country. The census of housing and population income and characteristics, and the special census of manufacturing, provide excellent source data for such comparative growth studies. Ready access to the economic growth data listed previously should enable the real estate appraiser to formulate accurate forecasts of what the future holds in store for a given community. The number of banks and their total deposits and savings reflect on a per capita basis the degree of well-being as well as the extent of optimism or pessimism that motivates the general economy. Construction volume in dollars and the number of building permits issued during a given period are excellent measures of speed of economic growth or decline. Registration statistics of automobiles and trucks, compared with state or national averages, provide further proof of conclusions supported by commercial indexes. Saturation measures of electric and telephone service on a per household basis are useful in ranking a community on the economic "totem pole." Most informative of all as a statistical measure of community standing, however, are retail expenditures, disposable income per household, and number of gainfully employed persons by type of employment.

Employment data should be analyzed as to the number and percentage engaged in primary occupations as compared with those employed in secondary or service establishments. A primary source of employment involves a product or service that is exported from the community and creates purchasing power from outside areas that supports service and community economic life generally. As a rule, each primary worker may support two secondary workers engaged as butchers, tailors, barbers, shopkeepers, and general servicers. Thus a new industry providing jobs for 100 family breadwinners in effect accounts for 200 more families which are needed to provide essential social, educational, economic, and recreational community services.

Generally, it is not too difficult to ascertain the status and past performance record of a city and to keep one's finger, so to speak, on the economic pulse of the community under study. Economic source data as a rule can be obtained from utility companies, which are called on to forecast community needs for many years into the future. State development agencies as well as local and state chambers of commerce take periodic inventories to ascertain the relative impact of economic growth on the city, the region, and the state. Appraisers should keep themselves well informed as to the economic health of their communities and be in a position, when compiling reports for appraisal clients, to support their judgments concerning the prospects for growth, decline, or stability of property values within the confines of a city over the economic life of the real estate for which they form value judgments.

Care must be taken not to rely too strongly on past performance. Every effort should be made to forecast accurately, on the basis of past trends, the prospects for continued economic growth as well as the anticipated rate of progress compared with past performance. The value of property, as previously emphasized, lies in the future; and the ups and downs of property income, and hence property worth, are closely tied to the economic strings of the city to which real property is irrevocably attached.

THE NATURE AND CHARACTER OF CITIES

Cities, broadly speaking, may be classified as *primary* and *secondary* urban centers. A primary community is one that has its own economic base, and whose existence is not dependent on the operations or welfare of other communities within the state or the metropolitan region. A secondary community, on the other hand, is in effect a satellite whose length and strength of orbit depends on the principal cities to which it owes its existence. These satellite communities are better known as "bedroom" cities where commuters (people who work where they would rather not or cannot afford to live) reside. The economic strength of a satellite community is entirely dependent on the strength of the primary community, of which it is often an unwilling part. To appraise property in such a community necessitates careful evaluation of the forces that keep the primary community operative.

Primary communities may be subclassified into cities which reflect their cause of urbanization, as follows:

Industrial cities	such as Detroit, Michigan, and Pittsburgh, Pennsylvania.
Commercial cities	such as Chicago, Illinois, and San Francisco, California.
Mining cities	such as Scranton, Pennsylvania, and Wheeling, West Virginia.
Resort cities	such as Miami Beach, Florida, and Atlantic City, New Jersey.
Political cities	such as Tallahassee, Florida, and Washington, D.C.
Educational cities	such as Chapel Hill, North Carolina, and Ann Arbor, Michigan.

Many communities have assumed a diverse economic base and may fall with equal importance into two or more subclassifications. Thus New York City is both industrial and commercial in character. Miami, Florida, which started as a resort city, is presently one of the most important commercial cities in the South, having one of the largest international airport facilities in the country. New Orleans, which served as the fishing and commercial center of Louisiana, is important today as an international shipping center with impressive harbor facilities and shipping tonnage.

In evaluating property within a city, it is important to gain a clear understanding not only of the city's origin but also of the economic base that presently and prospectively will support continued city growth and development. A city with a single dominant industry or service activity, no matter how prosperous currently, must be evaluated with caution. Having all its eggs in one basket is hazardous for a city, and technological changes or competition within the area may cause economic slumps that severely depress its property values. Even though the appraiser is unable to forecast with accuracy future changes in economic patterns, he or she must call potential value hazards to the attention of clients and reflect the concern of informed investors for the required yield which the market will deem necessary to attract investment and venture capital.

THE CITY'S PLAN AND LAND USE PATTERN

City planning is an art more often talked about than practiced. Most cities with a simple village origin grow like Topsy until economically costly growing pains call for hindsight actions which foresight actions could well have avoided. (The growth of Boston along its early cowpaths is a vivid example of this kind of chaotic growth.) Generally, the development of a city should be planned 10 or even 20 years in advance under a comprehensive land use plan. In judging a site's highest and best use, an appraiser must be familiar with its prescribed future use according to the comprehensive land use plan in addition to understanding its current zoned uses. Communities, like people, are dynamic in character, and their expanding or changing needs must be served through orderly expansion beyond the city's limits where necessary. Like a business enterprise, a city as a whole must prosper if it is to continue effectively as a going concern.

As a requisite to better understanding of a city's potential growth and development, the appraiser should inventory the physical and economic resources of the subject community and maintain an active file to keep such data up to date. The first step in the collection of pertinent data is to obtain an official city map on which the legal boundaries are delineated and the street pattern shown. Wherever possible, land use data about contiguous county areas should be obtained to observe facilities for street and utility service expansion. A well planned city, as a rule, reduces per capita urban operating costs and facilitates the ready flow of people and commerce during normal as well as rush hours.

Next in importance is checking the adequacy of land use patterns and city zoning in relation to public needs for sites suitable for improvements as follows:

Residential homes.
Commercial buildings.
Industrial parks and districts.
Public administrative and school buildings.
Recreational parks and playgrounds.

Residential areas should be free from natural hazards or those introduced by humans, and should provide the opportunity for privacy and enjoyment of the amenities of home ownership. Through streets should be routed around residential areas to reduce traffic flow and noise, especially during evening hours. Streets should be paved; curbs, gutters, and, when appropriate, sidewalks provided; and all essential utilities—including water, electricity, telephone, sanitation, and storm sewerage—made available for service connection. Effective zoning should call for uniform building setback, minimum plot width, and building construction and population-density regulations. Nonconforming uses of an industrial and commercial nature should especially be screened out by natural or artificial buffer zones, such as landscaped plantings. The degree to which good planning is lacking, and the extent to which private or public hazards are permitted to encroach on residential areas, will significantly affect the lifespan of the neighborhood and the duration of economic life throughout which property values are assured freedom from external obsolescence.

Commercial facilities—including retail stores, bank and office buildings, and wholesale establishments—should be grouped together in an orderly pattern, with ample off-street parking to permit uncrowded commerce and safe shopping. Spot and faulty business zoning impede orderly city growth and may adversely affect the value of surrounding property. Generally, areas chosen for commercial development are level, of even contour, and readily accessible by surface transportation. Commercial areas should also be strictly zoned and protected by building ordinances to promote public interests and to safeguard private ownership of one of a city's most valuable investments—the 100 percent shopping district.

Industrial sites, which prior to World War II were given little protection from encroachment by other supposedly higher uses, have often been hampered in potential development and in relation to their highest and best land use. Manufacturing, whether heavy or light, provides for many communities the "bread and butter" resources on which much of the secondary commercial and service industries depend. Planned industrial parks should play an important part in every master plan. Such industrial locations should be situated near major highways, railroad rights of way, waterways, and airports. Ready road and rail access, adequate utility service, and freedom to expand give assurance to established industries that they are wanted and respected for the part they play in the corporate structure of the city. In communities where residential, commercial, and industrial growth complement rather than encroach upon each other, the values of real estate will reflect the increased income stability and the longer productive lives of properties.

Public administration buildings, school buildings, and recreational parks and playgrounds should all be carefully planned and located to serve public needs adequately and effectively. Even quasi-public buildings such as churches, libraries, museums, and exhibition halls should be placed as near as possible to the community areas they serve. In political, educational, and resort cities, greater care must be taken in planning the location of public structures that may influence the character and extent of private building investment and thus indirectly influence the very structure of city growth. Familiarity with the principles of good city and regional planning will better enable the real estate appraiser to judge economic forecasts in the light of regional and state developments in which the subject community plays a part.

SUMMARY

In conducting a real estate valuation, an appraiser should keep in mind that all phases of the analysis must lead toward a clear and convincing conclusion of (1) the highest and best use and (2) the value of the appraised property.

An understanding of the effects of regional forces on real estate values is facilitated by first understanding why people came together to form villages, towns, and cities. Villages and cities were created during the preindustrial city era essentially for reasons of government, commerce, culture, religion, courts, and mutual protection. Over the years, such influences as trade routes, confluence of rivers, favorable elevation, proximity to raw materials, and deep water to aid transportation have influenced the locations of towns and cities.

Several urban spatial growth theories have been developed to explain the physical form of cities. These theories include the following.

The *concentric ring growth theory* was developed by Ernest W. Burgess in the 1920s. He divided his model city into five zones which began at the center and progressed outwardly. They are known as: (1) central business district, (2) transition zone, (3) low-income housing zone, (4) middle-to high-income housing zone, and (5) commuters' zone.

The *axial growth theory* was conceived by Richard M. Hurd in 1903. His model pointed out that residential areas tend to develop along the fastest transportation routes and subsequent growth occurs in the parts lying between these routes, resulting in a star-shaped city.

In 1939 Homer Hoyt introduced the *sector theory* which explained the internal structure and growth of American cities. His research revealed that nine considerations explained the direction and pattern of cities, especially residential neighborhoods.

Later, in 1945, Chauncey D. Harris and Edward L. Ullman observed clusters of fairly discrete land use activities which led to their *multiple-nuclei theory* of urban growth. They found that certain similar activities benefit from close proximity, whereas unlike activities are repulsed by other unlike activities.

Two types of regional analysis are sometimes used to analyze a region's economic health. One of these, economic base analysis, focuses on how a community earns its living. It breaks a community into two parts: basic and nonbasic industries. The second method, regional input-output analysis, is used to trace the impact of demand on a region's income and employment.

Since there is a direct relationship between population growth and rising real property values, the appraiser should understand a region's population shifts, deaths, births, and migratory patterns.

Generally, the economic growth of a community is best judged by comparison with other communities of like size and character within the same region. Yet, care must be taken to avoid placing undue emphasis on past economic performance.

Cities, in general, are classified either as *primary* or *secondary* urban centers. A primary community has its own economic base, whereas a secondary community is a satellite and its well-being depends on a nearby primary city.

In judging a site's highest and best use, an appraiser must be familiar with its prescribed future use according to the local comprehensive land use plan in addition to understanding its current zoned uses.

REVIEW QUESTIONS

1. Explain how the real estate cycle relates to general business downturns and recoveries.
2. How can the earlier causes of urbanization be applied to present regional analysis?
3. Briefly list the basic features of each of the urban growth theories.
4. Identify and discuss the urban growth theories that are useful in analyzing a region today.
5. Explain how the economic base analysis helps you understand regional economy.
6. What is the main purposes of regional economic and population analysis?
7. List economic measures of community growth in addition to those discussed in the chapter. Explain how these economic measures assist in the appraisal of real estate.

READING AND STUDY REFERENCES

ANDERSON, AUSTIN G. "Common Pitfalls in Real Estate Market Research," *Real Estate Finance* (Spring 1989), pp. 77–81.

BARRETT, G. VINCENT, and JOHN P. BLAIR. *How to Conduct and Analyze Real Estate Market and Feasibility Studies.* New York: Van Nostrand Reinhold Co., Inc., 1982. See Chapter 2, "How to Analyze Real Estate Markets."

CARN, NEIL E., and JOSEPH S. RABIANSKI. Chapter 23, "Nonsite-Specific Market Analysis," *The Real Estate Handbook*, 2nd ed. (Maury Seldin and James H. Boykin, eds.). Homewood, Ill.: Dow Jones-Irwin, 1990.

CARTES, CHARLES P. "Market Analysis: Its Interface with the Review, the Appraisal and the Feasibility Process," *Appraisal Review Journal* (Winter 1982), pp. 63–69.

FANNING, STEPHEN F., and JODY WINSLOW. "Guidelines for Defining the Scope of Market Analysis in Appraisal Assignments, *The Appraisal Journal* 56, no. 3 (October 1988), pp. 466–476.

HOYT, HOMER. "The Structure and Growth of American Cities Contrasted with the Structure of European and Asiatic Cities," *Urban Land* 18, no. 8 (September 1959).

HURD, RICHARD M. *Principles of City Land Values*, 3rd ed. New York: The Record and Guide, 1911. See particularly Chapters 2 and 5, "Location of Cities" and "Directions of Growth."

KELL, LAWRENCE A. Chapter 5, "Location Analysis," *Real Estate Counseling*, James H. Boykin, ed. Chicago: American Society of Real Estate Counselors, 1984.

MARTIN, W. B. "How to Predict Urban Growth Paths," *The Appraisal Journal* 52, no. 2 (April 1984), pp. 242–249.

MYERS, DOWELL. "Extended Forecasts of Housing Demand in Metropolitan Areas: The Coming Downtown," *The Appraisal Journal* 55, no. 2 (April 1987), pp. 266–278.

RATCLIFF, RICHARD U. *Real Estate Analysis*. New York: McGraw-Hill Book Company, 1961. See Chapters 2 and 4, "The Urban Setting" and "The Locational Basis of Real Estate Value."

TIEBOUT, CHARLES I. *The Community Economic Base Study*, Supplementary Paper 16. New York: Committee for Economic Development, 1962.

VANDELL, KERRY D. "Market Analysis: Can We Do Better?" *The Appraisal Journal* 56, no. 3 (July 1988), pp. 344–350.

6
Neighborhood Value Analysis

Learning Objectives

After reading this chapter, you should be able to:

- Understand the essentials of a neighborhood
- Discuss the neighborhood life cycle
- Identify the principal ways that neighborhoods are delineated
- Appreciate the nature of neighborhood characteristics
- Recognize amenities that enhance the appeal of residential neighborhoods
- Point out the major attributes of commercial and industrial districts

NEIGHBORHOOD DEFINED

In the past, neighborhood analysis has been distorted by two major misconceptions. The first was an idealized notion of what a neighborhood *should be* rather than what it *actually is*. Such phrases as "homogeneous grouping of people" or "similarity of backgrounds" do not necessarily describe residential neighborhoods as they exist and are not fully accurate for nonresidential districts. People of different backgrounds and different but usually compatible land use activities come together and remain together for various reasons. The other mistake of the past has been perpetuated by appraisers, mortgage lenders, and the federal government through a misunderstanding of the effect on property values by racial minorities. Some earlier "studies" implied with an apparent high degree of precision the negative effect of racial "infiltration," as it was once called.

Today, neighborhood analysis is enhanced through the use of a model that universally applies to all land use activities—residential as well as nonresidential. Therefore, a generalized definition of *a neighborhood is a bounded area wherein certain land use activities are attracted and retained by sets of linkages*. Ideally, these activities are compatible, but if they are not, there is still a neighborhood. Unquestionably, a neighborhood's economic and social strength is enhanced if its

97

activities are compatible. This relationship may be called its linkages.[1] "Linkages" are the "glue" that hold a neighborhood together. *Linkages may be thought of as external economies or centripetal forces. It is the periodic interaction between people or establishments that draw and hold them together.* Examples of linkages are where machine work is subcontracted by one business for another nearby business or where close proximity to legal or advertising services makes a particular location attractive for a small business unable to afford such specialized in-house staff. In a residential neighborhood, linkages may exist between the home, shopping, schools, social and religious centers, and place of employment.

Usually, it is not difficult to delineate a neighborhood, because of natural or artificial barriers that enclose it or because of physical attributes or development practices that characterize the area. In most planned communities, neighborhoods come into existence as a result of deliberate design by developers who, with the aid of deed restrictions, control the character, growth, and expansion of neighborhoods. In Figure 6.1, a desirable neighborhood has formed about a spring-fed creek that winds its way alongside a dual-lane, oak-tree-shaded boulevard. Mere size, of course, does not determine a neighborhood. However, the larger the size, the better the protection from infiltration by inharmonious land use influences or detrimental property uses. At the same time land use activities near the center of a large neighborhood or district sometimes are remote from desired supporting services.

THE NEIGHBORHOOD AGE CYCLE

An important step in the valuation process is the determination of the position of a neighborhood in its *age cycle.* All neighborhoods have a beginning, and most follow a life pattern that reflects growth, maturity, decline, and transition or rehabilitation as influenced by the socioeconomic forces that shape community land use patterns. A typical neighborhood age cycle may be diagrammed as in Figure 6.2. It should be noted that there generally are several recurring cycles in the life of a neighborhood. Moreover, the value trend may either be declining or increasing. Frequently, neighborhood property values decline to a point of fostering new uses which reverse the trend of declining values.

As indicated in Figure 6.2, the *development period* of any neighborhood is the period of growth. The length of time to reach neighborhood maturity will vary

---

[1]This concept is amply covered in the literature, but sometimes by different names. See, for example, Robert M. Haig and Roswell C. McCrea, "Major Economic Factors in Metropolitan Growth and Arrangement," *Regional Survey of New York and Its Environs,* Vol. 1 (New York: New York Regional Planning Committee, 1927), p. 37; Ernest M. Fisher and Robert M. Fisher, *Urban Real Estate* (New York: Henry Holt and Company, 1954), p. 324; R. L. Estell and R. Ogilvie Buchanan, *Industrial Activity and Economic Geography* (London: Hutchinson University Library, 1966), pp. 94–96; Alfred Weber, *Theory of the Location of Industry,* translated by C. J. Freidrich (Chicago: The University of Chicago Press, 1928), pp. 163–67; Edgar M. Hoover, *The Location of Economic Activity* (New York: McGraw-Hill Book Company, 1948), pp. 118, 120; Walter Isard, *Location and Space-Economy* (Cambridge, Mass.: Technology Press, MIT; New York: John Wiley and Sons, Inc., 1956), p. 182.

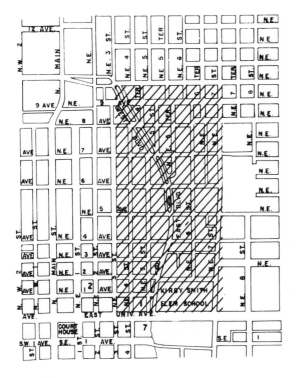

Figure 6.1 Highland Subdivision, Gainesville, Florida

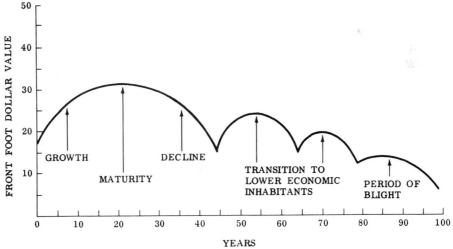

Figure 6.2 Typical Neighborhood Age Cycle

with the size of the area under development as well as its appeal and location, but 15 to 20 years is generally considered typical. Peak neighborhood values are reached during the period of maturity, when improvements generally are at their prime appearance. The length of the maturity period will vary with the kind and size of the community and the economic well-being of neighborhood residents and businesses. Generally, a period of 20 to 25 years may be regarded as a typical stretch of time during which a neighborhood remains static in quality.

As buildings pass the prime of their economic life, and as a new generation replaces the old, properties that no longer fulfill the needs of the original buyers are placed on the market and a new and generally lower economic class of buyers enters the area. This is the stage of neighborhood decline. At first, the trend of property values gradually becomes lower, as shown by the diagram in Figure 6.2. As demand for properties increases with the transition to the new class of residents (who tell their friends and relatives of the better residential district now available at costs they can all afford), demand pressure causes property values to rise again, and often to the heights reached in prior years. This cyclical economic behavior repeats with successions of transitory ownership changes until the neighborhood reaches a status of blight and prospective slum condition. At this stage, or in prior periods, public or private renewal efforts may change the character of a neighborhood to a higher and better use. Sometimes, older residential areas with modestly priced, but architecturally appealing, homes become fashionable for families who restore these structures. This process is known as *gentrification* as higher income families replace lower income residents who often are of a minority race. The same concept applies to nonresidential neighborhoods.

It is the appraiser's responsibility to determine the position of the neighborhood in its life cycle and to estimate the effect of neighborhood age and obsolescence on amenities of ownership or income from its use over the remaining economic life of the subject property. As will be demonstrated in Chapter 15, the income productive capacity of a property, as a rule, lessens with age; and under the impact of the forces of obsolescence, consideration must be given to the value effect of such contingencies by (1) stabilizing in the appraisal the anticipated declining income flow, (2) increasing the risk rate at which such prospective diminishing income must be capitalized, or (3) reflecting the rate of value decline in a higher capitalization rate. Frequently, new highways or bypasses have been constructed, diverting many of the former clients and customers away from a particular neighborhood. Eventually, alternative uses for these commercial businesses are developed and the buildings are rehabilitated as shown in Figure 6.3.

NEIGHBORHOOD CHARACTERISTICS

In judging the quality of a residential neighborhood the following physical, population, and economic factors warrant analysis:

    A. Physical features
        1. Location within the city.
        2. Nature of terrain.
        3. Nature and load-bearing capacity of soil.
        4. Features of natural beauty.
        5. Drainage facilities, both natural and fabricated.

Figure 6.3   Former Three-Bay Service Station Converted into a Savings and Loan Facility

   6. Street pattern and street improvements, including essential public
      utilities.
   7. Type of architecture and quality of housing.
   8. Nature, frequency, and cost of public transportation facilities.
   9. Proximity to schools, stores, and recreational facilities.
   10. Freedom from environmental hazards.
B. Population characteristics
   1. Types of residents—as to income and education.
   2. Living habits and care of homes.
   3. Attitude toward law and government.
   4. Homogeneity of cultural and civic interests.
   5. Age grouping and size of families.
C. Economic influences
   1. Extent (percentage) of development.
   2. Percentage of homes owner occupied.
   3. Professional or occupational means of earning a livelihood and income
      stability.
   4. Taxation and assessment levels, and tax burdens.
   5. Zoning and deed restrictions.
   6. Investment quality of area for VA, FHA, and institutional mortgage
      loan financing.
   7. Price range and rental value of neighborhood homes.

NEIGHBORHOOD BOUNDARIES

It is desirable to define the limits of the neighborhood wherein an appraised property is situated. There are several reasons for this delineation. By knowing the limits of a neighborhood, the search for comparable properties can be concentrated within a defined area. Further, a knowledge of neighborhood boundaries permits the appraiser to determine the present state of the neighborhood. Finally, it is possible to ascertain more accurately the highest and best use of the appraised property. It is important to note that neighborhood analysis is an essential link in the eventual conclusion of an appraised property's highest and best use and its value. It is not an overstatement to say "so goes the neighborhood, so goes the property." The desirability and in turn the value of a property are inextricably intertwined with the soundness of its neighborhood.

The question then arises: How can the boundaries of a neighborhood be identified? There are several ways to do this. The most obvious neighborhood boundaries are physical in nature (see Figure 6.1). Examples of physical boundaries are natural features such as rivers, changes in topography such as ravines or hills, or changes in soil conditions or natural growth (e.g., trees). Fabricated features can also establish neighborhood boundaries. Examples are railroad rights-of-way, expressways, streets, and major building complexes. Legal and governmental factors sometimes will shape a neighborhood. For example, the limits of a platted residential subdivision can set boundaries as well as can different zoning classifications, municipal boundaries, and the school districts in those cities where there is no forced busing of school-age children. A final type of neighborhood boundary is established by the price levels of residences. Generally, residential neighborhoods are fairly similar with regard to the price of lots, which in turn dictates the price of homes built, which finally sets the level of family income needed to live in various neighborhoods. The appraiser therefore needs to consciously identify neighborhood boundaries as an important step in arriving at the value of an appraised property.

LOCATION CHARACTERISTICS

The first step in the analysis of a neighborhood is to delineate the boundaries that encompass the area under value study. This can readily be done by identifying the names of streets that enclose the neighborhood on the north, south, east, and west. Generally, the boundaries of a neighborhood are not difficult to establish because of physical features—natural or artificial—that distinguish the area as a unit of development. Normally, the neighborhood is referred to by name as originally recorded on public plat records or by reference to a distinguishing natural feature that marks the area such as San Francisco's Telegraph Hill. Often a neighborhood, because of location within the city, acquires a favorable reputation which to status-seeking buyers enhances the location or status value of the area thus described.

The *terrain*, too, may influence development practices and should be described and noted as to its effect on value. For residential purposes, gently rolling land is preferable to a flat plateau or low-lying land. People, it seems, prefer to live on hillsides, which make possible the enjoyment of a more extensive view of a community's skyline. Elevations, and sometimes valleys, provide a sense of security which attracts residents to that location in preference to others. A flat terrain, on the other hand, is preferable for commercial and industrial development. It is costly and difficult to make building storefronts conform to sloping sidewalks, and an uneven area is hazardous in a wintery climate where ice and snow make travel on sloping streets dangerous. Thus the nature of the terrain may strongly influence the marketability of a site for a particular type of intended and permissible use.

Many appraisal reports are deficient in that reference to the *quality of soil* has been omitted. The reason for this oversight, no doubt, is that the "normal" load-bearing quality of the soil is taken for granted and that the quality of the soil for other purposes is considered of negligible importance. An appraiser, however, has no right to take anything for granted. It is his or her obligation to gather factual data and to report it without prejudice instilled by custom or personal preference. In commercial uses of land the presence of rock, quicksand, hard pan,[2] and high or low water levels may significantly influence the costs of construction and hence—since the income to land under a highest and best use is residual in character—the value of the land. Even for residential use, the quality of soil for lawn development and general landscaping may be of deciding importance to a purchaser.

Features of natural beauty that distinguish a neighborhood also deserve careful attention. Majestic trees that line an avenue or provide welcome shade in summer months add value to the abutting land far beyond the price of cords of wood that can be realized if the same trees (as is often, sadly, the case) are cut down and sold for lumber. The presence or nearness of creeks, streams, rivers, lakes, or even reservoirs enhances the value of sites to varying degrees, depending on land use, beauty of terrain, and utility of the waterways. In any case, the appraiser in formulating a final value decision should carefully inventory the influencing value features for a particular use which should interest the report reader.

Of increasing importance in suburban developments, where the extension of public sewerage facilities proves too costly, is the adequacy of soil drainage both natural and synthetic. The existence of hard pan or inadequate soil drainage as based on *soil percolation tests*[3] may cause a site or area to be declared unsafe for installation of sanitary septic tanks, and may result in the denial of building permits in order to safeguard public health. Drainage of surface or flood waters dur-

---

[2]Layers of dense sand or limestone that prevent the percolating (penetration) of surface waters to subsurface levels.

[3]Soil penetration or drainage tests taken by municipal, state, HUD, and other agencies to determine soil fitness for installation of private sanitary sewage systems.

ing periods of seasonal rains or storms also must be considered. Failure to do so is a serious omission of factual data, and may subject the appraiser to a lawsuit and court charges for professional negligence.

The impact of neighborhood *street patterns and street improvements*, including essential public utilities, must next be carefully evaluated. Subdivision cost studies confirm that development expenditures for road grading, paving, curbing, gutters, water mains, storm drains, and sanitary sewerage facilities may range from a minimum of 60 to as high as 90 percent of the value of a developed site. Conversely, the value of raw land may be as little as 10 and seldom more than 40 percent of the value of a fully developed residential site. The presence or absence of street improvements must therefore be emphasized and evaluated by market comparison studies, as demonstrated in Chapter 7. The street pattern, too, should be noted and its influence on value stressed. The grid street pattern which characterizes older neighborhoods, and which is still favored by some economy-minded builders and developers, is frowned on by modern planners and discouraged in proposed subdivisions submitted for loan approval to the VA or the FHA. Curvilinear streets and cul-de-sac avenues cause automobile traffic to slow down and usually limit their use to residents in the immediate area, creating greater enjoyment and safety for neighborhood occupants both young and old. Market prices confirm buyer preference for *safe* lot locations, and the appraiser must recognize this in the adjustment of comparable sales where neighborhood street patterns are unsatisfactory.

In judging the quality of a neighborhood, it is essential to observe the type of *architecture and the quality of housing.* In design, a distinction should be made between "homogeneity" and "monotony." It is the former that is preferable in residential neighborhoods. Pleasing and tasteful exterior dwelling design in an attractive setting enhances the appeal and market value of residences. A good neighborhood is not marred by irregular building setbacks, extremely unorthodox designs, and clashing periods of architecture. The appraiser should be conversant with the features and characteristics of basic architectural styles and be able to classify the ancestry of a residence at least in terms of its relationship to colonial, English, Latin, contemporary, or native-conventional periods of construction.

Although the automobile has diminished the importance of intracity transportation, nevertheless the quality of a neighborhood is enhanced by the ready availability of *public transportation.* Pedestrians are still the rule rather than the exception in community life, and the use of public surface transportation to reach schools, shopping, and recreational centers provides an essential convenience. In considering the value added by convenient public transportation, the type, frequency, reliability, and cost of service should be ascertained and reported. Generally, a neighborhood with ready accessibility to high-quality public transportation is preferable to a wider segment of the populace and deemed more valuable than one isolated from arteries of public surface travel.

Spreading decentralization, aided by the increasing use of electricity and electronics for the performance of essential household and even home office tasks, has encouraged the development of residential subdivisions far from the public conveniences offered to residents of central urban areas. Although efforts are made to provide essential public conveniences for these outlying developments through the construction of neighborhood shopping centers, schools, parks, and recreation areas, there is nevertheless a considerable time lag from the period of original neighborhood development to the period when sufficient neighborhood shopping facilities and schools become a reality. Years often elapse without such public conveniences, and the values of suburban sites will reflect their absence. An appraiser, therefore, must accurately report the distances in blocks or miles from the subject neighborhood to nearby schools, stores, and churches as well as to the central business area. He or she must also estimate the effect that distance from these public service facilities may have on the value of the subject property.

The last, but by no means the least, of the physical features that make or break a neighborhood from a value point of view is the relative freedom that residents of the area enjoy from *health hazards and other adverse environmental influences.* The danger of through automobile traffic was mentioned before. Other hazards to be checked are smoke, dust, noise, and the gradual infiltration of nonconforming land uses. A check of area residents, public officials, and the opinions of informed persons, along with a thorough neighborhood investigation, should disclose the absence or presence of neighborhood nuisances. Where evidence points to conditions that presently or potentially will impair the health or peace of area residents, the effects on the present value of neighborhood sites must be ascertained and disclosed in the section on area influences.

SOCIAL FORCES INFLUENCING NEIGHBORHOOD VALUES

People create value—hence the compatibility and congeniality of people in an area are important to sustain and enhance neighborhood desirability and property values. In a good-quality neighborhood there will be compatibility and a sense of personal security among residents as well as well maintained properties.

The role of the appraiser is to interpret the attitudes of buyers, sellers, tenants, and owners toward real estate in a neighborhood. The appraiser should never inject his or her own value biases or preferences. Also, the appraiser is obligated to reflect actual values in a neighborhood rather than to conjecture on the effect on value of a particular situation. Instead of noting that a neighborhood exhibits "pride of ownership," he or she should document the actual state of maintenance of properties and off-site improvements.

Inspecting the neighborhood and interviewing its residents will give additional value clues as to the *living habits* of residents and their *care of property.* These external evidences give the neighborhood a character of its own. Well-kept lawns, attractive landscaping, neat and well-maintained buildings, and clean, quiet thoroughfares all are important ingredients for stable property values.

Attitude toward government is another essential social trait that enters into a neighborhood quality rating. Ownership and possession of property are legally backed and sanctioned. Respect for law and judiciary opinions minimizes vandalism and the violation of constitutional rights to the quiet enjoyment of life, liberty, and property. Law-abiding citizens, too, will refrain from the illegal and illicit use of premises—use that undermines the moral character of the area. A breakdown in moral fiber, respect for law, and law enforcement itself destroys neighborhood value more swiftly than do the physical forces of wear, tear, decay, and the actions of the elements. A statement of the apparent attitude of local residents toward law, order, and government is an essential part of a report on property value.

Another social characteristic lending support to neighborhood stability and value is the relative *homogeneity of cultural interests.* Generally, this homogeneity is evidenced by friendly relations among neighbors, membership in the area's civic organizations, organized neighborhood social and cultural events, the extent of resident participation in social clubs, and the sharing of recreational facilities by residents of all ages. This social aspect of neighborhood population is, of course, closely linked to the homogeneity of occupational and professional economic interests, as will be shown in the following discussion.

Racial discrimination in appraisal and mortgage lending practices has occurred from a variety of causes—good intentions in making loans in sound neighborhoods, ignorance of actual economic facts, and slipshod analysis. The term *redlining* was once used by the Federal Housing Administration to indicate residential neighborhoods that had a history of septic tank failures. Later, the term assumed negative racial overtones. Mortgage lenders avoided making loans in such designated racial minority neighborhoods due to perceived high risks, but such lending practices actually accelerated the physical deterioration in these neighborhoods.

It is unlawful as well as unethical for an appraiser to discriminate in appraising real estate. The National Fair Housing Act, Title VIII, of the Civil Rights Act of 1968 prohibits discrimination in the sale, rental, or financing of real estate on the basis of race, color, religion, sex, or national origin.

In addition to avoiding discriminatory appraisal practices related to individuals as mentioned previously, the appraiser must avoid such unwarranted actions regarding a dwelling's age and location. Each property should be considered on its own merits, with the appraiser avoiding any arbitrary judgment that automatically places older residences or those in older neighborhoods at a disadvantage.

NEIGHBORHOOD ECONOMIC CHARACTERISTICS

A matter of important interest to mortgage lenders, and of prime concern to real estate investors, is the extent or percentage of neighborhood development. The image of investment failures and mass property foreclosures during the early 1930s—although more than a generation removed—is still much talked and read about in informed real estate circles. The danger then and the fear now are based on overexpansion caused by thinly supported hypothetical demands envisioned as a projection of a temporary "boom" psychology rather than a projection based on the analysis of long-term trends and socioeconomic resource studies. An area thinly developed or improved below 50 percent of its land capacity holds investment hazards which must be reflected in value estimates and stressed in appraisal report writing. Undeveloped sites, too, tempt owners and speculators into premature, hasty, and often faulty land utilization that may adversely affect the value of abutting and neighboring properties. The appraiser is duty-bound to remove the "blinders" that cause the uninformed to evaluate an apparent "jewel" of a property without an objective study of its situation.

If the neighborhood is of residential character, it is important to determine the number or percentage of total homes that are *owner occupied*. Tenants, no matter how desirable, are transient in character,[4] and frequent changes in the kind and composition of tenant families create a sense of insecurity and area instability which impairs the investment quality of a neighborhood. Tenants, too, lack a feeling of belonging, and generally their lack of pride of ownership is reflected in lax lawn and home care. Owner-occupancy status can readily be secured from public tax-record data or from tax officials, especially in states where homestead tax exemptions are accorded owner-occupants.

The frequency of *property turnover* and the percentage of home, apartment, or store vacancies provide another measure of economic rating. As a rule a neighborhood with well-established owner-occupants of long standing poses fewer investment risks than one characterized by frequent property transfers. Excessive property sales, no matter how valid the reason, create a feeling of investment insecurity or a climate of speculation, resulting in distorted market prices and often deferred maintenance for the properties involved. Since property values—unless otherwise stated—reflect the present worth of future rights to income, at least over the remaining economic life of property improvements,[5] the appraiser must take into account the influence of temporary price determinants while objectively predicting future value under anticipated typical market operations. Vacancies, too, if in excess of normal ratios varying from 2 to 7 percent of total space supply—depending on geographic location and kind of real property—must be analyzed with care. Excessive vacancies may indicate a glutting of the market or its becoming less appealing to owners, tenants, and investors.

The economic status of neighborhood occupants, their means of livelihood, and their income stability are of further economic importance. The predominant professional or occupational interests of area residents should be established. The order generally descends from executives to professionals (doctors, lawyers, etc.), junior executives, white-collar office workers, skilled mechanics, clerks, and skilled laborers. Although a neighborhood can normally be classified as housing one or more of the occupational or professional interest groups, it is the relative

---

[4]Studies of tenancy in metropolitan areas support the fact that the average tenant moves once each year.

[5]A shorter holding period generally typifies income-producing property resulting from federal income tax laws and mortgage terms.

income and status of the area occupants (assuming compatible social status) that matter most. Generally, there is a direct relationship between the range of annual earnings and the range of property values. Executives earning $100,000 to $125,000 annually generally seek homes in the price range $250,000 to $300,000. On the other hand, white-collar workers earning from $30,000 to $40,000 annually create a demand for housing in the $75,000 to $90,000 price range.[6] Of equal significance is income stability. Certain occupations, though lower on the scale of earning power (such as teachers and salaried technicians), enjoy greater job security and stability of income. Neighborhoods occupied by this group, or any similar group—such as retired persons—whose stability of income is relatively certain will experience greater stability in their level of property values. However, it is possible that in some neighborhoods of fixed-income residents property values will be adversely affected as rising utility bills prevent normal home maintenance due to lack of income.

The economic impact of property taxation and assessment levels and burdens must be carefully analyzed in the valuation process. Although property taxation is generally a matter for study and analysis as a political policy of county and city governments, it is a commonly recognized fact that tax differentials exist between most newer and older communities. Initially, new neighborhoods and even communities will have relatively low tax burdens. Fast-growing suburban neighborhoods often fit this pattern. They also are characterized by crowded schools and inadequate public services. Eventually, residents demand improved public services, with the result being tax rates increasing at a faster rate than in older established neighborhoods (or tax districts). The appraiser needs to anticipate such trends. Over the short term, municipal capital budgets for schools, parks, sewers, and streets provide an indication of these tax rate trends. Where such tax differentials exist, they must be noted and evaluated over the immediate years as being, at best, a form of community "good will." Conversely, neighborhoods may have been overburdened with heavy assessments for road and area improvements that have brought little if any benefits to the properties affected. To illustrate: In a court case, property owners in Miami Beach, Florida, challenged the right of the municipality to levy assessments for the widening of Indian Creek Drive. The property owners contended that the improvements were made to relieve congested traffic on another street, and that as a result of the widening the affected street had turned into a noisy thoroughfare that had caused neighboring values to lessen. The state supreme court, in a 4–3 decision, ruled against the city and in favor of the property owners by recognizing that benefits which may accrue from road widening in a residential area are questionable. The majority opinion at one point asked: "Whoever heard of making a traffic count to locate a home?" However, where uneconomic assessments are enforced the appraiser must estimate their effect (considering both amount and duration) on the market value of neighborhood properties.

[6]Housing affordability varies with mortgage down payment and interest rate along with a purchaser's other debt repayment obligations.

Since the typical buyer, contrary to accepted opinion, is not especially informed on matters concerning public zoning and private deed restrictions, it is the appraiser's responsibility to evaluate the benefits or detriments constituted by the presence or absence of protective zoning and private deed restrictions. Care must be taken to recognize that zoning by itself does not create value. For example, to zone an area for business counter to good planning or in excess of such land use demands may not only lower the value of the property so zoned but may also lessen the value of surrounding properties in the neighborhood. Zoning is designed to restrict *land* uses. Good zoning, however, does assure uniformity of land use and thus provides protection against inharmonious land uses which exploit the public good for purposes of excessive private gain. The presence, need, and adequacy of deed restrictions must also be evaluated. Zoning ordinances can often be rescinded or adversely amended. Deed restrictions, however, have stronger legal sanctions which attach to and run with the land and cannot be violated without consent of the property owners affected, as well as without compliance to stipulated contractual provisions under which land use exceptions may be made. The period of time during which deed restrictions are effective must be noted along with the permissible extension of existing deed restrictions where they are deemed essential to protect the character of the neighborhood over the economic life of the neighborhood improvements.

Of interest to investors and home owners, as well as being of value significance, is whether a neighborhood warrants approval for FHA, VA, or *institutional mortgage loan financing*. In recent years where an increasing number of marginal home buyers depend on high-ratio mortgage-to-value loans, the unavailability of government-underwritten or institutional loans—especially if caused by a lack of required neighborhood improvements such as sewerage, water, paving, and so on—may curb sales of residential properties to an extent where a buyers' market will reflect in lower prices the absence of liberal mortgage terms. The loss in property value in a restricted mortgage market is often far in excess of the costs of street and utility improvements the absence of which disqualifies the neighborhood for government-approved or conventional mortgage loans.

An important guide as to how well an appraised property fits in a neighborhood is the value range of residential homes. In fact, the first step in classifying a neighborhood is to establish the price range within which typical homes can be exchanged in the open market. It is this price range[7] that guides the appraiser in his or her selection of comparable properties to serve as a market guide for estimating the worth of a particular property in the subject neighborhood. Care must be taken not to attempt a narrowing of the range to the point where "guess-timating" becomes a strong temptation. As a rule, the spread of values may range from a minimum of 25 to a maximum of 50 percent of typical sale values. The appraiser thus may conclude a range, for instance, of $100,000 to $125,000. Although circumstances may warrant exceptions, it should be kept in mind that a

---

[7]The other major consideration is the similarity of comparable properties. This is truly the "yardstick" of value for the appraised property.

typical and not an extreme range is sought in categorizing a neighborhood. The actual, or imputed, rental value per month or per annum of typical neighborhood structures, too, is of interest. This information serves in helping to check market sales estimates against the capitalized value found under the income or earnings approach to value.

No appraisal is complete without a thorough analysis of the environmental forces and improvements that affect the value rating of a neighborhood. Every appraisal form in use currently provides for entry of data that aid the field appraiser in reaching a value conclusion concerning the quality of the area under study.

NEIGHBORHOOD ANALYSIS IN FORM REPORTS

Figure 6.4 shows those factors that the Federal Home Loan Mortgage Corporation (Fannie Mae) considers important in residential neighborhood analysis. Some of the key concerns revealed in this section of the "Uniform Residential Appraisal Report" are the demand for homes, development activity and trends, type of occupancy, typical age and price range of homes, proximity and adequacy of employment, neighborhood educational, shopping, and recreational facilities, and general appeal of the neighborhood to prospective purchasers. In using this section of the appraisal form, it should be remembered that the purpose of a neighborhood analysis is to identify an area that is subject to the same influences as the appraised property.

A neighborhood analysis should focus on all factors that influence value, such as economic, social, government, and environmental. The appraiser should be objective in considering factual information, noting any changes within the neighborhood that may affect the marketability of properties, such as known environmental hazards. The following will provide an explanation of each of the sections of the "Neighborhood" part of this form.

NEIGHBORHOOD

LOCATION	☐ Urban	☐ Suburban	☐ Rural
BUILT UP	☐ Over 75%	☐ 25-75%	☐ Under 25%
GROWTH RATE	☐ Rapid	☐ Stable	☐ Slow
PROPERTY VALUES	☐ Increasing	☐ Stable	☐ Declining
DEMAND/SUPPLY	☐ Shortage	☐ In Balance	☐ Over Supply
MARKETING TIME	☐ Under 3 Mos.	☐ 3-6 Mos.	☐ Over 6 Mos.

PRESENT LAND USE %	LAND USE CHANGE	PREDOMINANT OCCUPANCY	SINGLE FAMILY HOUSING PRICE $ (000)	AGE (yrs)
Single Family ____	Not Likely ☐	Owner ☐		
2-4 Family ____	Likely ☐	Tenant ☐	Low	____
Multi-family ____	In process ☐	Vacant (0-5%) ☐	High	____
Commercial ____	To: ____	Vacant (over 5%) ☐	Predominant	____
Industrial ____			–	
Vacant				

NEIGHBORHOOD ANALYSIS	Good	Avg	Fair	Poor
Employment Stability	☐	☐	☐	☐
Convenience to Employment	☐	☐	☐	☐
Convenience to Shopping	☐	☐	☐	☐
Convenience to Schools	☐	☐	☐	☐
Adequacy of Public Transportation	☐	☐	☐	☐
Recreation Facilities	☐	☐	☐	☐
Adequacy of Utilities	☐	☐	☐	☐
Property Compatibility	☐	☐	☐	☐
Protection from Detrimental Cond.	☐	☐	☐	☐
Police & Fire Protection	☐	☐	☐	☐
General Appearance of Properties	☐	☐	☐	☐
Appeal to Market	☐	☐	☐	☐

Note: Race or the racial composition of the neighborhood are not considered reliable appraisal factors.

COMMENTS ____________________

Figure 6.4 Neighborhood Analysis Grid Used by FHLMC and FNMA (10/86)

Location.   An appraised property's location must be identified either as urban, suburban, or rural. An urban location is one within a city; suburban is an area adjacent to a city; and rural relates to country locations. Although resort properties are sometimes intended for seasonal use, Fannie Mae will acquire loans on such properties only if they are suitable for year-round occupancy.

Built-up and growth rate.   This part indicates the percentage of a neighborhood's land that is developed. Areas that are under 25 percent built up do not qualify for maximum financing due to the higher risk associated with raw land, especially in a rural area. Areas that are between 25 and 75 percent built up are eligible for maximum financing if they have either stable or steady growth. Areas that are over 75 percent developed qualify for maximum financing if property values are not declining.

Property values.   Maximum mortgage financing is available only in neighborhoods where property values either are stable or increasing. If the values are declining, the appraiser is expected to comment on the cause and its effect on the appraised property's marketability.

Demand/supply and marketing time.   The appraiser is expected to comment on any signs of an oversupply of housing since this can adversely affect property values. Generally, six months is judged to be normal for the sale of a residence.

Present land use.   Residential property values usually are enhanced by the presence of other similar dwellings. Therefore, it is required that the appraiser indicate the relative percentages of developed land in a neighborhood put to such uses as single family or commercial.

Land use change.   Of concern to maintaining stable neighborhood property values is the nature of the neighborhood and its rate of change. Racial and ethnic composition are not legitimate indicators of future neighborhood property values. However, the appraiser should be alert to changes in land uses that may harm the appeal and value of residential properties. For example, the appraiser should note such changes as residential to commercial or owner- to tenant-occupied properties. Also affecting neighborhood values are dwelling occupancy levels.

Price range and predominant price.   The prevailing price range of homes in a neighborhood should be given by the appraiser, excluding exceptionally high or low prices. Against this price range, the appraised property can be classified as either typical, overimproved, or underimproved. It should be noted in the appraisal report why the property is an overimprovement and how an adjustment is made for this feature in the "sales comparison analysis" adjustment grid.

Age range and predominant age.   The appraiser should base his or her estimate of a neighborhood's age range on typical properties rather than exceptionally new or old properties. As a rule, residences that fit within the typical age range offer better security for loan purposes. However, well maintained older properties in conveniently located neighborhoods with appealing architectural features often are superior to newer homes in less accessible suburban locations.

Neighborhood analysis rating.   The items listed in this section are important to prospective home buyers. The appraiser must comment on any rating that is less than "average," explaining its impact on the subject property's marketability and value.

NEIGHBORHOOD ATTRIBUTES OF RETAIL DISTRICTS

Greater dependence by shoppers on private means of transportation has accelerated the development of suburban shopping centers where ready access and ample parking invite unhurried and carefree shopping. As a result, the relative importance of the central city as a retail entity has greatly waned over the past three decades. A scene typical of many downtowns is abandoned retail stores and frequently the exodus of one or more large department stores which have moved to suburbia. In the past 30 years the number of shopping centers in the United States has grown from 2,000 to 30,000. There are several different classifications of shopping centers. Following is a brief description of these different centers.

Convenience center.   These centers, often called neighborhood shopping centers, generally range in size from 30,000 to 40,000 square feet with a site of 3 to 5 acres. They are anchored by a food store or possibly a drugstore. Other typical tenants are pizza shops, beauty salons, dry cleaners, video stores, and yogurt shops. There may be self-service gasoline pumps. Key features of a convenience center are location and accessibility. Unquestionably, a successful convenience center must be located near its customers. The trade area typically is within a 2-mile radius and requires a population of 10,000 to 20,000. A daily vehicle volume of approximately 20,000 is desirable as well. Figure 6.5 depicts a convenience center site plan.

Community center.   Sometimes called a power center, this center generally contains 125,000 to 175,000 square feet of leasable space and may occupy from 10 to 20 acres, depending on market size and tenant mix. The trade area typically varies from 40,000 to 100,000 persons, drawing from a radius of 4 to 5 miles. Anchor tenants include a discount or specialty store. Other popular tenants in these centers include building supply stores, supermarkets, toy stores, drugstores, and apparel shops.

Regional center.   These destination shopping villages may vary in size from 300,000 to 1,000,000 square feet and be sited on parcels ranging from 25 to 100 acres. They typically require a trade area of at least 150,000 persons who are

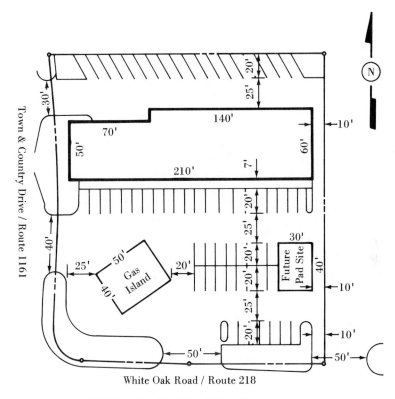

Figure 6.5 Retail Convenience Center Site Plan (Courtesy of Silver Convenience Centers, Fredericksburg, Virginia)

located within a 30-minute drive. A regional center generally will have two or more department store anchor tenants coupled with perhaps 50 to 100 stores.

Other types of shopping centers include super regional malls with over one million square feet of shopping space and usually three major department stores of 100,000 square feet each. Specialty centers may have no anchor tenants and feature off-price, discount, furniture, or other similar stores. These special centers often group at interchanges along major interstate highways.

OFFICE DISTRICTS

Office districts are composed of different types of users and the buildings may be classified according to their occupancy and usage. For instance, an office building may be (1) single tenancy, (2) multitenancy (see Figure 6.6), (3) special use, such as a medical building, (4) general-purpose building, and (5) ownership form if it is a condominium. In studying either a central office district or suburban office park, it should be viewed from the perspective of the tenant. The tenant will want to know how long it takes to commute to the district. Are parking lots nearby and

Figure 6.6 Modern Suburban Multitenancy Office Building (Courtesy of Pruitt Associates, Richmond, Virginia)

spaces reasonably priced? Is the district safe for employees and clients? Are rentals competitive? Are there ample supporting amenities such as restaurants, hotels, and shopping facilities?

INDUSTRIAL DISTRICT ATTRIBUTES

There exist today a large number of centrally located industrial districts. These earlier districts often are characterized by older multistoried buildings that front on city streets and alleys. These buildings were individually planned, built, and owned. The modern counterparts to these districts are planned industrial parks. Generally, there is one developer but numerous tenants and/or building owners. Increasingly, these parks contain office buildings and public facilities such as fire stations and technical schools along with the traditional manufacturing and distribution functions.

Some of the district or park attributes that are judged to be important for industrial activities are an ample supply of utilities (water, sewer, and source of power). Accessibility to markets, to sources of materials, subcontractors, a skilled work force, and adequate circulation and parking for trucks is needed. Access to alternative transportation is required for certain industries in the form of rail and airlines. Adequate public school systems, housing, shopping, and recreation and religious facilities are also desirable in order to attract and retain employees. Realistic zoning and building codes are expected to protect industrial districts from incompatible land uses and from inferior construction.

Most industrial parks are dominated by warehouse and distribution facilities rather than manufacturing establishments. Thus these modern parks tend to have low employment ratios (employees per square feet of building area). Sometimes, communities resist the development of warehouses since they provide relatively low employment opportunities and real estate tax revenue.

Industrial districts ideally should possess the following characteristics:

1. Reasonably level land outside of floodplains with no more than 5 percent slope, which is capable of being graded at a reasonable cost.

2. Direct access to railroad sidings, major trucking routes, cargo airports, and in some cases deep-water terminals.

3. Within easy commuting time of residential areas and accessible to transit and major thoroughfares directly connected to such labor pools.

4. Availability of adequate public utilities.

5. Compatibility with surrounding uses such as other industrial parks.

6. Locations where adequate on-site pretreatment of waste is possible for those industrial activities involving water-borne wastes.[8]

SUMMARY

A *neighborhood* is a bounded area wherein certain land use activities are attracted and retained by sets of linkages. *Linkages*, in turn, are thought of as external economies or centripetal forces. Further, linkages are the periodic interaction between people or establishments that draw and hold them together.

Neighborhoods have a life cycle which includes growth, maturity, decline, and transition or rehabilitation. The appraiser is responsible for determining the position of the neighborhood life cycle and for estimating the effect of neighborhood age and obsolescence on the amenities of ownership or income from its use over the remaining economic life of the subject property.

The quality of a neighborhood is revealed by its physical features, population characteristics, and economic influences.

The boundaries of a neighborhood may be identified by physical characteristics which either are natural or fabricated. Legal and governmental factors also may delineate a neighborhood. Sometimes, neighborhood boundaries are set by the price level of residences.

Influences on a neighborhood's appeal include its reputation, terrain, soil quality, soil drainage capability, architecture and quality of housing, availability of public transportation, and freedom from health hazards and other adverse environmental influences.

When using the Uniform Residential Appraisal Report, an appraiser must observe and note the following neighborhood characteristics: location, built-up and growth rate, property values, demand/supply and marketing time, present

[8]James H. Boykin, ed., *Industrial Real Estate*, 4th ed. (Washington, D.C.: Society of Industrial and Office Realtors, 1984), p. 94, citing F. Stuart Chapin, Jr., *Urban Land Use Planning*, 3rd ed. (Urbana, Ill.: University of Illinois Press, 1979), pp. 366–67.

land use, land use change, price range and predominant price, and age range and predominant age of properties.

In recent years, suburban shopping centers have grown at the expense of downtown retail districts. The suburban centers generally are identified as (1) convenience centers with 30,000 to 40,000 square feet of leasable store space, (2) community centers with 125,000 to 175,000 square feet, and (3) regional centers which may vary in size from 300,000 to 1,000,000 square feet.

In analyzing office districts, buildings should be classified according to their predominant occupancy and use, such as single tenancy, multitenancy, special use (such as a medical building), general-purpose building, and ownership form if it is a condominium.

Older, centrally located industrial districts largely have been replaced by suburban industrial and increasingly industrial-office parks. Ideally, these parks have level land outside of floodplains, direct access to transportation routes, availability of public utilities, compatible adjacent land uses, adequate on-site pretreatment of waste for those industrial activities involving water-borne wastes, and are convenient to labor pools.

REVIEW QUESTIONS

1. Briefly discuss two past errors made in neighborhood analysis.
2. Discuss and give examples of the "linkages" concept.
3. Why is it important to accurately perceive the phase of life cycle that a neighborhood is in at the date of appraisal?
4. List the several ways that a neighborhood can be delineated.
5. Drawing from your own observations, describe a neighborhood that has been revitalized. What factors were responsible for its economic upturn?
6. List 10 residential neighborhood characteristics that should be investigated by an appraiser.
7. Discuss the earlier justification for the practice of "redlining" and explain the fallacy of this practice when later applied to minority neighborhoods.
8. Discuss the importance of traffic analysis in residential, commercial, and industrial neighborhoods or districts.

READING AND STUDY REFERENCES

American Institute of Real Estate Appraisers. Chapter 8, "Neighborhoods and Districts," *The Appraisal of Real Estate*. Chicago: AIREA, 1987.

BLOCK, WILLIAM K. "Issues in the Assessment of Neighborhoods in Transition," *Assessment Digest* (May–June 1986), pp. 10–16.

BLOOM, GEORGE F., and HENRY S. HARRISON. Chapter 6, "Neighborhood Analysis," *Appraising the Single Family Residence*. Chicago: American Institute of Real Estate Appraisers, 1978.

BOYKIN, JAMES H. (consulting editor). Chapter 4, "Meeting the Demand for Industrial Space," *Industrial Real Estate*. Washington, D.C.: Society of Industrial and Office Realtors, 1984.

BOYKIN, JAMES H. "Neighborhood Analysis," *Financing Real Estate*. Lexington, Mass.: D.C. Heath and Company, 1979, pp. 433–444.

DELISLE, JAMES R. "Neighborhood Treatment in Residential Appraisal: A Behavioral Approach," *The Real Estate Appraiser and Analyst* (Summer 1984), pp. 31–35.

FARBER, JOSEPH. Chapter 13, "Counseling the Office Building Client," *Real Estate Counseling*, James H. Boykin, ed. Englewood Cliffs, N.J.: Prentice-Hall, Inc., 1984.

Federal National Mortgage Association. *Focus: Appraisal Guide*, Section 404 "Neighborhood Analysis." Washington, D.C.: Fannie Mae, 1988, pp. 13–19.

GREIDER, LINDA. "Secrets of Great Old Neighborhoods," *Historic Preservation* (February 1986), pp. 28–35.

HICKMAN, EDGAR P., JAMES P. GAINES, and JERRY F. INGRAM. "The Influence of Neighborhood Quality of Residential Property," *The Real Estate Appraiser and Analyst* (Summer 1984), pp. 36–42.

MELCHERT, DAVID, and JOEL L. NAROFF. "Central City Revitalization: A Predictive Model," *AREUEA Journal* (Spring 1987), pp. 664–683.

RING, ALFRED A., and JEROME J. DASSO. Chapter 11, "Urban-Area Structure and Highest and Best Use," *Real Estate Principles and Practices*, 10th ed. Englewood Cliffs, N.J.: Prentice-Hall, Inc., 1985.

7

Considerations in Site Analysis

Learning Objectives

After reading this chapter, you should be able to:

- Understand the purposes of site analysis
- Discuss the factors normally considered in analyzing a site
- Distinguish among the terms site, parcel, tract, and land
- Appreciate the different methods used to describe a site
- Apply the principle of marginal productivity to site analysis

This chapter focuses on sites and in particular on the physical, legal, and economic analysis of sites. All of this leads to judging the desirability and in turn the value of an appraised site. Although the term site is generally used in this chapter, it will be enlightening to the reader if four terms—site, tract, parcel, and land—are defined at this point:

> *Site.* A unit of land that is ready for its intended use. A site generally is a section of a larger holding, such as a subdivision. It has been prepared and serviced. That is, it has been surveyed, cleared, graded, and has the necessary drainage. Streets, curbs, gutters, sewer, water, and other public utilities, such as gas and electric lines, are in place.
>
> *Tract.* A comparatively large unit of land that has not been prepared for its eventual use. A site may be developed from a tract.
>
> *Parcel.* This unit of land is part of a larger holding, and under one ownership. It sometimes is used interchangeably with *tract.*
>
> *Land.* The meaning of this term is evasive even though sometimes it is used synonymously with the other terms listed previously. It may refer to the earth's surface, a region, natural resources, or a property. It is distinguished from *site* in its not having been developed for an intensive use (e.g., farmland versus shopping center site).

SITE ANALYSIS PRINCIPLES

Several of the value principles discussed in Chapter 3 are particularly relevant to site analysis. Determining the highest and best use is one of the two major reasons for site analysis. Thus the appraiser must keep his or her valuation objective in mind as the site and off-site influences are considered. Another concern is the principle of marginal productivity, which was previously illustrated using two different sites with varying depths. Although each additional foot of depth adds overall value to a site, its unit value contribution diminishes when the depth of the site extends beyond some optimum use point. To illustrate, the front part of a site is best improved with a retail building, whereas the rear is useful for parking, outside storage, or not at all.

In judging the utility and value of a site, the appraiser should consider the optimum site depth and size for a prospective use. These considerations will guide his or her selection of comparable sales to support the estimated value of the site. It is preferable to develop local depth and corner value relationships than to use depth and corner setback tables that may be empirically derived but for different circumstances at an earlier date in different municipalities, and possibly in another state.

Purpose of Site Analysis

A basic rule of mathematics is that "the sum of the parts equals the whole." This principle is sometimes violated in the case of appraising. Logically, each section of a report should relate to the final value reported. In fact, some of the parts (facts) considered have no relation to the whole (value estimate). Yet a basic premise of real property valuation is that every factor considered should relate to a property's highest and best use and its value. If it does not, it is superfluous and should be excluded. Similarly, the regional analysis should relate to the community analysis and in turn to the neighborhood and site analysis. If the appraiser keeps these interrelationships in mind, the appraisal product will be a coherent, accurate, and convincing report.

The *major purposes of site analysis* are to judge a property's highest and best use, its utility for prospective present and future uses, its market appeal, the remaining economic life of the improvements, and, finally, its value. All of these factors are influenced by physical, legal, and market constraints. This analysis essentially is undertaken to judge the usefulness of a site, which then may be translated into a measure of its value. Also, the type of analysis is undertaken to identify the boundaries of the property, any encroachments, and also to establish the rights to be appraised.

Site Identification

Every appraisal should include a legal description which definitely and unmistakably fixes the geographic location of the subject property. In urban areas, the legal description should be reinforced by street name and lot number and even the U.S. postal zip code for added reference. Within city limits and in suburban subdivisions, a description by lot, block, and section number as shown on a given page in a plat book on official record best serves this purpose. For property locations in suburban or rural areas, or where subdivision designations by lot and block numbers are unavailable, the appraiser should obtain accurate legal descriptions prepared under either the "metes and bounds" or government survey system.

Because of the technical competency required to derive directional bearings north, south, east, and west with accuracy to minutes and seconds of degrees, metes and bounds descriptions should be prepared only by registered land surveyors. In metes and bounds descriptions as shown in Figure 7.1, the bearings or course of a line of direction is the angle that line makes from the central point of departure parallel with a meridian. As shown in Figure 7.1, the bearing of any line cannot exceed 90 degrees. A line running almost due east might have a bearing of "north" 89 degrees east. If this same line were rotated 2 degrees in a clockwise direction, its bearing would become "south" 89 degrees east.

Bearings may be measured and described either from the magnetic north and south (in which case they are called *magnetic bearings*) or from a true astronomic meridian north and south (in which case they are called *true bearings*). The bearings of a given line as expressed under the two systems will differ by the amount of the magnetic declination for that date and locality.

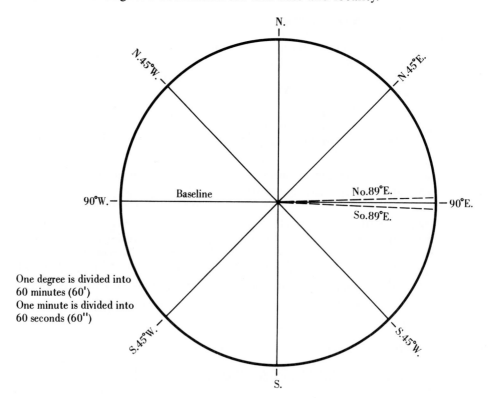

Figure 7.1   Metes and Bounds Descriptions

Rectangular Survey System

To make available accurate legal descriptions, particularly in western areas, the Continental Congress adopted in 1785 the rectangular survey of subdividing public lands. The primary purpose of this effort was to sell these lands in order to pay the tremendous public debt incurred by the colonies during the Revolutionary War. This western land was to be sold at public auction for a minimum price of one dollar per acre. Thomas Jefferson had a great influence on originating the rectangular system. This system is based on surveying lines running north and south, called *meridians*, and east and west, called *base lines*. These are established through the area to be surveyed and each is given a name and number by the Federal Land Office in Washington, D.C. A map showing the location of the several prime meridians and their base lines in the United States is shown in Figure 7.2.

Beginning at the intersection of the meridian and base lines, the surveyors divided the area between intersections into squares, called *checks*, 24 miles on each side. These squares were further subdivided into 16 areas each measuring 6 miles by 6 miles, called *townships*. The townships containing an area of 36 square miles were again subdivided into *sections*, each a square mile containing 640

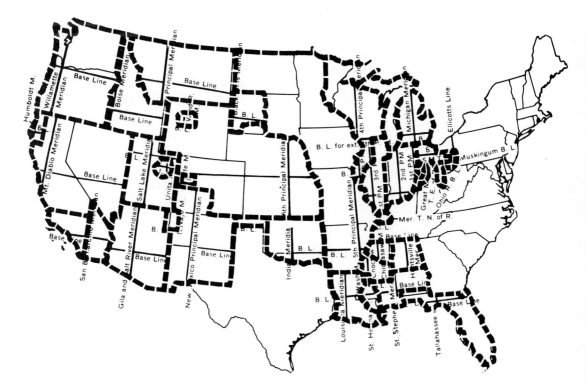

Figure 7.2 Map of Prime Meridians and Their Base Lines Within the United States

acres, and the sections were then divided into halves, quarters, or smaller subdivisions as the need called for to describe individual land holdings.[1]

To identify the various townships, the rows east and west and parallel to the base line were numbered as *tiers* 1, 2, and so on, north or south, of a given base line. The rows north and south and parallel to the meridians were called *ranges* and were numbered 1, 2, and so on, east or west of a principal or guide meridian. The numbering system is illustrated in Figure 7.3.

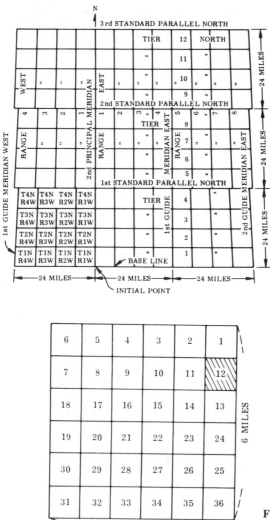

Figure 7.3 Illustration of Meridians, Base Lines, and Township

[1]For a full explanation of land surveying and property descriptions, see Chapter 3 of Jerome J. Dasso and Alfred A. Ring, *Real Estate Principles and Practices*, 11th ed. (Englewood Cliffs, N.J.: Prentice-Hall, Inc., 1989).

Owing to the spherical shape of the earth, the meridians converge as one goes north—the north side of a township is approximately 50 feet shorter than the south side. To correct this error, the government established certain principal meridians and others, called guide meridians, which are changed at each parallel to make allowances for the earth's curvature. This problem really concerns only the surveyor and is mentioned only so that the reader will not be confused in studying the diagram.

In describing a section, it is customary to state first the number of the section, then the township and range: "Section 12, Township 3 North, Range 2 East of the principal (named) meridian." It may be abbreviated "Sec. 12 T. 3N R. 2E, . . . County, State of . . . ."

The description of a part of a section is simple. For example, the plot A shown in Figure 7.4 is "West ½ of Southwest ¼, Sec. 12." The same diagram indicates the description of other parts of the section.

Metes and Bounds Method

This method of site or tract identification may be used with any of the other methods. It is especially prevalent in the states that formed the original 13 colonies, the South Atlantic states, and Texas. It describes a property's boundaries by giving the courses and distances. The *courses* are indicated by compass headings;

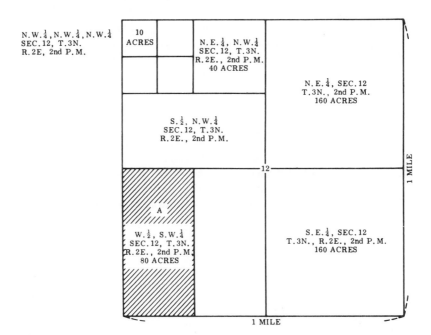

Figure 7.4 Divisions of a Section

distances in a given direction generally are measured in feet.[2] This lineal method is based on a boundary survey. It starts at a point of beginning, which usually is some distance from a point extended from a side property line to the center line of the abutting street or road. The boundary is traced around the site's perimeter and eventually returns to the point of beginning. The appraiser should be much more familiar with this technique than the city investor who once asked the owner of a rural tract: "What are these leaps and bounds that you've been talking about?". An example of this metes and bounds method is shown for lot 5 in Figure 7.5.

Monument Method

In many early surveys, a rural property's boundaries were fixed by reference to "monuments." These landmarks were such items as a neighbor's wooden fence or a particular tree, stream, or rock. Such references over time often disappeared or were relocated, causing confusion for later owners of the property. However, a monument may be either natural or fabricated; it is used to indicate a corner or change in direction of a property line. Earlier these were used without any measured distances between monuments. Later, this method included such measurements and greater use of artificial monuments such as iron stakes set by surveyors. An example of an earlier monument system is given in the following description. This illustration points out some of the potential problems in using the monument system, including changing directions of streams, replaced and relocated rock piles, trees dying over the years, and named and once-familiar landmarks being unrecognizable in successive generations.

The following description, taken from the Hartford, Connecticut, Probate Court records for 1812, will illustrate what is often encountered in early metes and bounds (boundary) surveys.

> 147 acres, 3 rods, and 19 rods after deducting whatever swamp, water, rock and road areas there may be included therein and all other lands of little or no value, the same being part of said deceased's 1280 acre colony grant, and the portion hereby set off being known as near to and on the other side of Black Oak Ridge, bounded and described more in particular as follows, to wit:—Commencing at a heap of stone, about a stone's throw from a certain small clump of alders, near a brook running down off from a rather high part of said ridge; thence, by a straight line to a certain marked white birch tree, about two or three times as far from a jog in a fence going around a ledge nearby; thence, by another straight line in a different direction, around said

---

[2] The following measurements commonly appeared in deeds for properties surveyed prior to this century:

1 link	7.92 inches	1 furlong	660 feet or 40 rods
1 rod	16½ feet or 25 links	1 acre	43,560 square feet,
1 chain	66 feet		160 square rods, or 10 square chains

In sixteenth-century England, an acre originally was defined as the amount of land a yoke of oxen could plow in a day, which was 4 perches (or rods) in breadth by 40 perches in length. See Appendix 6.

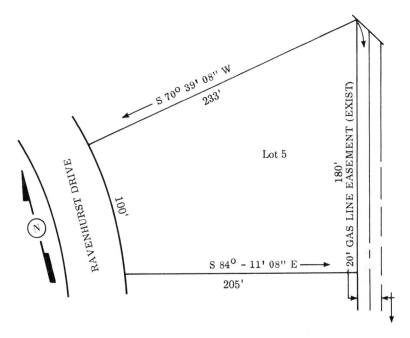

Figure 7.5 Illustrative Legal Description (Using Metes and Bounds)

ledge and the Great Swamp, so called; thence, in line of said lot in part and in part by another piece of fence which joins on to said line, and by an extension of the general run of said fence to a heap of stone near a surface rock; thence, as aforesaid, to the 'Horn,' so called, and passing around the same as aforesaid, as far as the 'Great Bend,' so called, and from thence to a squarish sort of a jog in another fence, and so on to a marked black oak tree with stones piled around it; thence, by another straight line in about a contrary direction and somewhere about parallel with the line around the ledge and the Great Swamp, to a stake and stone bounds not far off from the old Indian trail; thence, by another straight line on a course diagonally parallel, or nearly so, with 'Fox Hollow Run,' so called, to a certain marked red cedar tree out on a sandy sort of a plain; thence, by another straight line, in a different direction, to a certain marked yellow oak tree on the off side of a knoll with a flat stone laid against it; thence, after turning around in another direction, and by a sloping straight line to a certain heap of stone which is, by pacing, just 18 rods and about one half a rod more from the stump of the big hemlock tree where Philo Blake killed the bear; thence, to the corner begun at by two straight lines of about equal length, which are to be run by some skilled and competent surveyor, so as to include the area and acreage as herein before set forth.

Aerial Photography

A frequently overlooked and potentially valuable means for ascertaining the location of a parcel, especially an outlying tract, is aerial photography. A recent aerial photograph can be used to give an overview of a neighborhood, depict landmarks, and show different classes of land such as pasture and woodland. With the use of a polar plenimeter, it is possible to compute the area of the entire tract as well as individual sections. The scale (e.g., 1 inch = 800 feet) of the photograph is needed to make these computations.

Figures 7.6 and 7.7 depict the boundaries of a tract. By using the aerial photograph the appraiser can orientate himself or herself to the corners of the property on the road, be more accurate in inspecting the property based on landmarks shown on the photograph, and reveal the location of structures or land features that otherwise may have been overlooked. Some clients find aerial views of property to be informative.

Subdivision Method

Whenever a site is located in a platted subdivision, it should be identified with reference to that subdivision. For example, in Figure 7.8 the shaded lot on Ravenhurst Drive could be generally identified as being a certain distance southwest of Robious Road and so many feet southeast of the intersection of Ravenhurst Drive and Charter Drive. However, a more specific identification would be to identify it as Lot 5, Block A, Section I, Charter Woods, in Midlothian District, Chesterfield County, Virginia. Taking this description a step further, the appraiser would refer to the plat book and page where the lot is recorded in the courthouse of the local jurisdiction.

In addition to the subdivision method, a property is identified by its metes and bounds description on a sketch of the site. Reference to a recorded subdivision plat offers the advantage of giving an accurate measure of the boundary lines, quantity of land, any dedication of streets or easements, sources of title, and a statement of the liens on the property. An example of such reference follows:

Figure 7.6 Aerial View of Property

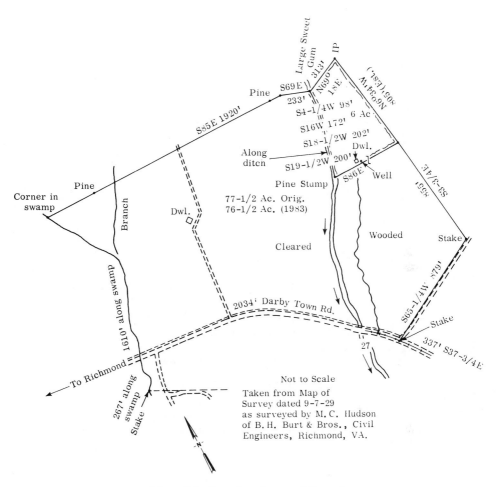

Figure 7.7 Boundary Survey of Property

All that certain lot, piece or parcel of land, with all improvements thereon, lying and being in Midlothian District, Chesterfield County, Virginia, known and designated as Lot 5, Block A, Section I, Charter Woods, as shown on a subdivision plat of Charter Woods, dated May 3, 1985 by J. K. Timmons and Associates, Inc., Engineers, Surveyors, Planners, said plat recorded May 16, 1985 in the Clerk's Office, Circuit Court of Chesterfield County, Virginia, in Plat Book 50, page 29, and reference to which is hereby made for a more particular description thereof.

Condominium Subdivision

Especially where condominiums are housed in a multistoried building, it becomes necessary to identify a property accurately, not only in the customary horizontal manner but vertically as well. The vertical part of the legal description may begin at a datum point on the ground and extend to elevations from the top of a unit's unfinished floor to the bottom of the unfinished ceiling. The space between ceiling and floor is part of the common area. Each unit is described in a master

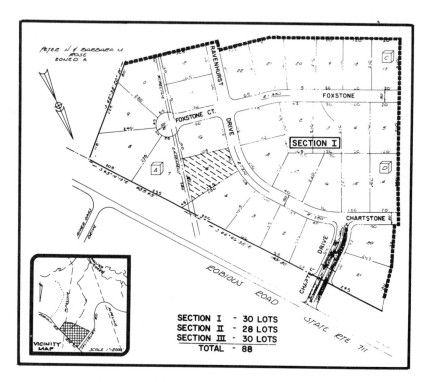

Figure 7.8 Subdivision Plat Showing One of Several Sections

deed for the entire development. Important, too, for identification purposes, is an identification of the common areas owned by each individual condominium owner. The joint ownership and maintenance of these common areas can influence the value of each individual property since ownership is extended beyond the actual residence and maintenance expenses may be burdensome. If parking spaces are owned in fee, they should be included in the legal description as well.

Street Address

This method is ordinarily used either by itself or, preferably, in conjunction with one of the other methods. It can only be used in municipalities where streets have been numbered. This system is weakened when several streets within a metropolis have the same name. Sometimes streets are renamed and renumbered. A safeguard, in view of these possibilities, is to include the U.S. postal zip code along with the street address.

To avoid any possible misunderstanding as to the exact location of the site under value study, it is recommended that a location sketch, such as that shown in Figure 7.9, be made a part of every appraisal report. This sketch should designate a prominent point of reference, such as a courthouse, police station, museum, or other well-known public building, and should indicate by reference to public roads or streets the direction and location of the subject property. Major commercial properties, such as shopping centers, also are helpful reference points. With

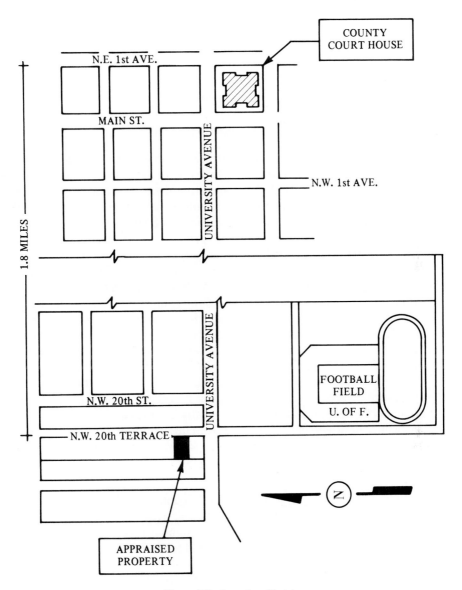

Figure 7.9 Location Sketch

the aid of this sketch, even a stranger to the community should be able to reach the location without difficulty. As shown, distances in blocks or miles should be noted to avoid further unnecessary delays in pinpointing the subject location.

The location, once accurately established, should then be analyzed in regard to

1. Nature of terrain and soil characteristics.
2. Size, depth, shape, and corner-lot location influences.

3. Street improvements and availability of essential public utilities.
4. Zoning, building, and deed restrictions.
5. Title considerations and encroachments.
6. Adjoining structures and land uses.
7. Landscaping, building, and subsurface land improvements.

NATURE OF TERRAIN AND SOIL CHARACTERISTICS

Site preparations and the cost of site developments differ with soil conditions and nature of terrain. Sites below street level may require filling; others, because of subsurface flaws, costly shoring; and still others, terracing to prevent washouts or construction of retaining walls to safeguard building foundations. Rock may have to be blasted or pilings driven where the load-bearing quality of the soil is deemed inadequate. Additional costs of site preparation, over and above those typically incurred in building construction, usually diminish the value of the land. This reduction in land value is in proportion to the extraordinary dollar outlays necessary because of adverse site conditions. Some sites, in fact, may prove so costly to prepare that the land is classified *submarginal* and defaulted in title to the city or county for tax-saving purposes, or deeded to public authorities for utilization—at public expense—as a park or for other recreational or community-use benefits. Conversely, a site, because of favorable orientation or natural terrain features, may bring about savings in construction or offer amenities that result in *situs qualities* (economic characteristics of land made or brought about by popular acceptance) over and above those typical for other neighborhood locations. In such instances it is the appraiser's task to estimate the construction cost savings, or to measure the added value resulting from demand preference for site locations possessing quality soil conditions or geographic orientation.

Terrain

Topographical analysis should be used to determine if the site is usable for the intended or prospective use. Is the terrain so irregular and steep as to prohibitively increase the site preparation costs and foundation costs for the building? The relationship of the terrain at street or road grade is important. If it is elevated several feet, steps will be necessary, which may reduce the appeal of the site for residential purposes for many prospective users. If, on the other hand, the site is below street grade, it may be equally unattractive and pose some problems in getting a vehicle onto the street. A site with some variation in topography, such as a gently rolling parcel, offers appeal for residential subdivision purposes. The variation in terrain adds interest and variation to the individual home sites. This premise is not true for commercial or industrial sites, however.

A site with some slope gradient facilitates surface water runoff. But if the slope is too great, there may be erosion problems. On the other hand, a flat site eliminates erosion problems but, depending on subsoil conditions, may cause standing water. Water standing under a house may in time cause rotting structural members.

In some areas it is particularly necessary for the appraiser to be aware of both the neighborhood's and the site's history. For example, the subdivision may have been built over coal mines or a sanitary landfill. Both could cause settling. Continual house repairs are associated with foundation and footings settling where there may be such unstable subsoil conditions. The additional threat to homes on a landfill site is the possible emission of methane gas. It can cause explosions and the property to be uninhabitable or certainly its value greatly reduced in the future.

Reference to a topographical map such as illustrated in Figure 7.10 will show the severity of terrain for an area and possibly an individual property. The terrain in the upper left corner of the figure rises to 2,200 feet above sea level at "The Knob," and declines to 1,400 feet along Lake Merriweather. Note as the contour lines become closer the terrain changes more abruptly. Also in this figure, each line represents a 20-foot change in terrain.

Soil

Soil surveys generally are available throughout the country. Although appraisers are not soil scientists, it is important that soil conditions be taken into account in judging the potential use and value of a site. Figure 7.11 is taken from a soil survey in Virginia. The illustration is included to point out the appearance of a soil survey map and to show a preliminary means for determining whether certain soils are fit for developmental purposes. In studying this soils classification map along with a description of the different classes of soil, it can be determined, for example, that WoB (Woodstown) has a seasonal high water table, is moderately suited for septic system drain fields, but is not suited for basements; it has a low shrink-swell potential. The SfA and SfB (Sassafras) is a well-drained soil and permeable; it is only slightly impaired for septic system drain fields and basements. Tm (Tidal Marsh) is generally composed of various combinations and layers of sandy, loamy, clayey, and mucky materials. It is constantly waterlogged and unsuitable for development or septic system drainage fields.

Another key consideration in site analysis is the combined effect of slope and subsoil conditions. A particular subsoil may be marginally suitable for development purposes for a level site. Yet when there is a slope, the same subsoil may be too unstable to support footings for a building.

Flood Hazard

Flood insurance has become important for the financing of residential property. For example, HUD, VA, FHLMC, and FNMA require flood insurance on single-family properties when they are located in a 100-year floodplain. An appraiser can obtain *flood hazard boundary maps* showing flood-prone areas in most communities. These maps are provided by the Federal Insurance Administration of the Federal Emergency Management Agency in Bethesda, Maryland. A flood-prone area is one where there is a risk of serious flooding at least once every 100 years. An example of a flood hazard boundary map for Ontario, Oregon, is shown in Figure 7.12.

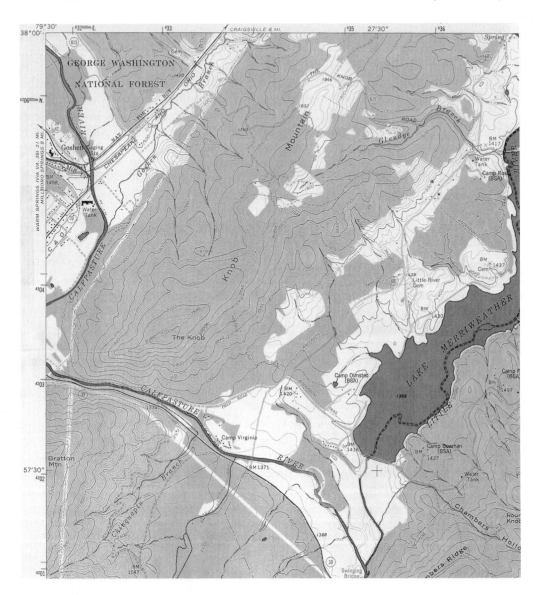

Figure 7.10 Topographical Map
Source: U.S. Department of the Interior, Geological Survey "Goshen Quadrangle, Virginia–Rockbridge Co."

Wetlands

Increasingly, appraisers are faced with the valuation of land that includes wetlands. *Wetlands* are defined as "those areas that are inundated or saturated by surface or ground water at a frequency and duration sufficient to support a prevalence of vegetation typically adapted for life in saturated soil conditions." Wetlands include obvious areas such as swamps, marshes, and bogs. Not always so

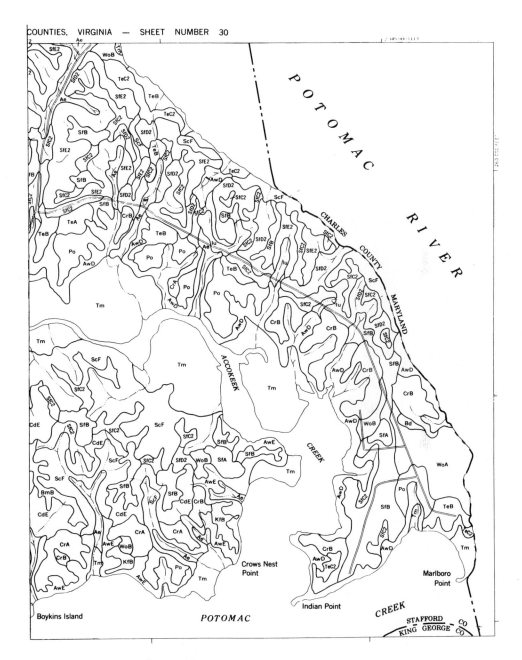

Figure 7.11 Soil Classification Map
Source: *Soil Survey: Stafford and King George Counties, Virginia,* U.S. Department of Agriculture in cooperation with Virginia Polytechnic Institute and State University (Washington, D.C.: Government Printing Office, 1974), sheet no. 30.

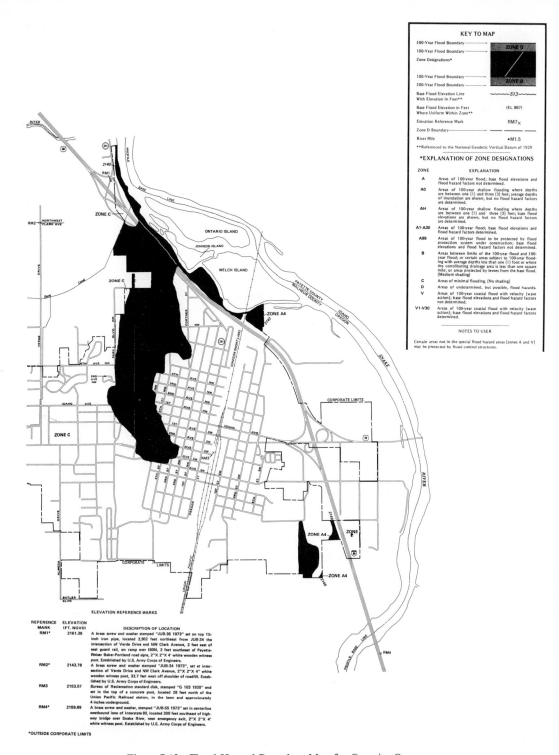

Figure 7.12 Flood Hazard Boundary Map for Ontario, Oregon

obvious are wetlands in bottomland forests, pine savannahs, and meadows. The U.S. Army Corps of Engineers considers three factors in determining if an area in question is a wetland: hydrology, vegetation, and soil, with the most emphasis being given to soil. Wetland hydrology refers to the existence of water on or in the soil for a sufficiently long period to significantly influence the plant types that occur on that land.

Although most real estate appraisers are not trained in the detection of wetlands, they nevertheless may be able to spot such areas by noting any of the following symptoms.

Hydrology.   Waterlogged soil; standing or flowing water for seven or more consecutive days during the growing season; "drift lines" or small piles of debris oriented in the direction of water movement through an area; debris lodged by the water in or against trees or other objects; water marks on trees or other erect objects; and thin layers of sediment deposits on leaves or other plants.

Vegetation.   These may include cattails, bulrushes, willows, mangroves, and sphagnum moss. Also, trees with shallow root systems, swollen trunks, or roots growing above the ground are good indications of wetlands.

Soil.   Hydric soil may be indicated by an abundance of decomposed plant material on the soil's surface; bluish-gray, brownish-black, or black as the predominant soil color 10 to 12 inches below the surface; and an odor resembling rotten eggs.

Appraisers must be cautious in not overstepping their valuation expertise by attempting to make definite wetland delineations. The best method in appraising wetlands or land containing some wetlands is use of comparable sales analysis. Other factors that might be considered are the cost of mitigation, extension of the development period by an owner having to deal with government agencies, and the risk of whether any development will be permitted by governmental bodies.[3]

Site Contamination

Clients are concerned about the prospect of acquiring a site that either cannot be utilized as planned or may incur unanticipated and large financial liabilities because of existing site contamination. Some possible sources of contamination include: leaking underground storage tanks, asbestos, formaldehyde-emitting products, PCBs (polychlorinated biphenyls) in electrical equipment such as transformers, and other toxic substances. Few real estate appraisers are trained in the detection of these environmental hazards and therefore should avoid giving unqualified opinions on such matters. If such substances are likely to be found on appraised sites, work between the environmental analyst and the appraiser should be coordinated so the appraiser has the environmentalist's report prior to completing his or her valuation which will consider the economic effects of any site contamination.

[3]Richard S. Hawrylak, "What You Should Know About Wetlands," *The Practical Real Estate Lawyer* (January 1991), pp. 60–61.

STREET IMPROVEMENTS AND AVAILABILITY OF ESSENTIAL PUBLIC UTILITIES

Street accessibility and the extent of street frontage are of substantial value importance for all urban land use activities. This is supported by the fact that the *unit value* for such sites is typically quoted on a front-foot rather than on a square-foot or acre basis, as is the case with industrial or agricultural land. This front-foot value is considerably enhanced where streets are properly improved and provide for service connections to essential public utilities. Street improvements recognized as adding value include paving, sidewalks, curbs, gutters, storm drains, sanitary sewage, and connections for water, gas, telephones, and electricity. Care must be taken to make certain that all improvements are fully paid. The value of a site is generally based on its "as is" condition on a given date. If assessments for street and capital improvements are outstanding, the present worth of the future dollar obligations must be subtracted from the site value derived under a "free and clear" assumption of land ownership. If, however, the appraiser is unable to determine whether such outstanding debt obligations and assessments are unpaid, including accrued taxes, up to the date of the appraisal, he or she should clearly note that the property is appraised as if free and clear of these debts. Where essential street improvements or public utilities are lacking, the appraiser must measure with care the "negative value" market reactions that penalize a site, often in excess of the cost of such utilities or road improvements.

The highest and best use and value of a site is strongly influenced by the availability and adequacy of public sewer systems. Alternatively, it should be determined whether the site is capable of supporting an individual septic system if public facilities are unavailable. The review of subsoil conditions, interview of municipal sanitary engineers, and a general knowledge of an area will generally disclose the probability of problems due to inadequate subsoil permeability. Sometimes subsoil conditions are such that it is prohibitively expensive either to build an on-site sewerage system or even to construct the building itself. Examples of this would be where there are outcroppings that require expensive and time-consuming rock blasting or unstable subsoil that requires pilings or substantial footings.

SHAPE, SIZE, DEPTH, AND CORNER LOCATION INFLUENCES

Shape and Size

Virtually every land use has an optimum site size and shape. In some cases, depth is important, whereas in other instances frontage is of greater significance. A business that depends on customers arriving in vehicles must have a site with sufficient frontage to allow comfortable braking distance and turning radius for its customers. For example, a service station typically needs at least 200 feet of road frontage.

Another example of the importance of adequate site size is residential sites that lack a community sewage removal system and water supply. In such cases the minimum site size is determined by the locally required health department distance between the well and septic system drain field. Further complicating this site size determination is the fact that the well generally needs to be uphill from the drain field and then there must be perhaps 100 feet of separation between any drain fields on adjoining properties. Also, there may be a dwelling setback requirement. In some cases a site does not have sufficient percolation capacity throughout to allow the drain field being placed where the owner prefers.

The importance of these factors being considered is shown in relation to a situation where a lot was purchased at a lake resort. The current owner had paid $15,000 for a lakefront site 12 years previously. Ordinarily, the value for such property would be considerably greater than the purchase price after 12 years. However, the developer failed to install a public water system, causing each individual lot owner to have to install his or her own well in addition to a septic system. After having considered all the various setback requirements, this particular lot had no value except to an adjoining property owner to assemble two lots in order to create one usable site. Instead of the property value increasing, lots were selling for only $300 to $500.

A site must be of a minimum size and shape to permit effective utilization in conformity with the principle of highest and best use under existing zoning, building, and deed restrictions. A site 10 feet wide and 100 feet deep in a residential area where building restrictions call for a minimum lot size of 10,000 square feet has no value except as it may attract offers from neighboring property owners who may, at a nominal price, be interested in adding this strip of land to their holdings. It is important, therefore, to ascertain whether a site under valuation meets minimum lot size requirements. The value of a rectangular site (if residential or commercial in character) depends on the number of front feet, along the abutting street, and on the depth of the lot in comparison to the standard for the neighborhood. The shape of the site also influences its use and value.

To illustrate: Assuming a standard lot depth of 100 feet in a given neighborhood and a front-foot lot value of $300 (as supported by market comparison of similar lot sales), a 100-foot-wide by 150-foot-deep lot is estimated to bring $100 \times \$300$, or $30,000, if exposed for sale. For every front foot added or subtracted from this lot, provided that the lot depth remains 150 feet, the value will increase or decrease by $300 in amount, as long as the same increment of utility is contributed or deducted by each foot added or subtracted for the standard lot. In many instances, however, lots are either substandard or in excess of a depth considered standard for the area. To measure the value influence of depth—in conformity with the principle that the front of a lot (because of street access and utility) is more valuable than the rear—depth rules have been devised to measure changes in value resulting from variations in depth.

In applying depth rules, it should be kept in mind that rules by themselves do not make value but rather reflect the market actions of typical buyers in a community. Then, too, rules applied should merit acceptance by professional appraisers in the area and prove acceptable in court practice.[4] Most of the depth rules have been devised as an aid to tax assessors to permit uniformity of value treatment. For individual appraisals, it is generally better for the appraiser to develop his or her own guidelines regarding the incremental unit of value added or deducted for nonstandard depth sites. Observations need to be made for different types of sites in different locations. To generalize for all categories of land is no better than using standardized depth tables.

Odd-Shaped Lot Valuation

Irregular-shaped sites often present a problem in appraising. Assuming no disutility because of odd shape and no impairment of utilization for a particular highest and best land employment program, an irregular site should be evaluated in accordance with the customary unit measure applied in practice for similar and regular-shaped lots, plus value allowance for odd-plot portions as demonstrated in Figure 7.13. Residential and commercial sites are generally evaluated in relation to the number of feet fronting on a street. Where the shape is a parallelogram as shown in Figure 7.13, usually no value adjustment is necessary for lot irregularity since the two triangles, marked *B* and *C*, in effect form a rectangle the combined value of which is equal to a rectangle of like street frontage.

Odd-shaped lots such as those shown in Figure 7.14 are valued as rectangular lots, plus the additional value of the triangular lots. Suppose, for example, a market study reveals that a triangular lot with its base fronting the street, such as Lot 2 in Figure 7.14, is worth 65 percent of a rectangular lot of the same frontage. A triangular lot with its apex on the street, such as Lot 1 in Figure 7.14, is worth 35 percent of a rectangular lot with a street frontage equal to the base of the triangle. To illustrate, assuming a value of $300 per front foot, the lots illustrated in Figure 7.14 would be appraised as shown below the figure. Importantly, each site must be appraised on the basis of local value patterns.

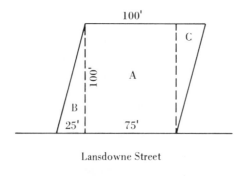

Lansdowne Street

Figure 7.13   Irregular-Shaped Lot

[4]During testimony in an Alabama District Court, a witness referred to the use of a "New York depth rule in measuring damages for land taken under eminent domain proceedings." Opposing counsel asked, "Why do ya'll use a Yankee rule in the Southland?" The jury got the message—at least so the verdict indicated.

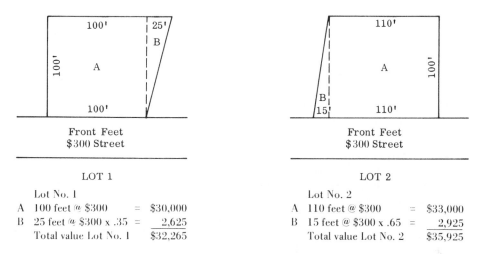

Figure 7.14   Lots with Different Triangular Sections

Corner Lot Valuation

With the increasing width of standard residential lots—from 20 and 25 feet to 100 feet or more in suburban subdivisions—the advantages which corner locations once offered in providing better light, more convenient access, and perhaps, greater privacy have diminished to a point where the additional hazards encountered at corner locations from automobile traffic have neutralized corner location advantages. In residential areas, therefore, the recommended appraisal practice is not to ascribe a value increment because of corner location, unless market sales in a community or area clearly demonstrate a preference for such locations.

Commercial corner locations, however, do have value advantages over inside lots because of greater accessibility, increased pedestrian traffic, better merchandise display, and store visibility from two street locations. Corner lots typically command higher rentals, and the net income available to land is higher at corner store locations whether they are under owner or tenant occupancy. Under the capitalized income approach—as will be demonstrated in Chapter 18—the added corner value is directly accounted for by capitalization of the increased income resulting from a favorable location. Under the sales comparison approach, however, comparison sales may include inside lots with adjustments being required to account for corner value influences. As stated previously, rules do not create value; nevertheless, they do offer, where tested by field practice, an opportunity to check value findings derived from other approaches to value. After a while, experienced appraisers will develop sufficient data to reveal the extent of corner premiums, if any, for different classes of property.

As a rule, the land closest to the corner benefits most from the corner location influences and the corner value premium diminishes to a negligible or fractional amount for the last portion of the corner lot. Assuming separate ownership of a corner lot as marked in Figure 7.15 and on the basis of empirical data, the corner value benefits would be derived as shown below the figure.

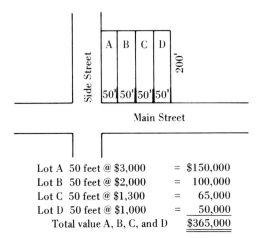

Lot A 50 feet @ $3,000   = $150,000
Lot B 50 feet @ $2,000   = 100,000
Lot C 50 feet @ $1,300   =   65,000
Lot D 50 feet @ $1,000   =   50,000
       Total value A, B, C, and D $365,000

Figure 7.15 Corner Influence on Value

Where the assembled lots, because of single ownership and unified control, permit more intensive utilization of the land, the added value increment is known as *plottage*. This plottage value is best measured either by capitalizing the actual or anticipated increased income attributable to an assembled property or by comparative analysis of sites of different sizes and utility. Considerable care must be exercised by the appraiser in using small sites to derive the value of a larger site. Due to the higher unit value, the smaller, more affordable comparable sale sites could overstate the value of the larger appraised parcel. Figure 7.16 shows how market-derived data can reveal value differentials resulting from plottage. Parcels A and B separately had modest highest and best uses and an average front-foot value of $763. Yet, when assembled into a larger parcel offering greater utility and a higher and better use, the front-foot value increased to $1,250. It could be said that the plottage value is $487 per front foot ($1,250 − $763).

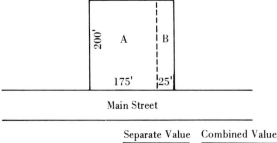

Main Street

	Separate Value	Combined Value
Lot A 175 feet @ $800	= $140,000	
Lot B 25 feet @ $500	= 12,500	
Total of separate site values	$152,000	
Combined value of parcels A and B		$250,000

Figure 7.16 Illustration of Plottage Concept

ZONING AND CONTRACTUAL LIMITATIONS ON OWNERSHIP

The highest and best use of land is often limited by the legal and permissible use for which a site may be developed. Again attention is called to the fact that zoning by itself does not create value. There must be a demand for land so zoned. If this demand is lacking, the period of years required for land to ripen into the highest and best use must be estimated and the value of future income discounted to the present value at an appropriate discount rate.

Often changes in the character of a neighborhood support a strong possibility that changes in zoning regulations will follow in order that land utilization can be adapted to dynamic community needs. Where this is the case, the appraiser should recognize such added value influences, provided that the current prices of similar land indicate investor expectation of higher and better land uses under anticipated changes in zoning or deed restrictions. It is improper, however, to use comparable sales with superior zoning without making an appropriate minus adjustment.

Contractual limitations on ownership are generally noted in deeds of record, and hence are referred to as *deed restrictions*. Such restrictions as a rule are initiated by developers for the protection of property owners, and are intended to govern future land utilization in conformity with preconceived building plans and in the interest of owners and users as a whole. Deed restrictions that go with or attach to the land may control items as follows: minimum lot sizes, maximum building area, building height, minimum building value, building setback requirements from front, side, and rear property lines, occupancy by single family, and other customary and reasonable limitations on ownership to safeguard property values.

Other contractual limitations that must be noted and evaluated by the appraiser include easements, leases, and mortgages. *Easements* are rights extended to others for ingress and egress over a property, or to air or subsurface rights for utility installation, soil removal, flood control, or mining operations. The effects of such easements on property value must be measured and accounted for in appraisal reporting. *Leases* give tenants, or lessees, the right to use land and its improvements for certain periods of time. In effect, leases create "split" interests that divide property values among the parties involved. Important too, leases may limit a property's highest and best use. The technique of appraising lease interests will be fully illustrated in Chapter 9. *Mortgages* in effect encumber a property. Where terms of the mortgage debt are at typical market rates of interest and for typical periods of years, there is no impact on property value. However, where mortgage contract terms are favorable or unfavorable as measured by market standards, there is a proportionate effect on the property's value.

Title Considerations and Encroachments

The appraiser, in seeking values, operates within the field of economics. He or she is cautioned not to usurp the functions or assume the responsibilities that are rightfully those of title companies, lawyers, architects, surveyors, or construction engineers. For appraisal purposes it must be assumed that the title to the subject property is free and clear, unless otherwise and expressly stated, and that no encumbrances restrict the full use of the property except those covered by zoning and deed restrictions as shown on public records. If the appraisal client, in addition to value, seeks assurance that the title is good and marketable or that lot measurements are accurate and the property is free from encroachments, qualified professionals in the respective fields should be consulted and the cost of their services added to the agreed-upon appraisal fee.

Furthermore, the validity of the title and the accuracy of survey lines and measurements for appraisal purposes must be assumed to be correct, except for encroachments and property use violations that are apparent at the time of field inspection. Where such violations or *easements* (rights for public ingress or egress to or over the site) are apparent, it is the appraiser's responsibility to report them and to estimate their effects on the value and marketability of the property.

Adjoining Structures and Land Uses

As the prospective highest and best use of the site is considered, it is important to visualize it in the context of adjoining properties. Will the prospective use be compatible with other nearby uses? Are the adjoining uses likely to cause market resistance to the subject property? Are the structures on adjacent properties inadequately maintained so that the potential of the appraised property is impaired? These factors must be seriously considered by the appraiser in a site analysis.

Site Improvements

All improvements classified as *fixtures* (previously defined in Chapter 3), the ownership of which legally "runs" with the land, must be inspected and appraised. To guard against errors and omissions, it is recommended that a plot plan be prepared as a guide for better appraisal reporting. The lot dimensions and lot improvements should be drawn to scale and in proportion to boundary line measurements that enclose the property. The plot plan should further show walks, driveways, and roof plans of the various structures on the property. This plan, together with pictures of the site and neighboring street and lot improvements, is deemed essential to effective site analysis in the appraisal process.

Other land improvements that should be inventoried and analyzed include landscaping and subsurface land improvements. Not all shrubs are classified as fixtures, and care must be taken to specify in the appraisal report the extent and amount to which landscaping contributed to total value. An allocation of 1, or at most 2, percent of final value for lawn sodding and foundation plantings may prove typical for most residential properties. Amounts expended in excess of 2 percent may not be a measure of market value, depending on the circumstances at the time the property is exposed for sale to typical buyers.

Subsurface improvements, too, must be judged according to their value influence. Underground utilities such as gas, telephone, sewerage, drainage, water, electricity, and steam piping are assets adding to site value. Other on-site improvements to be included in site valuation include paving, curbs, gutters, and sidewalk installation. (See the illustrative report in Appendix II.) When comparing comparable land sales care must be taken to adjust transaction prices to reflect the presence or absence of the various site improvements.

SUMMARY

Distinctions are made among the terms: site, tract, parcel, and land. *Site* is a unit of land that is ready for its intended use. *Tract* is a large unit of land that has not been prepared for its eventual use. *Parcel* is a large holding under one ownership and is used interchangeably with tract. *Land* is sometimes used synonymously with the previous terms, but is not yet developed for an intensive use.

The major purposes of site analysis are to judge a property's highest and best use, its utility for prospective present and future uses, its market appeal, the remaining economic life of the improvements, and, finally, its value.

Every appraisal should include a legal description which is accomplished by several methods. The *rectangular survey system*, used primarily west of the original 13 colonies, is based on survey lines running north and south, called meridians, and east and west, called base lines.

The *metes and bounds method* of site identification describes a property's boundaries by giving its courses and distances. Another method is the use of *monuments*. These "monuments" may have been trees, streams, or rocks which over the years have disappeared or been moved. *Aerial photography* can be useful in giving an overview of a neighborhood, depicting landmarks, as well as showing different classes of land such as pasture. The *subdivision method* is appropriate when identifying a site in a platted subdivision. It refers to a particular lot, block, section, and, of course, the subdivision.

Two final identification methods are *condominium subdivision* and *street address*. The former method, when used in multistoried buildings, utilizes both the traditional horizontal metes and bounds method plus a vertical reference. The street address method usually is a backup method and is best applied with a zip code in case there is more than one street having the same name.

Topographical analysis should be used to determine if the site is usable for an intended use. Soil surveys are available throughout the country. Although appraisers are not soil scientists, it is important that soil conditions be taken into account in judging the potential value of a site. Another form of site analysis is to indicate whether a site is within a 100-year floodplain. Increasingly, appraisers are faced with the valuation of land that includes wetlands. *Wetlands* are those areas that are inundated or saturated by surface or ground water at a frequency and duration sufficient to support a prevalence of vegetation typically adapted for life in saturated soil conditions. Another concern is the potential presence of on-site contamination.

In the appraisal of sites, the shape, size, depth, and corner location must be considered. Also, zoning and contractual limitations can alter the value of a site. The latter includes deed restrictions, easements, leases, and mortgages.

REVIEW QUESTIONS

1. Explain the relationship between chains and acres.
2. How many feet are there on each side of a square acre?
3. List three major concerns in conducting a site analysis.
4. Give an advantage and disadvantage of the monument method of site description.
5. Discuss the importance of a knowledge of soil conditions to a proper site analysis.
6. What do you judge to be an inherent weakness of depth tables?
7. What are the three factors considered by the U.S. Army Corps of Engineers in determining if an area in question is wetland?

READING AND STUDY REFERENCES

BABCOCK, RICHARD F., and CLIFFORD L. WEAVER. "Zoning City Neighborhoods," *Real Estate Issues* 5, no. 1 (Summer 1980), pp. 1–15.

BOYCE, BRYL N., and WILLIAM N. KINNARD, JR. Chapter 6, "Property Analysis," *Appraising Real Property.* Lexington, Mass.: Lexington Books, 1984, pp. 135–144.

FLOYD, CHARLES F. "Valuation of Flood Plain Lands for Stream Valley Parks," *The Appraisal Journal* 51, no. 2 (April 1983), pp. 202–210.

GROSS, SHELDON. "Market Research to Find and Evaluate Sites," *Realty* (December 31, 1985), pp. 48, 51.

HARDING, BRUCE. "Limitation of Land Use by Downzoning: The Appraiser's Dilemma along the California Coast," *The Appraisal Journal* 53, no. 1 (January 1985), pp. 58–65.

KNIPE, WILLIAM B., III. "Valuing the Probability of Rezoning," *The Appraisal Journal* 56, no. 2 (April 1988), pp. 217–222.

MILLER, RONALD D. "Exploring Possible Environmental Hazards: Serving Clients' Needs," *Environmental Watch* III, no. 3 (Fall 1990). Chicago: American Institute of Real Estate Appraisers, pp. 1, 4–6.

O'MALLEY, ROBERTA A., and JOYCE C. SHUMAN. "Warning: Environmental Hazards," *The Real Estate Appraiser and Analyst* 55, no. 3 (Fall 1989), pp. 4–9.

REENSTIERNA, ERIC. "The Appraisal of Wetlands," *The Real Estate Appraiser and Analyst* 46, no. 3 (May–June 1980), pp. 4–8.

SCRIBNER, DAVID. "The Key to Value Estimation: Highest and Best Use or Most Probable Use," *The Real Estate Appraiser* 44, no. 3 (May–June 1978), pp. 23–28.

SMITH, HALBERT C., and MARK R. MAURAIS. "Highest and Best Use in the Appraisal Profession," *The Real Estate Appraiser and Analyst* 46, no. 2 (March–April 1980), pp. 27–37.

SMITH, WALSTEIN. "Some Enchanting Easements," *The Appraisal Journal* 48, no. 4 (October 1980), pp. 527–539.

STEWART, LOWELL D. *Public Land Surveys.* New York: Arno Press, 1979 (a volume in the Arno Press collection "The Development of Public Land Law in the United States").

STRAIN, JOSEPH A. "Appraisal of Flowage Easements—Another Look," *The Appraisal Journal* 49, no. 4 (October 1981), pp. 580–586.

Wetlands: Basic Information for Appraisers. Chicago: American Institute of Real Estate Appraisers, June 1989, 16 pp.

8
Fundamentals of Land Valuation

Learning Objectives

After reading this chapter, you should be able to:

- Understand why separate site appraisals are sometimes required
- Distinguish among the five principal land appraisal methods and when each is appropriately used
- Recognize the major factors that influence land values
- Organize market data analysis on a systematic basis

Since nearly all sites differ from others because of geographic location, land improvement, size, shape, and other physical or economic attributes, it is important that a site—either vacant or improved—be evaluated as if free for development, in conformity with the principle of highest and best use. There are, of course, other reasons why the value of the land, as distinct from the improvements that it supports, must be known:

1. Local tax assessment regulations, in most jurisdictions, require the allocation of total property value to land, buildings, and other land improvements. This division aids the assessor in the allocation of units of value with greater consistency and uniformity. Improvements, too, are made subject to adjustment for loss in value due to depreciation, whereas land historically has tended to appreciate.

2. Federal Internal Revenue Service regulations also require the separation of land from improvement value for purposes of depreciation allowance on the latter.

3. Where land is not improved with structures that constitute the highest and best use, it is necessary to determine the value of land as if free and clear and to charge the improvements with value losses resulting from over-, under-, or faulty improvements.

4. For insurance purposes, a separation of land from value of building improvements (which are subject to fire and other hazards) is essential in order to measure accurately the nature and extent of insurable risks.

145

5. For investment purposes, a shift in land-to-building value ratio may prove important in measuring changes in the duration of economic building life for structures in a particular district.

6. Some appraisal techniques, as is the case of the depreciated cost and building residual income approaches to value, require separate handling of site and improvement value in the valuation process.

7. Unimproved or vacant land must be evaluated as available under a potential and legally permissible highest and best use.

8. For site leases that often require that the value of a site be specified as a basis for setting rental payments.

In estimating the value of land, reliance is placed on one or more of the following methods, or approaches:

1. Sales comparison approach.
2. Land residual earnings approach.
3. Subdivision development approach.
4. Ratio of site value to total property value.
5. Land value extraction method.

Generally, only one of these approaches to land value is preferred in a given valuation situation, although a second approach, if applicable and if appropriate data are available, may prove useful as a check for accuracy. For clarity, the various approaches to land value will be discussed as independent appraisal techniques. In practice, however, all valuation methods are related and based on market operations. The interrelationship of the various approaches to value will become apparent as the discussion of recommended appraisal procedures unfolds. A statistical valuation technique sometimes used is regression analysis. This method is discussed in Chapter 10.

SALES COMPARISON APPROACH

The most reliable method of estimating land value is based on a comparison of the subject property with similar properties in like locations which have sold recently. Where the market is active and sales are recent and similar in kind, the comparison approach yields satisfactory value estimates. The mechanics of the comparison approach are relatively simple, and no great skill is required to master the method. Yet, the reliability of this method is enhanced when the appraiser has a clear understanding of market influences on value and has made a thorough survey of comparable sales.

The first and most important requirement in the sales comparison approach to value is ready access to up-to-date sources of real property sales transactions. The sources of sales data in order of availability, accuracy, and convenience are as follows:

1. Tax assessor's record files.
2. County clerk's official public records, for example, deed books.
3. Appraiser's personal office files.
4. Other real estate appraisers.
5. Abstract or title insurance company records.
6. Real estate brokers' multiple listing or general sales record files.
7. Financial news or newspaper reporting services.

The appraiser may use one or more of these sources for sales data depending on appraisal volume and procedures adopted for maintenance of an appraisal plant file. There are often commercial sources of comparable sales data in most larger cities. In many communities copies of official deed records are made available by the county clerk's office at reasonable costs. Similarly, some real estate assessors' offices maintain such sales data for public use. This information, when promptly posted in geographic order or by alphabetical name of subdivision, furnishes a ready and convenient source for market sales information. Maintenance of such information, where available, keeps the appraiser abreast of market operations and thus provides him or her with ready information concerning volume of transfers, price trends, and community growth patterns.

Irrespective of the source from which sales record data are obtained, it is the appraiser's responsibility to verify the price and terms of sale by a personal or telephone interview with the buyer, the seller, or both. Real estate transactions historically are considered private in nature and public records may or may not reveal factual circumstances which "cushioned" or "sweetened" a sale. Interviewing the parties to the transaction, or informed persons such as lawyers or brokers who guided the sales, enables the appraiser to formulate judgments in adjusting market prices paid to the prices obtainable for the subject property were it exposed for sale in the open market. If a sale cannot be confirmed, or where the prices or terms are deliberately held secretive, it usually is best to disregard the transaction in favor of another and more reliable sale property. When applying the sales comparison approach to value, caution must be exercised in accepting state transfer taxes as reliable evidence of the transaction price. Legally, a deed is considered an instrument of "conveyance" in which the actual consideration agreed on in a prior and unrecorded contract need not be stipulated. Although most state laws require that revenue stamps (or the dollar amount of transfer taxes) based on the exact transaction price be attached to the deed, there are, nevertheless, circumstances under which these stamps do not indicate the price for which a property was exchanged. For instance:

1. A buyer may wish to give the impression that he or she paid an amount greater than the actual purchase price and for that reason affixes more revenue stamps than the law requires. There is no limit to the number or amount of stamps that may be purchased, and the municipal agent will gladly sell all the buyer wants. The attaching of excess stamps may be a device to have fu-

ture buyers believe that the property is worth a great deal more than the "bargain" price that was actually paid.

2. Sellers who must deliver the deed at the time of closing—with revenue or transfer fees indicated—may attempt, perhaps unlawfully, to save on this expenditure by paying a lower amount than the actual sale price calls for. The county or city deed recording clerk probably will not question the transaction price quoted by the seller, or the intent of the seller in paying a lower or higher transfer fee (tax) than the law requires.

3. Many states do not have deed revenue stamp laws, and even where such laws are in force the requirements regarding the balance of existing mortgages differ. In some states, only the cash portions of transactions need be considered, whereas in others, state revenue stamps representing the full consideration must be attached to the deed.

4. In the case of property exchanges, the interested parties may understate or overstate the transaction price for tax or other purposes which prove mutually advantageous.

Although in many jurisdictions the state transfer tax or grantor's tax reflects fairly well the actual transaction price of the property, the possible exceptions noted previously should be kept in mind when accepting state transfer tax data as evidence of market price or value. In most condemnation trials, too, revenue stamp data as evidence of market sale price are inadmissible or subject to challenge when introduced by an expert witness. To aid the appraiser in the analysis of market sales, a data report form such as shown in Figure 8.1 is recommended for use.

In securing information from courthouse or file records for entry on the work form, it should not be taken for granted that the date of title closing represents the date of sale. Often land is sold under a *contract for deed*,[1] in which case months and years may separate the date of contract from the date of title closing. The date of contract, in fact and in law, determines the time at which a meeting of minds took place, and it is that date which ideally serves as a basis for time adjustments reflecting changes in economic or market conditions up to the date of appraisal. Furthermore, the appraiser must make certain that the sale was concluded under objective, impersonal bargaining and that the terms of sale were fully disclosed. Sales from father to son or daughter or from one relative to another, or where circumstances indicate undisclosed terms and conditions, or where prices paid appear either unreasonable or questionable should be discarded in favor of other clear-cut, bona fide sale transactions.

Many multiple listing services (MLSs) show the percentage of sale prices to listing prices. In fact, some of these services report this relationship for different classes of properties, such as townhouses, industrial, and vacant land. Properties frequently sell for 92 to 97 percent of their listed prices. This relationship varies according to the state of the real estate market and with different classes of property, especially land. Where market data for comparable properties are scarce,

[1]An agreement under which transfer of title to the land is deferred until partial (periodic) payments aggregate the entire or agreed-upon amount of the purchase price.

Index Sales No. _____

Location _____

_____   Tax map and parcel _____

Seller _____   Area _____

Buyer _____   Frontage _____ Depth _____

Financing terms _____   Deed date _____

_____   Deed of record _____

_____   Deed book _____ Page _____

State transfer tax _____

Price indicated $ _____   Price shown $ _____

Price paid was $ _____   or $ _____ per _____

Sale as confirmed by _____

_____ on _____ at _____ AM/PM

The property was inspected by _____ on _____

Zoning _____   Allowable density _____

Public Utilities: Water _____ ,   Sanitary sewer _____ ,   Storm sewer _____ ,

         Gas _____ ,   Electricity _____ ,   Telephone _____

Unusual influences _____

_____

Land _____

_____

_____

Improvements _____

_____

_____

Assessed value: Land _____ ,   Improvements _____ ,   Year _____

Remarks and analysis of sale (continued on back, along with site sketch) _____

_____

Figure 8.1   Market Data Report Form

property listings may have to be used to provide additional evidence of market value. Moreover, appropriately selected listings can provide an upper limit of an appraised property's market value as well as an indication of the strength of the market. The latter is revealed by the number of days listed properties have been on the market.

Adjustment of Comparable Sales

Prior to comparatively analyzing the comparable site sales, it should be remembered that the adjustments always are made toward the appraised site. Stated differently, the adjustments are made from the known (sale price) toward the unknown (market value of subject). Some of the different adjustment techniques, such as percentage versus dollar adjustments, multiplication versus addition and subtraction of adjustments, and cash equivalency, are covered in detail in the following chapter.

Regardless of the method used to make adjustments in arriving at an estimate of the appraised site's value, the appraiser must always seek, first, to discover truly comparable sales and, second, to be thoroughly familiar with each sale. A factor that is sometimes misapplied in adjusting comparable sales is adjusting for conditions (physical and economic) that existed when the property was sold. Two examples will clearly illustrate the meaning of this statement. A site may have sold as an unfinished parcel, lacking its present zoning and curbs and gutters. Also, it may have sold in a "buyers' market," whereas at the date of appraisal, the market has strengthened to become a "sellers' market." Thus the appraiser must determine the physical and economic conditions that existed when the property was sold in addition to those existing on the appraisal date.

Elements of Comparison

To give a reasonable degree of order to the comparative analysis and the related adjustment process, sales analysis should be broken down into four categories. These are:

1. Date of sale.
2. Conditions of sale.
3. Location.
4. Physical features.

Date of sale.   Previously, it was stated that the appraiser must be thoroughly familiar with the physical and economic conditions that existed when the property sold. Although it is desirable to make time adjustments from the contract date, this date is not always readily available. The next best date to use is the deed date. Whenever possible, however, the appraiser should adjust from the contract date since this is the date that the buyer and seller had a "meeting of the minds." Unfortunately, too frequently more effort is expended on making adjustments rather than securing recent sales that require no time adjustments.

The appraiser has several options available in making time adjustments. Generally, it is advisable to use more than one method to ensure that a reasonable adjustment has been made. Perhaps the best indication of value change due to the passage of time is the sale and resale of the comparable sale site as shown in the following illustration. In using this method, care must be taken to ascertain whether any significant change has occurred in the property or neighborhood. Another method is to study several sites that have sold at different times in the same neighborhood. The third method is to consider general land value trends in the market. This observation lacks the precision of the other two methods.

Sale price (2/15/90)	$100,000
Sale price (8/17/92)	$106,000
Increase in price	$106,000 − $100,000 = $6,000 or 6%
Number of years from 2/15/90 to 8/17/92	2.5
Adjustment per year	6.0% ÷ 2.5 = +2.40%

Conditions of sale.   Several different factors can influence the price paid for a site. If these influences are too great or cannot be substantiated, it is best to delete such sales. Some of the conditions that can influence the price paid for a property are:

1. Unequal bargaining power of the two parties.
2. Favorable or unfavorable loan terms.
3. Unusually strong motivation either to buy or to sell a particular site.
4. Market conditions at sale date that differed sharply from prevailing conditions.

An example of buyer motivation that would cause an unusually high price to be paid is when a prospective buyer needs an adjoining site for business expansion purposes. In all likelihood, he or she would pay more for this site than for a similar site a block away. Such sales ordinarily are eliminated from consideration.

Location.   It might be argued that the best comparable sale is a sale of the appraised site with the second best comparable being an adjoining site. In this regard, the appraiser must *always* ascertain whether there have been recent sales of the appraised site. Usually such sales over the previous 2 to 5 years should be analyzed. The possibility of a location adjustment is greatly reduced when comparable sales near the appraised site are selected. In short, more reliable appraisals result from more thorough market analysis involving the selection of truly similar sale properties and less dependence on "judgment." When making location adjustments the off-site amenities and any differences in highest and best use must be taken into account.

Physical features.   Adjustments are made for any significant differences in physical features that would likely be detected by buyers and sellers of similar sites. The appraiser sometimes may be tempted to make adjustments for insignificant features that are of no consequence to persons trading in a particular class of real estate. Such unnecessary adjustments will cause the appraiser to report a distorted market value. As a result, the appraiser no longer is interpreting the actions of those who make up the real estate market.

A review of Chapter 7 will reveal the physical features for which adjustments *may be* necessary. Some of these features are differences in terrain, depth, frontage, soil conditions, shape, and drainage.

After a minimum of three or four comparable sales have been selected, confirmed, field inspected, and analyzed, the appraiser is in a position to transfer the individual sales data to an adjustment sheet for adjustment and correlation purposes to derive an estimate of market value for the subject property. Table 8.1 shows a sample adjustment sheet on which the derivation of a market value estimate for a residential site is illustrated. The property being appraised measures 110 feet along the street front, is 120 feet in depth, and has a depth/frontage ratio of 1.09. In this instance, it is compared with four reasonably similar market sale transactions that are adjusted to reflect and equalize for economically better or poorer conditions of the subject property as demonstrated.

TABLE 8.1 MARKET VALUE ADJUSTMENT SHEET

	Sales reference number			
	1	2	3	4
1. Date of sale	One month ago	Two months ago	Twelve months ago	Eight months ago
2. Indicated price	$56,000	$50,400	$46,400	$49,600
3. Size of lot	100' × 150'	80' × 200'	90' × 120'	100' × 90'
4. Price per front foot	$560	$630	$516	$496
5. Time adjustment factor	1.00	1.00	1.15	1.10
6. Unit price adjusted for time	$560	$630	$593	$546
7. Depth/frontage ratio	1.50	2.50	1.33	0.90
8. Depth adjustment	0.92	0.82	1.00	1.15
9. Unit price adjustment for depth	$515	$517	$693	$628
Subject property is rated as follows in regard to:				
10. Neighborhood	Same	Better	Same	Poorer
11. Location	Better	Same	Same	Same
12. Site facilities	Better	Same	Same	Poorer
13. Subject comparative percentage rating	1.10	1.05	1.00	0.90
14. Adjusted value	$567	$543	$593	$565
Market value correlation:				
15. Estimated (correlated unit value of land)	$560			
16. Value of subject site	110' × $560 = $61,600 rounded to $61,500			
17. Value adjusted for corner or plottage influences	None			
18. Final estimated land value	$61,500			

In following the step-by-step correlation of comparable market sales data as indicated in the market value adjustment sheet, it will become apparent that the accuracy of the final value conclusion reached depends largely on the exercise of sound appraisal judgment. This judgment cannot be gained by textbook reading or classroom study alone, but results from diligent application of the valuation principles in field practice. Disciplined systematic and thorough data compilation and analysis based on an inquiring and energetic mind are essential ingredients of good appraising.

The first entry on the summary sheet (Table 8.1) is the *date of sale* for each comparable property. This entry is important as a measure of elapsed time to the date of the appraisal. Consideration should be given where changes caused by economic forces influenced market value during the interval.

The second entry shows the *indicated price* paid for each sale property. This price often is based initially on the dollar amount of state transfer taxes posted in each deed. Where tax stamp information appears to be out of line, and where sale confirmation fails to yield supporting facts and explanations, the sale should be rejected in favor of another, more reliable source of market value.

The third entry notes *size of lot*. With the aid of these measurements the appraiser is in a position to compute the price paid per unit (front foot) of land, and to adjust unit value where necessary to compensate for variation in lot depth. Economic units, such as the number of apartment units permitted by zoning, may be used, too.

The fourth entry is the *price paid per front foot of land*. This amount is derived by dividing the total price paid (entry 2) by the number of front feet (entry 3) of the comparable lot.

The fifth entry indicates a *time adjustment factor*. If because of economic conditions, the comparable sale property would bring more or less were the sale to take place today (i.e., on the date of appraisal), an adjustment factor should indicate the percentage of increase or decrease as market conditions warrant. Where no adjustment is necessary, the entry is 1.00. A 5-percent-plus adjustment would be noted as 1.05. Plus or minus adjustments are allowable.

The time adjustment factor in entry 5 is then multiplied by the unit foot value given in entry 4, and the resulting *unit price adjusted for time* is then shown in entry 6. This time adjustment must not be made arbitrarily but rather must be based on considered study of market conditions—or at least on the opinions of *informed* persons such as experienced appraisers, builders, and realtors in the community.

The seventh entry is *depth/frontage ratio*. It is calculated by dividing a sale parcel's depth by its road frontage. It gives an indication of the comparative depth to frontage relationship, with a higher square unit (e.g., square foot) of value expected for sites that have comparatively less depth. Contrastingly, deeper sites generally command a higher price per front foot.

Entry 8 provides for *depth factor* consideration. Where all sales are of the same depth as the subject property, this and the following entry can be omitted from the adjustment sheet. However, whenever lot depth variations influence the price paid, the appraiser must adjust the figures accordingly and in conformity with appropriate depth value guidelines developed in the local market. The resulting calculation is entry 9 and is expressed in this example as sale price per front foot.

Entries 10, 11, and 12 constitute judgment conclusions concerning the relative quality of the subject property as compared with each comparable property in regard to (a) neighborhood, (b) location advantages, and (c) site facilities. Considering the status of the *subject* property as compared with the *sale* property, the appraiser establishes a quality rating for each of the features as being better, poorer, or the same. An overall percentage rating is then reached for the subject property (entry 13).

In arriving at a final estimated site value, some appraisers prefer to rate each feature on a percentage basis, and to multiply the separate percentage ratings for a weighted or combined average. There is danger, however, in this practice. Suppose that each of the features (i.e., time adjustment, neighborhood, and site facilities) is judged to be 50 percent when compared with the sale property; by multiplying 0.50 times 0.50 times 0.50, an overall average of 12.5 percent is obtained. This method has a tendency to overadjust for comparative deficiencies and to underadjust for superior features. To illustrate: Where one adjustment calls for a 50 percent minus rating and another adjustment calls for a 50 percent plus rating, it would appear logical that the two ratings should cancel out. By multiplying 0.50 by 1.50, the net result, however, is 75 percent, which clearly is an overadjustment on the minus side.

A second method is to add percentage adjustments—plus and minus—to overcome the errors derived by percentage multiplications.

In using this method, it is essential that market evidence is the basis for each separate adjustment. Otherwise, the final value will be the result of "guesstimating" rather than "estimating." A third method follows where the ratings are judged descriptively, and that only *one* final percentage quality rating is arrived at and entered as shown under entry 13 of the market summary sheet.

The overall quality percentage rating is then multiplied by the adjusted unit price (entry 9) of the comparable property to derive an estimated value per unit measure of land for the *subject* property. This value is listed in entry 14. The next step calls for correlating the adjusted values derived from four or more sales into a single estimate of unit value. This final unit value is found in entry 15. Correlation does not mean averaging but rather assigning judgment weights to each sale on the basis of compatibility, terms of sale, and reliability of sales data. The correlation procedure should be explained in the narrative section of the appraisal report as follows:

Sale 1 is located in the same block as the subject property, is identical in size, and required no time adjustment. A judgment weight of 50 percent was given to this sale. This weight implies to the client that this sale is of such similarity that 50 percent of the final value component is based on it.

Sale 2 is also located in the same block, but the property depth of this sale is nonstandard. For this reason a judgment weight of only 30 percent was given to this sale.

Sales 3 and 4 are in an adjacent neighborhood, and both sales required time adjustments of 1.15 percent and 1.10 percent, respectively. For these reasons the correlation weight assigned to these sales was 10 percent each.

The estimated value of the subject property is then derived as follows:

Index sales	Adjusted value	Weight of sale	Value component
1	$567	50	$284
2	543	30	163
3	593	10	59
4	565	10	57
			$563
	Rounded to $560		

The value of the subject site may then be derived by multiplying the number of front feet of land by the unit value as was done under entry 16. Similarly, adjustments for corner locations or plottage if called for should be made and noted under entry 17. The final estimate of land value, rounded to the nearest $500 (for sites in this value range), should then be listed in entry 18. The market value procedure as outlined, when applied with professional care, should yield accurate estimates that will reasonably reflect the market price that may be anticipated were the subject property exposed for sale in the open market on the date of appraisal.

Alternatively, the relative merits of each selected comparable sale may be discussed and followed by a selected final unit value such as $560. Whichever approach chosen should allow the reader to reach essentially the same value conclusion as derived by the appraiser. No valuation table, method, or procedure can ever serve as a substitute for diligent data compilation, careful analysis, and sound judgment sharpened by experience. Conversely, it is inconceivable that sound judgment can be exercised without a systematic data adjustment program such as that outlined previously.

LAND RESIDUAL EARNINGS APPROACH

In the final analysis, the value of all land is based on its productivity or income-producing capacity under a program of highest and best use. Whenever the sales comparison approach is inapplicable, either because of the absence of market transactions or the nonexistence of unimproved land in the subject or comparable areas, the appraiser may resort to the earnings or income approach to value. Land income, as discussed in Chapter 3, is residual in character. Costs of labor, management, maintenance, operations, and a competitive market return *on* and *of* the invested capital in improvements must be met first. What is left, if anything, under a program of highest and best use belongs to land. This residual income, when capitalized at an appropriate rate of interest, forms a capital sum of money that measures the *present* worth of the subject site.

To apply the income approach to land value, the appraiser cannot and must not assume that the existing building improvements necessarily constitute the highest and best use of the land. The appraiser, in fact, must undertake a land utilization study of the area and site and determine what type and size of improvement should be placed on the land in order to achieve its highest possible return and present value. Since few improvements—even when considered to represent the highest and best use—are in new condition, it is necessary under the income approach to land value to assume first a reasonable highest and best land use, and second that improvements *are* viewed in their current condition (and value).

The procedure for selecting the highest and best use and the process of capitalizing the residual income into a sum of present value can best be illustrated as follows. Suppose that a building site in a given community can be developed for residential purposes only under existing and reasonably anticipated zoning restrictions. Suppose, further, that preliminary analysis of neighborhood characteristics and of housing demand narrows the choice of possible and profitable site improvements to one of the following types of structures:

1. A single-story duplex building, each rental unit containing two bedrooms, dining-living room, kitchen, and tiled bath. Total improvement cost, $63,000.
2. A three-family apartment building, each apartment containing two bedrooms, dining-living room, kitchen, and tiled bath. Total improvement cost, $72,000.

Since the *highest* use of the building site was prescribed by zoning law for residential purposes, the determination still to be made is which of the alternate types of improvements described previously constitutes the *best* use. Under the definition of highest and best use, it is necessary to ascertain the income-producing capacity of the land under the alternative types of improvements and to find by the process of capitalization which income yields to the land its highest present value. Based on prevailing rentals of similar residences in comparable neighborhoods at $550 per month per four-room and bath duplex unit, and $500 per month per four-room and bath apartment unit, the procedure to derive land income and land value at a market rate of interest (R_L) of 10 percent is as shown in Table 8.2. This valuation procedure is one generally practiced by informed investors to determine the present worth of land under the income or earnings residual approach to land value. Based on the analysis, as illustrated, the conclusion can be drawn that the highest and best use of the building site under value study is a three-family apartment building to be constructed at a cost of $72,000 and renting at $500 per month per dwelling unit. Under this highest and best use, the land is worth $24,800. If the site were developed as a duplex site, both land income and land value would diminish.

The income attributable to each proposed building is based on a 10 percent return on the improvement plus an annual recapture rate of 2.5 percent. The latter figure is based on a forecast of a remaining economic life of 40 years

TABLE 8.2 ANALYSIS OF LAND INCOME AND LAND VALUE UNDER ALTERNATE TYPES OF IMPROVEMENTS

	Single-story duplex	Three-family apartment
Gross annual income		
Duplex units $550 × 2 × 12 (months)	$13,200	
Three-family apartment $500 × 3 × 12 (months)		$18,000
Less vacancy and collection losses at 5%	660	900
Effective gross income	$12,540	$17,100
Less operating expenses		
Management fee (7%)	$ 878	$ 1,197
Real estate taxes	1,212	1,693
Maintenance and repairs	630	940
Hazard insurance	210	340
Fuel and utilities	750	1,080
Janitor service		370
Total operating expenses	$ 3,680	$ 5,620
Net operating income	$ 8,860	$11,480
Less income attributable to buildings (I_B)		
Duplex $63,000 × 0.125 (0.10 + 0.025)	$ 7,875	
Apartments $72,000 × 0.125		$ 9,000
Net income remaining to land (I_L)	$ 985	$ 2,480
Value of land at 0.10% rate of capitalization (R_L)		
Duplex $985 ÷ 0.10	$ 9,850	
Apartment $2,480 ÷ 0.10		$24,800

(100% ÷ 40 years = 2.5%/year). The residual techniques of capitalization under the income approach to value are more fully described and demonstrated in Chapter 19.

SUBDIVISION DEVELOPMENT METHOD

Throughout the historical development of appraisal thought, and in the writing of most appraisal literature, the existence of land has been taken for granted. In effect, it is implied that land cannot be produced and hence should not be evaluated via the cost approach to value. This classical theory of land as being permanent, indestructible, immovable, and unique (heterogeneous) is valid only if applied to land in its natural state. The appraiser, however is concerned with "economic" land, modified and improved; and in this economic sense, such land *can* be produced, duplicated, and its situs qualities shifted to other locations.

Our ability to modify land and thereby produce land value is illustrated by the following story. A farmer, after years of grueling work cutting trees, pulling stumps, and plowing, had converted an overgrown forest into a fertile and productive farm. One day while harvesting he was talking with a city cousin who was mightily impressed by the lush appearance of the farm and said: "Aren't you lucky to own this land, which God created and presented as a gift to man." The farmer looked bemused at his calloused hands and replied: "It's true. But you should have seen this land when God had it all to himself."

Today, raw land as nature provided it rarely exists. Almost all land has been directly or indirectly modified by human beings. Direct modification has included the construction of buildings, fences, dikes, drainage canals, land filling and grading, and the conversion of forests into grazing, farming, or building sites. Land has been modified indirectly by the construction of access roads, bridges, canals, modes of rapid transportation, and other means of public improvements which increase land utility. In a negative respect, land values have suffered from soil, water, and air pollution as well as from high frequency of criminal acts on persons and property.

This appraisal method should be supported by use of the direct market sales approach whenever possible. It can be used in the appraisal of any kind of land as long as it has subdivision potential. That is, it is adaptable to residential, industrial, or commercial uses. Further, such land does not have to be immediately "ripe" for development, but the probable absorption period should be capable of an accurate estimate. Reasons that this method produces unrealistic value estimates include:

1. Inaccurate highest and best use analysis.
2. Failure to account for all the expenditures necessary to produce the forecast income.
3. Overstatement of income or failure to graduate the sales income as the marketing program progresses.
4. Incorrect selection and application of the discount rate.[2]

Where land is anticipated to ripen into higher economic uses, or where the conversion of farm or rur-urban (land in transition, being neither farm nor suburban in use or character) acreage into suburban building sites is justified by community growth and demand, the appraiser can logically and accurately apply the subdivision development approach to value.

The suggested steps in using this method are as follows:

1. Create a sound development plan.
2. Forecast a realistic pricing schedule.
3. Forecast accurately the absorption rate and mix of sites to be sold.
4. Accurately estimate the staging and expense of land development and related expenses.
5. Forecast marketing and related expenditures.
6. Estimate the annual real property taxes during the development and marketing periods.
7. Estimate a reasonable overhead and profit allowance.

[2]James H. Boykin, "Developmental Method of Land Appraisal," *The Appraisal Journal* (April 1976), p. 181.

8. Analyze the market to determine the appropriate discount rate expected by investors for this type of investment.

9. Select a discount rate that properly reflects the timing of the site sales.[3]

An appraisal assignment calls for finding the value of 50 acres of land which a subdivider seeks to purchase and develop into residential building sites. As a result of a highest and best land use study, it appears best to sub-divide the 50-acre tract into 150 lots each measuring 100 feet by 120 feet, or three lots per acre. Under this development plan the 150 building lots comprise 82.5 percent of the total land area, whereas the balance, or 17.5 percent of land, is deemed necessary for construction of streets, traffic isles, and other public uses. Based on study and analysis of comparable property sales, it is concluded that the lots can be marketed as follows:

First year: 40 lots at $30,000 each
Second year: 60 lots at $32,000 each
Third year: 50 lots at $35,000 each

The basic question answered by this technique is how much an inves-tor can afford to pay for an undeveloped site today in anticipation of a forecast development and marketing program. This appraisal method is il-lustrated in Table 8.3. This illustration does not include costs of sidewalks, extension of gas, electric, or telephone utilities, or expenditures for other public or recreational facilities. Should such expenditures be incurred by the developer, they must, of course, be added into the subdivision development method of land valuation.

SITE VALUE-TO-PROPERTY VALUE RATIO (ALLOCATION)

Under conditions where the sales comparison, land residual, or subdivision de-velopment approach to value are not applicable, an estimate of land value may be derived from a study of typical ratios of site value to total property value as indi-cated by comparable improved property sales. Under the highest and best utiliza-tion of land, studies disclose certain optimum land/property value ratios on which the appraiser may rely for value guidance. At the outset, stress is laid on the fact that ratios, like depth or corner land value rules, do not unfailingly indicate value but rather reflect typical land/property relationships which serve a useful purpose in the allocation of total value to the component parts of land and build-ing improvements.

Where land value equals improvement value, the ratio is said to be one-to-one, or the land-to-property ratio is said to be 50 percent. Commercial land in

[3]*Ibid.*, p. 186.

TABLE 8.3 APPRAISAL BY THE LAND DEVELOPMENTAL APPROACH

Income and Expenses	Year 1	Year 2	Year 3
Lot sales	$1,200,000	$1,920,000	$1,750,000
Less:			
Engineering	$101,250	—	—
Clearing	39,350	—	—
Roads and drainage	562,500	$131,750	$117,150
Water lines	118,100	89,200	68,600
Sanitary sewer (on- and off-site)	585,000	113,450	103,550
Entrance	30,000	—	—
Advertising	4,500	2,200	2,150
Real estate taxes	5,600	4,350	2,900
Mortgage interest	127,500	98,200	27,150
Project management	15,000	11,550	7,150
Overhead and profit (35% of lot sales)	420,000	672,000	612,500
	(2,008,800)	1,122,700	941,150
Value of net sales revenue	$ (808,800)	$ 797,300	$ 808,850

Present value of net sales revenue
(using a 10% end-of-year discount factor, see Table 16.1)

Year 1 $(808,800) × 0.909091 = $(735,273)
Year 2 $ 797,300 × 0.826446 = 658,925
Year 3   808,850 × 0.751315 = 607,701

Present value of raw acreage $ 531,353 rounded to $531,500

Present value per acre ($531,500 ÷ 50) $10,630

downtown areas is generally characterized by a low (but efficient) land-to-improvement ratio, and the ratio increases as the land is put to lower (less efficient) uses. Guiding ratios for a typical community may range as follows:

Land use	Land-to-property value ratio (%)
Commercial	20–50
Office	10–30
Residential	15–25
Apartment house	10–15
Industrial	5–10

Once a study of typical land uses within a community discloses a guiding relationship of site value ratios, the appraiser may use the results as a basis for or check on the accuracy of value findings by other and more direct appraisal methods. For instance, if typical residential properties are improved with buildings so as to create a 12 to 16 percent ratio, a property with a land/value ratio of as little as 5 percent or as high as 25 percent may connote over- or underdevelopment of the site. In either case, faulty improvement will cause a loss in building value reflected by the difference between actual and estimated potential value realizable under a program of highest and best site utilization.

This method seldom can stand by itself as an indication of site value. When used in a built-up, older residential neighborhood, the question that must be answered is: What was the market source of the ratio evidence? The irony of this method is that it is most accurately applied to new residential properties where there generally are abundant lot sales. Whenever ample site sales are available, this method is usually superfluous.

The site value results will likely be distorted if site value ratios for new properties are applied to older properties or ratios for properties in one neighborhood to another neighborhood. Nevertheless, it has its place in obtaining an initial idea of a site value. For example, the site value of an appraised site might be estimated as follows. Assume a typical land/value ratio of 20 percent, and that each of the sale properties is similar to the appraised site:

Sale number	Sale price	Land ratio	Site value
1	$150,000	× 0.20	$30,000
2	165,000	× 0.20	33,000
3	142,000	× 0.20	28,400
4	160,000	× 0.20	32,000
5	168,000	× 0.20	33,600

Thus the indicated range of values for the subject site is from $28,400 to $33,600. The appraiser, based on similarities in the improved property sales and the appraised property, would be expected to select a value within this $5,200 range.

LAND VALUE EXTRACTION METHOD

Sometimes it is necessary to use improved property sales to estimate an appraised site's value. This method is best applied when the value of the improvements have minimal value such as dilapidated or obsolete structures.

The land value extraction method involves the following steps:

1. Confirm sale price and inspect the improvements.
2. Estimate the salvage value of the improvements, less demolition expenses.
3. Deduct the net salvage value of improvements from the sale price.

The remainder is the value of the land. An example of the land value extraction method follows:

> A 16.70-acre industrially zoned parcel sold for $575,000. There were a 70-year-old abandoned frame dwelling and a dilapidated storage shed on the site which have a combined salvage value of $4,000. Neither structure is compatible with the property's zoning or highest and best use. Therefore, their value is limited to salvage value. It will cost $1,000 to demolish the structure and sort and remove the materials from the site. Thus the remaining land value is

Sale price	$575,000
Less salvage value	− 3,000
Land value	$572,000 or $34,251/acre

SUMMARY

Since nearly all sites differ from others in location, land improvement, size, shape, and other physical or economic attributes, sites must be analyzed separately and evaluated as if free for development in conformity with the principle of highest and best use. Some reasons why separate land valuations are needed include (1) local tax assessment regulations, (2) federal Internal Revenue Service regulations, (3) for highest and best use analysis, (4) for insurance purposes, (5) for investment purposes, (6) in applying certain appraisal techniques, and (7) to set site lease payments.

Five methods are available for the valuation of sites. These are (1) the sales comparison approach, (2) the land residual approach, (3) the land development approach, (4) the ratio of site value to total property value, and (5) the land value extraction method.

The *sales comparison method* involves the analysis of sales in four categories: (1) date of sale, (2) conditions of sale, (3) location, and (4) physical features. In using this method, it is essential that market evidence is the basis for each separate adjustment.

The *land residual approach* is based on converting the earnings available for a site into an indication of market value. The steps involved are to first estimate the net operating income available to land and improvements. Next, the earnings for improvements are deducted from the overall income, leaving the land income. This income is divided by a land capitalization rate to find its value.

The *subdivision development method* is applicable to any land that has subdivision potential including industrial, commercial, retail, and residential. It involves the following steps: (1) a sound development plan, (2) a realistic pricing schedule, (3) an accurate forecast of the absorption rate and mix of sites to be sold, (4) an accurate estimate of the land development staging and expenses, (5) forecast marketing and related expenses, (6) an annual estimate of real property taxes during the development and marketing periods, and (7) selection of the appropriate discount rate expected by investors that also reflects the timing of site sales.

The *site value-to-property value ratio method*, also called the allocation method, is used when the site value can be estimated from a study of typical ratios of site value to total property value as indicated by comparable improved property sales.

The final method is the *land value extraction method*, which involves three steps: (1) confirm the sale price and inspect the improvements, (2) estimate the salvage value of the improvements, less demolition expenses, and (3) deduct the net salvage value of improvements from the sale price. The remainder is the land value.

REVIEW QUESTIONS

1. List five purposes for making separate site appraisals.
2. Discuss four situations where the stated consideration in a deed may be inaccurate.
3. Explain why it is important for an appraiser to understand thoroughly the conditions that existed when a property sold.
4. Identify and discuss the number and type of adjustments that should be made by the appraiser.
5. Comparatively evaluate site appraisal via the sales comparison and land residual earnings methods.
6. Under what circumstances is it acceptable to use the subdivision development land appraisal method?
7. Two identical residences are erected on opposite sides of the same street. The same builder and identical building designs are employed. The contract specified that the builder should be compensated at a cost-plus-10-percent basis with a maximum expenditure of $100,000 per structure. The final costs were as follows: building A, $90,000; building B, $95,000. The higher cost of building B was caused by the existence of rock which had to be blasted out of place. The lot for each structure (75 feet by 150 feet) was purchased for $10,000. Based on the preceding data, discuss the following:
   (a) Do the buildings have different values? Explain.
   (b) Are the lots identical in value?
   (c) Classify the expenditure for blasting the rock.

READING AND STUDY REFERENCES

BOYCE, BYRL N., and WILLIAM N. KINNARD. Chapter 8, "Site Valuation," *Appraising Real Property*. Lexington, Mass.: Lexington Books, 1984.

CONSTAM, E. "Methodology of Water Lot Evaluation," *The Appraisal Journal* 45, no. 1 (January 1977), pp. 70–79.

DONOHO, MARK B. "Land Valuation in a Dormant Market," *The Appraisal Journal* (April 1988), pp. 200–204.

GAINES, JAMES P. "Industrial Land Valuation," *The Real Estate Appraiser and Analyst* 47, no. 4 (Winter 1981), pp. 5–9.

HOAGLAND, GARY. "Are the Mechanics of the Adjustment Process Correct?", *The Real Estate Appraiser and Analyst* 48, no. 1 (Spring 1982), pp. 59–61.

JANUARY, DAVID J. "Forecasting Lot Values Using Regression Analysis," *The Real Estate Appraiser and Analyst* 55, no. 3 (Fall 1989), pp. 61–72.

MAES, MARVIN A. "Subdivision Analysis: A Case Study," *The Appraisal Journal* 50, no. 1 (January 1982), pp. 100–112.

WALDRON, DELORIS M. "Analyzing Land Sales: A Case Study," *The Real Estate Appraiser and Analyst* (Fall 1988), pp. 34–40.

WILLIAMS, SCOTT R. "Problems with Percentage Adjustments," *The Real Estate Appraiser and Analyst* 48, no. 4 (Winter 1982), pp. 48–55.

9

SALES COMPARISON APPROACH TO VALUE

Learning Objectives

After reading this chapter, you should be able to:

- Comprehend the reason for and be able to adjust for nonstandard financing
- Appreciate the various methods of adjusting comparable sales to indicate the value of the appraised property
- Understand how to use linear regression as a means of adjusting prices of comparable sales properties
- Use the cash-equivalent sales analysis method
- Develop and properly use the gross income multiplier technique for estimating property value
- Distinguish between the GIM and EGIM
- Understand and apply paired data set analysis

For standardized goods and services, prices paid at "arm's-length" bargaining in an open and normal market provide a reliable *index* of value. As a rule, little difficulty is encountered in obtaining reasonably accurate estimates of market price quotations for commodities such as wheat, coffee, sugar, corn, eggs, poultry, or for bonds and stocks which are freely traded. The greater the dissimilarity of the product and the less frequent the trading, however, the greater the skill required to adjust for product differences in order to attain price comparability, and the greater the chances for error in the final estimate of value.

With real estate, which is heterogeneous in character, exact comparability seldom occurs, if only because of differences in the fixed geographical location of the property. It is possible, nevertheless, through study and analysis of market operations, to adjust for price effects caused by differences in physical characteristics in order to obtain economic equality essential to an accurate estimate of market value.

165

The greater the number and the more recent the sales of comparable properties analyzed, the greater the accuracy and the more convincing are the results obtained via the sales comparison approach to value. Ready access to market transaction source data is, therefore, of first importance. Most active appraisers maintain a market sales-data file as part of their appraisal plant, at least for the geographic area in which the majority of their appraisal assignments originate. The appraisal report file itself provides an important source of market transaction information. For example, an appraisal request may be received for a property in the same neighborhood, or better still in the same block, as another property that was recently appraised. Where office files are insufficient or incomplete, ready access to sales data must be had through other appraisers, brokers or agents, multiple listing services, abstract companies, county tax or record offices, or through commercial services which computerize sales data for multiuse research purposes. Abstract companies, for title search and title insurance application, maintain accurate records of property ownership and title transfer data which generally are filed in geographic or alphabetical order by legal descriptions for a county. Appraisers determine in time which of these data sources are most reliable and most economical.

VERIFICATION OF SALES

Market sale transactions should never be used as comparable sales unless the appraiser personally, or through a responsible assistant, has confirmed the sale and inquired into the circumstances causing the sale or affecting the transaction price. Verification usually can be obtained from the seller or purchaser of the property or the agent who handled its sale. Most parties involved in a sale will confirm a property's sale price, especially if informed that the sales information was obtained from public records and is to be used as one of several sales transactions in deriving an objective measure of value. Circumstances affecting the sale must be known, especially if extraordinary terms or conditions appear likely or if lack of objective, impersonal bargaining or forced-sale motivations are suspected. Where the sale was not clear cut, and when adjustments for conditions or terms of sale cannot readily and accurately be made, it probably is best to refrain from using the particular transactions and to select another and more reliable guide to market value.

Sale prices, too, should never be deduced solely from the amount of state transfer or seller tax cited in a deed of record. These tax references may be inaccurate. For example, in Virginia, the amount of the state recordation tax is based either on the amount of the consideration stated in the deed or the actual value of the property conveyed, whichever is higher. State recordation tax data, too, are deemed unreliable and unacceptable as evidence for an index of market value in most court jurisdictions, unless the sale price was directly confirmed by a party to the transaction. This recording tax information is not available in nondisclosure states.

PRICE ADJUSTMENTS FOR TIME AND TRANSFER TERMS

Price simply represents the amount paid for real property in terms of dollars. Before accepting price as bona fide evidence of value, however, it is essential that the appraiser verify the transaction in order to learn how closely the purchase price fulfills the definition of market value. The following conditions must be carefully scrutinized:

1. Relationship of the parties.
2. Date of sale.
3. Financial terms of sale.

Relationship of the Parties

The importance of the *relationship of the parties* is not always self-evident. Unless the buyer and the seller deal on a reasonably objective and impersonal basis, little reliance can be placed on their transaction as representing *typical* attitudes of market buyers and sellers. Thus a sale from father to son, or brother to sister, would hardly represent typical market transfers. Neither would sales from one corporation to a subsidiary company, nor from an employer to an employee and probably not between adjoining property owners be considered evidence of *market* value. Such sales, even though validly recorded on public records, must be disregarded in favor of impersonally objective transactions by sellers and buyers who have bartered freely and independently in an *open* market in which the sale was offered with knowledge of the property's potential uses and where its availability to all concerned is readily and widely known.

Date of Sale

Comparable sales selected for price analysis under the sales comparison approach to value must be adjusted, if necessary, to compensate for the effect of economic forces that influenced the real estate market during the time interval elapsed between the date of the comparable sale and the date of the subject property appraisal. Market prices of real estate are dynamic in character and move upward or downward with changes in building supply and demand, variations in business and real estate cycles, and changes in the value of money as a result of dollar inflation or deflation. The more recent the comparable sale, the better and the more reliable are the market comparison results. Sales that are six months old or older generally will need to be adjusted to reflect current market conditions, that is, to measure the change in value, if any, due to the passage of time since the sale occurred. The appraiser should ask himself or herself the question: Suppose that the comparable sale were exposed for sale today (on the date of the appraisal)— would it bring the same price at which it sold some time ago? If the answer is no, price adjustments are called for, and the reason for each must be explained in the narrative section of the appraisal report. Adjustments are generally shown in relation to 100 percent and applied as ratios of 1.00—such as 0.95, 1.02, 1.05, and so on—of prevailing market prices.

In analyzing market transactions, the *date of sale* is also of great importance. Appraisers as a rule rely on the date of the transaction as shown on the deed of record as evidence of the time of sale. It is possible that months, or even years, may elapse between the date of contract and the date of appraisal of a given property. However, it is not always possible to obtain this contract date and the deed date is used instead. This date is preferred over the date the deed is recorded since several weeks may pass before a deed is recorded.

Where it is evident that the terms of sale influenced the price at which the index property exchanged, price adjustments, too, are called for. Value, by market definition, is based on property transfer on a cash or cash-equivalent basis. Where the impact of terms is difficult to measure, or where the sale was not on an open and competitive basis, it is best to disregard the transaction and to select another for market comparison purposes.

Adjusting for Financing

Seldom, if ever, does a party buy real estate alone. The decision to acquire and to pay a particular price for real estate may be influenced by the perceived benefits generated by the property, its ability to shelter other passive income from income taxes, and also by the financing terms. Financing terms can either inflate or deflate the price that a party is willing to pay. The appraiser's dilemma is twofold: (1) being able to use a mathematical method that will logically account for out-of-the-ordinary financing terms, and (2) determining to some reasonable degree of satisfaction whether the market participants' behavior is reflected by this adjustment methodology. This adjustment method is known as "cash equivalency," which is a misnomer. Application of this method does not actually equate a sale price to the price expected from an all-cash purchase. Instead, the process is more accurately described as "prevailing financing equivalency." The appraiser seeks to identify any unusual financing and then adjust accordingly until the price reflects the price that probably would have been paid had prevailing or normal debt financing been used in the sale of a comparable property. In effect, this adjustment is made to determine the price the real estate itself would have brought in a sale involving normal financing. No adjustment is needed if the financing arrangements did not affect the price paid for the comparable property.

There is no universal agreement as to how this adjustment should be handled. The following examples illustrate how this adjustment can be applied.

Sale price	$130,000
Financing terms	$104,000 loan, 30 years, level monthly payments, 11% interest rate
Prevailing loan terms	25-year term and 12% interest rate with monthly installments

The question is how much a buyer would probably have paid for this property if it had been financed with a typical 25-year, 12 percent loan. The cash equivalency of the down payment of $26,000 needs no adjustment since this is already cash. The next step is to adjust the $104,000 loan to its prevailing financing equivalency by use of present worth factors as shown in Table 9.1. This adjustment is simply a means of computing the installment to amortize both the favorable and prevailing loans. The subject of present worth and finance mathematics is covered in more detail in Chapters 16 and 17.

Installment to amortize 1 at 11% for 30 years $\dfrac{0.009523}{0.010532} = 0.904197$
Installment to amortize 1 at 12% for 25 years

The value of the existing loan would be worth $94,036 ($104,000 × 0.904197). Stated differently, the 11 percent loan would be discounted by 9.58 percent (1.00 − .9042) in a 12 percent market. The adjusted sale price of this comparable sale would be

$$\begin{array}{r} \$ \ 26{,}000 \\ + \ 94{,}036 \\ \hline \$ \ 120{,}036 \text{ or } \$120{,}000 \text{ (rounded)} \end{array}$$

The prevailing financing equivalency (cash equivalency) can be calculated by two other methods as well. A variation of this method is to substitute dollars for the monthly payment rate. This payment information is found in mortgage payment schedules used by mortgage lenders and real estate brokers. It can also be calculated by multiplying the monthly payment rate (.009523) by the loan principal ($104,000). This method is shown as follows:

Monthly payment at 11% for 30 years $\dfrac{\$ \ 990.39}{\$1{,}095.33} = 0.904195$
Monthly payment at 12% for 25 years

The second alternative is to multiply the existing monthly mortgage payment by the monthly present worth of one per period factor (at the prevailing interest rate). This would be

Monthly payment (at 11%)	
0.009523 × $104,000	$ 990.39
times present worth of 1 per period	
(at 12%) (1/0.010532)	94.948728
Present value of mortgage	$ 94,036
plus down payment	26,000
Cash equivalency	$120,036

A relatively simple financing adjustment can be made when a seller pays any discount points that a buyer ordinarily would be expected to pay. For example, assume that in a given market, home purchasers are accustomed to paying one discount point[1] plus one loan origination point. However, the best available financing in the case of a particular comparable sale was six discount points plus the usual one point loan fee. In order to sell the $200,000 dwelling, the seller agreed to pay five discount points on behalf of the buyer. The buyer paid a $20,000 down payment. The cash equivalent is computed as follows:

[1]A discount point is equal to 1 percent of the face amount of a mortgage loan.

TABLE 9.1 MONTHLY PRESENT VALUE FACTORS

Year	11% interest			12% interest		
	Present value of 1 $V^n = \dfrac{1}{S^n}$	Present value of 1 per period $a_n = \dfrac{1-V^n}{i}$	Installment to amortize 1 $1/a_n = \dfrac{i}{1-V^n}$	Present value of 1 $V^n = \dfrac{1}{S^n}$	Present value of 1 per period $a_n = \dfrac{1-V^n}{i}$	Installment to amortize 1 $1/a_n = \dfrac{i}{1-V^n}$
1	0.896283	11.314564	0.088381	0.887449	11.255077	0.088848
2	0.803323	21.455618	0.046607	0.787566	21.243387	0.047073
3	0.720005	30.544874	0.032738	0.698924	30.107505	0.033214
4	0.645328	38.691421	0.025845	0.620260	37.973959	0.026333
5	0.578397	45.993033	0.021742	0.550449	44.955038	0.022244
6	0.518407	52.537346	0.019034	0.488496	51.150391	0.019550
7	0.464640	58.402903	0.017122	0.433515	56.648452	0.017652
8	0.416449	63.660103	0.015708	0.384722	61.527703	0.016252
9	0.373256	68.372043	0.014625	0.341422	65.857789	0.015184
10	0.334543	72.595274	0.013775	0.302994	69.700522	0.014347
11	0.299845	76.380486	0.013092	0.268892	73.110751	0.013677
12	0.268746	79.773108	0.012535	0.238628	76.137157	0.013134
13	0.240872	82.813858	0.012075	0.211770	78.822938	0.012686
14	0.215890	85.539231	0.011690	0.187935	81.206433	0.012314
15	0.193498	87.981936	0.011365	0.166783	83.321664	0.012001

16	0.173429	90.171292	0.011090	0.148011	85.198823	0.011787
17	0.155442	92.133575	0.010853	0.131352	86.864707	0.011512
18	0.139320	93.892336	0.010650	0.116569	88.343095	0.011319
19	0.124870	95.468684	0.010474	0.103449	89.655088	0.011153
20	0.111919	96.881538	0.010321	0.091805	90.819416	0.011010
21	0.100311	98.147855	0.010188	0.081473	91.852697	0.010886
22	0.089907	99.282835	0.010072	0.072303	92.769683	0.010779
23	0.080582	100.300097	0.009970	0.064165	93.583461	0.010685
24	0.072224	101.211853	0.009880	0.056943	94.305647	0.010603
25	0.064733	102.029043	0.009801	0.050534	94.946551	0.010532
26	0.058019	102.761477	0.009731	0.044846	95.515320	0.010469
27	0.052002	103.417946	0.009669	0.039799	96.020074	0.010414
28	0.046608	104.006327	0.009614	0.035319	96.468018	0.010366
29	0.041774	104.533684	0.009566	0.031344	96.865546	0.010323
30	0.037441	105.006345	0.009523	0.027816	97.218330	0.010286
31	0.033558	105.429983	0.009484	0.024685	97.531409	0.010253
32	0.030077	105.809682	0.009450	0.021907	97.809251	0.010223
33	0.026958	106.150002	0.009420	0.019441	98.055821	0.010198
34	0.024162	106.455022	0.009393	0.017253	98.274641	0.010175
35	0.021656	106.728408	0.009369	0.015311	98.468831	0.010155
36	0.019410	106.973440	0.009348	0.013588	98.641165	0.010137
37	0.017396	107.193057	0.009328	0.012058	98.794103	0.010122
38	0.015592	107.389896	0.009311	0.010701	98.929827	0.010108
39	0.013975	107.566320	0.009296	0.009497	99.050277	0.010095
40	0.012525	107.724446	0.009282	0.008428	99.157169	0.010084

Points paid by seller $180,000 × 0.05 = $9,000

Down payment	$ 20,000
Cash equivalent of mortgage ($180,000 − $9,000)	171,000
Cash equivalent for comparable sale	$191,000

The preceding methods are not completely realistic in the sense that the cash equivalency of the mortgage is computed as if the loans will be held by a purchaser for the entire mortgage term. In practice, residential mortgages are generally held for approximately 8 years at which time homes are sold or mortgages refinanced under new terms. Thus a more accurate reflection of residential buyer behavior regarding cash equivalency would be to discount the contracted mortgage payments over 8 years at the prevailing market rate (12%) rather than the previously presumed 25 years. Also, the unpaid mortgage balance at the end of the projected holding period should be discounted at the same rate. These values, when combined, indicate the cash equivalency of the mortgage as follows:

Monthly payment of 11%, 30 year,	$ 990.93	
$104,000 loan		
times present worth of 1 per period		
factor (12%, 8 years—see Table 9.1)	61.527703	
Value of loan payments over 8 years		$ 60,936
Monthly loan payment × PW of 1 per		
period at 11% for remaining		
loan term of 22 years		
($990.39 × 99.282835)		
= loan balance	$98,329	
Present worth of mortgage balance		
(12% for 8 years)		
($98,329 × 0.384722)		37,829
Cash equivalency of mortgage		$ 98,765
plus down payment		26,000
Cash equivalency of comparable sale		$124,765

This comparable sale would indicate an additional value of $4,729 over the prior method ($124,765 − $120,036) for the subject property since a more realistic holding period of 8 years was used.

An important point to remember when using this method is to determine whether the financing terms were known prior to the offer to purchase having been made. In the case of a loan assumption or seller-provided financing, the buyer certainly would be aware of these terms. Sometimes with third-party financing (such as a bank), the buyer does not know the exact terms and often they do not vary significantly from prevailing terms anyway. Finally, the appraiser should confirm with the buyer or seller whether the atypical financing terms affected the sale price of the comparable property.

MARKET COMPARISON ADJUSTMENT TECHNIQUES

The market approach to value as applied to the appraisal of unimproved land, and the adjustments necessary to equalize for differences in sale prices caused by neighborhood, location, and site advantages was illustrated and explained in Chapter 8. The market data report form shown in Figure 8.1 can with slight modification also be used for entry of improved property sales information from public records. The only suggested change in the form, as shown, is to provide for field entry of a description of the kind and condition of on-site improvements. To adjust for value differences attributable to variations in age, size, and quality of building construction, one of the following techniques may be employed:

1. Detailed property analysis technique.
2. Overall property rating technique.

The application of these market comparison techniques as applied to the subject property and to the comparable sales are for purposes of illustration based on building construction data obtained as follows:

Subject property. Frame construction, 1,450-square-foot area. Exterior walls of redwood siding. Three bedrooms, two tiled bathrooms, living room, kitchen, and dinette. One-car garage, screened porch, and concrete patio. Central forced-air ducted gas heating, vinyl floor covering over concrete slab, asphalt shingle roofing over 4-inch fiberglass insulation. Building condition good, deferred maintenance—none. Effective age 8 years. Lot value by market comparison, $27,000.

Comparable sale 1. Concrete block structure, 1,650-square-foot area, four bedrooms, three tiled baths, living-dining room combination, kitchen, and utility room. Carport storage area and open entrance porch. Central forced-air–oil-fired heating system. Terrazzo flooring over concrete slab subflooring. Asphalt shingle gable roof. No attic insulation. Building condition good, deferred maintenance (decorating) $1,800. Effective age 10 years. Lot value by market comparison, $30,000. Total sale price: $126,000. Date of sale: one month ago.

Comparable sale 2. Brick veneer over concrete block structure, 1,520-square-foot area. Three bedrooms, one tiled bath, living room, sunporch, and kitchen. One-car garage, open porch. Central oil heating and 3-ton air-conditioning system. Oak parquet flooring over plywood subflooring; house has crawl space. Asphalt shingle roof over 4-inch fiberglass insulation. Floored attic storage area. Condition good, no deferred maintenance. Effective age 12 years. Lot value by market comparison, $24,000. Total sale price: $135,000. Date of sale: current.

Comparable sale 3. Cedar-shingled frame structure, 1,400-square-foot area. Three bedrooms, den living-dining room, kitchen, and two partially tiled bathrooms. Two-car garage, open entrance porch. Wall-to-wall carpeting over plywood subflooring. Built-up roofing covered with crushed stone, 4-inch insulation, circulating gas heater, 36-inch attic fan. Built-in air-conditioning wall unit. Effective age 5 years. Deferred maintenance $600 (repaint kitchen, bath, and hallway areas). Lot value by market comparison, $27,000. Total sale price: $137,000. Date of sale: six months ago.

Comparable sale 4. Concrete block structure, stuccoed exterior, 1,550-square-foot area. Three bedrooms, one tiled bathroom, living room, kitchen, utility room, and screened porch. Two-car carport. Wall-to-wall carpeting over concrete slab subflooring. Asphalt shingle roof over 4-inch insulation, hip-roof construction, boxed eaves, 36-inch roof overhang. Central duct oil-fired–forced-air heating system. Built-in kitchen fan, electric wall heater in bathroom, and garbage disposal unit. Condition good, no deferred maintenance. Effective age 12 years. Lot value by market comparison, $31,500. Total sale price: $123,000. Date of sale: 20 months ago.

DETAILED PROPERTY ANALYSIS TECHNIQUE

After confirmation of the sale prices and terms of sale with respective buyers, sellers, or real estate brokers, the comparable (index) properties are inspected for size and details of construction in order that price adjustments can be performed to make each sale as nearly as possible comparable to the subject property. The appraiser, in effect, must ask as he or she considers differences in age, size, and quality of building construction: How much more or less will a typical purchaser pay—as compared with the subject property—because of the presence or absence of major construction features? Moreover, the appraiser's task is to interpret value as viewed by market participants—not to set value. The successful application of this technique requires:

1. Building construction know-how.
2. Detailed property inspection and keen observation.
3. Knowledge of construction costs and building unit prices.
4. Knowledge of typical buyer preferences and price reactions.
5. Recognition of changes in prices due to financing and passage of time.
6. Application of sound judgment to obtain reasonable results.

The adjustments required to bring about price comparability of the index sales with the subject property are shown in Table 9.2. The first adjustment equates differences in the time of sale. As noted, index properties 3 and 4 would bring $3,000 and $6,000 more if exposed for sale on the date of the appraisal as compared with sale prices realized six months and one year before, respectively. Atypical financing is the next item to be considered. Sale 4 was conveyed with the seller paying one discount point, or $1,000. Differences in lot value, based on recent sales, are adjusted next. Other adjustments reflect differences in the quantity and quality of building construction. The building area was equalized at a current building rate of $45.00 per square foot, exclusive of fixtures, heating, electrical, and plumbing costs in the kitchen and bathrooms. Further adjustments were cal-

TABLE 9.2 SALES PRICE ADJUSTMENT SCHEDULE BASED ON DETAILED
PROPERTY ANALYSIS

	Comparable sale number			
	1	2	3	4
Indicated price	$126,000	$135,000	$137,000	$ 123,000
Time adjustment	0	0	+3,000	+6,000
Financing	0	0	0	−1,000
Lot value difference	−3,000	+3,000	0	+4,500
Construction variations[a]				
Building area	−9,000	−3,150	+2,250	−4,500
Exterior walls	+4,650	−4,500	−1,000	+3,000
Interior finishes	+4,000	0	+1,500	0
Number of baths	−2,100	+2,100	0	+2,100
Tile in baths	0	+1,650	+1,800	+1,700
Roof construction	+1,800	+1,800	0	+1,200
Insulation	+1,050	0	0	0
Heating and cooling	0	−5,400	+3,600	0
Equipment	0	0	−2,550	−1,350
Finished flooring	0	0	−3,000	0
Attic area	0	−3,200	0	0
Garage construction	+3,000	0	−4,800	0
Porches and utility rooms	+1,800	+1,800	0	0
Building age	+3,000	+6,000	−3,000	+6,000
Building conditions	+3,450	0	+1,200	0
Net adjustment	$ +8,650	$ +100	$ −1,000	$+17,650
Adjusted sale price	$134,650	$135,100	$136,000	$ 140,650
Final indication of value	$ 135,000			

[a]Price variations are based on market evidence (not cost to install) of how much more or less buyers
are willing to pay for the presence or absence of construction features.

culated at estimated construction expenditures at time of construction new, less
accrued depreciation due to wear and use over the period of economic age of the
index property. Differences in economic ages were equated at uniform rates of 2.5
percent per year on the basis of straight-line accounting over an economic age
period of 40 years. Differences in building conditions were adjusted on the basis
of estimated expenditures to cure deferred maintenance. Based on these adjustments and weights assigned, in accordance with the importance of each sale as an
index of market value, a final estimate of $135,000 indicates the value for the
subject property under the sales comparison approach using the construction detail analysis technique.

The four comparable sales used in the sales comparison approach to value
were correlated in accordance with assigned judgment weights. The comparative
weight assigned to each of the four comparable sales is explained as follows, with
the most reliance given to sales 2 and 3.

Sale 1 required no time adjustment to update this sale for market changes in the price level of residential properties. This sale is located in a similar setting as the subject property, both being in the same neighborhood. Further, an opportunity to inspect this sale property with care made possible accurate adjustments for variations in building features and construction.

Sale 2 was a particularly good value indicator because this property is located in the same block as the subject property, and because it represents the most recent transaction of all the sales considered in the sales comparison approach to value. Sale 2 also comes reasonably close to the building area of the subject house (1,450 square feet, as compared with 1,503 square feet for the sale property). Similarity of building condition, too, made this sale superior to sales 3 and 4.

Sale 3 is located in a comparable neighborhood, 1/2 mile from the subject property. The sale took place one year ago and a time adjustment of $3,000 was made to reflect the estimated increase in market prices caused by rising property values in the community. Because of substantial variations in time of sale and location, this comparable sale was given less weight.

Sale 4, although most comparable as far as physical features are concerned, took place nearly 20 months ago, thus necessitating a time adjustment of $6,000. This sale, too, is located in a similar but distant neighborhood, causing a significant adjustment in the property lot value. Because of the substantial adjustments necessary to make this sale comparable, it is given the least weight of all the sales considered. (A summary of the sale prices and adjustments is provided in Table 9.3.)

The market approach to value under the construction detail analysis and price rating technique as illustrated is ideal, provided that good reasons are given for the use of the different correlation weights. The appraiser, in deciding on the degree of comparability among sale properties, should not rely on the net adjustments. A better guide of similarity is the number and total dollar amount of adjustments made for the selected sales. A sale may show a nominal net adjustment which resulted from a large number of offsetting plus and minus adjustments. As indicators of the appraised property's value, such sales are inferior to those requiring relatively few adjustments of lesser dollar amounts.

When applied with care, the sales comparison method produces accurate appraisal estimates. This method, however, can be used successfully only where the appraiser, through available internal or other source data, has construction features for each sale property readily at hand. In practice, few appraisers can afford the time required to complete a thorough field inspection of each comparable sale (assuming the owner's permission) used as an index to market value. Nor do appraisal fees customarily paid for appraisals of residential properties economically warrant the expenditure of effort necessary to secure and analyze essential market and construction data as outlined previously. For this reason a less detailed but still sufficiently accurate market comparison technique is recommended for appraisal purposes. An appraiser must always expend sufficient effort and time to assure clients of a reliable report insofar as possible.

TABLE 9.3 MARKET SALES PRICES AND ADJUSTMENT SUMMARY

Index sale number	Market price	Price adjustment	Indicated value
1	$126,000	$ +8,650	$134,650
2	135,000	+100	135,100
3	137,000	−1,000	136,000
4	123,000	+17,650	140,650

OVERALL PROPERTY RATING TECHNIQUE

Under this approach to value, market comparison is based on an overall judgment as to the percentage-value adjustment called for in order to make each index sale comparable with the subject property. The overall percentage applied to each property in turn is justified by a statement that the subject property is deemed better, poorer, or the same in relation to its construction as to type, size, features, age, and building condition. Since the subject property in every value problem represents X (unknown price), each index sale for comparison purposes is accepted as a measure of market forces of supply and demand equal to 100 percent at a given time and place. By adjusting the index rating upward or downward in accordance with the characteristics of the subject property, a market value estimate is derived. The greater the number of truly comparable index sales used for market analysis purposes, the greater, as a rule, the accuracy of the final value estimate.

The application of the overall property technique is demonstrated in Table 9.4. The judgment ratings shown are supported by property descriptions as detailed earlier, and are based on a general field inspection of the comparable sale properties. For the reader's benefit, further explanatory statements can be made in the appraisal report as follows:

> The subject property, as compared with improved sale 1, is poorer in type of construction because the sale property has four bedrooms and three fully tiled bathrooms as compared with the three bedrooms and two bathrooms contained in the subject building. The subject also is smaller in size, containing 1,450 square feet of area as compared with the 1,650-square-foot area of sale 1. The subject property is deemed better in construction features, age, and condition because it has an asbestos-shingled roof and rock-wool insulation compared with the asphalt-shingled roof without insulation of the sale property. The subject property has an effective age of 8 years; the sale property age is 10 years. The subject property is in good condition with no deferred maintenance. Improved sale 1 requires an expenditure of $1,800 to redecorate the interior. The overall adjustment rating for the subject property is estimated at 110 percent, with a resulting market value for the subject property of $135,500.

A like comparative analysis of each of the other index sales with the subject property aids the client for whom the report is prepared in following step by step the procedure and logic used by the appraiser in arriving at the final estimate and value conclusions. In arriving at a final indication of value, the relative merits of

TABLE 9.4 SALES PRICE ADJUSTMENT SCHEDULE BASED ON OVERALL
PROPERTY RATING TECHNIQUE

	Improved sale number			
	1	2	3	4
Indicated price	$126,000	$135,000	$137,000	$123,000
Time adjustment	0	0	+3,000	+6,000
Price adjustment for time	126,000	135,000	140,000	129,000
Lot value difference	−3,000	+3,000	0	−4,500
Adjusted price	123,000	138,000	140,000	124,500
Subject property rating in regard to:				
Construction				
Type	Poorer	Poorer	Poorer	Same
Size	Poorer	Poorer	Better	Poorer
Features	Better	Poorer	Same	Better
Age	Better	Better	Poorer	Better
Condition	Better	Same	Better	Same
Subject property percentage rating	1.10	1.00	0.95	1.15
Adjusted value	$135,300	$138,000	$133,000	$143,175

Comparable sales weights and
correlation

Index sale number	Adjusted market value	Weight of sale	Value components
1	$135,300	0.30	$ 40,590
2	138,000	0.40	55,200
3	133,000	0.20	26,600
4	143,175	0.10	14,318
			$136,708

Correlated market value—total
  Rounded to $136,708

each sale property should be noted. This can be done narratively as shown previously. Alternatively, higher numerical weights can be used to show the reliance placed by the appraiser on each of the comparable sales analyzed. An example of this method is shown at the bottom of Table 9.4.

Although the percentage adjustment method does not appear as refined as the dollar equalization method, the former method often is more realistic and in conformity with the thought processes that motivate buyers and sellers when bargaining. It must be kept in mind that appraising is an art and not a science, and that final estimates of value are deemed reasonably accurate if within 5 percent of the actual market value realized by a subsequent and open sale. Then, too, the sales comparison approach to value is rarely used alone. Generally, the depreciated cost approach and, where applicable, the capitalized income approach to value, or both, are used as checks on each other to ensure the accuracy of the final value estimate as certified in the appraisal report.

PERCENTAGE ADJUSTMENTS: THEIR USE AND LIMITATION

To achieve comparability and to adjust for price differences caused by variations in type, size, features, age, and condition of the improvements, most appraising practitioners apply percentage ratings to reflect superior or inferior market factor relationships. The use of a sequence of percentage ratings poses certain pitfalls and limitations. First, to ascribe to a number of structural deviations, precise percentage ratings such as 5 percent superior, 10 percent inferior, and so on, presumes appraising to be a science—which it is not. Then, too, an appraiser would be hard put to justify whether a given quality of construction should be rated exactly 10 percent or perhaps 9 or 11 percent superior. Thus it becomes extremely important for an appraiser to provide reasonable market-based support for each adjustment rather than to claim it was made based on "experience." Second, and more serious, is the mathematical distortion that results from giving equal weight to percentage minuses and percentage pluses when multiplying these individual adjustments. A given market value can decline only 100 percent but can possibly increase a million or more percent—perhaps large and long enough to reach the moon. To illustrate, a minus of 50 percent is not offset by a plus of 50 percent, for a multiplication of 0.50×1.50 equals 0.75. Third, use of multiplied separate percentage adjustments presumes an interrelationship that probably does not exist. For example, there certainly is no relationship between the time, location, and conditions of sale adjustments.

A preferred percentage adjustment method is to add and subtract each of the adjustments. This adjustment process is illustrated in the following example and also was covered in Chapter 8.

In making adjustments, it is recommended that the adjusted sale prices of the sale properties be made with reference to the appraised property in order to *reflect the inferiority or superiority of the appraised property.* An easy way to remember this adjustment process is to make a minus adjustment when the appraised property is inferior to the sale property. Similarly, a positive adjustment is called for when the subject property is superior to the comparable sales property. This logic is illustrated in the following example. A small commercial building sold for $500,000; the subject property has 10 feet less frontage than the sale property. Such frontage is worth $1,000 per front foot. However, the appraised property has a heating and air-conditioning system that is judged to be $50,000 superior to that serving the comparable sale property. Also, it contains an additional 500 square feet of building space which is judged to be worth $20,000. Thus these adjustments to the sale property reveal a value for the subject property as follows:

Sale price		$500,000
Frontage	$-10,000	
Heat and air conditioning	+50,000	+40,000
Building size		+20,000
Indicated value of subject property		$560,000

The value caused by the presence or lack of a physical item is the proper adjustment—not its cost. Ordinarily, time adjustments are made on a percentage basis, but physical and locational adjustments are made both on a percentage and dollar basis. Two key points for the appraiser to always remember are (1) his or her job is to reflect the attitudes of buyers and sellers and not his or her own biases, and (2) if the market participants do not consider certain features in arriving at a purchase price, then neither should the appraiser.

Order of Adjustments

There seems to be no consensus as to how adjustments should be made. Certainly, two initial adjustments should be made before physical or locational adjustments are undertaken. First, a sale should be adjusted to reveal the price that it probably would bring at the date of the appraisal. Generally, a sale and resale of the sale property at fairly recent dates can provide support for this adjustment. Care must be taken to ascertain if any physical improvements occurred in the interim. For example, a good part of the increase in the sale price may have resulted from modernization or perhaps a room having been added to the dwelling. The sale of similar properties at different times can also provide an indication of property appreciation. Next, the conditions influencing the sale such as buyer and seller motivation and financing terms should be considered and appropriately adjusted. Once having adjusted for these items, the appraiser knows the approximate price that the comparable sale would have brought in the current market. The next (and key) question is to determine the probable selling price of the appraised property. This is handled by adjusting for physical and locational value factors.

Paired Data Set Analysis

Paired data set analysis involves the selection of two or more comparable sales and isolating one value attribute (element of comparison) in a sale not found in the other sales in order to judge that attribute's effect on value. This process works providing the sales selected are sufficiently similar and individual value-influencing factors actually can be identified. This method sometimes is criticized as being almost impossible to implement because sales of real estate seldom have just one feature that stands out and can be assigned a value. Nevertheless, this method gives appraisers a technique when properly applied to similar sale properties that can provide market-based price adjustments instead of vague guesstimates. An example of its application follows for three, two-story office building comparable sales:

Feature	Subject	Sale 1	Sale 2	Sale 3
Sale price		$1,000,000	$ 940,000	$ 960,000
Air conditioning	Yes	Yes	No	Yes
Adjustment		0	+60,000	0
Elevator	Yes	Yes	Yes	No
Adjustment				+40,000
Adjusted sale price		$1,000,000	$1,000,000	$1,000,000

The subject property has both air conditioning and an elevator. In arriving at an indication of the subject property's market value, sales 1 and 2 are initially compared. The only difference is that sale 2 lacks air conditioning. It sold for $60,000 less than sale 1; therefore, an air-conditioning system is judged to be worth $60,000. Similarly, sales 1 and 3 are identical except for sale 3 having an elevator. A comparison of their respective sale prices implies a contributing value of $40,000 for an elevator.

REGRESSION ANALYSIS

In regression analysis a mathematical expression is developed so that property value can be expressed as a function of another variable or variables. These variables are known as the *independent* or explanatory *variables*. In its simplest form, one independent variable is used to explain the value of the dependent variable through the use of a straight-line or linear relationship. The statistical method known as *simple linear regression* fits a straight line to a set of data points. In graphical representation the independent or explanatory variable is plotted on the X (horizontal) axis and the dependent variable is plotted on the Y (vertical) axis. In real estate applications the dependent variable usually is property value or sale price which depends on the value of some independent variable such as street frontage. Table 9.5 illustrates the calculations required to estimate value when using this method.

The simple linear regression equation is[2]:

where $\hat{Y}$ $= a + bX$ ($\hat{Y}$ used to show the Y value is estimated)

a $= Y$ intercept, the point where the line intersects the Y axis

b = slope of the line, the amount Y would change if the value of X increases one unit

If the value of the slope is positive, then Y would increase as X increases. Correspondingly, if the slope is negative, then Y would decrease as X increases.

One should always plot the data to visually examine how well a straight line will fit the data. A numeric measure of how well the regression line describes the relation between the variables is the coefficient of determination, r^2. Its value ranges from 0 to 1 and measures the proportion of the variability of the dependent variable that is explained by the independent variable. If $r^2 = 0$, the independent variable explains none of the variability of Y. If $r^2 = 1$, the independent variable explains all of the variability of the dependent variable; hence if one knows the value of X, then by using the regression equation the value of Y can be determined exactly. It should be noted that if r has a positive value, then the X's

[2]The equations for determining a and b are not included because many calculators have the ability to calculate the values automatically. This line is often called the least squares line because of the method that is used to fit the line to the data. a and b cannot be determined precisely but instead have to be estimated. This is achieved by making use of the method of least squares. For more information on this subject, the interested reader should refer to John Neter, William Wasserman, and Michael H. Kutner, *Applied Linear Statistical Models*, 2nd ed. (Homewood, Ill.: Irwin, 1985), pp. 35–40.

TABLE 9.5   ILLUSTRATION OF SIMPLE LINEAR REGRESSION METHODOLOGY

SP	SP − $\overline{\text{SP}}$	FF	(FF − $\overline{\text{FF}}$)	(FF − $\overline{\text{FF}}$)²	(SP − $\overline{\text{SP}}$)(FF − $\overline{\text{FF}}$)
$ 37,500	$2,985	150	3.3	10.9	9,850.5
30,800	−3,715	140	−6.7	44.9	24,890.5
34,750	235	155	8.3	68.9	1,950.5
30,500	−4,015	132	−14.7	216.1	59,020.5
35,000	485	147	0.3	0.1	145.5
39,000	4,485	158	11.3	127.7	50,680.5
38,000	3,485	162	15.3	234.1	53,320.5
34,800	285	160	13.3	176.9	3,790.5
35,300	785	138	−8.7	75.7	−6,829.5
29,500	−5,015	125	−21.7	470.9	108,825.5
$345,150	0	1,467	0	1,426.2	305,645.0

$$\overline{\text{SP}} = \text{average sales price}$$
$$\overline{\text{FF}} = \text{average front feet}$$

$$\overline{\text{SP}} = \Sigma\,\text{SP}/n \qquad\qquad \overline{\text{FF}} = \Sigma\,\text{FF}/n$$
$$= \$345,150/10 \qquad\qquad\quad = 1,467/10$$
$$= \$34,515 \qquad\qquad\qquad\quad = 146.7$$

$$a = \overline{\text{SP}} - (b)(\overline{\text{FF}}) \qquad b = \frac{\Sigma(\text{SP} - \overline{\text{SP}})(\text{FF} - \overline{\text{FF}})}{\Sigma(\text{FF} - \overline{\text{FF}})^2}$$
$$= \$34,515 - (214.3)(146.7) \qquad\qquad = 305,645.0/1,426.2$$
$$= 3,077.2$$

$$\text{MV} = a + b(\text{FF})$$
$$= 3,077.2 + (214.3)(152) \qquad\qquad = 214.3$$
$$= \$35,650$$

and Y's are positively correlated. That is, Y increases in proportion to increases in X. Conversely, when the X's and Y's are negatively or inversely related, the Y value increases as the X value decreases. The resulting line is said to have a negative slope and r is negative.

The coefficient of determination (r^2) is the square of the correlation coefficient (r) and can easily be determined on a calculator. For example if $r = 0.5$, then $r^2 = 0.25$ and the simple linear regression line explains only 25 percent of the variability of Y, which is not sufficiently linear to warrant use of a linear equation.

An example of linear regression applied to real estate appraising follows:

Lot frontage, X (ft)	Sale price, Y
150	$37,500
140	30,800
155	34,750
132	30,500
147	35,000
158	39,000
162	38,000
160	34,800
138	35,300
125	29,500

Plotting these data produces the regression line shown in Figure 9.1. This plotting gives an initial idea as to whether there is a linear relationship between lot front-age and value.

By use of a programmable calculator, it can be determined that the value of the appraised site with 152 front feet is estimated to be $36,201. Using a calcula-tor, the value of r^2 is computed to be 0.67, which means that 67 percent of the var-iability of the sale prices for these data can be explained by knowing the lot frontage of each sale site.

The same results occur when using the linear regression equation. If neither method were used, the appraiser could approximate the estimated market value of the appraised site simply by plotting the front footage and sale price of each sale on a chart. The subject site's frontage would be lined up with a corresponding site price (or value) as shown by the dashed lines in Figure 9.1.

Multiple regression is a statistical technique that allows the analyst to take a step beyond linear regression in that more than one independent variable can be included in the analysis. When it is found that a variable such as lot frontage does not adequately explain the sale price of property, other variables may be included. For example, studies show that variables such as the house size, the number of bathrooms, and the physical age of the dwelling generally predict the probable value of the appraised residential property.

The multiple regression is a straightforward extension of linear regression. If the number of explanatory or independent variables is n, then the equation is

$$\hat{Y} = a + b_1 X_1 + b_2 X_2 + \cdots + b_n X_n$$

Solutions for the a's and b's can be obtained through the least squares method (see footnote 2 reference). Because of the computing power required, a small com-puter is needed to find the multiple linear regression equation for most problems. Most computer regression packages compute the coefficient of determination, denoted R^2 for multiple regression, in addition to the regression coefficients (i.e.,

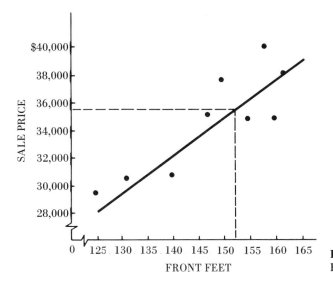

Figure 9.1 Plot of Sale Prices, Frontage, and Regression Line

the *a* and *b* values). As in simple linear regression it measures the proportion of the variation in *Y* that can be explained by the independent variables.

Interpreting the value of the regression coefficients for real estate problems is often very tricky. If the intercorrelations among the *n* independent variables are all zero, that is, they do not vary together, then *b* can be accurately interpreted as the amount of change in *Y* that would accompany a one-unit change in X_1. If X_1 is the square footage of a dwelling and X_2 is the number of baths, then these variables would tend to covary (change together). A large value for X_1 would generally be accompanied by a large value for X_2. Hence the correlation would be positive and the line would slope upward to the right. When explanatory variables covary in multiple regression, the data are said to be multicollinear. In the presence of multicollinearity one cannot accurately use the multiple regression coefficients to estimate the value contribution to *Y* that would accompany a one-unit change in a multicollinear independent variable. The regression equation itself is still accurate for prediction purposes even if multicollinearity exists. The difficulty exists in the interpretation of the coefficients.

The use of regression equations presents a well-established way of formally using a set of past data to help predict the sale price of a property based on the characteristics of the property. For example, consider a hypothetical regression equation

$$Y = 55,000 + 7X_1 + 1,850X_2$$
where
X_1 = dwelling square footage
X_2 = number of rooms

Suppose that a prediction is desired for the value of a property similar to those in the data set that generated the previous equation. This property has 1,500 square feet in the dwelling and eight rooms. Then $Y = 55,000 + 7(1,500) + 1,850(8) = \$80,300$.

SALES COMPARISON APPROACH FOR COMMERCIAL AND INDUSTRIAL PROPERTIES

The larger and more complex the physical improvements, the more detailed and difficult the sales comparison approach. Whereas with residential property the structure as a whole served as a basis for comparison, a more detailed and informative unit basis now must be devised to permit realistic comparison and logical adjustments for building differences caused by size, age, quality, and quantity of construction.

Sale price equalization is generally achieved by the unit comparison approach based on one or more of the following:

1. Price per square or cubic foot of building volume.
2. Price per square foot of net rentable area.

3. Price per apartment including land investment.
4. Price per room inclusive of bath, closet, and storage areas.
5. Gross annual or monthly income multiplier.
6. For special-purpose properties: for example, hospital, per bed; restaurant and theater, per seat.

For industrial, warehouse, or church buildings the cubic-foot method of comparison (assigning weight to the height of ceilings and the depth of the basement area) may yield more accurate results than the square-foot comparison approach to value. Care, however, must be taken to exclude land value from the total market price paid for the property when there is a significant variation in site sizes and to adjust the cubic-foot cost of each sale or index property for differences caused by age, quality and condition of building(s), economy of building size, and equipment features compared with the subject property. Where sale properties are selected with care, this sales comparison approach to value yields reliable results. The gross income multiplier, as explained later, can also be applied as a check on the direct and usually more accurate unit comparisons to value. The appraiser should observe the amount and finish of any office space, adequacy of parking and turning radius for trucks, as well as column spacing and overhead clearance in warehouses.

Apartment properties offer greater flexibility in the application of the unit comparison approach to value. Because of greater uniformity in construction design and building technique, and competitive demand and supply for apartment housing, it is readily possible to apply the unit comparison method more effectively on the basis of sale price[3] per apartment, per room as well as per square or cubic foot. All these various price unit indexes can then be rechecked by the gross annual multiplier for derivation of a market-correlated index of value for the property as a whole.

Given a subject property that is effectively in new condition, contains 110 apartments and 384 rooms, and has an effective gross income of $498,200, a sales recapitulation summary schedule for the estimation of market value may be constructed as shown in Table 9.6. The comparative analysis is relatively simple. The price paid for each comparable sale property is adjusted for changes attributed to the passage of time from the date of the sale transaction to the date of the appraisal. Next comes an important percentage adjustment that reflects, in the appraiser's judgment, the age and condition of each sale property as compared with the subject property. The adjusted sale prices are then allocated on a per apartment and a per room basis as shown. By correlating the derived units of measurement, giving greater judgment weights to sales that require little or no percentage adjustment, the appraised value of the subject property is obtained as demonstrated.

---

[3]Where building-to-total-property value ratios are markedly different, the appraiser may be justified in using a value unit measure with the land excluded. It then is added to the adjusted value of a comparable sale to indicate its fully adjusted value.

TABLE 9.6 SALES COMPARISON APPROACH FOR AN APARTMENT PROPERTY

	Comparable sale number			
	1	2	3	4
Sale price	$2,450,000	$2,392,000	$2,480,000	$3,025,000
Time adjustment	0	0	0	+10%
Adjusted price	$2,450,000	$2,392,000	$2,480,000	$3,327,500
Location adjustment[a]	+10%	+20%	0	−5%
Age and condition	0	−5%	+3%	+12%
Adjusted value	$2,695,000	$2,750,800	$2,554,400	$3,560,425
Number of apartments	100	112	95	138
Number of rooms	348	384	312	469
Adjusted sale price per apartment	$ 26,950	$ 24,561	$ 26,888	$ 25,800
Adjusted sale price per room	$ 7,744	$ 7,164	$ 8,187	$ 7,592
Effective gross income	$ 429,825	$ 410,996	$ 404,565	$ 527,000
Effective gross income multiplier (EGIM)	5.70	5.82	6.13	5.74

Indicated Market Value of Subject Property

1. 110 apartments at $26,500		$2,915,000
Indicated value—based on apartments		
2. 384 rooms at $7,500		$2,880,000
3. Effective gross income	$ 498,200	
Gross income multiplier[b]	5.75	
Indicated value—based on EGIM		$2,864,650
Correlated market value		$2,900,000

[a]A minus adjustment denotes that the subject property is inferior to a comparable sale, whereas a plus adjustment indicates the appraised property to be superior.

[b]Market indexes are based principally on sale 1, because no adjustment for age and condition of the building was necessary and the room and apartment counts were close to the subject property.

GROSS INCOME MULTIPLIER AS A GUIDE TO MARKET VALUE

When using this technique, the appraiser must apply it in the same manner that it is derived. For example, a GIM can be based on either gross potential income (assumes full occupancy) or effective gross income (allows for vacancy and collection losses). Thus, if a GIM is based on the actual occupancy of a sale building, it should be applied to the appraised property's actual or effective income. Sometimes, this multiplier is abbreviated EGIM. It may be more accurate to use effective gross income data, but not all property owners are able or willing to provide this rental information. Hence potential gross income and sale price are usually used to derive a GIM which is more accurately abbreviated PGIM.

The gross income multiplier (GIM) as a device to convert monthly or annual gross income into an expression of market value has gained popularity both as a rule of thumb and as an index of value. The gross income multiplier can serve a useful purpose when applied intelligently and with care.

At the outset, it should be realized that the use of the gross income multiplier should not be considered as part of the income or capitalization approach to value. To capitalize means to convert the estimated *net* operating income anticipated over the remaining economic life of the subject property or some other shorter holding period into a present value. The gross income multiplier does not give weight to the amounts of operating expense ratios or to variations in the remaining economic life of properties. In fact, the user of the multiplier may incorrectly assume that all properties within a given classification, such as residential, commercial, or industrial, are identical in operating characteristics and in their remaining productive life.

It may be fair to state that, by custom, many appraisers have been compelled to give recognition to the gross income multiplier as an index of value. In many areas, lay investors use the multiplier as a cardinal guide in judging the amount of property purchase offers. The multiplier is unscientific but, nevertheless, is a market phenomenon that cannot be ignored.

Not only should the GIM not be ignored, it should be used to the fullest extent possible. As with any research methodology, the results can be no better than the quality of data analyzed. It is argued that the gross income multiplier produces inaccurate results when the sale-rental properties possess different operating expense and land-value to property-value ratios, or is used for different aged properties. True, but there is no reason to expect reliable results in any approach to value when dissimilar data are considered. The key, then, is to compile a sufficient quantity of recent and similar transactions that have been confirmed by the appraiser. Instead of two or three comparables, perhaps 10 or 12 would be more in order—if available.

One study revealed that if appraisers in the study had used nothing but GIMs for their final figure, their appraisals, on the average, would have been within 0.1 percent of the final value estimates.[4] This study of real estate price/earnings also found that the average percentage difference between predicted sale price and actual sale price varied within a 4 percent and 8 percent range. This range is believed to be acceptable for most appraisers.[5]

By custom, the gross income multiplier is used for conversion of monthly rentals in establishing the value of residential properties and is applied to the annual gross income valuation of industrial and commercial properties. Studies disclose that multipliers vary from region to region, often among communities within a region—and conceivably among neighborhoods within a city. The multiplier is simply derived for any given area by relating market prices of a given class

---

[4]Richard U. Ratcliff, "Don't Underrate the Gross Income Multiplier," *The Appraisal Journal* 39, no. 2 (April 1971), p. 264.

[5]*Ibid.*, p. 269.

of properties which have recently sold to the gross income actually or hypothetically derived from these properties if offered for rent in the open, competitive market at the time of sale. For residential properties—using the four index sales described earlier—the procedure for obtaining and using the multiplier is as follows.

The market analysis detailed in Table 9.7 indicates a monthly multiplier of 135. This multiplier can now be applied to the actual or estimated rental of the subject property to yield a measure of market value. Based on an estimated rent of $1,000 per month, the resultant market value equals $135,000 ($1,000 × 135). Conversely, the multiplier may also prove useful in estimating market rentals for residential properties offered for lease. Given a market value of $135,000 and a prevailing monthly rent multiplier of 135, the expected market rent is $1,000 per month ($135,000 ÷ 135).

Advantages of the Gross Income Multiplier

The advantages of the GIM are (1) it typically is used by investors, (2) it is easily understood by investors and clients, and, perhaps most important, (3) it is based exclusively on actual market events. There is no esoteric, complicated, or unrealistic opinion involved in its derivation and use which often characterizes the depreciated cost and capitalized income approaches. The key to its successful use is in obtaining a sufficient number of truly comparable sale-rental properties that have sold and rented recently. It is important that both the sales and rental transactions be recent. Examples of the under- and overvalue distortion created by mismatched data are as follows for 12-unit apartment properties:

Example A. Old sale and recent rent
$250,000/$50,000 = 5.00

Example B. Recent sale and old rent
$300,000/$42,000 = 7.14

Example C. Recent sale and recent rent
$300,000/$50,000 = 6.00

TABLE 9.7   DERIVATION OF MONTHLY RENT MULTIPLIER FOR RESIDENTIAL PROPERTIES

Index sale number	Sale price	Actual or estimated monthly rental	Gross monthly multiplier
1	$126,000	$ 950	133
2	135,000	1,025	132
3	137,000	1,000	137
4	123,000	900	137
Averages	$130,250	$ 969	135

Carrying these examples further, suppose that the expected or prevailing rental for the subject 12-unit apartment building is $52,000. Applying each of the three GIMs derived previously produces the following value results:

A. 5.00 × $52,000 = $260,000
B. 7.14 × $52,000 = $371,280
C. 6.00 × $52,000 = $312,000

Disadvantages of the Gross Income Multiplier

As indicated, in the hands of an informed person, the multiplier may prove a useful aid in approximating prevailing market value. The professional appraiser, however, is well advised to use this valuation tool with caution for the following reasons. First, the multiplier converts into value *gross* income rather than *net* operating income. It is entirely possible that a property that produces a comparable gross income may yield minimal or even no net operating income because of excessive operating costs due to faulty construction or long-term lease agreements that favor the tenant(s). Also, the property may be inefficiently managed. In either case the existence of gross income gives an illusion of value that could not be justified by an expert appraiser. It is for this reason that users of the gross income multiplier should pay heed to the saying, "The accountant can estimate our gross, but only God can give us our net."

Second, the use of the multiplier assumes uniformity among properties in their operating expense ratios. Even among residential properties, where operating experience reveals similar expense outlays, individual properties may vary significantly from the norm as a result of differences in construction, quality of insulation, type of heating, amount of built-in equipment, equity of property taxation, and other causes. Again the key to successful use of this method is to compile a sufficient number of truly similar sale-rental properties.

Third, consideration of remaining economic life appears entirely ignored. It is a rare coincidence that properties selected as comparable sales are identical in relation to effective age, and a rarer coincidence still that the subject property should be of the same actual age as those of the comparable sales. Uninformed use of the gross multiplier would ascribe equal value to properties of equal income even though one may be in the last stages of its economic life and the other in new condition. Such properties are not comparable. Moreover, the gross income multiplier *never* provides for adjustment of differences in properties which are by nature dissimilar in character.

Fourth, care must be taken not to adjust the gross income, or the "raw" market prices, paid for comparable properties for age, condition, or location of the sale property. To do so will overadjust for physical, functional, or economic factors which both the renters and the investors have already considered in the price paid for rental and in the purchase amount offered for the property in its "as is" condition.

With these limitations in mind, the gross income multiplier may be used as a valuable input in the overall analysis that the appraiser makes in formulating and justifying his or her final estimate of market value.

SUMMARY

The sales comparison approach to value is well adapted to situations where there are an adequate number of similar properties which have recently sold. In using these sales, the appraiser should always try to verify each sale to confirm the relationship of the parties, date of sale, and the financial terms.

In analyzing comparable sales, it may be necessary to adjust a price if prices have changed between the time a comparable property sold and the subject property is appraised. Also, an adjustment is required if a sale property's price was influenced by financing terms. The "cash equivalency" method is available to handle this influence. The purpose of this adjustment is to reveal the price that a comparable property would have brought without the influence of atypical financing.

There are two basic ways to analyze sale properties under the sales comparison approach. These are the detailed property analysis and the overall property rating techniques. The first of these methods requires the appraiser to make a detailed analysis of all features in a property that influenced the price paid as well as transactional, location, and time influences. The second method, although also requiring a thorough familiarity with the sales and appraised properties, permits the appraiser to make an overall price adjustment in arriving at the appraised value of the subject property.

Percentages, as well as dollars, are used to adjust the differences between comparable sales and an appraised property. It is clearer and more accurate to make these adjustments by adding and subtracting the different percentage adjustments rather than multiplying each adjustment. In judging the reliability of sale properties, both the net adjusted difference as well as the total percentage adjustments should be noted.

The proper order of adjustments is initially to account for price changes due to the time lapse and financing terms. Next, physical and location differences are taken into account.

An appraisal technique used to isolate features influencing value is the paired data set analysis. It necessitates the use of similar sales. Another method of analyzing comparable sales is regression analysis. It is based on using independent variables such as building size or lot frontage to explain a dependent variable such as value. Its proper use requires the analysis of more sales than is typically used in traditional or nonstatistical sales analysis.

The sales comparison approach is adaptable to commercial and industrial properties, but it is somewhat more involved than with residential properties. One method used for appraising these properties is the gross income multiplier. Care must be exercised in applying it to either the potential or effective gross income, as required in a given situation. It is typically used by and is familiar to investors and is based on actual market events. Its disadvantages are that it is based on gross, rather than the usually more revealing net, operating income. Also, it fails to account for differences in operating expense ratios or remaining economic lives of properties.

REVIEW QUESTIONS

1. Compute the cash equivalency for a sale that sold for $200,000 and was financed with an 11 percent, 25-year, monthly installment 80 percent mortgage in a market where the prevailing terms were 12 percent, 20 years, and the same loan-to-value ratio. Assume these loans will be held until maturity.

2. Explain why a comparatively small net adjustment may not represent the most comparable sale.

3. Why should adjustments be made for time and conditions of sale prior to considering differences in physical and locational features?

4. (a) Briefly state the steps involved in paired data set analysis.
   (b) What two conditions must exist in order for this valuation process to work?

5. What problem occurs when applying a market-derived GIM to an appraised property's effective gross income?

6. Discuss the relative merits of the gross income multiplier as a means of estimating property value.

READING AND STUDY REFERENCES

CANNADAY, ROGER E. "How Should You Estimate and Provide Market Support for Adjustments in Single Family Appraisals?" *The Real Estate Appraiser and Analyst* 55, no. 4 (Winter 1989), pp. 43–54.

CHRISTENSEN, BARBARA. "Take the Guesstimating out of Adjustments," *The Appraisal Journal* 48, no. 2 (April 1980), pp. 255–260.

DELACY, P. BARTON. "Cash Equivalency in Residential Appraising," *The Appraisal Journal* 51, no. 1 (January 1983), pp. 81–88.

GIPE, GEORGE W. "Developing a Multiple Regression Model for Multi-family Residential Properties," *The Real Estate Appraiser* 42, no. 3 (May–June 1976), pp. 28–33.

GOOLSBY, WILLIAM C., JAMES A. GRAASKAMP, and TIMOTHY N. WARNER. "Cash Equivalent Value of Real Property," *The Real Estate Appraiser and Analyst* 49, no. 3 (Fall 1983), pp. 43–48.

HOAGLAND, GARY. "Are the Mechanics of the Adjustment Process Correct?" *The Real Estate Appraiser and Analyst* 48, no. 1 (Spring 1982), pp. 59–61.

KAMATH, RAVINDA R., and KENNETH R. YANTEK. "Linear Multiple Regression Analysis Applied to Valuation of Single Family Homes," *The Real Estate Appraiser and Analyst* 45, no. 5 (September–October 1979), pp. 36–41.

PARDUE, WILLIAM A., JR. "Checklist for Confirming Sales," *The Appraisal Journal* 54, no. 2 (April 1986), pp. 274–281.

PATCHIN, PETER J. "Valuation of Contaminated Properties," *The Appraisal Journal* 56, no. 1 (January 1988), pp. 7–16.

RATCLIFF, RICHARD U. "Don't Underestimate the Gross Income Multiplier," *The Appraisal Journal* 39, no. 2 (April 1971), pp. 264–271.

SCHWARTZ, ARTHUR L., JR. "Influences of Seller Financing upon Residential Property Sales Prices," *The Real Estate Appraisal and Analyst* 48, no. 4 (Winter 1982), pp. 35–38.

SIRMANS, G. STACY, C. F. SIRMANS, and STANLEY D. SMITH. "Adjusting Comparable Sales for Assumption Financing," *The Appraisal Journal* 52, no. 1 (January 1984), pp. 84–91.

SMITH, CHARLES A. "A Critique of Conventional Cash Equivalency Techniques in Stepped Rate/Stepped Payment Loans," *The Appraisal Journal* 58, no. 1 (January 1990), pp. 51–56.

SMITH, HALBERT C., and JOHN B. CORGEL. "Adjusting for Nonmarketing Financing: A Quick and Easy Method," *The Appraisal Journal* 52, no. 1 (January 1984), pp. 75–83.

WILLIAMS, SCOTT R. "Problems with Percentage Adjustments," *The Real Estate Appraiser and Analyst* 48, no. 4 (Winter 1982), pp. 48–53.

WILSON, ALBERT R. "Probable Financial Effect of Asbestos Removal on Real Estate," *The Appraisal Journal* 58, no. 3 (July 1989), pp. 378–391.

10
Building Construction and Plan Reading

Learning Objectives

After reading this chapter, you should be able to:

- Recognize the basic structural components of a residence and be able to distinguish the quality and condition of each
- Distinguish among the different roof designs
- Understand how roof pitch is calculated
- Appreciate the basic design components found in construction plans
- Sense the importance of written construction specifications
- Discuss the basic attributes of good floor planning
- Recognize the basics of building inspections

A competent appraiser, to be professionally qualified, must possess a working knowledge of building design and construction. As will be demonstrated, this knowledge is essential in the accurate application of each of the approaches to value as well as in deriving a reliable measure of accrued depreciation. Under the depreciated cost approach to value, knowledge of construction quantity and quality is essential in order that the applicable unit cost per square foot or per cubic foot can be computed to reproduce or replace the structure in new condition. Under the sales comparison approach to value, structural differences between the subject and the comparable properties must be recognized in order to make reasonable qualitative and quantitative value adjustments. Under the capitalized income approach, too, an estimate of remaining building life expectancy is sometimes necessary for correct capitalization of building income. Even an estimate of accrued depreciation cannot be made without an estimate of the effective structural age as reflected by a building's condition, its functional and locational obsolescence, and the structural resistance it offers to forces of wear, tear, and action of the elements.

BUILDING COMPONENTS

Figure 10.1 displays the principal structural components of a dwelling. Additionally, the anatomy of a building[1] may be studied in the order of its structural components as follows:

1. Footing, piers, and foundation walls.
2. Exterior walls.
3. Sub- and finish floor and framing.
4. Partition framing and interior walls.
5. Roof framing and roof cover finish.
6. Windows and doors—kind, quality.
7. Cabinetwork.
8. Plumbing and electric wiring.
9. Heating and air-conditioning systems.
10. Insulation and other improvements.

Footings, piers, and foundation walls as a rule are constructed in accordance with local or national BOCA (Building Officials and Code Administration International, Inc.) building codes. Footings generally consist of reinforced concrete that is poured on undisturbed soil below the frostline, as specified for the geographic area. The width of the footing generally must be at least twice that of the foundation wall to be supported. Foundation walls typically are of concrete blocks 8 by 8 by 16 inches in size. A recent innovation in foundation wall construction is the use of pressure-treated wood trusses. These trusses span each footing to form the floor system. Builders have begun to use this system because it saves time, money, and the problems involved in dealing with masonry subcontractors. Where needed for extra strength, reinforcing rods are placed at corner and wall supporting locations. Waterproofing is a requirement where subfloor or basement areas are subject to surface water penetration. The appraiser, unless informed of structural weaknesses, or unless he or she sees evidence of excessive settlement at the time of building inspection, assumes proper compliance with applicable construction codes in all foundation work. Where doubt exists, or conditions warrant it, a construction engineer should be called on to inspect the premises for building flaws and to render a certified report on which the appraiser may rely for value adjustments or repair expenditures.

Exterior walls are constructed in a variety of frame, metal, or masonry materials and generally in conformity with community customs and owner preferences. Again, unless evidence points otherwise, structural soundness must be assumed. The appraiser should chiefly be interested in cost differentials of the materials used, and in the comparative utility (or disutility) of exterior wall con-

[1]Since the bulk of building construction is residential rather than commercial or industrial in character, emphasis in this chapter for illustration purposes will be placed on the anatomy of a single-family building structure.

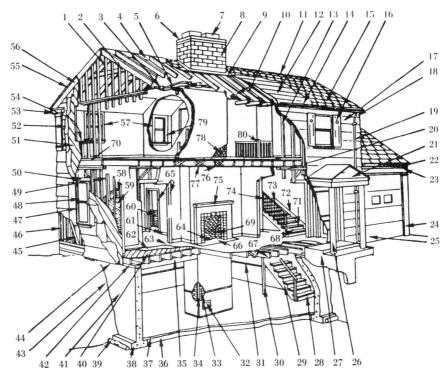

1 Gable stud	29 Stair stringer	57 Window casing
2 Collar beam	30 Girder post	58 Lath
3 Ceiling joist	31 Chair rail	59 Insulation
4 Ridge board	32 Cleanout door	60 Wainscoting
5 Insulation	33 Furring strips	61 Baseboard
6 Chimney cap	34 Corner stud	62 Building paper
7 Chimney pot	35 Girder	63 Finish floor
8 Chimney	36 Cinder or gravel fill	64 Ash dump
9 Chimney flashing	37 Concrete basement floor	65 Door trim
10 Rafters	38 Foundation wall footing	66 Fireplace hearth
11 Ridge	39 Foundation drain tile	67 Floor joists
12 Roof boards	40 Diagonal subflooring	68 Stair riser
13 Stud	41 Foundation wall	69 Fire brick
14 Gutter	42 Mud sill	70 Sole plate
15 Roofing	43 Backfill	71 Stair tread
16 Shutter	44 Termite shield	72 Finish stringer
17 Bevel siding	45 Corner brace	73 Stair rail
18 Downspout gooseneck	46 Corner studs	74 Balusters
19 Downspout	47 Window frame	75 Mantel
20 Double plate	48 Window light	76 Floor joist
21 Entrance canopy	49 Wall studs	77 Bridging
22 Garage cornice	50 Header	78 Metal lath
23 Frieze	51 Wall sheathing	79 Window sash
24 Door jamb	52 Building paper	80 Newel post
25 Garage door	53 Frieze or barge board	
26 Entrance post	54 Rough header	
27 Entrance platform	55 Cornice moulding	
28 Basement stair riser	56 Fascia board	

Figure 10.1 Anatomy of a Residential Building (Courtesy of Marshall and Swift, Los Angeles-revised by the authors.)

195

struction in relation to expenditures for building maintenance and repair. More expensive exterior wall material may be warranted from a value point of view (brick versus frame) where the additional construction cost does not exceed the present worth of anticipated dollar savings in building management and upkeep. Amenities offered by the attractiveness of exterior design or appearance must, of course, be considered as plus items in the value estimate.

Where exterior walls are of frame or of brick or stone veneer, the supporting wood framing consists of studs either 2 by 4 inches or 2 by 6 inches in size that rest on sills which are bolted or nailed to the foundation wall. In geographic areas where termite infestation is prevalent, soils enclosed by the foundation walls are poisoned by licensed pest exterminators and/or metal termite shields are placed on top of foundation walls and piers to safeguard against these wood-destroying subterranean pests.

In checking the kind and quality of *sub- and finish floor construction*, the appraiser should make certain that the underlying and surrounding soil shows no evidence of poor surface drainage and moisture in the crawl space or on the underside of the subflooring and that no telltale signs point to the existence of, or possible damage from, subterranean pests or surface varmints. The basement area should be checked for size, quality, and utility. Many residential buildings today are constructed without basements, and most throughout the Deep South and Far West are built on concrete slab poured directly on the ground without crawl space or excavation of any kind. This type of construction, in milder climates where ground frost presents no danger, may cost one-third as much as hardwood flooring built over a crawl space depending on the size of the building area. Where the frame subfloor is suspended, a check should be made of the size of girders, size and spacing of floor joists, proper cross bridging or solid blocking of joists (at least every 8 feet apart) to assure floor stability and creakproof construction. Subfloor plywood sheets generally are 1/2- to 3/4-inch tongue-and-groove plywood. Each sheet should have its longest dimension run perpendicular to the floor joists. The kind and quality of finished flooring should be noted, and inspected for uniformity of placement and appearance. Wall-to-wall carpet should be mounted over 1/2-inch or more foam padding for even and longer wear. Where rugs are intended as partial floor covering, the finished wood surface should be of hard clear wood strips or parquet wood tiles nailed over 4-by-8-foot plywood sheets or other subflooring. Kitchen floors generally are covered with grease-resistant vinyl sheet. Bathroom floors, for long-lasting use as well as appearance, are recommended to be finished with ceramic tile firmly cemented in place over concrete slab or plywood subflooring. Concrete flooring in basement, commercial, or industrial areas should be four inches in thickness and reinforced with continuous wire mesh.

Construction details of *partition framing and interior walls* should be considered. Particular checks should be made where exterior walls are of metal or masonry to discern whether the inside of these walls are fitted with furred strips of kiln-dried or moisture-treated wood to create airspace between the wall surface and the plaster or other interior wall finishes. This airspace is important wherever climatic conditions cause walls to sweat because of extreme differences in indoor-outdoor temperatures. Most brick walls today are brick veneer that is supported by a wood frame. The combination of the wood and vertical open spaces between bricks (weep holes) allows moisture buildup to be discharged. Where plaster is placed directly on the wall rather than on rock lath over furring strips, the appraiser should reflect this "economy" construction in his or her value estimate and possibly consider penalizing the property under functional obsolescence, especially in areas where lending companies reject such substandard construction for mortgage loan purposes. Interior finishes, too, should be noted for quality attributes. Where wood paneling is used, check for quality workmanship in the mitering of joints, and for type and grade of wood and excellence of finish. The height of walls from floor to ceiling is important, and where more or less than standard (generally 8 feet, but may be 9 feet for expensive homes) clearance, a plus or minus adjustment should be made to reflect the lack of, or increase in, resulting amenities to owner-occupants.

The type of *roof construction*, method of framing, and roof shingle or surface finishing should next be given due attention. Depending on the period of architecture, the principal roof types are as follows: flat (built-up), gable, hip, gambrel, mansard, or pyramid, as shown in Figure 10.2. A variation of the gable is the one and one-half story house with several front dormers and possibly a full or "shed" dormer across the rear. Where roofs are sloped and roof shingles are conventionally nailed (and not cemented), it is important that the rise in slope is not less than 3 inches for every 12 inches of horizontal distance, as shown in Figure 10.3. This relationship is expressed as "3 and 12." Roof pitches may range from low (3 and 12) to steep (e.g., 12 and 12, which is a 45-degree incline).

The higher the rise in slope, the costlier the roof construction—but the larger the attic area and the safer and more lasting the roof shingle coverage because of lessened wear and tear from rain, hail, snow, or tornadic winds. A rise in slope below 3 inches for every 12 inches permits rain and wind to drive under the shingles, weakening the shingle fastenings and the undercover roof seal. Ceiling joists and roof rafters should be at least 2 inches by 6 inches in size for residential

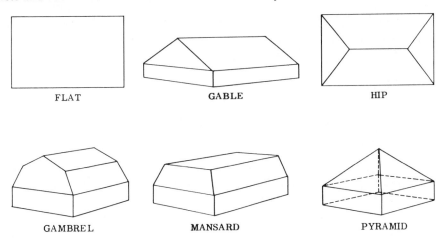

FLAT   GABLE   HIP

GAMBREL   MANSARD   PYRAMID

Figure 10.2 Roof Types

Figure 10.3   Roof Slope

buildings, and placed not less than 16 inches on center (from the center of one joist or rafter to the center of the adjacent joist or rafter). The trend is toward use of 2-by-4-inch wooden trusses, 2 feet on center. The roof extension, or eaves, should be at least 12 inches beyond the exterior wall surface, and larger where protection is sought from sun and rain for windows and exterior finishes. A typical roof section shows details as in Figure 10.4.

Windows and doors should be inspected to ascertain the manufacturer, the kind of wood or metal sash, the quality of fitting, and the extent of trouble-free operation. Weakness of construction or poor lintel support over wall openings manifests itself in plaster and wall cracks at corners of windows and doors. Where cracks are due to structural settlement, inspection of floor beams and piers should be made to determine the necessity for and cost of corrective repairs. Windows should be tested and checked for airtightness, and exterior doors should be fitted with full- or half-length screens and weatherstripped thresholds and frames. Window sills and stools, where of special construction and finish, should be noted as quality attributes which must be reflected specifically in the cost approach to value.

Windows generally are either double-hung or casement type and of wood sash in northern and midwestern states, and of jalousie or awning type and of aluminum sash in subtropical climate states. Jalousie windows are largely used in closed-in porches and in industrial and commercial buildings. Better home con-

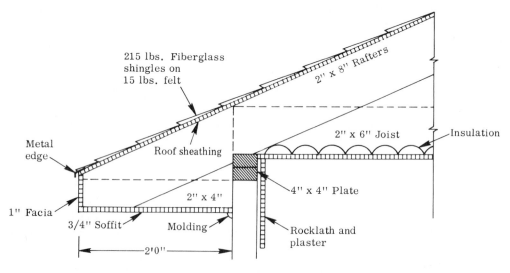

Figure 10.4   Roof Section View

struction practices confine window types to double-hung, casement, or awning manufacture. Triplex-pane windows are seldom justified except in the northern parts of the country; however, the duplex window is frequently found in the more temperate zones of the United States. Vinyl-clad wood is a superior type of window construction because the vinyl protects the exterior from deteriorating and the wood protects the interior from sweating. Ease of operation and weatherstripping are further marks of quality noticeable by careful inspection.

Sufficiency in number, size, and quality of *closets, built-ins, and cabinetwork* in general should be evaluated and described for the benefit of the report reader. Quality construction is apparent when closets are cedar-lined, fitted with switch-controlled lights, and contain carpentry details such as shoeracks and special shelf-and-rod arrangements. Sliding, louvered, or mirrored closet doors, too, may warrant special value consideration. Built-in vanities, bookcases, mantles, china closets, and extra kitchen cabinets that increase the functional utility and amenities of living must be itemized and considered for appraisal purposes.

Adequacy, convenience, and safety of *plumbing and electrical installations* are a *must* in a modern home. Each bathroom, unless back to back with another, should be separately vented with a PVC or polybutilane stack extending through the roof as well as have a window. Similar venting for the kitchen sink is a requirement. Water faucets should have individual valve shutoffs to permit emergency repairs or washer replacements. The piping should be checked as to the kind of metal (galvanized or copper) and whether water flow is adequate or impeded by inadequate pipe size or faulty construction. It is important, too, to ascertain whether sewage disposal is by a public, community, or individual septic tank system. In the latter case, the number and size of septic tanks and the condition of drain fields should be considered and reported. Increasing reliance on electrically operated household conveniences such as whirlpool bathtubs, ranges, refrigerators, dishwashers, garbage disposals, and washing machines makes proper and adequate wiring for regular lighting and power use of utmost importance. Modern construction calls for a three-wire (220-volt) panel wiring, of 100-ampere or greater capacity, and fitted with circuit breakers rather than old-fashioned fuses. Wall receptacles, six to nine feet spacing between each, should be conveniently located. Switches, whether conventional or mercury (silent) type, should be noted. All plumbing and wiring should be concealed, including wiring for telephone outlets to various rooms and television antenna connections.

Most often underestimated is the cost of an installed *heating and air-conditioning system.* In many southern and far-western homes, heat is supplied simply by a single gas, electric, or oil-fired space heater. Such a method of heating—no matter how warm the climate during most of the year—is inadequate and often unhealthy because of faulty venting or inadequate air circulation. The cost of central heating and air conditioning, with adequate duct and register controls, may vary from 2 to 3 percent of the total dwelling cost, depending on the quality of the system and the intricacy of the pipe or ductwork installation. This wide cost range is reason enough for an appraiser to confirm the kind and quality of heating and cooling, and to reflect the appropriate value attributes in his or her appraisal estimate. Air conditioning in many parts of our country has become a standard feature in new homes and care must be taken to study the demand for homes not equipped in order to reflect market value.

Last but not least, accessory building details should be inventoried. Included in this category are ceiling and wall insulation. The appraiser should note the type and form of insulation installed. It may be mineral wool, fiberglass, or cellulosic fiber and be installed loosely (hand poured or machine blown) or in the form of blankets or batts that fit between the floor joists, wall studs, or ceiling joists. Other choices are foam or rigid board insulation. The latter is usually used on basement walls. The symbol used to measure the insulating quality of a material is "R value." The higher the R value, the better the insulation. Different R values are expected for ceilings and walls and in different temperature zones of the country. For example, in temperate zones the following R values may be expected for fiberglass insulation: Walls (R-11, 3-1/2-inch thickness); ceiling (R-19, 6-to-6-1/2-inch, to R-30, 9-to-10-inch thickness). Also to be considered is the finished attic space, outdoor floodlighting, patios, landscaping, driveways, walks, porches, garages, stoves, refrigerators, laundry equipment, disposals, fireplaces, incinerators, elevators, storm sashes, fences, wells, water tanks, water softeners, water pumps, sprinkler systems, septic systems, and other related improvements.

PLAN READING FOR PROPOSED CONSTRUCTION

It is said that the best time to appraise a property is before it is built. Ideally, this would give the best protection to builders, investors, and home buyers. In practice, however, this precaution is not generally taken. It is often assumed by the public at large that cost and value are synonymous. Not until a resale takes place do errors come to light as to under-, over-, or faulty improvements and resultant value losses. Fortunately, as a protection to mortgage lenders, the practice of appraising proposed buildings prior to construction is mandatory—at least where governmental agencies or private institutional lenders are involved.

Every appraiser must be capable of analyzing building plans and specifications of materials in order to estimate the cost of constructing proposed improvements. Whether costs are warranted will depend on the kind and character of the described improvements in light of prevailing demand and market conditions, as was discussed in preceding chapters and as will be further outlined in chapters concerned with the depreciated cost, sales comparison, and capitalized income approaches to value.

Typical construction drawings, as a rule, contain the following:

1. Foundation plan.
2. Floor plan.
3. Elevations (i.e., front, rear, and side views).
4. Sectional views.
5. Mechanical, heating, and electrical plan layouts.

The *foundation plan* is generally drawn to a scale of 1/4 inch to 1 foot and provides the essential details concerning size of footings, size and dimensions of piers, and construction measurements and details of the subfloor area. Where the building foundation is of concrete slab, the plan will show the thickness of the slab, the kind and size of steel wire reinforcement, and areas where foundations are to be thickened for placement of load-bearing interior walls. Location of concrete expansion joints and foundation areas to be termite-shielded or soil-poisoned are also marked for ease of reference and worker's guide. Where basement area or subfloor crawl space is called for, the foundation plan will note the exact location and size of girders and beams as well as the kind and quality of floor joists—generally 2 by 8 or 2 by 10 inches in size and placed, as a rule, 12 or 16 inches on center, depending on the type of superstructure and the permissible building codes. A recent innovation in construction techniques is the use of plywood floor joists. They are straighter and easier to handle than conventional wood joists. Fewer joists are needed since they can be spaced on 2-foot centers.

The *floor plan* (see Figure 10.5) is an important guide to accurate building layout. From this plan, measurements are taken for the calculation of square-foot or cubic-foot space volume that serve as a basis for construction-cost estimating. The floor plan, as shown, indicates wall-to-wall dimensions, room sizes and expo-

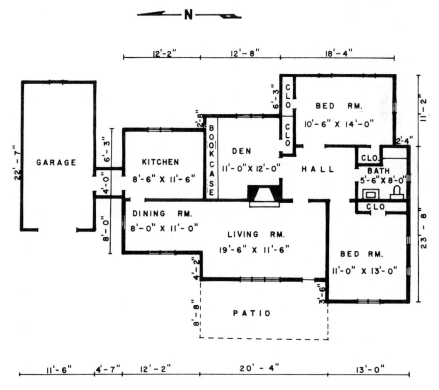

Figure 10.5 Floor Plan for Residential Structure

sures, and placement of windows, doors, partitions, fireplace, chimney, fixtures, cabinets, patio, breezeway, and attached garage. The floor plan is normally drawn to an exact scale of 1/4 inch to 1 foot and includes, where separate mechanical drawings are not called for, construction details concerning placement of lighting outlets, telephone jacks, plumbing, and heating fixtures.

Elevations show the exterior sides of a building as it appears after all structural work has been completed. As a rule, each building side is viewed by an elevation and, for identification, marked as north, south, east, and west or by structural designation as front, rear, left, and right side elevation. Symbols on elevation drawings indicate the kind of exterior materials, their placement, and the height of their construction. The type and slope of roof is noted, as well as the kind and placement of roof shingles. Type and placement of windows are detailed, as are other openings such as doors, dormers, vents, and skylights. Typical elevations, from which an overall view of the finished building can be obtained at a glance, are shown in Figure 10.6.

To provide a detailed guide to specific construction practices, sectional views of exterior and interior walls are made a part of every set of building plans. Sectional views permit detailed considerations of specific construction methods, from footings and subflooring to ceiling, attic, and roof construction. Special elevation drawings, too, are provided for built-in items such as bookcases, china closets, and kitchen cabinets.

THE IMPORTANCE OF WRITTEN SPECIFICATIONS

No matter how completely plans, elevations, and related drawings and sketches are prepared, they still would fail to convey an accurate picture of the structural elements to be incorporated in a building without the important and supplementary aid of written specifications (sometimes called "specifications of materials"). In fact, written instructions are deemed of greater importance than graphic illustrations, and where these two are in conflict it is the written word that is guiding and legally binding.

The reason for the importance of written specifications can be readily illustrated. Plans may indicate construction and placement of materials. In the specifications, however, structural quality and quantity are specifically spelled out. Thus the specifications may call for a concrete mix of one part cement, two parts sand, three parts stone, and a minimum supporting strength of 2,400 pounds per square inch at a time interval of 48 hours after pouring. Or the plans may show 2-by-6-inch floor joists placed 24 inches on center. The specifications will indicate the kind of timber—whether pine, oak, or other—and the grade of timber as rated in accordance with quality and manufacturer's tensile strength. Specifications, too, may stipulate whether timber is to be treated, processed for protection against termites, or kiln-dried to minimize shrinkage.

Specifications historically have served as a contract document between builder and owner, and are intended to avoid disputes or misunderstandings concerning the details of construction. Other and equally important purposes are to

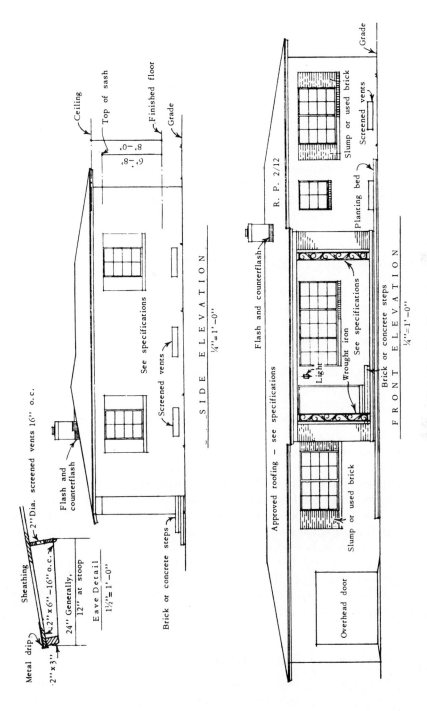

Figure 10.6 Dwelling Elevations

permit accurate estimating of required labor, quality of materials, and cost of contractors' and subcontractors' services in accordance with plan requirements. Specifications also safeguard against expensive omissions when construction costs are estimated and minimize construction delays due to misunderstanding of the building plans. Written specifications generally are prepared in one of two forms:

1. The narrative or report form.
2. The standard specification form.

For multiple-story residential and for commercial and industrial buildings, the narrative or report form is generally used. For a skyscraper, for instance, the specifications contain sufficient pages to comprise a book. An excerpt from a standard specification form for a single-family dwelling is shown in Figure 10.7.

COMPUTING BUILDING MEASUREMENTS

Depending on local custom and building practices, construction areas are quoted in terms of square-foot or cubic-foot measurements. The latter method of sizing a building is more accurate, since the height of a structure is measured from 6 inches below the finished surface of the lowest floor to and including the roof and attic area. Where given structures, such as residences, are of uniform height, however, the use and application of the square-foot method of costing a building is justified and yields accurate results, as will be demonstrated in Chapter 11. All building measurements are based on exterior rather than interior wall dimensions. House area and cost are based on overall square footage, not interior wall dimensions. Interior dimensions are useful for interior finish cost calculations and evaluation of room functionality.

In illustrating the procedure of "squaring" a building, reference is made to the building sketch shown in Figure 10.8 and is based on Figure 10.5. For computation purposes the floor area is divided into rectangular units.

Where cubic-foot measurements are required, an additional multiplication for each rectangular unit must be made in accordance with the building height taken from 6 inches below the finished basement floor to the outside measurement of a flat roof. Other roof plans must be computed to reflect the accurate cubic-foot volume of gable or other types of roof areas. For detailed illustrations and instructions on building measurements, reference can be made to the various cost services, which are identified in Chapter 11.

BASIC ATTRIBUTES OF GOOD FLOOR PLANNING

It is the appraiser's responsibility to develop and use sound judgment in classifying the attributes of good or poor floor planning, and to evaluate the effects on the marketability of the property with regard to layout and design or impaired functional utility. Where there is an imbalance in interior space allocation, the degree

PLUMBING:

FIXTURE	NUMBER	LOCATION	MAKE	MFR'S FIXTURE IDENTIFICATION NO.	SIZE	COLOR
Sink	1	kitchen	stainless steel	double bowl	32 x 21	ss
Lavatory	1	1st fl lav	ELJER	E1634	19 x 17	white
Water closet	3	baths	"	E5250	–	"
Bathtub	1	hall bath	"		60"	
Shower over tub	1	"			–	
Stall shower	1	mast. br			48"	
Laundry trays						
Lavatory	1	hall bath	ELJER			
"	1	mast. br	"			

△ ☐ Curtain rod   △ ☐ door   ☐ Shower pan: material _____

Water supply: ☐ public: ☐ community system: ☐ individual (private) system. ★

Sewage disposal: ☐ public: ☐ community system; ☐ individual (private) system. ★

★ *Show and describe individual system in complete detail in separate drawings and specifications according to requirements.*

House drain (inside): ☐ cast iron; ☐ tile; ☐ other _____ ABS/DWV _____ House sewer (outside): ☐ cast iron; ☐ tile; ☐ other _____

Water piping: ☐ galvanized steel; ☐ copper tubing; ☐ other _____ Sill cocks, number _____ 2

Domestic water heater type _____ elect, hi-recovery _____ make and model _____; heating capacity

_____ 36 _____ gph. 100° rise. Storage tank: material _____ glass lined _____; capacity _____ 50 _____ gallons.

Gas service: ☐ utility company; ☐ liq. pet. gas; ☐ other _____ Gas piping: ☐ cooking; ☐ house heating.

Footing drains connected to: ☐ storm sewer; ☐ sanitary sewer; ☐ dry well. Sump pump; make and model _____

_____ ; discharges into _____

DESCRIPTION OF MATERIALS
HUD-92005 (6-79)
VA Form 26-1852, Form FmHA 424-2

Figure 10.7 Plumbing Specifications

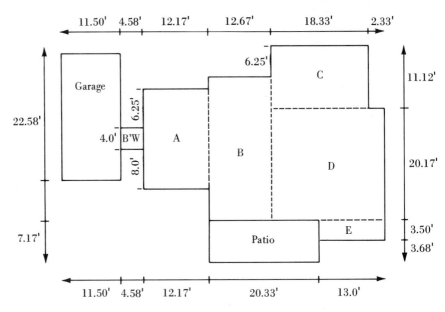

Figure 10.8 Building Sketch

of functional obsolescence will be reflected in sales resistance that is measurable in dollars.

Attributes of good floor planning which increase the amenities of residential structures and which make for more efficient use of space include the following:

1. Orientation of rooms to capture prevailing breezes, sunshine, and scenic views.
2. Proper placing of picture window and all other window areas to assure adequate light and fenestration for all rooms.
3. Provision for entrance hall or foyer (with guest-closet space) to shield living room from direct view and drafts.
4. Grouping of bed and bathroom areas to assure maximum privacy. A separate entrance to the bedroom wing or access without a view from or crossing of living room area is considered a must for upscale homes.
5. Proper functional layout of kitchen area to conserve steps in housekeeping.
6. Location of kitchen near entrance and side doors to minimize traffic flow through other parts of the house.
7. Adequate bedroom, linen, and storage closets and necessary utility space.
8. Proper wiring and location of household utility equipment and economical but adequate provision for central heating.
9. Accessibility to attic space area via conveniently located hatch or concealed stairway.

10. Minimum room sizes at least equal in square-foot area and dimensions as provided by minimum property standards for residential units adopted by local or statewide building codes.

Earlier minimum property standards prescribed by the Federal Housing Administration provided guidelines for room sizes and other architectural features of dwellings. Over the last several years FHA (U.S. Department of Housing and Urban Development) has moved away from establishing such standards and has allowed local requirements and nationally recognized standards to achieve these goals. Examples of current standards follow.

> A single-family dwelling shall have at least one room with a minimum of 150 square feet of floor area; other habitable rooms except the kitchen must have at least 70 square feet; the minimum dimension for all rooms except kitchen is 7 feet (unless mechanically vented); ceiling height, except kitchen, storage rooms and laundry rooms, shall have an average height of at least 7 feet 6 inches for at least 50 percent of the required area, no portion shall be less than 5 feet; every room or space intended for human occupancy shall have an exterior glazing (glass) area of not less than 8 percent of the floor area of the interior room or space, but not less than 25 square feet.[2]

The functional utility of commercial, industrial, or farm buildings can in like manner be tested by the principle of balance. In appraising large and multistory structures—especially if old or intricate in design—professional aid from contractors, builders, architects, or construction engineers may have to be obtained to report in detail on matters such as structural condition, deferred maintenance and repair, adequacy, safety and speed of elevators, and functional conditions which affect the cost of servicing the building. In some court jurisdictions appraisers are not qualified to testify as experts on matters concerning construction or the costs thereof, unless they are also licensed as building contractors, architects, or building engineers. Other matters of structural design affecting revenue, maintenance, management, and, possibly, the remaining economic building life include the following:

1. Adequacy of foyer, halls, and public areas to accommodate traffic flow of tenants, employees, and business clientele.
2. Proper washroom facilities assigned where possible for private use to minimize general janitorial services.
3. Modular construction that permits space repartitioning to suit tenant needs.
4. Good lighting and adequate, concealed telephone and electric wiring to serve anticipated maximum service loads.
5. Sufficiency of central heating under individual unit or zone control.
6. Capacity and readiness to supply air conditioning where competitively necessary.

[2]*The BOCA National Building Code 1987*, 10th ed. (Country Club Hills, Ill.: Building Officials and Code Administrators International, Inc., 1986), pp. 126–28.

7. High ratio of net rentable area as a percentage of total building area.
8. Adequate off-street parking.

In the appraisal of old structures, special care must be taken to recognize functional disutility. For example, structures built of thick masonry walls, which were designed under the old post-and-lintel system to support by sheer dead weight the stresses and strains of tall, multistory buildings, may offer as much as 10 percent less net rentable space than modern structures where exterior walls are built of steel or of steel-reinforced masonry.[3] In such instances, the capitalized income loss due to an outmoded type of construction will reflect the amount of accrued depreciation caused by this type of functional disutility.

IMPORTANCE OF CONSTRUCTION KNOWLEDGE

Since improvements on and to land comprise the major portion of total property value, it is important that the appraiser become thoroughly familiar with the essential details of building construction and building-plan reading. In this chapter the importance of construction principles and practices knowledge has been emphasized in order that the appraiser might effectively distinguish between and evaluate the vastly varied types of building improvements. Many books have been written on construction subjects, and many colleges and universities throughout the country offer courses in this important field of study. A qualified appraiser who seeks to serve the profession well should become familiar with the types of architecture and construction practices that typically prevail in the state or region in which he or she works. Reading and course work is important to lay a foundation for appraisal knowledge, but nothing can take the place of field experience gained from the inspection of buildings at various stages of construction. Every appraisal presents a challenge to inventory correctly the details of construction, and to evaluate accurately the utility of building improvements. Effective application of the construction guides discussed previously should contribute importantly to accurate consideration of building improvements under the depreciated cost, sales comparison, and income capitalization approaches to value, as will be demonstrated in succeeding chapters.

BUILDING INSPECTION

Certainly it is important in the appraisal of real property to understand construction. Equally important is to apply this knowledge in a thorough and systematic inspection of the appraised property. This section will focus only on the building. In Chapter 7 factors concerning site analysis are presented. The primary purpose of a building inspection is to determine its age, condition, and functional utility for its intended use. Without a clear understanding of these three factors, a com-

[3]Construction under the modern *birdcage* building method, where outer walls are mere protection sheaths, may offer further space advantages or construction-cost economies.

petent analysis of the market value of the appraised property via the three traditional approaches to value is virtually impossible.

Prior to inspecting a property, the appraiser should call the property owner or his or her representative to schedule an appointment for the inspection. The proper equipment should be taken by the appraiser. This includes a camera (usually a 35-millimeter camera), clipboard, 100-foot cloth or plastic measuring tape with a hook, pocket knife, and flashlight. On some assignments it is necessary to have protective clothing and waterproof boots. Prior to visiting the property, the appraiser should ask the owner to provide appropriate income-expense records, current real estate tax information, and plat and floor plans as well.

In making an inspection, it is desirable to use either a checklist or the Uniform Residential Report Form to be certain that all aspects of the building are recorded during the inspection. Some appraisers find it more convenient to use a hand-held dictating machine.

As the building is inspected, the appraiser should observe the design, traffic flow, privacy and access to the various parts of the building, and adequacy of mechanical services such as heat, air conditioning, plumbing, and electrical. Quality of construction, adequacy and convenience of storage, need for painting and repairs, termite infestation, and moisture in the basement or crawl space should all be noted. Before leaving the property, check to be certain that all required information and measurements have been obtained.

SUMMARY

A competent appraiser, to be professionally qualified, must have a working knowledge of building design and construction. In appraising proposed construction, the appraiser must be capable of analyzing building plans and specifications of materials and be able to estimate building costs from architectural specifications. Typical construction drawings contain the following: (1) foundation plan, (2) floor plan, (3) front, rear, and side elevations, (4) sectional views, and (5) mechanical, heating, and electrical plan layouts. Building specifications generally serve as a contract document between builder and owner and safeguard against expensive omissions when construction costs are estimated, and minimize construction delays due to the misunderstanding of building plans.

The appraiser should use sound judgment in classifying the attributes of good or poor floor planning, and evaluate the effects on the marketability of the property with regard to layout and design or impaired functional utility. This information can be obtained from a careful building inspection. The primary purpose of a building inspection is to determine its age, condition, and functional utility for its intended use.

REVIEW QUESTIONS

1. How can the rise (or pitch) of a roof affect the life of the shingles?
2. What aspect of a building does the "R value" measure?

3. What feature of a building do the elevations show?
4. List six attributes of good floor planning.
5. Of what importance are specifications of materials?
6. List five matters of structural design that affect revenue, maintenance, management, and possibly, the remaining economic life of a building.
7. Calculate the area of the (a) patio, (b) breezeway, (c) garage, and (d) dwelling shown in Figure 10.7 (rounding to the nearest square foot).

READING AND STUDY REFERENCES

ADDLESON, LYALL. *Building Failures: A Guide to Diagnosis, Remedy and Prevention.* London: Architectural Press, 1982.

American Institute of Real Estate Appraisers. Chapters 10 and 11, *The Appraisal of Real Estate*, 9th ed. Chicago: AIREA, 1987.

BARLOW, PHILIP MARC. "How to Make an Inspection," *The Appraisal Journal* (October 1985), pp. 606–616.

BLOOM, GEORGE F., and HENRY S. HARRISON. Chapter 10, "Improvement Description and Analysis," *Appraising the Single Family Residence.* Chicago: American Institute of Real Estate Appraisers, 1978.

BOYCE, BYRL N., and WILLIAM N. KINNARD, JR. "Improvements Analysis (Building Analysis)," *Appraising Real Property.* Lexington, Mass.: Lexington Books, 1984, pp. 144–159.

FOUTE, STEVEN J. "Appraising and Underwriting the Energy Efficient Home: The Energy Mortgage Value Method," *The Real Estate Appraiser and Analyst* 48, no. 1 (Spring 1982), pp. 5–9.

HARRISON, HENRY S. *Houses: The Illustrated Guide to Construction, Design and Systems.* Chicago: National Institute of Real Estate Brokers, 1973.

ISAKSON, HANS R. "Residential Energy Audits: A New Source of Appraisal Data," *The Appraisal Journal* 49, no. 1 (January 1981), pp. 74–84.

KIMBALL, WILLIAM J. "Measuring an Office Building—1+1=2.2," *The Appraisal Journal* 56, no. 1 (January 1988), pp. 39–44.

LENNON, MICHAEL P. "A Layman's Guide to Electrical Systems," *The Real Estate Appraiser and Analyst* 56, no. 1 (Spring 1990), pp. 29–40.

MULLER, EDWARD J. *Reading Architectural Working Drawings.* Englewood Cliffs, N.J.: Prentice-Hall, Inc., 1981.

OLIN, HAROLD B., JOHN L. SCHMIDT, and WALTER H. LEWIS. *Construction—Principles, Materials and Methods*, 4th ed. Chicago: Institute of Financial Education, 1980.

"Residential Inspection." Video 1/2 in. VHS. Chicago: Appraisal Institute, 1987.

WHITE, EDWARD L. "Appraising from Plans and Specifications," *The Real Estate Appraiser* 32, no. 6 (June 1966), pp. 13–26.

11

The Depreciated Cost
Approach: Cost Estimating

Learning Objectives

After reading this chapter, you should be able to:

- Distinguish between replacement and reproduction cost
- Appreciate when and when not to use the depreciated cost approach
- Understand the basic steps involved in the depreciated cost approach
- Discuss the relationship and differences between cost and value
- Explain and give examples of direct and indirect building costs
- Explain the different ways that current construction costs can be computed

STEPS IN THE DEPRECIATED COST APPROACH

The depreciated cost approach is a hybrid approach in that it is based partly on the sales comparison approach. The steps involved in this approach are outlined as follows:

1. Estimate the highest and best use of the site. This initial step provides a basis for selecting comparable site sales as well as later establishing a "yardstick" against which accrued depreciation of the improvements is measured.
2. Find the present cost of reproducing or replacing the building(s). This cost includes builder's entrepreneurial profit which is based on local market evidence. In order to accurately estimate this amount, the appraiser must understand building design and materials as well as be acquainted with cost estimating to a reasonable degree. The techniques for estimating construction costs are covered later in this chapter.
3. Estimate the total dollar amount of accrued depreciation from all causes. This depreciation is broken down into three categories: physical deterioration, functional obsolescence, and external obsolescence.

4. Subtract the dollar amount of accrued depreciation from the present reproduction or replacement cost. This difference, if computed accurately, ap-
   proximates the present value of the building(s).
5. Estimate the depreciated cost of any minor buildings and other on-site improvements, such as landscaping, fencing, and driveways. The key to this
   step is estimating the value that these improvements add to the overall value
   of the property rather than their cost.
6. Add the site value to the depreciated cost of the building(s) and other on-site
   improvements (steps 4 and 5). The resultant figure is the estimated value of
   the property via the depreciated cost approach.

PROS AND CONS OF THE DEPRECIATED COST APPROACH

Every method conceived either to measure or predict the value of real estate has
its proponents and opponents. The depreciated cost approach certainly has not
been spared this divided support. As forthrightly as possible, this section will lay
out the advantages and disadvantages of this method. The reader should attempt
to recognize that this, and the other approaches to finding value, has its relative
strengths and weaknesses and each approach should be used to its best advantage.

Advantages.   The advantages of this approach are as follows:

1. By inspecting a property and subsequently accounting for its cost new and
   value lost due to accrued depreciation, the appraiser enhances his or her
   ability to estimate the property's value via the sales comparison and capitalized income approaches.
2. It can be used to estimate the financial feasibility of a proposed property.
   That is, if the value indicated by the sales and income approaches equals or
   exceeds the current replacement cost plus builder's profit and land value,
   the property is feasible. The reverse situation implies infeasibility.
3. The same arguments advanced for a separate site value apply to use of this
   approach, which can provide a separate estimate of property value.
4. It can be used to provide an indication of value for special-purpose properties, new properties, or in those instances when there is a dearth of similar
   market transfers or rental data.
5. It is helpful when there are insufficient market data for the sales comparison
   approach to reveal the value differential for such items as differences in
   building size, heating–air-conditioning systems, or roof covering.

Disadvantages.   The major disadvantages of this method are as follows:

1. It requires great diligence in maintaining current data as well as in carefully
   recognizing differences in cost due to different sizes and quality of materials. Also, a careful identification and accounting for the various elements of
   accrued depreciation are required.

2. It fails to provide a truly independent estimate of market value. The site value, comprising perhaps 10 to 40 percent of a property's value, is estimated by use of comparable sales. Deductions for accrued depreciation generally are based on market evidence. Thus a great deal of the reported depreciation is generated by the analysis of sales of comparable sites and improved properties.
3. It is not well suited for old buildings. Appraisers often deplore using comparable sales that require net adjustments in excess of 15 to 20 percent. Yet the "adjustment" or deduction for accrued depreciation for an old building can easily reach 75 percent.
4. It can be an overly complicated approach that is suspect especially when the various deductions for supposed accrued depreciation are backed up by nothing more than such unconvincing statements as "the appraiser's experience" or "unfavorable consumer reaction to a particular building or neighborhood feature." Such practices can only weaken the depreciated cost approach and, in fact, the whole appraisal report.

COST VERSUS VALUE

Perhaps no single concept in real estate valuation gives rise to greater miscalculations by both nonappraisers and appraisers than the concept of *cost*. Cost and value are confused because expenditures in terms of labor and materials are necessary in order to supply goods or services in demand, and in the long run such expenditures must equal value if construction is to continue and prove economically rewarding. Also, since value without expenditure or cost of production is unthinkable, it would appear that the reliance on cost as a measure of value is justified.

There are a number of reasons, nevertheless, why care must be exercised before accepting cost as a measure of value.

1. Cost and value are only equal if, among other considerations, the property is new or proposed. Since improvements age physically from the day of construction, and since the functional and external forces of obsolescence are operating constantly because of changes in style, use, and demand, depreciation must be accounted for accurately and subtracted from cost as if new in order that *depreciated cost* may reflect a truer measure of value.
2. Cost and value are one and the same only where the improvements represent the highest and best use. Since many properties are under- or overimproved—or misimproved—cost and value may differ significantly.
3. Cost must be economically warranted if it is to equal value. To illustrate: Digging a hole in the ground for no purpose whatever except to satisfy a whim does not create value. In fact, the hole in the ground may constitute "negative" value because the hole may have to be filled again in order to make the site economically usable. Costs that are not justified cannot equal

value because no "informed" buyer will pay more for a good or service than is warranted at a given time or place and under prevailing economic conditions. The proverbial "hotel built in a desert" is an illustration of this.

Cost is always a measure of a past expenditure either of labor or materials or both, and always represents a measure of *past* expenditures. Value, on the other hand, is influenced in the future because value, by definition, constitutes the *present worth* of future rights and benefits. Stated somewhat differently, *cost* is the amount of money necessary to acquire or to create an item, while *value* represents its worth. There is merit to claiming that a prudent person would not pay more for a used property than the cost necessary to build the same structure without an unacceptable delay. However, there is absolutely no reason for the estimated depreciated cost of a property to set its upper limit of value. Value may be equal to or be more or less than cost.

DIRECT AND INDIRECT COSTS

In estimating the present construction cost of a structure, it is important that all associated costs be included. As a matter of convenience, total current construction cost (reproduction or replacement) may be identified as *direct* and *indirect* costs. *Direct costs* are labor and materials (sometimes called hard costs), which include:

1. Labor hired by the general contractors and subcontractors.
2. Materials used, beginning with site clearance to the final cleanup.
3. Equipment, leased or owned.
4. Temporary electric service.
5. Builder's overhead and profit.

Indirect costs (sometimes called soft costs), equally important as direct costs, may not be as apparent to persons unfamiliar with building construction. These supporting costs are:

1. Professional service fees, including legal, appraisal, financial feasibility, engineering, architectural, and surveying.
2. Construction and possibly permanent loan charges.
3. Property management commissions.
4. Project management fees.
5. Land lease rent, if appropriate.
6. Real estate taxes.
7. Project promotion charges.
8. Any other interim carrying costs.

In a normal market, when building supply and demand are in equilibrium, replacement cost in current dollars will set the ceiling of value—provided that the structure is new and conforms in design, size, and mode of construction with the principle of highest and best land use. As a first step in the field-data program, it is essential that the appraiser make a detailed inventory of the existing or proposed land and building improvements in order that an accurate estimate can be made of the cost to *replace* the utility of the structure under up-to-date but generally typical methods of building construction.

Even when costs are accounted for and deemed acceptable as an initial measure of value, it usually is *replacement* cost and not *reproduction* cost that must be considered in an estimation of value. The valid question facing an informed buyer or a professional appraiser is what it would cost to duplicate the subject improvements. *Duplication* means to recreate the utility or amenities that the property is expected to offer a typical buyer. Where modern methods of construction and design offer savings in both labor and material costs as compared with methods in vogue when the appraised structure was originally built, then present-day replacement costs should be used by the appraiser. Ceilings may be too high or too low, walls excessively thick or not properly reinforced, the floor plan outmoded or simply wasteful in space utilization, and convenient built-ins and energy-saving devices lacking. To reproduce such a structure—even on paper for hypothetical calculation of value—would be a wasteful practice. Even in condemnation trials, the law in most states requires the owner's property to be left intact in terms of *value*, and only a replacement of like improvements, or what typical buyers value as such in open market transactions, can effectively serve as the final guide to just compensation.

Replacement cost is defined as the current cost of building a structure that provides functional utility equal to the building being appraised. Further, it implies that modern materials, methods, and technology are used and as a result all components of functional obsolescence due to superadequate design or materials are excluded. This cost is less than the amount indicated by the reproduction cost method, implying that it is based on a modern building that affords utility equivalent to that provided by the appraised building. For example, if the reproduction cost for a building is $860,000 and the replacement cost is $800,000, then the $60,000 difference would be caused by superadequate functional obsolescence.

Reproduction cost is the cost of building an appraised structure in a manner that replicates the materials, design, layout, and quality of workmanship. In short, this cost involves rebuilding the subject structure with any inherent faulty design superadequacies and inefficiencies. It is an unrealistic method for older obsolete structures because virtually no one would waste money erecting such inefficient and expensive buildings. Reproduction costs of a replica building—using current labor and similar materials—rather than replacement costs generally are considered more accurate as an approach to value, but this may not necessarily be true since the appraiser will have to account for any functional obsolescence that has occurred. No doubt the purpose of the appraisal and the nature of the value problem will guide the appraiser in selecting the costing method which, at the proper time and place, will yield the most reliable results. The appraiser must be aware of which of these costs are implied in cost manuals or from any other source. Also, since the current value of a property ordinarily is sought, the appraiser is concerned with the present cost of building the structure, not with some earlier building cost. For relatively new structures, these two costs should be essentially the same.

There are two schools of appraisal thought on this subject. One holds that to apply replacement costs as a measure of value constitutes "lazy" appraising, inasmuch as some forms of functional obsolescence are not accounted for unless a reproduction cost estimate is first obtained. From this estimate of reproduction cost, subtraction should be made for all forms of accrued depreciation resulting from wear and tear, action of the elements, and functional and external obsolescence. Thus if the present building walls are of brick 24 inches thick, the reproduction cost adherents would estimate the cost to reproduce these walls even though modern methods of construction call for steel-reinforced walls with a maximum thickness of 12 inches. The other school of appraisal thought (to which these writers subscribe) maintains that it is wasteful to estimate reproduction cost when factual evidence supports the conclusion reached by typically informed buyers that replacement cost sets the ceiling of value, and that reference to costs of reproducing an outmoded replica is not a realistic approach to accurately measure value.

In choosing replacement cost rather than reproduction cost as a measure of value, the appraiser must take care not to double up depreciation losses. Such doubling of value losses takes place when faulty methods of construction or design are eliminated in the calculation of replacement cost and then included again in the estimate of accrued depreciation. To state it differently, where replacement costs are lower than reproduction costs of a subject property the estimate cannot be reduced again for functional faults which theoretically have been "cured" by using the lower cost estimate. Such practice distorts the facts and places a property as well as its owner in double jeopardy. The application of the depreciated cost approach and the technique of measuring accrued depreciation will be dealt with fully in later chapters.

The art of cost estimating is taught in vocational schools and in colleges of architecture and building construction. The cost estimator as a technician is generally not concerned with value. It is the appraiser's task to convert cost into value by considering the effect of market conditions and identifying the causes of accrued depreciation, as explained in Chapter 12. Cost estimating methods presently in use by architects, builders, and appraisers are classified as follows:

1. Quantity survey method.
2. Unit-in-place construction method.
3. The comparative unit method.
4. Cost indexing method.

QUANTITY SURVEY METHOD

This, the most comprehensive and detailed method of cost estimating, is preferred by architects in the costing of residential structures. Under this method, bids for major construction work are obtained by the general contractor from subcontractors and added together to derive a composite cost estimate. The final cost includes the total quantity of labor and materials plus overhead and profit for the general contractor. An illustration of this cost estimating method as applied to a single-family residence is shown in Table 11.1.

The quantity survey or subcontractors' method, if expertly applied, produces accurate results. The application, however, is often too time consuming and costly to be recommended for use for most appraisal assignments. In fact, it would take thoroughly trained cost estimators, who are conversant with the operational details and technology of the building industry, to apply this method with assurance and relative accuracy. The typical appraiser is by necessity, therefore, inclined to rely on simpler and more objective methods of cost calculation.

This method of cost estimating is useful for estimating costs of substitute materials, and for estimating construction additions or deletions from plans and specifications. Because of the difficulty in accurately reducing such costs as carpentry and finishing work to a unit basis, this method of cost estimating is only infrequently employed by builders and developers and is not recommended as a valuation tool for real estate appraisers.

UNIT-IN-PLACE CONSTRUCTION METHOD

This method, also called the segregated method, is introduced in Figures 11.1, 11.2, 11.3 and 11.4. It generally represents how most residential and small commercial property builders prepare their cost bids. This method permits appraisers to give separate attention to each of the three major building components with relative ease and accurate results. These three building components are (1) floor, (2) outside wall, and (3) roof. Most of the subbuilding components are placed for computational purposes in the floor category. These include foundation, framing, floor structure, floor structure and cover, ceiling, interior construction, plumbing, heating and cooling, and electrical. This method is based on installed costs, including labor and materials, and uses the different unit costs for each building component as installed. The source of the individual numbers in Figure 11.3 is based on bids received from subcontractors. These subcontractors may be responsible for site clearance (and well and septic system installation for outlying properties), excavation, foundation and masonry walls, carpentry, roofing, plumbing, and electrical. These trades are broken down even more in the segregated cost example mentioned previously.

Computing costs in this manner is simpler for appraisers to prepare and more readily understood by clients than the quantity survey method. There is a

TABLE 11.1 CONSTRUCTION COST ESTIMATE UNDER THE QUANTITY SURVEY OR SUBCONTRACTOR'S METHOD FOR A SINGLE-FAMILY RESIDENCE CONTAINING 1,000 SQUARE FEET OF BUILDING AREA

Building Description: Average quality two-bedroom, living room, kitchen and bath, brick veneer residential structure. Interior walls of frame and drywall. Asphalt-shingled roof with 4-inch in 12-inch over 2-inch fiberglass ceiling insulation. Concrete subflooring and carpeting. Aluminum double-hung windows. Equipped with 40-gallon automatic electric water heater, built-in electric range and oven, and 85,000-Btu oil-fired, forced-air central heating system. Construction methods and specifications to meet BOCA property standards for one-family living units.

Cost Breakdown

Cost component	Total, materials and labor
Architect's fee	$ 215
Permits and utility connections	420
Site clearing	444
Excavation	253
Foundation	748
Chimney-masonry	908
Exterior walls	486
Subflooring	3,800
Framing, carpentry	2,202
Roofing	7,519
Windows and doors	1,107
Lath and plaster	2,365
Finished flooring	4,465
Cabinetwork	3,379
Insulation	1,500
Painting	338
Plumbing	2,458
Heating	3,455
Electrical	3,168
Fixtures	1,635
Insurance	359
Miscellaneous	127
Field overhead—3%	422
Contractor's overhead & profit	2,647
Total	$44,420

Cost per square foot of building $44.42

similarity between the latter method and the unit-in-place method in that both are based on subcontractors' bids. However, the unit-in-place method is less detailed and more widely used by appraisers. None of these methods will produce acceptable results unless the appraiser thoroughly inspects the appraised building and judiciously compares the nature and quality of the building to the benchmark building in a cost manual or to figures provided by a local contractor. If the initial cost figures are inaccurate, the eventual depreciated cost in turn will be inaccurate.

THE COMPARATIVE UNIT METHOD

The comparative square- or cubic-foot method is used almost exclusively by appraisers and by builders and architects when cost estimates are needed quickly. Under this method, the applicable unit cost per square or cubic foot of a building is derived by dividing the total building costs of similar structures recently completed by the number of square or cubic feet contained within the exterior wall dimension of the building's structural surfaces—which may or may not include attics, dormers, basements, and subfloor areas. A variation of this cost estimating method is to extract the construction costs from the sale prices of recently built similar properties. For example, suppose a 3,000-square-foot new dwelling just sold for $250,000. Through interviews with the builder and project developer, the following information was revealed: lot value, $52,500; yard improvements and landscaping, $2,500. Thus the cost (assumed to equal value) for the dwelling is $195,000 ($250,000 − $55,000). When divided by the gross dwelling area of 3,000 square feet, a square-foot cost of $65.00 is indicated. Where the building to be costed is similar in size, design, quality, and quantity of construction of buildings completed within a three- to six-month period, the results obtained should prove quite accurate. The unit cost thus obtained is then multiplied by the total square- or cubic-foot space area, and to this total is added a percentage for architect's fees and builder's overhead and profit.

Figure 11.1   Two-Story Office Building (Courtesy of Marshall and Swift, Los Angeles, California)

FLOOR PLANS

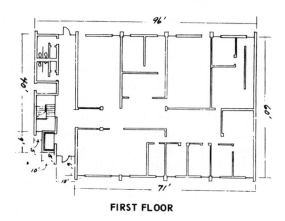

FIRST FLOOR

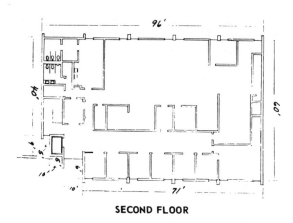

SECOND FLOOR

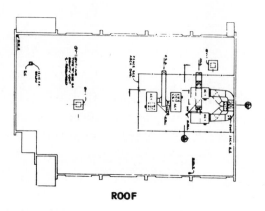

ROOF

Figure 11.1 (cont.)   Floor Plan of Two-Story Office Building (Courtesy of Marshall and Swift, Los Angeles, California)

SUBJECT BUILDING DESCRIPTION

OCCUPANCY:	Offices
BUILDING CLASS:	"C"
QUALITY:	Good
NUMBER OF STORIES:	Two
TOTAL HEIGHT:	26 feet
AVERAGE STORY HEIGHT:	13 feet
AVERAGE SINGLE FLOOR AREA:	5490 sq. ft.
FOUNDATION:	Continuous concrete footings and foundation for the bearing walls.
EXTERIOR WALLS:	Grouted 10" reinforced brick with pilasters. The exterior is face brick.
ROOF STRUCTURE:	1/2" plywood sheathing over 2" x 10" rafters 16" o.c.
ROOF COVER:	3 ply composition with tar and gravel.

FLOORS:	First floor: 4" concrete slab on the ground, with a vapor barrier.
	  25% quarry tile - 10% vinyl asbestos tile.
	  65% carpet over concrete slab, ceramic tile floors in restrooms.
	Second floor: 1-5/8" foamed concrete over sheathing.
	  Wood joists and sheathing. 60% vinyl asbestos tile.
	  40% carpet.

CEILING:	Acoustic tile on a suspended ceiling structure.
INTERIOR CONSTRUCTION:	Drywall construction, taped and spackled. Some Good quality hardwood plywood paneling on wood frame. Some concrete block partitions on first floor only. Ceramic tile wainscoting in restrooms. Wood cabinets with a laminated plastic countertop in employees lounge.
HEATING AND COOLING:	For the purpose of this example the building is considered to be in the central district in a moderate climate. It has a Package A. C. system.
ELECTRICAL:	Flex-conduit, typical outlets throughout. Recessed fluorescent fixtures.
PLUMBING:	Includes four restrooms, 8 toilets, 2 urinals, 6 lavatories, 1 kitchen sink, 2 service sinks, 30 gal. electric hot water heater for restrooms and lounge, 2 drinking fountains.
SPRINKLERS:	Fire extinguishers.
ELEVATORS:	One small office elevator with simple call system and push button control, four passenger cab with 2 stops.

Figure 11.2   Two-Story Office Building Description (Courtesy of Marshall and Swift, Los Angeles, California)

The principal difficulty and inaccuracy of the comparative costing method is that—except for large developments—no two buildings are exactly alike in type and quality of construction; and unless adjustments are made to reflect these differences, the margin of possible error may prove too great to make the estimate reliable as a guide to building costs. To minimize errors and to perfect this costing method, square- or cubic-foot cost is calculated for a *standard* or *base* building of a given size, exclusive of land costs, and adjustments are then made for differences in size, perimeter, or shape of building as well as for quality and quantity of features such as extra bathrooms, special flooring, fixtures, equipment, ceiling height, and other exceptional improvements. The application of the modified comparative method of cost estimating is demonstrated in Figure 11.5.

SEGREGATED COST FORM

For subscribers using the **MARSHALL VALUATION SERVICE** *Segregated Cost Method*

1. Subscriber making survey _____ Date _____ Name of Building _____
2. Located at _____ Owner _____

	Section 1 *OFFICE*	Section 2 _____	Section 3 _____
3. Occupancy			
4. Building class and quality . .	Cls. *C* Qual. *GOOD*	Cls. ____ Qual. ____	Cls. ____ Qual. ____
5. No. of stories & height per story .	No. *2* Ht. *13*	No. ____ Ht. ____	No. ____ Ht. ____
6. Age and condition	Age ____ Cond. ____	Age ____ Cond. ____	Age ____ Cond. ____

7. Region: Western _____ Central _✓_ Eastern _____
8. Climate: Mild _____ Moderate _✓_ Extreme _____

COST RANGE RATING NUMBERS							
Low	No 1	Average	No 2	Above Average	No 3	High	No 4

UNIT COSTS

FLOOR AREA COSTS

		NO	SECTION I	NO	SECTION II	NO	SECTION III
9.	Excavation *SITE PREP* @ $.12−2 (*SITE ADJ.− 2 STORIES*)	2	$.06				
10.	Foundation *BEARING* @ $1.35 × 1.02 (*HT.*) × .992 (*MULTI-STORY*)	2	1.37				
11.	Frame						
12.	Floor Structure = $1.44 + 50% *WOOD* = $2.20 + 50% *FOAMED CONC.* = $.29 50% *CONC.* + *VAPOR BARRIER*	3	3.93				
13.	Floor Cover *SEE NOTES*	⅔	2.75				
14.	Ceiling *CANE FIBER* @ $1.09 + *SUSPENDED* @ $1.03	3	2.12				
15.	Interior Construction 80% *FRAME* $0.36 + 20% *MASONRY* $2.80 = $13.16 × 1.05 (*HT.*)	3	3.82				
16.	Plumbing *OFFICE*	2	2.34				
17.	Sprinklers *NONE*						
18.	Heating, Cooling, Ventilating *PACKAGE A/C* = $4.63 × 1.03 (*HT.*)	⅔	4.77				
19.	Electrical *OFFICE*	3	6.67				
20.	_____ Total floor area unit costs move to line 27		$37.83				

WALL COSTS

		NO	SECTION I	NO	SECTION II	NO	SECTION III
21.	Exterior Walls 10" *BRICK* @ $16.13 + *FACE* @ $1.75 + *PILASTER* @ $.79 Move to line 28	3	$18.67				
22.	Wall Ornamentation _____ Move to line 29						

ROOF COSTS

		NO	SECTION I	NO	SECTION II	NO	SECTION III
23.	Roof Structure *WOOD JOIST − WOOD DECK*	3	$4.03				
24.	Roof Cover *BUILT-UP*	3	1.32				
25.	Trusses _____						
26.	_____ Total roof unit costs move total to line 30		$5.35				

FINAL CALCULATIONS

		from line	SECTION I			SECTION II			SECTION III		
			UNIT COST x	AREA =	TOTAL COST	UNIT COST x	AREA =	TOTAL COST	UNIT COST x	AREA =	TOTAL COST
27.	Floor Area Costs .	20	37.83 ×	10,980	$415,373	X	=		X	=	
28.	Exterior Walls . .	21	18.67 ×	8,112	= 151,451	X	=		X	=	
29.	Wall Ornamentation	22	X		=	X	=		X	=	
30.	Roof	26	5.35 ×	5,490	= 29,372	X	=		X	=	
31.	Section Sub Totals				$596,196						
32.	Number of Stories Multiplier		X		1.000	X			X		
33.	Section Totals				$596,196						
34.	Architect's Fees (Sec. 99/2)				1.069						
35.	Current Cost Multiplier (Sec. 99/3) . . .				1.00						
36.	Local Multiplier (Sec. 99/5 thru 8) . . .				1.05						
37.	Final Multiplier (Ln. 34 x Ln. 35 x Ln. 36)				1.122						
38.	Line 37 x Line 33				$668,932						
39.	LUMP SUMS (Ln. 45)				32,423						
40.	REPLACEMENT COST (Ln. 38 + Ln. 39).				$701,355						
41.	Depreciation % (Section 97)										
42.	Depreciation amount (Ln. 41 x Ln. 40) . .										
43.	DEPRECIATED COST (Ln. 40 − Ln. 42) .										

TOTAL OF ALL SECTIONS

44. Replacement Cost $ *701,355* _____ Depreciated Cost _____ Insurable Value _____

FORM 101 (Seg. Cost)   See back of form for drawings and area and insurable value calculations.

Figure 11.3 Unit-in-Place Cost Method (Courtesy of Marshall and Swift, Los Angeles, California)

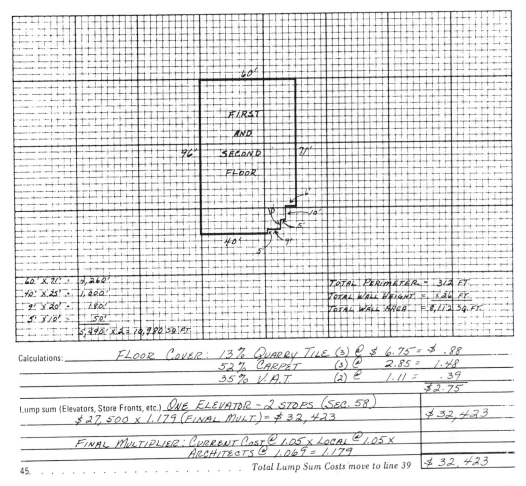

Figure 11.4 Comparative Unit Method (Courtesy of Marshall and Swift, Los Angeles, California)

ESTIMATING THE STANDARD OR BASE HOUSE

Since a comparison with anything in any field is best attained if a reliable standard of measure is available, a base building typical for a given geographic area is selected and priced under the quantity survey or unit-in-place method by competent, reliable, and active builders. Generally, specifications complying with local or state building codes are set up and given to at least two, preferably three, community builders for detailed cost estimating. The several estimates are then analyzed, checked, and correlated into one composite estimate representative of local building costs for the selected base building. The 1,000-square-foot house as described and estimated in Table 11.1 is used for purposes of illustration. Attention is called to the fact that items not normally included in a dwelling's base cost, such as special type of flooring, paneled walls, extra equipment, built-in cabinets, security system, radio-intercom system, and fireplaces, to name a few, must be

OFFICE AND MEDICAL OFFICE BUILDINGS
(CALCULATOR METHOD)

CLASS	TYPE	EXTERIOR WALLS	INTERIOR FINISH	LIGHTING, PLUMBING AND MECHANICAL	HEAT	COST Sq. M.	Cu. Ft.	Sq. Ft.
C	Excellent office	Steel frame, masonry and glass, stone ornamentation, top quality	Plaster, paneling, carpet and terrazzo, suspended ceilings	*Best fluorescent ceiling panels, tiled restrooms, good fixtures	Warm & cool air (zoned)	$ 884.48	$6.85	$82.17
	Good office	Steel frame or bearing walls, brick/conc. panels, some ornamentation	Plaster or drywall, good partitions, acoustic tile, carpet and vinyl	*Good fluorescent lighting, good restrooms and fixtures	Package A.C.	634.65	4.91	58.96
	Average office	Steel or concrete frame, or bearing walls, some trim	Paint, drywall partitions, acoustic tile, asphalt tile	*Fluorescent lighting, adequate outlets and plumbing	Forced air	458.12	3.55	42.56
	Low cost office	Masonry bearing walls, light rafters, very plain	Paint, few low cost partitions, acoustic tile, asphalt tile	Minimum office lighting and plumbing	Wall furnace	315.71	2.44	29.33
	Excellent medical	Steel frame, masonry and glass, ornamentation, top quality	Plaster, paneling, carpet and vinyl tile, acoustic plaster	*Fluorescent panels, air piping, X-ray rooms, good plumbing	Hot & chilled water (zoned)	1,005.36	7.78	93.40
	Good medical	Steel frame, masonry, best concrete panels, ornamentation	Plaster or drywall, good partitions, acoustic tile, carpet and vinyl	*Good fluorescent lighting, X-ray rooms, good plumbing	Warm & cool air (zoned)	763.06	5.91	70.89
	Average medical	Steel or concrete frame, or bearing walls, some trim	Plaster, drywall partitions, acoustic tile, vinyl asbestos	*Adequate lighting and outlets, adequate plumbing	Package A.C.	585.24	4.53	54.37
	Low cost medical	Masonry bearing walls, light rafters, very plain	Paint, cheap partitions, acoustic tile, asphalt tile	Minimum lighting and outlets, adequate plumbing	Forced air	446.81	3.46	41.51
D	Excellent office	Studs or steel columns, bar or web joists, brick or stone veneer	Best plaster, paneling, carpet and vinyl tile	*Fluorescent panels, many outlets, good tiled restrooms	Warm & cool air (zoned)	802.24	6.21	74.53
	Good office	Best stucco on good frame, brick or stone trim, good front	Plaster or drywall, good partitions, acoustic tile, carpet and vinyl	*Good fluorescent lighting, good restrooms and fixtures	Package A.C.	584.27	4.52	54.28
	Average office	Stucco or wood siding on wood studs, some trim	Drywall, acoustic tile, low cost carpet or asphalt tile	Adequate lighting and plumbing	Forced air	428.41	3.32	39.80
	Low cost office	Light stucco or siding on wood studs, very plain	Drywall, few partitions, acoustic tile, asphalt tile	Minimum lighting and plumbing	Wall furnace	299.24	2.32	27.80
	Low cost office	Pole frame, metal siding, lined and insulated	Drywall, few partitions, acoustic tile, asphalt tile	Minimum lighting and plumbing	Wall furnace	266.30	2.06	24.74
	Excellent medical	Studs or steel columns, bar or web joists, brick or stone veneer	Best plaster, paneling, carpet and vinyl tile	*Fluorescent panels, air piping, X-ray rooms, good plumbing	Warm & cool air (zoned)	885.45	6.86	82.26
	Good medical	Best stucco on good frame, good brick or stone trim	Plaster or drywall, good partitions, acoustic tile, carpet and vinyl	*Good fluorescent lighting, X-ray rooms, good plumbing	Warm & cool air (zoned)	708.59	5.49	65.83
	Average medical	Stucco or wood siding on wood studs, some trim	Drywall, acoustic tile, low cost carpet or asphalt tile	Adequate lighting and outlets, adequate plumbing	Package A.C.	537.12	4.16	49.90
	Low cost medical	Light stucco or siding on wood studs, very plain	Drywall, cheap partitions, acoustic tile, asphalt tile	Minimum lighting and outlets, adequate plumbing	Forced air	419.04	3.24	38.93
C-D	Basement offices	Plaster or drywall interior	Average office finish, acoustic tile, vinyl asbestos	Typical office lighting and plumbing	Forced air	341.76	2.65	31.75
	Bsmt. storage	Painted interior	Paint only, few partitions	Minimum lighting, drains	None	145.21	1.12	13.49
	Bsmt. parking	†Unfinished interior	Finished ceiling, concrete floor	Minimum lighting, drains	Ventilation	180.40	1.40	16.76
S	Mezzanine office	Not included	Enclosed, average office finish, acoustic tile soffit	Average office lighting and plumbing	In building cost	265.55	......	24.67
	Mezz, open	Not included	Open, finished floors and soffit	Average lighting, no plumbing	In building cost	147.14		13.67

† For fire-resistant Type I basements, with concrete slab separation under Class C, D or S units, add $2.95 per square foot ($31.75 per square meter).

Add .5% for each story over three, above ground, to all base costs, excluding mezzanines.

MULTISTORY BUILDINGS
*ELEVATORS — Buildings with elevators included in the base costs are marked with an asterisk (*). If none are found, deduct the following from the base costs for buildings on this page which are marked.

MEZZANINES
Do not use story height or area-perimeter multipliers with mezzanine costs.

	Sq. M.	Sq. Ft.		Sq. M.	Sq. Ft.		Sq. M.	Sq. Ft.
Excellent	$26.37	$2.45	Good	$15.61	$1.45	Average	$9.15	$ .85

SPRINKLERS
Add for sprinklers from Section 45.
Basements and mezzanines: add the cost of additional stops from Section 58.

Figure 11.4 (cont.) (Courtesy of Marshall and Swift, Los Angeles, California)

CALCULATOR COST FORM

For subscribers using the **MARSHALL VALUATION SERVICE** *Calculator Cost Method*

SQUARE FOOT COSTS

1. Subscriber making survey_____ Date of survey_____

2. Name of building_____ Owner _____

3. Located at _____

	SECTION I	SECTION II	SECTION III	SECTION IV
4. Occupancy	*OFFICE*			
5. Building class and quality	Cls. *C* Qual. *GOOD*	Cls._____ Qual._____	Cls._____ Qual._____	Cls._____ Qual._____
6. Exterior wall	*FACE BRICK*			
7. No. of stories & height per story.	No. *2* Ht. *13'*	No._____ Ht._____	No._____ Ht._____	No._____ Ht_____
8. Average floor area	*5490 SQ FT.*			
9. Average perimeter	*312 LIN. FT.*			
10. Age and condition	Age_____ Cond._____	Age_____ Cond_____	Age_____ Cond._____	Age_____ Cond_____

11. Region: Western_____ Central___*✓*___ Eastern_____

12. Climate: Mild_____ Moderate___*✓*___ Extreme_____

	SECTION I	SECTION II	SECTION III	SECTION IV
13. **Base Square Foot Cost**	*$ 58.96*			

SQUARE FOOT REFINEMENTS

		SECTION I			
14. Heating, cooling, ventilation	*PACKAGE A/C*	*BASE*			
15. Elevator deduction					
16. Miscellaneous					
17. .... Total lines 13 through 16		*$58.96*			

HEIGHT AND SIZE REFINEMENTS

	SECTION I
18. Number of stories-multiplier	*1.000*
19. Height per story-multiplier (see Line 7)	*1.023*
20. Floor area-perimeter multiplier (see Lines 8 and 9)	*.988*
21. ..... Combined height and size multiplier (Lines 18 x 19 x 20)	*1.011*

FINAL CALCULATIONS

	SECTION I	SECTION II	SECTION III	SECTION IV
22. Refined square foot cost (Line 17 x 21)	*$ 59.61*			
23. Current cost multiplier (Sect. 99 p. 3)	*1.00*			
24. Local multiplier (Sect. 99 p. 5 thru 8)	*1.05*			
25. Final sq. ft. cost (Line 22 x Line 23 x Line 24)..	*$ 62.59*			
26. Area (Back of this form)	*10,980 SQ. FT.*			
27. Line 25 x Line 26	*$ 687,238*			
28. Lump sums (Line 34)				
29. **Replacement Cost** (Line 27 + Line 28)	*$ 687,238*			
30. Depreciation % (Sect. 97)				
31. Depreciation amount (Line 29 x Line 30)				
32. **Depreciated Cost** (Line 29 - Line 31)				

TOTAL OF ALL SECTIONS

33. Replacement cost *$ 687,238*_____ Depreciated cost _____ Insurable value _____

FORM 1003 (Calc. Cost)

Figure 11.5 Comparative Unit Method (Courtesy of Marshall and Swift, Los Angeles, California)

separately priced and added to the basic unit cost at the time when adjustments are made to account for differences between the base or standard house and the subject house under cost study. This is similar to the practice of pricing automobiles where the costs of extras are added to the factory price of a "standard" model as quoted f.o.b. at the factory location.

Variations in unit cost most frequently encountered are caused by the following:

1. Differences in community construction costs and standards.
2. Differences in building size.
3. Quality of design and construction.
4. Added construction cost of built-in features.
5. Built-in fixtures and appliances.

Unit costs per square foot or cubic foot of building construction are generally available for metropolitan areas as well as for principal cities with populations of 100,000 persons or more from individual sources or commercial cost valuation services. For communities of lesser size, or where unit-building cost quotations are unavailable, it is necessary to adjust the best available and most reliable cost index for a given community in accordance with cost differentials known to exist between it and the community in which the subject property is located. As a rule, cost variations are ascribable to differences in wage rates, costs of locally delivered materials, local construction standards, and labor practices enforced in given areas. Assuming a cost average of 1.00 for the United States as a whole, location cost differentials for selected cities have been calculated by the *Marshall Valuation Service* as follows[1]:

Metropolitan area	Local cost modifier	Metropolitan area	Local cost modifier
Atlanta, Ga.	0.93	Jacksonville, Fla.	0.88
Atlantic City, N.J.	1.13	Las Vegas, Nev.	1.12
Augusta, Me.	1.03	Manhattan, N.Y.	1.42
Baltimore, Md.	1.04	Milwaukee, Wis.	1.11
Baton Rouge, La.	0.91	Minneapolis, Minn.	1.12
Bismarck, N.D.	0.98	Montreal, Quebec	1.38
Boston, Mass.	1.23	New Orleans, La.	0.93
Chicago, Ill.	1.18	Oklahoma City, Okla.	0.93
Cleveland, Ohio	1.14	Omaha, Nebr.	0.96
Dallas, Tex.	0.89	Philadelphia, Pa.	1.17
Denver, Colo.	0.98	Portland, Me.	1.05
Detroit, Mich.	1.14	Portland, Ore.	1.06
Flint, Mich.	1.09	Raleigh, N.C.	0.88
Greenville, S.C.	0.85	Richmond, Va.	0.94
Hartford, Conn.	1.20	Sacramento, Calif.	1.16
Indianapolis, Ind.	1.02	Winnipeg, Manitoba	1.39

[1]*Marshall Valuation Service*, Class S, Section 99, April 1991 insert (Los Angeles: Marshall and Swift Publication Company).

ESTIMATING COST NEW OF THE SUBJECT HOUSE

An essential prerequisite to the application of the cost approach is an accurate and detailed word picture of the appraised building and related improvements. Without full and firsthand knowledge of building construction features, it is not possible to compare effectively the subject house with the benchmark house, and to adjust applicable construction unit costs to reflect the differences. To illustrate the application of the comparative unit method of cost estimating where the square footage of building area is accepted as a unit of construction cost, it is assumed that the property under appraisal consists of a building site 100 feet by 125 feet valued by comparison at $20,000, and that the new building improvements are described in Figure 11.6. Based on the building data, the property value under the depreciated cost approach is derived in the following manner:

Depreciated cost approach to value

**Base cost per square foot for benchmark average quality
house, Table 11.1 (1,000 sq ft)**   **$44.42**
**Adjustment for size and shape, subject house[2]
(1,214 sq ft) = 1.03**

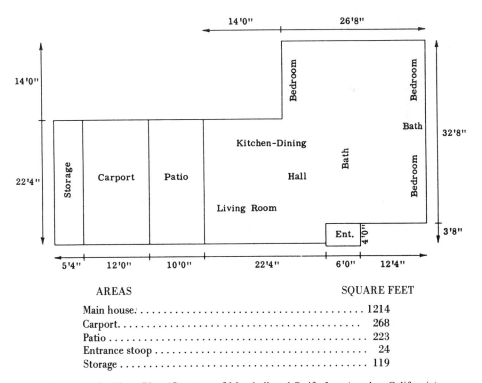

AREAS	SQUARE FEET
Main house.	1214
Carport	268
Patio	223
Entrance stoop	24
Storage	119

Figure 11.6   Floor Plan (Courtesy of Marshall and Swift, Los Angeles, California)

[2]See Table 11.3 for variations in base costs due to building size and shape.

Adjustment for cost variation due to
location = 1.09
Adjusted cost of subject house
$44.42 × 1.12 $49.75

     All cost data are provided to illustrate application of the depreciated cost approach to value (Table 11.2). In practice the appraiser must consult applicable local builders' services or use current national building cost references and adjust these to reflect construction costs. For items not listed, the appraiser should con-

TABLE 11.2   COST ADJUSTMENTS FOR VARIATION FROM STANDARD CONSTRUCTION

Item	Amount
Extra bathroom with full tile	$ 2,025
Sliding glass doors (2)	630
Extra windows, 2 at $195	390
Extra interior doors, 2 at $210	420
Garbage disposal	225
Kitchen exhaust fan and hood	165
Bathroom fan, 8 in.	120
Bath wall heater	360
Built-in bookcase	650
Built-in vanity	415
Double kitchen sink	200
Washing machine connections	375
Extra kitchen cabinets and counter	410
Extra closet	180
Gutters and downspouts	890
Extra construction details and finishes	735
Total extras	$ 8,290
Cost of extras per square foot ($8,290 ÷ 1,214)	$ 683
Adjusted square foot cost—subject house ($49.75 + $6.83)	$ 56.58

Cost calculations

Cost of:	Main house	1,214 sq ft at $56.58	$68,687
	Carport	268 sq ft at $ 8.25	2,211
	Patio	223 sq ft at $ 9.00	2,007
	Entrance	24 sq ft at $20.00	480
	Storage	119 sq ft at $18.25	2,172
	Total costs of improvements		$75,557
Add value:	Venetian blinds		$ 700
	Landscaping		1,250
	Walks and driveway		790
	Land—by comparison		20,000
	Total value via depreciated cost approach[a]		$98,297
	Rounded to $98,300		

[a]No accrued depreciation deducted due to new construction and for simplicity of example.

tact a building contractor or a building supply agency to obtain the missing cost data. Attention is called also to the necessity of adjusting the base cost per square foot of a building to account for variations in building size and shape. The adjustment factor for building floor area and shape is shown in Table 11.3 for dwellings of a rectangular or slightly irregular shape and varying building sizes. The base or standard house, as a rule, is rectangular in shape. Where architectural design calls for an elongated L-type or a ranch-type residence, the extra number of feet of perimeter wall must be reflected in the cost estimate. To illustrate: A structure 20 feet by 20 feet and a structure 40 feet by 10 feet both contain 400 square feet of building area. However, the latter requires 100 feet of perimeter wall as compared with 80 feet of perimeter wall for the former. The cost of the perimeter wall per lineal foot (inclusive of exterior and interior wall finishes) varies depending on the type of construction.

The comparative unit building cost method, as demonstrated, provides a speedy and fairly accurate means for obtaining value estimates for appraisal purposes. Where variations in ceiling heights or building practices necessitate cost quotations on a cubic-foot rather than a square-foot basis, this costing method can be converted by adding the third, or height, dimension and dividing total building costs by the number of cubic-foot units contained in the base house.

With experience and years of appraisal practice, an ever-expanding file of building cost material and construction data can be accumulated. This, as part of the overall appraisal plan, should prove a valuable aid in perfecting appraisal cost estimates. It is important, of course, to keep building construction costs up to date. It is suggested that a check of overall labor and material costs and practices be made at least every six months, or preferably every three months.

TABLE 11.3 SINGLE-FAMILY FLOOR AREA—
SHAPE MULTIPLIERS

Building size (sq ft)	Rectangular or slightly irregular
800	1.085
1,000	1.054
1,200	1.030
1,400	1.009
1,600	0.992
1,800	0.977
2,000	0.964
2,400	0.941
2,800	0.923
3,200	0.907
3,600	0.893
4,000	0.881
4,400	0.870
4,800	0.860

Source: *Marshall Valuation Service* (Los Angeles: Marshall and Swift, February 1991), Sec. 12, p. 13.

From the replacement or reproduction cost estimate, as is the case with existing structures, a deduction must be made for accrued depreciation caused by age, wear and tear, and action of the elements. For a detailed study of the causes of depreciation, and the various methods in use for estimating and accounting purposes, the reader is referred to Chapter 12.

The format of the depreciated cost approach for existing buildings is recommended as outlined in Table 11.4. The example given in Table 11.2 excluded deductions for accrued depreciation for simplicity in introducing this concept.

COST INDEXING METHOD

Some assignments may involve buildings for which it is difficult to estimate the current construction cost. If the original date of construction and the cost of construction are known, the appraiser can index the original cost to the date of appraisal to provide a check on the current replacement or reproduction cost. Care must be exercised in ascertaining the accuracy of the original cost. Cost information provided by building permits usually is inadequate and tends to understate actual costs.

Suppose, for example, that the appraised dwelling was built in 1966 at a cost of $38,360. A check on building cost indexes (usually included in commercial cost service publications) shows that the 1966 index was 385.48; the present index is 1,649.1. Thus, by comparing the two indexes, the present reproduction cost is estimated to be $164,100:

$$\left(\frac{1,649.1}{385.48}\right) \ (\$38,360) = \$164,106$$

TABLE 11.4   COST APPROACH FORMAT

Current reproduction cost: all building improvements inclusive of all direct and indirect costs, including builder's overhead and profit		$_____
Less: Accrued depreciation (see Schedule)		
1. Deferred maintenance	$_____	
2. Incurable physical deterioration, postponed	_____	
3. Incurable loss due to age of structure, incurable	_____	
4. Functional obsolescence, curable	_____	
5. Functional obsolescence, incurable	_____	
6. External obsolescence	_____	
Total accrued depreciation		$_____
Depreciated reproduction cost		_____
Add value: land, by comparison		_____
Landscaping		_____
Walks and drive		_____
Other land improvements (fences, etc.)		_____
Total value via depreciated cost approach		$_____

COMMERCIAL COST SERVICES

The depreciated cost approach, as a measure of value, becomes increasingly tenuous as the size and age of a structure increase. Therefore, this approach is recommended for use primarily as an overall check of the reliability of other market measures of value or where the depreciated cost approach—as is the case with fire insurance or with special-purpose properties—represents the principal if not the only measure of value.

Few appraisers, unless they also are trained cost specialists, contract builders, or construction engineers, are capable of estimating with any degree of accuracy the costs of proposed construction or the replacement costs of complex commercial, industrial, or special-purpose-use structures. In such cases, it is best for an appraiser to rely on comparative cost studies made available on a periodic updated subscription basis by commercial cost services such as the *Boeckh Building Valuation Manual*, published by the American Appraisal Associates, 525 East Michigan Street, Milwaukee, Wisconsin 53201, three volumes covering residential and agricultural, commercial, and industrial and institutional buildings; *Marshall Valuation Service*, published by Marshall and Swift Publication Company, 1617 Beverly Boulevard, P.O. Box 26307, Los Angeles, California 90026–9954, a looseleaf service giving the replacement cost of buildings and improvements; or *Residential Cost Handbook*, also published by Marshall and Swift Publication Company. The latter is a looseleaf presentation of localized square-foot and segregated replacement costs. Both Boeckh and Marshall and Swift offer telephone-accessible computer-based cost routines. The preparation of a single-family-dwelling cost estimate may take less than three minutes. An example of one of these computer printouts is shown in Figure 11.7. In these and other more regional or localized cost services, information typically is published for the following classes of buildings:

Apartments.
Hotels, motels, and clubs.
Offices, banks, and lofts.
Stores and shopping centers.
Warehouses.
Garages and service stations.
Theaters.
Educational and public buildings.
Industrial structures.
Hospitals and churches.
Restaurants, bowling alleys, and stadiums.
Other special-purpose buildings.

The commercial cost units generally are quoted on a base cost (i.e., cubic foot) basis exclusive of foundation and excavation costs and exclusive of architects' fees and builders' overhead and profit allowances. The latter costs generally range from 15 to 20 percent of the quoted base costs, which must be further adjusted to reflect local conditions, which vary due to differences in labor, material,

AMERICAN APPRAISAL ASSOCIATES, INC

06/19/91

POLICY NUMBER: 12345   12/91
PROPERTY OWNER: MR. J.J. JONES COST AS OF: 3/91
PROPERTY ADDRESS: 4321 AMERICAN AVENUE #006860
        HOMETOWN, WI 53200

RESIDENCE DESCRIPTION
 CONSTRUCTION: CLASS C 100%
 # OF STORIES: 1-STORY   100%
 OCCUPANCY: SINGLE-FAMILY
 EXTERIOR WALL: CATEGORY I 50% CATEGORY II 50%
 AREA: 2100 SQUARE FEET OF GROUND FLOOR AREA
 BASEMENT: 2100 SQUARE FEET

BASE RESIDENCE WALL CATEGORY I,II	70,350
ADD FOR BASEMENT	7,830
BASE RESIDENCE COST	78,180
AREA/PERIMETER RATIO FACTOR	1.00
ADJUSTED BASE RESIDENCE COST	78,180

ADDITIONAL FEATURES
DECK	1,400
FIREPLACE	2,575
HALF BATH	850
FULL BATH	1,850
GARAGE(S)	7,600
AIR CONDITIONING	3,150
CUSTOM BUILT-INS	2,850

   COUNTER COOKTOP, OVEN, BATHROOM HEATER
   POWER ATTIC VENTILATOR
   SECURITY AND FIRE ALARM

TOTAL ADDITIONAL FEATURES	20,275

TOTAL BASE COST	98,455
CLASS-LOCATION MULTIPLIER	1.59
LOCAL REPLACEMENT COST NEW	156,543
TOTAL	156,543

INSURED AMOUNT	150,000
% OF INSURANCE TO REPLACEMENT COST NEW	96%

BOECKH SYSTEM, A PRODUCT OF AMERICAN APPRAISAL ASSOCI-
ATES, INC.

ABOVE COSTS INCLUDE LABOR AND MATERIAL, NORMAL PROFIT
AND OVERHEAD AS OF DATE OF REPORT. COSTS REPRESENT GEN-
ERAL ESTIMATES NOT TO BE CONSIDERED A DETAILED QUANTITY
SURVEY.

Figure 11.7 Computerized Building Cost Estimate (Courtesy of BOECKH, an operating
unit of American Appraisal Associates, Inc., Milwaukee, Wisconsin)

sales tax, insurance and finance costs, and building construction regulations. It is possible to obtain these cost data from computerized services, saving the appraiser considerable time. Nevertheless, the appraiser must check the figures for reasonableness.

It is deemed a "must" that every appraiser subscribe to at least one major cost service, and further subscribe to a competent market newsletter or economic business publication that keeps the appraiser informed of national and state laws and general market conditions which may have an impact on building construction costs.

Building cost services, at best, serve as a guide to the establishment of replacement costs when the building is in "new" condition. The difficult task of estimating accrued depreciation remains a major valuation task. For a more detailed study of the causes and measures of accrued depreciation, the reader is referred to Chapter 12.

SUMMARY

The steps involved in the depreciated cost approach are as follows:

1. Estimate the highest and best use of the site.
2. Find the present cost of replacing or reproducing the building(s).
3. Estimate the total dollar amount of accrued depreciation from all causes.
4. Subtract the dollar amount of accrued depreciation from the present reproduction or replacement cost.
5. Estimate the depreciated cost of any minor buildings and other on-site improvements.
6. Add the site value to the depreciated cost of the building(s) and other on-site improvements.

The depreciated cost approach has both advantages as well as disadvantages. The advantages are as follows. (1) By having thoroughly inspected a property and analyzed its accrued depreciation, an appraiser can better use the other two approaches to value. (2) It can be used to estimate the financial feasibility of a proposed property. (3) It provides a separate value estimate of building value. (4) It can provide an indication of value for special-purpose properties. (5) It can assist in making value adjustments for building components.

Its disadvantages are as follows. (1) It requires great effort in maintaining current cost data and in accounting for various elements of accrued depreciation. (2) It does not provide an independent measure of market value. (3) It is not well suited for old buildings. (4) It can be overly complicated with results backed up solely by "the appraiser's experience."

Cost and value differ. *Cost* is the amount of money necessary to acquire or to create an item, whereas *value* represents its worth. Cost can be broken down into direct and indirect components. *Direct costs* include labor and materials, whereas *indirect costs* include professional services, finance charges, and real estate taxes.

The two types of construction costs are replacement and reproduction. *Replacement cost* is the current cost of building a structure that provides functional utility equal to the building being appraised and built with modern materials and according to current standards. *Reproduction cost* is the cost of building an appraised structure in a manner that replicates the materials, design, layout, and quality of workmanship.

The four principal cost estimating methods are (1) quantity survey method, (2) unit-in-place method, (3) comparative unit method, and (4) cost indexing method.

The *quantity survey method* of cost estimating is the most comprehensive and detailed method. The typical appraiser prefers simpler, less time-consuming methods.

The *unit-in-place construction method*, also called the segregated method, permits appraisers to give separate attention to each of the three major building components with relative ease and accurate results. These three building components are: floor, outside wall, and roof. Computing costs in this manner is simpler for appraisers to prepare and more readily understood by clients than the quantity survey method.

The *comparative unit method* is used almost exclusively by appraisers and by builders and architects when cost estimates are needed quickly. Under this method, the applicable unit cost per square or cubic foot of a building is derived by dividing the total building costs of similar structures recently completed by the number of square or cubic feet contained within the exterior wall dimensions of the building's structural surfaces.

Variations in unit cost contained in national cost manuals and local costs frequently are caused by (1) differences in community construction costs and standards, (2) differences in building size, (3) quality of design and construction, (4) added construction cost of built-in features, and (5) built-in fixtures and appliances.

The *cost indexing method* is applicable when the original date of construction and the cost of construction are known. The present cost new of the appraised building is estimated by comparing the ratio of the original cost index to the current index and then multiplying the answer by the original construction cost.

REVIEW QUESTIONS

1. Briefly explain how the estimation of a site's highest and best use relates to the estimated depreciated cost of the building.
2. (a) List the single most important advantage and disadvantage of the depreciated cost approach.
   (b) Explain your reasoning for these choices.

3. Give a short definition of accrued depreciation.

4. What is the principal difference between direct and indirect construction costs?

5. Give the respective advantages of replacement and reproduction costs.

6. List one advantage and one disadvantage of each of the four methods of estimating the current construction cost of a building.

READING AND STUDY REFERENCES

American Institute of Real Estate Appraisers. Chapter 16, "Building Cost Estimates," *The Appraisal of Real Estate*. Chicago: AIREA, 1987.

DERBES, MAX J., JR. "Is the Cost Approach Obsolete?" *The Appraisal Journal* 50, no. 4 (October 1982), pp. 581–590.

ENTREKEN, HENRY C., JR., and STEVEN D. KAPPLIN. "More Applications of the Cost Approach," *The Real Estate Appraiser* 43, no. 6 (November–December 1977), pp. 13–15.

SACKMAN, JULIUS L. "The Limitations of the Cost Approach," *The Appraisal Journal* 36, no. 1 (January 1968), pp. 53–63.

TREADWELL, DONALD H. "Replacement of What?" *The Appraisal Journal* 58, no. 2 (April 1990), pp. 239–248.

ZIMMERMAN, PAUL. "Reproduction Cost New Is "Cute," *The Real Estate Appraiser* 40, no. 4 (July–August 1974), pp. 43–47.

12
The Depreciated Cost Approach: Measuring Accrued Depreciation

___

Learning Objectives

After reading this chapter, you should be able to:

- Define and give examples of each of the forms of accrued depreciation
- Distinguish between accrued depreciation and amortization
- Understand the difference between economic life and physical life
- Compute accrued depreciation using several different methods

A *loss* in value—from any cause—as measured by the difference between replacement (or reproduction) cost new of a property in current dollars and the market value of the same property is classed as *accrued depreciation*. In fact, it is possible that a property may appreciate rather than depreciate, as is the case when abnormal scarcity exacts a market premium for possession or where uniqueness (classification as antique) makes the property a collector's item. Appreciation may also be apparent, rather than real, where inflation has diminished the purchasing power of the dollar. Nevertheless, appreciation is the exception rather than the rule and its causes and measures will not be dealt with in this chapter.

In appraisal practice, it is an established maxim that an estimate of value via the depreciated cost approach is no more accurate than the underlying estimate of depreciation through which measures of cost are converted into measures of value. The difficulties encountered in obtaining accurate dollar expressions of accrued depreciation are generally based on lack of sound appraisal judgment, faulty cost estimate, incorrect methodology, or insufficient research essential to an evaluation of the causes of a loss in value of a given property at a specific time and place. Judgment is a subjective mental attitude difficult to teach and which generally must be developed through experience and maturation of thinking. In this chapter an attempt is made to outline and discuss the theory underlying the causes of accrued depreciation and to explain and demonstrate the methods most suitable in measuring the resultant losses in value.

DEPRECIATION VERSUS AMORTIZATION

It is the appraiser's task to estimate the amount of accrued depreciation without concern as to whether depreciation reserves have been established to compensate the owner for losses in the value of the original investment. It is on this point that recognition should be given to the differences in the functions of, and the responsibilities assumed by, the accountant versus the appraiser. The accountant, with the aid of effective bookkeeping, traces and records the *history* of dollar expenditures for capital outlays and those spent for maintenance and operation of an enterprise or property. The accountant is principally concerned with the *original cost*, and his or her interest in value (in current dollars) is, as a rule, incidental and secondary. The appraiser, on the other hand, is principally interested in the *present worth* of future rights to income which flow from the productive use of the subject property. The original or historical cost of the property are data that may be gathered by the appraiser in order to be fully informed, but the importance of such data is secondary, if not negligible, in the valuation process. What someone pays for a property may or may not be equivalent to value. In fact, the property may have been given to the present owner, purchased at a token price from a friend or a relative, or bought so long ago at a price that bears little relation to the property's present market value.

Once an estimate of value is ascertained and certified to by an appraiser, his or her task, generally, is completed. The accountant may take over from here to check the book value against the market value reported by the appraiser, and to make or recommend changes in accounting procedure to accelerate or decelerate depreciation reserve provisions.

It would prove less confusing and contribute to greater clarity of thinking if in practice and in literature all reference to reserve provisions for the recapture of investment capital were classified as *amortization* rather than *depreciation*. The term "future depreciation" is a misnomer. The best that one can do is provide for the recapture of anticipated value losses in accordance with a preselected schedule of capital amortization, which at the investment rate of interest will equal in amount the replacement cost of the subject property at the end of its economic life. A schedule of amortization of an investment of $50,000 over an economic investment life of 30 years is illustrated in Appendix V. The cumulative amount of capital recapture, computed at an investment interest rate of 10 percent, represents at the end of a given period of years depreciation as an amount or *book depreciation* derived under the annuity or debt amortization method, as will be explained more fully later. This concept may be applied to the systematic reduction of mortgage debt or in structuring lease payments for retiring a capital investment. The computation of accrued depreciation at any given time first necessitates an estimation of value. Thus, if we know that the present replacement cost of a residential property is $100,000, and that market sales of like properties in "as is" condition are $75,000, accrued depreciation is found to be $25,000 or 25 percent ($100,000–$75,000/$100,000).

It is important to recognize that accrued depreciation is a loss in market value from *all* causes and that this loss, measured in a lump sum, is automatically reflected in the prices that similar properties sell for in the open market. The same holds true when value is derived under the capitalized income approach. Old properties, as a rule, produce less net operating income than like properties when in new condition. The income from old properties, too, must be capitalized at a higher rate. As in the sales comparison approach, the difference between the dollar amount as represented by present replacement cost and the value derived by capitalization of income for the property in an "as is" condition measures the loss in value (accrued depreciation) from all causes. Thus, under the sales comparison and capitalized income approaches to value, the appraiser is freed from the responsibility of making a separate estimate of accrued depreciation. The market, through lower prices and reduced rental income, automatically reflects the property's diminished utility from all causes, be they age, wear and tear, actions of natural or synthetic elements, or functional or external obsolescence. Only under the depreciated cost approach to value is the appraiser compelled to estimate independently and directly the amounts ascribable to the various causes that have lessened value as a result of age, and so on. For this reason the cost approach is deemed the least accurate measure of value. The accuracy of the depreciated cost approach in fact is no more reliable than the appraiser's measure of accrued depreciation as revealed by a rigorous analysis of pertinent market influences.

DEPRECIATION THEORY

Accrued depreciation is defined as a loss in value from any cause. The principal causes are recognized as follows[1]:

1. Physical deterioration.
2. Functional obsolescence.
3. External obsolescence.

These causes may be further subclassified for purposes of identification as follows:

Physical Deterioration

1. Wear and tear through use.
2. Action of the elements (including the ravages of storms and extreme temperatures), age, and destruction by termites and other wood-boring insects.

---

[1]A more detailed list of the causes of accrued depreciation is given in Table 12.1. Most of these items are based on a speech by Robert V. McCurdy, MAI, CRE in Atlantic City, New Jersey, in 1958. The source of this list is William S. Harps, Chapter 28, "Depreciated Cost Approach to Value," in *The Real Estate Handbook*, 2nd ed., Maury Seldin and James H. Boykin, eds. (Homewood, Ill.: Dow Jones-Irwin, 1990), pp. 479–80.

3. Structural impairment through neglect, fire, water, explosion, and vandalism.

Functional Obsolescence

1. *Faulty design.* Ceilings too high or too low; improper location of kitchen, bathroom, bedrooms, and other rooms; wasted space; and general disutility arising from poor floor planning.
2. *Inadequacy of structural facilities.* Ceilings and walls not insulated; inadequate wiring, plumbing, heating, fenestration, and other functional deficiencies which limit effective utilization of the property as a whole.
3. *Superadequacy of structural facilities.* Oversized heating or cooling systems; oversized plumbing and electric wiring; excessive number of closets, bathrooms, and built-in facilities; and exterior walls built in excess of normal structural or safety standards.
4. *Outmoded equipment.* Old-fashioned cast-iron tub and kitchen sink; exposed wiring and plumbing; coal-burning kitchen stove; undersized water heater; and expensive-to-operate air conditioning system.

External Obsolescence

1. *Neighborhood hazards and nuisances.* Heavy traffic flow, smoke, dust, noise, offensive odors, or incompatible land uses.
2. *Down zoning and reduced highest and best land uses.* Lower land uses and less valuable zoning regulations impair utility of use and ownership.
3. *Over- or underimprovement of land.* A $200,000 home in a $100,000 neighborhood or a $100,000 home in a $200,000 neighborhood lessen overall property value as a result of violation of prevailing site (land)-to-property value ratios.
4. *Decreasing demand.* Population shifts, depression, periods of overbuilding, or other economic factors that lessen demand as reflected in lower property values.

ECONOMIC LIFE VERSUS PHYSICAL LIFE

An economically productive property must produce an income over and above the expenditures necessary to operate and maintain the property. In turn, when a property ceases to be productive, it may have reached the end of its economic life. A structure thus may conceivably be physically sound but economically dead and constitute a financial burden on the land on which it rests. In dynamic societies, more properties are torn down to make room for more economically productive replacements than fall down.

Economic life is the productive life of a building measured from when it was built to when it economically encumbers the site and its optimum use. That is, at the end of a building's economic life, the building has no value and its presence actually reduces the site's value. Typically, the economic life of a well-constructed improvement will vary from 50 to 60 years. It is true that many buildings reach chronological ages well beyond that age figure, but experience discloses that most buildings at the ripe old age of 50 years either must be demolished or modernized and generally rejuvenated to warrant their continued existence. Capital improvements generally extend the remaining economic life of a building or, conversely, lower its effective age. Properties with identical chronological age may differ significantly in their effective age depending on quality of construction, maintenance practice, operational care, and expenditures made for capital improvements or modernization. Thus it may be concluded that the *effective age* of a building is based partly on its actual age, but more importantly, on its comparative utility, physical condition, and expected remaining life expectancy. These determinants of effective age are based on other similar properties. If, for example, the appraised property has been unusually well maintained, is in an appealing neighborhood, or if it has been renovated, its actual age could be 40 years, but its effective age is only 25 years. The converse is true of a building that has suffered hard use or been neglected. A term used to describe a building's remaining productive life is *remaining economic life* (REL).

To determine the effective age on which calculations of accrued depreciation are based, the appraiser subtracts from the total (typical) economic life for the appraised building his or her estimate of the remaining economic life over which the structure is deemed to be productive. This estimate, as a rule, is derived after careful field inspection and a conclusion of the present condition of the building.

To illustrate: Assuming a total economic life of 50 years and an estimated remaining economic life of 35 years[2], the effective age is judged to be 15 years. These age relationships are shown as follows:

Total expected economic building life	50 years
Remaining (estimated) economic building life	35 years
Effective age of building	15 years

In using the effective age to estimate accrued depreciation, it should be noted that in its simplest form, this method accounts for all forms of physical deterioration and obsolescence. For example, suppose that the reproduction cost of a building is $140,000, the remaining economic life is 26 years, the total economic life is judged to be 45 years and the difference of 19 years is the effective age. Then the total accrued depreciation is computed as follows:

$$(\$140,000)(19/45) = \underline{\underline{\$59,111}}$$

The actual or chronological age of the structure is, of course, of interest to the appraiser. The *physical* or *actual life* of a building is simply the time that has passed from the date of its completion to the date of the appraisal. For instance,

[2]The remaining economic life can also be measured by the period over which a competitive net return is received by typical real estate investors. Actions of such investors in how long they allow buildings to continue in productive service is far more significant than how they may claim they will act.

judgment based on field study supports an effective age of 15 years, but building history may disclose a chronological age of 30 years. In this case, structural improvements may have been added or substantial rehabilitation must have taken place.[3] *Chronological age*,[4] too, is important in calculating structural decrepitude resulting from wear and aging of the building's supporting structures, and for estimating the effective age of component building parts such as roof covering, plumbing, electrical wiring, and heating equipment—which have a limited service life, generally shorter than the remaining economic life of the property as a whole, and for which a replacement reserve must be established under the category "physical deterioration: deferred curable," as demonstrated later.

There are three principal methods of measuring accrued depreciation:

1. The economic age-life method.
2. The breakdown, or observed condition, method.
3. The market extracted method.

Each of these methods is discussed in the remainder of this chapter.

ECONOMIC AGE-LIFE METHOD

The *economic age-life method* of estimating accrued depreciation is based upon establishing a ratio between the effective age and the total economic life of improvements. Having done this, the ratio is then multiplied by either the replacement or reproduction cost new of the building improvements at the date of appraisal:

$$\frac{\text{Effective age}}{\text{Total economic life}} \times \text{Replacement or reproduction cost}$$

Using numbers, this method is utilized as shown in Table 12.1.

[3]An alternative technique for estimating the actual age of a building depicts the age of the original section of a building plus any subsequent additions. This method, called the *weighted average age* method, lists the ages of each of a building's various sections, and assigns a weight in proportion to the ratio of that section's area to the building's total area. It is uniform, objective, and simple in comparison to the effective age method and can also be used in the sales comparison method. An example of this method, taken from James H. Boykin, *Industrial Potential of the Central City* (Washington, D.C.: Urban Land Institute, 1973), pp. 27–29, follows:

(a) Year section completed	(b) Age of section	(c) Area of section (sq ft)	(d) Ratio of section to building area	(e) Weighted age of each section (b) × (d)
1930	60	10,000	0.22	13.20
1980	10	25,000	0.56	5.60
1985	5	10,000	0.22	1.10
Total area		45,000	1.00	19.90 or
Weighted average age of building as of 1990				20 years

[4]Physical, chronological, and actual age are interchangeable terms.

TABLE 12.1 DEPRECIATED COST APPROACH VIA AGE-LIFE METHOD

Total economic life	50 years	
Effective age	15 years	
Remaining economic life	35 years	
Replacement cost new	$110,000	
Less accrued depreciation (15/50 = 30%)	33,000	
Depreciated cost of improvements		$77,000
Add: Land value by market comparison		18,000
Walks and driveway		1,000
Landscaping		700
Total indicated value via age-life method depreciation approach		$96,700

This method offers the advantages of simplicity and adaptability to a wide variety of property classifications. However, it has some drawbacks, including: it is based on economic life and effective age—both being difficult to estimate accurately; it relies solely on a straight-line pattern of accrued depreciation; it uses an overall rather than component measure of depreciation; and it fails to distinguish either between curable or incurable obsolescence or short-life or long-life structural components.

The economic age-life method concept provides the basis for measuring physical deterioration-incurable in the breakdown method (Tables 12.3 and 12.4). Additionally, it is refined under the modified economic age-life method. The *modified economic age-life method* provides an estimate of accrued depreciation by applying a ratio of effective age to total economic life times cost new of improvements—after having deducted value loss from curable physical deterioration and functional obsolescence (see Table 12.3). This modified method offers the principal advantage of reflecting the behavior of most sellers who would correct such building deficiencies prior to selling a property. Also, the cost of correcting these curable deficiencies usually can be estimated rather accurately. It suffers the same drawbacks as previously discussed about the economic age-life method. An example of this modified method is given in Table 12.2 and is based on the same data as contained in Table 12.1.

THE BREAKDOWN, OR OBSERVED CONDITION, METHOD

The *breakdown*, or *observed condition*, method is so named because (1) under this method each component of accrued depreciation is separately broken down, measured, and deducted from the cost new of a structure, and (2) field inspection and observation are essential in the gathering of depreciation data. The breakdown method is an *applied* method that yields informative and accurate results if professionally compiled. Under this method the causes of depreciation are analyzed as shown in Table 12.3.

TABLE 12.2   DEPRECIATED COST APPROACH VIA MODIFIED AGE-LIFE METHOD

Replacement cost new		$110,000
Less: Physical deterioration-curable	$1,250	
Functional obsolescence-curable	1,050	2,300
Depreciated cost after allowance for curable items		$107,700
Less accrued depreciation after allowance for physical and functional		
curable (15/50=30% × $107,700)		32,310
Depreciated cost of improvements		$ 75,390
Add: Land value by market comparison		18,000
Walks and driveway		1,000
Landscaping		700
Total value by modified age-life depreciation method		$ 95,090

The forms of accrued depreciation measured under the breakdown method are:

1. Physical deterioration
   a. Curable
      (1) Deferred maintenance
      (2) Curable postponed
   b. Incurable
2. Functional obsolescence
   a. Curable
   b. Incurable
3. External Obsolescence
   a. Incurable

Physical Deterioration-Curable

Under this heading, based on careful and detailed inspection, a listing is made of all deferred maintenance and repairs necessary to bring the structure into first-class operating order. The test of curability is based on (1) the necessity to cure defects to provide for efficient (economical) operation, and (2) the cost to cure relative to value added or the increase in net operating income for the property as a whole. Provision is also made for depreciation reserves necessary to cover anticipated expenditures for capital items and major units of maintenance which must be replaced or refurbished periodically. The latter items include heating system, roofing, plumbing, electrical wiring, periodic painting, appliances, and refinishing of exterior and interior surfaces. Prices for maintenance and repair work need to be obtained from service personnel and subcontractors who typically engage in this type of work. (For illustration of this and other sections of the observed depreciation schedules, see Table 12.6.) In addition to deferred maintenance which requires immediate attention, another form of curable physical deterioration is *curable postponed*. This depreciation is calculated as a percentage of cost new and measured by the economic age-life method.

TABLE 12.3 CLASSIFICATION OF DEPRECIATION AND OBSOLESCENCE

Physical-curable[a]
  Worn roof covering
  Rusted downspouts and gutters
  Broken or worn walks and drives
  Poor maintenance of exterior walls
  Worn trim
  Worn floors
  Worn wall finish
  Worn trim finish
  Worn bath fixtures
  Worn kitchen fixtures
  Worn plumbing and water supplies
  Worn and overaged heating and ventilating equipment
  Worn electrical switches and fixtures
  Cracked basement floor
  Badly maintained garage
  General wear and tear that is economically curable
Physical-incurable
  Loss in value resulting from the wearing out of irreplaceable items
  Damage to concealed foundations, exterior walls, load-bearing members of roof
  Structural defects
Functional obsolescence-curable[a]
  Crack or failure in foundations having other causes than structural defects or poor
    workmanship
  Undersized and weak roof members
  Insufficient downspouts and gutters
  Walks and drives not in place or insufficient
  Inadequacy or absence of baths
  Obsolete bath fixtures
  Fixtures or finish below neighborhood standards
  Poor kitchen layout
  Inadequate kitchen cabinets
  Obsolete kitchen fixtures
  Obsolete plumbing and water supply system
  Inadequate plumbing and water supply system
  Inadequate or insufficient heating and ventilating
  Obsolete heating and ventilating system
  Inadequate electrical wiring
  Outdated electrical fixtures
  Insufficient electrical service
Functional obsolescence-incurable
  Oversized foundations
  Cracked foundations
  Oversized roof members
  Column spaces too narrow for efficient parking layout
  Halls too narrow (may be curable)
  Inadequate or no insulation (may be curable)
  Roof covering substantially better than those of neighborhood
  Roof covering substantially worse than those of neighborhood
  Eccentric trim
  Poor workmanship in halls
  Poor workmanship in structural framing, oversized or undersized structural framing
  Oversized, undersized, or poor workmanship in floor and roof slabs

Overimprovement or poor quality of workmanship in finished floor
Poor quality and workmanship in walls
Poor quality and workmanship in trim
Bath fixtures above neighborhood standard
Kitchen equipment above neighborhood standard
Plumbing and water supply system above neighborhood standard
Superadequacy in heating and ventilating
Superadequacy in electrical wiring
Garage too small or superadequate
Architecture poor or unusual—bad floor plan, excessive ceiling height, poor plot plan
Overadequacy or underadequacy of capacity of plant
Excessive wall thickness
Any functional characteristic of a building which has become nonfunctional by
    reason of new materials or products such as double pane or thermal windows,
    new techniques, or decreased costs
External obsolescence
Structural overimprovement or underimprovement for neighborhood
Nuisances such as smoke, dirt, noise, odor, traffic, zoning, change in use, rent control,
    excessive taxes, and inadequate transportation, shopping, schools, and parks
Local, regional, and national legislation
Changes in economic conditions such as overbuilt apartment market

---

[a]These items are curable only if economically justified. Therefore, economic feasibility is the crucial test, not physical possibility.

Physical Deterioration-Incurable

Under this part of the depreciation estimate, an attempt is made to measure the accrued loss in dollars due to wear and tear of long-lived structural load-bearing parts of the building improvements. Since the supporting parts of a structure such as footings, foundations, and supporting walls and partitions are economically as well as mechanically incurable (without tearing down the building), the appraiser must establish a pro rata estimate of the expired portions of the various substructures in relation to their total unit replacement cost—in place. This can be accomplished by one of two alternative suggested methods:

1. The overall component value method.
2. The individual component value method.

    Under the overall component value method, the appraiser applies the estimated accrued percentage loss of the substructural component parts to the replacement cost estimate of such parts as shown in Table 12.4.

    The individual component method is similar to the preceding method except that it applies a depreciation rate to each of the components considered. Often, this method is applied only to short-lived items of a structure. Examples are roofing, carpeting, electrical, plumbing, and the mechanical parts of heating and air-conditioning systems. Using the previous information plus data on short-lived items, this method might appear as shown in Table 12.5. The total physical deterioration is higher in Table 12.5 than in 12.4 because three short-lived items are included in the latter table.

TABLE 12.4 OVERALL COMPONENT VALUE METHOD

Component-structural parts	Replacement cost	
Excavation	$ 2,400	
Footings	4,800	
Walls	19,800	
Partitions	7,200	
Roof construction	4,200	
Beams and joints	5,700	
Piers	1,320	
Total		$45,420
Add: 8% architectural costs		3,634
12% overhead and profit		5,450
Total components replacement costs		$54,504
Estimated observed incurable physical depreciation 15%[a]		8,176

[a]Based on ratio of effective age to normal life span of building improvements (9 years/60 years).

As demonstrated, the overall and individual component value methods of measuring accrued physical deterioration-incurable can be effectively applied as measures of physical-incurable depreciation.[5]

Functional Obsolescence-Curable

Under this heading, the appraiser lists recommended modernization and improvements which are essential and economically justified (or feasible) and which would be found in a new and comparable building. Into this category generally fall expenditures for modernization of bathrooms, kitchen, insulation, central heating, additional closets, and other built-in fixtures. Whether such improvements are warranted, and thus curable, depends on market demand and on compliance with the principle of contribution. Cost estimates to modernize items are obtained from building contractors or subcontractors who specialize in the areas of construction involved. Care must be taken not to duplicate estimated outlays. If, for instance, it is considered that the bathroom and kitchen require modernization, and the cost of painting and decorating these rooms is included in the modernization estimate, this expenditure must be excluded from physical deterioration-curable, under which category repainting of the entire structure may have been called for.

Functional Obsolescence-Incurable

This item of the depreciation schedule rests heavily on the application of sound appraisal judgment. An attempt is made here to reflect the sales resistance en-

[5]Whichever computational process is employed for measuring incurable physical deterioration, great care must be taken in the estimation of the total as well as the remaining economic life of the improvements that are being appraised.

TABLE 12.5   INDIVIDUAL COMPONENT VALUE METHOD

Component-structural parts	Replacement cost	Effective age	Normal life span	Deterioration percent	Deterioration dollars
Excavation	$ 2,400	9	60	15	$ 360
Footings	4,800	9	60	15	720
Walls	19,800	9	60	15	2,970
Partitions	7,200	9	60	15	1,080
Roof construction	4,200	9	60	15	630
Beams and joists	5,700	9	60	15	856
Piers	1,320	9	60	15	198
Roof cover	2,900	10	20	50	1,450
Heating–air conditioning	7,200	8	15	53	3,816
Carpeting	4,000	10	12	83	3,320
Total replacement cost	$59,520[a]				
Total physical deterioration-incurable					$15,400

[a]Architectural costs and overhead and profit omitted for simplicity.

countered from typical buyers as a result of flaws deemed economically incurable such as poor floor planning, lack of privacy, or low ceilings. This sales resistance is generally measured either in rounded dollars—$100, $500, $1,000, and so on—or as a percentage of total replacement costs new—1 percent, 5 percent, 10 percent, and so on.

The test of whether a structural component suffers from incurable rather than curable functional obsolescence is the economic feasibility of taking such corrective measures.

External Obsolescence-Incurable

Losses resulting from external obsolescence are always caused by forces outside of the structure but within the immediate market environment of the property. Since the typical property owner cannot control these outside forces, the resultant losses are classified as "incurable." The economic loss ascribable to the subject location, as compared with a neighborhood free from such environmental hazards or nuisances, is determined by capitalizing the actual or estimated rental loss through the use of a rent multiplier for residential buildings (see Chapter 9) or through the use of the capitalization process for income-producing properties as explained in Chapter 17. Since the estimated depreciation should aggregate losses ascribable only to the building improvements, care must be taken to exclude losses attributable to the land. This is accomplished by multiplying the capitalized income loss (depreciation) resulting from external forces by the typical ratio that building improvements bear to the value of the property as a whole, including the land. To do otherwise would penalize the land twice—once here and then again under the market comparison approach to land value, under which the external hazard or nuisance would also be reflected. For application of the depreciation procedure to reflect external obsolescence, see the demonstration schedule in Table 12.6.

MARKET EXTRACTED DEPRECIATION

This method accounts for all aspects of accrued depreciation. It might be argued that it is not as precise as the engineering breakdown method. However, in reality it is probably as accurate but offers the advantage of being market derived and easily understood by clients. This method is particularly well adapted to larger projects where a greater number of similar properties are being appraised.

The steps in this method are outlined as follows:

1. Locate, thoroughly inspect, and confirm sale prices of comparable improved properties.
2. By use of lot sales, estimate the value of each underlying site; this value is deducted along with the estimated value of minor site improvements (step 1 less step 2).
3. Compute the area of each sale building and then estimate the current reproduction (or replacement) cost.
4. Deduct the sale price allocated to the building from the current construction cost; this difference is the total accrued depreciation.
5. Divide the total accrued depreciation by the reproduction (or replacement) cost of the building to find the overall rate of depreciation.
6. Divide the overall accrued depreciation rate by the physical age to give the annual rate of depreciation. This annualized depreciation should be applied only to properties of similar age and physical characteristics.

TABLE 12.6 DEMONSTRATION SCHEDULE OF THE BREAKDOWN METHOD FOR MEASURING ACCRUED DEPRECIATION

Building statistics based on field observation indicate the following:		
Effective age	15 years	
Remaining economic life	35 years	
Replacement cost—new	$110,000	
Physical deterioration		
Curable		
Deferred maintenance		
Exterior painting	$ 1,800	
Repair porch screening	240	
Paint kitchen, bath, and hall	720	
Scrape and refinish floors	810	
Replace vinyl floor covering in kitchen	480	
Total deferred maintenance		$ 4,050

Postponed

Roof shingles 20% of $2,100	$ 420	
Interior painting 40% of $1,500	600	
Heating unit 40% of $2,250	900	
Plumbing and wiring 20% of $3,600	720	
Total postponed curable deterioration	$ 2,640	

Incurable

Based on overall component method (Table 12.4)	$ 8,176	
Total physical deterioration		$14,866

Functional obsolescence

Curable

Modernize bathroom (exclusive of painting)	$ 1,320	
Insulate ceiling	690	
Total functional-curable	$ 2,010	

Incurable

Sales resistance due to low 7.5-foot ceilings and poor floor plan (lack of privacy in bedroom areas); building value loss, measured via rent loss allocated to building (130 GIM × $100) (80%)

Total functional incurable	10,400	
Total functional obsolesence		$12,410

External obsolescence

Incurable

Rental loss due to heavy traffic and road hazards and noise $90 per month, $90 times monthly rent multiplier for area = $90 × 130 = $11,700
Ratio of land value to property value is 20%. Loss of rental value attributable to building is 80% of $11,700

	9,360
Total estimate of accrued depreciation	$36,636
Percentage accrued depreciation $36,636 ÷ $110,000	33.31%

Value via depreciated cost approach

Estimated replacement cost new (buildings)	$110,000	
Less accrued depreciation	36,636	
Depreciated replacement cost		$73,364
Add: Land value by market comparison		18,000
Walks and driveway		1,000
Landscaping		700
Total value via depreciated cost approach		$93,064
Rounded to $93,000		

This depreciation extraction method is illustrated as follows:

1. Sale price	$100,000
2. Less site value (and minor on-site improvements)	20,000
Building value	$ 80,000
3. Current reproduction cost (2,800 sq ft at $50/sq ft)	140,000
4. Total accrued depreciation ($140,000 − $80,000)	60,000
5. Overall rate of depreciation ($60,000 ÷ $140,000)	42.86%
6. Annual rate of accrued depreciation (42.86% ÷ 17 years)	2.52

DEPRECIATION ESTIMATES: THEIR LIMITS OF USE

Fortunately for the professional appraiser, estimating accrued depreciation directly is usually of secondary importance.[6] In fact, depreciation cannot accurately be determined until value is known. Then, by comparing present worth with estimated cost new, the amount of accrued depreciation is fixed with certainty. However, this "back door" approach is based on the current value of a property rather than providing an indication of the present value. Under the sales comparison and capitalized income approaches to value, as will be explained in other chapters, depreciation as a separate measure is of little importance. The appraiser's problem is to find the value of the subject property by comparison with comparable properties which have sold in recent times, or by capitalizing the net operating income for the subject property over the remaining economic life of the property or some generally accepted holding period. Once this value is found, the appraiser's task is, as a rule, completed. It should be noted that adjustments may be required to reflect accrued depreciation in the sales comparison approach, whereas this value loss is accounted for in the market rentals in the capitalized income approach. Only where the depreciated cost approach is deemed of importance must accrued depreciation—as a separate calculation—be taken into account. The depreciated cost approach is a most useful tool in the appraisal process, but in the hands of uninformed or unskilled appraisers it can result in grossly misleading calculations. A closing precaution: Use depreciation estimates with care. Each of the methods for measuring accrued depreciation covered herein are capable of providing accurate value estimates when properly used. This is especially true in markets where there is near equilibrium between supply and demand for a given class of real estate and the improvements represent the highest and best use of the subject site.

[6]The relative merits of the depreciated cost approach, covered in Chapter 11, should be reviewed now.

SUMMARY

Accrued depreciation is a loss in value from any cause—as measured by the difference between replacement or reproduction cost new of a property in current dollars and the market value of the same property.

The accountant is principally concerned with the *original cost*, and his or her interest in value is, as a rule, secondary. The appraiser, on the other hand, is principally interested in the *present worth* of future rights to income which flow from the productive use of a subject property. *Amortization* refers to reserve provisions for the recapture of investment capital.

The principal causes of accrued depreciation are (1) physical deterioration, (2) functional obsolescence, and (3) external obsolescence. Each of these three forms of accrued depreciation contain both curable and incurable deterioration/obsolescence except external obsolescence which includes only incurable obsolescence. The causes of loss in value for each of these forms of accrued depreciation are further subdivided as follows.

Physical deterioration: (1) wear and tear through use, (2) action of the elements and destruction by wood-boring insects, and (3) structural impairment through neglect, fire, water, and so on.

Functional obsolescence: (1) faulty design, (2) inadequacy of structural facilities, (3) superadequacy of structural facilities, and (4) outmoded equipment.

External obsolescence: (1) neighborhood hazards and nuisances, (2) down zoning and reduced highest and best use, (3) over- or underimprovement of land, and (4) decreasing demand.

Economic life is the productive life of a building measured from when it was built to when it economically encumbers the site and its optimum use. *Remaining economic life* describes a building's remaining productive life. *Effective age* of a building is based partly on its actual age, but more importantly, on its comparative utility, physical condition, and expected remaining life. Effective age of a building is equal to its total expected economic life minus its remaining economic life.

The three principal methods of measuring accrued depreciation are (1) the age-life method, (2) the breakdown, or observed condition, method, and (3) the market extracted method.

Under the breakdown, or observed condition, method each component of accrued depreciation is separately broken down, measured, and deducted from the cost new of a structure. The age-life method of estimating accrued depreciation is based upon establishing a ratio between the effective age and the total economic life of improvements. Having done this, the ratio is then multiplied by either the replacement or reproduction cost new of the building improvements at the date of appraisal. The market extracted depreciation method accounts for all forms of accrued depreciation and is based on deducting the lot value and value of minor site improvements from the sale price of an improved property. Next, this residual building value is subtracted from the current cost new of the structure. The difference is the accrued depreciation which can then be expressed as a percentage by dividing this amount by the current cost new of the building.

REVIEW QUESTIONS

1. Discuss the similarity and differences between accrued depreciation and amortization.
2. List three causes of each of the different forms of accrued depreciation. How do you think a prospective property owner or tenant would account for each of these deficiencies in terms of rent or sale price?
3. For investment purposes why is economic life more important than physical life?
4. Compute the value of a property with a lot worth $15,000; current replacement cost is $120,000; effective age is 15 years; and remaining economic life is 45 years.
5. What is the principal criterion used to determine whether a building suffers from curable versus incurable physical deterioration?
6. Define and give five examples of functional obsolescence-curable.
7. Outline the steps involved in estimating market value via the breakdown or observed method.
8. Find the depreciated cost and dollar amount of depreciation of a comparable sale dwelling based on the following facts: sale price, $125,000; value of site and minor on-site improvements, $28,000; current reproduction cost, $135,000. If the dwelling was built 14 years ago, what is the annual depreciation rate?
9. A real estate investor sold two parcels of property; one was an office building for which she received $175,000 and on which she made a capital gain of 25 percent; the other was an apartment building for which she received $175,000 and on which she suffered a loss of 25 percent. How much did the seller gain or lose? Show all computations.

READING AND STUDY REFERENCES

American Institute of Real Estate Appraisers. Chapter 17, "Accrued Depreciation," *The Appraisal of Real Estate*. Chicago: AIREA, 1987.

BOTTUM, MACKENZIE. "Estimating Economic Obsolescence in Supply-Saturated Office Markets," *The Appraisal Journal* 56, no. 4 (October 1988), pp. 451–455.

CALVANICO, JOSEPH J. "Economic Obsolescence of Manufacturing Facilities," *The Real Estate Appraiser and Analyst* (Spring 1989), pp. 58–59.

CORGEL, JOHN B., and HALBERT C. SMITH. "The Concept of Economic Life in the Residential Appraisal Process: A Summary of Findings," *The Real Estate Appraiser and Analyst* 48, no. 4 (Winter 1982), pp. 4–11.

EPLEY, DONALD R., and JAMES H. BOYKIN. Chapter 5, "Estimate of Value by the Cost Approach," *Basic Income Property Appraisal*. Reading, Mass.: Addison-Wesley Publishing Co., Inc., 1983.

GORDON, WILLIAM S. "Incurable Functional Obsolescence Due to the Lack of an Item: Is It Possible?" *The Real Estate Appraiser and Analyst* 48, no. 2 (Summer 1982), pp. 32–35.

HARPS, WILLIAM S. Chapter 28, "Depreciated Cost Approach to Value," *The Real Estate Handbook*, Maury Seldin and James H. Boykin, eds. Homewood, Ill.: Dow Jones-Irwin, 1989.

KLAASEN, ROMAIN L. "Fickle Obsolescence," *The Appraisal Journal* 57, no. 3 (July 1989), pp. 327–337.

TREADWELL, DONALD H. "Intricacies of the Cost Approach in the Appraisal of Major Industrial Properties," *The Appraisal Journal* 56, no. 1 (January 1988), pp. 70–79.

INCOME-EXPENSE ANALYSIS AND CAPITALIZATION

13

Income Forecasting and Analysis

Learning Objectives

After reading this chapter, you should be able to:

- Sense the fallacy of using average rather than actual income in estimating value
- Understand why typical management is assumed in conducting market value appraisals
- Appreciate the necessity of recognizing the probable future income pattern for both comparable and appraised properties
- Distinguish between potential gross income and effective gross income
- Define the term "net operating income"
- Be aware of the need for the appraiser to undertake a comprehensive lease analysis
- Recognize different conditions that can distort rental income

One of the basic characteristics that a commodity must have to possess value is *utility*.[1] Everything else remaining equal, the greater the utility, the greater the value. One of the best measures of utility is the amount of rental income that a property can command in an open and competitive market at a given time and place.

As emphasized previously, valuation, especially under the capitalized income approach, necessitates that an estimate be made of the present worth of future rights to income. The term *future* in this definition of value imposes on the appraiser an obligation to forecast with reasonable accuracy the pattern of income expectancy that may be anticipated over the remaining economic life of the subject property, or in most instances, a shorter holding period. Forecasting in any enterprise is fraught with hazards, as is testified to by the thousands of busi-

---

[1]Utility as used here refers to the power of a good to satisfy human wants or to render service or to produce income to its owner. See Chapter 1 for a discussion of value characteristics.

ness failures and bankruptcies reported every year. But forecast the appraiser must, or change to another profession in which he or she can search the annals of history, looking backward with reasonable certainty rather than forward into a realm of economic uncertainty. Every business venture requires prediction of future operations, and every property is improved in anticipation of estimated revenue from rental or owner use.

The accuracy of income predictions increases inversely with the length of the time period considered. As a rule, income for the year ahead can be established with a high degree of certainty. Income for the second, third, and fourth years ahead can be forecast with reasonable dependability; but thereafter, and to the end of the economic life of a property (extending up to 50 or more years), the accuracy of the forecast becomes tenuous. Fortunately, under the capitalization process the early and relatively accurate years of income forecasting are accorded substantial weight in the valuation process, with the importance of latter years diminishing as indicators of value. To illustrate this point, we will assume that two properties, A and B, are estimated to yield equal annual net operating incomes of $1,000 each, but that property A has an economic life of 50 years and property B, one of 100 years. At 8 percent interest, applying the present worth of 1 per period factor,[2] property A is worth $1,000 × 12.233, or $12,233, whereas property B is valued at $1,000 × 12.494, or $12,494. The difference is $261, or approximately 2 percent of the value of property A. In this instance, a 100 percent difference in the time span has practically no impact on the value estimate of the two properties.

INCOME AS A MEASURE OF VALUE

Income, especially for industrial and commercial properties, is an important index of value since income is essentially what an investor buys. Care must be taken to consider only income that is ascribable to the property under typical management. Income that is attributable to superior management or goodwill attaches to people or to the business and not to the property for which an estimate of value is sought. The techniques of capitalizing income into a sum of present value will be discussed fully in Chapters 15 through 20. This chapter introduces the basic principles underlying income forecasting.

Property income in previous references has been characterized as a "stream." The words "income stream" were deliberately chosen to create in the minds of both reader and appraiser a pictorial concept of the ups and downs of dynamic income productivity. Nothing is static, as the principle of change has taught us. Past income experiences may indicate a certain trend, and present income flow may substantiate this trend; nevertheless, the anticipated future income expectancy may radically differ on the basis of important changes in national, regional, and local business activity—of which the real estate market is a part. Income forecasting must not, however, be thought of as crystal ball gazing. The subject property in nearly all instances can be classified as belonging to a certain group of properties for which income experience data are known from prior

[2]Present and future worth functions are covered in detail in Chapter 16.

appraisal analysis or from study data published by management, accounting, or appraisal institutes. If experience data are unobtainable from file or published sources, a rental or income flow study of similar, or *benchmark*, properties (comparable properties from which value indexes are derived) must be undertaken as a guide to income forecasting.

The key income for appraisal purposes is usually *net operating income*, the income remaining after all operating expenses and replacement reserves have been accounted for but, as a rule, before deductions are made for mortgage debt service. A deduction for accrued depreciation is not made either. This deduction is not necessary since tenants and landlords already have adjusted the rent in view of the present state of the property.

ACTUAL VERSUS AVERAGE INCOME

Reliance on *average* rather than *actual* anticipated income, under the income approach to value, may result in substantial errors in the appraisal estimate. This is clearly demonstrated in the analysis of the two income-producing properties shown in Table 13.1.

In this illustration two income-producing properties with identical total and average incomes were discounted over a period of 10 years to a present worth at a rate of 10 percent interest. Property A, with a total income of $5,500 and an average annual income of $550 ($5,500 ÷ 10), yields a present value of $2,903.56. Property B, though experiencing the same total and average income—but derived from a reversed income pattern, as compared with property A—yields a present worth of $3,855.39, or a sum over 30 percent greater than that derived from prop-

TABLE 13.1   ANALYSIS OF PRESENT WORTH OF TWO INCOME-PRODUCING PROPERTIES WITH IDENTICAL TOTAL AND AVERAGE INCOMES—UNDER DIVERGENT INCOME ASSUMPTIONS

Years	Net income Property A	Net income Property B	Present worth factor 10 percent[a]	Present value Property A	Present value Property B
1	$ 100	$1,000	0.9091	$ 90.91	$ 909.10
2	200	900	0.8264	165.28	743.76
3	300	800	0.7513	225.39	601.04
4	400	700	0.6830	273.20	478.10
5	500	600	0.6209	310.45	372.54
6	600	500	0.5645	338.70	282.25
7	700	400	0.5132	359.24	205.28
8	800	300	0.4665	373.20	139.95
9	900	200	0.4241	381.69	84.82
10	1,000	100	0.3855	385.50	38.55
Total	$5,500	$5,500		$2,903.56	$3,855.39
Average	550	550		100%	133%

[a]See Table 16.1 for the source of these present worth factors.

erty A. The difference in valuation is a direct result of the nature of the income flow and the degree of time preference expressed in the discount rate. A dollar due one year from today has a greater value than one due ten years from today because the early dollar may be put to work for a period of nine years, and the revenue that this capital amount earns is reflected in the higher present value.[3] The difference in value estimate of the two diverse income-producing properties will vary directly, of course, with the discount rate employed in the discounted income approach shown in Table 13.1—decreasing with higher rates, and increasing with lower rates.

It may be argued that the illustration offered is extreme in nature and that it does not conform to general practice or experience. Perhaps so. But insistence on the use of unweighted income averages in the process of discounting is dangerous and may, as demonstrated, result in a substantial error in the value estimate. It is good to keep in mind that as a rule realty, because of its heterogeneous nature and fixity of location, may vary sharply in revenue productivity and hence in quantity and quality of income flow. Some income from real estate is ascending because land and, indirectly, its improvements are ripening into more productive use. Other properties may exhibit declining yields due to transition into lower uses, particularly during the last stages of their economic life cycle.

MARKET VERSUS CONTRACT RENTS

Too much importance is often placed, especially by amateur appraisers and "guesstimators," on past or present income or lease commitments. The present, it must be remembered, is merely a fleeting moment dividing the past from the future. Properties may be underimproved, overimproved, or faultily managed, or income may be attributable to personal skill or business operations rather than to the property itself.

Generally, it is the appraiser's duty when seeking market value to evaluate a property as if owned under fee simple title, free from all encumbrances except for use limitations imposed by public authorities and deed restrictions shown on public records. Exceptions arise, such as assignments involving the valuation of a leased fee, leasehold, or other partial interests. The property, too, must be considered in the light of its earning capacity in conformity with the principle of highest and best use. After value under these normal conditions has been established, appropriate adjustments should be made to reflect the economic advantages or disadvantages ascribable to limited contractual agreements or temporary managerial operating policies.

Market rent, which should form the basis of value, is defined as that amount of rent the appraised property probably would command at the date of appraisal. It usually is revealed by rentals being paid for similar space.

Contract rent, on the other hand, is that rental income actually paid for space as a result of a lease which binds owners and tenants for a stipulated future

[3]This example introduces the discounted cash flow concept which will be developed more fully later in the book.

time. This contract rent may be the same, greater, or less than the prevailing market rent that a property might reasonably expect.

IMPORTANCE OF TYPICAL MANAGEMENT

All property must be considered to be under some form of management, either by the owner himself or herself or by a professional manager. In either case, operating expenses must reflect a charge—whether or not actually paid—for the expenditure of time and effort customarily employed in operation and property supervision. Such managerial costs, as will be shown in the following chapter, are generally considered a percentage of revenue and vary from 5 to 10 percent of realized revenues or rent collections.

In forecasting income, it is important to consider property productivity under the operation of *typical* management. To do otherwise would ascribe to the property a value that is influenced by personal characteristics of the management. By *typical* management is meant that which most frequently prevails in the ownership and use of given types of properties. Income considerations, too, are based on typical future managerial practices. This does not mean that the effects of past managerial control and operation which linger on are not to be considered under the income approach to value. Exceptional management during past years may, like business goodwill, be the cause of excess income extending over several years. *Excess rent* is defined as the amount that contract rent exceeds market rent. Poor management during past years, on the other hand, may burden future operations as a result of deferred maintenance, or may reduce future income because of rental concessions. Reduced rental income may also result from glutted markets. Long-term leases made in such markets cause future rentals to be depressed below prevailing rentals as markets recover. *Rent deficiency* is that amount by which contract rent is less than market rent.

ESTIMATING THE QUANTITY OF INCOME FLOW

The amount of revenue generally varies with the size of the building, quality of construction, neighborhood, location and site characteristics, and amount and quality of furnishings and fixtures. Industrial property will produce revenue in proportion to the number of square feet of area offered for lease. The availability of railroad siding, highway access, and proximity to market and to community facilities will directly affect the quantity of rental payments offered per unit of space. The unit of income and value for commercial property is based on the number of either square feet or front feet of land in the property—depending on business use and land location—and the number of square feet of building area. Apartment buildings produce revenue on a per room or per apartment basis depending on local market customs. Single residences are rented on an overall property basis by the month. The analytical procedure for estimating the income of a subject property will be explained later in connection with the preparation of a rental schedule.

Income takes different patterns, as will be discussed later in the section "Future Payment Provisions." These patterns may be level, straight-line change, step-up or step-down variable such as in a percentage lease, or may occur at the end of a holding period when the property is sold and the seller receives the net proceeds from the sale. The appraiser's initial task is to recognize and forecast the future income pattern that the appraised property will probably experience. This task becomes complicated for a large multitenant office building where rents vary by size and location of space within the building and according to lease origination and termination dates. An electronic spreadsheet such as that shown in Figure 13.1 can be especially helpful with this task. Next, the appraiser must be prepared to convert the forecast income pattern into an estimate of present value.

The logic employed in forecasting anticipated loss or rise in the flow of income appears highly questionable without leases in place for the duration of the forecast period. Extreme care must be taken in forecasting future changes in income patterns as a basis for judging the present worth of a property. A fundamental question is: How can future income be more accurately predicted than the present rent or value of a property? Furthermore, an income decline based on an equal percentage curve should be used only when income is supportable by actual real estate market operations. If the income flow—on the basis of study of similar properties—is expected to change, then it is the appraiser's clear-cut responsibility to forecast the pattern of this change and to capitalize the changing returns accurately and professionally. Often, too, attempts are made to stabilize future returns by arithmetic averaging. Such a procedure is both unsupportable and unrealistic, since early dollar returns under discounting procedure have greater weight in relation to present value than equal dollar returns in late property life.

An early and noteworthy attempt to measure income decline by classes and kinds of real property was made by Frederick M. Babcock in *The Valuation of Real Estate.*[4] In practice, the mathematical theory underlying Babcock's premises proved difficult to explain and more difficult for practitioners and laypersons alike to understand. Consequently, little is currently known—and still less is applied—of Babcock's declining income premise findings. A more direct and mathematically less cumbersome method of accounting for income flow variations will be explained later.

Study of past and present income behavior of various types of properties should enable an appraiser to forecast income expectancy as affected by building age and the space competition of new construction. The diagram shown in Figure 13.2 illustrates an anticipated income pattern of a 16-unit apartment building in a moderate-size community. Omitted from this example is the economic rental in dollars for the property. Only the value of the expected relationship between building and land income is illustrated.

Figure 13.2, supported by income experience data of comparable buildings, indicates that earnings on completion of improvements and full occupancy will remain stable for an operating period of about 5 years. Its rental income then is

---

[4]Frederick M. Babcock, Chapter 27, *The Valuation of Real Estate* (New York: McGraw-Hill Book Company, 1932).

expected to rise in two increments through year 30. Building age and obsolescence as well as anticipated competition from other apartments are expected to cause a decline in building income at that life stage of approximately 25 percent. Income at this lower level is expected to prevail for a period of 10 years, at which time (year 40) continued obsolescence and supply competition for similar properties will cause a further drop in income of about 10 percent, or to a level of 55 percent of the income earned during the middle years of property life. Had the market land rent risen as shown by the dashed line instead of the solid line, the economic life of the building would have been shortened from 50 years to 40 years. For more on this subject, see the highest and best use section in Chapter 3.

To capitalize this changing income flow does not require special mathematical skill or the use of special capitalization tables. Each level of future income is merely converted into a sum of present worth and discounted to the date of the appraisal. The recommended procedure for capitalizing either stable, declining, or rising income will be demonstrated and explained in Chapter 17.

QUALITY AND DURATION OF INCOME

The value of property varies not only with the quantity or amount of rental income, but also with income quality and its duration. The *quality of income* generally depends on the financial strength of tenants and the stability of economic conditions in the subject market area. As a matter of practice, differences in the quality of income among properties should not be reflected in upward or downward adjustments of the amount of anticipated income. Quality differentials instead should be a matter for separate and analytical considerations in the selection of the applicable rate at which the net operating income is to be capitalized. The analysis and correlation of market rates of interest for purposes of selecting or constructing rates of capitalization will be demonstrated and discussed in Chapter 15.

The *duration of income* is that period over which the forecast rental income is expected to continue. It is directly proportional to the remaining economic life of the building improvements or perhaps to the holding period projected by typical investors. The income attributable to land under fee simple ownership is sometimes mistakenly thought to extend at the same level into perpetuity. In actuality, it has generally been found to rise over a period of time. Improvements, however, are subject to physical wear, tear, and the forces of obsolescence, and income to be derived from employment of depreciable assets will cease when their value reaches zero. In predicting the economic life span of property improvements, the appraiser must consider:

1. The physical and functional characteristics of the building improvements.
2. The external economic forces that operate on the demand side for the kind of utility or amenity offered by the subject improvement.

	Year 1	Year 2	Year 3	Year 4	Year 5	Year 6	Year 7
INCOME:							
GROSS POTENTIAL RENTS	$1,524,060	$1,600,263	$1,680,276	$1,764,290	$1,852,504	$1,945,130	$2,042,386
LESS: MANAGEMENT UNITS	(10,080)	(10,584)	(11,113)	(11,669)	(12,252)	(12,865)	(13,508)
POTENTIAL COLLECTIONS	$1,513,980	$1,589,679	$1,669,163	$1,752,621	$1,840,252	$1,932,265	$2,028,878
VACANCY LOSS	(209,367)	(200,714)	(178,612)	(122,683)	(128,818)	(135,259)	(142,021)
CREDIT LOSS	(37,850)	(31,794)	(25,037)	(21,908)	(23,003)	(24,153)	(25,361)
RENTAL INCOME	$1,266,764	$1,357,171	$1,465,514	$1,608,030	$1,688,431	$1,772,853	$1,861,496
LAUNDRY AND OTHER INCOME	25,335	27,143	29,310	32,161	33,769	35,457	37,230
TOTAL INCOME	$1,292,099	$1,384,315	$1,494,824	$1,640,190	$1,722,200	$1,808,310	$1,898,725
OPERATING EXPENSES:							
REAL ESTATE TAXES	$69,950	$73,448	$77,120	$80,976	$85,025	$89,276	$93,740
OTHER TAXES	1,000	1,050	1,103	1,158	1,216	1,276	1,340
INSURANCE	19,500	20,475	21,499	22,574	23,702	24,887	26,132
UTILITIES:							
WATER AND SEWER	90,000	94,500	99,225	104,186	109,396	114,865	120,609
GAS	2,400	2,520	2,646	2,778	2,917	3,063	3,216
ELECTRICITY	27,600	28,980	30,429	31,950	33,548	35,225	36,987
REPAIRS AND MAINTENANCE:							
MECHANICAL & APPLIANCE	18,000	18,900	19,845	20,837	21,879	22,973	24,122
GENERAL/MISC. REPAIRS	48,000	50,400	52,920	55,566	58,344	61,262	64,325
REPAIR LABOR	72,000	75,600	79,380	83,349	87,516	91,892	96,487

	Year 1	Year 2	Year 3	Year 4	Year 5	Year 6	Year 7
LAWN & SNOW	25,000	26,250	27,563	28,941	30,388	31,907	33,502
PEST CONTROL	3,000	3,150	3,308	3,473	3,647	3,829	4,020
POOL MAINTENANCE	10,000	10,500	11,025	11,576	12,155	12,763	13,401
MANAGEMENT FEES	63,338	67,859	73,276	80,401	84,422	88,643	93,075
REFUSE SERVICE	9,000	9,450	9,923	10,419	10,940	11,487	12,061
RESIDENT MANAGER	51,000	53,550	56,228	59,039	61,991	65,090	68,345
JANITORIAL EXPENSE	1,600	1,680	1,764	1,852	1,945	2,042	2,144
APT PAINTING/CLEANING (net)	45,000	47,250	49,613	52,093	54,698	57,433	60,304
OFFICE/ADMINISTRATIVE	12,000	12,600	13,230	13,892	14,586	15,315	16,081
ADVERTISING AND PROMOTION	25,842	27,134	28,491	29,915	31,411	32,982	34,631
OTHER/MISCELLANEOUS	7,200	7,560	7,938	8,335	8,752	9,189	9,649
TOTAL OPERATING EXPENSES	$601,430	$632,855	$666,522	$703,310	$738,476	$775,400	$814,169
NET OPERATING INCOME	$690,669	$751,460	$828,302	$936,880	$983,724	$1,032,910	$1,084,556
LESS: DEBT SERVICE (NET)	$492,624	$588,204	$631,064	$631,064	$631,064	$631,064	$631,064
CASH FLOW	$198,045	$163,256	$197,238	$305,816	$352,660	$401,847	$453,492
OVERALL RETURN (Ro) =	11.8%	10.5%	10.7%	11.6%	11.9%	12.2%	12.6%
CASH-ON-CASH RETURN (Re) =	33.8%	22.7%	27.0%	29.0%	28.5%	28.0%	27.7%

Figure 13.1 Seven-Year Pro Forma Operating Statement for a 300-Unit Garden Apartment Complex

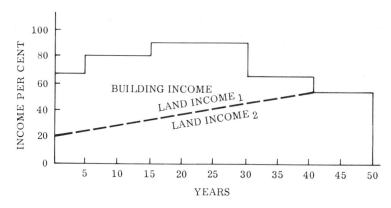

Figure 13.2   Forecast Income Flow for an Apartment Property Over an Economic Life of 50 Years

The physical characteristics set the outer limit of duration of economic life. Therefore, the type of architecture, the quality of materials used, the workmanship employed, and the physical conditions of maintenance and repair must be considered in establishing the maximum number of years of economic life. More important as a mortality factor, however, are the environing economic forces that cause building obsolescence. Otherwise identical improvements will have different economic lives depending on their location within or among communities. In rapidly growing cities, building obsolescence is accelerated as a result of rapid changes in land use and consequent significant increases in land value. For example, the 100 percent business location in a city may shift a distance of several blocks as a result of new and redevelopment construction activity. The impacts of the automobile, community decentralization, development of suburban shopping centers, and location of new industries and office parks in suburban areas are largely responsible for shifting land values and increased economic mortality of office and retail buildings in central business locations.

Where buildings are relatively new, errors in the prediction of remaining building life have a generally minor effect on the overall estimate of total property value. This is true for two reasons: first, because of the relatively minor weight given to the value of distant future income in the discounting or capitalization process; and second, because increased building obsolescence has historically been accompanied by rising land values which often more than compensate for the future value decline of the building. Where buildings are in middle or late life, however, an error in the anticipated duration of income may importantly affect the value estimate. To predict accurately the remaining economic building life requires judgment based on intimate knowledge of community and neighborhood forces affecting property value, as detailed in Chapters 5 and 6. It is for this reason, among others, that property appraising as an applied art is largely limited to local practitioners who keep their fingers on the economic pulse of their community. Also, the difficulty of accurately making such long-term forecasts is another reason that appraisers often prefer using a shorter holding period that reflects investor practices.

RENTAL SCHEDULE CONSTRUCTION AND ANALYSIS

In forecasting income for existing or proposed properties, the appraiser must look to the market for income experience data of properties comparable to the one under appraisal. Through cooperating brokers, appraisers, or property management firms, it is possible to secure rental amounts paid on a per room, per apartment, or square-foot basis for residential rental properties, and a square-foot or front-foot basis for commercial or business properties. With the aid of this information, the appraiser can construct a rental schedule which—after adjustments for differences in building age, construction, materials and design, attributes of location, and site facilities—can serve as a basis for rental estimates of the subject property.

Rental schedules for the various units of space to be offered are most realistically established on a market comparative basis. This is effectively done by rating the subject property in relation to like properties in similar neighborhoods for which accurate rental data are available. Comparison is generally made with a number of typical space units, and price adjustments for the subject property are based on quantitative and qualitative differences. For example, in the pricing of an apartment unit, consideration should be given to the following: area of floor space, number of bathrooms, quality of construction, amount of decorative features, efficiency of interior layout, type and quality of elevator service, nature and quality of janitorial services, reputation of the property, adequacy of on-site parking, recreational facilities, responsibility for utility expenses, and tenant security. In addition, the location of the building in relation to public conveniences and the quality rating of neighborhood and recent trends must both be considered. If a detailed comparison is made for each similar rental unit, a fairly accurate and reliable rental schedule for appraisal purposes can be established.

LEASE ANALYSIS

The ability to conduct a comprehensive lease analysis is an essential skill that should be mastered by any competent appraiser. This analysis can become quite tedious for a large multitenant office building such as those depicted in Figure 13.3. Investors generally ascertain the strength of each tenant and his or her obligation to pay rent for a specified term. When sophisticated owners and tenants understand the intricacies of an executed lease agreement and the appraiser only knows the property rents for so many dollars a square foot, then the appraiser is incapable of providing a fully informed service.

For an appraiser to understand completely the responsibilities of the parties to a lease and be able to accurately note exactly how much a tenant pays, he or she must study the executed lease, accompanying exhibits, and any amendments. Some of the major lease provisions that affect the amount paid by tenants are covered in the following examples. It is advisable to include in the addenda of an appraisal report a lease summary for each tenant such as shown in Figure 13.4. This summary provides a basis for lease analysis. From this information the ap-

Figure 13.3   High-Rise Office Building Complex (Courtesy of James Center, Richmond, Virginia)

praiser can array the leases according to expiration dates. This will show the distribution of rental revenue according to date of lease, the percentage increase in rentals, and the rents paid by the most recently made leases.

Area of Leased Premises

Different classes of buildings and those in different regions tend to be measured differently. The following examples will demonstrate the importance of the appraiser fully understanding how the demised premises (space identified as being leased to a tenant) are measured. Otherwise, the income applied to the appraised property probably will either be under- or overstated.

1. A multitenant office building with several tenants on a given floor would probably have the rentable area exclude exterior and corridor walls as well as public washrooms, halls, stairways, elevator, and mechanical shafts.

2. For a tenant occupying an entire floor, the area might be computed as within the exterior walls but exclude areas common to other tenants, such as elevator and stairway space.

XYZ Drug Store Chain, Inc.

Date of Lease: December 14, 1990

Demised Premises: 56′ × 120′ = 6,720 square feet.

Term: Rent payments begin when ABC Supermarkets, Inc. is open for business and all common areas have been completed with adequate lighting installed and operational; target for meeting all commencement requirements is November 1, 1992. Lease term is 10 lease years, plus the right to renew lease for 6 successive 5-year renewal periods.

Minimum Rent: $55,440 per year against percentage rent during the original term, followed by the following annual minimum rents during each of the subsequent six option periods: $57,120; $58,800; $60,480; $63,840; $67,200; and $70,560. Rents are payable monthly.

Percentage Rent: 2% of tenant's gross sales in each lease year, less any minimum rent payments made.

Security Deposit: None mentioned in lease.

Additional Rent: Tenant will pay its proportionate share (i.e., in the ratio of the gross square foot area in the premises to the aggregate of the gross square foot area in all buildings in the shopping center) of the actual real estate taxes, maintenance expenses of the common areas, and premiums for fire and extended coverage insurance and liability insurance on the shopping center.

Construction of Demised Premises: Landlord shall deliver to tenant the premises constructed in conformity with requirements described in tenant's prototype plans and specification (which are approximately 100 pages in length).

Repairs by Landlord: Landlord shall maintain in good condition and repair the roof, sprinkler system, if any, structural and exterior portions of the premises, including foundation, bearing walls and columns, utility lines outside the premises and permanently installed in walls or floors inside the premises. Landlord shall also make repairs to all interior walls, ceilings, floors and floor coverings when such repairs are made necessary because of faulty construction or landlord's failure to keep the premises in proper repair.

Figure 13.4   Shopping Center Store Lease Summary

3. If the leased area is computed from exterior walls, the *building efficiency* or ratio of occupied space to gross area becomes a consideration, that is, usable versus gross area.

4. It is possible for one office building to include exterior wall dimensions in computing leasable square footage where area for offices in another building may include one-half the thickness of exterior or interior partition walls.

Factors Influencing Rental Levels

In addition to carefully ascertaining the actual leased area for the comparable and appraised properties, the appraiser should be aware of other conditions that distort rentals. The following list contains examples of some conditions that, if not recognized by the appraiser, could result in an erroneous income being applied to the subject property:

1. Part of the rental income diverted away from the lessor may go to the mortgagee as the result of a participation loan. Thus consider rent paid rather than net rent received by owner.

2. Tenant improvements may cause an apparently low rental since this expenditure in effect is amortized by the tenant along with each rent payment. Examples of the work installed and paid by a tenant include finished ceilings and walls, interior painting, floor covering, trade fixtures, and heating, ventilating, and air-conditioning system.

3. Managerial competence of the owner or his agent can affect the level of vacancies, income, expenses, and maintenance.

4. Concessions made by either the lessor or lessee can affect rental levels. Examples are (a) where a tenant agrees not to engage in a similar business for a specific period of time and perhaps within a geographic radius of its present location, (b) special features provided by the lessor such as free draperies, or (c) free rent which generally is given at the beginning of the lease term and must be converted into effective rent for appraisal purposes.

5. Netness of leases and expense "stops" can give the illusion of different rental levels.

Netness of Lease

Every lease is different. Nevertheless, the appraiser should be familiar with certain generalized leasing practices. For instance, short-term leases (up to one year) tend to be gross leases. This means that the owner pays all the operating expenses. At the other extreme, the expense burden tends to shift from the owner to the tenant for long-term leases (in excess of five years). Although the following schedule does not hold true in all cases, it outlines the conventional means of identifying expense responsibilities under leases.

Types of Leases

Type of lease	Expense responsibility
Gross	Owner pays all expenses.
Net	Tenant pays all or part of future real estate tax increases after the base year.
Net net	In addition to taxes, the tenant pays all or part of insurance expenses; these premiums may be plate glass, boiler, fire, and extended coverage or public liability.
Net net net (also called absolute net)	In addition to taxes and insurance, the tenant agrees to pay all or part of the maintenance costs, which may be interior, exterior, or both.

Never should the appraiser assume that he or she understands "who pays what and when" or the netness of a lease simply from the interviewed party stating that it is a net or some other type of lease. For example, sometimes a net lease is confused with an absolute net lease. The best precaution is to read the lease.

Future Payment Provisions

A truism in commercial property is that virtually every lease is different. This section presents the basic ways that lease payments are structured. It should be remembered, however, that a lease may combine several of these future payment clauses. Most of the following payment provisions are included to minimize erosion in the owner's profits after the initial year of a multiyear lease.

Flat rental. This type of lease typically is used for small commercial properties and apartments. It usually is for a one-year term. To extend the fixed rental beyond one year is inequitable for either the owner or the tenant. This type of lease, which at one time enjoyed wide use and popularity, has come—at least for long-term leasing—into gradual disuse. The reason, no doubt, is the steadily declining purchasing power of the dollar. Where future rental payments are fixed in amount—a declining dollar value deprives the property (or fee) owner of a fair return in proportion to the value of his or her property as measured in terms of constant dollars. In fact, the inability to increase rentals in time will adversely affect a property's value.

Graded rent clause. This multiyear lease actually is a series of flat rental payments, rising in stair-step fashion as shown in the following example. Thus it sometimes is called a step-up lease. This form of lease is intended to give the land user an opportunity to lighten operating expense burdens during the early formative years of his or her business enterprise and to give the landlord an opportunity to participate in future business growth through successively higher rental payments as shown in the following example. Such lease agreements must be cautiously evaluated, since excessive rental payments historically have proved a prime cause of business failure and resultant bankruptcy of tenants.

Occasionally, it may be fashioned in a step-down manner for a property that is losing its appeal or for one in a deteriorating neighborhood. A variation of this lease is one where future-year payments are scheduled to increase by a predetermined percentage amount.

Years	Monthly rental
1–5	$2,000
6–10	2,400
11–15	3,000
16–20	3,600

Index clause. This provision allows the owner to enjoy the benefits of inflation by having rentals track some specified price index, such as the Consumer Price Index (CPI). Rental income is periodically adjusted in accordance with such a published index. Sometimes it is set at a percentage of the CPI change, such as 75 percent. Tenants sometimes criticize this rent adjustor because it bears little relationship to actual building operating costs. An example of an index clause follows.

> ... commencing on the first year of the renewal term and yearly thereafter shall be $15,152.17 (for improvements) plus an amount determined by multiplying the sum of $53,060.00 by a fraction, the numerator of which shall be the Consumer Price Index for the last month of the previous lease year, and the denominator of such fraction shall be the Consumer Price Index for March 1992 (when original lease began), less one-half of the increase over $53,060.00. In no event shall the application of the Consumer Price Index reduce the monthly rental to be paid during the extended term below $4,421.67.

Escalator clause. An escalator clause increases the tenant's operating expense burden. Conversely, it arrests the amount of expense paid by the owners. Hence it is sometimes called an "expense stop" or "pass through" and was previously covered in the discussion of netness of leases. Often, the tenant will require that a ceiling be placed on the amount of expenses shifted to him or her from the owner. An example of a real estate and utility expense stop for a 229-unit apartment project follows.

> The tenant agrees that the monthly rent stipulated in the lease shall be adjusted to reflect any increase in the cost to the landlord for increases in real estate taxes and utilities. The cost shall be prorated monthly one-two hundred and twenty-ninth of the cost increase to the project.

Percentage clause. This type of rent provision usually applies to retail businesses, including restaurants. It is made up of two parts: (1) base rent and (2) percentage rent. Ordinarily, the base rent will be paid regardless of the volume of the tenant's business. The percentage rent, as shown in the following example, varies according to the level of the tenant's sales. The appraiser should disregard any potential income from percentage or overage rentals unless there is convincing evidence provided by operating histories of the subject or similar retail businesses. Percentage rentals may range from as low as 1.25 percent of gross sales for department stores or supermarkets to 5 to 10 percent for small tenants such as camera shops and costume jewelry stores.

Minimum annual rental:

Year	Rental
1	$22,800
2	24,000
3	25,200

Plus percentage rental at 5 1/2% of gross annual sales in excess of

Year	Gross annual sales
1	$414,545.45
2	436,363.64
3	458,181.82

This type of rent provision also includes as additional rental common area maintenance and merchants' association promotion fund.

Sale and lease-back.   The "sale and lease-back" contract agreement has gained wide popularity with owners of large industrial and commercial properties. Under this form of agreement the owner, in return for full value, conveys title to his or her property by deed to a real estate investor or an institutional lender—generally a life insurance company or pension fund—and leases back the property for a long term.

Under provisions of the lease the former owner becomes the lessee and agrees to pay an absolute net rent as well as all operating expenses, which include real estate taxes, property insurance, maintenance, and essential replacements.

The sale and lease-back transaction has many advantages as a mode of real estate ownership and tenant operations:

1. The seller (user of real estate) obtains the full cash value of the property which, as a rule, is twice the amount that could be obtained under mortgage financing and this without the burdensome provisions of mortgage debt clauses and the possible threat of foreclosure in case of nonpayment of interest or principal.
2. The seller is able to reinvest the cash in his business enterprise in which as a "specialist" he has greater skill to increase net operating earnings. The sale, too, increases flexibility of capital investment and mobility of the enterprise in case expansion or relocation becomes necessary.
3. The seller, often, secures substantial tax advantages. If the sale yields a price less than the book value of the property, the loss can be reflected in income tax reporting. Also, the entire amount paid for rent becomes a business expense, whereas under mortgage borrowing only the interest portion of the debt and capital recovery (depreciation) are tax-deductible items.

The purchaser also gains advantages which make the sale and lease-back transaction financially profitable to her:

1. Since the lessee assumes all operating expenses and burden of management, the net income (rent) provides a rate of return generally more favorable than that obtainable under a mortgage debt arrangement.
2. Equity ownership provides an excellent hedge against inflation. If the property enhances in value during its investment life, it is the investor who will benefit in the long run.

The advantages to buyer and seller under a sale and lease-back transaction as outlined previously are not all-inclusive, but are sufficiently substantial to make consideration of this type of real estate financing worthy of serious and profitable consideration.

OWNER'S INCOME STATEMENTS AND ADJUSTMENTS

In the appraisal of existing properties, it is customary to request that the owner furnish an operating statement for at least the three prior years. This statement can be analyzed and reconstructed in conformity with income expectancy under typical property management standards and sound appraisal practices.

The income data supplied by the owner are generally labeled *as reported.* The income as reported by the owner for the three-or-more-year period is then modified to reflect typical operations, with the amounts used for appraisal purposes then labeled *as adjusted.*[5] Where adjustments reflect more than the rounding of dollar amounts, it is essential that a full explanation be given in the body of the valuation report or added as a footnote. Typical adjustments may show rental income for the owner- or janitor-occupied apartment, or they may reflect increases or decreases in existing rentals where such rentals are out of line with market rental comparisons.

Owners' statements also generally reflect rentals on an as-is basis and thus include built-in vacancies and rent-collection losses, if any. To indicate operation under typical management, it is preferable to estimate gross revenue collectible under 100 percent occupancy and then to subtract for normal vacancy and collection losses that prevail for this type of property in the community market area. Generally, vacancy and collection deductions are calculated as a percentage of potential gross revenue, varying from a minimum of 2 percent to as high as 50 percent in summer resort areas. In college towns or neighborhoods, where school enrollment declines during the summer months, vacancy ratios in apartments that cater to students and faculty personnel must be calculated to indicate *collectible* rather than *potential* income.

In appraisal terminology, the amount left after deductions for vacancy and collection losses are made is referred to as *effective gross income.* Even in rare instances where owners report no vacancies or collection loses over past years, the

---

[5]See Chapter 14 for a suggested method to adjust reported operating incomes and expenses.

appraiser must provide for such contingencies in accordance with typical loss ratios reported for similar competitive properties. The exception, of course, would be where an entire property is under firm lease to a responsible tenant over a period of years.

In forecasting income for capitalization in the estimation of value of proposed construction, or in the estimation of land value under a hypothetical highest and best use, care must be taken to account for land income and deferred rental income during the period of construction. The present worth of such phased-in income, discounted at the rate of interest applicable to the type of property, provides a value as of the date of the appraisal. Consideration, too, must be given to high vacancy ratios during initial months or years of the property's operation. Typical sound management calls for careful tenant selection, and larger office and business properties may require periods of two or more years to reach full occupancy. Absorption rates of competitive space in a submarket will reveal an appropriate absorption period for the subject property. Such deferment of revenue also must be accounted for in the valuation process via the income approach.

INCOME ADJUSTMENT FOR CHANGES IN THE PURCHASING POWER OF THE DOLLAR

Fortunately for the real estate appraiser, the anticipated income stream forecast over the remaining economic life of a property need not be adjusted for possible changes in the purchasing power of the dollar. As previously indicated, future income, through the process of capitalization, is converted into a sum of present dollars for which the property is to be exchanged on the open market. Assuming freedom from mortgage debts and other financial encumbrances as well as freedom from restrictions on income such as rent control, a property is deemed competitively free to adjust itself to future changes in the purchasing power of the dollar. However, in a study of income performance over many past years, or in accepting the historical income flow of similar properties as a guide to the forecasting of an anticipated income flow for a given property, it is necessary to adjust past income to reflect changes in the purchasing power of the dollar. This can readily be done with the aid of price level indices published by the U.S. Bureau of Labor Statistics. Thus a rising income stream over 30 or more elapsed years may actually, after dollar purchasing power adjustment, disclose a declining trend in real operating income. Care must be taken, however, to restrict the use of dollar purchasing power adjustment factors to past income only. Where future income is sluggish in adjusting itself to market dollar forces of inflation or deflation—as in the case of long-term lease arrangements—it is best to reflect this rigidity in income flow as a factor of negative income quality, and to adjust the rate of capitalization by an appropriate increase in the risk factor component of the rate of capitalization. A study of the income-to-price relationship of similarly affected properties will disclose directly the rate of capitalization applied by investors to like properties in the open market. For a full discussion of the derivation of capitalization rates, the reader is referred to Chapter 15.

SUMMARY

Generally, the value of real estate increases as rental income rises. The accuracy of income predictions increases inversely with the length of the time period considered. Net operating income usually is the income analyzed in order to arrive at a property's value. *Net operating income* is the income remaining after deductions have been made for all operating expenses and reserves for replacements.

More accurate value estimates tend to be produced by use of actual anticipated income rather than average income estimates. A value estimate also may be based either on market or contract rent. *Market rent* is defined as that amount of rent the appraised property will command at the date of appraisal. *Contract rent* is that rental income actually paid for space as a result of a lease which binds owners and tenants for a stipulated future time.

Real property ordinarily should be appraised on the basis of typical management. Otherwise, value attributable to management is incorrectly ascribed to the property.

Excess rent is defined as the amount that contract rent exceeds market rent. Conversely, *rent deficiency* is that amount by which contract rent is less than market rent.

The value of property varies not only with the quantity of rental income, but also with income quality and its duration. The *quality of income* generally depends on the financial strength of tenants. The *duration of income* is that period over which the forecast rental income is expected to continue.

A *lease summary* provides a basis for lease analysis. It should contain such information as tenant identification, date of lease, identification and area of demised premises, minimum and percentage rent as well as any additional rent such as pro rata amount of real estate taxes, security deposit, construction of demised premises, and repairs by landlord.

Any of the following conditions, if not recognized by the appraiser, could result in erroneous income being estimated for the subject property:

1. An owner may not receive all of the rent paid by a tenant due to part of it going to the mortgagee who is providing a participation loan on the property.
2. Tenant improvements may cause an apparently low rental since this expenditure is being amortized with each rent payment.
3. Managerial competence can affect the property's income and expense performance.
4. Netness of leases and expense "stops" can give the illusion of different rental levels.
5. Concessions made by either the lessor or lessee can affect rental levels.

Leases vary in the amount of expenses paid either by the tenant or landlord. This shift in expenses ranges from a gross lease where the owner pays all operating expenses to an absolute net lease where all of the operating expenses are paid by the tenant. The latter type of provision is associated with long-term leases.

Real estate leases may be classified according to the manner in which payments are structured. The following list includes the most common future payment provisions. The *flat rental* provision is associated with short-term leases where the same rental is paid each year. A *graded rent clause* provides for a series of flat rental payments, rising in stair-step fashion. Sometimes, in the latter years of a property's life, the income pattern is reversed in a step-down manner. An *index clause* allows rental income to be periodically adjusted in accordance with a published index such as the Consumer Price Index. An *escalator clause*, also known as an expense stop or pass through, increases the tenant's operating expense burden as specified operating expenses rise. A *percentage clause* usually is used with retail establishments. It has two parts—the base rent and the percentage rent. The latter increases as a tenant's business increases. A *sale and lease-back* provision provides for an owner to sell a property for full value to an investor and then simultaneously lease it back.

Appraisers, in analyzing an income-expense statement provided by a property owner, usually need to reconstruct it to accurately reflect relevant income and expenses. The income remaining after deducting for vacancy and collection losses is known as *effective gross income.*

REVIEW QUESTIONS

1. Define market and contract rent. Under what conditions are they equivalent?
2. Review Figure 13.1 and explain how rising land income and declining building income can shorten the remaining economic life of a building.
3. List at least five items that should be considered by an appraiser in estimating the amount of market (economic) rent for a rental property.
4. Why should the appraiser recognize unusually high vacancy levels during the "rent-up" period for new properties if a 3 to 7 percent vacancy level can be expected a year after completion?
5. How can a failure to account accurately for the actual leased area for comparable rental properties distort the market rental used for the appraised property?
6. Give the general expense responsibility pattern between lessor and lessee for short- and long-term leases.
7. How can a knowledge of future payment provisions in leases improve the accuracy of an appraisal report?
8. Brown bought a building from which he anticipates receiving, at the time of purchase, $8,000 annually in net operating income. Ten years later, having maintained the building in full repair, his yearly operating income remained at $8,000. He anticipates the same level of income throughout the future service life of this building. Has the passage of time, assuming all other things remain equal, affected the value of this building? Explain.
9. Explain why under the income approach to value the appraiser must consider past managerial practices.
10. In the valuation process what significance should the appraiser attach to (a) present income, (b) past income, and (c) anticipated income?

READING AND STUDY REFERENCES

BARNES, KENNETH A. "Rental Concessions and Value," *The Appraisal Journal* 54, no. 2 (April 1986), pp. 167–176.

BOYKIN, JAMES H. "Future Payment Clauses," Chapter 19, "Lease Financing," *Financing Real Estate*. Lexington, Mass.: D.C. Heath and Company, 1979, pp. 495–500.

BOYKIN, JAMES H. Chapter 22, "Property Income and Life Cycles," *The Real Estate Handbook*, Maury Seldin and James H. Boykin, eds. Homewood, Ill.: Dow Jones-Irwin, 1990.

DAL SANTO, JACQUELYN. "Valuation Concerns in the Appraisal of Covenants Not to Compete," *The Appraisal Journal* 59, no. 1 (January 1991), pp. 111–114.

ELLWOOD, L. W. "The Income Forecast: Straight Line or Curve?" *The Appraisal Journal* 39, no. 2 (April 1971), pp. 51–55.

FORD, STEVEN W. "The Impact of Escalations and Additional Rent on Commercial Leases," *Real Estate Accounting and Taxation* (Winter 1987), pp. 43–52.

FRIEDMAN, JACK P., and NICHOLAS ORDWAY. Chapter 8, "Income Estimating and Forecasting," *Income Property Appraisal and Analysis*. Reston, Va.: Reston Publishing Co., Inc., 1981.

14
Operating Expense Forecasting and Analysis

Learning Objectives

After reading this chapter, you should be able to:

- Distinguish between income deductions and operating expenses
- Understand how net operating income can and sometimes needs to be derived for an appraised property without having the actual real estate tax statement
- Be familiar with the major published sources of income-expense data for different types of real estate
- Reconstruct an owner's operating expense statement
- Discern the difference between capital and operating expenditures
- Understand the pros and cons of using reserves for replacements and be familiar with several ways of setting up such reserves

The development and use of the gross income multiplier (see Chapter 9) seems to bypass completely the need for operating expense forecasting and analysis. Professional appraisers nevertheless should not neglect this important phase of the capitalized income approach to value. Failure to analyze expense schedules and property operating performance may be the cause of substantial errors in the final estimate of value. Moreover, it is not always possible to use the GIM due to lack of comparable sales and rental data.

Neglect of operating expense data analysis often is based on the belief that properties of given classifications—residential, apartments, office buildings, and so on—are characterized by similar expense-to-income ratios. This assumption ignores differences in types of buildings, quality of construction, building size, age of improvements, architectural design, building features, vacancy ratios, location characteristics, length of leases, and types of tenants. Since net operating income is the basis of value, under the capitalized income approach, failure to forecast anticipated operating expenses accurately is bound to be reflected in grossly unreliable appraisal reporting.

INCOME DEDUCTIONS VERSUS OPERATING EXPENSES

An understanding of accounting procedures proves helpful in identifying and classifying expenditures which are personal in character, or which are of the nature of income deductions as opposed to expenditures that are essential to the operation of a property. Confusion often arises because of differences in treatment of certain expenses under conventional profit and loss accounting as compared with income and expense classification for appraisal purposes. Two of the most important outlays incurred in connection with ownership of real property are (1) mortgage interest and mortgage amortization payments and (2) allowances for investment losses due to depreciation (capital recovery) of the property. There is no question concerning the fact that under conventional tax accounting both of these expenditures—that is, mortgage interest and depreciation charges—are costs of ownership. But in the appraisal of real property, mortgage interest charges are considered operating costs only when evaluating the *equity* (that is, the owner's interest in the property exclusive of the mortgage lien). When borrowing funds, an investor, as a rule, engages in *trading on the equity.* Under such circumstances the investor finds it profitable to borrow funds at interest rates lower than the property is expected to earn as an operating entity. In deriving gains from interest differentials between the rate of property earnings and the cost of borrowing money, the owner is assuming investment risks for which—if his or her efforts are successful—he or she is being appropriately compensated. But such financial dealings are personal in character (a business venture within itself) and must be classified as income deductions and not as expenditures essential to the operation of a property. The price of a given parcel of investment real estate generally varies with the terms and conditions of sale, but its value must be measured in relation to net operating income derived under typical management, free and clear of all encumbrances, including mortgage liens.

Measuring depreciation either for federal income tax reasons or corporate purposes does not necessarily relate to a property's actual monetary loss in value. Moreover, under the capitalized income approach it is superfluous to enter an amount for such depreciation. The property owner and tenants already have recognized the physical state of the leased building in the rental payment.

INCOME TAX AND PROPERTY TAX CONSIDERATIONS

Personal and corporate income taxes, too, must be excluded as costs of operation when valuing real property. Income tax payments vary with the income brackets into which the taxable earnings of individuals and corporations fall. Such payments are important to a purchaser of property and may influence his or her decision as to whether to buy a given property; but its value must be found free and clear of such personal considerations. Otherwise, the practice of real estate appraising would lose its general applicability as a guide to market value. That is, market value would vary according to the particular financial status of each prospective purchaser.

Real estate (property) taxes are correctly classified as an operating expense. The omission of property taxes would overstate the net operating income used for capitalization purposes and, as a consequence, the answer sought in the valuation assignment. On important occasions, however, the value to be used for tax purposes is at issue, as in the case of a *tax certiorari* proceeding.[1] To include as an operating expense a tax payment made on what is believed to be an excessive assessment would lower both net operating income and value, as compared with the market value that would prevail under equalized tax assessment practices. Where value for tax purposes is at issue—and this is an exception rather than a rule—property taxes as an amount can also be excluded from the operating expense schedule, and taxes as a rate (percentage per hundred dollars of assessed value) can be added to the rate of capitalization. In such instances the appraiser excludes an operating expense amount which depends on the value sought. Thus, if the rate of capitalization is 8 percent and the rate of taxation based on market value is 20 mills, or 2 percent, value for tax purposes can be derived by capitalizing net operating income before property taxes by a combined rate of 10 percent. This method is also applicable for proposed construction where the real estate taxes are unknown. Suppose, for instance, that the forecast net operating income (excluding real estate taxes) for a proposed property is $28,000 annually. Further, the market-derived overall capitalization rate is 12 percent. If the tax rate is 2 percent, the estimated value is as follows:

$$\$28,000 \div 0.14 = \$200,000$$

The application of a real estate tax appeal valuation problem will be demonstrated in connection with review question 10 at the end of the chapter.

CLASSIFICATION OF OPERATING EXPENSES

In nearly all appraisal assignments it becomes necessary to reconstruct operating expense schedules and to adjust—over the forecast income period—expenditures in accordance with those estimated to be incurred under typical management and operation. This requires knowledge of property maintenance, as well as the analysis of operating performance of comparable properties in similar locations.

Operating expense schedules generally are arranged for recording of costs under the following headings:

1. Fixed charges.
2. Variable expenses.
3. Reserves for replacement.

Fixed charges are those which as a rule vary little, if at all, with occupancy from year to year. This category includes property taxes and insurance for fire, theft, and comprehensive hazards.

[1]If an owner believes that the assessed value of his or her property is too high, and is unable to secure a reduction upon protest to the tax officials, he or she can appeal to the courts. Such a court case is known as a *certiorari* or tax appeal proceeding.

Variable expenses include expenditures for periodic maintenance, management, janitorial services, heating, utilities, repairs, and miscellaneous building supplies. These expenses tend to vary with the level of tenant occupancy.

Reserves for replacement cover outlays on a pro rata basis of the estimated service life of furnishings and fixtures. For instance, if an apartment building contains 20 refrigerators each having an estimated service life of 10 years, the reserve for replacement in this case would call for expense provision equal to costs of two refrigerators annually. Similarly, if each of the 20 apartments is decorated once every fourth year, annual provision would include the cost of 20 divided by four—or five apartments typically would be decorated during any one year. Where exterior fronts, roofing, and plumbing are replaced at service-life intervals, like provision would be made, generally on a straight-line accounting basis.

It is recommended that operating expense schedules be reconstructed in accordance with the accounting procedure followed by a group such as the International Building Owners and Managers Association. This permits comparison of expense estimates with those typically incurred for similar properties and as reported annually by the association in its BOMA *Building Experience Exchange Report*, available through the Washington office of the association. A listing of several income-expense sources is given at the end of this chapter. Cost comparisons for office buildings can readily be made from these reports on a per-square-foot basis of rentable space for the following items:

Operating expenses. Cleaning including trash removal, repairs and maintenance, utilities, roads/grounds/security, and administrative.

Fixed expenses. Real estate taxes, building insurance, personal property tax, and other taxes.

Leasing expenses. Advertising/promotion, commissions, professional fees, tenant alterations, buy-outs, and other leasing.

A good source for apartment income-expense data is *Income/Expense Analysis—Conventional Apartments*, which is published annually by the Institute of Real Estate Management. This publication presents trends in apartment building operations and includes income and operating cost data and tenant turnover data for various types of apartment buildings by selected metropolitan areas, region, and by age. An example of an income-expense presentation is shown in Table 14.1.

Typical income and operating expenditures for garden apartment buildings, based on an annual survey by the Institute of Real Estate Management, are classified by square feet of rentable area and median percentage of gross possible total income in Table 14.1.

For operating expense data and comparative performance statistics of hotels, informative reports are published by Pannell Kerr Forster, Accountants and Auditors.[2]

Detailed data for major cities given for average hotel revenues and expenditures include the following:

[2]*Trends in the Hotel Industry, USA Edition 1989.* (Houston, Tex.: Pannell Kerr Forster).

TABLE 14.1 COMPARISON OF MEDIAN INCOME AND OPERATING COSTS FOR GARDEN APARTMENT BUILDINGS UNFURNISHED, UNITED STATES, 1989

	Median $/sq ft (rentable area)	Median percentage of GPI
Income		
Rents		
Apartments	5.70	97.3
Garage/parking	0.13	2.0
Stores/offices	0.08	2.2
Gross possible rents	5.71	97.5
Vacancies/rent loss	0.46	7.4
Total rents collected	5.19	89.4
Other income	0.16	2.6
Gross possible income	5.89	100.0
Total collections	5.39	92.6
Expenses		
Management fee	0.27	4.6
Other administrative	0.40	6.8
Subtotal administrative	0.68	11.3
Supplies	0.02	0.3
Heating fuel		
CA[a] only	0.04	0.7
CA and apartments	0.21	3.4
Electricity		
CA only	0.10	1.7
CA and apartments	0.11	1.8
Water/sewer		
CA only	0.10	1.7
CA and apartments	0.17	2.7
Gas		
CA only	0.03	0.4
CA and apartments	0.11	1.7
Building services	0.07	1.1
Other operating	0.03	0.6
Subtotal operating	0.53	9.2
Security	0.02	0.4
Grounds maintenance	0.13	2.1
Maintenance—repair	0.22	3.7
Painting/decorating-interior	0.14	2.4
Subtotal maintenance	0.53	8.9
Real estate taxes	0.46	7.6
Other taxes/fees/permits	0.01	0.1
Insurance	0.11	1.8
Subtotal tax and insurance	0.59	9.8
Recreational/amenities	0.02	0.4
Other payroll	0.31	5.2
Total all expenses	2.56	42.9
Net operating income	2.68	45.6
Number of buildings in sample	740	743

[a]CA denotes common areas.
Source: *Income/Expense Analysis—Conventional Apartments* (Chicago: Institute of Real Estate Management, 1990), p. 22.

Revenues.
Departmental costs and expenses.
Undistributed operating expenses.
Property taxes and insurance.
Percentage of occupancy.
Average daily rate per occupied room.
Average room size.

This report provides statistics for 1,000 hotels and motels in the United States. It emphasizes trends of hotel and motel income and expenses, earnings on capitalization, occupancy ratios, room rates, and disposition of the hotel dollar. These facilities are analyzed according to type and operations, showing 20-year trends. For purposes of hotel and motel appraising, this publication offers important statistical data which are most useful in a study of comparative income and expense performance. A summary of selected motel revenue and expenses is shown in Table 14.2.

OPERATING EXPENSE SCHEDULE RECONSTRUCTION

An owner's typical expense statement for a 20-unit apartment house may contain information as shown in Table 14.3. A reconstructed owner's operating expense statement for appraisal report analysis and valuation of the subject property is presented in Table 14.4. The reference numbers noted in the reconstructed operating expense statement are a guide to explanatory footnotes as follows:

1. Revenue was adjusted upward in the amount of $6,000 to include rental value of $500 per month for an apartment occupied by the resident janitor.
2. Vacancy and collection losses, based on a community rental study and records of the local Association of Realtors, typically amount to 5 percent of gross income at 100 percent occupancy. This rental loss was provided to cover vacancy contingencies over the forecast income period for the property.
3. Insurance coverage was increased to 80 percent of coinsurance requirements.
4. Management costs for comparable properties equal 6 percent of effective gross revenue (sometimes called collectible rent). Subject building is owner managed.
5. Janitorial expenses were adjusted to include cost (income forgone) of apartment furnished for his use.
6. Miscellaneous supplies for cleaning were estimated at a cost of $25 for each of the 20 apartments.
7. Miscellaneous repairs increased to equal typical expenditures estimated at 3 percent of potential gross income.
8. Refrigerator expenses adjusted to provide for two per year at $850 each. Service life is 10 years, or $20 \div 10 = 2$.

TABLE 14.2 185 MOTELS WITHOUT RESTAURANTS
SELECTED REVENUE AND EXPENSE ITEMS—20-YEAR TREND

	Year							
	1969	1974	1979	1984	1985	1986	1987	1988
Ratios to total revenues:								
Total operated departments' income	70.4%	69.3%	74.7%	76.5%	74.7%	74.9%	75.2%	73.7%
Income after property taxes and insurance[a]	42.0	33.9	40.2	43.5	43.2	41.7	40.5	37.3
Property taxes and insurance	6.4	7.7	5.3	3.5	3.5	4.7	5.0	5.1
Payroll and related costs	18.9	24.3	23.7	19.7	21.4	19.4	18.1	18.0
Dollars per available room:								
Total revenues	$3,727	$4,277	$7,916	$8,871	$10,674	$9,996	$10,364	$10,171
Income after property taxes and insurance[a]	1,749	1,535	3,182	3,860	4,623	4,170	4,178	3,717
Percentage of occupancy	76.3%	65.9%	68.2%	61.8%	69.1%	66.2%	66.1%	63.8%
Average room rate	$14.07	$17.76	$29.50	$36.98	$37.39	$38.91	$40.64	$41.37

[a]The income after property taxes and insurance, wherever it appears in this study, is before deducting depreciation, rent, interest, amortization, and income taxes.
Source: *Trends in the Hotel Industry USA Edition 1989* (Houston, Tex.: Pannell Kerr Forster, 1989), Figure 43, p. 81.

TABLE 14.3   OWNER'S OPERATING EXPENSE STATEMENT FOR THE YEAR 19__

Revenue			$111,150
Operating expenses:			
Taxes		$11,250	
Insurance			
Fire	$1,350		
Theft	225		
Liability	180		
		1,755	
Maintenance			
Janitor—exclusive of apartment		4,500	
Heat—oil		5,400	
Water		675	
Electricity		1,000	
Repairs—miscellaneous		900	
Elevator—contract		1,800	
Replacements			
1 refrigerator		850	
1 stove		600	
Decorating—6 apartments		4,000	
Mortgage—interest		2,700	
Amortization		2,250	
Paving assessment		4,500	
Depreciation		10,000	
Total operating expenses			$ 52,180
Net operating income			$ 58,970

9. Stove replacement adjusted to provide for purchase of two per year at $600 each.

10. Decorating expenses were adjusted to provide for refurbishing each apartment once every four years at a cost of $540 each.

11. Roof replacement required once every 20 years at a cost of $36,000 (5 percent of $36,000 = $1,800).

12. Plumbing and electrical replacements based on the service life of fixtures of 20 years, or 5 percent of $72,000 = $3,600.

13. Lobby and hall furnishings at a cost of $8,000 are replaceable every 10 years, or at a cost of $800 per year.

14. Other expenses shown in the owner's statement were omitted as follows:
    (a) Mortgage interest and amortization payments are income deductions, not property expenses. Financing arrangements benefit the owner and not the subject property.
    (b) Paving assessments are capital improvement outlays which increase the value of the property.
    (c) Depreciation is included as a rate of return to the property owner in the building rate of capitalization. To include it here would provide a dual return.

TABLE 14.4 RECONSTRUCTED OPERATING EXPENSE STATEMENT FOR THE YEAR 19___

	As reported	As adjusted	Reference
Potential gross income	$111,150	$117,150	1
Vacancy and collection losses 5%		5,858	2
Effective gross income		$111,292	
Operating expenses			
Fixed expenses			
Taxes	11,250	11,250	
Insurance	1,755	2,140	3
Maintenance costs			
Management 6%		6,678	4
Janitor	4,500	10,500	5
Heat	5,400	5,400	
Water	675	675	
Electricity	1,000	1,000	
Miscellaneous—supplies		500	6
Elevator—contract service	1,800	1,800	
Miscellaneous—repairs	900	3,515	7
Replacements			
Refrigerators	850	1,700	8
Stoves	600	1,200	9
Decorating	4,000	2,700	10
Roof replacement		1,800	11
Plumbing and electrical		3,600	12
Furniture—lobby and halls		800	13
Other expenses	19,450	—	14
Total operating expenses	$ 52,180	$ 55,258	
Net operating income		$ 56,034	15

Operating expense ratio $55,258 \div $111,293 = 50\%$
Operating expense ratio (using PGI) $55,258 \div $117,150 = 47\%$

15. It is recommended that the net operating income used be that income expected for the appraised property as of the date of appraisal. Operating expenses should be as of the same date. Use of "stabilized net operating income" is an unclear concept since it may be for the early years of a loan, the typical investor's holding period, or for some other future period.

RESERVES FOR REPLACEMENTS

This is a troublesome part of the appraisal process. In this section the issues are explored and the relative merits of the different ways of handling this phase are presented. Each reader will need to decide on the most applicable handling of replacement reserves. The opposite positions on this issue are:

1. (*Pro*) Any wasting asset with a useful life less than the remaining life of the building will need to be replaced—maybe more than once. If the stated operating expenses fail to recognize these future expenses on an annualized

basis, the net operating income and in turn the appraised value of the subject property will be overstated.

2. (*Con*) Most investors do not include an entry for replacement reserves. In fact, one study revealed that 58 percent of real estate investors did not include such provision for replacements.[3] This argument goes on to say that if investors do not recognize this future expense in their statements, but only pay for such replacements when they occur, then appraisers are not faithfully representing the real estate market when this "artificial" entry is made in their appraisal reports.

One point is certainly clear: Appraisers should know whether income-expense records for comparable income and sale properties either include or exclude replacement reserves. Ignorance of this information will distort the expense ratio, net operating income, and appraised value of the subject property.

If replacement reserves are included, there are three basic ways of handling them.[4]

Method 1. Identify the short-lived items that must be replaced during the remaining economic life of the building; determine how many times the item will need to be replaced; estimate its cost; determine the total cost; and finally determine the annualized average replacement cost as follows:

Item	Expected life (years)	Number of replacements $\times$	Cost per replacement =	Total cost	Average annual replacement cost
Roofing	20	2	$10,000	$20,000	$400[a]

[a]$20,000 ÷ 50 years.

Method 2. It can be argued that method 1 is illogical since it places as much weight on an item to be replaced in 40 years as one requiring replacement in 20 years. Thus a more appropriate means would be to recognize the time value of money by finding the present worth of these future replacements via the sinking fund factor. This process only considers the first replacement, but it could just as well include the present worth of subsequent replacements. Applying a 10 percent discount rate to the preceding example produces the following annual roofing replacement reserve requirement, which is considerably less than that given by the previous method:

[3]Robert H. Zerbst and Gary W. Eldred, "The Specification of Net Operating Income," *The Real Estate Appraiser and Analyst* (November–December 1979), p. 43, citing Kenneth M. Lusht, *The Behavior of Appraisers in Valuing Multifamily Property*, unpublished report sponsored by the Society of Real Estate Appraisers Foundation.

[4]For more detail, see Jay C. Troxel, "Replacement Reserves Reviewed," *The Real Estate Appraiser* (September–October 1974), pp. 44–47.

Item	Expected life (years)	Cost of replacement	10 percent sinking fund factor	Annual requirement
Roofing	20	$10,000	0.017460	$174.60

Method 3.   Consistent with the trend of analyzing income streams over typical investors' holding periods, it seems reasonable to forecast reserve replacements over a like period instead of the remaining economic life of the improvements. It seems far more reasonable to include income, expenses, and reserves of a 5- to 10-year holding period than to go beyond this time frame. Why include a replacement reserve for 20 to 40 years if the investor will likely sell the property prior to the end of this longer period? To make the inclusion of these reserves even more realistic, a sinking fund method is preferable to an average annual cost method. This method then would exclude such longer-life items as a 20-year roof, but include shorter-term replaceable building components such as carpeting, refrigerators, ranges, decorating, interior improvements for leased space, and parking lots:

Item	Expected life (years)	Cost of replacement	10 percent sinking fund factor	Annual requirement
Refrigerators	7	$8,500	0.105405	$895.94

For greater accuracy in appraisal reporting and to provide assurance that income and expense forecasting reflects the feasible performance capacity of the subject property, it is recommended that the appraiser analyze, whenever possible, income and expense accounting statements for a period of at least three full years. Income or expenditures in any one year may not prove to be indicative of normal operations. Analysis of several years of property operating performance will enable the appraiser to "normalize" operating expense trends and to forecast with greater accuracy the anticipated income stream for the forecast income period of the appraised property.

THE SIGNIFICANCE OF OPERATING EXPENSE RATIOS

Although revenue and operating expenses are independently estimated, a definite relationship exists between them. The amount of rental income for given types of properties varies directly with the amount and quality of services, furnishings, and facilities offered the tenants. Increased revenue from superior conveniences and amenities provided occupants is in turn based on higher operating outlays to supply these services. Characteristically, however, although gross revenue rises and falls in proportion to percentage of occupancy, operating expenses are relatively inflexible. Property taxes and insurance payments do not diminish, even where the property at times is 100 percent vacant. Heating, cooling, and janitorial services, too, remain relatively constant. Except for managerial service cost—which is considered a percentage of the effective gross revenue—other expense charges are relatively inflexible.

The inelasticity of operating expenses impairs the amount of net operating income that is derived from properties with high operating expense ratios. To illustrate: Suppose that two properties, A and B, each yield a net operating income of $20,000 as follows:

	Property A	Property B
Effective gross income	$100,000	$40,000
Operating expense	80,000	20,000
Net operating income	$ 20,000	$20,000

Property A, as shown, has an operating ratio (operating expenses divided by effective gross revenue) of 80 percent. The operating ratio for property B is 50 percent. A decline in gross revenue of only 10 percent will, for property A, cause a decrease of 50 percent in the available net operating income. A decrease of 20 percent in revenue will wipe out property A's net operating income entirely. Property B, however, will experience a much less drastic decline in its net income. A decrease of 10 and 20 percent in revenue causes only a drop of 20 and 40 percent, respectively, in the net operating income of property B. High operating ratios thus impair the amount of anticipated income. Increased risk of operation as measured by high operating ratios necessitates, as will be explained more fully in the following chapter, a selection of a higher rate of capitalization—which in turn results in a lower value estimate of the property. Everything else remaining equal, the income stream of $20,000 from property B is worth more than the identical income anticipated from property A, the difference in value being a direct reflection of the investor's unwillingness to gamble with economically sensitive income returns.

Knowledge of typical operating expense ratios is helpful in judging the efficiency of building operating performance and value. If typical residential properties indicate prevailing operating ratios between 35 and 40 percent of effective gross income, an operating ratio of 55 percent for a subject property should be cause for inquiry to ascertain the reason for such poor performance. Many factors such as poor construction, mismanagement, glutted market, and neighborhood decline may underlie the increased economic hazards reflected by the excessive operating ratio.

Typical operating expense ratios for various types of properties may fall into the following percentage ranges:

Residential, single-family structures	35–40%
Apartment buildings—garden	40–50%
Apartment buildings—automatic elevator	45–55%
Office buildings	40–60%
Store and loft buildings	50–60%
Retail	15–30%

These expense ratios vary from area to area with local rental customs and community building use regulations. Like other rules of thumb, operating ratios should not be used as a prime measure of value, but rather should serve as an indicator to judge the reasonableness of the results obtained through reconstruction of owner's income and expense operating statements. An excessively high—or unusually low—operating ratio may be a warning sign that reanalysis of income-expense data is warranted to safeguard against possible errors.

Several caveats are in order regarding use of operating-expense ratios. First, the appraiser must understand how it was computed for a comparable property. Was it based on the ratio of operating expenses (with or without replacement reserves) to potential gross income or to effective gross income? Once having determined how it was computed, it should be applied to the appraised property in the same manner. For example, if it was based on the comparable property's effective gross income, it should then be applied to the subject's effective gross income. For some buildings, such as office buildings, it may be more accurate to rely on operating expenses per square foot of leasable area rather than expense ratios.

Without some knowledge of the comparable property, a sizable error could occur when applying the derived operating ratio to the subject property. Some factors that could distort the ratio are:

1. Different building designs can cause different expense ratios.
2. Buildings of different ages or in different locations can experience different income levels but the same square-foot expenses.
3. The netness of leases can alter the share of expenses borne by the lessor and in turn affect the operating expense ratio.

CAPITAL EXPENDITURES

Care should also be taken in the analysis of operating expenses to exclude outlays or investments for capital improvements. Additions of porches, bathrooms, carports, or utility rooms, for instance, increase property value. As a rule improvements of this kind also increase the utility and appeal of the property and produce greater rentals or amenities for the occupying owner. The test of whether an expenditure is a true operating expense or not rests on the nature of the expenditure and the necessity of the outlay in relation to the operating care and maintenance of the property. Intimate knowledge of the operating performance of the various property types for which appraisal opinions are to be rendered is a prerequisite to sound and professional appraisal practice.

SUMMARY

Failure to analyze expense schedules and property operating performance may be the cause of substantial errors in the final estimate of value. Operating expense-to-income ratios vary according to differences in types of buildings, quality of construction, building size, age of improvements, architectural design, building features, vacancy ratios, location characteristics, length of leases, and type of tenants.

Certain expenses are considered in conventional profit and loss accounting but not in classifying income and expenses for appraisal purposes. Although mortgage payments and allowances for depreciation are important deductions for accounting purposes, they generally are excluded in valuing real property. Moreover, accounting either for federal income tax or corporate purposes does not necessarily relate to a property's actual monetary loss in value. Personal and corporate income taxes, too, must be excluded as costs of building operation.

The three categories of operating expenses are:

Fixed charges such as property taxes and insurance premiums which vary little, if at all, with changing occupancy levels.

Variable expenses generally vary in accordance with the level of tenant occupancy and include such expenses as periodic maintenance, management, janitorial services, heating, utilities, repairs, and building supplies.

Reserves for replacement cover outlays on a pro rata basis for the estimated service life of furnishings and fixtures that will last a shorter time than a building's remaining economic life. Examples include refrigerators, stoves, roofing, floor covering, plumbing, and heating and air-conditioning systems.

A property owner will prepare income-expense statements to serve his or her particular objectives. These objectives as well as the assumptions and methods used in preparing an owner's statement often do not fulfill the standards for real estate appraising. Hence appraisers reconstruct owners' real estate income-expense statements to meet these valuation standards.

Appraisers must know whether income-expense records for comparable income and sale properties either include or exclude replacement reserves. The argument for including reserves for replacements is that if the stated operating expenses fail to recognize these future expenses on an annualized basis, the net operating income and in turn the appraised value of the subject property will be overstated. The argument against including these reserves is that most investors do not include an entry for replacement reserves and for the appraiser to do so results in an "artificial" entry in the appraisal report.

The amount of rental income for given types of properties varies directly with the amount and quality of services, furnishings, and facilities offered tenants. Therefore, knowledge of typical operating expense ratios is helpful in judging the efficiency of building operating performance and value.

Capital expenditures should be excluded from operating expense statements. These expenses increase property value rather than maintain the condition of the property for its intended purpose.

REVIEW QUESTIONS

1. List three items that may appear in an owner's income-expense statement that should be disallowed for appraisal purposes.
2. Briefly distinguish between fixed charges and variable or maintenance expenses.
3. List arguments for and against inclusion of reserves for replacements.
4. Prepare an example of how the value of a property can be estimated via capitalized net operating income using the real estate tax rate in lieu of real estate taxes expressed in dollars.
5. Give three ways that an inaccurate operating expense ratio can distort the estimated net operating income of an appraised property.
6. Identify the several methods of setting up replacement reserves. Select a method that you prefer and explain the reasoning for your choice.
7. Two properties have the following income schedules:

	Property A	Property B
Revenue	$100,000	$40,000
Operating expense	80,000	20,000
Net operating income	$ 20,000	$20,000

Which property has greater value? Why? Explain your reasoning.

8. Based on the following facts, determine the correct net operating income for the apartment property:
   (a) Building contains 40 apartments renting at $300.00 (average rental) each month. Remaining building life is estimated at 40 years.
   (b) Observation reveals that vacancy and collection losses currently average 10 percent for competitive properties.
   (c) Property management fees for this type of property typically average 5 percent of effective gross income in this market.
   (d) The following expenses are listed for the calendar year:

Taxes on land and building	$14,400
Power and light	1,200
Depreciation provision	9,600
Repairs	4,800
Renovating and painting	7,200
Janitor expense	1,200
Extermination	360
Replacements:	
40 ranges (8-year life)	18,000
40 refrigerators (12-year life)	36,000
New roof	6,600
Legal fees	720
Corporation tax	1,800
Income taxes	2,100
Mortgage interest	7,200
Mortgage amortization	6,000
Management fees	7,200
Water	2,700
Fire insurance (three-year policy)	3,600
Paving assessment	2,400
Promotion and advertising	1,500

9. In estimating capitalizable net operating income for office or apartment properties, should depreciation expense be subtracted from effective gross revenue? Explain your reasons fully.

10. A skyscraper office building on Madison Avenue in New York City was assessed for $20,500,000, and the property tax at $3.00 per $100 of assessed value or $615,000. The owners claimed overassessment and instituted appeal proceedings to reduce taxes in conformity with fair market value. Assuming a land value of $5,000,000, a net operating income after real estate taxes (as billed) of $1,600,000, a discount rate of 9.0 percent, and an annual recapture rate of 2.5 percent, determine the following:
    (a) The capitalized value of the property (see Chapter 17).
    (b) Property taxes based on this value.
    (c) Net operating income after (fair) taxes.

READING AND STUDY REFERENCES

American Institute of Real Estate Appraisers. "Operating Expenses," *The Appraisal of Real Estate*. Chicago: AIREA, 1987, pp. 445–453.

EPLEY, DONALD R., and JAMES H. BOYKIN. Chapter 8, "Estimate of Net Operating Income, I," *Basic Income Property Appraisal*. Reading, Mass.: Addison-Wesley Publishing Co., Inc., 1983.

HINES, MARY ALICE. Chapter 11, "Income Approach: Estimation of Revenue and Expenses," *Real Estate Appraisal*. New York: Macmillan Publishing Company, 1981.

MANN, GEORGE R. "Replacement Allowance: Modified Sinking Fund Method," *The Appraisal Journal* 53, no. 4 (October 1990), pp. 486–493.

SLACK, THEODORE C. "How to Find the Real Estate Taxes When You Don't Yet Know the Assessment," *The Real Estate Appraiser and Analyst* 50, no. 3 (Fall 1984), pp. 19–20.

TROXEL, JAY C. "Replacement Reserves Reviewed," *The Real Estate Appraiser* 40, no. 5 (September–October 1974), pp. 44–47.

LISTING OF PUBLISHED INCOME-EXPENSE SOURCES

Building Owners and Managers Association International. *Experience Exchange Report: Income/Expense Analysis for Office Buildings*. 1201 New York Avenue NW, Suite 300, Washington, DC 20005.

Institute of Real Estate Management. *Income/Expense Analysis: Apartments*. 430 North Michigan Avenue, Chicago, IL 60611 (annual operating costs by region, metropolis, and building type).

Institute of Real Estate Management. *Income/Expense Analysis: Office Buildings (Downtown and Suburban)* (annual operating data for different categories of buildings by national, regional, and metropolitan areas).

Institute of Real Estate Management. *Expense Analysis: Condominiums, Cooperatives and PUDs* (annual data on over 40 expense categories; metropolitan, regional, and national statistics).

National Retail Merchants Association, Controllers' Congress. *Department Store and Specialty Store Merchandising and Operating Results.* 100 West 31st Street, New York, NY 10001 (annual merchandising results such as financial ratios, operating data, and merchandising data).

Pannell Kerr Forster. *Trends in the Hotel Industry International and USA Editions.* 262 North Belt East, Suite 300, Houston, TX 77060 (annual income-expense data and operating ratios by region).

Urban Land Institute. *Dollars and Cents of Shopping Centers.* 625 Indiana Avenue NW, Washington, DC 20077–1555 (published every three years and containing income-expense data by type of shopping center and tenant).

15

Determining the Rate of Capitalization

Learning Objectives

After reading this chapter, you should be able to:

- Appreciate the primary motivation for the purchase of real property
- Recognize and discuss the relationship among the various rates of return
- Define and give examples of each rate of return
- Compute an overall capitalization rate using any of the different techniques presented herein
- Distinguish between interest rates and capitalization rates applied to physical and financial components of real estate
- Develop and properly use capitalization rates applied to net operating income

The most important, perhaps the most controversial, and often the weakest phase of property valuation revolves about the procedure for the determination of a market rate of capitalization through which estimated future net operating income is converted into an estimate of present value. The capitalization rate acts as a conversion mechanism to convert periodic income into an estimate of present value.

There is an inverse relationship between capitalization rates and value. That is, the lower the capitalization rate, the higher the value per dollar of income. Of course, the opposite effect occurs as progressively higher capitalization rates are applied to property income. Just as important is the magnification of value that results from apparently modest differences in capitalization rates. This relationship is shown in Table 15.1 and emphasizes the care required by appraisers in deriving capitalization rates. It is shown in Table 15.1 that a one-half percent error in selecting a capitalization rate causes a value variance of $47,019 to $52,632, and a one percent error results in a value difference of $100,251.

TABLE 15.1   VALUE DISTORTION CAUSE BY RATE SELECTION ERROR

Income	Capitalization rate (%)	Value	Value difference
$100,000	9.50	$1,052,632	$52,632
100,000	10.00	1,000,000	47,619
100,000	10.50	952,381	

The basic relationship of income to value through the use of a rate or recip-rocal conversion factor is expressed by the formulas $V = I/R$ or $V = I \times F$. To find present value, income is divided by a rate and multiplied by a factor.

In these formulas the symbols used represent the following:

V = present worth of future rights to income

I = property income (usually annual)

R = rate of capitalization applicable to the conversion of income (over holding period, limited property life, or in perpetuity) into value

F = reciprocal of capitalization rate (a convenience factor employed to convert income into value by process of multiplication rather than division; usually, a factor is used to convert gross income to value and a rate is used to convert net operating income to value)

Whenever two of the factors represented by the symbols in the foregoing for-mulas are known, the third or unknown factor can be calculated mathematically. Thus, if value and income amounts are known, the capitalization rate or the re-ciprocal rate factor (multiplier) can be calculated by application of the formulas $R = I/V$ or $F = V/I$. Similarly, applicable income is ascertained by use of the for-mulas $I = V \times R$ or $I = V/F$. Figure 15.1 provides handy memory tools for ready appraisal reference. These pie charts are used by covering the desired quantity (e.g., V); the equation is completed by the remaining two symbols which in this case are I divided by R.

Appraisers often spend hours if not days in the analysis of income and oper-ating expense statements in order to estimate accurately the net operating income essential to market (investment) value. By comparison, relatively little time is employed in the selection of the applicable capitalization rate even though an error of only 1 percentage point (e.g., use of 8 percent in place of a 7 percent rate) causes an error of 12.5 percent in the final estimate of value. It seems advisable, therefore, to spend less time on auditing of minor accounts and more time on the study of market indexes which offer an insight into capitalization rates expected by investors.

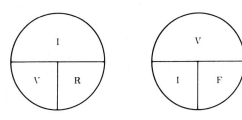

Figure 15.1 Income-Value-Rate and Factor Relation Charts

Why is it so difficult to derive a correct rate of capitalization? This is a question often raised. The answer revolves about the problems encountered in ferreting out accurate information for objective analysis of the varied and numerous subjective reasons motivating buyers to purchase properties at given prices and times. But even if buyer motives were known, it is still essential to extract reliable and accurate information concerning the net operating income of a subject property.

Generally, real property is purchased for one or more of the following reasons:

1. *Investment.* In this classification fall all buyers who intend to hold property for its income or, if vacant land, to develop it into an income-producing investment.

2. *Owners' use or pleasure.* Under this category fall home owners, store owners, and other individuals who acquire property for purposes other than investment or speculation. In such cases property utility in terms of income-producing capacity must be estimated.

3. *Speculation.* This classification includes those whose principal motive in buying is to profit from the resale of the property at some future time. Properties purchased for speculation, such as vacant land, may produce no income at all; in fact, the income may be negative, in the form of outlays for taxes and related costs of ownership.

4. *Investment and speculation.* This type of purchase is often motivated by the desire to improve the income tax position of the buyer. The buyer anticipates rental income during the holding period followed by a profit upon resale.

Where speculation or motives other than investment buying are prime reasons for a purchase, the sale price of the property in relation to its income may offer little aid to the appraiser in his or her search for applicable market rates of capitalization. In fact, such sales, if used, may prove highly misleading as indicators of prevailing yields on real estate investment. This can be illustrated by a hypothetical sale as follows:

Suppose that 40 acres of suburban property is purchased at a price of $1,000 per acre in anticipation that it will increase to $4,000 per acre in 10 years' time. Suppose, further, that the land is rented for cattle-grazing purposes and produces a rent just equal to taxes and miscellaneous outlays, leaving a zero operating income. Under traditional analysis where the appraiser relates current income to current market prices, the resultant rate of capitalization would be zero since no net income is realized by the purchaser. Should this property, however, sell for $4,000 per acre as anticipated 10 years later, the resultant increment in value represents a yield of nearly 15 percent per annum. Reference to a compound annuity table will confirm that $1.00 invested at 15 percent compound interest will grow to $4.05 in 10 years' time. The necessity to consider both appreciation and depreciation of the investment during the period of ownership is most essential and will be given more detailed consideration later in this chapter and in Chapter 20.

Although difficult, it generally is necessary in selecting a rate of capitalization for the appraiser to thoroughly analyze investment property sales in the community. Real estate transactions are traditionally private and confidential in nature and factual income data are often difficult to obtain. More difficult still is obtaining sales that could be usefully employed for income analysis.

Although real estate as a commodity is local in character, the financing and purchase of real estate—both for investment and speculative purposes—have characteristics of a national market. The mobility of credit and the flexibility of investment buying with income reserves and surpluses accumulated by insurance companies, investment firms, and labor union pension funds have—as is the case with "arbitrage" in the stock and commodity markets—channeled funds into community areas where the investment returns in relation to capital risks are highest. The existence of a national real estate investment market makes available for real properties national income and rate-of-return statistics which are compiled by investment firms and real estate analysts. These national indices of investment yields, when adjusted for community and regional risks for given classes of real properties, can be used as effective guides in judging the reasonableness of rates of capitalization secured from market analysis of comparable sales.

Even though an appraiser may not readily translate capital market trends into capitalization rates, a familiarity with these markets, inflationary trends, and federal monetary and fiscal policy are desirable to providing astute services to clients. Since institutional investors, such as life insurance companies, are primarily obligated to protect the financial interests of their investors or policyholders, they seek investments that balance risk and yield. As a consequence, they invest in real estate only when it is competitive with stocks, bonds, and securities. Therefore, competition exists between real estate and nonrealty alternatives. If an appraiser is aware of the yields on these alternative investments, he or she has a sound basis for developing real estate capitalization rates.

Historically, mortgage lenders have sought a "real" earnings rate of about 3 percentage points over the anticipated rate of inflation. Thus mortgage interest rates ordinarily would be pegged to the *expected* inflation rate. An understanding of inflationary trends as related to mortgage interest rates assumes major significance since most of the capital involved in real estate investments is debt capital. A fairly close pattern generally exists between prevailing mortgage constants and overall capitalization rates. Similarly, since federal monetary policy, as administered by the Federal Reserve System, strongly influences interest rates, it behooves appraisers to be able to anticipate market conditions that will probably prompt intervention in the nation's economy by the Federal Reserve System. Important as well is the fact that in order for a capitalization rate to be supportable it must be similar to returns provided by equivalent investments.

TYPES OF RATES OF RETURN

The types of and purposes served by various types of rates in common use today will be discussed next. Appraisers should be able to recognize and differentiate among the following:

1. Interest rate, i.
2. Capitalization rate, R.
3. Overall capitalization rate, R_o.
4. Building capitalization rate, R_B.
5. Land capitalization rate, R_L.
6. Amortization rate, or sinking fund factor, $1/S_{\overline{n}}$.
7. Mortgage rate, R_M.
8. Equity dividend rate, R_E.
9. Equity yield rate, Y_E.
10. Property yield rate, Y_o.
11. Composite capitalization rate.

(i) Interest Rate

The *interest rate* is in effect a measure of the cost of money and represents "wages" paid for the use of capital. It is a return on the investment and must be high enough to attract capital to a particular kind of investment. The interest rate defined is based on the continued and unimpaired existence of the property as an investment entity. The rate does not include any provision for recapture. The interest rate is a market phenomenon and varies in amount with the supply and demand of money, and with the quality characteristics of the investment property. The interest rate as a composite annual return per dollar of investment is influenced by the following market forces:

1. Rate of interest on government bonds on guaranteed bank deposits.
2. Burden of management or cost of maintaining the investment, including bookkeeping, rent collecting, inspection, and fund supervision expenses.
3. Relative liquidity of the investment for conversion into cash.
4. Risk of loss of income and investment due to competition or operation of economic forces as reflected by the phase of the business cycle.

(R) Cap Rate Defined

The *capitalization rate* expresses in percentage form the relationship between the net operating income of a property and the value or price at which the property sold. The rate of capitalization is always a composite of (1) an interest rate and (2) an amortization rate of the investment when the future value is expected to decline. In instances where the investment or any part of it will maintain its level of value into perpetuity, the rate of amortization for either that part or for the investment as a whole is zero.

The interest rate (or risk rate) and the capitalization rate are often used interchangeably as if their meaning were one and the same. It is this kind of loose thinking that confuses the uninformed and leads to erroneous value conclusions. It is true that where amortization of the investment need not be provided for, the rate of interest and the rate of capitalization are identical. But even in such cases it is best to be consistent and to speak of a capitalization rate rather than an interest rate when converting income into value. The latter term should be used only when reference is made to a return on the investment representing "wages" paid for the use of capital. It would also contribute to clarity of thinking if the term *capitalization rate*, whenever used in appraisal practice, were modified to indicate whether use is made of this rate as an overall (R_o), a building (R_B), or a land (R_L) rate of capitalization.

The *overall capitalization rate* (R_o) is a ratio indicating the relationship of net operating income of the entire property (land and building) to the value or price of the entire property. The overall rate of capitalization is, as a rule, always greater than the land rate of capitalization and less than the building rate of capitalization. To illustrate: If a building valued at $320,000 produces a net income of $38,400, the building rate of capitalization is $38,400 ÷ $320,000, or 12 percent. If the land on which this building stands is valued at $80,000 and yields an income of $7,200, the land rate of capitalization is $7,200 ÷ $80,000, or 9 percent. The overall capitalization rate would be obtained by dividing the combined land and building (property) income by the combined land and building (property) value. In this illustration the overall rate equals $45,600 ÷ $400,000, or 11.4 percent. This overall rate can then be checked by weighting the building and the land (split) rates of capitalization on the basis of a building-to-property ratio of 80 percent and a land-to-property ratio of 20 percent as follows:

Building capitalization rate, 0.12×0.80	0.096
Land capitalization rate, 0.09×0.20	0.018
Total property, or overall, capitalization rate	0.114, or 11.4 percent

When property income (for both land and building) is converted directly into value by use of an overall rate of capitalization, the method of valuation is called *direct capitalization*. The direct method of capitalization is not recommended for use when other and more precise methods of capitalization, as will be demonstrated in the following chapters, are available. The use of an overall rate assumes that the subject property is identical in building characteristics, building age, and land-to-building value ratio to the comparable properties from which the overall rate was derived. This in practice is rarely the case.

The *building capitalization rate* (R_B) is a ratio of building net operating income to the value of the building. Since building income must cover both a return on the investment and amortization of the building investment over the remaining economic life of the building or the forecast holding period, the capitalization rate applicable to the building must also be a composite rate which includes these two investment components. The rate of amortization generally is based on one of the depreciation methods explained in Chapter 11. To illustrate: If the rate of interest for a building investment is 9 percent and the rate of amortization is 2 percent (straight-line depreciation based on 50-year remaining life), the building capitalization rate is 9 percent plus 2 percent, or 11 percent. As the remaining building life shortens, the building rate of capitalization will increase—assuming no change in the rate of interest. To illustrate: Where the remaining economic life is estimated at 20 years, the straight-line rate of amortization is 5 percent (100% ÷ 20 years). This rate, when added to the 9 percent rate of interest, equals a 14 percent building rate of capitalization.

The *land capitalization rate* (R_L) is a ratio of net operating income derived from land to the value or price paid for the land. If property rights are held in fee simple ownership and income from land is assumed to extend into perpetuity, then no provision need be made for recapture of the land investment. However, where land is subject to depletion of its mineral or other resources, its value is expected to decline due to external forces, or where ownership is for a period of years as in a leasehold estate, a rate of annual recapture must be calculated and added to the rate of interest to provide for a return of the land investment over the projection period. In some instances, the value of a site is expected to increase over the forecast income period, causing a lowered overall capitalization rate (R_o). In appraisal problems in which the capitalization of land income involves perpetuity, the land capitalization rate and the land interest rate are the same.

The *amortization rate* $(1/S_{\overline{n}|})$ provides for a return or recapture of an investment over the economic life of the property. This rate is sometimes known as the sinking fund factor and may be applied over a shorter period than a structure's remaining economic life. This annual rate of recapture is based, as a rule, on one of the theoretical, or age-life, methods explained in Chapter 11. The selection of the appropriate rate at which an investment is to be amortized is most important because of the impact that differences in rates have on capitalized value. This is illustrated by the amortization provisions necessary to recapture an investment over a 25-year-life period as follows:

Method	*Rate of amortization*
Straight line	0.040
Sinking fund (4%)[1]	0.024

The straight-line method of providing for future depreciation as compared with the annuity method, as shown previously, requires nearly two times the dollar provisions necessary under the latter method. Considering the important differences in leverage that small differences in rates of capitalization cause in the results obtained under the capitalized income approach to value, it is evident that the selection of the method and rate of amortization must be undertaken with great care.

In practice, the sinking fund method of capital recapture is rarely used except in mortgage amortization. Where the straight-line method of recapture is applied to reflect a declining income stream over the life of the investment, the declining income may be stabilized and capitalized under the annuity, or Inwood method, for identical appraisal results. Except for short-lived properties or for provision of reserves for the replacement of furniture and fixtures, the use of the straight-line method of capitalization is not recommended.

The *mortgage rate* (R_M), frequently called mortgage constant, is a term associated with level payment mortgages. It, however, can apply to variable payment mortgages as well. It expresses a constant relationship between annual mortgage payments (including interest and amortization) and the original amount of a loan; an example of this, using dollars, is

[1]See the calculator keystroke sequence in Chapter 16.

$$R_M = \frac{\text{Monthly mortgage payments} \times 12}{\text{Original mortgage principal}}$$

$$= \frac{\$1,000 \times 12}{\$100,00}$$

$$= 0.1200$$

The *equity dividend rate* (R_E) complements the mortgage rate. Two different equity rates exist and will be discussed at length in Chapter 20. The equity dividend rate is a postmortgage debt service rate; that is, it relates cash flow income to the original equity or down payment made by an investor and sometimes is called "cash on cash."

The other equity rate is the *equity yield rate* (Y_E), which accounts for "cash on cash" plus any forecast future change in value, such as might occur upon sale of the property. Thus this rate accounts for total return to the equity position over a projection period.

The *property yield rate* (Y_o) combines the rate derived from NOI/SP and future changes in value. This rate equals the overall capitalization rate (R_o) when there is no change in value during the projection period. It can also apply to past sale transactions and rental performance.

The *composite capitalization rate* is of relatively recent origin. This rate is applied in the capitalization of an income stream over a relatively short period of ownership of about 10 to 15 years at a preselected yield to the equity owner rather than a rate applicable to the property as an investment entity. The composite rate, as will be more fully demonstrated in Chapter 20, is precalculated to provide the desired equity yield—as influenced by mortgage interest rates and amortization terms, and anticipated percentage depreciation or appreciation of the property as a whole over the ownership or projection period. In effect, the equity yield as reflected in the composite rate is that rate at which the present worth of the stabilized income stream plus the present worth of the equity reversion at time of sale equals the equity (cash) value of the property, exclusive of the mortgage debt, on date of purchase. Composite rates of capitalization for selected yield and mortgage interest rates over typical mortgage terms and ownership life periods earlier were precomputed and published as "Ellwood tables."[2] Today, similar results are achieved by use of calculators.

CAPITALIZATION RATE SELECTION METHODS

If rates used to convert periodic income into an estimate of value are to have any relevance or credibility, they must be based on thorough market analysis. An appraiser may find any of the capitalization rates by analyzing market transaction data under one or more of the following rate-selection methods:

1. Band-of-investment method.
2. Mortgage terms method.

[2]L. W. Ellwood, *Ellwood Tables for Real Estate Appraising and Financing* (Chicago: American Institute of Real Estate Appraisers, 1977).

3. Market extracted overall capitalization rate.
4. Market extracted building and land capitalization rates.
5. Gross income multiplier derivation of R_o.
6. Overall capitalization rate with different income-value patterns.
   (a) Level income with changing value.
   (b) Straight-line change in income and value.
   (c) Constant income and value change.
7. R_o via simplified mortgage-equity analysis.

Band-of-Investment Method

Until recent years, this technique was used to compute the interest rate—the rate that measures the return on the investment in the land and improvements. Added to this rate was the annual recapture rate for the improvements. The recapture period generally was the forecast remaining economic life of these improvements over which the "return of" the investment would occur. An example of this method involves a property for which the available mortgage financing is: 12 percent interest, 75 percent loan-to-value ratio, 25-year first mortgage; a 15-year 14 percent second mortgage due in 5 years, with a 20 percent loan-to-value ratio; the owner's desired equity return is 10 percent; the expected remaining economic life of the building is 50 years.

Therefore, the building (not property) capitalization rate (R_B) is computed as follows:

$0.75 \times 0.12 =$	0.0900
$0.20 \times 0.14 =$	0.0280
$0.05 \times 0.10 =$	0.0050
Total interest rate	0.1230
Plus recapture rate (1/50 years)	0.0200
Building capitalization rate	0.1430

This same information can be used to calculate an overall capitalization rate (R_o), assuming that the land and building value-to-property value ratios are known. To continue this example, assume that 20 percent of the total property value is allocated to the site. The R_o is then computed as follows:

$$0.20 \times 0.1230 = 0.0246$$
$$0.80 \times 0.1430 = 0.1144$$
$$R_o \qquad\qquad\quad 0.1390$$

A variation of the foregoing version of the band-of-investment method is to add the weighted rates for the debt and equity positions for an investment. The mortgage rate (R_M) or loan constant, which provides for a return on and of the mortgage, is substituted for the mortgage interest. The return of the debt capital is provided through amortization. Added to this mortgage rate is the equity dividend rate (R_E), which includes a return to the borrower after all property operating expenses have been paid and mortgage debt service has been satisfied. The equity dividend rate is based on the appraiser surveying investors involved and the type and age of property being appraised. Using the same information used previously, and assuming that investors usually expect a 10 percent equity dividend rate on cash flow, the overall capitalization rate is computed as follows:

$$0.75 \times 0.126387^3 = 0.094790$$
$$0.20 \times 0.159809 = 0.031962$$
$$0.05 \times 0.100000 = \underline{0.005000}$$
$$R_o = 0.131752$$

Rounded to 0.1318

Mortgage Terms Method

A method popularized in the late 1970s by Ronald E. Gettel fully recognizes all aspects of mortgage financing for the class of property under consideration. That is, it accounts for the loan-to-value ratio (M), mortgage rate (R_M), and the debt coverage ratio (DCR), which is expressed as NOI/DS, with NOI being net operating income and DS being the annual mortgage payments. The equation is $R_o = (M)(R_M)(DCR)$. Although this equation indirectly accounts for the equity position, it has been criticized as being lender dominated and failing to account for future equity benefits.[4]

This method can be illustrated by an example that assumes a 75 percent loan-to-value ratio, a 12 percent monthly installment 30-year loan with a 5-year balloon, and a debt coverage ratio of 1.30. The R_o then is found to be

$$R_o = (0.75)(0.123434)(1.30)$$
$$= 0.1203$$

Market Extracted Overall Capitalization Rate

This form of direct capitalization is based on the appraiser obtaining accurate rental information on recently sold comparable properties. This method has several variants. Ideally, the net operating income data are available as of the date of sale. Sometimes, it is not possible to obtain this needed information, so the appraiser must begin with the potential gross income, apply a vacancy and collection loss factor that the buyer or seller generally can provide, and then apply an operating expense ratio (OER) in order to produce an estimate of the sale property's net operating income.

In obtaining these market data, comparables should be used that are similar to the appraised property with respect to

---

[3]R_M, allowing for interest and amortization; the keystroke sequence is given in Chapter 10. Also see Appendix V, the table entitled "Annual Constants for Monthly Mortgage Payments." Use 12 percent, 25-year loan term and 14 percent, 15-year loan term mortgages.

[4]For example, see Kenneth M. Lusht and Robert H. Zerbst, "Valuing Income Property in an Inflationary Environment," *The Real Estate Appraiser and Analyst* (July–August 1980), p. 14, and Roy C. Schaeffer, "DCR: An Appraisal Gate Crasher," *The Appraisal Journal* (April 1982), pp. 195–203.

1. Building age.
2. Operating expense ratio.
3. Building design.
4. Building usage.
5. Land-to-property value ratio.

Two examples of this method follow:

Example 1

Sale	NOI	Sale price	R_o
1	$41,500	$350,000	0.1186
2	38,090	325,000	0.1172
3	50,635	410,000	0.1235
4	46,460	383,000	0.1213

Example 2

Sale	PGI	−	Vacancy and collection ratio	=	EGI	×	1-OER	=	NOI	÷	Sale price	=	R_o
1	$52,000		0.05($2,600)		$49,400		0.55		$27,170		$260,000		0.1045
2	61,500		0.04($2,460)		59,040		0.50		29,520		287,150		0.1028
3	47,360		0.10($4,736)		42,624		0.55		23,443		221,600		0.1058

The equity dividend rate can also be derived by a variation of this method. Discussion of this technique will be covered generally later in this chapter and in detail in Chapter 20.

Market Extracted Building and Land Capitalization Rates

Inaccurate valuations can occur from the use of overall capitalization rates. Such misleading results are associated with comparable properties that are dissimilar to the appraised property in size, age, land-to-total property value ratio, and building usage. This problem can be avoided by extracting either the building (R_B) or the land (R_L) capitalization rates from an overall rate and then applying either of these to an appraised property. The following example illustrates how this procedure operates.

Assume that the following four comparable property sales are being analyzed:

Improved sale 1. Sale price, $500,000; NOI, $60,000; estimated site value ratio, 25 percent.

Improved sale 2. Sale price, $600,000; NOI, $73,800; estimated site value ratio, 15 percent.

Improved sale 3. Sale price, $520,000; NOI, $60,424; estimated site value ratio, 40 percent.

Land sale 1. Sale price, $450,000; NOI, $45,000.

Land sale 2. Sale price, $250,000; NOI, $25,000.

The R_B may be solved for by use of the equation

$$R_B = [(I_o) - (V_L \times R_L)]/V_B,$$

or if the value of the building is unknown, the following grid may be used.

Sale	Component	Value ratio		Capitalization rate		Weighted rate
1	Property	1.00	×	0.1200	=	0.1200
	Land	0.25	×	0.1000	=	0.0250
	Building	0.75		R_B		0.0950
	$R_B = 0.0950/0.75$					
	$= 0.1267$[a]					
2	Property	1.00	×	0.1230	=	0.1230
	Land	0.15	×	0.1000	=	0.0150
	Building	0.85		R_B		0.1080
	$R_B = 0.1080/0.85$					
	$= 0.1271$					
3	Property	1.00	×	0.1162	=	0.1162
	Land	0.40	×	0.1000	=	0.0400
	Building	0.60		R_B		0.0762
	$R_B = 0.0762/0.60$					
	$= 0.1270$					

[a]Calculated as follows: $\dfrac{0.75 \times R_B}{0.75} = \dfrac{0.0950}{0.75}$

A building capitalization rate of 12.70 percent and a land capitalization rate of 10.00 percent are thus indicated for the subject property.

Gross Income Multiplier Derivation of R_o

Seldom, if ever, are appraisers blessed with an abundance of perfect market data from which to derive an estimate of market value. In fact, if such information were readily available, there would be little need for the appraiser's skills of compiling and analyzing real estate market data. Faced with imperfect and often scant information related to market value, appraisers need a variety of means to accurately appraise real property. One such method is available when the appraiser is unable to obtain more information on a property than its sale price, date and terms of sale, physical description, operating expense ratio (OER), and effective gross income multiplier (EGIM). An operating expense ratio (OER) is computed by dividing a property's operating expense by its effective gross income. When the OER is deducted from 1, the result is the net income ratio (NIR). From this information the appraiser can derive an overall capitalization rate (R_o). The equation for this computation is

$$R_o = \frac{\text{NIR}}{\text{EGIM}}$$

Suppose, for example, that a comparable property with an effective gross income of $145,500 recently sold for $800,000. An operating expense ratio (OER) of 45 percent is typical for this type and age of property. The overall capitalization rate is

$$\text{EGIM} = \$800,000/\$145,500$$
$$= 5.5$$
$$R_o = \frac{1 - 0.45}{5.5}$$
$$= \frac{0.55}{5.5}$$
$$= 10.0\%$$

Overall Capitalization Rates with Different Income-Value Patterns

The inevitable task of the appraiser is to understand the attitudes and concerns of real estate investors and users concerning real estate. These concerns pertain to both the measurement and prediction of value. In order to measure value competently, the appraiser must be able to anticipate future trends since investors and home owners consider real estate in such terms. This section contains three possible ways that future income and value patterns can occur. Overall capitalization rates can be derived from these future patterns.

Level income with changing value.   The lease terms may specify a fixed rental (flat rental) over a specified term while the value of the property itself changes. This change could be either positive or negative depending on market forces. Prospective purchasers may either pay a discounted price, reflecting adverse neighborhood or general market conditions, or pay a premium in anticipation of improved conditions caused by such factors as rezoning, traffic rerouting, or unusually low vacancy rates for this type of property.

The basic equation to account for change is

$R_o = Y_o - \Delta a$

R_o = overall capitalization rate

Y_o = property yield rate,[5] which reflects current income, anticipated future income, and value changes

Δ = total value change over the projection period

---

[5] The reader is cautioned to avoid incorrectly mixing equity and property yield rates with overall capitalization and equity dividend rates. The proper combinations are $R_o = Y_o - \Delta a$ and $R_E = Y_E - \Delta a$.

a = annualizer or factor that converts total value change to the desired periodic rate of change which usually is annual

The basic equation is adapted to a level income and changing future value where R_o and Y_o are as defined previously, but Δ is the total expected value change during the forecast income period (n), and a is the sinking fund factor ($1/S_{\overline{n}}$) computed at the yield rate over the forecast income period.

An application of this method would be as follows. The appraised property is subject to a 10-year lease that specifies an absolute net annual income of $80,000; the property value is forecast to increase by 40 percent during this 10-year period; and market analysis shows that investors typically expect a 10 percent property yield:

$$R_o = Y_o - \Delta a$$
$$= 0.10 - (0.40)(0.062745)$$
$$= 0.10 - 0.025098$$
$$= 0.074902$$

Note: R_o is less than Y_o when the property value is expected to appreciate. R_o is greater than Y_o when the property value is expected to depreciate. The reason that R_o is lower when there is appreciation is because the owner can recapture a part of his or her investment through resale of the property instead of solely from rental income. Also, R_o equals Y_o when there is no change in value ($\Delta = 0$).

Suppose now that the same property is expected to decline in value by 40 percent during the 10-year forecast period. Notice the difference in R_o in the two examples:

$$R_o = 0.10 - (-0.40)(0.062745)$$
$$= 0.10 + 0.025098$$
$$= 0.125098$$

Straight-line change in income and value.   A variation of the foregoing income change pattern would apply to a step-up lease where the rental income increases (or declines) by the same dollar amount each successive year. Similarly, the value is expected to trace a parallel path. Usually, this method is based on a forecast annual constant dollar increase or decrease in property value and a parallel rental income change. Figure 15.2 depicts a constant change of $200 annually.

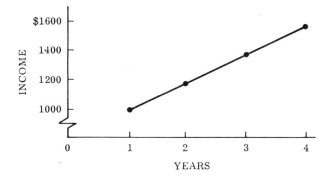

Figure 15.2   Constant Income Change Chart

Instead of using a sinking fund factor as in the previous example, the annualizer (a) is now the reciprocal of the forecast income period (n). Using the preceding figures, the overall capitalization rate is found as follows:

$$R_o = Y_o - (\Delta)\,(1/n)$$
$$= 0.10 - (0.40)(1/10)$$
$$= 0.10 - 0.04$$
$$= 0.06$$

Constant income and value change.   When both the property income and value are expected to change at a constant (exponential) rate, the solution for R_o is quite simple. This income-value change curve is nothing more than the same percentage rate of change each year for a predetermined time, such as an annual increase of 5 percent for 10 years. The annualizer then becomes the annual compound rate of change (CR) as follows and as illustrated in Figure 15.3:

$$R_o = Y_o - \text{CR}$$
$$= 0.10 - 0.05$$
$$= 0.05$$

R_o via Simplified Mortgage-Equity Analysis

An overall capitalization rate can be extracted from market data in a manner similar to that described previously for the physical value components, land and building. In this case, the initial step is to ascertain an appropriate equity dividend rate (R_E), based on an overall capitalization rate and prevailing mortgage terms for a given type of property. Once having computed several market-derived equity dividend rates (R_E), the appropriate mortgage terms are determined for

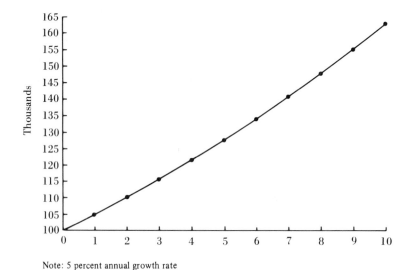

Note: 5 percent annual growth rate

Figure 15.3 Exponential Value Change Chart

the appraised property. Next, an overall capitalization rate is derived and applied to the appraised property's net operating income.

This method is illustrated with the following example:

Sale 1. Sale price, $1,000,000; net operating income, $120,000; mortgage loan terms, 75 percent first mortgage (or deed of trust), 25-year term, monthly installments, 13 percent interest.

Sale 2. Sale price, $900,000; net operating income, $104,490; mortgage loan terms, 75 percent first mortgage, 30-year term with a 10-year balloon, monthly installments, 12.75 percent interest.

Sale 3. Sale price, $875,000; net operating income, $109,290; mortgage loan terms, 80 percent first mortgage, 30-year term, monthly installments, 13.50 percent interest.

Sale	Component	Value ratio		Capitalization rate		Weighted rate
1	Property	1.00	×	0.1200	=	0.1200
	Mortgage	0.75	×	0.1353	=	0.1015
	Equity	0.25		R_E		0.0185
	$R_B = 0.0185/0.25$					
	$= 0.0740$					
2	Property	1.00	×	0.1161	=	0.1161
	Mortgage	0.75	×	0.1304	=	0.0978
	Equity	0.25		R_E		0.0183
	$R_B = 0.0183/0.25$					
	$= 0.0732$					
3	Property	1.00	×	0.1249	=	0.1249
	Mortgage	0.80	×	0.1374	=	0.1100
	Equity	0.20		R_E		0.0149
	$R_B = 0.0149/0.20$					
	$= 0.0745$					
		Rounded to 0.0740				

It is possible to secure a 75 percent loan-to-value, 25-year, 12.50 percent loan for the subject property. Based on these loan terms and the market-derived equity dividend rate, an overall capitalization rate is computed as follows:

Component	Value ratio	Capitalization rate	Weighted rate
Mortgage	0.75	0.1308	0.0981
Equity	0.25	0.0740	0.0185
Property	1.00	R_o	0.1166
	$R_o = 0.1166$		

SUMMARY

The capitalization rate acts as a conversion mechanism to convert periodic income into an estimate of present value. There is an inverse relationship between capitalization rate and value. This relationship can be seen in the basic capitalization equation $V = I/R$.

The basic reasons for purchasing real estate are (1) investment, (2) owner's use or pleasure, (3) speculation, or (4) investment and speculation.

The several types of rates of return currently in use include:

1. *Amortization rate*, or sinking fund rate, provides for the recapture of an investment over the economic life of that property.
2. *Building capitalization rate* is the ratio of building net operating income to the value of the building.
3. *Capitalization rate* expresses the relationship between a property's net operating income and its value; it consists of an interest rate and an amortization rate.
4. *Interest rate* is a measure of the cost of money and does not include a provision for investment recapture.
5. *Land capitalization rate* is the ratio of net operating income derived from land to the land value.
6. *Mortgage rate*, or mortgage constant, expresses a constant relationship between annual mortgage payments (including principal and interest) and the original loan amount.
7. *Overall capitalization rate* is the ratio between net operating income and the value of an entire property.

Equity dividend rate relates cash flow income to the original equity or down payment made by an investor and sometimes is called "cash on cash."

Property yield rate combines the rate derived from NOI/sale price and changes in property value. It equals the overall capitalization rate when there is no change in property value.

Composite capitalization rate is a rate developed over an income projection period and is influenced by mortgage interest rates, amortization terms, and anticipated percentage change in property value over the projection period.

Appraisers typically will compute a capitalization rate by use of one of the following methods.

The band-of-investment capitalization method is based on the sum of the weighted mortgage and equity or building and land capitalization rates.

The mortgage terms method produces an overall capitalization rate from the product of the loan-to-value ratio, mortgage rate, and debt coverage ratio appropriate for a given type of property.

The market extracted overall capitalization rate is usually based on a ratio of net operating income to the sale price of recently sold properties, that is, net operating income divided by sale price.

   The market extracted building and land capitalization rates can avoid the inaccurate results that sometimes result from preparing overall capitalization rates without regard to differences between comparable properties and the appraised property. This problem is avoided by extracting either the building or land capitalization rates from an overall rate and then applying either to the appraised property.

   The gross income multiplier derivation of R_o results from dividing a property's net operating income ratio by its effective gross income multiplier. Effective gross income is potential gross income minus vacancy and collection losses and net income ratio equals 1 minus the operating expense ratio.

   It is possible to estimate capitalization rates by recognizing or predicting future value and income patterns. The three techniques used to prepare these rates are based on the basic equation, $R = Y - \Delta a$, and are described as follows.

   Level income with changing value is used to calculate a capitalization rate by deducting from a yield rate an annual rate of change which is measured by multiplying the overall percentage value change by a sinking fund factor.

   Straight-line change in income and value produces a capitalization rate by deducting from a yield rate an annualized rate of value change which is calculated by multiplying the overall value change by the reciprocal of the value projection period for the appraised property.

   Constant income and value change allow the computation of a capitalization rate to be made by deducting from the yield rate the annual compound rate of change.

   R_o via simplified mortgage-equity analysis results from extracting weighted equity dividend rates from the overall capitalization rates of several comparable sale properties. Each of these weighted equity dividend rates is then divided by the equity value ratio to reveal the equity dividend rates (R_E) for each comparable sale. The selected R_E is then applied to the subject property along with the appropriate mortgage terms to reveal an overall capitalization rate.

REVIEW QUESTIONS

1. Distinguish between and relate amortization rate and mortgage rate.
2. Explain how a capitalization rate is applied differently from a factor in estimating value.
3. Modify the equation $V = I/R$ to find R and I.
4. Explain the basic difference between an equity dividend and an equity yield rate.
5. Given mortgage terms of 75 percent loan-to-value, 13 percent interest, monthly payments, 20-year term, and a market-determined equity dividend rate of 7 percent, solve for R_o, indicating whether it should be applied to NOI or BTCF.
6. Using the same mortgage terms given in question 5, and an NOI of $46,000 and annual debt service of $36,800, compute the R_o.

7. A client has asked you to indicate the appropriate R_o for a property for which the annual potential gross income is $25,000, vacancy and collection losses are 6 percent, the operating expense ratio is 40 percent, and the sale price is $117,500.

8. What is the R_o for a property for which both the income and value are expected to decline by 20 percent on a straight-line basis over the next 10 years? Investors in this type of property usually expect a property yield of 11 percent.

9. Derive the R_B from the following two sales transactions. Improved sale—price, $550,000; NOI, $77,000; site value ratio, 15 percent. Land sale—price, $100,000; NOI, $12,000.

10. Assume that the net income from the ownership of land is $2,000 and that the current capitalization rate is 10 percent. Assume further that a tax of $200 is levied on this land, which reduces the net income to $1,800. Compute the following:
    (a) The land value prior to payment of the tax.
    (b) The land value after the tax levy.
    (c) The amount of value reduction caused by this tax if the capitalization rate falls to 8 percent.

11. Explain what is meant by (a) overall capitalization rate and (b) fractional rate.

12. Compute the overall capitalization rates from the following data:

Property A	Land value	$ 2,500 Capitalization rate	6%
	Building value	7,500 Capitalization rate	8%
	Total value	$10,000 Capitalization rate	?
Property B	Land value	$ 5,000 Capitalization rate	6%
	Building value	5,000 Capitalization rate	9%
	Total value	$10,000 Capitalization rate	?
Property C	Land value	$ 7,500 Capitalization rate	7%
	Building value	2,500 Capitalization rate	9%
	Total value	$10,000 Capitalization rate	?

13. Briefly explain the difference between the overall capitalization rate and the property yield rate.

READING AND STUDY REFERENCES

AKERSON, CHARLES B. Lessons 5, 8, and 10, "Direct Capitalization," "Discounting Procedures and Income/Value Patterns," and "Applied Discounting," *Capitalization Theory and Techniques Study Guide*. Chicago: American Institute of Real Estate Appraisers, 1984.

American Institute of Real Estate Appraisers. Chapters 20 and 21, "Direct Capitalization" and "Yield Capitalization—Theory and Basic Applications," *The Appraisal of Real Estate*, 8th ed. Chicago: AIREA, 1987.

BROWN, RALPH J., and DENNIS A. JOHNSON. "Inflation, Valuation, and the Discount Rate," *The Appraisal Journal* 48, no. 4 (October 1980), pp. 549–555.

EPLEY, DONALD R., and JAMES H. BOYKIN. Chapters 9–11, *Basic Income Property Appraisal*. Reading, Mass.: Addison-Wesley Publishing Co., Inc., 1983.

FISHER, JEFFREY D., and ANTHONY B. SAUNDERS. "Capitalization Rates and Market Information," *The Appraisal Journal* 49, no. 2 (April 1981), pp. 186–198.

GIBBONS, JAMES E. "Financial Views," *The Appraisal Journal* 51, no. 4 (October 1983), pp. 600–609.

MASON, ROBERT C. "Present Worth in Present Dollars," *The Appraisal Journal* 51, no. 3 (July 1983), pp. 415–421.

PETERSON, CHARLES H. "Are Capitalization Rates Obsolete?" *The Appraisal Journal* 49, no. 2 (April 1981), pp. 179–184.

16
Compound Interest and Discounting

Learning Objectives

After reading this chapter, you should be able to:

- Compute all present and future worth functions as a means of estimating value or amortized installments
- See the interrelationships among the present and future worth functions
- Solve problems involving compound interest and discounting via tables or financial calculators
- Become generally familiar with the Inwood, Hoskold, and Ellwood premises
- Understand how mortgage installments are allocated between principal amortization and interest on remaining principal
- Interpolate numerical results in order to reach more accurate findings

An understanding of mathematics as applied to compound interest functions is an important basic tool of property appraising. The entire concept of value is based on a determination of the present worth of future (dollar) rights to income. To convert future income, or, for that matter, future commitments (liabilities) into a sum of present worth or present liability requires not only the application of mathematics but also a knowledge of the functions and purposes served by established financial tables.

There are several types of special-purpose financial tables in current use. Each table is designed as an aid in solving often-repeated problems and in saving the user the laborious work and time that basic calculations would otherwise require. In recent years, it has become possible to conveniently derive the financial factors via financial calculators. In this and succeeding chapters, reference will be made to calculator keystroke sequences to facilitate calculations of present and future values. Reference will also be made to special-purpose tables of which a professional appraiser should have knowledge as an expert in his or her field—

even though he or she may seldom use such tables. Among the special tables sometimes used for professional appraisers are the following:

1. Inwood (coefficient) table.
2. Hoskold (sinking fund) premise table.
3. Ellwood (investment) tables.

A brief description of the derivation and function of each of the previously mentioned special-purpose tables will be given following a detailed explanation and demonstration of standard tables which are in general use and which serve as basic tools in appraisal practice. These standard tables are as follows:

1. *Compound amount of 1, S^n.* This future value function answers the basic question: How much will a dollar invested today grow to in n periods at a given rate of interest? The equation used to express this relationship is

$$S^n = (1 + i)^n$$

2. *Future worth of 1 per period, S_n.* This future value function answers the question: To what amount will a dollar deposited at the end of each period grow in n periods at a given rate of interest? This relationship is expressed symbolically as

$$S_{\overline{n}|} = \frac{S^n - 1}{i}$$

3. *Sinking fund factor, $1/S_{\overline{n}|}$.* This future value function answers the question: How much must be deposited at the end of each period at compound interest to accumulate a dollar in n periods? The expression for this factor is

$$\frac{1}{S_{\overline{n}|}} = \frac{i}{S^n - 1}$$

4. *Present worth of 1, V^n.* This present value factor, sometimes called a reversion factor, provides an answer to the question: What is the present worth of the right to receive a dollar in n periods in the future at a given rate of interest? The equation expressing this function is

$$V^n = 1/S^n$$

5. *Present worth of 1 per period, $a_{\overline{n}|}$.* This present value factor, also known as the Inwood factor, answers the question: How much is the present worth of the right to receive a dollar at the end of each period for n periods at a given rate of interest? The equation for this function is

$$a_{\overline{n}|} = \frac{1 - V^n}{i}$$

6. *Installment to amortize 1, $1/a_{\overline{n}|}$.* This present value factor, also called mortgage rate (R_M) or annual mortgage constant, answers the question: How much must be paid in periodic payments to amortize a dollar, including principal and interest, in n periods at a given rate of interest? It is expressed in equation form as

$$\frac{1}{a_{\overline{n}|}} = \frac{i}{1 - V^n}$$

Before examining each of the future and present value functions, the reader should note the interrelationship among them. The basis of all these functions is the compound amount of 1. Knowing the equation for this function $(1 + i)^n$ permits the reader to solve for all the others. It should further be observed that functions 1 and 4, 2 and 3, and 5 and 6 are reciprocals of one another. For example, referring to Table 16.1, it can be seen that S^n for 15 years is 4.177248. The reciprocal $(1 \div 4.177248)$ is the value of V^n, which is 0.239392.

Another important relationship to be remembered is I = *nominal annual interest rate*, which is the stated annual interest rate, and i = *effective periodic interest rate*, which is the nominal annual interest rate divided by the number of payments per year [e.g., $0.10 \div 4$ payments a year = $0.025(i)$].

COMPOUND AMOUNT OF 1

This compound interest function (table) rightfully may be called the mother function, from which all basic future and present worth functions used in appraisal practice are derived. An understanding of this function and its derivation is most important, for it will permit the ready computation of rates and factors contained in all the other five functions mentioned previously. The ability to construct a compound interest or discount factor, too, may fill a vital need—especially at times when prepared tables at required interest rates are not available. At the outset, the reader is cautioned to keep in mind that interest tables do not make valuations; they are merely tools in the appraisal process, furnishing, as needed, ready-made calculations.

The compound amount of 1 interest table is based on the premise that $1 deposited at the beginning of a period—usually a year—earns interest that accrues during the period and which becomes part of the principal at the end of that period or the beginning of the second interest period. The interest earned during the second year is again added to become part of the principal on which interest is earned during the third period. This continues for the number of required periods of interest compounding called for in the appraisal problem. The interest earned and added to the principal during each period increases in geometric progression, as is evident from the equation $S^n = (1 + i)^n$. The symbols in this equation represent the following:

S^n = original investment plus the compound interest accumulations
i = rate of interest used for period (effective interest rate)
n = periods of compounding

A compound amount of 1 table at 10 percent is displayed in Table 16.1 (a monthly installment variation is found in Appendix V). The derivation of this table is illustrated in Table 16.2.

If the appraiser is interested in knowing the amount to which $1.00 will grow at 10 percent annual compound interest over a five-year period, he or she merely refers to the compound interest rate table at that rate and for that period and finds the amount as 1.610510. If the original amount is $200, the compounded principal and interest equals $200 × 1.610510, or $322.10.

Typical Use of Compound Interest Table

An investor purchased a property five years ago for $10,000. If this property is to be sold today, how much must the owner realize in order to have his original investment returned plus 10 percent annual compound interest? Assuming for purposes of this illustration there are no other capital or expense outlays and no change in the purchasing power of the dollar, the answer is $10,000 × 1.610510, or $16,105.10. The value would have been even higher if the compounding occurred more frequently than annually.

Calculator Solution

Rather than rely on financial tables, the appraiser often will find it more convenient to use a financial calculator to compute present and future worth functions. In solving for the future worth of 1 at 10 percent for five years, the keystroke sequence (this and subsequent keystroke sequences are compatible with the Hewlett-Packard 12C and 38C calculators; some readers will want to use other calculators such as the HP 17BII and 19BII) is

$$5 \boxed{n} \; 10 \boxed{i} \; 1 \boxed{\text{CHS}} \quad \boxed{\text{PV}} \quad \boxed{\text{FV}}$$

The answer is 1.610510. The preceding squares represent the calculator keys, beginning with n which represents the number of years; i is interest; CHS is pressed to change the sign, representing a capital outflow—it also allows the final answer to be positive; PV is the present value; and FV is the future value. The required interest rate (10) and number of years (5) must be entered by pressing the appropriate keys.

The future worth of 1 can be computed still another way by calculator, using the exponential factor. Begin with the basic expression of $(1 + i)^n$, which in this example is $(1.10)^5$. The keystroke sequence is

$$1.1 \boxed{\text{ENTER}} \; 5 \boxed{y^x}$$

It should be noted that any answer found for the future worth of 1 can then be substituted into the equations for the other functions—assuming that the same term and interest rate are used.

FUTURE WORTH OF 1 PER PERIOD

The function explained previously applies to a single sum either invested at the beginning, or anticipated at the end, of a given time. The remaining tables, except Table 16.4, to be explained and demonstrated apply to periodic payments called annuities. An *annuity* is defined as a *series of periodic payments usually, but not necessarily, equal in amount*. An annuity income stream must be both scheduled and predictable. Annuity payments or earnings can occur either at the beginning of each period (advance rental payments) or at the end of each period, such as mortgage payments. An annuity payment made at the beginning of each period is

TABLE 16.1 FUTURE AND PRESENT VALUE USING 10 PERCENT ANNUAL INTEREST

	1 Compound amount of 1 $S^n = (1+i)^n$	2 Future worth of 1 per period $S_{\overline{n}|} = \dfrac{S^n - 1}{i}$	3 Sinking fund factor $1/S_{\overline{n}|} = \dfrac{i}{S^n - 1}$	4 Present value of 1 $V^n = \dfrac{1}{S^n}$	5 Present value of 1 per period $a_{\overline{n}|} = \dfrac{1 - V^n}{i}$	6 Installment to amortize 1 $1/a_{\overline{n}|} = \dfrac{i}{1 - V^n}$
Months						
0	1.000000	—	—	1.000000	—	—
1	1.008333	—	—	0.991736	—	—
2	1.016667	—	—	0.983607	—	—
3	1.025000	—	—	0.975610	—	—
4	1.033333	—	—	0.967742	—	—
5	1.041667	—	—	0.960000	—	—
6	1.050000	—	—	0.952381	—	—
7	1.058333	—	—	0.944882	—	—
8	1.066667	—	—	0.937500	—	—
9	1.075000	—	—	0.930233	—	—
10	1.083333	—	—	0.923077	—	—
11	1.091667	—	—	0.916031	—	—
Years						
1	1.100000	1.000000	1.000000	0.909091	0.909091	1.100000
2	1.210000	2.100000	0.476190	0.826446	1.735537	0.576190
3	1.331000	3.310000	0.302115	0.751315	2.486852	0.402115
4	1.464100	4.641000	0.215471	0.683013	3.169865	0.315471
5	1.610510	6.105100	0.163797	0.620921	3.790787	0.263797
6	1.771561	7.715610	0.129607	0.564474	4.355261	0.229607
7	1.948717	9.487171	0.105405	0.513158	4.868419	0.205405
8	2.143589	11.435888	0.087444	0.466507	5.334926	0.187444
9	2.357948	13.579477	0.073641	0.424098	5.759024	0.173641
10	2.593742	15.937425	0.062745	0.385543	6.144567	0.162745
11	2.853117	18.531167	0.053963	0.350494	6.495061	0.153963
12	3.138428	21.384284	0.046763	0.318631	6.813692	0.146763
13	3.452271	24.522712	0.040779	0.289664	7.103356	0.140779

14	3.797498	27.974983	0.035746	0.263331	7.366687	0.135746
15	4.177248	31.772482	0.031474	0.239392	7.606080	0.131474
16	4.594973	35.949730	0.027817	0.217629	7.823709	0.127817
17	5.054470	40.544703	0.024664	0.197845	8.021553	0.124664
18	5.559917	45.599173	0.021930	0.179859	8.201412	0.121930
19	6.115909	51.159090	0.019547	0.163508	8.364920	0.119547
20	6.727500	57.274999	0.017460	0.148644	8.513564	0.117460
21	7.400250	64.002499	0.015624	0.135131	8.648694	0.115624
22	8.140275	71.402749	0.014005	0.122846	8.771540	0.114005
23	8.954302	79.543024	0.012572	0.111678	8.883218	0.112572
24	9.849733	88.497327	0.011300	0.101526	8.984744	0.111300
25	10.834706	98.347059	0.010168	0.092296	9.077040	0.110168
26	11.918177	109.181765	0.009159	0.083905	9.160945	0.109159
27	13.109994	121.099942	0.008258	0.076278	9.237223	0.108258
28	14.420994	134.209936	0.007451	0.069343	9.306567	0.107451
29	15.863093	148.630930	0.006728	0.063039	9.369606	0.106728
30	17.449402	164.494023	0.006079	0.057309	9.426914	0.106079
31	19.194342	181.943425	0.005496	0.052099	9.479013	0.105496
32	21.113777	201.137767	0.004972	0.047362	9.526376	0.104972
33	23.225154	222.251544	0.004499	0.043057	9.569432	0.104499
34	25.547670	245.476699	0.004074	0.039143	9.608575	0.104074
35	28.102437	271.024368	0.003690	0.035584	9.644159	0.103690
36	30.912681	299.126805	0.003343	0.032349	9.676508	0.103343
37	34.003949	330.039486	0.003030	0.029408	9.705917	0.103030
38	37.404343	364.043434	0.002747	0.026735	9.732651	0.102747
39	41.144778	401.447778	0.002491	0.024304	9.756956	0.102491
40	45.259256	442.592556	0.002259	0.022095	9.779051	0.102259
41	49.785181	487.851811	0.002050	0.020086	9.799137	0.102050
42	54.763699	537.636992	0.001860	0.018260	9.817397	0.101860
43	60.240069	592.400692	0.001688	0.016600	9.833998	0.101688
44	66.264076	652.640761	0.001532	0.015091	9.849089	0.101532
45	72.890484	718.904837	0.001391	0.013719	9.862808	0.101391
46	80.179532	791.795321	0.001263	0.012472	9.875280	0.101263
47	88.197485	871.974853	0.001147	0.011338	9.886618	0.101147
48	97.017234	960.172338	0.001041	0.010307	9.896926	0.101041
49	106.718957	1057.189572	0.000946	0.009370	9.906296	0.100946
50	117.390853	1163.908529	0.000859	0.008519	9.914814	0.100859

TABLE 16.2 DERIVATION OF ANNUAL COMPOUND AMOUNT OF 1 AT 10 PERCENT INTEREST

n periods	Amount at beginning	Interest at 10 percent	Amount at end	Progression formula
1	1.000000	0.100000	1.100000	$1 + i$
2	1.100000	0.110000	1.210000	$(1 + i)^2$
3	1.210000	0.121000	1.331000	$(1 + i)^3$
4	1.331000	0.133100	1.464100	$(1 + i)^4$
5	1.464100	0.146410	1.610510	$(1 + i)^5$
...				
49	97.017234	9.701723	106.718957	$(1 + i)^{49}$
50	106.178957	10.671896	117.390853	$(1 + i)^{50}$

called an *annuity due*. An annuity payment made at the end of each year is called an *ordinary annuity*. Since advance income payments are the exception rather than the rule, emphasis is given here to the development and explanation of the future worth of an *ordinary annuity* table. Such a table is in effect an addition of the compound interest amounts of each *payment* over the periods (years) that each payment remains invested. To illustrate: Suppose that periodic payments of $1.00 are made annually at the end of each period for five years. If the interest rate at which these annuity payments are to be compounded is 10 percent, the total sum of these payments, plus interest earned, can be derived with the aid of the compound amount of 1 table, as shown in Figure 16.1.

The last payment under an ordinary annuity is made at the end of the last period and thus accumulates no interest, as shown in Figure 16.1. The next-to-the-last payment is invested for a one-year period, the one before that for a two-

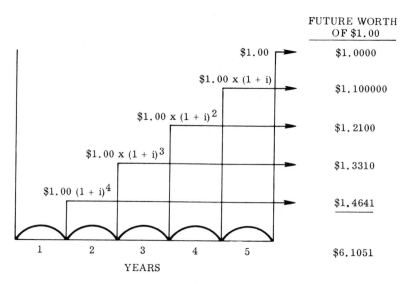

Figure 16.1 Construction of Future Worth of $1 per Period over a Five-Year Period—at 10 Percent Compound Interest

year period, and so on. As an equation, the sum total of the compound amount of an ordinary annuity may be expressed as follows:

$$S_{n5} = 1 + (1 + i) + (1 + i)^2 + (1 + i)^3 + (1 + i)^4 + (1 + i)^5$$

The construction of a future worth of an ordinary annuity table in relation to the compound amount of 1 table is shown in Table 16.3.

Typical Use of Future Worth of 1 per Period Table

Suppose that operating costs on a vacant property covering taxes, insurance, and related maintenance amounted to $500 per annum over a five-year period. How much must the property owner add to the compounded amount of his or her original investment to recover the expenditures plus 10 percent interest? By reference to the future worth of 1 table, the answer is derived by simply multiplying the periodic outlays of $500 by the fifth-year factor of 6.1051. This equals a sum of $3,052.55.

To illustrate further: Suppose that a person has an opportunity to purchase a property in five years. The required down payment will be $10,000. This prospective investor is able to deposit $1,500 at the end of each year in an account paying interest at the rate of 10 percent annually. Will he have accumulated the $10,000 down payment? The answer is found by multiplying the annual deposit by the five-year future worth of 1 per period factor:

$$\$1,500 \times 6.1051 = \$9,157.65$$

Hence the person will be unable to purchase the property requiring a $10,000 down payment.

Calculator Solution

Substituting a financial calculator, such as the HP 12C, for Table 16.1, it also is possible to solve for $S_{\overline{n}}$. Suppose that you desire to find how much you would have accumulated at the end of 15 years if you deposited $1 per year and it earned 10 percent annually. The proper keystrokes are as follows:

$$15 \boxed{n}\ 10 \boxed{i}\ 1 \boxed{\text{CHS}} \boxed{\text{PMT}} \boxed{\text{FV}} = 31.772482$$

This number corresponds with the 10 percent, 15-year future worth of 1 per period factor. If the periodic deposit was some other amount, such as $1,000, the answer would be $1,000 × 31.772482, or $31,772.48.

TABLE 16.3 DERIVATION OF A FUTURE WORTH OF 1 AT 10 PERCENT INTEREST UNDER ORDINARY ANNUITY PAYMENTS

n periods (end of period)	Compound amount of 1	Cumulative amounts future worth of 1
1	1.100000	1.000000
2	1.210000	2.100000
3	1.331000	3.310000
4	1.464100	4.641000
5	1.610510	6.105100

SINKING FUND (AMORTIZATION) FACTOR

In all valuation problems in which buildings or other types of property have limited economic lives, provisions must be made for the amortization of that portion of the investment which is consumed annually by use or lessened in value by other causes of depreciation. In instances where the annual provisions for amortization can be set aside in a sinking fund to accumulate at a given rate of interest over the economic life of the property, or where the periodic amortization provisions can be reinvested in similar investment properties at a given rate of interest, it is necessary to calculate the amount of annual provisions for amortization—or to know the rate per dollar of investment that must be set aside to provide for a return of capital. A useful and ready-made table, known as a sinking fund or amortization table, gives annuity amounts at various rates of compound interest whose future value is 1. To illustrate: If an amount of $1.00 is to be accumulated at 10 percent compound interest over a period of four years, how much must be set aside annually? The amount whose future value is $1 at 10 percent can be found by reference to the sinking fund factor column of Table 16.1. The amount as indicated opposite the fourth-year period is 0.215471 or $0.215471 per dollar of investment value. If the property is worth $10,000, the amount to be set aside annually over a four-year period at 10 percent interest to equal this sum is $10,000 × 0.215471, or $2,154.71.

The sinking fund or amortization rate table has a reciprocal relationship to the future worth of 1 per period table. Thus any factor at a given rate shown in the future worth of an annuity table, when divided into 1, will yield a sinking fund factor of 1 at the same rate of interest. This reciprocal relationship and derivation of the sinking fund function at 10 percent interest is demonstrated in Table 16.4.

Typical Use of Sinking Fund Table

A building worth $200,000 is to be amortized over a period of 40 years at 10 percent interest. For appraisal purposes, the following information may be required:

1. The rate of the annual amortization provision.
2. The amount of the annual amortization provision.

TABLE 16.4   DERIVATION OF A SINKING FUND AT 10 PERCENT COMPOUND INTEREST

n periods (end of period)	Future worth of 1 per period	Reciprocal of future worth or sinking fund rate
1	1.000000	1.000000
2	2.100000	0.476190
3	3.310000	0.302115
4	4.641000	0.215471
5	6.105100	0.163797
. . .		
49	1,057.189572	0.000946
50	1,163.908529	0.000859

3. Proof that the amount computed is correct.
4. The accumulated amount of amortization at the end of 30 years of building life.
5. The percentage of accrued depreciation at the end of 30 years.

The preceding information may be obtained as follows:

1. The rate of annual amortization is found in the sinking fund column (see Table 16.1), and the rate indicated under 10 percent opposite 40 years is 0.002259.
2. The amount of the annual amortization provision is $200,000 × 0.002259, or $451.80.
3. Proof: $451.80 × 442.592556 (future worth of an ordinary annuity over 40 years at 10 percent interest) equals $200,000 (rounded).
4. The amount of amortization at the end of 30 years will be $451.80 × 164.494023 (future worth of 1 per period over 30 years at 10 percent interest), which equals $74,318.40.
5. The percentage of accrued depreciation can be derived by (a) dividing $74,318.40 by the total value of $200,000 or (b) multiplying the sinking fund rate of 0.002259 (40-year factor) by the future worth of 1 per period rate of 164.494023 (30-year factor). Either method of calculation will yield identical answers of 37.16 percent.

Calculator Solution

Greater flexibility and speed can generally be achieved through use of a handheld calculator in seeking a sinking fund value. For example, to determine the amount that would have to be set aside at the end of each year in order to accumulate $25,000 at the end of 12 years in an account earning 10 percent annually, the calculations would be as follows:

12 $\boxed{n}$ 10 $\boxed{i}$ 25000 $\boxed{\text{CHS}}$ $\boxed{\text{FV}}$ $\boxed{\text{PMT}}$

The annual deposit is found to be $1,169.08. This answer can be checked by dividing $1,169.08 by $25,000, which equals 0.046763 (see Table 16.1).

PRESENT WORTH OF 1

In appraisal practice, it is often known that a certain amount either will become due or be earned in a given number of years from now. The question confronting the appraiser then may be: What is the present worth of this amount today? The present worth of 1 column shown in Table 16.1 provides the answer at selected years for the amount of $1.00. If X dollars are involved, the amount shown for $1.00 is merely multiplied by X. The present worth of a sum due in the future may be defined as that amount today which if invested at compound interest over the period involved will grow to that sum at the interest rate specified.

The present worth of 1 table in effect bears a reciprocal relationship to the compound amount of 1 table. To illustrate: If $1.00 at 10 percent will grow to $1.10 at the end of one year, then $1.00 due one year from a given date has a present worth at 10 percent interest (discount) of $1.00 × 1/1.10 = $1.00 × 0.909091, or $0.91. If $1.00 is due two years from today at 10 percent, the answer is secured by multiplying $1.00 × 1/1.21 or $1.00 × 0.826446 = $0.83. The equation for the present value of an amount then becomes PV = FV/(1 + i)^n. In this equation PV is the present worth in dollars and FV is the sum due at a future time. The construction of the present worth table is illustrated in Table 16.5.

Typical Use of Present Worth of 1 Table

Suppose at the time of purchase of a property it is known that the porch floor must be replaced five years hence. The cost of this replacement is estimated at $2,000. The question is: How much should be subtracted from the purchase price to provide for this future expenditure? If the interest rate is 10 percent, the answer is $2,000 × 0.620921, or $1,241.84. Proof: If $1,241.84 is invested today at 10 percent compound interest, this amount at the end of the five-year period will grow to $1,241.84 × 1.610510 (compound amount of 1 at 10 percent), or $2,000.

To illustrate further: Suppose that a property is under a 50-year lease and will at the expiration of the lease period have an estimated worth of $50,000. What is the present value of this reversionary right at a rate of 10 percent interest?

TABLE 16.5 DERIVATION OF PRESENT WORTH OF 1 AT 10 PERCENT COMPOUND (DISCOUNT) INTEREST

n periods	Compound amount of 1	Present worth of 1[a]	Factor formula
1	1.100000	0.909091	$\frac{1}{1+i}$
2	1.210000	0.826446	$\frac{1}{(1+i)^2}$
3	1.331000	0.751315	$\frac{1}{(1+i)^3}$
4	1.464100	0.683013	$\frac{1}{(1+i)^4}$
5	1.610510	0.620921	$\frac{1}{(1+i)^5}$
...			
49	106.718957	0.009370	$\frac{1}{(1+i)^{49}}$
50	117.390853	0.008519	$\frac{1}{(1+i)^{50}}$

[a]Reciprocal of compound amount of 1.

The answer is $50,000 × 0.008519, or $425.95. To prove this answer: If $425.95 is multiplied by the compound amount of 1 at 10 percent interest for 50 years (117.390853), the total will equal a sum of $50,000.

Calculator Solution

The reversionary value of a future single amount can be found via calculator. Assume that a party wants to know how much they should pay today for the right to purchase a property for $100,000 in eight years; a 10 percent discount rate would be appropriate for this type of property. The process is as follows:

$$8 \boxed{n}\ 10 \boxed{i}\ 100000 \boxed{\text{CHS}}\quad \boxed{\text{FV}}\quad \boxed{\text{PV}}$$

which equals $46,650.74. Still another way of solving for this value would be as follows:

$$1.1 \boxed{\text{ENTER}}\ 8 \boxed{y^x}\quad \boxed{1/x}\ 100000 \boxed{\times}$$

This alternative method provides the reciprocal of the future worth of 1.

PRESENT WORTH OF 1 PER PERIOD

This table is used more than any other in appraisal practice. It provides factors indicating the present worth of an ordinary annuity of 1 (income receivable at the end of a period). Most income payments or earnings obtained from the use of real property have the characteristics of an annuity. To find the present worth of an income stream under the earnings approach to value, it is necessary only to convert (capitalize) the estimated annual earnings into a sum of present value by use of this table. The procedure for converting estimated net operating income into value and the techniques of capitalization will be explained in succeeding chapters. In this chapter effort will be made to explain the derivation of the present worth of 1 per period table and to demonstrate its use.

It will be recalled that the present worth of 1 table provided discount factors for the measurement of present value of a single payment or sum of money due at some future time. In effect an annuity is merely a series of future income payments, and the sum total of the present worth of all payments can be derived as demonstrated in Figure 16.2. Assuming an annual income of $1.00 at the end of each year for a period of five years and an interest rate of 10 percent, the present worth of this annuity can be computed as shown in Figure 16.2.

The equation for deriving the present value of an annuity may be constructed as follows:

$$a_{\overline{n}|} = (1 + i)^{-1} + (1 + i)^{-2} + (1 + i)^{-3} + (1 + i)^{-4} + (1 + i)^{-5} + (1 + i)^{-n}$$

This equation is mathematically reduced to

$$a_{\overline{n}|} = (1 + i)^{-n} = \frac{1}{(1 + i)^n}$$

The present worth table of 1 per annum at compound interest can be constructed in relation to the present worth of 1 function in Table 16.1.

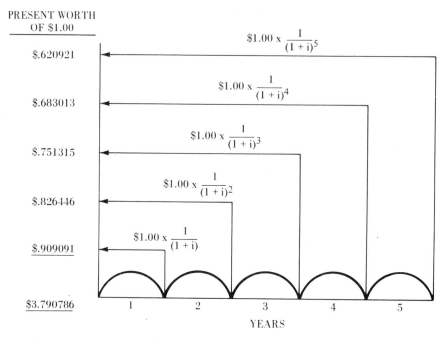

PRESENT WORTH
OF $1.00

$.620921

$.683013

$.751315

$.826446

$.909091

$3.790786

$1.00 x $\frac{1}{(1+i)^5}$

$1.00 x $\frac{1}{(1+i)^4}$

$1.00 x $\frac{1}{(1+i)^3}$

$1.00 x $\frac{1}{(1+i)^2}$

$1.00 x $\frac{1}{(1+i)}$

1   2   3   4   5

YEARS

Figure 16.2 Construction of Present Worth of an Ordinary Annuity of $1.00 over a Five-Year
Period—at 10 Percent Compound Interest

Inspection of Table 16.6 will disclose that the increase in the present worth
of an annuity is at a diminishing rate as future and equal periodic payments are
added.

At a rate of 10 percent interest, the present worth of an annuity of $1.00 ex-
tending into perpetuity equals 1/0.10, or $10. Proof: If a sum of $10 is invested, or
deposited with a bank that pays 10 percent interest, the annual income as long as
the deposit is kept intact (into perpetuity) is $10 × 0.10, or $1.00. The perpetuity
factor for a sum of $1.00 at any rate of interest is merely the sum of $1.00 divided
by the rate of interest as in Table 16.7.

TABLE 16.6 DERIVATION OF PRESENT WORTH OF 1 PER ANNUM AT 10 PERCENT
INTEREST PAYMENTS AT END OF PERIOD

n periods	Present worth of 1	Cumulative present worth of 1 per annum
1	0.909091	0.909091
2	0.826446	1.735537
3	0.751315	2.486852
4	0.683013	3.169865
5	0.620921	3.790787
. . .		
49	0.009370	9.906296
50	0.008519	9.914814

TABLE 16.7 RELATIONSHIP OF INTEREST RATES AND PERPETUITY FACTORS

Income	÷	Rate of interest	=	Perpetuity factor
$1.00		0.06		16.67
1.00		0.08		12.50
1.00		0.10		10.00
1.00		0.12		8.33

Thus where income (as is the case with most land) is anticipated to extend unendingly into the future (i.e., perpetuity), the value of such income is obtained by dividing it by the applicable market-determined capitalization rate or, conversely, multiplying same by the perpetuity (rate reciprocal) factor as demonstrated previously.

Typical Use of Present Worth of 1 per Period Table

Suppose that a five-year lease calls for net rental payments at the end of each year in the amount of $1,000. If this lease is offered for sale and the rate of interest is 10 percent, what is the present value of this series of income payments? The answer is $1,000 × 3.790787 (present worth of 1 per period, see Table 16.1), which equals a sum of $3,790.79. Or, suppose that a property in new condition is estimated to yield $10,000 net annually over a remaining building life of 50 years: What is the present value of this level annuity? Answer: $10,000 × 9.914814, or $99,148.14.

Calculator Solution

Instead of finding the present worth of a level annuity by use of financial tables, the calculator can be used to find $a_{\overline{n}|}$. Suppose, for instance, that an appraiser has been asked to find the present value of an annual net rental income of $2,500, discounted at 10 percent for the next 25 years. The current value would be computed as follows:

$$25 \boxed{n} \quad 10 \boxed{i} \quad 2500 \boxed{\text{CHS}} \quad \boxed{\text{PMT}} \quad \boxed{\text{PV}}$$

The present value of this level income stream is found to be $22,692.60. The answer is proven correct by comparing the calculation $22,692.60/$2,500 (9.077040) to the present value of 1 per period for 10 percent and 25 years in Table 16.1.

INSTALLMENT TO AMORTIZE 1

The installment to amortize 1 can apply to several real estate situations. Frequently, an appraiser is asked how much net operating income a property of a given value must produce in order to provide a fair return on the investment and amortization of the investment over the economic life of the property, or for the lease term, at market rates of interest. Whenever a mortgage loan is applied for, it must be calculated in advance how much the periodic payments amount to in order to yield interest on the mortgage and a return of the loan principal over the term of the mortgage. Where the value of a property or the amount of a loan is known, the annuity income—or loan payment per dollar of present value—can be obtained from a special table in which the amounts, whose present value is 1, are calculated at selected rates of interest. A table of this type is shown in column six of Table 16.1.

The annuity payment table for an installment to amortize 1 has a reciprocal relationship to the present worth of an annuity of 1 table and may be constructed as in Table 16.8.

Typical Use of Installment to Amortize 1 Table

Suppose that a property is worth $30,000 and has an economic life of 50 years. How much must this property return as net operating income annually to provide interest and amortization at 10 percent interest? The annuity necessary to warrant an amount whose present value is 1 at 10 percent interest is 0.100859 (see Table 16.1). Multiplying this amount by $30,000 gives the answer of $3,025.77. The rate of 0.100859 used in this illustration is in fact a composite of the effective interest rate on the investment, or 0.10 plus the sinking fund rate for 50 years at 10 percent, or 0.00859.

To derive the amount whose present value is 1 for a four-year period at 10 percent interest, all that is necessary (if this special table is not available) is to make reference to a sinking fund table and to add the effective rate of interest to the rate shown as follows: The sinking fund rate for four years at 10 percent = 0.215471 + 0.10 interest equals 0.315471, which is the annual amount necessary to provide a return *on* and *of* an investment of $1.00 for a four-year period at 10 percent interest.

A table showing the installment to amortize 1 is especially useful in connection with mortgage loan financing. This table provides the exact amounts that must be repaid over the loan period at given rates of interest for every dollar borrowed. Attention is called to the fact that interest and amortization payments on

TABLE 16.8 DERIVATION OF ANNUITY PAYMENT FOR INSTALLMENT
TO AMORTIZE 1 AT 10 PERCENT INTEREST

n periods (end of period)	Present worth of 1 per period	Reciprocal of present worth of 1 per period
1	0.909091	1.1000000
2	1.735537	0.576190
3	2.486852	0.402115
4	3.169865	0.315471
5	3.790787	0.263797
...		
49	9.906296	0.100946
50	9.914814	0.100859

mortgage loans are generally computed over monthly rather than annual periods of time. When this is the case the interest rate must be divided in the same proportion that the year is divided into smaller parts. To illustrate: If a $10,000 mortgage is made at 6 percent over 20 years and is to be amortized monthly, the 20-year loan period is multiplied by 12 (months of the year) to obtain 240 monthly payment periods. Similarly, the annual interest of 0.06 must be divided by 12 to obtain the rate per payment period, which in this case is 0.005, or 1/2 of 1 percent. By reference to a table showing the amount whose present value is 1, the payment per $1.00 is obtained opposite 240 (n) periods under the "1/2 percent interest" column. This amount is 0.007165. Multiplying this rate of payment per $1.00 of loan by $10,000 indicates that monthly payments of $71.65 will be necessary to pay interest at the annual rate of 6 percent (1/2 percent each month) and to amortize the $10,000 over a period of 240 months. An amortization schedule for the first three months of this loan would show entries as in Table 16.9.

The various interest and annuity tables discussed in this chapter must be thoroughly understood by all professional appraisers. A complete book of financial tables[1] and a good financial (preferably printing) calculator should be part of every appraisal office. Small electronic computers have become an integral part of many real estate appraisal offices. Further illustrations and applications of the various interest and annuity tables will be encountered in the chapters dealing with capitalization methods and techniques.

Calculator Solution

Three different calculator methods will be given to determine the periodic installment required to amortize a capital investment—either debt, equity, or total property value. The first method is best applied to annual installments as will be shown, assuming that the mortgage term is 25 years, the installments are made

TABLE 16.9 AMORTIZATION SCHEDULE OF A MORTGAGE LOAN OF $10,000 PROVIDING MONTHLY AMORTIZATION OVER A 20-YEAR PERIOD AT 6 PERCENT INTEREST

Year and month	Monthly payment	Interest at 0.005 per period	Amortization of loan	Remaining loan balance
				$10,000.00
0–1	$ 71.65	$ 50.00	$ 21.65	9,978.35
0–2	71.65	49.89	21.76	9,956.59
0–3	71.65	49.78	21.87	9,934.72
. . .	. . .	. . .	. . .	. . .
20-year totals	$17,196.00	$7,196.00	$10,000	0

[1]For instance, *Financial Compound Interest and Annuity Tables*, 6th ed. (Boston: Financial Publishing Co., 1980); James J. Mason, ed. and compiler, *American Institute of Real Estate Appraisers Financial Tables* (Chicago: American Institute of Real Estate Appraisers, 1981); Paul R. Goebel and Norman G. Miller, *Handbook of Mortgage Mathematics and Financial Tables* (Englewood Cliffs, N.J.: Prentice-Hall, Inc., 1981).

annually, the mortgage is for $100,000, and interest compounds at the annual rate of 10 percent. Thus the annual principal and interest payment is

25 | n | 10 | i | 100000 | CHS | | PV | | PMT | = $11,016.81

Had the installments been payable on a monthly basis, one of the two following methods could have been used.

Method 1

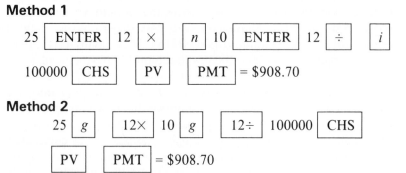

25 | ENTER | 12 | $\times$ | | n | 10 | ENTER | 12 | $\div$ | | i

100000 | CHS | | PV | | PMT | = $908.70

Method 2

25 | g | | 12$\times$ | 10 | g | | 12$\div$ | 100000 | CHS

| PV | | PMT | = $908.70

THE IMPORTANCE OF LOGARITHMIC FUNCTIONS

At the outset of this chapter, it was stated that the basic compound interest table derived by the formula $S^n = (1 + i)^n$ is the mother table from which all other interest tables explained previously can be readily derived. It is important, therefore, that professional appraisers learn how to compute the compound amount of 1. Occasions arise when prepared tables at required percentages are not available, or where unusually long property life spans go beyond the number of compound periods covered in available table publications. The capitalization of income from a hydroelectric power dam, or the computation of its reversionary value when its economic life is judged to be 200 or more years, may be such an instance.

To find the compound amount of 1 requires raising the amount of 1 plus the rate of interest (at which 1 is to be compounded) to a power equal to that of the number of interest periods involved. To find the compound amount of 1 at 10 percent interest over a period of five years—$(1 + i)^5$—it is necessary to raise 1.10 to the fifth power, as follows:

$$1.00 \times 1.10 = 1.100000 \qquad 1.331000 \times 1.10 = 1.464100$$
$$1.10 \times 1.10 = 1.210000 \qquad 1.464100 \times 1.10 = 1.610510$$
$$1.21 \times 1.10 = 1.331000$$

To raise 1.10 to a power of 50, or 500, or higher by simple arithmetic would be a most laborious if not an impossible task. A number, however, can be raised to any conceivable power with relative ease through the use of logarithmic tables or with a calculator having natural and common logarithm keys.

It is not intended in this chapter to teach the use of logarithmic tables or to explain the principle underlying the theory of logarithms or its geometric functions. All that is intended is to state briefly the purposes that logarithmic tables serve and to recommend that interested students or professional appraisers unacquainted with these tables acquire a set, together with instructions for their use, through a bookstore or library.

A logarithm expresses a number in decimals of the power of 10. Adding the log of 1.10 to the log of 1.10 has the same effect as raising 1.10 to the second power; 20 times the log of 1.10 in effect raises 1.10 to its twentieth power. To find the compound amount of $(1.10)^{50}$ merely requires looking up the log of 1.10, multiplying by 50, and looking up the antilog to obtain the answer sought. To illustrate:

$$\text{Log of } 0.10 = 0.041393$$
$$\text{Log} \quad 0.041393 \times 50 = 2.069634$$
$$\text{Antilog} \quad 2.069634 = 117.390853$$

The amount of 117.390853 thus obtained equals the amount shown under the compound amount of 1 table at 10 percent interest opposite the n, or time period of 50. Possession of a calculator with logarithmic capability, working knowledge of its application, and familiarity with logarithmic tables are highly recommended, if not essential, to all practicing appraisers.

SPECIAL APPLICATIONS OF COMPOUNDING AND DISCOUNTING

No table, however complete, will handle every situation confronting the real estate appraiser. This section is included to expand the scope of these present and future worth functions. Presented herein are techniques for

1. Solving for intermediate period values.
2. Extending functions beyond the capacity of tables.
3. Interpolating for intermediate values.
4. Converting end-of-period to beginning-of-period payments.
5. Valuing deferred payments.
6. Solving mortgage problems.

Intermediate Period Values

There will be times when the value of an intermediate or odd period is required. For example, the appraiser may want to know the present worth of $100,000, discounted at 10 percent annually for 25½ years. In using the tables to solve for this value, it must be remembered that the *rule of exponents* states that exponents are added and factors are multiplied. Exponents may be thought of as years, for example (25 + 0.5), and factors are the value under a particular present or future worth function for a given year and specified interest rate. For 10 percent, this would be 0.092296 (25 years) and 0.952381 (6 months). By multiplying these factors, the present worth of 1 at 10 percent for 25½ years is determined to be 0.087901. A visual inspection of Table 16.1 shows that this factor lies between the 25- and 26-year present worth of 1 factors.

A *very important point* to remember when trying to find intermediate values or in extending the tables for the present worth of 1 per period is that the initial computations must be for the present worth of 1 or its reciprocal, compound amount of 1. That factor then is substituted into the equation

$$a_{\overline{n}|} = \frac{1 - V^n}{i}$$

The same process applies for the future worth of 1 per period. The initial calculations must be made for the compound amount of 1. This computed factor is then substituted into the future value of 1 per period equation. Illustrating this method for the present value of 1 per period with the previously computed factor, we see that the 25½-year 10 percent value of $a_{\overline{n}|}$ is

$$\frac{1 - V^n}{i} = \frac{1 - 0.087901}{0.10} = 9.120990$$

A quick perusal of Table 16.1 reveals that this factor is midway between the present value of 1 per period factors for 25 and 26 years.

Extending Table Functions

The previously mentioned law of exponents applies to tabular extensions. Also, the initial calculations should be made either for the compound amount of 1 or present value of 1 with the answers then being substituted into the future or present value of 1 per period equations. Assume, for example, a client wants to know the present value of a 75-year $10,000 annual income stream discounted at 10 percent annually. Any combination of reversion factors totaling 75 years will provide the first step. In this case, factors for 50 and 25 years are used.

Step 1

$$V^n = 0.008519 \times 0.092296$$
$$= 0.000786$$

Step 2

$$a_{\overline{n}|} = \frac{1 - 0.000786}{0.10}$$
$$= 9.992137$$

Step 3

$$PV = 9.992137 \times \$10,000$$
$$= \$99,921.37$$

Interpolating Intermediate Values

In some instances, it may not be possible to derive intermediate values via tables. Still, more precision is desired than simply giving a range of values. This is where a knowledge of interpolation is beneficial. This method sometimes is called the rule of proportional parts.

Suppose that a property sold for $400,000 and at the date of sale had a net operating income of $53,342, which is expected to continue for the next 15 years.

From this information, a present worth of 1 per period factor of 7.498781 is computed ($400,000 ÷ $53,342).

You are interested in the exact discount rate that pertains to this situation. The first step is to bracket the computed present worth of 1 ($a_{\overline{n}}$) factor. These 9 and 11 percent factor values are found in Appendix V. Next, solve for the discount rate that corresponds to the $a_{\overline{n}}$ for a particular property as follows:

	Discount rate		$a_{\overline{n}}$
	0.09	8.060688	8.060688
	Target factor	7.498781	
	0.11		7.190870
Difference	0.02	0.561907	0.869818

$$DR = 0.09 + 0.02 \,(0.561907/0.869818)$$
$$= 0.09 + 0.02 \,(0.646005)$$
$$= 0.09 + 0.012920$$
$$= 0.102920, \text{ or } 10.29\%$$

Converting End-of-Period to Beginning-of-Period Payments

Present and future worth tables are traditionally set up on the basis of payments being received at the end of a period (EOP). This rationale fits the premise under which mortgage payments are made. However, rental payments usually are paid at the beginning of a period (BOP). To convert EOP payments to BOP payments, the steps are as follows:

1. Compute EOP present worth of 1 per period factor.
2. Convert EOP factor to BOP factor by multiplying it by $1 + i$, remembering that i is the effective interest rate or the nominal interest rate divided by the number of installments per year.

Assume that an investor wants to know the present worth of a level income stream of $1,000 annually, received at the beginning of each year over 20 years, and discounted at 10 percent. The solution is as follows:

$$PV = \$1,000 \times 8.513564 \times 1.10$$
$$= 9,364.92$$

If the rental income were received monthly in advance, the present value would be

$$PV = (\$1,000/12)(103.624619)(1 + 0.10/12)$$
$$= (\$83.33)(103.624619)(1.008333)$$
$$= \$8,707.00$$

The calculator solution is as follows:

g	BEG	20	g	n	10	g	i

83.33	PMT	PV

The first two keystrokes are done to convert the payments to the beginning of the period (also see the corresponding table in Appendix V).

Some financial calculators allow for BOP payments simply by shifting a key to denote this form of payment rather than EOP payments.

Valuing Deferred Payments

A type of lease discussed in a previous chapter is one in which future payments are staged in stair-step fashion. Since the income stream is irregular, customary use of the present value of 1 per period is negated. However, a variation of the level annuity method is possible. That is, future income at different levels can be discounted to reveal the present value.

Assume, for example, that a property is subject to a lease where the rent payments are received at the end of each year; for the first 5 years the annual rental is $2,000; for the next 5 years, it advances to $2,500 annually; the discount rate is 10 percent.

The present value is found by using the Table 16.1 factors as follows:

3.790787 × $2,000	$ 7,581.57
+ (6.144567 − 3.790787)($2,500)	5,884.45
PW of 1 per period for years 1 to 10	$13,466.02

The procedure in using this method is to first multiply the present worth of 1 per period for the first period (e.g., first five years) by the annual income to be received during this period. Next, the annual income for the next period is multiplied by the difference in the factor for the last year of the second period and the factor used for the first period. Proof of the correctness of this second-period calculation is shown by calculating the present worth of 1 factors for years 6 through 10 and comparing the total to the difference of the present worth of 1 per period factors for years 10 and 5. The comparative results follow:

1. Present worth of 1 (years 6 through 10):

$$
\begin{array}{r}
0.564474 \\
+\ 0.513158 \\
+\ 0.466507 \\
+\ 0.424098 \\
+\ 0.385543 \\
\hline
2.353780
\end{array}
$$

2. Present worth of 1 per period (year 10 − year 5):

$$
\begin{array}{r}
6.144567 \\
-\ 3.790787 \\
\hline
2.353780
\end{array}
$$

One other comment is in order regarding the present value of deferred income. The simplest way of converting end-of-period income to beginning-of-period income in order to estimate present value is (1) to solve for present value under the premise that the income is received at EOP and (2) to adjust the preliminary answer in (1) by multiplying it by $1 + i$. Applied to the preceding example,

$$PW = \$13,466.02 \times 1.10 = \$14,812.62$$

By use of the HP 12C calculator the present worth of this two-phase income is calculated as follows:

$$\boxed{10}\ \boxed{i}\ \boxed{2000}\ \boxed{g}\quad \boxed{CFj}\ \boxed{5}\ \boxed{g}\quad \boxed{Nj}$$

$$\boxed{2500}\ \boxed{g}\quad \boxed{CFj}\ \boxed{5}\ \boxed{g}\quad \boxed{Nj}\quad \boxed{f}\quad \boxed{NPV}$$

read $13,466.02

Mortgage Problems

A problem often occurs when a party prepares to sell its property. That is, before it can judge the net proceeds from a sale, the remaining balance of the loan must be ascertained.[2] Several methods can be used, but all stem from the amount of the mortgage payments. For each of the following methods, assume monthly installments; 10 percent interest; original principal, $100,000; original loan term, 25 years; remaining loan term, 15 years (see Appendix V).

1. $$\text{Remaining loan balance} = (\$100,000)\left(\frac{0.009087}{0.010746}\right)$$
    $$= \$100,000 \times 0.845617$$
    $$= \$84,561.70$$

    This step compares the installment factor for the full loan term to the remaining loan term.

2. Find the monthly mortgage payment for 25-year and for 15-year loan terms; next divide the monthly payment for 15 years into that used for 25 years; this percentage is then multiplied by the original amount of the mortgage.

    Monthly payment for 25-year loan = $100,000 × 0.009087
    Monthly payment for 15-year loan = $100,000 × 0.010746

    $$\text{Remaining loan balance} = (\$100,00)\left(\frac{\$908.70}{\$1,074.60}\right)$$
    $$= \$100,000 \times 0.845617$$
    $$= \$84,561.70$$

SPECIAL-PURPOSE TABLES

To permit ready and more rapid conversion of operating income into value, a number of special-purpose tables have been developed and published for use by property appraisers. Although all value problems can be solved without reference to precomputed tables and it is often advisable not to employ or rely on special-

---

[2]Equity buildup via loan amortization is the complement of the remaining loan balance.

purpose tables, especially when testifying in court as an expert witness,[3] neverthe-less, there may be certain assignments in which the appraiser will find it advantageous to be acquainted with such tables, their derivation, and with cir-cumstances under which such tables may be correctly applied.

The Inwood (Coefficient) Table

This is the oldest, best known, and most frequently applied capitalization table. This table in essence is a summation of the present worth of $1.00 for each of the future years in which a level income (same amount each year) is expected over the remaining economic life of a property. The Inwood factor, which is the same as the present value of 1 per period covered earlier, for a sum of $1.00 to be received over a period of 40 years at 10 percent is 9.779051. This factor is precomputed as shown in Table 16.1 and is obtained by addition of the present worth of $1 at 10 percent, $1/1.10 + 1/(1.10)^2 + 1/(1.10)^3 + \cdots + 1/(1.10)^{40}$, or by the shortcut method under which the rate of interest is added to the sinking fund factor at the same rate for the number of years over which the income is to be capitalized. This rate combination is then divided into the sum of 1.00. The reciprocal thus ob-tained is the Inwood factor. To illustrate: An interest rate of 0.10 plus a sinking fund factor at 10 percent for 40 years of 0.002259 equals a capitalization rate of 0.102259. The reciprocal of this rate is 1/0.102259, which equals the Inwood fac-tor of 9.779051. To capitalize an estimated level income of $1,000 per year for a period of 40 years under the Inwood method at 10 percent interest requires only the multiplication of $1,000 by the Inwood factor of 9.779051 to obtain the pres-ent value of the property in the amount of $9,779.05. Thus the Inwood factor con-verts a level future income stream to a present value by use of a single discount rate.

The Hoskold Factor Table

The Hoskold annuity factor is constructed in a fashion similar to the Inwood an-nuity factor. The only difference between these two methods of capitalization is that the sinking fund rate of depreciation or recapture is always at a lower, lesser, or "safe" rate than the rate of interest employed as a return on the invested capi-tal. This latter rate sometimes is known as a "speculative" rate. To illustrate: If the rate of interest is found to be 10 percent and the "safe" rate of capital recapture is 5 percent, the rate of capitalization for an income stream over a period of 40 years is 10 percent plus 0.008278 (5% sinking fund factor) or a total capitalization rate of 0.108278. The Hoskold factor is merely the reciprocal of the rate of capitaliza-tion or 1 ÷ 0.108278, which equals 9.235486. Thus an income of $1,000 due each year over a period of 40 years is worth, under the Hoskold method of valuation at the rates stated previously, the sum of $1,000 × 9.235486, or $9,235.49.

---

[3]Experience has shown that laypersons and jurors have difficulty in understanding the use and purpose of complex mathematical tables and as a result become wary of the findings and judge the person's integrity rather than the accuracy of the mechanisms of valuation.

Ellwood Tables

These precomputed rates or coefficients were derived under the band-of-investment rate method to reflect mathematically varying combinations of mortgage and equity ratios over investment or ownership life periods of 1 to 30 years at preselected mortgage interest and equity yield rates. Ellwood tables were not intended to be applied in the conventional valuation of real property, where the sale represents a cash or cash-equivalent transaction. Rather, the Ellwood tables were intended for use in the valuation of *equity* investments where a major part of the total property is encumbered with a level-payment mortgage which is scheduled to be amortized monthly over a number of years at a stipulated rate of interest. With the aid of the Ellwood tables, an appraiser can readily compute the cash outlay that is warranted for the purchase of the equity interest in a property. This cash outlay must equal at stipulated (market-determined) equity yield rates the present worth of future rights to income and capital payments as follows:

1. The present worth of the stabilized cash flow—left after mortgage payments covering interest and amortization of principal are met—during the ownership period of the property.
2. The present worth of the cash reversion to which the owner is entitled. This is the selling price less the amount of the remaining mortgage principal that is due at the time of sale.

The derivation and application of the precomputed Ellwood tables will be more fully explained and illustrated along with other equity capitalization techniques in Chapter 20. With the availability of reasonably priced microcomputers, appraisers increasingly have become less dependent on these tables.

SUMMARY

The use of compound interest and discounting is an integral part of appraising income property. There are six principal functions available for this effort with three being future worth functions and the other three being present worth functions. Each of the functions is summarized as follows.

The *compound amount of 1* is used to determine the amount a dollar invested today will grow to in *n* periods at a given rate of interest.

The *future worth of 1 per period* reveals the amount that a dollar deposited at the end of each period will grow to in *n* periods at a given rate of interest.

The *sinking fund factor* reveals how much must be deposited at the end of each period at compound interest to accumulate a dollar in n periods.

The *present worth of 1*, sometimes called a reversion factor, provides the present worth of the right to receive a dollar in *n* periods in the future at a given rate of interest.

The *present worth of 1 per period*, or Inwood factor, determines the present worth of the right to receive a dollar at the end of each period for *n* periods at a given rate of interest.

The *installment to amortize 1*, or mortgage constant, is used to determine how much must be paid in periodic payments to amortize a dollar, including principal and interest, in n periods at a given rate of interest.

In addition to having an understanding of compound interest tables and financial calculators, it is advisable for appraisers to have a basic grasp of logarithmic functions as well.

Sometimes it is necessary to make special calculations that are not directly shown in financial tables. Examples of these calculations include finding intermediate period values, extending table functions, interpolating intermediate values, converting end-of-period payments to beginning-of-period payments, valuing deferred payments, and solving mortgage problems such as loan balances.

Three other special purpose tables are the Inwood table, the Hoskold factor table, and the Ellwood tables. The Inwood table is used to convert a level future income stream to a present value by use of a single discount rate. The Hoskold factor table is similar to the Inwood table except that it employs two rates—the speculative rate to value the income stream and the safe rate which is a lower rate used to compute the sinking fund rate of recapture. The Ellwood tables contain rates derived under the band-of-investment method to reflect mathematically varying combinations of mortgage and equity rates of varying periods at preselected mortgage interest and equity yield rates.

REVIEW QUESTIONS

1. Given a 10 percent annual interest rate and a 22-year term, compute the future worth of 1 per period and sinking fund factor by substituting the compound amount of 1 factor into each of these two equations.

2. To compute an intermediate (odd period) value or extend the tables from the future-present worth table, either of two factors must first be computed. Identify both of these factors.

3. How much must be deposited at the end of each year, compounded at 10 percent annually, to grow to $10,000 at the end of 12 years?

4. If an investor were to deposit $5,000 today, assuming 10 percent annual compounding, to what amount would this grow at the end of 16 years?

5. Would your client have accumulated $10,000 through loan amortization on a 25-year, $75,000, 10 percent annual installment mortgage at the end of the eighth year? How much equity would have been built up?

6. Compute the present value of a property available for purchase in 65 years for $600,000, discounted at 10 percent annually.

7. What is the present worth of a $4,000 annual income stream receivable at the beginning of the year over the next 15 years? Assume that a 10 percent annual discount rate is applicable.

8. Find the current value of the following lease income that is received at the end of the year and discounted at 10 percent annually: years 1 to 3, $10,000; years 4 to 6, $12,000; years 7 to 9, $13,500.

9. B has paid $100 in taxes each year on a vacant lot which he purchased 10 years ago for $3,000. Assuming interest rates at 9 percent, how much is his total investment to date (see the corresponding table in Appendix V)?

10. **(a)** Explain what is meant by "present value of an annuity."
    (b) What is the present value of $1.00 due each year for a period of three years, discounted at 10 percent annually?

11. Capitalize the following at 10 percent:
    (a) An income flow (annuity) of $500 per annum for 15 years.
    (b) An income flow (annuity) of $500 per annum for 100 years.
    (c) An income flow of $500 per annum in perpetuity.

12. If $1,000 is to be accumulated under the sinking fund method over a period of 20 years, how much must be placed annually into the fund if the compound interest rate is 10 percent?

13. Set up a schedule of amortization for a 10 percent, eight-year, $10,000, monthly installment mortgage and show *all* captions, headings, and entries for the first two months.

14. An apartment house which represents the highest and best use has been completed at a cost of $750,000. The land has been owned by the developer for many years and its value is unknown. The anticipated net operating income from this improvement, which has an estimated economic life of 40 years, is as follows:

First year	$47,500
Second year	60,000
Third year and thereafter	
for 37 years	70,000

Based on an interest rate of 10 percent for the entire property, determine the appraised value of this property. Use the Inwood method of capitalization.

READING AND STUDY REFERENCES

BOYKIN, JAMES H. "Seeking the Elusive Discount Rate," *The Appraisal Journal* 59, no. 3 (July 1990), pp. 328–333.

ELLWOOD, L. W. *Ellwood Tables for Real Estate Appraising and Financing*, 4th ed. Chicago: American Institute of Real Estate Appraisers, 1977.

EPLEY, DONALD R., and JAMES H. BOYKIN. Chapter 6, "Discounting and Compounding," *Basic Income Property Appraisal*. Reading, Mass.: Addison-Wesley Publishing Co., Inc., 1983.

FRIEDMAN, JACK, P., and NICHOLAS ORDWAY. Chapters 2 and 3, *Income Property Appraisal and Analysis*. Reston, Va.: Reston Publishing Co., Inc., 1981.

HONNOLD, KEITH L. "The Link Between Discount Rates and Capitalization Rate: Revisited," *The Appraisal Journal* 58, no. 2 (April 1990), pp. 190–195.

JONES, ROBERT N., and STEPHEN D. ROACH. "Valuation of Long-Term Leases," *The Appraisal Journal* 57, no. 4 (October 1989), pp. 451–459.

KINCHELOE, STEPHEN C. "The Weighted Average Cost of Capital," *The Appraisal Journal* 58, no. 1 (January 1990), pp. 88–95.

MASON, JAMES J. (ed. and compiler). *American Institute of Real Estate Appraisers Financial Tables*. Chicago: American Institute of Real Estate Appraisers, 1981.

MASON, ROBERT C. "Discount Rate Derivation," *The Appraisal Journal* 57, no. 1 (January 1989), pp. 79–87.

SLAY, KELLEY D. "The Capitalization Rate, the Discount Rate, and Projected Growth in Value," *The Appraisal Journal* 59, no. 3 (July 1990), pp. 324–327.

17
Income Capitalization Methods

Learning Objectives

After reading this chapter, you should be able to:

- Understand the reciprocal relationship between capitalization rates and discount factors
- Capitalize an income stream that is forecast to extend into perpetuity
- Use several methods for capitalizing income over a specific time period
- Explain how periodic recapture is set up via the straight-line and annuity methods
- Appreciate the complementary nature of the present worth of the income to the land user and the fee owner's reversionary interest
- Use the discounted cash flow technique in deriving an equity yield rate
- Distinguish among the net present value, internal rate of return, and modified internal rate of return concepts

Appraising, under the income approach to value, calls for aptitude and skill in applying the capitalization process. *Capitalization* of income means to convert or to process earnings anticipated from typical operation of a property into a sum of present worth (capital value). Mathematically, the basic relationship of income to value is expressed by the formula

$$V = I/R \quad \text{or} \quad V = I \times F$$

The symbols used in these alternate direct capitalization formulas are defined as follows:

V = present worth of future rights to income

I = net operating income *before* cost recovery for income tax purposes and mortgage payments on the investment

R = rate of capitalization—a summation of the rate of interest plus the rate of amortization $(i + a)$

F = valuation or capitalization factor—a reciprocal of R

Use of the formula $V = I/R$ or $V = I \times F$ generally is optional, as far as the appraiser is concerned, since both equations will yield identical value conclusions. However, it is recommended that in the selection of a capitalization method, consideration be given to the technical level of understanding of the valuation report reader and that the income and capitalization data be presented in logical sequence and simple mathematical style.

The basic value formula $V = I/R$ is applicable to all appraisal problems involving capitalization of future rights to income. Care, however, must be taken to match income and rates of capitalization in relation to each particular valuation assignment. Thus, if the value of an entire property in fee simple ownership is sought, I_o in the capitalization formula must represent total property income and R_o the total (or overall) property rate at which a fair return *on* and *of* the investment is anticipated. Similarly, if the value of a fractional interest is at issue, both income and the rate of capitalization must be consistently related to that portion of the property, as will be demonstrated later.

CAPITALIZATION OF INCOME EXTENDING INTO PERPETUITY

The generally indestructible physical characteristics of land permit consideration of income derived from use of land as extending into perpetuity, without termination. There are times when land loses its value due to physical deterioration, such as from erosion or soil depletion. Other value losses may result from economic causes such as traffic rerouting. Improvements placed on land have finite economic lives, but new improvements can replace old ones, and the cycle of replacement for all practical activities can be conceived as extending on into infinity.

To illustrate the application of the capitalization process to income extending into perpetuity, it is assumed that a constant, or level, flow of income in the amount of $1,000 annually is to be converted into value at an interest rate of 10 percent. Applying the formula $V = I/R$, the value obtained equals $1,000 ÷ 0.10 = $10,000. The correctness of this answer can be proven by transposing the basic value formula to find income, or I. In this instance, $I = V \times R$ = $10,000 \times 0.10 = $1,000, or the amount necessary annually (into perpetuity) to support a value of $10,000 at a risk (interest) rate of 10 percent. The value of $10,000 could also be obtained by use of the formula $V = I \times F$. Since F is the reciprocal of R, the valuation factor is obtained by dividing 1.00 by the rate at which the income is to be capitalized. In this instance $1.00 ÷ 0.10$ equals a perpetuity factor of 10. Thus $1,000 \times 10 = $10,000, a sum equal to that obtained under the alternate capitalization formula used previously.

Perpetuity factors at any rate of interest or fraction thereof are derived by simply dividing 1.00 by the rate used for capitalization purposes. With the aid of these valuation factors, land value is readily obtained by a simple process of multiplication, as demonstrated previously. Perpetuity factors at selected rates of interest are indicated in Table 17.1.

TABLE 17.1 PERPETUITY FACTORS FOR
CAPITALIZATION OF NET OPERATING
INCOME AT SELECTED RATES OF INTEREST

Rate	Perpetuity factor
0.04	25.00
0.05	20.00
0.06	16.67
0.07	14.29
0.08	12.50
0.09	11.11
0.10	10.00

CAPITALIZATION OF NONPERPETUITY INCOME

In the valuation of building improvements or property interests with terminal lives, provision must be made to write off, or amortize, the investment over the remaining economic life of the property. The methods of capitalization used in appraisal practice are named in accordance with the method under which future value recapture, or amortization, is to be provided.

When use of the reciprocal formula $V = I \times F$ is deemed more practical or convenient, specially prepared factor tables can be applied. In such instances, the capitalization factor method used takes its name from the person who compiled or who popularized the use of the ready-made factor table in question. Using the same order as the capitalization methods listed previously, the reciprocal or income conversion methods available for valuation of nonperpetuity income are as follows:

1. Ring factor table of capitalization.[1]
2. Hoskold factor table of capitalization.
3. Inwood factor table of capitalization.

The various methods of capitalization yield value conclusions that differ importantly from one another, as will be demonstrated. Consequently, great care must be taken to select the appropriate method that reflects the market actions of typical investors. Under no circumstances should the selection of a method of capitalization be contingent on the value to be found. Instead, a particular method should be chosen that will most accurately measure the present value under given circumstances. Identical incomes produce different values under the methods of capitalization discussed here because of differences in the amount of income set aside under each method to recapture (amortize) the investment value. Everything else remaining equal, the greater the amount that is set aside out of a fixed sum of annual income for amortization purposes, the less total in-

[1]This factor table, for selected rates of interest, was developed by one of the authors and first published in the April 1960 issue of the *Appraisal Journal*, American Institute of Real Estate Appraisers. An excerpt from this table is given in Appendix V.

come that remains for the interest earnings on which property value depends. When future recapture is calculated under the formula $V = I/R$, the capitalization methods most frequently applied are known as

1. Straight-line capitalization.
2. Sinking fund capitalization.
3. Annuity capitalization.

To illustrate the traditional use of capitalization methods, a simple valuation problem will be assumed, based on the following property and income data:

1. A net operating income of $50,000 per year.
2. A remaining economic life of 40 years.
3. A 10 percent rate of interest.
4. A sinking fund rate of 5 percent.
5. An annuity rate of 10 percent.
6. A straight-line rate of depreciation of 2 1/2 percent over a period of 40 years.

The Straight-Line Method of Capitalization

Based on the straight-line method, and using the formula $V = I/R$, the value of a $50,000 net operating income may be derived. The annual income is estimated to be received over an investment life period of 40 years; similar investments typically earn an interest rate of 10 percent. The first step is to substitute income and rate data for the symbols in the value formula. The capitalization equation is then $V = \$50,000$ divided by 0.125 (0.10 interest plus 0.025 annual rate of amortization), giving a present worth of $400,000. The accuracy of this value is proven by application of the interest and amortization rates as follows:

10% return on $400,000	$40,000
2.5% amortization allowance on $400,000	10,000
Total required annual income	$50,000

Using the Ring factor table of capitalization and the formula $V = I \times F$, the appraiser can obtain identical value results. Reference to this table (see Appendix V) discloses under the 10 percent rate of capitalization, and opposite 40 years, a present worth factor per dollar of income of 8.00000. Multiplying the income expectancy of $50,000 by the Ring factor of 8.00000 (1 ÷ 0.1250) produces a value of $400,000, which is identical to the value found under the $V = I/R$ rate formula given previously.

It is well to emphasize that the appraiser selects by way of market analysis the applicable rate of interest as well as the method and rate of recapture. No matter which method of capitalization is selected by the appraiser, the ratio that the rate of recapture bears to the combined rate of capitalization always represents the percentage of net operating income that should be labeled "provision for recapture" in the operating expense schedule. Under the straight-line method of capitalization, amortization of the investment is provided in equal annual amounts—but as increasing percentages of the remaining value. This can be observed in the entries derived over the first three years of income life for the investment of $400,000 as shown in Table 17.2.

In appraisal practice, the use of the straight-line method of capital recapture is often justified by the assumption that income from the investment will decline as the property ages in direct proportion to the reduced interest earnings derived from the remaining value of the investment at the end of each year. Thus, if the remaining value decreases by $10,000 annually, as shown in Table 17.2, income is expected to decrease annually by 10 percent of $10,000, or in the amount of $1,000 over the 40-year economic-income-life period. Based on declining income under this assumption and under the straight-line method of capitalization, a schedule of amortization would produce entries as shown in Table 17.3.

The assumption that net operating income will decline in precise amounts, as indicated in Table 17.3, is difficult to substantiate. Furthermore, it is not orthodox mathematical practice to reflect an anticipated decline in the numerator of the equation ($V = I/R$) by an upward adjustment of the denominator of the value equation. If income is expected to decline over the life of the investment, why not stabilize the future income stream to reflect this decline rather than tamper with the interest or annuity rate by means of which *all* income should be capitalized? To illustrate: If an income of $50,000 per year over a life period of 40 years is expected to decline annually over its remaining economic life, many appraisers at present capitalize this income flow by dividing $50,000 by the rate of interest plus the straight-line rate of recapture, or given a rate of 10 percent and a

TABLE 17.2 AMORTIZATION FOR A $400,000 INVESTMENT OVER A 40-YEAR PERIOD AT 10 PERCENT INTEREST UNDER THE STRAIGHT-LINE METHOD

End of year	Annual income	10 percent interest	2.5 percent amortization	Remaining value
1	$ 50,000	$ 40,000[a]	$ 10,000	$390,000
2	50,000	40,000	10,000	380,000
3	50,000	40,000	10,000	370,000
. . .	. . .	. . .	. . .	. . .
40	50,000	40,000	10,000	0
Total	$2,000,000	$1,600,000	$400,000	

[a]$0.10 \times $400,000; similarly, the annual amortization figure is based on $0.025 \times $400,000.

TABLE 17.3 DECLINING INCOME UNDER STRAIGHT-LINE CAPITALIZATION

Year	Annual income	10 percent interest on value balance	2.5 percent amortization	Remaining value
				$400,000
1	$50,000	$40,000	$10,000	
2	49,000	39,000	10,000	
3	48,000	38,000	10,000	

rate of recapture of 2.5 percent the indicated value is obtained as follows: $50,000 ÷ 0.125 = $400,000.

The same value, however, can be obtained by stabilizing this declining income stream to an amount of $40,904. Capitalizing this *stabilized* income of $40,904[2] by use of the 10 percent Inwood factor for 40 years of 9.779, or the inverse annuity rate of 0.102260, an identical value of $400,000 is obtained. To stabilize a declining income stream (under the straight-line premise), all the appraiser needs to do is to divide the annuity rate of capitalization at the selected interest rate by the straight-line rate of capitalization. In the illustration given previously, the 10 percent annuity rate for 40 years is 0.102260 (see Table 16.1), and the straight-line rate of capitalization is 0.125. Dividing the former rate by the latter yields a quotient of 81.808 percent. This is the stabilized income flow per dollar of income, which, when capitalized by the Inwood factor or the annuity rate (reciprocal of Inwood factor), will give identical value results as those obtained under straight-line capitalization. An even more accurate procedure for forecasting and capitalizing a declining income stream will be demonstrated under the annuity method of capitalization.

Most properties are purchased and financed up to 80 or more percent of value by means of a mortgage which is invariably amortized under the compound interest or Inwood annuity method of financing. If the Inwood or annuity method is applicable to 80 or more percent of property value, one must seriously question the accuracy of straight-line recapture and straight-line capitalization when applied to the property as a whole.

The use of the straight-line method of capitalization, however, may be justified for income to be realized over comparatively short periods of an investment life, or where typical investment practices clearly warrant the use of straight-line amortization. For income-producing properties with economic life periods extending over more than 10 years, and where declining incomes can be estimated or stabilized with a fair degree of accuracy by market comparison study, the use of the straight-line method of capitalization is not recommended unless it accurately depicts the future income stream.

The Sinking Fund Method of Capitalization

This method of capitalization is based on the premise that the investor has no access or control over the amounts set aside for amortization of the investment and that provisions for capital replacement can be accumulated in a fund, earning compound interest at a safe, or bank, rate of interest. Employing the same valuation data as previously used under straight-line capitalization, the value of a $50,000 income for a period of 40 years at 10 percent interest is derived under the sinking fund (3 percent) rate method as follows: $V = I/R = $50,000 divided by 0.1132624 (0.10 interest plus 0.0132624[3] amortization at 3 percent interest),

---

[2]Computed as follows: ($50,000)(81.808%); 81.808 percent is based on 0.102260 ÷ 0.125 as explained in this paragraph.

[3]This rate was obtained from a sinking fund table at 3 percent interest. (See Chapter 16 for both the mathematical and calculator solutions.)

which equals a present worth of $441,452.77. The accuracy of this value is proven by the application of interest and amortization rates as follows:

10% return on $441,452.77	$44,145.28
1.32624% annual sinking fund requirements on	
$441,452.77	5,854.72
Total required annual earnings	$50,000.00

The annual depreciation allowance of $5,854.72, if invested at compound interest at a 3 percent rate over a 40-year period, will equal an amount of $441,452.77 ($5,854.72 × 75.401260).

The sinking fund method of capitalization perhaps is better designed to serve accounting rather than appraisal purposes. As a rule investment buyers of real property have access to all the net operating income derived from operation of such property and typically do not set up a fund for amortization of equity interests. The sinking fund method also does not provide for declining income as a property ages. It is possible, of course, to consider that the amounts accumulated in the sinking fund are available for reinvestment and that the annual income will decline in proportion to interest earnings on the remaining value, as was the case under straight-line amortization. The assumption, however, to consider accumulated depreciation returns, under this method of capitalization, as available for reinvestment violates the concept of a "fund" on which the sinking fund or Hoskold method of capitalization is founded.

The Annuity Method of Capitalization

This method of capitalization is similar in all respects to the sinking fund method except that no fund is established in which the annual amortization provisions are to accumulate. Instead, the periodic payments for amortization of investment capital are made available to the property user or owner for immediate reinvestment in similar or other types of property. The rates of earning for both the property as a whole, and for portions of the investment returned each year through amortization provisions—and which are available for reinvestment—are considered as one and the same.

To illustrate again by use of the formula $V = I/R$, the value of a $50,000 income for a life period of 40 years at 7 percent interest is $50,000 divided by 0.075009 (0.07 percent interest plus 0.005009, the amortization rate at 7 percent), which equals a present worth of $666,586.68. The accuracy of this value conclusion can be proved as follows:

7% return on $666,586.68	$46,661.07
0.005009 amortization allowance on	
$666,586.68	3,338.93
Total required annual earnings	$50,000.00

The annual income of $50,000, if reinvested at a compound interest of 7 percent over a 40-year period, will equal the original investment of $666,586.68.

The application of the annuity method, too, can be simplified by use of the formula $V = I \times F$ and the Inwood table method of capitalization (covered in Chapter 16). By reference to the Inwood table, a factor of 13.33171 is obtained under the 7 percent interest column opposite 40 years of income life. Alternatively, the following keystroke sequence produces the same results:

$$40 \boxed{n} \ 7 \boxed{i} \ 50000 \boxed{\text{CHS}} \ \boxed{\text{PMT}} \ \boxed{\text{PV}}$$

Multiplying this factor by the income of $50,000 gives a present value of $666,585.44, which is essentially identical with that obtained under the annuity method of capitalization. The Inwood premise table and the present worth of an annuity of 1 table are one and the same. Amortization of the investment value of $666,586.68 derived under the annuity, or Inwood, method of capitalization is indicated by entries over the first three years of investment life as shown in Table 17.4. Study of the amortization schedule given in Table 17.4 will reveal that although the annual income remains stable, the interest or net income on the investment is declining annually. The original investment differs slightly from the previous amount due to rounding.

It is often and erroneously held that the annuity method of capitalization should be applied only to a constant or "level" income flow, or to annuities which are equal in amount throughout the economic life of the investment property. As will be demonstrated, the annuity, or Inwood, method of capitalization can effectively be applied whether the income flow is increasing, decreasing, or a combination of both. Even deficit income occasionally incurred—as during initial stages of investment operation—can be capitalized by the annuity method and amortized out of future earnings. This topic is covered in more detail in Chapter 18.

To illustrate the application of the annuity capitalization method to a declining income expectancy from a typical apartment property, it is assumed that field studies of comparable properties support a conclusion that a most probable pattern of income over the economic life expectancy of 50 years will be as follows:

First 5 years	$10,000
Next 15 years	9,000
Next 10 years	7,500
Next 10 years	6,500
Last 10 years	5,500

TABLE 17.4 AMORTIZATION FOR AN INVESTMENT OF $666,585.71 OVER A 40-YEAR PERIOD AT 7 PERCENT INTEREST UNDER THE ANNUITY METHOD

Year	Annual income	7 percent interest	Amortization	Remaining value
				$666,585.71
1	$ 50,000	$ 46,660.98	$ 3,339.02	663,246.69
2	50,000	46,427.25	3,572.75	659,673.94
3	50,000	46,177.15	3,822.85	655,851.09
. . .	. . .	. . .	. . .	. . .
40	. . .	. . .	. . .	. . .
Total	$2,000,000	$1,333,464.29	$666,585.71	

The present worth of this declining income stream at 7 percent interest is capitalized with the aid of conventional interest and discount tables as will be shown.

The same value conclusion can also be obtained by application of the Inwood factors exclusively, as shown in Table 17.5. The reader can see how the present worth of an annuity of 1 and reversion factors are also used in Table 17.5 in computing the present worth of a declining income stream. Table 17.6 provides the factors used in Table 17.5. The first part of Table 17.5 illustrates the combined use of the present worth of an annuity of 1 and the present worth of 1 in computing the present worth of a series of deferred payments. This value is calculated by multiplying the multiyear income (e.g., $9,000 a year for years 6 through 20) by the product of the present worth of the annuity of 1 factor for the number of years in that period (15 years) and the present worth of 1 factor for the number of years elapsed in the prior period or periods (5 years). The second part of Table 17.5 permits calculation of the present worth of such income by multiplying the

TABLE 17.5 CAPITALIZATION OF DECLINING INCOME VIA INWOOD PREMISE USING TWO DIFFERENT METHODS

Income period	Income expectancy	×	Present worth of annuity of 1	×	Reversion factor (PW of 1)	=	Present value
1–5	$10,000		4.1002		1.0000		$ 41,002
6–20	9,000		9.1079		0.7130		58,445
21–30	7,500		7.0236		0.2584		13,612
31–40	6,500		7.0236		0.1314		5,999
41–50	5,500		7.0236		0.0668		2,580
Total present value							$121,638

Income period	Income expectancy	Inwood factor	Fractional factors	Present value
1–5	$10,000	—	4.1002	$ 41,002
6–20	9,000	(10.5940− 4.1002)	6.4938	58,445
21–30	7,500	(12.4090−10.5940)	1.8150	13,612
31–40	6,500	(13.3317−12.4090)	0.9227	5,999
41–50	5,500	(13.8007−13.3317)	0.4690	2,580
Total present value				$121,638

TABLE 17.6 SELECTED 7 PERCENT PRESENT WORTH FACTORS

Year	Present worth of annuity of 1	Reversion factor (PW of 1)
5	4.1002	0.7130
10	7.0236	0.5083
15	9.1079	0.3624
20	10.5940	0.2584
30	12.4090	0.1314
40	13.3317	0.0668
50	13.8007	0.0339

income by the difference of the present worth of the annuity of 1 factors for the total elapsed years and the years already accounted for in prior income stages. This latter method is discussed in more detail under "Valuing Deferred Payments" in Chapter 16.

Where appraisers prefer to stabilize income rather than report detailed valuation results in stages of declining or increasing amounts as shown previously, this stabilization can readily be accomplished by transposing the formula $V = I/R$ to $I = V \times R$. By multiplying the present value derived from the declining income flow in the amount of $121,638 by the 7 percent capitalization annuity rate of 0.07245985 (0.07 interest plus 0.00245985 amortization at 7 percent for 50 years), a level income flow of $8,813.87 is obtained. A schedule of amortization can now be established using the declining income estimates—or the stabilized income amount—as computed previously. In both instances the income flow over the 50-year economic life period will yield an income of 7 percent on the remaining value balances and amortize the investment value of $121,638 under the annuity method of capitalization.

The annuity method of capitalization is almost always used in connection with capitalization of land income where the period of land ownership does not extend into perpetuity, as is the case under leasehold operation. When the reversionary interest of the fee owner (to whom the land reverts at the end of the lease period) is discounted at the same rate at which the income received by the tenant is capitalized, the value of the parts (into which land ownership is divided) will always equal the value of the land as a whole. Assuming a land value of $100,000 and a discount rate of 6 percent, the value of the split interests at 10-year intervals over a 100-year period is derived as shown in Tables 17.7 and 17.8.

The importance of early years of income life as compared with ownership and income privileges that lie in the distant future can be judged effectively by inspection of the foregoing tables. At 6 percent interest and under the annuity method of capitalization, the present worth of the income flow over the first 20 years equals 68.8 percent of total property value as compared with 100 percent for income rights that extend into perpetuity. The first 40 years represent 90.3

TABLE 17.7   PRESENT WORTH OF INCOME FLOW TO LAND USER AT 6 PERCENT

Years	Income	6 percent Inwood factor	Present worth of income	Percentage of total value
10	$6,000	7.360087	$44,161	44.2
20	6,000	11.469921	68,820	68.8
30	6,000	13.764831	82,589	82.6
40	6,000	15.046297	90,278	90.3
50	6,000	15.761861	94,571	94.6
60	6,000	16.161428	96,969	97.0
70	6,000	16.384544	98,307	98.3
80	6,000	16.509131	99,055	99.1
90	6,000	16.578699	99,472	99.5
100	6,000	16.617546	99,705	99.7

TABLE 17.8 PRESENT WORTH OF FEE OWNER'S REVERSIONARY INTEREST AT 6 PERCENT

Years	Value of land	Present worth factor	Present value of reversion land	Percentage of total value
10	$100,000	0.558395	$55,840	55.8
20	100,000	0.311805	31,181	31.2
30	100,000	0.174110	17,411	17.4
40	100,000	0.097222	9,722	9.7
50	100,000	0.054288	5,429	5.4
60	100,000	0.030314	3,031	3.0
70	100,000	0.016927	1,693	1.7
80	100,000	0.009452	945	0.9
90	100,000	0.005278	528	0.5
100	100,000	0.002947	295	0.3

percent of total property value, and rights extending beyond 80 years and into perpetuity have a present worth of less than 1 percent of total value.

DISCOUNTED CASH FLOW

Capitalization is a process for converting periodic future income into an estimated present value. This income conversion process can occur in a variety of ways such as discussed earlier in this chapter as well as in Chapters 15 and 16. It is essential that the appraiser be familiar with a variety of methods as well as know when to apply each method. Earlier, the discounted income from a graduated or step lease was explained. Other variations of irregular income streams require that a substitute for the Inwood factor, which usually is used to discount level income streams, be found (for more on this topic, see Chapter 18). Several possible situations require this alternative analysis. It may be that the appraiser is required to find (1) the present worth of an income stream that changes annually, (2) the present worth of a changing income stream as well as the need to account for the down payment and eventual net sales proceeds, or (3) whether a prospective investment is likely to fulfill an investor's yield criteria.

The majority of institutional real estate investors now use DCF, particularly the internal rate of return (IRR) before taxes. An even higher proportion use this form of DCF on an after-tax basis. Appropriately, increasing numbers of appraisers have begun to include DCF analysis in reports on income properties. With greater accessibility to microcomputers and well-designed software, appraisers can be expected to perform both before- and after-tax analyses. The latter is very important for investment and financial feasibility analyses.

The initial example involves computing the present worth of an income stream that is scheduled to change annually. It can be computed by use of the present worth of 1 (reversion) factors. Assume that the appropriate discount rate is 10 percent, as shown in Table 16.1. The annual cash flows (which could just as well have been net operating income) are as follows: year 1, $10,000; year 2,

$20,000; year 3, $30,000; year 4, $40,000; year 5, $50,000; year 6, $60,000; year 7, $70,000. To find the present value of these individual cash flows, each must be discounted by the corresponding present worth factor (see Table 17.9). Assume that the income is received at the end of each year.

As can be seen in the preceding example, an advantage of the discounted cash flow (DCF) method is its ability to be sensitive to the time value of money. That is, it measures the present worth of variable income when it is received rather than on the less accurate average income basis. At the same time, an inherent weakness of this method is that it is usually based on subjectively derived future forecasts of income and expenses. As in all capitalization techniques, diligence is required in selecting the discount rate(s).

Now suppose that the property being analyzed is a proposed structure and consequently is not expected to achieve a stabilized occupancy until the third year. Also, the buyer must make a down payment of $25,000 when the property is purchased. At the end of the fifth year, it is forecast that the net sales proceeds will be $200,000. A 10 percent annual rate of return is necessary to attract investors to this type of venture. The annual income is: year 1, minus $50,000; year 2, minus $15,000; year 3, $60,000; year 4, $65,000; year 5, $70,000.

The estimated value of this property is shown in Table 17.10.

Suppose that the previous investment required an initial equity contribution of $75,000 and the expected net sale proceeds were $50,000. Would this be a financially acceptable investment if the investor required a 10 percent equity yield? The answer is "yes" since there is a positive net present value. Look at Table 17.11.

The net present value (NPV) is the difference between the present value of the positive cash flows and the present value of the negative cash flows. This concept (outlined in Tables 17.10 and 17.11) might be thought of as a "go–no go" test of financial feasibility. Certain prescribed conditions, such as projected income, expenses, initial and final equity, as well as the investor's desired equity yield rate, are applied. If under these preset conditions the NPV is equal to or greater than zero (as found previously), the investment is feasible. If not, it is judged to be infeasible. In the preceding example, the investment would be acceptable to the investor.

TABLE 17.9 PRESENT WORTH VIA DISCOUNTED CASH FLOW METHOD AT 10 PERCENT ANNUALLY

Year	Cash flows	×	PW of 1	=	Present worth
1	$10,000		0.909091		$ 9,091
2	20,000		0.826446		16,529
3	30,000		0.751315		22,539
4	40,000		0.683013		27,321
5	50,000		0.620921		31,046
6	60,000		0.564474		33,868
7	70,000		0.513158		35,921
Total present worth					$176,315

Discounted Cash Flow

351

TABLE 17.10 PRESENT WORTH OF INVESTMENT WITH POSITIVE AND NEGATIVE CASH FLOWS

Year	Cash flow	×	PW of 1	=	Present worth
0	$(25,000)		1		$ (25,000)
1	(50,000)		0.909091		(45,455)
2	(15,000)		0.826446		(12,397)
3	60,000		0.751315		45,079
4	65,000		0.683013		44,396
5	$200,000[a] + 70,000		0.620921		167,649
Net present value					$ 174,272

[a]Rather than multiply the PW of 1 for five years by the cash flow and net sales proceeds separately, the dollar values of each have been combined.

TABLE 17.11 INVESTMENT WITH DOWNPAYMENT AND MIXED CASH FLOWS

Year	Cash flow	×	PW of 1	=	Present worth
0	$(75,000)		1		$(75,000)
1	(50,000)		0.909091		(45,455)
2	(15,000)		0.826446		(12,397)
3	60,000		0.751315		45,079
4	120,000		0.683013		44,396
5	($50,000 + $70,000)		0.620921		74,511
Net present value					$ 31,134

Internal Rate of Return

Upon receiving this net present value information, the client may now decide that he would like to know the exact return on his investment. The process for finding the exact investment return is called the *internal rate of return* (IRR). *The internal rate of return is that discount rate which equates all future income inflows and outflows.* Since it encompasses all returns on and of value, it may also be referred to as a yield rate. An assumption underlying the IRR method is that the property earnings are reinvested at the computed internal rate of return.

Since the NPV is greater than zero, the total return rate or IRR is known to be in excess of 10 percent. Finding the IRR is an iterative or trial-and-error process. This iterative process is simply repeating calculations until a more refined answer occurs. The objective of internal rate of return calculations is to find that discount rate which causes the outflows to equal the inflows. At this point, the internal rate of return is that discount rate which causes the net present value to equal zero. If the discounted cash flows exceed zero, a higher discount should be used. The reverse procedure applies when the discounted cash flows are less than zero.

It may be necessary to interpolate to determine the exact IRR, as will be shown. Also, a financial calculator can be used. This alternative will also be illustrated as well. A higher discount rate must be selected since the NPV is greater than zero.

By using the foregoing process, or a financial calculator, the net present value at 18 percent can be found:

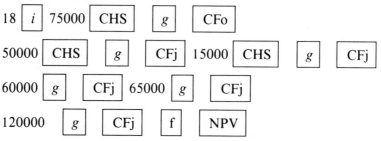

Answer: ($5,648)

Thus the IRR lies between 10 and 18 percent, but is much closer to 18 percent than 10 percent. By use of interpolation the *approximate* answer can be found. It should be remembered that more accurate results will occur when the trial run rates are relatively close to the actual rate, such as 10 and 11 percent.

	Rate		NPV
	0.10	$31,134	$31,134
	IRR	0	
	0.18		(5,648)
Difference	0.08	$31,134	$36,782

$$IRR = 0.10 + 0.08 \ (\$31{,}134/\$36{,}782)$$
$$= 0.10 + 0.08 \ (0.8464)$$
$$= \underline{\underline{0.1677}}$$

Similarly, the IRR can more easily and accurately be found by financial calculator by continuing the preceding keystroke sequence as follows:

$$\boxed{f} \quad \boxed{IRR} = \underline{0.1654}$$

Modified Internal Rate of Return

A drawback of the traditional internal rate of return is that it assumes that all cash flows are reinvested at the computed yield rate (IRR). Further, it is limited by the number of times the sign of the cash flows change (+ or −). Every time the sign changes, there is the potential for another answer.

The modified internal rate of return (MIRR) is the adjusted rate found by compounding the periodic income forward at the cost of capital rate, then computing the rate that will discount this future value to equal the cost of the investment.

The notion of using a separate reinvestment rate is associated with the Hoskold capitalization method which holds that the recaptured part of income should be viewed as being reinvested at a "safe rate." No two investors treat their income precisely the same. Yet, smaller amounts of income not needed to meet property repair and replacement commitments normally are deposited in a savings account until a larger sum has been accumulated. The larger sum may then be invested in higher yield investments such as short-term bonds or certificates of deposit while awaiting another real estate (or other) venture.

The procedure for using the MIRR method is demonstrated as follows, using the information contained in Table 17.11. The reinvestment rate is assumed to be 5 percent. The MIRR may be expressed as

$$n \sqrt{\frac{FV_{CF}}{PV_E}} - 1$$

where n = projection period
FV_{CF} = future value of periodic cash flows
PV_E = initial equity, or down payment

Cash flows	$\times$	FW 1/per (5%)	$=$	FW	Accumulation period
$ (50,000)		1.2155		$ (60,775)	4
(15,000)		1.1576		(17,364)	3
60,000		1.1025		66,150	2
65,000		1.0500		68,250	1
120,000		1.0000		120,000	0
				$176,261	

$$5 \sqrt{\frac{176,261}{75,000}} - 1$$

or

2.3501 | ENTER | 5 | 1/x | | y^x | 1 | $-$

MIRR = 18.64%

An alternative method of calculating the MIRR is

5i	4n	50,000 PV	FV			
	3n	15,000 PV	FV	+		
	2n	60,000 CHS	PV	FV	+	
	1n	65,000 CHS	PV	FV	+	
	0n	120,000 CHS	PV	FV	+	(read 176,260)

FV   75,000   CHS   PV   5n   i
MIRR = 18.64%

SUMMARY

The income approach to value calls for application of the capitalization process and use of the basic formula $V = I/R$ or $V = I \times F$. The first formula gives the appraiser a choice of three methods of capitalization, commonly known as

1. The straight-line method.
2. The sinking fund method.
3. The annuity method.

Where the latter formula is applied, specially prepared factor tables are available. These factor tables are reciprocals of the rates found under the straight-line, sinking fund, and annuity rate methods of capitalization and are in the order given previously:

1. The Ring factor table.
2. The Hoskold factor table.
3. The Inwood factor table.

To illustrate the application of the rate and factor methods of capitalization, the following data are assumed: a net operating income of $1,000 per annum over an economic life period of 40 years, a rate of interest of 7 percent, and a 3 percent sinking fund earnings rate. Based on these income rate and property life data, value estimates are obtained as follows:

Straight line

1. Straight-line rate capitalization:
$$V = I/R = \$1,000 \div 0.095 = \$10,526.32$$
$$(0.07 + 0.025)$$

2. Ring factor capitalization:
$$V = I \times F = \$1,000 \times 10.52632 = \$10,526.32$$
$$(1/0.095)$$

Sinking fund at 3 percent

1. Sinking fund rate capitalization:
$$V = I/R = \$1,000 \div 0.0832624 = \$12,010.22$$
$$(0.07 + 0.0132624)$$

2. Hoskold factor capitalization:
$$V = I \times F = \$1,000 \times 12.01022 = \$12,010.22$$
$$(1/\text{sinking fund capitalization rate})$$

Annuity method

1. Annuity method rate capitalization:
$$V = I/R = \$1,000 \div 0.07500913 = \$13,331.71$$
$$(0.07 + \text{sinking fund factor @ } 0.07)$$

2. Inwood capitalization:
$$V = I \times F = \$1,000 \times 13.33171 = \$13,331.71$$
$$(1/\text{annuity rate})$$

The values obtained under the respective methods of capitalization vary from a low of $10,526.32 under the straight-line method to a high of $13,331.71 under the annuity method for identical income streams of $1,000 capitalized at a 7 percent rate of interest. The difference in value is entirely due to differences in the amounts of income (expressed as a rate per dollar) set aside for amortization purposes under each capitalization method. The greater the portion of net operating income that is reserved for depreciation anticipated over the economic life span of the property, the lesser the amount that remains for interest earnings—and, as a consequence, the smaller the capital value.

In appraisal practice, only one method of capitalization can best be applied in a particular valuation assignment. The selection of the appropriate method of capitalization should not be made haphazardly, nor should the choice be influenced by attempts to obtain high, low, or conservative value estimates. Rather it is the appraiser's duty to study earnings-to-price relationships at which comparable properties have exchanged in the open market and to use rates as well as methods of capitalization which reflect typical market practices and operations.

REVIEW QUESTIONS

1. How can a capitalization factor be converted into a perpetuity factor?
2. What is the value of a property that has an annual income of $10,000 for 25 years, using a 10 percent annual discount rate and a 5 percent owner's reinvestment rate (sinking fund) using the sinking fund premise?
3. Calculate the value of the income stream for the property in question 2 using the annuity method of capitalization; use a 10 percent annual discount rate.
4. Discuss the reasoning behind the different values found by use of the sinking fund and annuity capitalization methods.
5. Compute the value of the property in question 2 using the present worth of 1 per period factor (Inwood) and compare the results to the answer found in question 3.
6. Explain how the NPV concept is similar to as well as different from IRR.
7. A building which was constructed 40 years ago is located in a strong central business district and has shown profitable operating returns throughout its entire history. It is now proposed to modernize the structure at a cost of $150,000. The land has a value of $200,000. Taxes are estimated at $14,500 per annum after modernization. An appraisal of the structure made from plans indicates that after modernization, the building will be worth $250,000. Depreciation has been charged in the past at 2 1/2 percent and will be charged at the same rate in the future. The present owner, who has owned the property since the building was originally constructed, expects to hold the property and seeks a return of 9 percent net on her investment.
   (a) On the basis of a land investment of $200,000, what is the owner's net investment after remodeling?
   (b) What is the net rental required to pay 9 percent and to liquidate the owner's depreciable investment in 40 years?

Assuming that the property is placed on the market and is sold at its value, not its cost:

(c) What net rental would a prudent buyer require assuming a 9 percent return and liquidation of her depreciable investment in 25 years?

(d) Explain how a prudent buyer would establish an equitable *net* rent.

READING AND STUDY REFERENCES

CHESTER, BRIAN A. "Partitioning the Pre-Tax IRR," *The Appraisal Journal* 54, no. 2 (April 1986), pp. 177–187.

DOTZOUR, MARK G., and DONALD R. LEVI. "Partitioning the After-Tax IRR for Better Analysis," *The Real Estate Appraiser and Analyst* (Spring 1989), pp. 60–66.

GRISSOM, TERRY V., and JAMES L. KUHLE. "An Alternative Cash Flow Method for Real Estate Analysis," *The Real Estate Appraiser and Analyst* 49, no. 4 (Winter 1983), pp. 52–58.

HINES, MARY ALICE. Chapter 12, *Real Estate Appraisal*. New York: Macmillan Publishing Company, 1981.

KORPACZ, PETER F., and MARK I. ROTH. "Changing Emphasis in Appraisal Techniques: The Transition to Discounted Cash Flow," *The Appraisal Journal* 51, no. 1 (January 1983), pp. 21–44.

MARTIN, VERNON, III. "Reviewing Discounted Cash Flow Analyses," *The Appraisal Journal* 58, no. 1 (January 1990), pp. 83–87.

STEELE, ROBERT A. "A Recipe for Good Cash Flow Analysis," *The Appraisal Journal* 57, no. 2 (April 1989), pp. 156–165.

18
Physical Residual Techniques of Capitalization

Learning Objectives

After reading this chapter, you should be able to:

- Determine which of the physical residual techniques of capitalization is most applicable in determining an estimate of value under given circumstances
- Be more aware of the comparative strengths and weaknesses of each of the physical residual techniques
- Outline the steps involved in each residual technique
- Use the appropriate residual technique along with the different future income and value premises to fit a particular appraisal assignment
- Understand why a given future income-value change assumption produces higher or lower values than do alternative methods

In the previous chapter discussion of the income approach to value was limited to application of the methods of capitalization. Separate treatment was given to the valuation procedure for perpetuity income derived from land and nonperpetuity income derived from either land or building improvements. To promote better understanding of the different methods of capitalization, it was assumed that income from land and income from buildings and their respective values can readily be obtained as separate entities, and that summation of the values of the parts will yield an estimate of the value of the entire property.

In everyday practice, when improvements are placed on land to make land productive in conformity with the principle of highest and best use, an economic merger takes place that weds the investment parts into an economic unit as a whole. Physically, we can describe the nature and character of land, and, separately, the amount, kind, and quality of the improvements—but rental income derived from a tenant is a product of the joint property and not an aggregate of its parts. Yet in valuation procedure it becomes necessary to isolate the income attributable to the parts in order to ascertain whether land, in fact, is developed to its highest and best use, and if not, the extent to which value losses are ascribable to the improvements as a measure of functional or external obsolescence. Likewise, there are other instances where the separate values of a mortgage and equity must be ascertained. This subject will be considered later in Chapter 20.

In all appraising problems where land and building improvements form an integral whole from which net operating income is derived, the appraiser may consider (1) the land residual, (2) the building residual, or (3) the property residual techniques of valuation. Which appraisal technique to apply is not a matter of arbitrary selection but rather one dependent on the nature of the property and valuation data. Where land is developed under a program of highest and best use, and where the improvements are in new condition, it is logical to determine the amount of net operating income necessary to yield a prevailing (market) risk rate on the value of the building—plus the amounts which are necessary to amortize the depreciable building investment. The amount of income left is then residual to the land and forms the basis for an estimation of land value via the capitalized income approach. Where land is vacant and available for use, the *land residual technique* permits study of alternative (hypothetical) land uses in order to determine which use over a period of years produces the highest residual land income and hence the highest present value of the land.

Often land is developed with improvements considered to be in middle or late economic life or which do not represent the highest and best use of the site. Wherever possible in such situations, the value of the land should be estimated by either the sales comparison method or by a hypothetical analysis of land uses and capitalization of land income on the basis of its highest and best use. Once the value of land is known, the income attributable to land at going rates of interest can be determined, and the balance of the net operating income becomes residual to the building improvements. By capitalization of the residual income under the appropriate method of income conversion, the value of the building is obtained. The *building residual technique* of capitalization also serves a highly useful purpose in cases where community growth or shifting land uses cause rapid increases in land value and, conversely, accelerates building obsolescence. Where, under this technique of valuation, the net operating income barely covers the income necessary to yield a fair return on the rising value of the land, the appraiser can report the approaching end of a building's economic life and the necessity to plan for reconstruction or rehabilitation to maintain a future flow of income and to preserve the financial integrity of the property as a going investment.

In some instances where buildings are old and land is of a specialized nature, or in a location where neither market transactions nor income analysis makes possible a reasonably accurate estimate of land value, it is necessary to treat the property as an integral whole and to apply the *property residual technique* of valuation. In such instances care must be taken not to use the straight-line or sinking fund methods of capitalization, since both of these methods for the duration of the property life apply to land a rate of amortization that is inconsistent with basic theory and practice underlying the valuation of land. Land values typically increase rather than decline over time. If the property residual technique is deemed applicable, the appraiser should estimate with care the pattern of income flow anticipated over the economic life span (or projected holding period) of the property and convert this income stream into a present value estimate under the annuity method of capitalization. To the capitalized value of the property income must then be added the present, or reversionary, worth of the land based on land value when such land is free for sale or use at the end of the economic life (or projected holding period) of the subject property. Since only the reversionary worth of estimated future land value is added to the capitalized value of property income, errors in the estimated land value are minimized under this technique of capitalization.

THE RESIDUAL CHARACTER OF LAND

As explained in Chapter 8, the value of land is dependent on its use in combination with labor and capital investment, and the highest value of land is reached at a point when a site achieves its highest and best use. Land can be assigned a value by studying similar sites that have sold recently in the open market. Yet, economic comparability via the sales comparison approach is based partly on judgment and sometimes is difficult to achieve—especially where land is found to be best suited for agricultural, industrial, or special-purpose commercial uses. But even where market transactions are considered reliable indices of value, a check on the accuracy of market forces generally necessitates the application of the capitalized income approach to value.

Economically, land is residual in character. This means that the factors of labor and capital, when combined with land, must be compensated first or they will cease to function. The balance of income that remains is thus residual (left over) to land. It is this residual income which, under highest and best utilization, forms the logical basis for land value.

In appraisal practice, land is found either vacant and available for immediate or prospective use or in different stages of utilization. Because of this, various capitalization techniques had to be developed to strengthen the order of income priority of the production factors, as warranted under ever-changing socioeconomic circumstances. The techniques of capitalization which are generally applied in appraisal practice, and which will be fully explained and demonstrated, are the

1. Land residual technique.
2. Building residual technique.
3. Property residual technique.

LAND RESIDUAL TECHNIQUE

Where buildings are new and their values are known or can be estimated with reasonable accuracy, the land residual technique is used for estimating land value and for obtaining the value of the property as a whole. Also, it is well applied to such newer properties where the building makes up a large part of the total value. Hence any possibility of error occurring in the land value estimate will have only a minimum effect on the overall estimated property value. Generally, this technique of separating property net operating income into sums attributable to land and buildings is used either when the land is vacant—or assumed to be vacant—and available for development under its highest and best use, or is actually improved with a new building that constitutes the highest and best utilization of a property.

Where the property is vacant or assumed to be vacant, it is the appraiser's responsibility to visualize, specify, and support the kind of land improvements that will yield a residual income stream to the land which, when appropriately capitalized, results in the highest present value of the land. This generally involves appraising for highest and best use purposes, since the specified improvements in fact may not be built at the time of valuation—or even in the immediate future. Nevertheless, if this capitalization technique is to be accurately applied, the appraiser must carry out the following steps:

1. Describe and justify the type (architecture), kind (materials used), and quality of improvements that are recommended for construction under a program of highest and best land use.
2. Accurately estimate, or ascertain, dependable bids for construction costs of building and related land improvements complete in all respects and ready for operation as of a given date.
3. Estimate the effective gross revenue that can reasonably be obtained under typical management and operation.
4. Estimate the operating expenses to be incurred under typical management, and by subtracting these from the effective gross revenue derive the net operating income before interest and amortization payments.
5. Derive by market study and analysis the risk rate[1] at which land and building income is to be capitalized.
6. Select the method of capitalization and determine the economic life expectancy of the building investment or holding period based on the market actions of typical investors who have purchased similar properties.

Where the land is already improved under a program of highest and best use, and where the buildings are in new condition and in operating order, steps 1 and 2 may be eliminated. To illustrate the application of the land residual technique under straight-line and annuity methods of capitalization, the following assumptions are made:

---

[1]The risk rate is defined as that earnings rate required by investors; it provides for a periodic return on an investment.

1. Value of building improvements	$100,000
2. Estimated remaining economic life	50 years
3. Risk rate	10%
4. Net operating income	$ 15,000

1. Land Residual Technique: Straight-Line Capitalization

Net operating income		$15,000
Building capitalization rate (R_B):		
Interest rate	0.10	
Recapture rate (100% ÷ 50)	0.02	
Total building rate	0.12	
Building income (I_B):		
$I = V \times R = \$100,000 \times 0.12$		$12,000
Land income (I_L):		$ 3,000
Land capitalization rate (R_L) 0.10		
Land value, $V = I/R = \$3,000 \div 0.10$		$30,000
Property value:		
Land	$ 30,000	
Building	100,000	
Total	$130,000	

2. Land Residual Technique: Annuity Method Capitalization

Net operating income		$15,000
Building rate of capitalization:		
Risk rate	0.10	
Amortization rate (sinking fund factor, 10%)[2]	0.000859	
Total rate	0.100859	
Income attributable to building:		
$I = V \times R = \$100,000 \times 0.100859$		10,086
Income attributable to land:		$ 4,914
Land rate of capitalization 0.10		
Land value, $V = I/R = \$4,914 \div 0.10$		$49,140
Property value:		
Land	$ 49,140	
Building	100,000	
Total	$149,140	

[2]See Table 16.1 as well as other sections of that chapter for calculator keystrokes for finding sinking fund factors.

Note that a higher value results from use of the annuity method, which is based on a level income stream. On the other hand, the straight-line capitalization method assumes that both the building value and income will decline.

3. Land Residual Technique: Changing Income and Value Premise

There are instances when neither the income nor the value of the land and building are expected to remain level over a given forecast period. It is also possible that the income will remain constant while the land value increases (or declines) and the building value declines (or increases). Moreover, it may be that the change in land or building value will occur on either a linear or exponential basis. When change occurs on a *linear (or straight line) basis*, it increases or decreases by the same dollar amount each year. Alternatively, *exponential change* implies the value changes by the same percentage amount each period.

The generalized equation used to account for these changes in arriving at a capitalization rate is

$$R = Y - \Delta a$$

where R = capitalization rate, such as R_o, R_L, or R_B
   Y = equity or property yield rate (allowing for anticipated future value changes)
   Δ = overall value change during the forecast period
   a = annualizer (factor that converts overall change to annual rate of change)

The three major possibilities regarding changing incomes and values are

1. Income stream remains level while value changes.
2. Both income and value will change linearly.
3. Both income and value will change exponentially.

Level income and changing value.   This income-value pattern necessitates annualizing the overall value change by use of a sinking fund factor computed at the equity yield rate for the forecast period. The equation then becomes

$$R = Y - \Delta(1/S_{\overline{n}|})$$

An example of this method follows where the appraiser is retained to find the value of a property under the following circumstances:

1. Level annual net operating income	$ 15,000
2. Yield rate	10%
3. Forecast period	20 years
4. Expected land value change	+100%
5. Expected building value change	−20%
6. Estimated building value	$130,000

Net operating income $(I_L + I_B)$	$ 15,000
− Building income $(I_B)^3$ ($130,000)(0.10 + 0.20 × 0.017460)	13,454
= Land income (I_L)	$ 1,546
Capitalized at R_L ($1,546/0.10 − 1 × 0.017460)	
= Land value	$ 18,730
+ Building value	130,000
= Property value	$148,730

Income and value changing linearly.   If both the income and value of a property are expected to change on a straight-line basis, the capitalization equation is modified as follows:

$$R = Y - \Delta(1/n)$$

That is, the annualizer (a) is the reciprocal of the forecast period. Thus the property value would now be estimated as follows:

Net operating income $(I_L + I_B)$	$ 15,000
− Building income $(I_B)^3$ ($130,000)(0.10 + 0.20 × 0.05)	14,300
= Land income (I_L)	$ 700
Capitalized at R_L ($700/0.10 − 1 × 0.05)	
= Land value	$ 14,000
+ Building value	130,000
= Property value	$144,000

Income and value changing exponentially.   When the income and property value are forecast to change at the same annual percentage rate, that rate of change replaces both Δ and a. Thus the capitalization equation can be restated as

$$R = Y - CR$$

with CR being the annual compounded rate of change. Usually this annual rate is given in problems, but it may have to be computed as shown in this example. Under this premise, the property data given previously would be processed as follows:

[3]

$$R_B = \frac{\Delta I \times Y}{\Delta I + Y} = \frac{(0.20/20)(0.10)}{0.20/20 + 0.10} = \frac{0.001000}{0.110000} = 0.009091$$

and

$$R_L = \frac{(1.0/20)(0.10)}{1.0/20 + 0.10} = \frac{0.005000}{0.150000} = 0.033333$$

Net operating income	$ 15,000
− Building income $(I_B)^3$	
($130,000)(0.10 + 0.009091)	14,182
= Land income (I_L)	$ 818
Capitalized at R_L	
($818/0.10 − 0.033333)	
= Land value	$ 12,270
+ Building value	130,000
= Property value	$142,270

It can readily be seen that varying expectations of future income and value produce different present value estimates. Therefore, considerable care must be given in the forecasting of these future outcomes.

Somewhat different values were indicated by each of the preceding methods, which were based on different income and value assumptions. These estimated values varied as follows:

Level income and changing value	$148,730
Income and value changing linearly	144,000
Income and value changing exponentially	142,270

These variations again point up the professional necessity of selecting with great care the method under which an income flow is to be capitalized. Usually, a property's net operating income will not remain constant over the entire period of economic life, nor is it appropriate to provide for income decline through a rate of amortization as covered in the first section of this chapter. Where the income flow pattern and value changes can be estimated with reasonable certainty, one of the alternative methods of capitalization suggested in the second and third sections can be counted on to produce consistent, logical, and professionally defendable value estimates.

BUILDING RESIDUAL TECHNIQUE

Where land value is known—or can be established with reasonable certainty under the market approach to value or under the capitalization of ground lease income—the appraiser can determine the portion of total net operating income that is attributable to the *known* quantity, the land, and make the balance residual to the *unknown* quantity, which in this instance is the building. Generally, the building residual technique of capitalization is applicable when the building improvements are substantially depreciated, do not conform to standards which represent the highest and best use of the land, or the cost new of the building as well as the depreciated cost are difficult to estimate.

To apply the building residual technique, the appraiser must obtain or estimate the following:

1. The land value by market, income, or preferably both approaches to value.
2. Estimate the effective gross revenue obtainable under typical management.
3. Estimate the operating property expenditures and derive the net operating income—net, as always, before mortgage interest and amortization charges.
4. Derive the risk rate at which land and building income is to be capitalized.
5. Select the method of capitalization, and determine the remaining economic life expectancy of the building improvements or the income forecast period.

To illustrate the application of the building residual technique under the straight-line and annuity methods of capitalization, the following assumptions are made:

1. Value of land	$50,000
2. Estimated remaining economic life	30 years
3. Rate of land and building interest	10%
4. Net operating income	$15,000

1. Building Residual Technique: Straight-Line Capitalization

Net operating income		$15,000
Income attributable to land:		
$I = V \times R = \$50,000 \times 0.10$		5,000
Income attributable to building		$10,000
Building rate of capitalization:		
Interest rate	0.10	
Amortization rate (100% ÷ 30)	0.033333	
Total rate	0.133333	
Building value:		
$V = I/R = \$10,000 \div 0.133333$		$75,000
Property value:		
Land value	$ 50,000	
Building value	75,000	
Total	$125,000	

2. Building Residual Technique: Annuity Method of Capitalization

Net operating income	$15,000
Income attributable to land:	
$I = V \times R = \$50,000 \times 0.10$	5,000
Income attributable to building	$10,000

Building rate of capitalization:

Interest rate	0.10
Amortization rate (sinking fund factor, 10%)	0.006079
Total rate	0.106079

Building value:

$V = I/R = \$10{,}000 \div 0.106079$ $94{,}269$

Property value:

Land value	$ 50,000
Building	94,269
Total	$144,269

3. Building Residual Technique: Straight-Line Expense Recapture Method of Capitalization[4]

Net operating income	$ 15,000
Income to land $50,000 × 0.10	5,000
Income to building—before recapture	$ 10,000

Recapture of building: $\dfrac{0.033333}{0.133333} = 0.249998$

and $10,000 × 0.249998	2,500
Building income—after recapture	$ 7,500
Residual value of building, $7,500 ÷ 0.10	$ 75,000
Add value of land	50,000
Total property value	$125,000

4. Building Residual Technique: Annuity Expense Recapture Method of Capitalization[5]

Net operating income	$ 15,000
Income to land $50,000 × 0.10	5,000
Income to building—before recapture	$ 10,000

Recapture on building: $\dfrac{0.006079}{0.106079} = 0.057306$

and $10,000 × 0.057306	573
Building income—after recapture	$ 9,427
Residual value of building, $9,427 ÷ 0.10	$ 94,270
Add value of land	50,000
Total property value	$144,270

[4]The recapture rate is derived from the division of the annual straight-line building amortization rate by the straight-line annual building capitalization rate.

[5]This expense method deducts an annual depreciation expense from the building income (before depreciation) to give the building income after expenses. The annual depreciation rate is determined by dividing the sinking fund factor by the corresponding partial payment factor (at 10 percent for 30 years).

As illustrated, under the building residual technique the land value of $50,000 is held constant and the building value varies depending on the method of capitalization employed. The straight-line method, again, results in the lowest value—in this case, $125,000—for the building, and the annuity method results in the highest value, $144,270. Logically, an identical income stream should not produce different values. Again, the reasons for the differences are found in the methods used for providing for future building value recapture or amortization. The higher amounts set aside under straight-line amortization leave less net income available as interest earnings, hence the lower value. For long-lived properties, there can be only one correct method of amortization. The choice of four different methods has long proved confusing to laypersons and real estate practitioners alike. Where a reasonably accurate estimate of future earnings can be made either on a declining, rising, or stabilized income basis, the annuity method of capitalization gives results that are consistent with monetary compound interest theory and practice (see Chapter 17).

5. Building Residual Technique: Changing Income and Value Premise

Level income and changing value.   Continuing with the example used previously under the land residual technique, we can find the present value of a property using the building residual technique. The prior example was based on a level annual income of $15,000, a 10% yield rate, a 20-year projection period, with the land value forecast to double and the building value projected to decline 20 percent. Initially, it is expected that the income will remain level (probably due to lease requirements) while the value of the property's land and building components is forecast to change during the forecast period.

The same data used previously apply to this example except that the value of the site is judged to be $18,750; the building value is unknown. The value of the property is estimated as follows:

Net operating income $(I_L + I_B)$		$15,000
$-$ Land income (I_L)		
($18,750)(0.10 $-$ 1 $\times$ 0.017460)		1,548
$=$ Building income (I_B)		$13,452
Capitalized at R_B		
($13,452/0.10 + 0.20 $\times$ 0.017460)		
$=$ Building value	$129,981	
$+$ Land value	18,750	
$=$ Property value	$148,731	

Income and value changing linearly.   This example is similar to the previous land residual except that now the value of the land has already been estimated at $14,000, and the value of the building is now sought as follows:

Net operating income $(I_L + I_B)$		$15,000
− Land income (I_B)		
($14,000)(0.10 − 1 × 0.05)		700
− Building income (I_B)		$14,300
($14,300/0.10 + 0.20 × 0.05)		
= Building value	$130,000	
+ Land value	14,000	
= Property value	$144,000	

Income and value changing exponentially. Assume that both the income and values will change on a compound interest basis. Beginning with an estimated land value of $12,270, the residual building value remains to be ascertained, as follows[6]:

Net operating income		$15,000
− Land income		
($12,270)(0.10 − 0.033333)		818
= Building income		$14,182
Capitalized at R_B		
($14,182/0.10 + 0.009091)		
= Building value	$130,002	
+ Land value	12,270	
= Property value	$142,272	

PROPERTY RESIDUAL TECHNIQUE

Occasionally, valuation problems arise in which total property income is difficult to allocate to either land or building. This may be the case where building improvements are old and where there is doubt as to whether they constitute the highest and best land use. Then, too, market sales of comparable sites may not be available, and hypothetical analysis of land income and land value may be of doubtful validity because of the location or specialized character of the land. Under such circumstances the appraiser may find the application of the property residual technique a useful valuation tool.

This method is frequently used without being identified as the property residual technique. Instead, it is called the Inwood plus reversion method. However identified, the total present property value is the addition of the present value of the presumed level income stream and the present value of the land and possibly building value at some future date. It is often used to estimate the leased fee value of property under a long-term lease.

In view of the extreme uncertainty of estimating the future income and value at the end of a building's remaining economic life, a shorter forecast term

[6]Land and building incomes and corresponding rates were computed previously under the land residual example.

has been substituted in recent years. This alternative forecast period generally co-incides with the period that investors tend to hold a particular class of property. Additionally, this method has become more realistic by providing for several possible future income and value patterns. A criticism of this technique is the dependency of the present value estimate on a long-term future value estimate (i.e., the reversionary value).

To employ the property residual technique, the appraiser must ascertain or decide on the following:

1. An estimate of the effective gross revenue that is obtainable under typical management.
2. An estimate of the net operating income—net before loan interest and amortization charges.
3. The rate at which the property income is to be capitalized.
4. The method of capitalization to be applied over the remaining economic life of the property or the shorter holding period.
5. An estimate of the probable property value at the end of the forecast income period. This may include land and building or just the building.

With the aid of these data, the property residual technique can be applied. For illustration purposes the following initially will be assumed:

1. Risk rate	10%
2. Building economic life	30 years
3. Net operating income	$15,000
4. Estimated reversionary land value	$40,000

Based on these assumptions, the property residual technique will be applied under straight-line and annuity methods of capitalization. Later, different assumptions will be used.

1. Property Residual Technique: Straight-Line Capitalization

Net operating income		$ 15,000
Property rate of capitalization:		
Interest rate	0.10	
Amortization rate	0.033333	
Total rate	0.133333	
Value of property income:		
$V = I/R = \$15,000 \div 0.133333$		$112,500
or $V = I \times F = \$15,000 \times 7.500019$		
(Ring factor)		

Reversionary value of land:
$40,000 × 0.057309
(10% for 30 years)   2,292
Property value:
  Value of property income $112,500
  Present reversionary value of land   2,292
  Total $114,792

2. Property Residual Technique: Annuity Method Capitalization

Net operating income $ 15,000
Property rate of capitalization:
  Interest rate   0.10
  Amortization rate (sinking fund factor,
    10%)   0.006079
  Total rate   0.106079
Value of property income:
  $V = I/R = \$15,000 \div 0.106079 =$ $141,404
  or $V = I \times F = \$15,000 \times 9.426914$
  (Inwood)
Present worth of land (reversion)
  $40,000 × 0.057309   2,292
Property value:
  Value of property income $141,404
  Present reversionary value of land   2,292
  Total $143,696

The property residual technique, too, produces value results that differ importantly, depending on the method of capitalization used to provide for amortization of a nonperpetuity property investment. Again, the low value under the straight-line provision results because this method subtracts the highest annual amounts from the income stream for estimated losses due to future depreciation.

Appraisers are cautioned against careless or inopportune use of the property residual technique of valuation where a straight-line rate of amortization is combined with the risk rate to form a rate of capitalization. The application of a straight-line amortization rate to total property income in effect applies a rate of depreciation to the land in excess of that sanctioned by sound appraisal practice for a period extending over the life of the building. Thus the longer the economic life of the property, the greater the error in the estimate of value under the straight-line (and sinking fund) method of capitalization. The built-in errors can readily be detected by reference to the value results obtained previously under the building residual and property residual techniques. It will be noted that for both techniques the basic income, building, and land value data are identical as follows: net operating income, $15,000; building or property life, 30 years; land value, $50,000; and 10 percent risk rate. The value results obtained on the basis of these identical assumptions compare as follows:

Method of capitalization	Building residual	Property residual
Straight line	$125,000	$114,792
Annuity	144,270	143,696

Only under the annuity method of capitalization are similar value results consistently obtained using both residual techniques, where the underlying income and property data remain equal. The substantial error under the straight-line method points up, once more, the fallacy of mixing an interest-bearing rate of capitalization with a noninterest-bearing rate of amortization.

Nevertheless, the property residual technique under the annuity, or Inwood, method of capitalization serves a useful appraising function. There are occasions when neither land nor building value can be obtained with reasonable accuracy. Under such circumstances the application of either the land or building residual techniques is inappropriate. If these techniques are used, they will magnify the basic error where the value of land or building is assumed. The property residual technique, it may be pointed out, also assumes a land or property value in the distant future. Does not such an unreliable forecast invalidate the use of this method also? It does not, because in the property residual technique only the reversionary (present worth)—not the full—value of the land (or property) is included in the appraisal estimate. The effect of a possible error in computing the future value of the land is thus minimized, if not neutralized. To illustrate: Assume that in the preceding problem the land value proved to be $40,000 instead of $50,000. What is the impact of this $10,000 error on the present value estimate? The answer is as follows:

I. Assumed land value of $40,000
    1. Value of property income (given previously) $141,404
    2. Reversionary land value ($40,000 × 0.057309)   2,292
        Total property value $143,696

II. Assumed land value of $50,000
    1. Value of property income as before $141,404
    2. Reversionary land value ($50,000 × 0.057309)   2,865
        Total property value $144,269

The difference in the two appraisals is $573, or approximately 4/10 of 1 percent of the present value estimate. Since appraisals of such magnitude as those derived previously are generally rounded off to the nearest thousand dollars, the present value effect of the error of $10,000 in the assumed land value, 30 years moved from the date of the appraisal, is of little present worth consequence.

3. Property Residual Technique: Changing Income and Value Premise

The previously presented equation, $R = Y - \Delta a$, can also be applied to the property residual technique. The results are more likely to represent actual investor behavior when a typical holding period is used instead of the longer remaining economic life of the improvements.

Level income and changing value.   The same income and yield rate used previously are used here. However, a shorter forecast period is used along with an overall future property value.

1. Level annual net operating income	$15,000
2. Yield rate	10%
3. Forecast period	8 years
4. Expected property value change	+25%

$$R = 0.10 - 0.25 \times 0.087444$$
$$= 0.078139$$
$$V = \$15{,}000/0.078139$$
$$= \underline{\underline{\$191{,}966}}$$

Income and value changing linearly.   Suppose now that the same first-year NOI, yield rate, and forecast period apply. However, the annual change in income is expected to average $750 during the forecast period. At the end of this eight-year period, the property is expected to be worth $250,000. Using preprinted tables or the following equation, the present worth of the income stream can be computed. Initially, the present worth of 1 per period factor is found:

$$PW = (d + hn)a_{\overline{n}} - \frac{h(n - a_{\overline{n}})}{i}$$

where d = starting income at the end of year 1
 h = annual increase or decrease after year 1
 n = number of years in forecast period
 $a_{\overline{n}}$ = present worth of 1 per period for a level annuity
 i = effective interest rate

$$PW = (1 + 750/15{,}000 \times 8)(5.334926) - \frac{750/15{,}000(8 - 5.334926)}{0.10}$$

$$= (1 + 0.05 \times 8)(5.334926) - \frac{0.05(8 - 5.334926)}{0.10}$$

$$= 7.468896 - 1.332537$$
$$= 6.136359$$
$$PW = 6.136359 \times \ \$15{,}000 \quad = \$ \ 92{,}045$$
$$+ 0.466507 \times \$250{,}000 = \underline{116{,}627}$$
$$\underline{\underline{\$208{,}672}}$$

Income and value changing exponentially.[7]   The previous data are used again, but now assume that the income and value are expected to rise 5 percent annually compounded over the eight-year forecast period. Again, preprinted tables may be used to find the present worth of 1 per period factor, assuming a compound growth rate, or the following equation can be used to produce the same results:

$$a_{\overline{n}|} = \frac{1 - [(1 + x)^n/(1 + i)^n]}{i - x}$$

where x is the annual rate of change and i is the annual discount rate.

$$a_{\overline{n}|} = \frac{1 - [(1 + 0.05)^8/(+ 0.10)^8]}{0.10 - 0.05}$$

$$= \frac{1 - [1.477455/2.143589]}{0.05}$$

$$= \frac{0.310756}{0.05}$$

$$= 6.215120$$

$$PW = 6.215120 \times \$15,000 \quad = \$\ 93,227$$
$$+ 0.466507 \times \$250,000 = \underline{\ 116,627}$$
$$\underline{\underline{\$209,854}}$$

Accurate Forecast of Income Period Required

As mentioned previously, it is usually difficult to forecast accurately that future time when the improvements may become worthless. Neighborhoods often change as a result of unanticipated changes in zoning, traffic and land use patterns, and construction materials and technology. Thus one of the most important aspects of the property residual techniques is to forecast accurately the holding period or the remaining economic life of the improvements. A crucial part of this estimate is the probable value of the property (land or land and improvements). Of course, a longer term produces a higher present value of the income stream.

The following two examples show how quite different value estimates can result from using different forecast periods. Different future values would produce even more noticeable variations in present value estimates.

Example 1

Net operating income (level)	$ 15,000
Forecast period	10 years
Future property value	$100,000
Discount rate	10%

---

[7]Variations of the exponential and the previous linear equations are also found in Charles B. Akerson, *Capitalization Theory and Techniques Study Guide* (Chicago: American Institute of Real Estate Appraisers, 1984), pp. 154–55.

Present value of 10-year level income stream

$15,000 × 6.144567	$ 92,169
+ Present value of 10-year reversion	
$100,000 × 0.385543	38,554
= Total property value	$130,723

Example 2

Net operating income (level)	$ 15,000
Forecast period	40 years
Future property value	$100,000
Discount rate	10%
Present value of 40-year level income stream	
$15,000 × 9.779051	$146,686
+ Present value of 40-year reversion	
$100,000 × 0.022095	2,210
= Total property value	$148,896

SUMMARY

It is possible, and sometimes necessary, for real estate appraisers to consider the (1) land residual, (2) building residual, or (3) property residual techniques in valuing real property.

The *land residual technique* is best applied in estimating land value and total property value when buildings are new and their values can be estimated with reasonable accuracy. The *building residual technique* is applicable when site value can be accurately estimated, the buildings are substantially depreciated, do not conform to standards that represent the highest and best use of the site, or the cost new of the building as well as the depreciated cost are difficult to estimate. The *property residual technique* is used when it is difficult to allocate property income to either the building or the site. In such circumstances, there may be no valid recent comparable land sales available, the improvements are old, and there is difficulty in judging the highest and best land use.

Each of these methods may utilize either the straight-line or annuity methods of capitalization. Moreover, the appropriate capitalization rate may be computed using the equation $R = Y - \Delta a$, when there are any of the following income-value patterns:

1. Level income and changing value.
2. Income and value changing on a straight-line (constant amount) basis.
3. Income and value changing on a compounded (exponential) basis.

In using the residual techniques, it is important that the appraiser carefully choose the appropriate technique. Care should be exercised, as well, in selecting the method that best reflects the anticipated future income and value pattern.

REVIEW QUESTIONS

1. List the relative merits of the three physical residual techniques of capitalization.
2. Find the present worth of a property under the following conditions: current NOI, $25,000; present value of improvements, $150,000; expected remaining economic life of improvements, 20 years; typical risk rate, 10 percent.
3. Compute the current value of a 15-year level annual rental income of $50,000, plus the value of the same property that will be available for purchase in 15 years for $300,000. The appropriate yield rate is 10 percent.
4. What is the present value of a property under the following conditions? NOI, $75,000; forecast period, 10 years; yield rate, 10 percent; building value is expected to increase by 10 percent and the site by 80 percent on a straight-line basis during this period; the building currently is judged to be worth $100,000.
5. What would be the estimated current value of a property which has a site worth $200,000 and current net operating income of $90,000? Other relevant information is: remaining lease period, 9 years; expected yield rate, 10 percent; land value is forecast to increase by 30 percent while the building value should increase by 3 percent. Both income and values are expected to change on a compounded basis.
6. Advise your client as to the present market value of the following property: annual first year NOI, $50,000; yield rate, 10 percent; holding period for investor, 12 years; annual income is set by the lease to rise an average of $2,500 during the holding period.
7. There are three physical residual methods of processing the net operating income from a property. Assume that you are appraising an old four-story brick-and-frame, furnished apartment property, on a $20,000 lot, and that you have found that the property for some time to come should produce a net operating income of $12,000. Further assume that the furnishings in use in the building have a 10-year remaining useful life, that 10 percent is to be earned on their present value of $11,000, that 8 percent is an acceptable rate of interest return, and that the building has a remaining economic life of 25 years.
   (a) Which one of the residual methods do you use in arriving at an estimate of the value to assign to the structure?
   (b) What is the indicated value of the structure? Show your computations. Use the straight-line method of capitalization.
8. An improved property sold for $150,000. Of this, $25,000 was imputed to land. The stabilized net operating income was $14,000 per annum. The building has a remaining life of 20 years; 6 percent is required to attract capital to land investment of this type. Problem: Find rates applicable to the building as follows:
   (a) Building rate of capitalization.
   (b) Interest rate under straight-line recapture—for building only.
   (c) Interest rate under Inwood premise valuation—for building only.

READING AND STUDY REFERENCES

AKERSON, CHARLES B. *Capitalization Theory and Techniques Study Guide.* Chicago: American Institute of Real Estate Appraisers, 1984, pp. 71–76.

American Institute of Real Estate Appraisers. *The Appraisal of Real Estate,* 9th ed. Chicago: AIREA, 1987, pp. 478–480, 498–504.

EPLEY, DONALD R., and JAMES H. BOYKIN. Chapters 14–16, *Basic Income Property Appraisal*. Reading, Mass.: Addison-Wesley Publishing Co., Inc., 1983.

FRIEDMAN, JACK P., and NICHOLAS ORDWAY. Chapter 6, *Income Property Appraisal and Analysis*. Reston, Va.: Reston Publishing Co., Inc., 1981.

HINES, MARY ALICE. *Real Estate Appraisal*. New York: Macmillan Publishing Company, 1981, pp. 280–287.

19

Leasehold Estates and Leased Fee Appraising[1]

Learning Objectives

After reading this chapter, you should be able to:

- Distinguish among leased fee, leasehold estate, and fee simple interest
- Identify the expenses that a tenant typically pays under a long-term ground lease
- Understand how to value a leased fee interest in a property under different conditions
- Appraise a leasehold estate in real property
- Understand how a sandwich lease is comprised and how to appraise this interest in real property

Owners of income-producing real estate often find it profitable to permit others to lease the property at a stipulated fee, or *rental*. Where this is the case, the parties to the transaction enter into an agreement, called a *lease*, which establishes the landlord and tenant relationship. When properly drawn and executed the lease becomes a legal contract binding the parties in accordance with specified terms as to length of possession, use of property, and payments due at periodic intervals.

Broadly speaking, leases are classified as either *short term* or *long term* in duration. This division, based on length of time and terms of use, is rather arbitrary. Generally, however, leases extending over 10 or more years may appropriately be referred to as having long-term lease characteristics. Such leases, as a

---

[1]The term *leased fee* as used in this chapter refers to the owner's interest and rights in the property subject to conditions and terms of a written or oral lease agreement. The term *leasehold estate* refers to the tenant's rights—over periods of months or years—to benefit from the use of the property in accordance with a written or oral agreement and the payment of a stipulated periodic rental. The *fee simple interest* is the unencumbered value of a property, the value of which is suggested by prevailing market rentals rather than by any value resulting from existing leases.

rule, are lengthy documents containing many special provisions and landlord-tenant covenants.

Lease agreements are further subclassified as to type, depending on the methods used to determine the amount of periodic rent payments. The most frequently used types of leases are the following, which are covered in detail in Chapter 13:

1. Flat, or fixed, rental leases.
2. Graded, or step-up, rental leases.
3. Index clause leases.
4. Escalator leases.
5. Percentage-of-gross-sales leases.
6. Sale and lease-back contract.

IMPORTANCE OF LEASE PROVISIONS

To appraise a leasehold interest or a leased fee estate requires careful study of lease provisions in order to establish the respective rights of parties and their obligations concerning costs of property maintenance and operation. The landlord, for instance, may own both land and building improvements and agree to pay property taxes, hazard insurance, and expenditures for maintenance of building improvements. Interior costs of decorating, repair, and costs of utilities, on the other hand, may be borne by the tenant.

Many long-term leases are for the rental of unimproved land and are called *ground leases*. Agreements of this type usually provide for construction of a building by the tenant. Under ground-lease terms, the tenant as a rule pays all taxes and other maintenance charges, leaving the landlord with *net* rental income. Ground leases generally provide for disposition of the building at the end of the term. The building, although erected at the expense of the tenant, legally becomes real property and is—unless otherwise provided for—the property of the landlord, subject to the tenant's right of possession for the term of the lease. At the end of the lease term the building improvements revert to the landlord or the landlord generally, as agreed on, either pays the tenant a stipulated or appraised value for the building or renews the lease at his or her option. Before a tenant enters into a long-term ground lease, he or she should make certain that his or her income from use of the property covers the following items:

1. The ground rent payable to the owner.
2. Taxes of all kinds and assessments for local improvements.
3. Premiums on policies of insurance against fire, liability suits, workers' compensation claims, and plate-glass damage.
4. Charges for water, heat, light, and power.
5. Labor and repairs—including all charges for upkeep, maintenance, and service to the tenant.

6. Interest on the construction loan while the building is being erected.

7. An amount sufficient to amortize the cost of the building during the term of the lease or by the end of the last renewal of the lease.

8. A sufficient amount over and above all the foregoing charges to compensate the operator for his or her services and the risk involved in the enterprise.[2]

COMPONENT INTEREST VALUATION

A lease in effect divides the *bundle of property rights* and transfers the rights to use for a designated period of time from the owner to the tenant. Often the tenant in turn subleases a part or all of his or her lease interests and thus becomes sandwiched between the owner—to whom he or she is obligated under the terms of the basic, or original, lease—and the user, or subtenant, of the property, from whom he or she obtains rental payments for the term of the sublease. In fact, the subsidiary leases between tenant and subtenant are actually called *sandwich leases* and are evaluated under the income approach in the same manner as other nonperpetuity rights to income.

Leased fee and leasehold interests are valued by the annuity and discounted cash flow methods of capitalization. The contract rent as specified by the lease terms provides a definite and thus predictable income flow. Although the same cannot be said for the income flow derived from operation of the property and out of which the tenant discharges his or her contract rent obligations, the leasehold interest in appraisal practice usually is capitalized under the annuity method. This is a step in the right direction, for the logic which sanctions use of the annuity method for appraisal of leasehold interests diminishes the need for the straight-line and sinking fund methods of capitalization for fee appraising.

In the appraisal of component interests, it is found that as a general rule the value of the sum of the parts of a property equals the value of the property as a whole. There are exceptions to this rule, and the appraiser must be alert to recognize conditions under which the value of the sum of the parts may be more or less than the value of the entire property—under free and clear ownership. The summation value of component interests is greater where the contract rent agreed on by a financially strong tenant exceeds the market rent that the property is estimated to produce at the time of appraisal. Such excessive income nevertheless may have to be separated and capitalized at higher risk rates of interest, for even financially strong tenants seek to correct inequities. Where lease terms are restrictive to the point that the tenant is unable to make effective use of the property, the reduced income flow would cause the value of the parts to be less than the overall value of the unencumbered property.

In lease appraisal assignments it is advisable to derive the value of the entire property first, as if unencumbered and free for operation under unrestricted fee

[2]For a detailed analysis of leases and leasing, refer to Alfred A. Ring and Jerome J. Dasso, *Real Estate Principles and Practices*, 10th ed. (Englewood Cliffs, N.J.: Prentice-Hall, Inc., 1985), Chapter 24, and James H. Boykin and Richard L. Haney, Jr., *Financing Real Estate*, 2nd ed. (Englewood Cliffs, N.J.: Prentice-Hall, Inc., 1993), Chapter 20.

simple ownership. This total value can then serve as a benchmark against which the reasonableness of the value of the parts can be judged. Failure to follow this procedure deprives the appraiser of necessary checks and balances.

It is also of interest to point out that when the contract rent and prevailing market rent are one and the same—assuming for purposes of illustration that the landlord furnishes both land and building improvements—the tenant's interest in the property is of zero value. One might ask why would anyone want to lease a property if the rental paid leaves no monetary interest or value to the leasehold. The answer is obvious: The land or improved property is leased merely as a vehicle for other business operations (selling merchandise, for instance) from which the tenant makes his or her profit. In all equity, the landowner should get the full return equal to the market rent attributable to his or her property investment. Many large business concerns in fact prefer to lease rather than own in order not to tie up thousands of dollars in real estate investments. Such money generally can be more profitably invested in operations in which management has the know-how and skill to make higher returns on capital investment.

LEASED FEE VALUATION

The rights of a landlord or *leased fee interest* under the terms of a lease are basically twofold:

> *First*, the landlord is entitled to receive the contract rent agreed on under terms of the lease for the duration of the lease period.
>
> *Second*, the landlord is entitled to repossession of the land and all permanent improvements thereon in accordance with the lease terms. The right to repossess, better known as the reversionary right, reunites the component interests into fee simple ownership on termination or breach of the lease.

In all leased fee valuations, both of these interests or rights of the fee owner must be considered even though the reversionary rights under extremely long-term (99 years) leasing may prove of little value consequence.

To demonstrate appraisal practices in leased fee and leasehold valuations, three types of long-term leases will be presented for analysis as follows:

1. A *fixed-rental* lease with a nationally known company. Under the terms of this lease, the contract rents specified exceed the warranted market rent attributable to the property if free and clear.
2. A *step-up ground* lease, under which contract rentals prove inadequate to yield a fair return on the market value of the property.
3. An *advance-payment* lease, providing for reversion of land and building improvements at the termination of the lease.

Illustration 1—Fixed-rental lease.   A building site in the downtown area of an industrial community was leased 20 years ago to a national concern for a period of 40 years at a fixed rental of $32,000 per year. The current market value of the land is estimated at $300,000, and the rate of capitalization for similar land investments is established at 10 percent. The building, which was erected by the tenant, is expected to have no value at the end of the lease term. Based on these facts, the value of the leased fee is derived as follows:

Value of the land by market comparison		$300,000
Land rate of capitalization, 10%		
Contract rent	$ 32,000	
Market rent, $I = V \times R$ ($300,000 \times 0.10$)	30,000	
Excess rent	$ 2,000	
Present worth of market rent for the remaining 20 years at 10%		
$V = I \times F$ (Inwood) = $30,000 \times 8.513564$		255,407
Present worth of excess rent for 20 years at 12%[3]		
$V = I \times F = \$2,000 \times 7.469444$		14,939
Reversionary land value	$300,000	
Present worth of all rent		$270,346
Present worth factor—20 years at 10% = 0.148644		
Present worth of reversion ($300,000 \times 0.148644$)		44,593
Total value of leased fee		$314,939

In this illustration the value of the leased fee exceeds the market value of the land precisely by the capitalized amount of the excess rentals. Based on the present value of the market rent and the present value of the reversion, the total of the parts equals the value of the property as a whole. Attention is also called to the fact that the excess rental, though committed for payment by a reliable national concern, was capitalized at a 12 percent rate of interest to indicate the greater risk attached to this excess income. National concerns of good repute—even banks—have closed down in times of stress. Bankruptcy, for instance, would terminate the lease, and in such a contingency only the market rent could be counted on to support property value. The selection of the risk rate is a matter of judgment based on general economic conditions, the reputation and history of the leasing firm, and the extent and nature of product and space competition.

Illustration 2—Step-up ground lease.   A city block measuring 200 feet by 200 feet was leased 30 years ago for a period of 99 years. The step-up lease calls for rental payments as follows:

---

[3]The likelihood that excess rent may not continue for the period of the lease term (e.g., the lessee may become bankrupt or attempt to break the lease) warrants application of a higher risk rate to this portion of the total income.

First 25 years	$16,000
Next 25 years	18,000
Next 20 years	20,000
Last 29 years	22,000

The sales comparison approach shows that the site on the date of appraisal has a market value of $200,000. It is estimated that this value will remain stable and that this amount may be anticipated at the time of land reversion. The discount rate for similar investments typically is 10 percent. Based on these facts and using the Inwood factor method of capitalization, the value of the leased fee is obtained as shown:

Value of land by market comparison	$200,000
Land rate of capitalization, 10%	
Present worth of rental income (69 remaining years):	
$18,000 for first 20 years at 10 percent	
interest equals:	
$18,000 × 8.513564	153,244
$20,000 for next 20 years at 10 percent	
interest deferred for 20 years equals:	
[4]$20,000 × 8.513564 = $170,271 × 0.148644	25,310
$22,000 for balance of 29 years at 10 percent	
interest deferred for 40 years equals:	
[5]$22,000 × 9.369606 = $206,131 × 0.022095	4,554
Present worth of contract rent	$183,108
Add: Reversionary rights to land value of	
$200,000, 69 years removed at 10 percent, equals:	
[6]$200,000 × 0.001393	279
Total value of leased fee	$183,387

The value derived previously can also be obtained by use of the 10 percent Inwood factors exclusively without reference to the deferment factors:

Present worth of $18,000 per year for 20 years at 10% equals:	
$18,000 × 8.513564	$153,244

[4]See Table 16.1 which shows 8.513564 and 0.148644 to be the present worth of 1 per period and the present worth of 1 factor for 20 years, respectively.

[5]The 10 percent present worth of 1 per period factor is for 29 years and the present worth of 1 factor is for 40 years. Note that each present worth of 1 per period factor is selected for the end of each intermediate period and the present worth of 1 factor is chosen for the total deferred period.

[6]The 10 percent present worth of 1 factor is for 69 years.

Present worth of $20,000 per year from
  21st year to 40th year:

40-year factor	9.779051	
Less 20-year factor	8.513564	
Factor for next 20 years	1.265487	
$20,000 × 1.265487		25,310

Present worth of $22,000 per year from
  41st year to 69th year:

69-year factor	9.986071	
Less 40-year factor	9.779051	
Factor for last 29 years	0.207020	
$22,000 × 0.207020		4,554
Present worth of contract rent		$183,108
(Add land reversion as before)		279
Total value of leased fee		$183,387

In this second illustration the lease as originally drawn covered a period of 99 years. On the date of appraisal, 30 years of the total lease period had elapsed and no consideration was given either to past rights or past obligations. The value of the leased fee interest as derived previously reflects only the present worth of future rights to income. Attention, too, is called to the fact that the value of the lessor's interest of $183,387 is less than the value of $200,000, which this property would warrant if free from lease obligations. The loss in value in this instance is entirely due to lease term provisions under which the contract rent paid is less than the market rent that the property can produce under a program of highest and best land use. The lessor's loss is, of course, the lessee's gain whenever the value of the sum of the parts equals the value of the property as a whole.

Illustration 3—Advance-payment lease. A single-story building containing three stores in a business district is leased for period of 30 years. The net rent payable annually in advance is $16,540—the same as prevailing market rentals. The tenant is to pay all taxes, insurance, and related costs of maintenance and repair, and to return the property in operating condition subject only to ordinary wear and tear from building age and use. The value of the land free and clear is $65,000, but should be $140,000 at the end of the lease; the building currently is worth $110,000. At the termination of the lease period, accrued building depreciation is estimated to have been 60 percent. Based on these facts and an interest rate of 10 percent, the value of the leased fee is derived as follows:

Contract rent (for 30 years)	$ 16,540
Present worth of 1 per annum	× 10.369605
(advance payment) at 10% interest (9.426914 × 1.10)	

Present worth of contract rent		$171,513
Add reversionary value:		
Land	$140,000	
Building (40%)	44,000	
Total	$184,000	
Present worth of 1 at 10%	× 0.057309	
Present worth of reversion		10,545
Total value of leased fee		$182,058

In this illustration the value of the leased fee exceeds the present value of the land and building by $7,058. This difference in value is caused by lease provisions which are favorable for the landlord and by the anticipated future increase in site value.

VALUATION OF LEASEHOLDS

Theoretically, in a free and competitive market the lessee's interest in a property should be of zero value. Leasehold profits, as previously explained, should be derived from operation of the business in which it specializes and not from the lease. In practice, however, lease terms are relatively inflexible and, as a consequence, contract rent is greater or lesser than the prevailing market rent the property yields under highest and best use and unencumbered fee simple ownership. To the extent that contract rent exceeds market rent, the lessee is transferring value from property he or she owns in buildings or business to the landlord or fee owner. Conversely, where contract rent is less than market rent the landlord transfers part of his or her property-value interest to the tenant.

In appraisal practice the value of a leasehold is often obtained by subtracting the value of the leased fee from the value of the property as if free and clear from contract obligations. This shortcut procedure for leasehold valuation is not always recommended, because an error in calculation of the leased fee interest automatically transfers this error to the leasehold estate whenever value of the parts is considered equal to the value of the whole. For this reason efforts should always be made to establish leasehold values independently by separate discounting of the future rights to leasehold income (positive or negative) into a sum of present value.

The tenant or user of the property has the right to use the property in accordance with the lease terms and to receive the market rent that the property produces under its highest and best use. Out of this market rental, the tenant pays the contract rent; that which remains, if anything, over the lease period forms the basis for the value of the leasehold estate. To demonstrate the application of leasehold valuation, reference is made to the three illustrations cited previously as follows:

Illustration 1

Market rent of property	$30,000
Contract rent per lease	32,000
Deficit rent from property	($ 2,000)
Capitalized value of deficit leasehold income:	
$V = I \times F = \$2,000 \times 7.469444$	($14,939)

The deficit income was discounted at a rate of 12 percent. (The rate used must be supported by market analysis of yields for comparable properties.)

To prove the accuracy of the leasehold valuation, a check can now be made as follows:

Valuation of leased fee (given previously)	$314,939
Add value of leasehold estate (*deficit*)	(14,939)
Value of entire property	$300,000

Illustration 2.   This illustration demonstrates a method which may be used to compute the value of a fee estate—the full unencumbered value of real property. This fee value is the sum of the values of the leasehold and leased fee interests.

Remaining term of leasehold	69 years	
Market rental	$20,000	
First 20 years:		
Market rent	$20,000	
Contract rent	18,000	
Excess rent	$ 2,000	
Discounted at 11%[7]		$ 15,927
$V = I \times F = \$2,000 \times 7.963328$		
Next 20 years:		
Market rent	$20,000	
Contract rent	20,000	
Excess rent	None	
Capitalized value		None
Last 29 years:		
Market rent	$20,000	
Contract rent	22,000	
Deficit rent	($ 2,000)	

[7]The discount (or yield) rate applied to the tenant's (lessee) interest in this illustration was selected for demonstration purposes. In practice a study of leasehold sales or market yield rates at which tenants are attracted to comparable investment properties is necessary to support the applicable yield rates.

Capitalized at rate of 11% interest

69-year (Inwood) factor	9.084128
40-year (Inwood) factor	8.951051
29-year factor—used	0.133077
Value = $I \times F$ = $(2,000) $\times$ 0.133077	(266)
Value of leasehold estate	$ 15,661

Value check:

Appraised leased fee value (given previously)	$183,387
Plus appraised value of leasehold estate	15,661
Value of entire fee simple interest	$199,048

The combined value derived previously is slightly lower than the value of the property under fee simple ownership. This discrepancy is caused by selection of discount rates—rounded to the nearest quarter of 1 percent—used in the capitalization of component property interests. The final value estimate should comply with market expressions of value, which generally are rounded to the nearest $500 or $1,000, depending on the value of the investment. In the preceding case, appraisal findings would probably be reported as follows:

Leased fee	$184,000
Leasehold estate	16,000
Total value of property	$200,000

Illustration 3.   In this illustration lease provisions for the contract rent match the market rent. Ordinarily in such instances the value of the leasehold estate would be zero. However, business custom and accounting practices typically provide for rental payments at the end of the payment period. This shift in the payment period results in a present worth gain for the leased fee, and a consequent loss to the leasehold estate, as follows:

1. Contract rent for 30 years paid annually in advance	$ 16,540
Present worth—advance—of annuity of 1 at 10%	$\times$ 10.369605
Present value of contract rent	$ 171,513
2. Contract rent for 30 years paid annually at end of year	$ 16,540
Present worth—end-of-year factor (10%)	$\times$ 9.426914
Present value of contract rent	$ 155,921
Deficit (negative) value of leasehold estate due to lease payments made in advance	$(15,592)

SANDWICH LEASE VALUATION

A *sandwich lease* occurs where a leasehold interest is subleased to a third party, the original lessee becomes a sublessor, and is both legally and economically sandwiched between the fee owner—to whom the property reverts at the termination of the original lease—and the user, or sublessee, to whom the leasehold was transferred under separate and specific contract provisions. Investors may find it profitable to acquire long-term ground leases, develop the land, erect building improvements, and sublease the property to one or more tenants for part of or the entire period of the original lease term.

The contract rights and obligations of the sandwich leasehold estate normally are clearly spelled out, and the rights to income are under the annuity, or Inwood, method in the same manner as demonstrated in the three illustrations shown previously. Care must be taken to derive the net rental to which the sandwich owner is entitled and to discount this net income (the difference between the contract rent received from the sublessee and the contract rent paid to the fee owner) at the appropriate risk rate. Dividing a fee interest into one or more leasehold interests also divides property value in accordance with the terms of income distribution and the relative risk of the component ownership. The general rule that the sum of the parts equals the whole prevails. Differences in rates of interest applied to different levels of ownership merely reflect a redistribution of the risk of rights to income under the terms of the lease agreements. The fee owner, like a first mortgagee, occupies a preferred risk position. The sandwich leaseholder has a contractual position similar to that of a second mortgagee, and the discount rate assigned to this second priority of income is appropriately higher. The user of the property must rely on income from operations of the property, and he or she assumes all the risks that accompany equity ownership.

To illustrate the application of the income approach to value a property under a sandwich lease agreement, the following data will be used as a basis for appraisal purposes.

A lease from Stem to Bloom was made 30 years ago, for a term of 80 years. Rental payments were agreed upon as follows:

First 20 years	$ 8,000
Next 20 years	10,000
Last 40 years	12,000

Ten years after the date of the original lease, Bloom completed a building at a cost of $320,000 and subleased the property to Petal for a period of 70 years. Rental payments on a step-up basis were agreed upon as follows:

First 25 years	$36,000
Next 25 years	40,000
Last 20 years	44,000

The property on a free-and-clear basis is estimated to have a market value on the date of appraisal of $280,000 for improvements and $320,000 for land, a total of $600,000. The prevailing market rent is estimated at $48,000. Market analysis indicates risk rates of interest of 7 percent for the leased fee, 8 percent for the sandwich leasehold, and 10 percent for the top leasehold. The lease and improvements have a 50-year remaining life.[8] Based on these data the value of the respective interests is derived as follows:

1. *Leased fee* at 7 percent discount rate:

Contract rent for 10 years,	
$10,000 × 7.0236	$ 70,236
(PW factor for 10 years)	
Contract rent for 40 years,	
$12,000 × 6.771 (50-year factor	
minus 10-year factor or	
13.8007 − 7.0236)	81,252
Present worth of reversion (50 years)	
$320,000 × 0.03395	10,863
Total value of leased fee	$162,351

2. *Sandwich lease* at 8 percent discount rate:

Net contract rent for first 5 years,
$26,000 ($36,000 − $10,000)
Net contract rent for next 5 years,
$30,000 ($40,000 − $10,000)
Net contract rent for next 20 years,
$28,000 ($40,000 − $12,000)
Net contract rent for last 20 years,
$32,000 ($44,000 − $12,000)

Value:	
$26,000 × 3.9927 (PW factor—first 5 years)	$103,810
$30,000 × 2.7174 next 5 years (6.7101 − 3.9927)	81,521
$28,000 × 4.5477 next 20 years (11.2578 − 6.7101)	127,335
$32,000 × 0.9757 last 20 years (12.2335 − 11.2578)	31,222
Total value of sandwich leasehold	$343,888

[8]In calculating the years remaining under both the original (prime) lease and the sublease, remember that under the original lease, 50 years remain with 10 years at $10,000 and 40 years at $12,000. When considering the sublease, there are 50 years remaining with annual rentals as follows: 5 years at $36,000; 25 years at $40,000; and 20 years at $44,000.

3. *Top leasehold* at 10 percent discount rate:

Net income for 5 years, $12,000
($48,000 − $36,000)
Net income for 25 years, $8,000
($48,000 − $40,000)
Net income for 20 years, $4,000
($48,000 − $44,000)
Value:

$12,000 × 3.7908 (PW factor—5 years)	$ 45,489
$8,000 × 5.6361 next 25 years	
(9.4269 − 3.7908)	45,089
$4,000 × 0.4879 last 20 years	
(9.9148 − 9.4269)	1,952
Total value of top leasehold	$ 92,530

Combined value of lease interests:

Leased fee	$162,351
Sandwich leasehold	343,888
Top leasehold	92,530
Total	$598,769

In appraisal practice the preceding value results might be rounded and reported as follows:

Leased fee	$163,000
Sandwich leasehold	344,000
Top leasehold	93,000
Total	$600,000

SUMMARY

A lease agreement is a formal, legally binding contract between two or more parties providing for a division of the bundle of rights between the owner of the fee, or landlord, and the leasehold user, or tenant. Under lease terms, definite or determinable rental payments are agreed on and paid at designated time intervals (monthly, quarterly, semiannually, or annually) in advance or at the end of each payment period.

The landlord, or *fee owner*, generally is entitled to the contract rent for the duration of the lease and to the reversion of the land and improvements—the latter as specified under the lease contract terms. The tenant, or *leasehold estate owner*, is entitled to the market rent, out of which he or she pays the contract rent. The difference between the market and contract rent constitutes the net income upon which the *value of the leasehold* is based. Under a sandwich lease agreement a further division of the leasehold interest is agreed upon and a third, or sandwich leasehold, interest is established. The value of this *sandwich interest* is based on the difference between the contract rent obtained from the top leaseholder and the contract rent paid to the owner of the leased fee.

It is the appraiser's responsibility to examine the lease agreements carefully, to evaluate the property under free-and-clear ownership, to establish the risk rates of interest applicable to the component property interests, and to determine, by capitalization of income under the annuity, or Inwood, method, the value of the various interests or rights to the property. Under typical circumstances, the combined value of the various interests should equal the value of the property as a whole—unencumbered. Where the sum of the parts does not equal the value of the whole (property), an explanation must be offered to substantiate the validity and accuracy of the value findings. As in all valuation problems, accuracy of factual data and soundness of appraisal judgment—rather than mathematical skill—are basic to accurate and reliable value conclusions.

REVIEW QUESTIONS

1. Explain why it is desirable to calculate the value of the unencumbered fee interest prior to estimating the value of either the leased fee or leasehold interest.
2. Identify the two rights of a landlord under a lease.
3. Find the value of the leased fee under the following conditions:

Sale price of property at end of lease	$100,000
Risk rate for comparable properties	10%
Risk rate for excess rent	13%
Contract rent	$ 15,000
Market rent	$ 14,000
Lease term	10 years

4. Compute the present worth of a property under the following conditions:

Discount rate	10%
Value of property at end of lease	$200,000

Income received at beginning of each year
Annual rental income:

Year 1	$1,000
Year 2	1,200
Years 3–5	1,500
Years 6–10	2,200

5. (a) Compute the value of the leasehold estate under the following conditions:

Market rent	$10,000
Contract rent	$ 8,000
Discount rate	10%
Lease term	5 years

   (b) Assuming that the value of the leased fee is $90,293, what is the overall fee simple property value?

6. (a) Define a sandwich leasehold.

(b) Calculate the value of the (1) leased fee interest, (2) sandwich leasehold, and (3) sublessee's interest under the following lease provisions:

Present property value	$ 70,000
Value of land at end of lease	$100,000
Remaining lease term	7 years
Annual net end-of-year contract rental income	$ 2,000
Expected rate of return	10%
Annual rent paid by subtenant	$ 3,000
Discount rate for sandwich lease	12%

7. X leased a vacant lot which he is using as a commercial parking lot. The lease calls for an annual payment of $600 per annum. X has been paying on this leasehold for a period of five years. If the interest rate is 7 percent, what is the full value of this leasehold to date?

8. Mrs. A is the fee owner of a vacant lot. She enters into a ground lease with Mr. B for a term of 50 years. The net ground rental reserved in the lease by Mrs. A is

$ 9,000 per year during the first 5 years.
  10,000 per year during the next 10 years.
  12,000 per year during the remainder of the term.

Mr. B, the lessee, erected a building on the leased land at a highest and best use cost of $200,000. Assume that you have appraised the market value of the freehold (i.e., the market value of the entire property—land and building as a unit) lease-free 10 years later and found the total market value of the property to be $400,000. You are to appraise the market value of the leased fee (the interest of the lessor, Mrs. A) and also appraise the value of the leasehold (the lessee's interest, Mr. B) as of today, 10 years after the date of the lease. After having made an analysis of the site, you have concluded that the land, if vacant, as of the date of the appraisal has a market value of $240,000 and is not expected to change over the remainder of the lease term, and that ground leases for 25 years or more in this vicinity are customarily based on a net yield of 6 percent. What is the indicated market value of

(a) The lessor's interest?

(b) The lessee's interest?

Assume that the building has a total economic life of 40 years from the date of its completion.

9. Mrs. A, the fee owner of a parcel of vacant land, leased the property to Mr. B for a term of 50 years at a net rent of $3,000 per year. Mr. B immediately erected a commercial building on the lot and five years later, subleased to Mr. C at a rent of $8,000 per year net, for 45 years. The vacant lot has a market value of $75,000. The market rental value of the property is $12,000 per year net. As of today (15 years after the date of the original lease from A to B) on a 10 percent basis for all three parties' interests, and assuming the building to be valueless at the end of the lease:

(a) What is the value of the interest of Mrs. A?

(b) What is the value of the interest of Mr. B?

(c) What is the value of the interest of Mr. C?

Show your computations.

READING AND STUDY REFERENCES

CARR, M. REBECCA. "Appraisal of a Sandwich Leasehold Interest," *Real Estate Valuation Guide* 18, no. 211 (1989).

EPLEY, DONALD R., and JAMES H. BOYKIN. *Basic Income Property Appraisal.* Reading, Mass.: Addison-Wesley Publishing Co., Inc., 1983, pp. 385–387.

FREE, ROBERT L. "The Appraisal of Sandwich Leases," *The Appraisal Journal* 26, no. 3 (July 1958), pp. 354–359.

HINES, MARY ALICE. Chapter 15, *Real Estate Appraisal.* New York: Macmillan Publishing Company, 1981.

JONES, ROBERT N., and STEPHEN D. ROACH. "Valuation of Long-Term Leases," *The Appraisal Journal* 57, no. 4 (October 1989), pp. 451–459.

RING, ALFRED A., and JEROME J. DASSO. Chapter 24, *Real Estate Principles and Practices.* Englewood Cliffs, N.J.: Prentice-Hall, Inc., 1985.

RODGERS, THOMAS. "Valuation of a Leased Fee Interest," *The Appraisal Journal* 57, no. 1 (January 1989), pp. 36–50.

20
Mortgage-Equity Appraising

Learning Objectives

After reading this chapter, you should be able to:

- Distinguish between a market value appraisal and a mortgage-equity appraisal
- Appreciate the effects of leveraged debt financing on equity yield
- Determine the difference between equity dividend rate and equity yield rate
- Understand how an anticipated future value change alters equity yield rates
- Discuss the fundamentals of the Ellwood method of mortgage-equity capitalization

Ever since the introduction of the *Ellwood Tables for Real Estate Appraising and Financing* in 1967, a keen interest has developed among professional appraisers in the application of increasingly sophisticated capitalization methods which will accurately reflect yields that accrue to equity investors under mortgage debt financing of real property. Although Ellwood's precomputed tables for mortgage-equity financing are of relatively recent origin, the concept of "leverage," or trading on the equity for purposes of increasing owners' interest earnings on cash investment, is as old as civilization. In fact, mortgage lending—although referred to as being evil—dates back to Biblical days (see Nehemiah, Chapter 5, verses 1 to 9). Extensive use of credit, however, as a major source of real estate financing did not become popular until the beginning of the twentieth century.

TRADING ON THE EQUITY

Apart from the necessity to borrow funds, probably the greatest justification for incurring indebtedness is to be found in the principle of trading on the equity (leverage). According to the principle, it is economically advisable to borrow funds when the use of such funds brings a higher rate of return than the rate, or cost, of borrowing.

Two related terms also should be clearly understood. The *equity dividend rate* is the investor's earnings rate which is often known as a "cash-on-cash" rate. This rate is based on either the investor's down payment or subsequent equity buildup divided into the annual cash flow. The investor's equity can be expected to increase as the mortgage principal is periodically reduced with each payment. The divisor may also include value increases resulting from appreciation. The *equity yield rate* accounts for the cash-on-cash return covered previously plus the anticipated net sale proceeds when the property is sold. Sometimes the forecast extends instead to the time the property is expected to be refinanced, and these net financing proceeds to the owner are included in the rate calculation.

The steps involved in computing an equity dividend rate are as follows:

Step		*Computation*
1		Potential gross income
2	minus	Vacancy and collection losses
3	equals	Effective gross income
4	minus	Operating expenses
5	equals	Net operating income
6	minus	Annual mortgage debt service
7	equals	Cash flow (before taxes)

Equity dividend rate = cash flow (step 7) divided by owner's equity

To illustrate: Assume that a property costing $100,000 brings in a gross rental of $20,000 per annum and that this property was purchased for all cash and thus is free and clear of monetary encumbrances. If the taxes, repairs, and other operating expenses amount to $7,000 annually, the net operating income is $13,000, or 13 percent on the owner's investment. Now suppose that the owner mortgages the property for $50,000 at 12 percent interest per annum. The annual mortgage payments on $50,000[1] amounting to $6,172 would reduce the cash flow to $6,828; but since the owner's equity investment is now only $50,000, his equity rate of return has increased from 13 percent to 13.7 percent per annum. Suppose, further, that a mortgage in the amount of $75,000 was obtainable at 12 percent. The annual debt service on this indebtedness would increase to $9,258 ($75,000 × 0.1234) and, conversely, would decrease the cash flow to equity to $3,742. This income, however, in relation to the equity investment of $25,000, represents an equity dividend—as a result of trading on the equity (often called leverage)—at a rate of 15 percent per annum. To recapitulate:

---

[1]Assumes a $50,000, 30-year, 12 percent, monthly installment mortgage which results in an annual mortgage constant of 12.34 percent.

	Case 1	Case 2
Investment value	$100,000	$100,000
Net income to property	$ 13,000	$ 13,000
Overall capitalization rate	13%	13%
Mortgage loan	$ 50,000	$ 75,000
Loan debt service at 12%	$ 6,172	$ 9,258
Equity value	$ 50,000	$ 25,000
Equity cash flow	$ 6,828	$ 3,742
Equity dividend rate	13.7%	15.0%

The previous illustration emphasizes at the outset of this chapter the distinction between the earnings capacity of a property under free-and-clear ownership and equity dividends (cash on cash) obtainable under favorable mortgage debt financing or "trading on the equity." Thus, although the preceding property earns a maximum rate of 13 percent per annum, the equity yield through use of leverage can be increased as noted before. More favorable loan terms would have increased the equity return even more. Trading on the equity does not increase the earnings of the property but rather compensates the borrower for the additional risks assumed in securing the safety of borrowed funds and in guaranteeing the priority of interest and amortization payments to which the lender—under the financial mortgage agreement—has a legal claim.

When property is unimproved, or inadequately improved, borrowing to erect a suitable improvement is invariably an advantage providing there is sufficient demand for the completed space. The land may be valuable, but it will yield its economic rent only when improved with a building; and it is often a financial advantage to obtain a mortgage loan to pay all or part of the cost of such building. Suppose that a parcel of unimproved land is worth $100,000. The taxes amount to $2,000, and the loss of interest on the money (sometimes called opportunity cost) invested in land is 10.0 percent or $10,000, a total annual loss of $12,000 to the owner. To avoid this loss, the owner puts up a building costing $300,000, and she borrows this whole amount on a mortgage at 10.0 percent.[2] The land and building together produce a rent income of $67,000, and the taxes and other operating charges are $27,000, leaving a net rental of $40,000. Out of this net annual rental, $31,593 is annual debt service on the money borrowed, leaving $8,407 for the equity owner—this being 8.4 percent on her cash investment, which is still $100,000. She has, therefore, stopped her loss on the undeveloped land and now has a postdebt service income of $8,407.

It is probable that in cases of this kind, the amount of depreciation recapture of the building would be represented by a corresponding annual payment to reduce the amount of the mortgage over the years of the indebtedness. More

[2]Assumes a 10 percent, 30-year, monthly installment mortgage, resulting in an annual mortgage constant of 10.53 percent ($31,593/$300,000).

likely, the amount of depreciation permitted as a write-off under the IRS Tax Code will provide a tax shelter (tax-free income) to the extent that allowable deductions exceed mortgage amortization. The equity portion of the total investment can increase in value in two ways: mortgage amortization and property value appreciation. The total amount of equity realized or recaptured at the time of property sale, if greater than the original equity investment, further increases the equity yield.

PROPERTY APPRAISING VERSUS EQUITY APPRAISING

Prior to illustrating the application of the mortgage-equity method of capitalization, it is essential that the appraiser fully realizes the distinction that must be made between valuation of real property as an economic whole or entity, and valuation of the "equity investment" under market-regulated mortgage-equity methods of financing.

Market value is best defined as the "present worth of future rights to income." To be accurate, market value must be based on income produced under:

1. Fee simple ownership, irrespective of financial or lease encumbrances.[3]
2. Typical property management.
3. Utilization of property at its highest and best use.

Once market value has been established, on the basis of typical financial terms, the "price" that the investor is warranted in paying for the property can be ascertained by adding or subtracting from market value the benefits or detriments attributable to personal or financial attributes such as reputation, or extraordinary management (goodwill), title encumbrances (good or bad leases, easements, and so on), and favorable or unfavorable financial terms of sale. To do otherwise would inject price-influencing personal motivation into the capitalization process and cloud, if not prevent, objective analysis and price adjustment of comparable sales in order to derive an accurate measure of the present worth of the subject property.

Those who apply and defend the mortgage-equity method of capitalization as a means for estimating property value reject the idea that property should be appraised as though free and clear of financial encumbrances. Instead it is claimed that the investor will secure as much of the purchase price as the "traffic will bear" through mortgage debt financing at rates and terms prevailing in the market. Further, it is refuted that value must be based on income derived over the economic life of the property; rather it is deemed an accepted and observable fact that the customary period of ownership is short lived—8 to 12 years—and that income projections should, therefore, be of equally short-term duration. At the termination of the investment life, the property is sold, the remaining equity investment (sale price less remaining mortgage debt) reverts back to the owner, and the cycle of ownership from a cash-in to a cash-out position is completed.

[3]Market value may also be estimated for other interests such as leased fee interest where an owner wants to know the value of his or her property subject to long-term, nonmarket leases.

Failure to differentiate between the mortgage-equity "price" methods of capitalization and the more conventional income "value" methods of capitalization, as explained previously, is responsible for the confusion found not only among earnest students of appraising but also among most professional appraisers who find themselves lost in mathematical equations. Semantics, too, aggravate the issue at hand. Whereas value should represent the "present" worth of future rights to income and be free from the influences of dollar inflation or deflation (income and value when unencumbered will rise and fall like a ship at sea with the level of prices), the mortgage-equity approach to value yields a "price" that includes the benefits of the terms of financing, the impact of leverage, and the inflationary or deflationary effects on equity investment which result in net sales proceeds. Further complicating matters is the fact that under the conventional method of income capitalization, the appraiser is given the option to use, as he or she deems best applicable, the straight-line, curved-line, or annuity residual techniques of determining land and building value as demonstrated in Chapter 18. Under the mortgage-equity method of capitalization, the appraiser is restricted to the use of an overall rate of capitalization and to the conversion of a "stabilized" or level income derived for the property as a whole rather than for land and improvements as separate and distinct value parts.

To illustrate the application of the mortgage-equity method of capitalization, the following appraisal problem is presented:

A department store property has been leased to a national chain for a term of 10 years at a rental of $50,000 per annum. Owner's taxes, insurance, and exterior maintenance costs total $12,000 per year, leaving a net operating income in the amount of $38,000. Mortgage money of $270,000 can be obtained to finance the purchase of this property at 11 percent interest with full amortization over 25 years payable monthly in the amount of $2,646, or $31,756 per year covering mortgage interest and amortization. The property is anticipated to increase in value over the 10-year ownership period, rising from $360,000 purchase price to $400,000. The owner seeks an appraisal of this income property specifying an equity yield of 10 percent.

Solution

1. Net operating income $ 38,000
2. Mortgage interest and
   principal—annual   31,756
3. Equity income—cash flow $ 6,244
4. Present value of equity
   income of $1.00 at 10%
   compound interest—

Inwood factor, 10-year period	6.1446	
Present worth of equity income for 10-year period $2,533 × 6.1446		$ 38,367
5. Sale price of property	$400,000	
6. Remaining value of mortgage:		
(a) Monthly mortgage payments	$2,646	
(b) Remaining payment period—15 years— Inwood factor for 180 months at rate 11% per annum	87.9819	
(c) Mortgage balance on date of sale $2,646 × 87.9819	$232,800	
7. Value of equity on date of sale	$167,200	
8. Reversionary value:		
(a) Present worth of $1.00 at 10% for income due 10 years from date of appraisal	0.3855	
9. Present worth of reversion $82,553 × 0.3855		$ 64,463
10. Total present value of equity at 10% interest		102,830
11. Add mortgage loan value on date of appraisal		270,000
12. Total value of property		$372,830
13. Overall capitalization rate $R = I/V = \$38,000 \div$ $\$372,830 = 10.19\%$		

The distribution of net operating income to equity and level mortgage payments, and the changing relationship between the mortgage amortization and mortgage interest components over the 10-year ownership period, are shown graphically in Figure 20.1. By the end of the tenth year, the loan amortization has grown from 6.46 percent of the first monthly mortgage payment to 19.2 percent of the monthly mortgage payment. The pattern of changes in capital formation caused by property appreciation, declining mortgage debt balances, and increasing equity over the ownership period are presented in Figure 20.2.

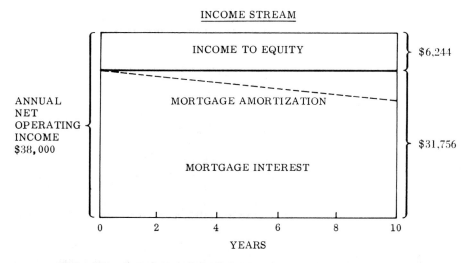

Figure 20.1   Changing relationship between loan interest and amortization

Solving for Equity Yield Rate (Y_e)

In the preceding example the equity yield rate was specified by the investor. The yield rate can also be obtained from market study of comparable properties. Where a sale price is firm and the mortgage terms and rate are known, the equity yield rate can be obtained by analysis as follows.

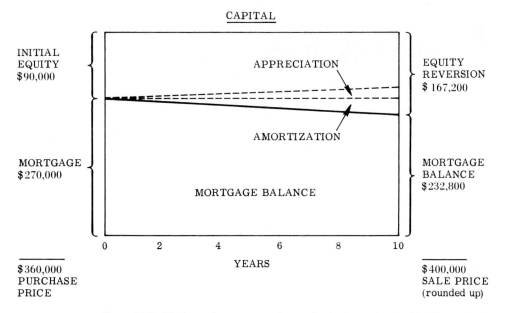

Figure 20.2   Equity and mortgage values at beginning and end of holding period

Suppose that a property was bought 8 years ago for $300,000. Of this purchase price, $200,000 was financed by a 25-year monthly installment mortgage at 10 percent interest. The level mortgage payments totaled $21,804 per year. The average annual net operating income produced by this property during the term of ownership was $30,000. The property brought on the date of sale—8 years from the date of purchase—a price of $275,000. What is the yield on the equity's investment?

Solution

1. Original purchase price		$300,000
2. Mortgage loan		200,000
3. Original cash investment		$100,000
4. Sales price—8 years later		$275,000
5. Mortgage balance—8 years later:		
(a) Monthly level payments	$ 1,817	
(b) Inwood factor 10% for 17 years	97.9230	
Mortgage balance $1,817 × 97.9230		$177,926
6. Reversion to equity on date of sale		$ 97,074
7. Income from property		30,000
8. Mortgage loan payments		21,804
9. Income to equity (cash flow) annually "Trial"[4] interest yield rate of 7%		$ 8,196
10. Present worth of income stream at 7% $8,196 × 5.9713 (Inwood factor for 8 years)		$ 48,941
11. Present worth of reversion at 7% $97,074 × 0.5820 (PW of $1.00 for 8 years)		56,497
12. Total value of equity indicated by yield rate of 7%		$105,438

Trial yield, using 8%

[4]In using this iterative or trial-and-error method in choosing a trial yield rate, a guide for the initial selection is as follows: $Y_E = R_E + \Delta a$ (assuming straight-line change and ignoring the value of the income stream)

$$Y_E = \$8,196/\$100,000 + (\$97,074 - \$100,000/\$100,000)$$
$$= 8.2\% + (-\$2,926/\$100,000)$$
$$= 8.2\% - 2.9\%$$
$$= 5.3\%$$

To allow for the value of the income stream, an adjustment of 1 or 2 percentage points would give an initial trial yield calculation at 6 or 7 percent. This method is useful in providing a starting point but not in giving a final yield figure. A more direct method, involving a financial calculator, is shown later in this chapter.

13. Present worth of income stream at 8%
$8,196 × 5.747 (Inwood factor for 8 years)   47,102
14. Present worth of reversion at 8%
$97,074 × 0.5403 (PW of $1.00 for 8 years)   52,449
Total value of equity indicated by yield rate
of 8% $ 99,551

To determine the precise yield rate that falls between 7 and 8 percent, it is necessary to interpolate as follows:

Value of equity at 7% interest $105,438
Value of equity at 8% interest   99,551

Difference caused by 1% rate of interest $ 5,887
Value of equity at 7% interest   105,438
Value of equity at X% interest   100,000
Difference of 7% over X% $ 5,438

Thus the actual rate is 5,438 ÷ 5,887 of 1 percent above the yield rate of 7 percent or 0.00924. This fractional rate when added to the trial rate 0.07 determines an exact yield rate of 0.0792 or 7.92 percent.

Finding Present Value at a Given Y_E

Suppose that the appraiser is called on to ascertain the amount that the property for which a yield rate of 7.92 percent was computed previously should have sold for in order to yield a 10 percent rate of interest to the owner. The answer would be derived as follows:

1. Value of income stream at 10%
$8,196 × 5.335 (8-year Inwood factor at 10%) $ 43,726
2. Present value of property reversion
$100,000 less $43,726   56,274
3. Future worth of property 8 years hence is
$56,274 × 2.144 (FW of $1.00 at 10%)   120,651
4. Add mortgage loan balance on date of sale
(see previous illustration)   177,926
5. Sale price of property to yield 10% interest
to owner $298,577

Conversely, it could be asked how much the owner should have paid for the property on the date of purchase to yield an interest rate of 10 percent where the anticipated future sale price of $275,000, the equity reversion of $97,074, and all other factors given in the preceding problem remain constant.

Solution

1. Present value of income stream at 10% as previously
   ($8,196 × 5.335) $ 43,726
2. Present worth of reversion at 10%
   $97,074 × 0.4665   45,285
3. Value of equity cash investment to yield 10% $ 89,011
4. Add amount of original mortgage loan of   200,000
5. Purchase price of property to yield 10% on equity investment $289,011

The previous illustrations support the fact that the equity yield which comparable sales support or an investor demands is that rate at which the stabilized cash flow to equity when discounted to present worth over the years of ownership plus the present worth of the equity reversionary interests (sale price less mortgage balance) at the time of resale equal the cash value[5] of the equity on the date of initial purchase. It should be held clearly in mind that since a property's income-producing capacity is unaffected by the terms of financing, the interest yield to an owner will vary with his or her ability to obtain the best bargain possible by "trading on the equity," that is, by obtaining the largest possible mortgage in relation to total property value at the lowest possible rate of interest over the longest possible years which are short of the economic life of the property.

As demonstrated previously, given a level income and a stated purchase price at appraised value, the equity yield rate will increase or decrease with appreciation or depreciation of the property over the ownership period. The impact on the equity yield rates resulting from property price increases or decreases can best be visualized by graphic presentation as shown in Figure 20.3.

This relationship can also be seen by use of the equation $Y_E = R_E + \Delta a$, assuming that $R_E = 0.10$ and (1) $\Delta a = +0.03$ and (2) $\Delta a = -0.02$. Then

$$Y_E = 0.10 + 0.03, \text{ or } 0.13 \text{ and alternatively}$$
$$Y_E = 0.10 - 0.02, \text{ or } 0.08$$

Assume that your client has expressed interest in a property currently available for sale for a price of $200,000 and which will be rented under an absolute net lease for the next eight years for $15,000 annually. You have been asked to advise her of the expected equity yield (Y_E) under the following projected sale prices: (1) $240,000 (+20%); (2) $200,000 (no change); (3) $190,000 (−5%); (4) $180,000 (−10%).

One method of solving this problem is by use of a financial calculator, using the following keystroke sequence, beginning with the first projection:

$$Y_E = 8 \boxed{n}\ 200000\ \boxed{\text{CHS}}\quad \boxed{\text{PV}}\ 240000\ \boxed{\text{FV}}\ 15000$$

$$\boxed{\text{PMT}}\quad \boxed{i} = 9.29\%$$

[5]The cash value of equity is the cash amount paid for the property over and above the existing mortgage debt on the date of purchase of the subject property.

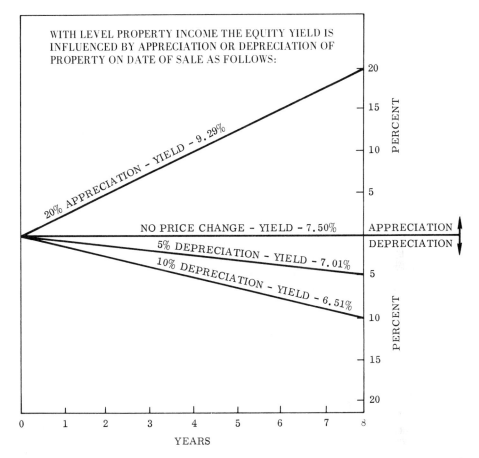

WITH LEVEL PROPERTY INCOME THE EQUITY YIELD IS INFLUENCED BY APPRECIATION OR DEPRECIATION OF PROPERTY ON DATE OF SALE AS FOLLOWS:

20% APPRECIATION - YIELD - 9.29%

NO PRICE CHANGE - YIELD - 7.50%

5% DEPRECIATION - YIELD - 7.01%

10% DEPRECIATION - YIELD - 6.51%

APPRECIATION

DEPRECIATION

PERCENT

PERCENT

YEARS

Figure 20.3   Prospects for yield on equity investment based on five- and eight-year holding periods

Equity yields for all four projections are

Yield for eight-year holding period:

+20% change in value	9.29%
No change in value	7.50%
−5% change in value	7.01%
−10% change in value	6.51%

Another way of looking at this situation is the property would have to increase in value by 20 percent over the next eight years in order to achieve a 9.29 percent equity yield. Yet a yield of 6.51 percent could be expected even if the property declined in value by 10 percent.

An investor may ask advice on still two other sets of conditions: (1) What yield would be realized if the property changed at the same average rate of value as shown previously, but was held only for five years? (2) What sale price would be necessary to produce a desired yield of 12 percent over five years (a) including the rental income and (b) without the rental income?

Using the same keystroke sequence as presented previously, the forecast yield rates would be as shown as follows as well as in Figure 20.3. For example, with an annual average rate of appreciation of 2.50 percent over 5 years, Y_E would be

| 5 | n | 200000 | CHS | | PV | 225000 | FV | 15000 | PMT |

| i | = 9.57%

Yield for five-year holding period:

+ 12.50% (+20% ÷ 8 yrs = 2.50%/yr)	Y_E = 9.57%
No change in value	Y_E = 7.50%
−3.13% (−0.63%/yr)	Y_E = 6.96%
−6.25% (−1.25%/yr)	Y_E = 6.40%

It is more profitable if the property is sold after five years if the property appreciates. There is no difference if the property value does not change, but slightly higher yields may be expected by holding the property for eight years if it is expected to decline in value. The widest yield margin is under the 2.50 percent annual appreciation.

The second question asked was what sale price would be required to produce a 12 percent equity yield over five years.

The answer for part (a) is $257,176, computed as follows:

| 5 | n | 12 | i | 200000 | CHS | | PV | 15000 | PMT | | FV |

The answer for part (b) is $352,468 computed as in part (a), but excluding the annual rent. The same answer is found by multiplying $200,000 by the future worth of 1 factor for 12% and 5 years as well as raising 1.12 to the power of 5 and then multiplying the result by $200,000.

MORTGAGE LOAN BALANCE

Sometimes it is necessary in appraising real estate to ascertain the loan balance(s), especially when estimating equity yield upon sale of the property. Another question that is sometimes raised is: "How much interest did I pay on my mortgage in a given year?" Answers can be provided to both of these questions as follows.

Example 1. Find the remaining loan balance on a 25-year, $100,000 mortgage at the end of 10 years. The interest rate is 10 percent, and payments are made on an annual basis.

There are several ways to solve for a loan balance. The one suggested here uses the installment to amortize 1 (loan constant) found in Table 16.1. The numerator is the factor for the full term, and the denominator is the factor for the remaining loan term (15 years). The latter factor should be easy to remember by associating it with the remaining loan balance.

$$\text{Loan balance} = \$100,000 \times \frac{0.110168}{0.131474} = \$83,795$$

The solution to this problem using a financial calculator is

| f | | FIN | 25 | n | 10 | i | 100000 | CHS | | PV |

| PMT | 10 | n | | FV | = $83,795 |

Example 2. Suppose now that same client wants to know (a) how much equity was accumulated during the tenth year as a result of loan amortization, and (b) how much interest was paid during the tenth year of the loan.

(a) Total annual loan payment
($100,000 × 0.110168) $11,016.80

Loan balance at end of year 9
(same as beginning of year 10)[6]
$\dfrac{0.110168 \ (1/a_{\overline{n}} \ 25 \ \text{yr})}{0.127817 \ (a/a_{\overline{n}} \ 16 \ \text{yr})}$ = 0.861920

minus loan balance at end of year 10
$\dfrac{0.110168 \ (1/a_{\overline{n}} \ 25 \ \text{yr})}{0.131474 \ (a/a_{\overline{n}} \ 15 \ \text{yr})}$ = 0.837945

equals loan amortization in year 10   0.023975
times original loan amount $100,000

Equity accumulation in year 10   = $2,397.50

(b) If the total annual level mortgage
installment (principal and interest) is $11,016.80
and the principal reduction is $ 2,397.50

then the interest paid in year 10 is $ 8,619.30

Alternatively, this calculation can be handled using a financial calculator as follows:

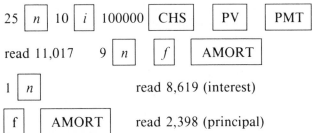

| 25 | n | 10 | i | 100000 | CHS | | PV | | PMT |

read 11,017   9 | n | | f | | AMORT |

1 | n | read 8,619 (interest)

| f | | AMORT | read 2,398 (principal)

To check the accuracy of the calculated amounts of interest and principal paid during the tenth year, add the two preceding amounts. The total is $11,017 which equals the previous calculation for the annual mortgage payment.

[6]The 16-year factor complements the 9-year factor to equal the total loan term of 25 years.

ELLWOOD'S TABLES FOR CAPITALIZATION

The solutions to the equity yield problems, as demonstrated previously in the mortgage-equity method of capitalization, were obtained without aid of any formulas or specially derived coefficients or factors other than those found in the standard compound interest tables such as presented and illustrated in Chapter 16 or by use of a financial calculator. Special-purpose tables such as those named Babcock, Inwood, Hoskold, Ring, and Ellwood are sometimes useful in the valuation process, for they are intended to save considerable work time in the appraisal process by offering precomputed rates, factors, or income derivations applicable to an amount or percentage of $1.00. Having established the impact of a method of capitalization on the value of an income stream of $1.00, the appraiser can readily compute the value of X dollars by multiplication or division, as the case might be, by simple reference to the appropriate factor table. In recent years, many commercial mortgage lenders have begun to place more emphasis on appraisers using discounted cash flow methodology in their valuation reports.

L. W. Ellwood, who for many years served as supervisor in the Mortgage Loan Division of the New York Life Insurance Company, developed, by following essentially the same mathematical steps as illustrated in the equity value problems given previously, precomputed "overall rates of capitalization" which permit ready and instant capitalization of a stabilized income stream over specified years of ownership periods at market-determined mortgage loan terms and prevailing equity yield rates applicable to the subject property.

The basic formula applied by Ellwood[7] in the development of precomputed (mortgage-equity-leveraged) rates of capitalization is as follows:

$$R = Y - MC + (\text{dep. } 1/S_n) \text{ or } (- \text{ app. } 1/S_n)$$

where R = overall rate of capitalization

Y = equity yield rate demanded by prudent investors

M = ratio of mortgage to total investment (i.e., 70%, 80%, etc.)

C = mortgage coefficient (This coefficient is derived by the formula $C = Y + (P \times 1/S_n) - R_m$. Here Y represents the equity yield; P, the percentage of the loan paid off[8]; $1/S_n$, the sinking fund factor at the equity yield rate for a given projection period or n years of ownership; and R_M, the annual level mortgage loan payment per dollar debt which sometimes is called the mortgage loan constant rate.)

$1/S_n$ = sinking fund factor at equity yield rate, which is multiplied by the percentage of appreciation or depreciation estimated to occur over the years of ownership (This derived portion of the sinking

[7] L. W. Ellwood, *Ellwood Tables for Real Estate Appraising and Financing* (Chicago: American Institute of Real Estate Appraisers, 1967).

[8] P also can be computed by the equation

$$P = \frac{R_m - I}{R_{mp} - I}$$

with R_m being the mortgage rate for the full loan term, R_{mp} the mortgage rate for the projection or holding period, and I the nominal interest rate.

fund factor is added in case of depreciation and subtracted in case of property appreciation.)

To demonstrate the development of a "band-of-investment" mortgage-equity-weighted rate of capitalization, the following market-derived data are applied:

1. Mortgage loan funds available over 25-year loan period for 70 percent of value at 10 percent interest compounded monthly.
2. Equity yield is 12 percent on cash investment.
3. Ownership period from the date of purchase to the date of sale is 10 years.
4. Net operating income is $57,360.
5. Depreciation is estimated at 1.5 percent per year or a total of 15 percent over the 10-year period.

Solution

$$R = Y - MC + \text{dep. } 1/S_n$$
$$= 0.12 - (0.70 \times 0.019754^*) + (0.15 \times 0.056984)$$
$$= 0.12 - 0.013828 + 0.008548$$
$$= 0.114720$$
$$^*C = Y + (P^9 \times 1/S_n{}^{10}) - R_m$$
$$= 0.12 + (0.154387 \times 0.056984) - 0.109044^{11}$$
$$= 0.12 + 0.008798 - 0.109044$$
$$= 0.019754$$

Value of property $57,360 ÷ 0.114720	$500,000
Mortgage loan at 70%	350,000
Equity cash investment	$150,000
Proof:	
Total income	$ 57,360
Debt service payments	
$350,000 × 0.109044 (mortgage constant)	38,165
Cash flow to equity	$ 19,195
Present worth of cash flow at	
12% = $19,195 × 5.650223	
(Inwood factor)	$108,456

Present worth of reversion, 12%, 10		
years	$425,000	
($500,000 less 15%) less mortgage		
balance of (0.845613 × $350,000)	295,965	
	$129,035	

[9]1.00 – (monthly mortgage payments of 0.009087) per $1.00 loan × Inwood factor for 180 months at 10 percent of 93.057439 = 0.845613 remaining mortgage principal, or 0.154387 per dollar of loan paid off in 10 years.

[10]Sinking fund factor for 10 years at 12 percent = 0.056984.

[11]Mortgage constant payment per month of 0.009087 × 12 = annual constant of 0.109044.

$129,035 \times 0.321973$ (PW of 1 at 12%)   41,546

Total present value of equity $150,002

    Rounded to $150,000

      The value of $500,000 as obtained previously, based on an income stream of $57,360 per annum to be derived from a property to be owned over a period of 10 years where 70 percent mortgage funds can be obtained at 10 percent interest over 25-year loan periods and where equity yields must bring 12 percent to the owner-investor, could have been capitalized directly by reference to an Ellwood table for real estate appraising and financing or could have been computed by the long method or formula method as demonstrated previously. The important thing is that the appraiser knows the methods for computing value under the mortgage-equity method of capitalization, and understands the difference between "property appraising" free and clear of debt encumbrances and mortgage-equity valuation to reflect leveraged income derived from "trading on the equity."

      A popular variation of the Ellwood mortgage-equity technique was developed by Charles B. Akerson and is known either as the "Ellwood without algebra" or "Akerson" approach for deriving an overall capitalization rate. It is divided into three tiers as follows:

Tier 1	Loan-to-value ratio $(M) \times$ mortgage rate (R_M)
	plus equity-to-value ratio $(EQ/V) \times$ equity yield rate (Y_E)
Tier 2	minus equity buildup
	$(M \times P \times 1/S_n)$
	equals basic capitalization rate (r)
Tier 3	Adjust for depreciation or appreciation
	(i.e., + dep and − app. $\times 1/S_n)$
	equals overall capitalization rate (R_o)

      Using the same information presented in the previous Ellwood example, the solution is as follows:

1. 0.70×0.109044 0.076331

     $+ 0.30 \times 0.12$ 0.036000

                                                  0.112331

2. $- (0.70 \times 0.154387 \times 0.056984)$ 0.006158

                             $r \;= 0.106173$

3. $+ 0.15 \times 0.056984$ 0.008548

                           $R_o = 0.114721$

      As can be seen, this method provides the same indicated overall capitalization rate (R_o) as the somewhat more difficult Ellwood formula.

SUMMARY

It is most important that a clear distinction be made between property appraising on the one hand, and mortgage-equity appraising on the other. In the former case, the appraiser is charged with the responsibility to estimate "objectively" the present worth of a property which is or can be placed to its highest and best use and which is managed in accordance with practices deemed typical in the market area. A property thus utilized can conceivably have only one market value but may, because of available alternate means of mortgage-equity financing and wide differences in buyers' abilities to trade on the equity, have a substantial range of values to different individual or corporate owners.

For the sake of clarity as well as for professional purity in appraisal theory and practice, it is strongly recommended that value be estimated first on a free-and-clear basis (i.e., free of all encumbrances); and second, on a basis that reflects available terms of financing, tax shelter opportunities, and other tax or ownership benefits that accrue to a specific owner or a group of owners. Such value report presentation will then enable the client to see the value of the property both unencumbered and subject to specified financing or lease terms.

The impact of trading on the equity caused by increasing mortgage loan leverage can cause a diminished equity dividend rate where there is sufficient net operating income to support the loan payments adequately, shown as follows:

	Example			
	1	2	3	4
Market value	$100,000	$100,000	$100,000	$100,000
Net operating income	$ 10,000	$ 10,000	$ 10,000	$ 10,000
Overall capitalization rate	10%	10%	10%	10%
Mortgage loan	$ 60,000	$ 70,000	$ 80,000	$ 90,000
Annual debt service at 10.90% constant	$ 6,540	$ 7,630	$ 8,720	$ 9,810
Debt coverage ratio	1.53	1.31	1.15	1.02
Income to equity	$ 3,460	$ 2,370	$ 1,280	$ 190
Cash value of equity	$ 40,000	$ 30,000	$ 20,000	$ 10,000
Equity dividend rate	8.7%	7.9%	6.4%	1.9%

Thus, although the property income and property value remain constant, equity dividend rates decreased from 8.7 percent to 1.9 percent depending on mortgage-equity ratios or leverages. If the interest rate applicable to the mortgage loan can be lowered because of an owner's increased security status, the equity dividend rate will become inversely higher.

Tables for mortgage-equity appraising are most useful in measuring quickly by reference to a precomputed table the effects of "leverage" or trading on the equity and in ascertaining the income tax impact as well as the financial investment cash requirements of the equity owner. Care, however, must be taken not to confuse equity appraising with property appraising where the "present worth" of land and building improvements are to be the measure of market value versus estimated value of the equity position plus the outstanding loan balance.

REVIEW QUESTIONS

1. Explain how the term "equity yield rate" differs from equity dividend rate.
2. Outline the steps necessary to compute equity dividend rate.
3. Solve for the present property value under the following conditions: Investor seeks a 10 percent equity yield rate; level annual net income to owner is $50,000 for the next 10 years; at the end of this period, the property is expected to rise from the beginning value of $200,000 to $300,000; a 25-year, 75 percent loan to value, annual installment loan with 10 percent interest is available. Use the mortgage-equity method in solving for the value.
4. Compute the amount of equity built up by a borrower on a $190,000, 30-year, 10 percent monthly installment loan after the first 6 years.
5. How much interest would have been paid on the mortgage in question 4 during the fifteenth year?
6. Using a financial calculator, determine which of the following two investments would produce the highest equity yield:

   Property A. Current purchase price, $500,000; forecast net sales price at the end of 10 years, $600,000; annual gross income, $90,000; forecast average annual operating expenses, $36,500.

   Property B. Purchase price, $425,000; expected net sale proceeds at the end of 8 years, $500,000; annual net operating income, $31,000.

7. By use of the Ellwood (or Akerson) capitalization rate formula, find the present value of a property that is subject to the following conditions: loan terms—25 years, 80 percent loan ratio, 10 percent interest rate, annual installments; expected equity yield, 14 percent; holding period, 5 years; net operating income, $48,000; appreciation during holding period, 10 percent.
8. Define: (a) equity income and (b) trading on the equity.
9. An 11 percent first mortgage in the amount of $10,000 is to be amortized monthly over 15 years. How much is due per month?
10. A commercial property producing a stabilized annual income of $60,000 is offered for sale to the Goodrich Investment Corporation. The purchase is subject to an existing 25-year amortizing mortgage of $300,000 financed at 12 percent interest. The monthly level mortgage payments amount to $3,160. The Goodrich Investment Corporation seeks an equity return of 10 percent over an ownership period of 10 years. The property is estimated to realize $500,000 on the date of sale. The unpaid mortgage balance 10 years from now will be $263,400. Problem: Find the purchase price that will yield a 10 percent return.
11. A property is offered to the Upland Corporation for $400,000. There is an existing 20-year $280,000 mortgage at 10 percent interest. Level debt service payments equal $2,702.06 per month. The property is scheduled to be held for a period of five years. The annual stabilized property income is $45,000. Depreciation is estimated at 1.5 percent per year. Problem: Find the yield to the Upland Corporation.

12. How much of the original loan principal of $100,000 would have been paid off on a 10 percent, 25-year mortgage after 15 years? Assume annual installments.

READING AND STUDY REFERENCES

AKERSON, CHARLES B. Chapters 11–13, *Capitalization Theory and Techniques Study Guide.* Chicago: American Institute of Real Estate Appraisers, 1984.

BOYKIN, JAMES H., and RICHARD L. HANEY, JR. Chapter 10, *Financing Real Estate.* Englewood Cliffs, N.J.: Prentice-Hall, Inc., 1993.

EPLEY, DONALD R., and JAMES H. BOYKIN. Chapters 9 and 10, *Basic Income Property Appraisal.* Reading, Mass.: Addison-Wesley Publishing Co., Inc., 1983.

GIBBONS, JAMES E. "Equity Yield," *The Appraisal Journal* 48, no. 1 (January 1980), pp. 31–56.

GIBBONS, JAMES E. "Mortgage Equity Capitalization: Ellwood Method," *The Appraisal Journal* 34, no. 2 (April 1966), pp. 196–202.

KNOPP, PAUL J., and JOSEPH S. FIORE. "The Mortgage Equity Capitalization Technique for Nonlevel Income Streams," *The Real Estate Appraiser and Analyst* (Summer 1989), pp. 78–88.

OLLMAN, ROGER, and DAVID H. TRAHAN. "Valuation of Equity Interests of Leveraged Properties," *The Appraisal Journal* 59, no. 3 (July 1991), pp. 338–347.

SIRMANS, C. F., and BOBBY NEWSOME. "Mortgage-Equity Valuation and Alternative Financing," *The Appraisal Journal* 52, no. 2 (October 1984), pp. 528–538.

21

Condemnation Appraising
Practices and Procedures

Learning Objectives

After reading this chapter, you should be able to:

- Discuss the nature and limitations of the power of eminent domain
- Recognize the due process of law associated with the use of eminent domain
- Appreciate the meaning of "just compensation" as related to the process of eminent domain
- Explain the basic steps involved in the appraisal of a property subject to a partial taking
- Understand the causes of monetary damages to a remainder property when there is a partial taking

Ownership of real property is widely distributed, and is cherished by millions of American home owners and real estate investors. This right to use and control property is legally recognized and is given express protection by the U.S. Constitution. As explained more fully in Chapter 3, property ownership is conceived of as a _bundle of rights_ in which the individual sticks that make up this bundle confer on an owner the following privileges:

TAXATION
POLICE POWER
EMINENT DOMAIN

1. To enter upon the premises or decline to enter.
2. To use the realty or decline to use it.
3. To sell the property rights wholly or separately or refuse to dispose of them.
4. To lease or decline to lease.
5. To donate, dispose by will, or give away the property interest—partially or totally.
6. To have peaceful possession and quiet enjoyment.

These rights to the control and enjoyment of property under allodial owner-ship are inviolate and exclusive, except for the superior and sovereign rights of government exercised for the mutual welfare of the community, state, or nation. These sovereign powers are exercised to safeguard the health, welfare, and moral-ity of the public at large and are enforced as needed by taxation, police-power reg-ulations, and the acquisition of property under the sovereign right of eminent domain.

POWER OF EMINENT DOMAIN

In the final analysis, the strength of private ownership is derived from the strength and power of a sovereign government formed to enforce and protect such rights as are vested in the individual under constitutional guardianship. It is fun-damental, therefore, that rights essential to the maintenance and welfare of soci-ety must be paramount to those claimed by individuals in the pursuit of their separate interests. The right to expropriate private property for public use is le-gally known as the power of *eminent domain*. This power is well defined in 10 Cal. Juris. Sec. 2 as follows:

> Eminent domain is the right of the people or government to take private property for public use, whenever the exigencies of the public cannot be adequately met and pro-vided for in any other way. . . . Eminent domain is justifiable only because the power makes for the common benefit.

To prevent arbitrary and confiscatory taking of private property by legisla-tive or executive decree, the drafters of the U.S. Constitution provided safeguards which U.S. courts throughout history have zealously enforced. These safeguards read as follows:

1. *Fifth Amendment*, ". . . nor shall private property be taken for public use, without just compensation."
2. *Fourteenth Amendment*, Section 1, ". . . nor shall any state deprive any per-son of life, liberty, or property without due process of law. . . ."

Individual states, generally, have patterned their respective constitutions to safeguard against the taking of private property except where (1) public necessity has been shown, (2) due process of law is followed, and (3) just compensation is paid to the owner.

DUE PROCESS OF LAW

The acquisition of private property in a condemnation action must conform to legal processes established under law. Procedures vary among states and within federal jurisdictions, but generally petition for taking of private property must provide more or less for the following:

1. Authority and necessity of taking.
2. Indication of public use for which land is condemned.
3. Survey of land and description.
4. Complaint and summons of owners.
5. Identification of the interest to be acquired.
6. Necessary parties defendant.
7. Legal testimony before proper tribunal.
8. Petition that property be condemned.

Unless the prescribed legal steps are carefully followed, due process may be declared lacking, and the condemnation action invalidated on account of error or omission of proceeding. Constitutional or statutory provisions by the various states further detail due process to include the following:

1. Process, service, and publication of public action.
2. Trial procedures.
3. Form of verdict by court in jury trials.
4. Appeal and review by court appeal.
5. Allocation of cost of proceedings.
6. Payment into court prior to taking.

JUST COMPENSATION

The payment of just compensation for the taking of property under eminent domain proceedings is assured by constitutional guaranty. The right to such payments is not questioned. The crux of the problem is a determination of the amount of payments due and the valuation procedure on which such payments are based.

Just compensation generally is restricted to the value of the property physically taken, and to offset a loss in value, if any, to the remaining parcel on account of severance of a part from the unity of a whole property. In evaluating just compensation, care must be taken to exclude losses incurred by the exercise of the police power of government, which in most states and legal jurisdictions are not compensable. Thus losses incurred through changes in zoning, change in level or grade of roads, construction, or elimination of public improvements and business losses in general are not compensated unless specifically provided for under statutory law or permissible under court instruction. Only losses attributable to the property as a result of physical taking, and as measured by a loss of value subsequent to the taking, are generally permitted as evidence for a court determination of just compensation.

MEANING OF VALUE

Value has many meanings to many persons (see Chapter 1). Because of the failure of the appraisal profession until recently[1] to establish a clear-cut definition of value based on the laws of economics (specifically, the law of supply and demand), higher courts filled the void and interpreted value for purposes of litigation. Most courts have held value to mean *market value* or its equivalent—a warranted market price obtainable as a result of open and free bartering between willing, able, ready, and informed buyers and sellers.

The definition of market value most frequently quoted in court proceedings and accepted for publication is based on a California court decision and reads:

Most Probable Price

> Market value is the highest price estimated in terms of money which a property will bring if exposed for sale in the open market, allowing a reasonable time to find a purchaser who buys with knowledge of all the uses to which it is adapted and for which it is capable of being used.[2]

The emphasis on market price as evidence of market value is further shown by another court decision which reads as follows:

> The market value of land taken for a public use is the price for which it could have been sold by a person desirous of selling to a person willing to buy, neither acting under compulsion and both exercising intelligent judgment.[3]

The "willing buyer, willing seller" concept so frequently stressed in conventional appraisal practice generally eliminates the use of condemnation-related conveyances as indicators of market value. This is so because the seller as a rule is *not* willing to sell and, in fact, is seeking relief in court.

Court decisions appear to sustain the principle of equity in condemnation under which the property owner is to be left whole in terms of dollars. It is the court's intention to leave his or her cash position, as measured by the value of his or her property before and after the taking, intact.

MEASURES OF VALUE

Where, as a result of condemnation for public use, an owner is deprived of *all* his or her real property holdings at a given location, the loss in value must equal the value of the entire property. Little difficulty, as a rule, is encountered by professional appraisers in estimating the market value of an entire property in accordance with prevailing appraising principles and practices and as outlined in preceding chapters. Generally, the things to be considered in a determination of

[1]See footnote 4, Chapter 1.
[2]Based on *People v. Ricciardi*, 23 Cal.2d 390, 144 p. 2d 799 (1943).
[3]*Baltimore and Ohio Railroad Company v. Bonafield's Heirs*, 90 SE 868, 79 W.Va. 287.

market value, and as gleaned from a condensation of court decisions, include among others the following[4]:

1. A view of the premises and its surroundings.
2. A description of the physical characteristics of the property and its situation in relation to the points of importance in the neighborhood.
3. The price at which the land was bought, if sufficiently recent to throw light on the present value.
4. The price at which similar neighboring land has sold, at or about the time of taking.
5. The opinion of expert witnesses.
6. A consideration of the uses for which the land is adapted and for which it is available.
7. The cost of the improvements less depreciation, if they are such as to increase the market value of the land.
8. The net income from the land, if the land is devoted to one of the uses to which it could be most advantageously and profitably applied.

It is in _partial_ taking that substantial differences arise among opposing expert witnesses as to value losses resulting from expropriation plus losses inflicted on the remainder of the property because of property _severance_.

The steps essential to a measurement of value losses in case of partial taking of real property are as follows:

1. Estimate the value of the property under consideration as a whole, free from encumbrances and restrictions imposed by the proposed facility. This market value is to be based on a cash or cash-equivalent market transaction.
2. Estimate the value of the part taken. If these are individual parts of the property, such as bushes or sheds, the value that these objects add to the property is the basis for compensation—not their replacement cost.
3. Deduct item 2 from item 1 to reveal the value of the remaining property as if unaffected by the proposed public improvement.
4. Estimate the value of the remaining parcel as a result of the acquisition and nature of the public improvement.
5. Estimate the damages, if any, caused to the remainder property as a result of severance of the part taken under the power of eminent domain (item 3 less item 4).
6. Add the value of the part taken to any damages the remainder suffered; this will be the total just compensation.

These six steps are illustrated by use of numbers in the following example:

[4]Julius L. Sackman, _Nichols' The Law of Eminent Domain_ (New York: Matthew Bender and Company, Inc., 1981), Vol. 4, Secs. 12.2–12.3142.

1. Value of the whole property	$250,000
2. Less value of the part taken	50,000
3. Value of remainder—unaffected by taking	$200,000
4. Value of remainder as affected by taking	175,000
5. Damages	$ 25,000
6. Total just compensation (item 2 + item 5)	$ 75,000

The value of the part taken, plus damages, if any, resulting from severance, comprises the amount due the owner as just compensation. This amount, however, cannot logically exceed the value of the entire property prior to taking as calculated under the first step. In the valuation of the part taken, courts have ruled that the part under appraisal must be evaluated as a part of the whole and not as a freestanding and separate parcel. A strip of land 5 feet deep and 100 feet long may have little value if offered for sale and use; but the same strip of land may make an important contribution to value if added to a parcel 95 feet deep in an area where a minimum depth of 100 feet is necessary under zoning regulations for a given highest and best land use. In considering what constitutes the whole property where several parcels are under one ownership at a given location, the appraiser should be guided by court-proved rules which establish economic unity in accordance with

1. Contiguity of location (a continuous, unbroken tract).
2. Unity of ownership.
3. Unity of use as evidenced by economic unity (utility) rather than physical unity.

In the estimation of value for the property as a whole, land and improvements must also be considered as an integral whole and not as independent and unrelated parts. Only after value for the entire property has been ascertained can allocation logically be made to fractional portions of the land or to land and buildings as respective parts. To illustrate: Where one-half of a tract of land is taken, and where the value of the entire tract is estimated to be $20,000, the value of the part taken—as a part of the whole—is deemed to be $10,000. However, if the two halves of the tract of land under value consideration were offered for sale as separate parcels, each may bring only $6,000 because of size and the resultant change in the economically feasible highest and best land use. Courts have consistently ruled that an owner's property must be left economically whole in terms of value and in the illustration cited previously would rule on—or instruct the jury to consider—the value of the land taken as a part of the whole and not as a separate parcel unrelated to the owner's entire property from which it is taken. The methods used most frequently in the valuation of property where there is a partial taking are:

1. The equal-unit-value (plus severance damages, if any) method.
2. The before-and-after valuation method.

The *equal-unit-value method*, often referred to as the *square-foot method* of land valuation, is a compromise designed to distribute the value of the whole over the physical units contained in the entire parcel affected by the taking. Otherwise, in the condemnation of a strip of land for street-widening purposes, it may be argued that the front part of a lot is more valuable than the rear portion which is remote from access and thus considered less serviceable. Opponents, on the other hand, may argue—and rightfully so—that the economic effect of condemnation of a strip of land for road-widening purposes is simply to reduce the lot in depth, leaving street rights and frontage intact. The economic effect of taking thus is deemed to be from the rear of the property rather than from the front area where the physical severance is to take place. Under the equal-unit-value method, the value of the part taken is intended to be in the same ratio that the physical units of land taken bear to the total land units of the property as a whole.

Suppose, for example, that a 5-acre vacant parcel is worth $10,000 an acre and a 0.10-acre strip is taken along the existing road to expand the width of the right of way. Assuming that the road widening causes no loss in value to the remainder parcel, the total just compensation under this premise would be $1,000 (0.10 acre × $10,000).

The *before-and-after method* of land valuation appears to be more equitable in measuring value losses sustained by the condemnee (landowner). This method, however, may unavoidably include benefits accruing to a property as a result of the proposed public improvements. For this reason, this method of valuation is used more often as a check on the accuracy of valuation obtained by the equal-unit-value (plus severance damages, if any) method rather than as an independent measure of just compensation. In practice, the procedure generally followed in estimating an owner's compensation is to compare the property values before and after the effects of the partial taking, allowing for the net difference between the benefits and damages. In some state jurisdictions, such as in Florida, consideration of benefits resulting from proposed public improvements is specifically ruled out by constitutional or statutory provisions. The appropriate measure of just compensation payable to the landowner is the loss in value to his or her property and not the benefits gained by the condemning authority.

The taking of a part of an owner's property often causes value losses to the remainder property as a result of *severance*. To minimize such severance losses, legislation in many states permits condemning authorities to offset damages caused by severance against benefits (value increments) brought about by the public improvements (for which the property was partially taken). Under no circumstances, however, should value benefits be given consideration in estimating the value of the part (or whole) of a property taken under eminent domain proceedings. Figure 21.1 illustrates three types of damaged remainder parcels.

SEVERANCE DAMAGE

In brief, *severance damage* constitutes a loss in value of the part of a property remaining after a taking as compared with the value of the remainder when considered as a part of the whole property. Severance damage in essence is a measure of

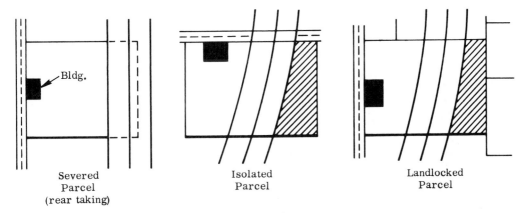

Severed
Parcel
(rear taking)

Isolated
Parcel

Landlocked
Parcel

Figure 21.1   Types of damaged parcels

depreciation attributable to a remainder property as a result of one or more of the following:

1. Change in highest and best use of the property subsequent to the taking.
2. Expenditures necessary to restore or protect the property from hazards caused by the taking of property.
3. Increased cost of operation or, conversely, a lowering of net operating income on which value is based.
4. Impaired accessibility or change of road grade with respect to the remainder.

Where a strip of land is acquired for construction of a limited access highway across an industrial property and the remainder land is cut off from railroad sidings and road access, a change in the highest and best use to a lower and possibly agricultural land use is likely. The difference in value under the prevailing use prior to land taking, as compared with the highest and best use subsequent to the land taking, constitutes the amount of severance to which the owner is entitled as just compensation in addition to the value of the land taken.

Where, as a result of the taking, expenditures are incurred to make repairs on remaining improvements—or where, for instance, fencing is necessary to guard cattle against the hazards of a proposed railroad right-of-way—such expenditures are recognized as severance damage for which compensation is due. It is important to recognize that severance damages claimed against the building improvements because of road hazards or the destruction of amenities caused by increased proximity to a new road right-of-way can logically be incurred only for the remaining useful (economic) life of the building and cannot extend into perpetuity as is the case with damage to land.

Without actual case studies of similar situations, appraisers unfortunately are forced to rely too much on "judgment." Figure 21.2 shows an example of a partial taking at a proposed interstate highway interchange in the state of Washington. Construction of the interchange caused enhancement rather than damages to the remaining property. In fact, the "after" value of the 27.36 acres

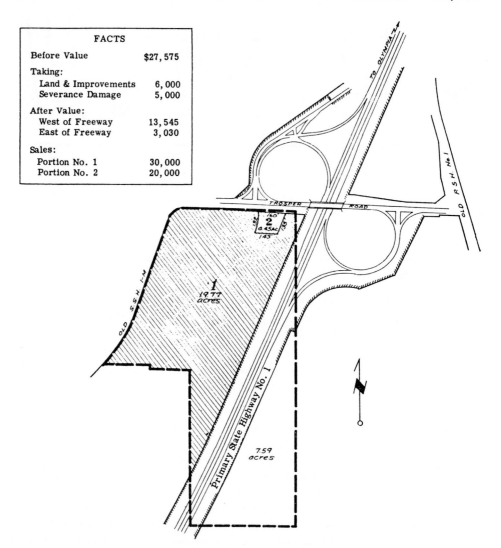

FACTS	
Before Value	$27,575
Taking:	
Land & Improvements	6,000
Severance Damage	5,000
After Value:	
West of Freeway	13,545
East of Freeway	3,030
Sales:	
Portion No. 1	30,000
Portion No. 2	20,000

Figure 21.2   Severance damage study interchange
Source: American Association of State Highway and Transportation Officials, *Acquisition for Right-of-Way* (Washington, D.C.: American Association of State, Highway and Transportation Officials, 1962), p. 660.

exceeded the value of the original 36 acres. Therefore, the appraisal provided unwarranted compensation to the landowner.

TREATMENT OF BENEFITS

Public improvements generally are intended to create benefits for the community as a whole, and specifically for the area in which the improvements are directly located. These benefits, although rarely mutually exclusive, must for purposes of court presentation be identified as follows:

1. Benefits which accrue to the community as a whole, and which in a few states such as Alabama, New Mexico, New York, North Carolina, South Carolina, Virginia, and Wisconsin, are permitted as "offset" against damages claimed as a result of the taking of private property. In other state jurisdictions, however, general benefits must be excluded from consideration in the determination of both the value of the part taken and in the loss of value suffered as a result of the taking by the remainder property.

2. Special benefits which accrue to the adjoining properties, and particularly to the property for which severance damages are claimed. In some states special benefits may be set off against both the value of the part taken and the damages claimed to the remainder property. In other states only the damages to the remainder or severed land may be reduced by the value of such special benefits as are directly related to the pubic improvements for which the taking of property was authorized.

CONSEQUENTIAL DAMAGE

Broadly speaking, *consequential damage* to property includes all damages suffered by a property owner, including the loss attributable to severance. In practice, however, the term has come to denote damage suffered by owners as a result of proposed public improvements where no real property is physically taken. A change in road grade, the construction of a bridge, the bypassing of a town, the relocation of a road, the construction of a sewage treatment plant—all are instances where neighboring or abutting property owners may suffer losses due to a diminution in the value of their property. Such losses, if ascribable to the exercise of the police power of government, are not compensable. It seems inequitable that some owners, where there is some taking of physical land, are compensated for consequential damages which contribute to a lowering of value of the remainder property, whereas other owners suffering like damage—but where there is no taking of property—are left without recourse for compensation. Often suit is brought by owners so affected, and their action at court is termed *inverse condemnation*. That is, a suit is instituted by them for relief under the laws of equity rather than by the condemnor as is the case in usual eminent domain court action. It is seldom that compensation is judicially ordered in such instances unless property losses can directly be linked to the physical taking of an owner's property.

EXCESS CONDEMNATION

Public improvements in general, and road improvements in particular, create benefits that often cause a substantial increase in the value of abutting and neighboring lands. When such value increments are substantial, an attempt is made, where permissible under law, to channel the benefits through public authority for the good of all within the state or community. Construction of parks, parkways, recreation centers, and planned public buildings are instances of this. In New York excess condemnation is permissible under state law. Thus, if it is estimated that the value benefits of a proposed garden parkway may extend up to 500 feet on either side of a 100-foot limited access roadbed, condemning authorities may acquire by eminent domain action a strip of land 1,100 feet in width. After completion of the parkway, the adjacent land may be leased for concessionary use by restaurant and service station chain operators, or the land may be resold to private owners at prices which may recoup the enhanced land value. Such gains may go far to offset the costs of construction, betterments, and capital improvements. The entire theory of excess condemnation is still in the development stage. Wisely used, this practice could prevent windfall gains by land speculators and place much-needed public improvement programs on a self-liquidating, pay-as-you-go financial basis.

THE EXPERT WITNESS

Increasingly, professional appraisers are called on to testify as expert witnesses in condemnation trials. Many facetious definitions of an "expert" are given. He has been called "a person 50 or more miles away from home," or, "someone who has learned to carry a briefcase with dignity." Such definitions are offered to belittle professional skill that usually can be acquired only through years of hard work and study, field experience, careful preparation, and training. The late George Schmutz, a leader in the appraisal field, defined an expert witness as

> one who is possessed of peculiar knowledge and experience that are not common to persons generally, and who has an opinion based upon such knowledge and experience that is peculiarly fitted for assisting the court, or jury, in determining an issue, such as the amount of damage measured in terms of dollars.[5]

This definition implies that the appraiser, as an expert, merely testifies as to his or her *opinion* of value. It is the court or jury that *determines* value. Appraisers must firmly keep this distinction in mind, or they will jeopardize their case by being accused of usurping the functions of both court and jury. Whereas an expert can express opinions and conclusions based on facts, laypersons as a rule are restricted to confining their testimony to recitation of statements concerning facts.

Before accepting an assignment to serve as an expert witness, the appraiser must make certain that he or she will be allowed to testify as an *independent* agent, free from bias and pressure to produce a "favorable" opinion. Unfortunately, many clients through their advocate attorneys shop around for "experts" whose judgment can be swayed. Professional appraisers are subject to censure on ethical and moral grounds if they serve as advocates rather than as free and independent analysts. Appraisal fees, too, should be based on time, expense, and degree of professional responsibility assumed, and should *not* be made contingent on the value reported, the amount of the verdict, or the winning of a case.

[5]George L. Schmutz, revised by Edwin M. Rams, *Condemnation Appraisal Handbook* (Englewood Cliffs, N.J.: Prentice-Hall, Inc., 1963), p. 360.

PRETRIAL PREPARATION

Testimony to be offered by an expert witness should be backed by a detailed appraisal report in which the value conclusions reached are fully documented. The report need not be and generally is not submitted as a court exhibit, and it cannot be demanded for inspection by the opposing counsel unless the report is referred to and used as a basis for testifying under direct examination. Comprehensive appraisal preparation permits the client's lawyer to become familiar with the factual details and the technical terminology peculiar to the case. Visual aids, where possible, should be employed. Subdivision maps, photographs, plot plans, market, sales, depreciated cost, and capitalized income summary sheets should be submitted for court exhibit and to facilitate one's data presentation at the time of the trial.

It is good, too, for the appraiser and trial attorney to agree on the order of data presentation, and to outline the questions and answers to be asked and given during direct examination. The sequence of questions asked generally falls into categories pertaining to

1. Qualifications of witness.
2. Examination of subject property.
3. Method used in arriving at an estimate of value.
4. Opinion of value.

Care should be taken to present in a simple but an impressive manner the qualifications of the expert witness. Even when opposing counsel stipulates that, in the interest of time, he or she accepts the witness as qualified to testify as an expert, the client's lawyer should nevertheless—if only for the court's benefit—qualify the witness as an expert in his or her field. It is the jury or court that sets the value, and the witness's testimony bears greater weight if extensive experience and knowledge in the field of property appraising back up the expert's findings.

Expert's Background

Qualifying questions should inform the court as to the expert's background and experience on such points as

1. Occupation.
2. Place and geographic extent of business or profession.
3. Education and degrees earned.
4. Membership in professional associations and state licensure.
5. Years of experience as an appraiser.
6. Types of clients served.
7. Types of properties appraised.
8. Appraisal courses completed or taught.
9. Publication of appraisal articles.

10. Experience in related fields of real estate brokerage and property management.

Demonstrated Familiarity with Property

The questions asked pertaining to the examination of the subject property should establish a thorough familiarity with the details of land and site improvements. Here the direct testimony should bring forth answers to such questions as

1. Please describe and clearly identify the subject property.
2. When did you last inspect the property?
3. Have you examined the building plans and specifications for estimating cost of reproduction of the improvements?
4. What is the age of the structure and what methods were used to determine accrued depreciation?
5. Have you compared the subject property with other similar properties that have sold in recent times?
6. Did you verify the income experience of this property? Have expenditures been verified?
7. What is the present and foreseeable future highest and best use of the subject property?

The next group of questions under direct examination explores the method used in arriving at an estimate of value. Since any testimony offered at this stage of the court proceedings is subject to rebuttal during cross-examination, the appraiser should be careful not to present details of estimating that later may be questioned to pinpoint errors of judgment or of facts. Care must also be taken so as not to testify that value was derived by the summation method; that is, an estimation of the value of the lot separately, to which was then added the value of the improvements less accrued depreciation. Land and buildings thereon are merged as an operating unit and any division of the whole into arbitrary parts in some state jurisdictions may be charged as constituting *hypothetical* appraising, which is contrary to accepted valuation theory and practice.

It is best to generalize and to explain in simple, nontechnical words the methods used in estimating value. The appraiser, for instance, may state: "I have examined the property; considered its location within the neighborhood; inspected the site; checked public records for legal description and zoning, deed restrictions, and assessment data; studied comparable sales and analyzed other general and specific factual data deemed essential to the formation of a professional opinion of value."

It is advisable, too, at this point for counsel to request that the witness describe and explain the comparable sales which he or she considered in formulating an estimate of market value. The witness should request permission to refer to a large subdivision or area map, which should be marked for identification as a court exhibit that jurors may study and to which they may refer during their deliberation. On this map the subject property should be prominently marked in color and the sale properties clearly numbered and marked in different colors. As each sale property is identified, the transaction price should be stated, the seller and buyer named, the date of sale specified, and the terms of sale at which the transaction closed given. The appraiser should make certain that each sale was verified with the purchaser, seller, or real estate broker as to the date of sale, transaction price, and terms of sale. Under no circumstances is it wise to rely on the state transfer tax as evidence of market prices at which the comparable sales exchanged. Even if this tax information posted in the deed book is considered accurate, the jury or court could be adversely influenced by lack of sale confirmation and by admission from the witness that revenue stamps can readily and legally be overstated to deliberately mislead those who rely on such evidence as a guide to market value. The witness may be discredited by failing to learn through interviewing a party to the sale that there were circumstances that distorted the price paid for the property.

The final category of questions concerns the *opinion* of value. Counsel as a rule asks: "As a result of your investigation, and by reason of your experience, have you formed an opinion of value for the subject [identify by name] property as of a specified date [date of taking]?" The witness, of course, answers in the affirmative. Counsel then may ask the witness to state his or her professional opinion concerning:

1. Value of the entire property as a whole.
2. Value of the part taken when considered as a part of the whole or as a separate parcel when such testimony is deemed advantageous to the interests of the condemnee.
3. Value of the remainder considered as part of the property as a whole.
4. Value of the remainder as a separate parcel after the taking of a part of the whole property.
5. Severance damage attributable to the remainder property, if any (item 3 less item 4).

DIRECT EXAMINATION

Where permissible, expert opinion may relate directly to the value of the entire property before the taking and the value of the remainder after the taking. This simplifies proceedings and yields directly the amount of compensation (the difference between before-and-after value as a result of condemnation) to which the owner is entitled to cover both the taking of a part of his or her property and the severance damages, if any, caused to the remainder. The appraiser must, of course, be prepared to testify as to the extent and possible effects of potential benefits caused by the public improvements, provided such questions are raised with the permission of the court (and undoubtedly over the objection of counsel for the condemnee).

Following the statement of value opinion, the expert witness generally is called on to give a reason for the conclusions reached either as to the value of the property as a whole or the allocation of this value to the parts and the severance damages resulting as a consequence. The answer merely calls for a summary of the important conclusions reached as a result of the appraisal investigation and a reemphasis of the sales comparison, depreciated cost, or capitalized income approaches which support the expert opinion.

CROSS-EXAMINATION

It is under cross-examination that the competence of the appraiser and his or her quality as an expert witness come to light. Many appraisers—although thorough, diligent, and accurate in their value findings—lack personality, experience on the witness stand, diction, and the ease that flows from a broad educational background. Such witnesses, through indecision, lack of confidence, and inability to think quickly on their feet may undo in a few minutes the work of many days or weeks of preparation. Other witnesses have an oversized ego which causes them to falter or to explode when—directly or by implication—their integrity or competence is questioned. Fear of seeing their findings exposed to ruthless analysis and their community reputation jolted by clever lawyers who go all out to destroy the effectiveness of their testimony keeps many otherwise qualified professional appraisers from accepting assignments that require their defense of these findings in court.

Yet those who enter the appraisal profession should be trained to take the stand as expert witnesses. As a first step, personal fear must be overcome and confidence acquired by taking due care in the process of estimating value as a means of aiding the court in reaching a just decision. The court and jurors usually frown on personal abuse and on tricky behavior unbecoming to the legal profession. Witnesses should remind themselves that their counsel is their partner, that unfair or misleading questions will be objected to when raised, and that the court and jurors are intelligent observers seeking truth rather than entertainment by a pyrotechnical display of legal skill.

The witness should listen to questions earnestly and carefully. Where the intent of the question is not clear, a clarification should be asked for. Answers should be short, simple, polite, and directed to the jury or court. When yes or no answers are requested, the witness should comply but ask permission to explain an answer when clarification is deemed essential. To illustrate, a series of yes or no questions may be as follows:

1. Are you representing the condemnee?
2. Have you served him or her professionally previously?
3. Are you paid by him or her for your services?
4. You would not be testifying without promise of pay, would you?
5. Your opinion of value is bought, is it not?

Certainly, questions 4 and 5 should be explained, since bias is implied that may influence the court's decision. To question 4 the witness should add that as a member of the appraisal profession he is not accustomed to volunteering his services, and that as an independent fee appraiser he gladly serves all who call on him for professional aid. To question 5 the witness, after a firm "no," should state that although his services are paid for, his opinion of value is based on facts gathered and studied during the course of the investigation, and that the findings and opinions stated would be the same no matter who engaged his services or agreed to defray professional costs and fees.

The cross-examiner must be expected to do all in his or her power to attempt to weaken or even discredit the value testimony of the opposing expert witness. Questions asked are generally designed to cast doubt where possible on such matters as

1. Adequacy of experience or education.
2. Familiarity with the subject property or subject area and neighborhood.
3. Adequate preparation or omission of relevant data.
4. Freedom from bias or incompetence.
5. Correctness of computations or validity of valuation premises.

In preparing his or her valuation report and in planning the sequence of testimony, the appraiser, with the aid of a lawyer, should anticipate probable questions that may be raised during cross-examination and be ready to offer clear and convincing answers. The following 13 guides can be invaluable as to the proper conduct of appraisers giving expert testimony in court:

1. Never lie or be evasive.
2. Never exaggerate the "highest and best use."
3. Never testify to a dictated appraisal.
4. Carefully examine and evaluate all comparable sales.
5. Avoid capitalizing hypothetical income on vacant land.
6. Judiciously exercise your right to explain your answer.
7. Avoid giving the false appearance of infallibility.
8. Always remember that you are an impartial witness, not an advocate.
9. Your testimony should be the same if appearing for the opposing party.
10. Think carefully before you respond to questions.
11. If you do not know the answer to a question, say so. In other words, neither guess nor answer questions in areas in which you have no expertise.
12. Always avoid allowing an opposing attorney to put words in your mouth. Restate his or her questions so that they accurately describe the issue being examined.
13. Always remember to control your temper on cross-examination and retain a sense of humor. Likewise, do not argue with opposing counsel.

SUMMARY

The power of eminent domain allows public bodies to acquire private property for the common benefit of the general public. In order to safeguard private property rights, state laws require that in the exercise of eminent domain (1) public necessity has been shown, (2) due process of law is followed, and (3) just compensation is paid to the owner. Unless the prescribed legal steps are followed carefully, due process may be declared lacking, and the condemnation action invalidated.

The payment of just compensation for the taking of property under eminent domain proceedings is assured by constitutional guaranty (Fifth and Fourteenth Amendments). *Just compensation* to a property owner generally includes payment for the value of the property taken plus any loss in value to the remainder property.

Market value, for eminent domain purposes, generally is defined as the highest price in terms of money that a property will bring if exposed for sale in the open market, allowing a reasonable time to find a purchaser who buys with knowledge of all the uses to which it is adapted and for which it is capable of being used.

Typically, there are six steps involved in estimating the total just compensation due a property owner in cases of partial takings. These steps are (1) value the whole property, (2) deduct the value of the part taken, which equals (3) value of the remainder, unaffected by the taking, (4) value the remainder as affected by the taking, (5) value the damages as measured by deducting item 4 from item 3, (6) which equals the total just compensation (item 2 plus item 5).

Two frequently used methods in the valuation of property where there is a partial taking are (1) the equal-unit-value method and (2) the before-and-after valuation method. Under the equal-unit-value method, the value of the part taken is intended to be in the same ratio that the physical units of land taken bear to the total land units of the property as a whole. The before-and-after method compares the property values before and after the effects of the partial taking, allowing for the net difference between the benefits and damages.

Severance damage is a loss in value to the part of a property remaining after a taking as compared with the value of the remainder when considered as a part of the whole property. This form of damage may result from change to a lower highest and best use, restoration expenses, increased operating costs or reduced property income, or change in road grade and impaired accessibility.

Consequential damages are a loss in property value that may occur through the exercise of police power. In such instances, no compensation is due the property owner. Some government agencies utilize *excess condemnation* as a means of acquiring land in excess of the actual need of a right of way as a means of recouping part of the cost of right of way construction. The excess lands are sold by the agency to other parties.

Appraisers are often called upon to give expert testimony in courts of law in eminent domain cases. Prior to presenting such testimony, the appraiser must be thoroughly familiar with the subject property as well as with all factors affecting its value. There are two phases in these court proceedings. First, the appraiser undergoes direct examination by his or her own attorney. This phase is followed by cross-examination by an attorney who represents the opposing side in the case. This attorney will endeavor to discredit the appraiser as a witness by raising questions about the adequacy of his or her valuation education, training or experience, lack of familiarity with the property or local market, inadequate appraisal report preparation, or detection of errors in computations or valuation premises.

REVIEW QUESTIONS

1. Explain why public bodies have been given the power of eminent domain.
2. List eight legal requirements that generally must be followed by governmental bodies to protect private property rights when the power of eminent domain is used.
3. Define the term "just compensation."
4. Explain how the conventional definition of market value generally prohibits the use of eminent domain conveyances as valid indicators of market value.
5. Give your interpretation of the court-proved rules used to establish economic unity of a condemned property.
6. Briefly explain the before-and-after rule for valuing land for eminent domain purposes.
7. How do consequential damages relate to just compensation for a property owner?

READING AND STUDY REFERENCES

American Association of State Highway and Transportation Officials. *Acquisition for Right-of-Way.* Washington, D.C.: Association Committee on Right-of-Way, 1962.

BAEN, JOHN S., THERESA H. WALLER, and NEIL G. WALLER. "Real Estate Professionals as Expert Witnesses," *The Appraisal Journal* 56, no. 1 (January 1988), pp. 80–88.

BAILEY, DONALD. "Appraisal of Real Estate for Purposes of Condemnation," *The Real Estate Appraiser and Analyst* (Summer 1989), pp. 10–17.

CHRISTENSEN, BARBARA. "How to Be a Winning Witness," *The Real Estate Appraiser and Analyst* 47, no. 3 (Fall 1981), pp. 23–24.

COREY, EDWARD A. "Easement Valuation Along Highway Frontage," *The Real Estate Appraiser and Analyst* (Spring 1989), pp. 15–18.

EPLEY, DONALD R., and JAMES H. BOYKIN. Chapter 19, *Basic Income Property Appraisal.* Reading, Mass.: Addison-Wesley Publishing Co., Inc., 1983.

HUXTABLE, RICHARD L. "Eminent Domain Is Traced to Biblical Times," *Right of Way* (May 1979), pp. 24–27.

KELLOUGH, W. R. "Impact Analysis of Electrical Transmission Lines," *Right of Way* (December 1980), pp. 19–25.

KENNER, GIDEON. "Remedies in Inverse Condemnation: A New Ball Game?" *Right of Way* (July 1979), pp. 9–10.

ROBERTS, THOMAS L. "Valuation of Project Enhancement in Eminent Domain," *The Appraisal Journal* 50, no. 2 (April 1982), pp. 220–227.

WISE, FLOYD. "Steps Given for Trial Preparation," *Right of Way* (April 1981), pp. 20–22.

22
Appraisal Report Writing

Learning Objectives

After reading this chapter, you should be able to:

- Understand the steps involved in planning and performing an appraisal assignment
- Discuss several purposes for which appraisals are made
- Explain the logic of the value reconciliation stage of an appraisal report
- Outline the essential parts of a narrative appraisal report
- Appreciate professional standards for appraisal reports
- Comparatively discuss the similarities and differences between a narrative and preprinted form report
- Improve your ability to write an appraisal report

During the past half-century, real estate appraising has developed into a well-defined practice engaged in professionally by thousands of qualified appraisers. Owners and investors in real property—including banking institutions, insurance companies, government agencies, brokerage firms, and commercial and industrial institutions—have come to rely on this profession as a reliable guide to property value. Annually, thousands of businesspeople attend appraisal seminars and extension courses conducted under the auspices of professional real estate valuation organizations. With the advent of state licensing requirements, even more appraisers have returned to the classroom in order to obtain their license or certification. An ever-increasing number of colleges and universities offer courses in real property valuation for degree credit and on an extension and short-course basis.

APPRAISAL PROCESS

Real estate appraising is patterned in accordance with well-defined ground rules, which as a whole are contained in an orderly plan of action known as the *appraisal process*. It is with the aid of this process that the professional appraiser seeks to reach a sound conclusion or estimate of value. The orderly steps and considerations of the appraisal process include the following:

---

1. Determine the appraisal problem.
2. Determine the purpose which the appraisal is to serve.
3. Secure a full and accurate description of the property to be appraised.
4. Make a preliminary estimate of the time, labor, and expense involved in the completion of the appraisal assignment and secure a written request for the appraisal services in which should be stated the fee agreed on for services to be rendered.
5. Plan the appraisal, assign the work details, and assemble the essential appraisal data.
6. Make a study of the general economic, social, and political influences that bear on the value of the property to be appraised.
7. Analyze the appraisal data and reach a value conclusion under each of the following approaches to value: depreciated cost, sales comparison, and capitalized income.
8. Reconcile the value findings.
9. Submit the appraisal report.

The first and most important step in the process is to *determine the appraisal problem*. Some owners, buyers, or investors are not only interested in obtaining an accurate estimate of value but also expect information regarding ownership or title interests, rights of tenants, property encroachments, claims of mortgagees and other lienors including tax liens, conditions shown by accurate survey, code violations, and soil contamination. The appraiser should not accept the valuation assignment unless the client clearly understands the limits of the appraiser's professional responsibility and the area of study to which his or her specialized knowledge is confined. The appraiser, in essence, practices in the field of land economics—for value is in fact the heart of economics. Appraisers should not consider themselves lawyers, architects, builders, engineers, soil scientists, surveyors, or title abstractors. If their clients request information in these specialized fields, authority should be secured to engage such qualified experts as the problem necessitates, arranging for independent compensation of the outside firms or individuals called on for the specified service. Unless otherwise stated, appraisers must assume (1) that a title is held in fee simple and that no legal claims, easements, restrictions, or other rights affect the title or use of the property except those stated to the appraiser by the client; (2) that the title and valuation are subject to corrections which an accurate survey of the property may reveal; (3) that the sale of the property will be on a cash or cash-equivalent basis, since either good or cumbersome financial arrangements do affect the price at which the property may sell in the market; and (4) that no responsibility can be taken by the appraiser for matters legal in character.

Some valuation problems, too, require special owner or tenant cooperation or aid from neighboring property owners, or users. Where such is the case, the assignment must be accepted contingent on the cooperation of the parties involved. Only when the problem is clearly defined, and its limits are known and understood, should an appraiser proceed with the subsequent steps of the appraisal process.

Next, it is essential that the appraiser be provided with a clear statement as to the *purpose that the appraisal is to serve*. Even though only one value can exist for market purposes at a given time and place, different valuation purposes may warrant greater stress being given to one of the three value approaches—or the inclusion of special appraisal details in the valuation report. It can readily be seen that different interests are served if the valuation is for any one of the following purposes:

1. Purchase, sale, or exchange of property.
2. Fire insurance or hazard underwriting.
3. Valuation for utility rate determination.
4. Investment or mortgage loan security.
5. Inheritance tax, property tax, or assessments.
6. Inventory or accrued depreciation.
7. Equity appraising or financing.

As different interests are served, different valuation points should be emphasized in an appraisal report. For instance, a report for fire insurance purposes would principally stress replacement costs as evidence of value, and the report would detail with great accuracy the construction features and material elements that make up the property improvements. For mortgage loan purposes, on the other hand, property income, its remaining economic life, and its ready marketability would receive major stress—with replacement cost, less depreciation, merely serving as a ceiling of value beyond which lenders, as a rule, are restricted or unwilling to go.

To avoid possible misunderstanding or claims that the purpose of the appraisal influenced the value found, the professional appraiser should not only include a clear statement of the purpose that the appraisal is to serve but also a clear-cut definition of the *value* as used in his or her report. Failure to do so may cause serious misunderstanding and, where warranted, even disciplinary action under the standards of professional practice to which all professional appraisers subscribe. The date of the appraisal, too, should be fixed and prominently stated. Values are subject to constant shifts because the laws of supply and demand operate in a dynamic society which experiences sudden and often unexpected changes. Then, too, value for specific purposes such as eminent domain may have to be stated as of a given day in the past.

A *full and accurate description of the property* is next in order. Not only must the exact limits of the physical area under appraisal be known, but the full legal property description must be cited in order to leave no doubt as to the precise location and identity of the real property covered in the valuation report. Although various kinds of property descriptions may be used, it is best to rely on the one shown in the last deed of record. Should property analysis disclose encumbrances that limit in any way an owner's rights under fee simple title or impede the utilization of the property under a program of highest and best use, then such financial encumbrances on ownership or use limitations must be clearly identified and the impact on value of such limitations made clear to the reader of the appraisal report.

Before proceeding with the valuation assignment, it is essential that the appraiser make a *preliminary but careful estimate of the time, labor, and expense involved in completing the appraisal request.* This preliminary estimate should serve as a guide in setting a fair appraisal fee commensurate with the responsibility and valuation services to be provided. Never should the fee be a percentage of the value findings. Where the recommended fee, for instance, is one-half of one percent of property value, the warranted appraisal fee on a $20,000 property would be $100. This method of service fee determination, however, appears illogical and is subject to censure on ethical grounds. The temptations would indeed be great to boost value findings as a means of increasing appraisal fees. It is unethical for appraisers to accept an engagement to appraise a property if the employment or fee is contingent on reporting a predetermined or specified amount of value, or is otherwise contingent upon any finding to be reported.

Once a fair fee has been ascertained, the client should be so informed. If the fee, as generally is the case, proves acceptable, the appraiser should request *written confirmation of the professional assignment and the fee* should be stipulated in the letter of request or should be noted by the appraiser in his or her letter of acceptance. The fee seldom covers any appearance or testimony by the appraiser before a court, commission, or other body; to avoid later dispute, this should be clearly understood at the time of engagement and stated in the appraisal report itself.

When the appraisal assignment and service fee are mutually agreed on, steps are taken to *plan the work details and to assemble the essential appraisal data.* Much of the necessary general data pertaining to social, political, and economic influences on the value are directly obtainable from office (appraisal plant) files or may be taken from previous appraisal reports in which the general value comments are deemed sufficiently recent and applicable to be of interest to the case at hand. Automated data retrieval systems have greatly enhanced this phase of the appraisal process in recent years. General data bearing on the value of the subject property and not available from the appraisal plant should be secured whenever possible from primary sources. Data applicable to the site, improvements, and immediate environment must be obtained through personal inspection and through a detailed inventory of the neighborhood, site, and improvement data that bear directly or indirectly on property values. Many forms have been devised by private firms and governmental agencies to aid the appraiser in the laborious task of gathering field data to ensure that no important matter pertaining to the property is inadvertently omitted.

VALUE RECONCILIATION

Once the general and specific data applicable to the subject property are assembled, the appraiser proceeds with an analysis of the data under each of the value approaches—market sales comparison, capitalized income, and depreciated cost. Although the importance of each of the three approaches to value may vary, depending on the kind of property and the purpose that the appraisal is to serve, nevertheless, it is important to consider each approach to value as a separate entity under the appraisal process and to reach independent value conclusions in relation to replacement costs less accrued depreciation, market sales of comparable properties, and capitalization of net operating income derived from property operation under typical ownership and management. These independent but related indications of value must then be reconciled (correlated) as the appraiser's considered judgment of final value estimate.

Reconciliation of the value estimates should under no circumstances be considered as a mathematical process involving mere averaging of the estimates derived under the independent value approaches. Rather, *reconciliation* is the careful weighing of the initial value results on the basis of accuracy and completeness of data and in light of market conditions that prevail on the date of the appraisal. Whenever significant differences exist in the estimates derived under the three value approaches, the appraiser, as a first step, should review the data assembled under each approach and check the mathematical procedures that underlie the answer. Under the depreciated cost approach, for instance, a recheck should be made of the size of the structure and the quantity of square or cubic feet reported. The cost factor, too, may be in error or inapplicable to the type and kind of structure under appraisal. More likely than not, the error may rest in the derivation of the amount of accrued depreciation. The economic age may have been misstated or an omission may have been made in the listing and weighing of the causes that account for total accrued depreciation. Under the sales comparison approach, judgment errors are easily committed. The transaction prices of the comparable properties may not reflect true property values, or the properties selected may not represent real comparability. Too, the judgment weights assigned may warrant a careful recheck. The capitalized income approach is also fraught with appraising pitfalls. The revenue flow may be over- or understated, allowances for vacancy and collection losses may have been omitted, operating expenses may not reflect operation under competent and efficient management, the remaining life of the property may be in error—and so may be the rate of capitalization—which especially warrants close inspection as to its appropriateness. The application of a rate of 8 percent instead of 9 percent may not appear serious to the uninformed, but the value results would differ by approximately 11 to 12.5 percent depending on which rate is the appropriate one.

If, after carefully rechecking the steps in each approach, significant differences still exist in the value estimates, the appraiser must consider the results in the light of the problem and the purposes that the appraisal is to serve. Thus, for mortgage loan purposes, the income-producing capacity of the property is all-important. For inheritance tax, condemnation, or sale purposes, the market data (provided the market is sufficiently active) should be given greatest stress. For fire insurance, the replacement cost may prove all-important. It is in the reconciliation of the value estimates where there can be no substitute for the experience, skill, and judgment of the appraiser. It is the human factor in the equation that causes real estate appraising to be more of a skilled art than an objective science.

THE APPRAISAL REPORT

The final step in the appraisal process is the preparation of a comprehensive appraisal report. At one time an oral opinion or a letter of valuation sufficed. Such practices, however, are frowned on today and professional appraisers generally furnish their clients with a narrative or appropriate form appraisal report in which their value findings, along with the contingent conditions on which the appraisal is based, are clearly set forth. No particular style of report is always recommended. A good report, nevertheless, is one in which the data presented are so convincingly analyzed that the reader inevitably is led to the same value conclusions as those reached by the appraiser. As a rule, the data should be sufficiently self-explanatory to permit the reader or client to follow the appraiser's reasoning. In order for this to happen, the appraiser first must clearly understand what needs to be said in the report.

Figure 22.1 (page 436) lists essentials for a well-written and comprehensive appraisal report.

PROFESSIONAL STANDARDS FOR APPRAISAL REPORTS

The most universally accepted professional appraisal standards are the *Uniform Standards of Professional Appraisal Practice* which are published by the Appraisal Foundation. Under Standard 2, it is asserted that "In reporting the results of a real property appraisal an appraiser must communicate each analysis, opinion, and conclusion in a manner that is not misleading."[1] A summary of the five standards rules for this standard follows:

2-1 Written or oral real property appraisal reports must:
  (a) *Clearly and accurately set forth the appraisal in a manner that will not be misleading.* Since most reports are used and relied upon by third parties, communications considered adequate by the appraiser's client may not be sufficient. An appraiser must take extreme care to make certain that his or her reports will not be misleading in the marketplace or to the public.
  (b) *Contain sufficient information to enable the person(s) who receive or rely on the report to understand it properly.* All reports, both written and oral, must clearly and accurately present the analyses, opinions, and conclusions of the appraiser in sufficient depth and detail to address adequately the significance of the specific appraisal problem.

---

[1]The Appraisal Foundation, *Uniform Standards of Professional Appraisal Practice* (Washington, D.C.: The Appraisal Foundation, 1990), p. B-15.

Section I: Introduction

1. A letter of transmittal in which the value findings and the effective date of the appraisal are recorded. This letter, too, should state the number of pages contained in the report in order to forestall possible deletion of important pages or insertion of data by unauthorized persons.
2. A table of contents which permits quick reference to particular report material.
3. Two clear and preferably large (8-by-10 inch) photographs showing front and side views of the property appraised.
4. A statement as to the purpose of the appraisal and definition of the term *value* as used by the appraiser.

Section II: Description of Relevant Facts

5. A statement of the property rights appraised.
6. A statement of the highest and best use of the property as if unimproved, and whether the present improvements meet this use.
7. An executive summary of important conclusions, particularly those in which the report reader has a prime interest: taxes, assessments, operating income, operating expenses, and value.
8. A complete and accurate legal description.
9. An analysis of the general social, political, and economic influences on value, particularly in reference to the region, the city, and the neighborhood.
10. A factual presentation of site, building, and property data. An inventory should be presented of the important site utilities and building construction features.

Section III: Analyses and Conclusions

11. An explanation of the appraisal process and the methods by which the value conclusions were derived.
12. An analysis of the depreciated cost approach to value, followed by schedules showing unit cost derivations and depreciation calculations.
13. An analysis of the sales comparison approach to value. Separate comparative tables should be included showing sales considered in arriving at the market value of (1) the land and (2) the property as a unified whole.
14. An analysis of the capitalized income approach to value, showing sources of revenue, allowances due to anticipated vacancies and collection losses, operating expenses, rates of capitalization, and the process employed in converting the anticipated income into a present sum of value.
15. A reconciliation of the value estimates derived under the cost, market, and income approaches to value. The weights, if any, assigned to each approach or the methods of selection of one estimate in preference to another should be clearly set forth and explained.

16. A statement of limiting conditions in which the appraiser sets forth the areas—as in fields of surveying, engineering, or law—in which he or she disclaims liability.

17. A certification of value in which the appraiser professionally warrants his or her findings and disclaims any personal interest in the property that could possibly influence his or her value findings.

18. A statement of qualifications of the appraiser, setting forth briefly his or her educational, professional background, and experience qualifications allowing him or her to render value opinions.

Section IV: Addenda

19. Addenda material containing some or all of the following: location sketch of the property, a plot plan, floor plan, and a subdivision map and city map on which markings indicate the subject property in relation to important business and civic centers; also, where deemed of interest, additional photographs of neighboring properties and street views, showing improvements north, south, east, and west of the subject property.

Figure 22.1   Essentials for a narrative appraisal report

(c) *Clearly and accurately disclose any extraordinary assumption or limiting condition that directly affects the appraisal and indicate its impact on value.* Examples of extraordinary assumptions or conditions might include items such as the execution of a pending lease agreement, atypical financing, or completion of on-site or off-site improvements. In a written report the disclosure would be required in conjunction with statements of each opinion or conclusion that is affected.

2-2 Each written real property appraisal report must:

(a) *Identify and describe the real estate being appraised.*

(b) *Identify the real property interest being appraised.*

These two requirements are essential elements in any report. Identifying the real estate can be accomplished by any combination of a legal description, address, map reference, copy of a survey or map, property sketch, and/or photographs. A property sketch and photographs also provide some description of the real estate in addition to written comments about the physical attributes of the real estate. Identifying the real property rights being appraised requires a direct statement substantiated as needed by copies or summaries of legal descriptions or other documents setting forth any encumbrances.

(c) *State the purpose of the appraisal.*

(d) *Define the value to be estimated.*

(e) *Set forth the effective date of the appraisal and the date of the report.*

These three requirements call for clear disclosure to the reader of a report the "why, what, and when" surrounding the appraisal. The purpose of the appraisal is used to include both the task involved and the rationale for the appraisal. Defining the value to be estimated requires both an appropriately referenced definition and any comments needed to clearly indicate to the reader how the definition is being applied. The effective date of the appraisal establishes the context for the value estimate, whereas the date of the report indicates whether the perspective of the appraiser on the market conditions as of the effective date of the appraisal was prospective, current, or retrospective.

(f) *Describe the extent of the process of collecting, confirming, and reporting data.* This requirement is designed to protect third parties whose reliance on an appraisal report may be affected by the extent of the appraiser's investigation, that is, the process of collecting, confirming, and reporting data.

(g) *Set forth all assumptions and limiting conditions that affect the analyses, opinions, and conclusions.* It is suggested that assumptions and limiting conditions be grouped together in an identified section of the report.

(h) *Set forth the information considered, the appraisal procedures followed, and the reasoning that supports the analyses, opinions, and conclusions.* This requirement calls for the appraiser to summarize the data considered and the procedures that were followed. Each item must be addressed in the depth and detail required by its significance to the appraisal. The appraiser must be certain that sufficient information is provided so that the client, the users of the report, and the public will understand it and will not be misled or confused. The substantive content of the report, not its size, determines its compliance with this specific reporting guideline.

(i) *Set forth the appraiser's opinion of the highest and best use of the real estate, when such an opinion is necessary and appropriate.* A written report shall contain a statement of the appraiser's opinion as to the highest and best use of the real estate, unless an opinion as to highest and best use is unnecessary, for example, insurance valuation or value in use appraisals. If an opinion as to highest and best use is required, the reasoning in support of the opinion must also be included.

(j) *Explain and support the exclusion of any of the usual valuation approaches.*

(k) *Set forth any additional information that may be appropriate to show compliance with, or clearly identify and explain permitted departures from, the requirements of Standard 1* (see Chapter 23). This requirement calls for a written appraisal report or other written communication concerning the results of an appraisal to contain sufficient information to indicate that the appraiser complied with the requirements of Standard 1, including the requirements governing any permitted departures from the appraisal guidelines. The amount of detail required will vary with the significance of the information to the appraisal.

Information considered and analyzed in compliance with Standards Rule 1-5 (see Chapter 23) is significant information that deserves comment in any report. If such information is unobtainable, comment on the efforts undertaken by the appraiser to obtain the information is required.

(l) *Include a signed certification in accordance with Standards Rule 2-3.*

2-3 *Each written real property appraisal report must contain a certification that is similar in content to the following form:*

I certify that, to the best of my knowledge and belief,:
- The statements of fact contained in this report are true and correct.
- The reported analyses, opinions, and conclusions are limited only by the reported assumptions and limiting conditions, and are my personal, unbiased professional analyses, opinions, and conclusions.
- I have no (or the specified) present or prospective interest in the property that is the subject of this report, and I have no (or the specified) personal interest or bias with respect to the parties involved.
- My compensation is not contingent upon the reporting of a predetermined value or direction in value that favors the cause of the client, the amount of the value estimate, the attainment of a stipulated result, or the occurrence of a subsequent event.
- My analyses, opinions, and conclusions were developed, and this report has been prepared, in conformity with the Uniform Standards of Professional Appraisal Practice.
- I have (or have not) made a personal inspection of the property that is the subject of this report. (If more than one person signs the report, this certification must clearly specify which individuals did and which individuals did not make a personal inspection of the appraised property.)
- No one provided significant professional assistance to the person signing this report. (If there are exceptions, the name of each individual providing significant professional assistance must be stated.)

2-4 *To the extent that it is both possible and appropriate, each oral real property appraisal report (including expert testimony) must address the substantive matters set forth in Standards Rule 2-2.* In addition to complying with the requirements of Standards Rule 2-1, an appraiser making an oral report must use his or her best efforts to address each of the substantive matters in Standards Rule 2-2. Testimony of an appraiser concerning his or her analyses, opinions, and conclusions is an oral report in which the appraiser must comply with the requirements of this standards rule.

2-5 *An appraiser who signs a real property appraisal report prepared by another, even under the label of "review appraiser," must accept full responsibility for the contents of the report.* This requirement is directed to the employer or supervisor signing the report of an employee or subcontractor. The employer or supervisor signing the report is as responsible as the individual preparing the appraisal for the content and conclusions of the appraisal and the report. Using a conditional label next to the signature of the employer or supervisor or signing a form report on the line over the words "review appraiser" does not exempt that individual from adherence to these standards.[2]

SUGGESTIONS FOR IMPROVED REPORT WRITING

A hallmark of professionalism is a well-crafted work product. For real estate appraisers, this product is valuation counsel which usually is presented in the form of a written report. This section contains suggestions for improving appraisal reports. Ideas are offered on recognizing frequently misused words and phrases and how to simplify expressions, reduce wordiness, use unbiased language, and eliminate redundancies.

Frequently Misused Words and Phrases

Misused	*Correct*
and etc.	etc.
different than	different from
He ought to surely decide	He ought surely to decide

(This is a split infinitive where an adverb is improperly placed between *to* and its verb.)

in back of	behind
inside of	within
irregardless	regardless
nowhere near	not nearly
those kind of sales	that kind or those kinds of sales

Misused words

accept (to take)

except (to omit)

affect (to influence)

effect (result)

between (use when discussing two items)

among (use when discussing three or more things)

capital (money or wealth)

capitol (legislative building or statehouse)

complement (something that completes)

compliment (to flatter)

farther (refers to distance)

further (additionally or moreover)

fewer (refers to things that can be counted)

less (refers to things that cannot be counted)

it's (contraction of it is)

[2]This section is based on Standard 2 of the *Uniform Standards of Professional Appraisal Practice.* Permission to use this material granted by the Appraisal Foundation.

its (possessive pronoun)
principal (sum of money or head of a school)
principle (a basic law or rule)
respectively (in the order named)
respectfully (showing respect)
site (place, such as homesite)
sight (a view or to view)
cite (quoting an authoritative source)
stationary (immovable)
stationery (writing paper)
than (expresses a choice)
then (at that time)

Simplify word or expression

Complex	Simple
ascertain	find out or learn
endeavor	try
execute	do
henceforth	after this
inundate	flood
subsequent	later
terminate	end
transpire	happen
utilize	use
viz	namely

Reduce wordiness

Wordy	Concise
after the conclusion of	after
arrive at	reach
at the present time	now or at present
Attached please find	Attached is
each of these	each
effects an improvement	improves
for a total of	for
fully cognizant of	aware
in a careful manner	carefully
inasmuch as	since
in connection with	by, for, in
in the neighborhood of	about or approximately
in view of the fact that	because or since
is of the opinion that	believe, judge, or estimate
it is recommended that consideration be given to	I recommend that

not in a position	cannot or unable
subsequent to	after
under consideration	considering or considered
whether or not	whether

Use unbiased language

Avoid	*Preferred term*
authoress	author
foreman	supervisor
lady executive	executive
man hours	staff hours
man made	manufactured or fabricated
manpower	personnel

Eliminate redundancies

Redundancy	*Simplified*
and moreover	moreover
assemble together	assemble
basic fundamentals	fundamentals
brown in color	brown
close proximity	close
consensus of opinion	consensus
depreciated in value	depreciated
exact same	same
few in number	few
important essentials	essentials
positively certain	certain
surrounded on all sides	surrounded
true facts	facts[3]

THE DEMONSTRATION APPRAISAL REPORT

Students of real estate appraising at many colleges and candidates who seek professional affiliation with such organizations as the Appraisal Institute are required to submit, in partial fulfillment of prerequisites for the respective professional membership designations,[4] fully documented narrative appraisal re-

[3]Several of the examples used in this section were taken from the references listed at the end of the chapter.

[4]Professional appraisal designations are awarded by the following organizations: American Society of Appraisers, Appraisal Institute, American Society of Farm Managers and Rural Appraisers, Appraisal Institute of Canada, International Association of Assessing Officers, International Right of Way Association, National Association of Independent Fee Appraisers, and National Society of Real Estate Appraisers.

ports of various types of real property. This is required to demonstrate their competence and soundness of judgment in the compilation and interpretation of valuation data and the logical presentation of such data in report form.

The difference between a demonstration and a professional narrative appraisal report lies mainly in the requirement that all data sources, sequence, and analysis of pertinent facts and value conclusions must be documented and justified in a demonstration appraisal report. Whereas the professional appraiser may, on the basis of experience and reputation, reach certain conclusions or make certain assumptions, the student appraiser must follow step-by-step orderly reporting and miss no link in welding the chain of value conclusions. A professional appraiser may categorically stipulate that a capitalization rate of 10 percent is deemed applicable to the subject property, or that the cost of reproduction of building improvement is estimated at $90.00 per square foot, and offer no evidence to support these statements. It nevertheless is advisable that professional reports contain such supporting data. A student appraiser cannot rely on personal skill, maturity of judgment, or years of appraisal experience to justify assumptions or conclusions. The reader of the demonstration report must literally be led along the path of the appraisal process and given an opportunity to judge the technical skill of the writer on the basis of sufficiency of report data, soundness of data interpretation, and extent to which the value conclusions reached are warranted.

NARRATIVE APPRAISAL REPORT

Appraisers are often required to prepare narrative appraisal reports such as presented in Appendix II. These reports customarily are written for nonresidential appraisals. Well prepared reports are characterized by

1. Being logical and orderly.
2. Being clear, direct, yet comprehensive.
3. Being readable.
4. Avoiding use of the first person.
5. Using appropriate words, summaries, and illustrations.
6. Using positive rather than noncommittal language.
7. Using thorough research that is convincingly and accurately presented.
8. Using language that is readily understood by and inoffensive to the client.

It is highly desirable to have another person proofread an appraiser's report. A second person is more likely to spot arithmetical errors as well as unclear phrases and omissions. In writing, the appraiser should always concentrate on "expressing" rather than "impressing." Suggestions for reports were offered in the previous section.

LETTER OR ABBREVIATED REPORT

A letter report generally fails to qualify as a true appraisal report because it does not include the steps leading to the appraiser's value conclusion. Even a form report contains this background information. Often the motivation for preparing such "reports" is that the client wants a report at the lowest possible cost. After having received such a report, the client may find it unusable for loan or sale purposes. In effect, he or she is told that it is inferior, which casts an unfavorable light on both the appraiser and the profession. Thus this form of appraisal digest is discouraged. If, for some reason, it is used, the appraiser should retain in his or her files all the pertinent calculations and analysis that would support the reported value and permit writing of a full narrative or form report.

This type of report may be used when a client wants a value update from a previous, fully documented appraisal. The updated report should include by reference all of the background data, market conditions, assumptions, and limiting conditions contained in the original report which was prepared for the same client.

According to the Uniform Standards of Professional Appraisal Practice, an appraiser, before entering into an assignment for appraisal services, should carefully consider the purpose of the report. Great caution should be taken to determine whether the scope of the appraisal service will be so limited that the resulting analysis, opinion, or conclusion will tend to mislead or confuse the client, the users of the report, or the public.

LETTER OF OPINION

This is not a genuine appraisal report, but instead, it is a preliminary opinion based on limited analysis. The value estimate usually is expressed as a range of values. A difficulty with the letter report is that the reported value range may be altered upon a more thorough investigation. If used, the appraiser must clearly indicate that this is a (1) preliminary finding, and (2) it may change once a complete appraisal has been prepared.

SHORT-FORM APPRAISAL REPORTING

Government agencies and lending institutions prefer standardized form reports in connection with routine appraising of properties offered as loan collateral. Although such forms leave little room for justification of appraisal judgment, uniformity of data reporting facilitates loan processing and supervision on the basis of comparability of report features in relation to minimum standards that properties must meet to prove acceptable. An appraisal form widely used for reporting on residential properties by mortgage lenders is the Uniform Residential Appraisal Report (see Figure 22.2).

In using this standardized appraisal form, the appraiser has an opportunity to include additional explanatory material such as a dwelling's floor plan. Notice

UNIFORM RESIDENTIAL APPRAISAL REPORT   File No. 481

Property Description & Analysis

SUBJECT

Property Address	Census Tract 1004.03
City Chester County Chesterfield State VA Zip Code 23831	
Legal Description	
Owner/Occupant Vacant Map Ref. 58-C-24	
Sale Price $ N/A Date of Sale 8/91	PROP RIGHTS APPRAISED
Loan charges/concessions paid by seller $ 0	X Fee Simple
R.E. Taxes $ 2,158.20 Tax Year 1991 HOA $/Mo. 10.00	Leasehold
Lender/Client	Condominium (HUD/VA)
	X De Minimus PUD

LENDER DISCRETIONARY USE
Sale Price $ ___ Date ___ Mortgage Amount $ ___ Mortgage Type ___ Discount Points and Other Concessions Paid by Seller $ ___ Source ___

NEIGHBORHOOD

				NEIGHBORHOOD ANALYSIS	Good	Avg.	Fair	Poor
LOCATION	Urban	X Suburban	Rural	Employment Stability	X			
BUILT UP	Over 75%	X 25-75%	Under 25%	Convenience to Employment		X		
GROWTH RATE	Rapid	X Stable	Slow	Convenience to Shopping	X			
PROPERTY VALUES	Increasing	X Stable	Declining	Convenience to Schools			X	
DEMAND/SUPPLY	Shortage	In Balance	X Over Supply	Adequacy of Public Transportation			X	
MARKETING TIME	Under 3 Mos.	3-6 Mos.	X Over 6 Mos.	Recreation Facilities	X			

PRESENT LAND USE %: Single Family 65, 2-4 Family 0, Multi-family 5, Commercial 10, Industrial 20, Vacant 0

LAND USE CHANGE: Not likely; X Likely; In process; To:

PREDOMINANT OCCUPANCY: Owner; X Tenant; Vacant (0-5%); X Vacant (over 5%)

SINGLE FAMILY HOUSING: PRICE $(000) 175 Low, 750 High, Predominant 225 — AGE (yrs) New, 3, 1

Adequacy of Utilities X; Property Compatibility X; Protection from Detrimental Conditions X(Fair); Police & Fire Protection X; General Appearance of Properties X; Appeal to Market X(Poor)

Note: Race or the racial composition of a neighborhood are not considered reliable appraisal factors.

COMMENTS: Rivers Bend on the James is a planned unit development of residential, commercial and industrial uses located in the Enon area of Chesterfield off Rt 10. There is easy access to the I-295 extension, Chester and Hopewell. Initial sales activity has been steady with recreational facilities including golf course, tennis courts, pool and clubhouse planned.

SITE

Dimensions 95.0'x34.51'225.69'x113.95'x195.0'
Site Area Irregular
Zoning Classification Residential
HIGHEST & BEST USE: Present Use Yes

Corner Lot No   Zoning Compliance Yes   Other Use No

Topography Level; Size Average for area; Shape Irregular; Drainage Average; View Average; Landscaping Average; Driveway Gravel; Apparent Easements Normal utility; FEMA Flood Hazard Yes* No X; FEMA Map/Zone

UTILITIES: Electricity X, Gas X, Water X, Sanitary Sewer X, Storm Sewer X

SITE IMPROVEMENTS: Street Asphalt (Public X), Curb/Gutter None, Sidewalk None, Street Lights None, Alley None

COMMENTS (Apparent adverse easements, encroachments, special assessments, slide areas, etc.): Mostly open site with established lawn and mature hardwoods - no adverse conditions noted.

IMPROVEMENTS

GENERAL DESCRIPTION: Units One, Stories Two, Type (Det/Att) Detached, Design (Style) 2 Story, Existing Yes, Proposed No, Under Construction No, Age (Yrs.) New, Effective Age (Yrs.) New

EXTERIOR DESCRIPTION: Foundation Brk & Blk, Exterior Walls Brk/Frame, Roof Surface Cedar, Gutters & Dwnspts. None, Window Type DH Wood, Storm Sash Insulated, Screens No, Manufactured House No

FOUNDATION: Slab, Crawl Space Yes, Basement No, Sump Pump No, Dampness No, Settlement No, Infestation *None Ntd *Recommend Insp by Experts.

BASEMENT: Area Sq. Ft. 0, % Finished, Ceiling, Walls, Floor, Outside Entry

INSULATION: Roof; Ceiling X; Walls X; Floor X; None; Adequacy Avg X; Energy Efficient Items: Insulated Windows

GARAGE: Yes

ROOMS:

ROOMS	Foyer	Living	Dining	Kitchen	Den	Family Rm	Rec. Rm	Bedrooms	# Baths	Laundry	Other	Area Sq. Ft.
Basement												
Level 1	1	1	1	1		1			.50	1		1,192
Level 2								4	2.00			1,435

Figure 22.2 Uniform residential appraisal report

the important information that is included in this appraisal report. For instance, the appraiser is able to describe the neighborhood and its growth trends (see "Neighborhood Analysis in Form Reports" in Chapter 6). A brief physical description of the appraised property is allowed, followed by a brief depreciated cost approach. The most space is allotted for the direct market comparison approach since this usually is the most reliable method for single-family-residence apprais-

| Finished area above grade contains: | | 8 Rooms; | | 4 Bedroom(s); | | 2.5 Bath(s); | | 2,627 Square Feet of Gross Living Area | | | | |

INTERIOR / AUTO / COMMENTS

SURFACES	Materials/Condition	HEATING		KITCHEN EQUIP		ATTIC		IMPROVEMENT ANALYSIS	Good	Avg.	Fair	Poor
Floors	HW/Carpet– New	Type	F/A	Refrigerator		None		Quality of Construction	X			
Walls	Drywall – New	Fuel	Gas	Range/Oven	X	Stairs		Condition of Improvements	X			
Trim/Finish	Good – New	Condition	New	Disposal	X	Drop Stair	X	Room Sizes/Layout		X		
Bath Floor	Ceramic – New	Adequacy	Good	Dishwasher	X	Scuttle		Closets and Storage		X		
Bath Wainscot	Marble – New	COOLING		Fan/Hood	X	Floor		Energy Efficiency		X		
Doors	6 Panel – New	Central	Yes	Compactor		Heated		Plumbing - Adequacy & Condition	X			
		Other	No	Washer/Dryer		Finished		Electrical - Adequacy & Condition	X			
		Condition	New	Microwave	X			Kitchen Cabinets - Adequacy & Condition		X		
Fireplace(s)	Masonry # 1	Adequacy	Good	Intercom				Compatibility to Neighborhood	X			
CAR STORAGE:	Garage X	Attached	X	Adequate	X	House Entry	X	Appeal & Marketability	X			
No. Cars 2.00	Carport	Detached		Inadequate		Outside Entry	X	Estimated Remaining Economic Life			65	Yrs.
Condition New	None	Built-In		Electric Door	X	Basement Entry	X	Estimated Remaining Physical Life			65	Yrs.

Additional features: Whirlpool tub, 9.0' ceilings main level, ceramic floor in foyer and kitchen, 1 skylight, 6 ceiling fans, 2 story foyer, 14.0' x 16.0' deck.

Depreciation (Physical, functional and external inadequacies, repairs needed, modernization, etc.): The improvements are complete.

General market conditions and prevalence and impact in subject/market area regarding loan discounts, interest buydowns and concessions: Sales activity is moderate in Rivers Bend with stable interest rates and ample mortgage funds. Cash or conventional financing is typical, with seller concessions not common in this price range and market.

Freddie Mac Form 70 10/86   Fannie Mae 1004 10/86

Valuation Section

Purpose of Appraisal is to estimate Market Value as defined in the Certification & Statement of Limiting Conditions.

COST APPROACH

BUILDING SKETCH (SHOW GROSS LIVING AREA ABOVE GRADE)
If for Freddie Mac or Fannie Mae, show only square foot calculations and cost approach comments.

```
36.00  X  26.00  X  1.00  =    936.00   /1
13.80  X   2.00  X  1.00  =     27.60   /1
16.20  X  11.50  X  1.00  =    186.30   /1
 7.00  X   6.00  X  1.00  =     42.00   /1
36.00  X  26.00  X  1.00  =    936.00   /2
13.80  X   2.00  X  1.00  =     27.60   /2
22.00  X  11.60  X  1.00  =    255.20   /2
16.20  X  11.50  X  1.00  =    186.30   /2
 8.00  X   2.00  X  1.00  =     16.00   /2
 4.50  X   3.00  X  1.00  =     13.50   /2
GROSS LIVING AREA (rounded) =  2,627.00  SF
```

ESTIMATED REPRODUCTION COST - NEW - OF IMPROVEMENTS

Dwelling 2,627 Sq. Ft. @ $ 55.00	= $	144,485
Sq. Ft. @ $	=	
Extras Fireplace	=	4,500
Special Energy Efficient Items Central Air	=	5,300
Porches, Patios, etc. Deck	=	2,016
Garage/Carport 484 Sq. Ft. @ $ 25.00	=	12,100
Total Estimated Cost New	= $	168,401

	Physical	Functional	External
Less			
Depreciation New			

Depreciation New	= $	
Depreciated Value of Improvements	= $	168,401
Site Imp. "as is" (driveway, landscaping, etc.)	= $	2,500
ESTIMATED SITE VALUE	= $	40,000
(If leasehold, show only leasehold value.)		
INDICATED VALUE BY COST APPROACH	= $	210,901

(Not Required by Freddie Mac and Fannie Mae)

Does property conform to applicable HUD/VA property standards?   [X] Yes [ ] No

If No, explain:

Construction Warranty	[X] Yes [ ] No
Name of Warranty Program	Builder Warranty
Warranty Coverage Expires	1 Year

Figure 22.2 (cont.)

als. Minimal emphasis is assigned to the income (gross income multiplier) approach, which often lacks sufficient data to permit use of this method.

SUMMARY

The principal guide used in preparing real estate appraisal reports is the appraisal process. The *appraisal process* is an orderly plan of action used by appraisers to reach a sound estimate of real property value. Clients have many different purposes for retaining appraisers. Thus it is compelling that a clearly worded state-

The undersigned has recited three recent sales of properties most similar and proximate to the subject and has considered these in the market analysis. The description includes a dollar adjustment, reflecting market reaction to those items of significant variation between the subject and comparable properties. If a significant item in the comparable property is superior to, or more favorable than, the subject property a minus (-) adjustment is made, thus reducing the indicated value of subject; if a significant item in the comparable is inferior to, or less favorable than, the subject property, a plus (+) adjustment is made, thus increasing the indicated value of the subject.

ITEM	SUBJECT	COMPARABLE NO. 1		COMPARABLE NO. 2		COMPARABLE NO. 3	
Address		105 Redbird Dr.		12905 Scrimshaw Court		112 Scrimshaw Ct.	
Proximity to Subject		Same Subdivision		Same Subdivision		Same Subdivision	
Sales Price	N/A	190,000		230,632		215,550	
Price/Gross Living Area		77.84		91.05		67.36	
Data Source	Inspection	Office Data Bank		Office Data Bank		Office Data Bank	
VALUE ADJUSTMENTS	DESCRIPTION	DESCRIPTION	+ (-) $ Adjustment	DESCRIPTION	+ (-) $ Adjustment	DESCRIPTION	+ (-) $ Adjustment
Sales or Financing Concessions		Conventional		Conventional		Conventional	
Date of Sale/Time	8/91	7/91		5/91		4/91	
Location	Good	Similar		Similar		Similar	
Site/View	Average	Superior	−5,000	Superior	−10,000	Superior	−5,000
Design and Appeal	Br-Fr 2 Sty	Frame 2 Sty	+7,800	Frame 2 Sty	+7,800	Frame 2 Sty	+7,800
Quality of Construction	Good	Inferior	+5,200	Inferior	−13,000	Similar	
Age	New	Similar		Similar		Similar	
Condition	New	Similar		Similar		Similar	
Above Grade Room Count	Total 8 · Bdrms 4 · Baths 2.5	Total 8 · Bdrms 4 · Baths 2.5		Total 8 · Bdrms 4 · Baths 2.5		Total 9 · Bdrms 4 · Baths 2.5	
Gross Living Area	2,627 Sq. Ft.	2,441 Sq. Ft.	+5,580	2,533 Sq. Ft.	+2,820	3,200 Sq. Ft.	−14,325
Basement & Finished Rooms Below Grade	No Bsmt.	Similar		Similar		Similar	
Functional Utility	Average	Similar		Similar		Similar	
Heating/Cooling	Central	Similar		Similar		Similar	
Garage/Carport	2 Car Garage	Similar		Similar		Similar	
Porches, Patio, Pools, etc.	Deck	Similar		Similar		Similar	
Special Energy Efficient Items	Insulated Windows	Similar		Similar		Similar	
Fireplace(s)	1 Fireplace	Similar		Similar		Similar	
Other (e.g. kitchen equip., remodeling)	Mod. Kitchen	Similar		Similar		Similar	
Net Adj. (total)		X + - $	13,580	+ X - $	12,380	+ X - $	11,525
Indicated Value of Subject		$	203,580	$	218,252	$	204,025

Comments on Sales Comparison　Sale #1: More lot value, all frame, not as custom, less square footage. Sale #2: More lot value, all frame, more custom, less square footage. Sale #3: More lot value, all frame, more square footage.

INDICATED VALUE BY SALES COMPARISON APPROACH .... $ 205,000

INDICATED VALUE BY INCOME APPROACH (If Applicable) Estimated Market Rent $ _____ /Mo. x Gross Rent Multiplier _____ = $ _____

This appraisal is made [X] "as is" ☐ subject to the repairs, alterations, inspections or conditions listed below ☐ completion per plans and specifications

Comments and Conditions:　The subject lot transferred in February of 1989 for $33,000.

Final Reconciliation:　The market approach is recognized as the most reliable indicator of value and is given the most weight in the final analysis. The income approach, due to a lack of sufficient and reliable neighborhood rental data, is given no consideration.

This appraisal is based upon the above requirements, the certification, contingent and limiting conditions, and Market Value definition that are stated in

☐ FmHA, HUD, &/or VA Instructions.

[X] Freddie Mac Form 439 (Rev 7/86)/Fannie Mae Form 1004B (Rev 7/86) filed with client　　August 9, 19 91　　[X] attached

I (WE) ESTIMATE THE MARKET VALUE, AS DEFINED, OF THE SUBJECT PROPERTY AS OF　August 9, 19 91 to be $　205,000

I (We) certify: that to the best of my (our) knowledge and belief the facts and data used herein are true and correct; that I (we) personally inspected the subject property, both inside and out, and have made an exterior inspection of all comparable sales cited in this report; and that I (we) have no undisclosed interest, present or prospective therein.

APPRAISER(S)	REVIEW APPRAISER (If applicable)		
Signature *Sarah C. Hoffman*	Signature *Mark B. Reed*	☐ Did [X] Did Not	Inspect Property
Name　Sarah C. Hoffman, SRA	Name　Mark B. Reed, MAI		

Freddie Mac Form 70 10/86　　　　　　　　　　　　　　　　　　　　　　　Fannie Mac 1004 10/86

Figure 22.2 (cont.)

ment of the purpose of the appraisal be set forth in the report. In order to avoid a misunderstanding, an appraisal report should include a definition of the value appraised, identification of the interest(s) appraised, and the effective date of the appraisal.

In reaching a defined value estimate, it is necessary to account for general economic, social, and political influences that bear on the value of the appraised property. Additionally, a thorough description of the subject property must be presented. Once these steps have been completed, the appraiser is ready to use any of the three customary approaches to value to arrive at independent value indications. Next, in the reconciliation phase each of the approaches to value is checked for accuracy and completeness of data in light of prevailing market conditions at the date of the appraisal.

A well written and comprehensive appraisal report consists of four sections: (1) introduction, (2) description of relevant facts, (3) analyses and conclusions, and (4) addenda. Well prepared narrative appraisal reports also are characterized by

1. Being logical and orderly.
2. Being clear, direct, yet comprehensive.
3. Being readable.
4. Avoiding use of the first person.
5. Using appropriate words, summaries, and illustrations.
6. Using positive rather than noncommittal language.
7. Using thorough research that is convincingly and accurately presented.
8. Using language that is readily understood by and inoffensive to the client.

An appraiser must report the results of his or her analysis in a manner that is not misleading. An appropriate set of guidelines available to assist appraisers in this effort are Standard 2 of the Uniform Standards of Professional Appraisal Practice. This standard governs the form and content of appraisal reports.

A well prepared appraisal report enhances the reputation of a real estate appraiser. Such reports are achieved when appropriate data are carefully analyzed while selecting the correct words and phrases.

REVIEW QUESTIONS

1. (a) Define the term "appraisal process."
   (b) How does an understanding of this process benefit the appraiser?
2. List four assumptions that appraisers will ordinarily make regarding appraisals.
3. Explain why an appraiser should define the appraised value in his or her report.
4. Discuss the nature of the reconciliation process in an appraisal report.
5. Briefly outline the steps involved in the "Analyses and Conclusions" section of an appraisal.

6. List several characteristics of a well written appraisal report.

7. Why is use of the letter report discouraged by professional appraisers?

8. Distinguish between the terms "certification" and "limiting conditions."

9. List the two items generally included in the "purpose of the appraisal."

10. What, if any, responsibility does an appraiser who signs a real property appraisal report prepared by another have with regard to the contents of the report?

11. Correct the following sentences, using preferred phrases and words.
    (a) The appraiser stated that the fuel storage tank in back of the dwelling was nowhere near the size of the one next to the garage.
    (b) Irregardless of the extent of inundation, the comparable cite sale should be utilized in this appraisal report.
    (c) Most similar properties sell in the neighborhood of $100 per square foot.
    (d) Comparable land sales surrounded on all sides by paved roads are few in number.

READING AND STUDY REFERENCES

American Institute of Real Estate Appraisers. Chapter 24, "The Appraisal Report," *The Appraisal of Real Estate*, 9th ed. Chicago: AIREA, 1987.

GOLEN, STEVEN P., C. GLENN PEARCE, and ROSS FIGGINS. *Report Writing for Business and Industry*. New York: John Wiley and Sons, 1985.

KUIPER, SHIRLEY, and CHERYL M. LUKE. *Report Writing with Microcomputer Applications*. Cincinnati: South-Western Publishing Company, 1992.

LESIKAR, RAYMOND V. and JOHN D. PETTIT, JR. *Report Writing for Business*, 8th ed. Homewood, Ill.: Richard D. Irvin, Inc., 1991.

OWENS, ROBERT W. "Critical Reading of Appraisal Reports," *Real Estate Review* 21, no. 1 (Spring 1991), pp. 26–31.

PARDUE, WILLIAM P., JR. "Writing Effective Appraisal Reports," *The Appraisal Journal* 58, no. 1 (January 1990), pp. 16–22.

23
Professional Appraisal Standards

Learning Objectives

After reading this chapter, you should be able to:

- Recognize the essentials underlying professional conduct
- Appreciate the purposes of standards of professional conduct
- Discuss the appraiser's rules of conduct
- Understand the evolution of professional standards and state appraiser regulations
- Apply the Uniform Standards of Professional Appraisal Practice in the development of an appraisal report

The field of real estate *appraising* has come a long way since value judgments were chiefly rendered by real estate brokers to facilitate the meeting of minds in connection with buyer-seller transactions. Today there exists an ever-increasing demand for accurate valuation services on the part of industry, business, governmental agencies, and related professions. This growth and development of technical and ethical appraising standards is in no small measure due to the individual efforts of leading appraisers who have won great respect for their profession by insistence that value findings be expressed in detailed, logical, and comprehensive narrative reports. Nevertheless, no matter how great the technical skill ascribable to a given field of specialization, it is adherence to an ideal that causes an individual, or a profession, ultimately to become favorably recognized by society.

PROFESSIONAL STANDARDS AND RESPONSIBILITIES

The older professional callings in the fields of medicine, law, and the chemical and biological sciences have conclusively demonstrated that worthwhile achievements—and public acceptance of the status of members as experts or scientists—are founded on unselfish devotion to a cause. Basically, the essentials that underlie professional conduct are:

1. Integrity.
2. Intellect.
3. Education.
4. Judgment.

The Bible asserts that we cannot live by bread alone. This implies that economic activities in any field of human endeavor need to be supplemented and guided by social and moral considerations. *Integrity* is an inner force that flows from a wholesome personal and professional philosophy of life which inspires trust and confidence in others. Integrity is akin to honor and service, and both are basic to a genuine sincerity of purpose in the discharge of professional responsibility. It is integrity that propels people to render their best service, independent of the financial reward offered to solve a given problem or to report on findings or investigations.

The service motive, to be fruitful, must be reinforced with *intellect*. This is the power of reasoning as distinguished from the faculty of absorbing knowledge. Without intellect, the power of knowing gained from study and experience remains limited. Some people are by nature blessed, it seems, with more intellect than are others. But unless such talents are put to use, atrophy—a form of mental rigor mortis—may rob the possessor of this native advantage.

Important as these sources of professional strength are, integrity and intellect cannot stand alone. Both of these qualities must be supplemented by *education*. One must consciously make efforts to discipline his or her mind through study and instruction. The art of learning is essential in order for professionals to keep abreast of modern developments in theory and in practice. Education, it should be emphasized, need not always be formal in character. Although study in college or trade school is economical and efficient in the long run, informal education can be gained through experience, intensive reading, attendance at seminars, workshops, and through related organizational and professional activities. It is in this area of self-study that professional groups render their most valuable service to fellow members.

Judgment, the final ingredient that characterizes a professional person, is the ability to consider and weigh relevant data in order to reach a sound and reasonable conclusion. Of the qualities that go to make up a professional person, judgment is the most difficult to cultivate. Judgment cannot readily be transferred from one person to another. Experience has proved to be the best teacher of judgment.

IMPORTANCE OF PROFESSIONAL CONDUCT

The more specialized a given activity and the greater the required personal skill, the less the public appears to know about the quality and technical phases of the service rendered. To safeguard the general public against the malpractices of the few and to promote the general interest of its members, professional societies are formed. Through them, intensive efforts are made to develop and maintain high standards of conduct.

As an organized profession, appraising dates back only to the year 1932, when the American Institute of Real Estate Appraisers was founded. But even before its founding, its predecessor organization—the National Association of Real Estate Boards—in 1929 published the "Standards of Appraisal Practice for Realtors, Appraisers and Appraisal Committees of Member Boards" (see footnote 36, Chapter 2). In 1935, another group of specialists organized the Society of Real Estate Appraisers. These organizations, international in scope, merged in 1991 to become the Appraisal Institute. Since 1935, other organizations that embrace valuation on a broader scale have been founded. For example, the members of the American Society of Appraisers are interested in the technical appraising of industrial plant equipment, securities, intangibles, and chattel fixtures.

Although real estate appraising has developed during the past 50 years into the most specialized branch of the real estate business, relatively few practitioners have achieved true professional standing. This is because relatively few real estate firms or individuals devote their working time exclusively to real estate appraising. Many appraisers depend on other income from collateral interests in brokerage, investment, management, or mortgage-financing fields of the real estate business. The collateral activities are by no means deemed a handicap, for the best known and most respected appraisers often are those who have had a broad background in related real estate activities and whose judgments are tempered by wide and personal experience in the varied phases of the real estate business. However, professional status can be claimed only by those who devote their full time and specialized energies to activities that sharpen their value judgments, strengthen their value know-how, and enhance the integrity and quality of their services to clients and to the general public. Some persons would argue that a step was taken in this direction when the Appraisal Institute in 1991 became independent of the National Association of Realtors.

PROFESSIONAL QUALIFICATIONS

Although ever-greater stress is placed on adequate selection and analysis of appraisal data, the value conclusions reached by valuation practitioners constitute at best an informed estimate, the soundness of which largely depends on the quality of judgment possessed by the appraiser. To perfect the practice of real estate appraising and to safeguard against incompetence, appraisal societies are setting ever higher standards as requisites for membership. For instance, to be eligible for membership in the Appraisal Institute, and thus be privileged to use the MAI designation after his or her name, a candidate must have a minimum of five years of creditable appraisal experience, possess a four-year college education, submit acceptable appraisal reports covering different classes of income-producing real estate, and must pass several written examinations in order to demonstrate the ability to cope with valuation theory questions and case study problems. There are several alternatives to writing one of the two narrative reports, such as a doctoral dissertation or published article. Even when meeting these requirements, a candidate may still be short of the points required for membership unless he or she has a college education, more than five years' appraising practice, and collateral business experience, and unless he or she submits additional appraisal reports or requests additional examinations to satisfy the credit points set as a minimum by the admissions committee of the Appraisal Institute. These stringent admission requirements account for the fact that the Appraisal Institute has fewer than 5,000 MAI members. Many times more than the number of professional appraisers now practicing are needed, however, if the demand for competent real property valuation services is to be met adequately. To this end, a comprehensive nationwide educational program is sponsored by the Appraisal Institute in cooperation with leading universities and colleges throughout the nation.

STANDARDS OF PROFESSIONAL CONDUCT

All professional societies have established rules of conduct or codes of ethics. Generally, rules of conduct are intended not only to safeguard the interests of individual members from one another but also to assure the public of professional services that will instill confidence and bring honor to the profession at large. To assure this, membership is restricted to those of proven technical competence who are known for adherence to high moral standards and a display of unquestionable personal integrity. Rules of conduct, by and large, are promulgated to promote the common good by protecting:

1. The interest of the public.
2. The interest of the client.
3. The interest of fellow members and the profession at large.

The *interest of the public* is deemed adversely affected whenever the appraiser fails to act as an independent agent. It is true that the appraiser must be hired by someone, and that he or she owes loyalty to the principal, but the value findings must not be slanted or biased because of it. Value found must be objective and independent of the client's cause or the compensation paid for services rendered. Based on premises clearly set forth in the body of the appraisal report, the value conclusions reached must be objectively supported no matter whose cause is being served.

In the interest of the public, the appraiser must be careful to base value on factual and reliable data and not on hypothetical assumptions or on questionable and uncertain future benefits. To ignore legal property-use restrictions, or to base value on hoped-for changes in area zoning, is a violation of public trust. The appraisal report must be well written for the benefit of the uninformed reader, who will act on the findings in good faith. Care must also be taken not to appraise fractional parts of a property, especially where the sum of the parts appraised as if independent property units does not equal the value of the entire property as an integral whole. Fractional appraising is deemed unethical whenever the report—intentionally or otherwise—misleads the reader.

The appraiser would also be guilty of professional misconduct if he or she should accept an assignment for valuation of a property in which he or she has an undisclosed financial interest. No one can serve two masters and serve them well, especially where a conflict of interests beclouds the independence of action on which objective value must rest to be publicly acceptable.

The *interests of the client* impose further obligations on the professional appraiser. The most important of these is not to reveal the value findings to anyone unless specifically authorized to do so by the client or compelled to do so by court order. Communications between appraiser and client are not privileged under common law as are those of physicians, clergy, and lawyers. Nevertheless, every precaution must be taken to keep a client's trust confidential and to protect his or her interests at all times.

Clients, too, have a right to expect that an appraiser will not accept an assignment for which he or she has no previous experience or for which he or she is not qualified professionally. It would be considered a violation of professional trust for an appraiser to accept an assignment to evaluate a citrus grove or an industrial park if his or her previous appraisal experience was limited to urban residential properties. Appraisers can, of course, affiliate themselves with other members of the profession who are qualified to render the specialized service, provided that the client is duly informed and the appraisal report discloses the cooperative efforts of the parties involved.

Appraisers must take care to keep their client's relationship aboveboard. The fees charged should bear a reasonable relationship to the quantity and character of service, and to the professional responsibility assumed in the discharge of the assignment. As a rule, fees should be calculated on a per diem basis for professional personnel employed, plus direct and indirect expenses chargeable to the assignment. It is considered unethical to accept a commission in lieu of a stipulated fee or to accept gifts and services or undisclosed payments. To do so destroys the standing of appraisers as independent members of their profession in the eyes of the public. Such conduct, of course, casts a shadow on all who strive diligently to uphold and enhance the dignity of this specialized calling.

The *interest of the members and the profession at large*, too, are guided by written and implied rules of conduct. Most professional organizations deem it unethical for members to conduct themselves in such a manner as to prejudice the professional status or reputation of other members or that of the association under whose auspices they practice. Appraisers thus should not solicit assignments or advertise professional attainments or services except as authorized and in a dignified manner. Generally, announcements are limited to business cards, directory listings, and newspaper notices containing only the member's name, professional designation, telephone number, and business address.

It generally is ill advised to offer services when it is known that the assignment will go to the lowest bidder. Service is two-dimensional: qualitative as well as quantitative. Bidding suggests uniformity of product service which in practice does not exist. Experience, judgment, skill, integrity, and education are intangible ingredients which are difficult to subject to measurement under standard specifications in accordance with which service is to be performed. Some government agencies nevertheless request bids and award appraisal contracts on the basis of cost, without due consideration of the experience, skill, and reputation which affect the quality of the service sought.

APPRAISER'S RULES OF CONDUCT

Whether a real estate appraiser belongs to one or more of the leading appraisal institutes or societies, he or she should be aware of and adhere to the guiding rules of conduct on which the growth and development of appraisal service as a professional calling depend. Under these rules, the appraiser must:

1. *Willingly share knowledge and professional experiences.* No one can live unto himself or herself alone. Exchange of experiences and knowledge enriches performance, creates mutual trust, and inspires public confidence. Cooperation, especially through affiliation with professional organizations, has increased the demand significantly for specialized appraisal service during the past 20 years. Members are urged to publish research findings and to participate in educational seminars and workshops in which new theories and practices can be explored and tested. It is in the field of education that professional organizations have made their greatest contributions.

2. *Encourage higher standards and service performance.* The transition from oral and letter reporting to preparation of lengthy and detailed narrative reports in which value conclusions are logically derived and supported is largely due to friendly competition encouraged among professional appraisers to promote higher performance standards. Professional service, if worthy of its name, should be documented and rendered with pride. It is facetiously said that doctors bury their mistakes, but appraisers exhibit theirs for all to see. Increased stress on higher standards and service performance will weed out the incompetent and create interest among the college-trained to share in the challenging opportunities that appraisal service promises to offer in the years to come.

3. *Never speak ill or disparagingly about a fellow appraiser.* Greatness cannot be achieved by pulling others down. One does not become taller by making others smaller. Disparaging talk—even when warranted—leaves a bitter taste, often traced to envy. How much more cheerful and impressive it is to subscribe to the theory that all persons, including fellow competitors, are striving to do well in accordance with their talents and abilities. In the long run, reputation based on quality performance standards will bring the best people to the top in a free and competitive society.

4. *Seek no unfair advantage.* It is disappointing that many otherwise informed people still subscribe to the erroneous philosophy that the goods of the world or of a nation, or the income derived from a service, are all as limited in quantity as is the size of a given pie. To secure a larger slice, those who

hold to this philosophy must necessarily connive to shrink the shares of others, or freeze them out entirely. Progress in all phases of life, as well as our high standard of living, is proof that bigger pies—and not more slices of an existing pie—increase the wealth of a nation. This is apparent in most professions, too, where despite increasing membership, work loads and work opportunities have not diminished.

5. *Avoid controversy.* Do not wash soiled linen in public. There is a saying that you may win an argument, but you may lose a friend. The professional person should avoid arguments, but when unavoidable, disputes should not be aired in public. More often than not, differences of opinion arise because of misunderstandings, statements of half-truth, or quotations taken out of context. Where differences of opinion do arise they can generally be resolved in a civil manner and under circumstances wherein honorable persons can agree to disagree.

6. *Abide by rules and regulations and encourage opportunities for professional education.* Most people are understandably rebellious at heart and inclined to disregard rules and regulations when such seem to work against them. We naturally seek to be free from fetters. We want to enjoy rights, but we object to obligations. Yet rights cannot exist without obligations. The right to free speech imposes the obligation to allow others to do likewise. Rights without obligations lead to anarchy and chaos. Rules and regulations are intended to maximize the common good either of a people or of a given clan or profession. Every individual gain is obtained at a sacrifice of social costs. Control of some sort is needed to keep a balance between incentive (profit) motives and those aimed at the exploitation of the weak, uninformed, or the public at large. Violations of rules and regulations and unprofessional conduct are often traceable to ignorance or lack of understanding. Enlightenment through education has proved the bulwark of professionalism. Every support should be given to efforts intended to spread the gospel of professional truth and knowledge.

7. *Keep confidential matters entrusted in good faith.* Every code of ethics, from the oldest to the youngest professions, stresses the importance of "privileged communication." It seems to bolster one's ego to possess information that others long to know, and it is the devilish urge to be magnanimous by sharing such important matters with others that inclines the weak to discuss private matters with the wrong people. The golden rule should have special meaning to persons of professional status. Once a trust is violated, it is difficult to regain public confidence. Worse still, a breach of conduct undermines strength of character and may lead to misfeasance in client relations that may have serious repercussions to individual practitioners and to the profession.

8. *Never undermine a fellow practitioner's professional relations with others or attempt to create an exclusionary appraisal practice in one's community.* Experience in all parts of the country supports the conclusion that the demand for qualified appraisers outruns the available supply. Commercial banks, in-

surance firms, business establishments, investors, and industry rely increasingly on independent appraisers for guidance in their loan and investment policies. Healthy competition is good for trade as well as for professional growth and development. In a progressive society, standing still means going backward. An attempt to keep qualified practitioners from serving the community is a sign of weakness and stagnation. A "let-the-best-person-win" philosophy is essential to keeping good people at the top.

9. *Conduct work so as to achieve a high regard in one's community and make fellow members of the appraisal profession thankful for one's wholesome influence.* There are many things in life that money cannot buy, and reputation is among them. Unfortunately, too many people consider short-run monetary gains without thoughtful deliberation as to the long-term effects of their actions. Where love of work, interest, and service are prime considerations in the discharge of professional duty, success is bound to follow. The sense of a job well done in an atmosphere of confidence and public recognition provides the lasting compensation that is reflected in a firm's shield of honor. Appraisers should strive to carry this shield on without blemish from one generation to another.

UNIFORM STANDARDS OF PROFESSIONAL APPRAISAL PRACTICE[1]

Beginning in the early 1980s, the mortgage portfolios of financial institutions began to deteriorate. Residential mortgage loan foreclosures increased, going from 0.38 percent to 0.81 percent between 1980 and 1985 for all home mortgages. The Veterans Administration estimated that in fiscal 1985 from 10 to 40 percent of its $420 million loan guarantee program suffered losses as a result of inadequate real estate appraisals. Similarly, during the July 1984–September 1985 interval, FNMA sold over 4,300 properties acquired via default at prices averaging 22 percent less than the original appraised value.[2] To arrest this problem, in 1986 the Federal Home Loan Bank Board issued a memorandum known as "R-41c, Appraisal Policies and Practices of Insured Institutions." R-41c provided certain appraisal guidelines or standards that were expected to be followed in all real estate appraisals for federally insured savings and loan associations and service corporations. This memorandum followed a similar effort in 1982 known as Memorandum R-41b.

Probably the most significant event for the appraisal field in the mid-1980s was the Congressional hearings in December 1985 which were chaired by Congressman Doug Barnard of Georgia. These hearings, entitled "Impact of Faulty and Fraudulent Real Estate Appraisals on Federally Insured Financial Institutions and Related Agencies of the Federal Government" set the stage for state reg-

[1]This section is based on the publication, *Uniform Standards of Professional Appraisal Practice* (Washington, D.C.: The Appraisal Foundation, 1990).

[2]James H. Boykin, "Solving Appraisal-Related Mortgage Problems," *The MGIC Newsletter* (Milwaukee: Mortgage Guaranty Insurance Corporation, September/October 1987), p. 1.

ulation of real estate appraisers. After some delays, the regulations resulting from the mandate of Title 11 of the Federal Financial Institutions Reform, Recovery and Enforcement Act of 1989 became effective in 1992 and 1993. The basic idea behind this national-state regulatory system was a three-part body. The initial body was the Real Estate Appraisal Foundation which is responsible for funding and making appointments to its two boards. The Real Estate Appraisal Standards Board develops and promulgates uniform appraisal standards, whereas the Qualifications Board develops education, experience, and examination criteria to be used in the licensing and certification of appraisers in the various states.

The Uniform Standards of Professional Appraisal Practice (USPAP) include 10 separate standards with Standards 6 through 10 focusing on mass appraisal, personal property appraisal and reporting, and business appraisal and reporting. The first five standards are more basic to general real estate appraisal and analysis and include the following topics: real estate appraisal and reporting, review appraisal, and real estate analysis and reporting. Standard 2, dealing with real estate appraisal and reporting, was covered in Chapter 22. An overview of the remaining four standards follows.

Standard 1 requires that in making an appraisal an appraiser must be aware of, understand, and correctly use recognized methods to develop a credible report. Further, the appraiser must neither commit an error that substantially affects an appraisal nor provide appraisal services in a careless or negligent manner.

In developing a real estate appraisal, an appraiser must observe the following specific guidelines when applicable:

1. Adequately identify the real estate and the real property interest under consideration, define the purpose and intended use of the appraisal, consider the scope of the appraisal, describe any limiting conditions, and identify the effective date of the appraisal.

2. Define the value being considered.

3. Consider easements, restrictions, encumbrances, leases, special assessments, and other items of a similar nature.

4. Identify and consider personal property, fixtures, or intangible items that are not real property but included in the appraisal.

5. Consider the effect on use and value of existing land use regulations, reasonably probable changes in such regulations, economic demand, physical adaptability of the property, neighborhood trends, and the highest and best use of the property.

6. Recognize that land is appraised as though vacant and available for development to its highest and best use and that the appraisal of improvements is based on their contribution to the site.

7. Value the site by an appropriate method.

8. Collect, verify, analyze, and reconcile: comparable cost data needed to estimate the cost new of the improvements, comparable data needed to estimate accrued depreciation, comparable sales data available to estimate the market rental and value of the appraised property, comparable operating ex-

pense data to estimate the operating expenses, and comparable data needed to estimate the capitalization or discount rates.

9. Base projections of future rent and expenses on reasonably clear and appropriate data.

10. Refrain from estimating the value of the whole property solely by adding together the individual values of the various estates.

11. Consider the effect on value of anticipated public or private improvements, located either on or off site, to the extent that market actions reflect such anticipated improvements as of the effective appraisal date.

12. Identify and consider appropriate procedures and market information such as physical, functional, and external market factors required to make an appraisal.

13. Appraise proposed improvements only after considering: (a) plans, specifications, or other related documents; (b) evidence indicating the probable completion time of the proposed improvements; and (c) evidence supporting development costs, anticipated earnings, occupancy projections, and anticipated competition at date of completion.

14. Consider any current agreement of sale, option, or listing of the property being appraised, if such information is normally available to the appraiser.

15. Consider any prior sales of the appraised property between the appraisal date and (a) one year for one- to four-family residential properties and (b) three years for other property.

16. Consider and reconcile the quantity and quality of data analyzed within the approaches used and the applicability of such approaches.

Standard 3 requires that an appraiser in reviewing an appraisal and reporting the results must form an opinion as to the adequacy and appropriateness of the report being reviewed and must clearly state the nature of the review process followed and observe the following guidelines:

1. Identify the report being reviewed, the real property interest being appraised, the effective date of the opinion in the report being reviewed, and the date of the review.

2. Identify the scope of the review process to be conducted.

3. Form an opinion as to the adequacy and relevance of the data and the propriety of any adjustments to the data.

4. Form an opinion as to the appropriateness of the appraisal methods used and present reasons for any disagreement.

5. Form an opinion concerning the correctness and appropriateness of the analyses, opinions, and conclusions in the report being reviewed and show the reasons for any disagreement.

6. Disclose the nature, extent, and detail of the review process undertaken.

7. Disclose the information that must be considered in points 1 through 5.

8. Separate the review function from any other function.

Standards 4 and 5 focus on using recognized methods and techniques in developing and reporting the results of a real estate analysis. These two standards are similar to USPAP Standards 1 and 2 in some respects, but differ in such areas where the analyst must: identify clearly the client's objectives; identify alternative courses of action and the optimum course to achieve the client's objective; define and delineate the market area; and analyze current and potential changes in supply and its effect on demand. In making real estate cash flow and investment analysis, the analyst is expected to consider income and expenses and financing availability and terms in order to properly analyze the cash flow returns and reversion to the specified investment position over a projected time period. In preparing a real estate feasibility analysis, an analyst is required to prepare a complete market analysis and apply the results of this analysis to alternative courses of action to achieve a client's objective.

Standard 5 is similar to Standard 2 in that it requires the analyst to set forth clearly and accurately the analysis in a manner that will not be misleading. The analyst must give his or her final conclusion or recommendations as well as include a signed certification which states among other things that to the best of the analyst's knowledge the statements of fact are true and accurate, the conclusions are his or her unbiased professional opinions, he or she has no interest in the property or interest or bias regarding the parties involved; his or her compensation is not, unless otherwise explained, contingent on an action resulting from the analysis; specifies who has personally inspected the property; and that no one provided significant professional assistance to the person signing the report.

SUMMARY

Professional conduct has as its basis four traits; these are integrity, intellect, education, and judgment. *Integrity* is an inner force that flows from a wholesome personal and professional philosophy of life which inspires trust and confidence in others. *Intellect* is the power of reasoning. *Education* is essential in order for professionals to keep abreast of modern developments in theory and in practice. *Judgment* is the ability to consider and weigh relevant data in order to reach a sound and reasonable conclusion.

Generally, rules of conduct of professional real estate appraisal societies focus on the protection of the interests of the public, the client, and of fellow members and the profession at large. The public interest is protected when appraisers base their value findings on factual and reliable data, consider legal property-use restrictions, prepare well written reports, avoid appraising fractional interests when the results may be misleading, and fully disclose any financial interest in the appraised property.

The interest of the client is protected when appraisers keep the results of their work confidential, the appraiser is properly qualified to handle an assignment, and the fee bears a reasonable relationship to the nature of the service provided.

The interests of fellow members and the profession at large are protected by the ethical conduct of appraisers. Assignments and advertising should always be handled in a dignified manner.

The nine rules of appraiser's conduct are that the appraiser must:

1. Willingly share knowledge and professional experience.
2. Encourage higher standards and service performance.
3. Never speak ill or disparagingly about a fellow appraiser.
4. Seek no unfair advantage.
5. Avoid controversy.
6. Abide by rules and regulations and encourage opportunities for professional education.
7. Keep confidential matters entrusted in good faith.
8. Never undermine a fellow practitioner's professional relations with others or attempt to create an exclusionary appraisal practice in one's community.
9. Conduct work so as to achieve a high regard in one's community and make fellow members of the appraisal profession thankful for one's wholesome influence.

An outgrowth of the cooperative efforts of nine North American appraisal organizations was the establishment of national real estate valuation standards known as the "Uniform Standards of Professional Appraisal Practice." The first five of these ten standards focus on the preparation and reporting of appraisals, reviews of appraisals, and real estate analysis. Each of these standards provides specific guidelines as to how to develop and prepare proper real estate appraisals, reviews, and analyses.

REVIEW QUESTIONS

1. How does education play a role in professional conduct?
2. Explain the real estate appraiser's responsibility to the public.
3. Why should an appraiser avoid speaking disparagingly of a fellow professional?
4. Why do you think an appraiser is obligated to maintain a confidential relationship with his or her clients?
5. Describe the responsibilities of the Real Estate Appraisal Foundation, Real Estate Appraisal Standards Board, and the Qualifications Board.
6. Under Standard 1 of USPAP, what factors must an appraiser consider in the valuation of proposed improvements?
7. What basic responsibility does a review appraiser have under Standard 3 of USPAP?
8. How do USPAP analysis Standards 4 and 5 differ from appraisal Standards 1 and 2?

READING AND STUDY REFERENCES

American Institute of Real Estate Appraisers. Appendix A "Professional Practice," *The Appraisal of Real Estate*, 8th ed. Chicago: AIREA, 1987.

BOYCE, BYRL R., and WILLIAM N. KINNARD, JR. "Professionalism and Ethics," *Appraising Real Property*. Lexington, Mass.: Lexington Books, 1984, pp. 400–403.

BOYKIN, JAMES H. "Solving Appraisal-Related Mortgage Problems," *The MGIC Newsletter*. Milwaukee: Mortgage Guaranty Insurance Corporation, September/October 1987, pp. 1–3.

DORSEY, THOMAS A. "Ethics, Appraisal Standards, and Client Relationships," *The Real Estate Appraiser and Analyst* 53, no. 3 (Fall/Winter 1987), pp. 22–25.

JOHNSON, LINDA L., and CHRISTINE LOUCKS. "The Effect of Certification and Licensure on Appraisers and Users of Appraisers," *The Appraisal Journal* 56, no. 4 (October 1988), pp. 548–555.

OWENS, ROBERT W. "Increased Accountability in the Appraisal Profession," *The Appraisal Journal* 59, no. 3 (July 1990), pp. 347–352.

The Appraisal Foundation. *Uniform Standards of Professional Appraisal Practice*. Washington, D.C.: The Appraisal Foundation, 1990.

I
Glossary

Accrued depreciation. A loss in value from any cause—as measured by the difference between replacement or reproduction cost new of a property in current dollars and the market value of the same property.

Amortization rate. A sinking fund rate that provides for the recapture of an investment over the economic life of a property.

Annuity. A periodic return on an investment, receivable at regular intervals either in advance or postpaid.

Anticipation of future benefits. A principle which holds that the present value of a real property is based on users' and owners' perceptions of the nature, magnitude, and duration of its expected future benefits.

Appraisal process. An orderly plan of action used by appraisers to reach a sound estimate of real property value.

Balance. A principle which asserts that value is created and maintained in proportion to supply and demand of a particular property type and in relation to consumer preference for on-site amenities in relation to a property's function.

Band-of-investment method. A capitalization rate that is based on the sum of the weighted mortgage and equity or building and land capitalization rates.

Building capitalization rate. The ratio of building net operating income to the value of the building.

Bundle of rights. The "bundle" contains all the individual interests essential to fee simple ownership, including the right to use or not to use the property, the right to lease all or parts of the property (air rights, surface rights, mineral rights, easements, and rights-of-way), the right to sell or not to sell, and the right to donate or grant the property to others as a gift.

Capacity. Refers to the ability of land to absorb capital outlays profitably.

Capitalization. A process for converting future income into an estimated present value.

Capitalization rate. Expresses the relationship between a property's net operating income and its value; it consists of an interest rate and an amortization rate.

Cash equivalency. Refers to typical financing terms: equity down payment plus mortgage loan amounts which were available to a typical purchaser when a particular comparable sale property was conveyed. (Also see prevailing financing equivalency.)

463

Cash-on-cash rate. See equity dividend rate.

Comparative advantage. A country should produce those goods in which it has the greatest comparative advantage and least comparative disadvantage with other countries.

Composite capitalization rate. A rate developed over an income projection period and influenced by mortgage interest rates, amortization terms, and anticipated percentage change in property value over the projection period.

Compound amount of 1. Used to determine the amount a dollar invested today will grow to in n periods at a given rate of interest.

Conformity. A principle which states that a property's value is maximized when it conforms to the surrounding properties, neighborhood, and tastes and desires of prospective users and purchasers.

Consequential damages. A loss in property value that may occur through the exercise of police power. In such instances, no compensation is due the property owner.

Consistent use. This principle holds that both the site and improvements must be valued for the same use.

Contract for deed. An agreement under which transfer of title to the land is deferred until partial (periodic) payments aggregate the entire or agreed-upon amount of the purchase price.

Contract rent. Rental income actually paid for space as a result of a lease which binds owners and tenants for a stipulated future time.

Cost. The amount of money necessary to acquire or to create an item.

Deed restrictions. Contractual limitations on ownership which generally are noted in deeds of record.

Demand. An economic concept that implies not only the presence of a "need" but also the existence of monetary power to fill that need.

Direct costs. Include construction labor and materials.

Discount point. Equal to 1 percent of the face amount of a mortgage loan.

Easements. Rights extended to others for ingress and egress over a property, or to air or subsurface rights for utility installation, soil removal, flood control, or mining operations.

Economic base analysis. Focuses on how a community earns its living. The economic base of a community is broken down into two parts: basic (export) industries and nonbasic (service) industries.

Economic life. The productive life of a building measured from when it was built to when it economically encumbers the site and its optimum use.

Effective age. Age of a building that is based partly on its actual age, but more importantly, on its comparative utility, physical condition, and expected remaining life expectancy.

Effective gross income. The income remaining after deducting for vacancy and collection losses.

Efficiency. Refers to a measure of profitability as represented by the ratio of dollar input (capital improvements) to dollar land output in terms of residual income.

Eminent domain. The power inherent in a governmental body to "take" an owner's land, or any part of it (air rights, road easements, etc.) by due process of law, when the necessity arises.

Equity dividend rate. Relates cash flow income to the original equity or down payment made by an investor and sometimes is called "cash on cash."

Equity yield rate. Accounts for the cash-on-cash return, or equity dividend rate, plus the anticipated net sale proceeds when the property is sold.

Escalator clause. Also known as an expense stop or pass through, increases the tenant's operating expense burden as specified operating expenses rise.

Escheat. Provides for the reversion or escheat of land to the state when an owner of land dies and leaves no heirs or fails to dispose of the land by will.

Excess condemnation. A means of acquiring land in excess of the actual need of a right-of-way as a means of recouping part of the cost of right-of-way construction.

Excess rent. The amount that contract rent exceeds market rent.

External obsolescence. Loss in value caused by (1) neighborhood hazards and nuisances, (2) down zoning and reduced highest and best use, (3) over- or underimprovement of land, and (4) decreasing demand.

Fee simple. The largest possible estate in real property.

Fee simple interest. The unencumbered value of a property which is suggested by prevailing market rentals rather than by any value resulting from existing leases.

Fixed charges. Property taxes and insurance premiums which vary little, if at all, with changing occupancy levels.

Fixture. Personal property that is attached or used in such a manner that it is considered to be part of the real estate.

Flat rental. A provision that is associated with short-term leases where the same rental is paid each year.

Functional obsolescence. Loss in value caused by (1) faulty design, (2) inadequacy of structural facilities, (3) superadequacy of structural facilities, and (4) outmoded equipment.

Future worth of 1 per period. Reveals the amount that a dollar deposited at the end of each period will grow to in n periods at a given rate of interest.

Graded rent clause. Provides for a series of flat rental payments, rising in stairstep fashion. Sometimes, in the latter years of a property's life, the income pattern is reversed in a step-down manner.

Highest and best use. That use or succession of available, legal, and physically permitted uses for which there is sufficient demand that produces the highest present site value.

Index clause. Allows rental income to be periodically adjusted in accordance with a published index such as the Consumer Price Index.

Indirect costs. Include professional services, finance charges, and real estate taxes.

Installment to amortize 1, or mortgage constant. Used to determine how much must be paid in periodic payments to amortize a dollar, including principal and interest, in *n* periods at a given rate of interest.

Interest rate. A measure of the cost of money and does not include a provision for investment recapture.

Internal rate of return. That discount rate which causes all future income inflows and outflows to equal the initial investment.

Just compensation. Payment for the value of an owner's property taken plus any loss in value to the remainder property.

Land. Sometimes used synonymously with site, tract, and parcel, but is not yet developed for an intensive use.

Land capitalization rate. A ratio of the net operating income derived from land to the land value.

Land residual approach. Converts the earnings available for a site into an indication of market value.

Leased fee. Refers to the owner's interest and rights in the property subject to conditions and terms of a written or oral lease agreement.

Leasehold estate. Refers to the tenant's right—over periods of months or years—to benefit from the use of the property in accordance with a lease and the payment of a stipulated periodic rental.

Linkages. External economies or centripetal forces. It is the periodic interaction between people or establishments that draw and hold them together.

Marginal productivity (principle of contribution). Concerned with the value that the presence of a property component contributes to the overall value of that property or the reduction in the overall property value caused by the absence of the component.

Market rent. That amount of rent the appraised property will command at the date of appraisal.

Market value. The most probable price that a property should bring in a competitive and open market under all conditions requisite to a fair sale, the buyer and seller each acting prudently and knowledgeably, and assuming the price is not affected by undue stimulus.

Modified internal rate of return. The adjusted rate found by compounding the periodic income forward at the cost of capital rate, then computing the rate that will discount this future value to equal the cost of the investment.

Mortgage rate. Also known as a mortgage constant, it expresses a constant relationship between annual mortgage payments (including principal and interest) and the original loan amount.

Most probable use. The use to which the land and building would most likely be put.

Neighborhood. A bounded area wherein certain land use activities are attracted and retained by sets of linkages.

Net operating income. The income remaining after all operating expenses and replacement reserves have been accounted for, but as a rule, before deductions are made for mortgage debt service.

Net present value. The difference between the present value of the positive cash flows and the present value of the negative cash flows.

Overall capitalization rate. A ratio between the net operating income and the value of an entire property.

Parcel. A large holding under one ownership; is used interchangeably with *tract*.

Percentage clause. Usually used with retail establishments. It has two parts: the base rent and the percentage rent. The latter increases as a tenant's business increases.

Physical deterioration. Loss in value caused by (1) wear and tear through use, (2) action of the elements and from wood-boring insects, and (3) structural impairment through neglect, fire, water, and so on.

Police power. A sovereign power inherent in state government and exercised or delegated by it to the village, city, county, or other governing agency to restrict the use of real property in order to protect the wellbeing of its citizens.

Present worth of 1, sometimes called a reversion factor. Provides the present worth of the right to receive a dollar in *n* periods in the future at a given rate of interest.

Present worth of 1 per period, or Inwood factor. Determines the present worth of the right to receive a dollar at the end of each period for *n* periods at a given rate of interest.

Prevailing financing equivalency. A process where the appraiser seeks to identify any unusual financing and then adjust accordingly until the price reflects the price that probably would have been paid had prevailing or normal debt financing been used in the sale of a comparable property.

Price. Represents the amount paid for real property in terms of dollars.

Primary city. A community that has its own economic base.

Probable price. The price a property is likely to bring within a given time frame and the economic environment in which the sale is expected to occur.

Property. An intangible concept, being the right to own or possess wealth and to put it to legal uses if one wishes.

Property yield rate. Combines the rate derived from NOI/sale price and changes in property value.

Real estate. Land, together with all improvements that are permanently affixed thereto.

Real property. The rights, interests, and benefits associated with the ownership of real estate.

Reconciliation. The careful weighing of the initial value results on the basis of accuracy and completeness of data and in the light of market conditions that prevail on the date of the appraisal.

Remaining economic life. Describes a building's remaining productive life.

Rent deficiency. That amount by which contract rent is less than market rent.

Replacement cost. The current cost of building a structure that provides functional utility equal to the building being appraised and built with modern materials and according to current standards.

Reproduction cost. The cost of building an appraised structure in a manner that replicates the materials, design, layout, and quality of workmanship.

Reserves for replacement. Cover outlays on a pro rata basis for the estimated service life of furnishings and fixtures that will last a shorter time than a building's remaining economic life.

R value. A symbol used to measure the insulating quality of material, such as R-19. Higher R values indicate better insulation.

Sale and lease-back. A lease provision that provides for an owner to sell a property for full value to an investor and then simultaneously lease it back.

Sandwich lease. The subsidiary lease between a tenant and subtenant.

Scarcity. A relative term, and must be considered in relation to demand and supply and the alternate uses—present or prospective—to which the good or service may be put.

Secondary city. A satellite community whose wellbeing depends on a nearby primary city.

Severance damage. A loss in value to the part of a property remaining after a taking as compared with the value of the remainder when considered as a part of the whole property.

Simple linear regression. A statistical method which fits a straight line to a set of data points.

Sinking fund factor. Reveals how much must be deposited at the end of each period at compound interest to accumulate a dollar in n periods.

Site. A unit of land that is ready for its intended use.

Soil percolation test. Usually made by a government agency to determine soil fitness for installation of private sanitary sewage systems.

Substitution. A principle which establishes an upper limit of value that is set by the cost of acquiring an equally desirable substitute property, provided such can be obtained without undue or costly delay.

Supply and demand. A principle which holds that price tends to vary directly according to demand and inversely proportional to supply: that is, higher prices will be paid when there is strong demand for a good.

Tract. A large unit of land that has not been prepared for its eventual use.

Transferability. A legal concept that must be considered in the estimation of property value. Even though the characteristics of utility, scarcity, and demand are present, if the property cannot be transferred in whole or in part, market value cannot exist.

Utility. The power of a good to render a service or fill a need.

Value

    Appraised value. Value estimated by an appraiser.

    Assessed value. Used for tax purposes and is based on fair market value estimated by assessors.

    Book value. An accounting value; acquisition cost plus capital improvements less depreciation reserves.

    Capital value. Value of fixed assets used in business.

    Cash value. Value associated with an all-cash purchase.

    Depreciated value. Value remaining after depreciation is deducted from the original acquisition price.

    Economic value. Value associated with a useful object that is scarce and capable of measurement.

    Exchange value. Value expressed in terms of other goods offered in exchange, usually money.

    Extrinsic value. Value determined by persons who wish to purchase a property.

    Face value. Value set forth in a security, such as a bond, stock, or mortgage.

    Fair value. A transaction price that is fair to all parties of the transfer.

    Improved value. Value of a property after on-site construction is completed.

    Insurable value. Actual cash value of improvements subject to damage from fire or other destructive hazards and excludes such items as site, excavation, pilings, and underground drains.

    Intrinsic value. Value inherent in the object itself, such as a precious metal.

    Investment value. Established by an individual investor, based on his or her particular criteria which may differ from those of the market in general.

    Leasehold value. A tenant's value in a property as a result of favorable lease terms.

    Liquidation value. Distress price received by owner without benefit of usual market exposure; sometimes called "forced sale value."

    Mortgage loan value. Based on a percentage of market value or other mortgage underwriting standards.

    Nuisance value. Price paid to gain relief from an objectionable situation, such as a derelict adjoining property.

    Potential value. Based on occurrence of some future event such as a proposed plan for a future development.

    Real value. In contrast to potential value; excludes value increment due to speculative future events.

    Rental value. Value as a function of a property having been leased.

Replacement value. Sum of money necessary to rebuild a structure if destroyed by fire or earthquake.

Sales value. Based on the price that a property might bring upon being sold.

Salvage value. Price paid for a property or its improvements, taking into account cost of removal of the structure, including delays.

Speculative value. A hoped-for price that an investor expects based on an influential event such as rezoning or population or economic growth.

Stable value. Assumes unchanging market and property conditions.

Use value. Based on the profitability of a property's present and anticipated uses.

Warranted value. Equivalent to market value, but seldom used.

Value in use. The value of a property for a specific use, which usually is its present use.

Variable expenses. Generally vary in accordance with the level of tenant occupancy and include such expenses as periodic maintenance, management, janitorial services, heating, utilities, repairs, and building supplies.

Wealth. All tangible and useful things owned by human beings which have attributes of economic value.

Wetlands. Those areas that are inundated or saturated by surface or ground water at a frequency and duration sufficient to support a prevalence of vegetation typically adapted for life in saturated soil conditions.

MARKET VALUE APPRAISAL OF THE
KEEGAN'S MILL APARTMENTS
11500 KEEGAN'S RIDGE
HOUSTON, HARRIS COUNTY, TEXAS
ASSET NAME: KEEGAN'S MILL APARTMENTS
LN/REO NUMBER: 29-0013613

Prepared for:

MR. ROSS PHILLIPS
SENIOR REVIEW APPRAISER
NCNB/UFSA SAB
1160 DAIRY ASHFORD, THIRD FLOOR
HOUSTON, TEXAS 77079

Prepared by:

LOVE & SCHULZ
Real Estate Consultants and Appraisers
3555 Timmons Lane, Suite 730
Houston, Texas 77027

471

Love & Schulz

Real Estate Consultants & Appraisers

A. Scruggs Love, Jr., MAI, CRE
Gerald Burke Schulz, MAI

3555 Timmons Lane, Suite 730
Houston, Texas 77027
(713) 850-1850

Post Office Box 460308
San Antonio, Texas 78246
(512) 590-7355

August 23, 1990

Mr. Ross Phillips
Senior Review Appraiser
NCNB/UFSA SAB
1160 Dairy Ashford, Third Floor
Houston, Texas 77079

Re: Keegan's Mill Rental Apartments
located at 11500 Keegan's Ridge, Houston,
Harris County, Texas.

Asset Name: Keegan's Mill Apts.
LN/REO Number: 29-0013613

Dear Mr. Phillips: *Fee Simple Interest*

At your request, we have completed an investigation and analysis for the
purpose of estimating the market value of the fee simple interest of the above
referenced property, as is, as of August 1, 1990.

The subject property is an existing two story, 318 unit apartment complex
containing approximately 218,016 net rentable square feet, in 21 apartment
buildings. The subject improvements also include a building containing the
office and club house, one pool, two tennis courts, and four laundry rooms.
This is an individually metered (tenant pays electric) project. The subject
property is situated on an irregularly shaped tract of land which contains
9.233 acres, or 402,189 square feet.

It has been our intention to prepare our narrative report in conformity with
our interpretation of the Resolution Trust Corporation's Uniform Appraisal

marketing PERIOD

Standards and Requirements dated December, 1989. We have valued the property in its "as is" condition. The subject property is currently experiencing 92% occupancy, which is above the average occupancy for the submarket. It is our opinion that the subject property will have a marketing period of approximately one year.

> It often is advisable to indicate the total number of pages in a report to reduce the chance of subsequent alterations by unauthorized persons.

We are not qualified to detect or identify hazardous substances which may, or may not, be present on, or in, this property. The presence of hazardous materials may affect value, and we have appraised this property assuming that there are no hazardous substances present. We have no reason to suspect the presence of hazardous substances, but we do urge the user of this report to obtain the services of specialists for the purpose of conducting an environmental audit.

Your attention is directed to the contingent and limiting conditions, which are contained in the body of this report, for a more thorough understanding of the conditions upon which the value conclusion contained herein was based. The physical inspection of the site and comparable sales and the analysis that forms the basis of our value conclusion was made by the undersigned.

Based upon the facts and analyses contained in this report, the market value of the fee simple interest, as is, as of August 1, 1990, was:

FOUR MILLION DOLLARS
($4,000,000)

The purpose of this letter is to transmit the following appraisal report which contains the data and analyses utilized to form our market value conclusions. Thank you for the opportunity to work with you on this appraisal assignment.

Respectfully submitted,

Gerald Burke Schulz, MAI

Julie W. Ashby

90-002: JWA\jez

Northwesterly view of the subject property as seen from Keegan's Ridge Drive.
Office/clubhouse is on the left.

Street scene looking south along Keegan's Ridge Drive.
Subject complex is on the right.

SUMMARY OF SALIENT FACTS AND CONCLUSIONS

This section gives a client an opportunity to gain an overview of the appraisal report prior to a detailed reading.

Property Identification: Keegan's Mill Apartments, 11500
                                      Keegan's Ridge, Houston, Harris County,
                                      Texas.

| | Location: | West line of Keegan's Ridge, south of Keegan's Bayou, with additional frontage along the south line of Ruffino Road. |

Location: West line of Keegan's Ridge, south of Keegan's Bayou, with additional frontage along the south line of Ruffino Road.

Key Map: 569 D

Effective Date of Appraisal: August 1, 1990

Purpose: To estimate the market value of the fee simple interest, in its "as is" condition.

Interest Appraised: Fee simple interest

Land Area: 9.233 acres, or 402,189 square feet

Shape of Tract: Irregular

Improvements: An existing two story, 318 unit apartment complex containing approximately 218,016 net rentable square feet in 21 apartment buildings, four laundry rooms, an office/club house building, pool, and two tennis courts. This is an individually metered (tenant pays electric) project. The unit mix is presented below:

Salient Fact Information

	Unit type	No. units	Size (sq.ft.)	Area (sq.ft.)
A	1BR/1BA	160	602	96,320
B	1BR/1BA	78	680	53,040
B-2	2BR/2BA (den)	16	1,059	16,944
C	2BR/1BA	48	796	38,208
D	2BR/2BA	16	844	13,504
Total		318		218,016

Gross Building Area: 223,302 SF
Average Unit Size: 686 SF
Density: 34.44 units per acre
Year Built: 1978

Highest and Best Use:

As Vacant: Hold for future multi-family development.

As Improved: Multi-family development.

Zoning: None

Occupancy: 92% as of the date of appraisal

Average Rent: $.40 PSF per month

Estimated Deferred Maintenance: $50,000 or $157 per unit

Estimated Marketing Period: One year

Value Indications:

Land Value:	$1,000,000, or $2.50 PSF of land area
Cost Approach:	$4,770,000
Direct Sales Comparison:	$4,085,000
Income Approach:	$3,980,000
Market Value:	$4,000,000, ($12,579 per unit; $18.35 per square foot NRA).

A table of contents should precede any report in excess of 5 to 10 pages. Importantly, each page should be numbered to facilitate reference to particular pages. Pagination is especially helpful when a client and appraiser discuss a report by telephone. It also reduces the possibility of pages being placed out of order.

Table of Contents

LETTER OF TRANSMITTAL 00
PHOTOGRAPHS OF THE APPRAISED PROPERTY 00
SUMMARY OF SALIENT FACTS AND CONCLUSIONS 00
TABLE OF CONTENTS 00
IDENTIFICATION OF PROPERTY 00
LEGAL DESCRIPTION 00
PURPOSE AND DATE OF THE APPRAISAL 00
FUNCTION OF THE APPRAISAL 00
SCOPE OF THE APPRAISAL 00
PROPERTY RIGHTS APPRAISED 00
DEFINITION OF VALUE AND INTEREST APPRAISED 00
REGIONAL ANALYSIS 00
APARTMENT MARKET OVERVIEW 00
NEIGHBORHOOD ANALYSIS 00
SITE ANALYSIS 00
DESCRIPTION OF THE IMPROVEMENTS 00
ANALYSIS OF IMPROVEMENTS 00
REAL PROPERTY ASSESSMENTS AND TAXES 00
HIGHEST AND BEST USE 00
MARKETABILITY 00
VALUATION ANALYSIS 00
COST APPROACH 00
SALES COMPARISON APPROACH 00
INCOME CAPITALIZATION APPROACH 00
RECONCILIATION AND FINAL VALUE ESTIMATE 00
CERTIFICATE 00
QUALIFICATIONS 00
ADDENDUM 00

It generally is advisable to place detailed sales, lease, and other such background data in an addendum. The client can study these detailed sections after considering the summary data in the body of the report.

Legal Descriptions
Floor Plans
Building Plans
Vacant Land Sales
Operating Statements
Rent Roll
Letter of Engagement
RTC Uniform Appraisal Instructions to Appraisers for RTC Real Estate
    Properties
NCNB/UFSA Appraisal Requirements

IDENTIFICATION OF PROPERTY

The subject property is an existing 318 unit, rental, garden apartment complex, located along the west line of Keegan's Ridge, south of Keegan's Bayou and north of West Bellfort. The tract also has frontage on the south line of Ruffino Road. It is situated approximately fifteen miles southwest of the Houston central business district. The street address of the subject property is 11500 Keegan's Ridge, Houston, Texas.

LEGAL DESCRIPTION

The subject property consists of two irregularly shaped tracts of land, which are legally described as follows:

Tract I

5.5000 acres of land of the James Alston Survey, Abstract 100, Harris County, Texas, and also being out of a certain 60.6097 acre tract recorded in Volume 7462, Page 107, H.C.D.R.

Tract II

A tract of land containing 3.7330 acres out of the James Alston Survey, Abstract 100, Harris County, Texas, and also being out of a certain 60.6097 acre tract recorded in Volume 7462, Page 107, H.C.D.R.

A metes and bounds description of each tract is included in the addendum.

PURPOSE AND DATE OF THE APPRAISAL

The purpose of this appraisal is to estimate the market value of the fee simple interest, as is, as of August 1, 1990.

FUNCTION OF THE APPRAISAL

It is our understanding that the function of this appraisal is to estimate the market value for asset valuation purposes for the client.

SCOPE OF THE APPRAISAL

This is a complete narrative report in accordance with the reporting requirements of the American Institute of Real Estate Appraisers and the Uniform Standards of Professional Appraisal Practice (USPAP). An inspection of the subject property and surrounding area was undertaken. Data were then compiled concerning comparable sales and rentals in the subject property area. Sources used for data compilation include both public and private sources such as tax records, deed records,

Realtors, lenders, appraisers, and governmental authorities. The analysis includes the cost approach, market data (sales comparison) approach, and income capitalization approach.

PROPERTY RIGHTS APPRAISED

The property rights appraised are those constituting the fee simple interest in the subject property subject to the short-term residential leases in effect as of the date of appraisal.

DEFINITION OF VALUE AND INTEREST APPRAISED

According to the Resolution Trust Corporation's *Uniform Appraisal Instructions to Appraisers*, published November, 1989, market value may be defined as follows:

> *The most probable price which a property should bring in a competitive and open market under all conditions requisite to a fair sale, the buyer and seller each acting prudently, knowledgeably and assuming the price is not affected by undue stimulus. Implicit in this definition is the consummation of a sale, as of a specified date, and the passing of title from seller to buyer under conditions whereby:*
>
> **a.** *buyer and seller are typically motivated;*
> **b.** *both parties are well informed or well advised, and each acting in what he considers his own best interest;*
> **c.** *a reasonable time is allowed for exposure in the open market;*
> **d.** *payment is made in terms of cash in U.S. dollars or in terms of financial arrangements comparable thereto; and*
> **e.** *the price represents the normal consideration for the property sold unaffected by special or creative financing or sales concessions granted by anyone associated with the sale.*[1]

Fee simple estate is defined as:

> *Absolute ownership unencumbered by any other interest or estate subject only to the four powers of government.*[2]

REGIONAL ANALYSIS

The subject property is located in the Consolidated Metropolitan Statistical Area (CMSA) which encompasses seven counties including Harris, Fort Bend, Liberty, Montgomery, Waller, Galveston, and Brazoria counties. The City of Houston is the focal point of this region, being the nation's fourth most populated city and largest in the South and Southwest.

[1]*Appraisal Policies and Practices of Insured Institutions and Service Corporation*, published by the Federal Home Loan Bank Board, No. 87, 12 CFR Parts 563 and 571, page 81.

[2]American Institute of Real Estate Appraisers, *The Dictionary of Real Estate Appraisal*, Second Edition (Chicago, 1989), Page 120.

The greater Houston area or the CMSA dependency on the petrochemical industry is apparent by its growth from 1978 to 1982. Houston was historically viewed as an oil-dependent city. After going through a six-year period of depressed oil prices, this dependency has diminished to some extent.

Social/Governmental Forces

The following chart presents a demographic profile of the subject region and numerically shows the growth patterns of the area. This information has been provided by the Houston-Galveston Area Council (HGAC) and is based on population data from the 1980 census. Estimates for 1990, 2000, and 2010 were based on the 1980 census data and 1988 estimates per the HGAC.

Population	1980	1985	1990	2000	2010
Brazoria	169,578	197,164	198,178	235,821	282,384
Chambers	18,538	20,148	20,215	24,440	29,617
Fort Bend	130,846	192,487	206,120	281,270	346,214
Galveston	195,930	224,149	224,169	264,120	313,533
Harris	2,409,544	2,711,730	2,712,765	3,160,005	3,716,947
Liberty	47,088	61,164	61,186	72,890	86,809
Montgomery	128,487	165,863	166,051	218,671	290,043
Waller	19,798	25,185	25,269	30,442	40,851
8 Counties	3,119,818	3,597,890	3,613,953	4,287,659	5,106,398
Annually Compounded Percent Change		2.89%	0.09%	1.72%	1.76 %

Employment	1980	1985	1990	2000	2010
Brazoria	63,382	58,802	59,456	73,503	88,926
Chambers	6,695	2,293	7,024	9,392	12,455
Fort Bend	34,284	37,767	41,652	62,682	87,432
Galveston	68,069	68,842	68,929	74,932	80,955
Harris	1,297,209	1,368,067	1,397,532	1,735,073	2,105,331
Liberty	12,357	11,952	12,250	15,517	19,180
Montgomery	24,072	35,377	40,181	61,456	84,442
Waller	4,962	6,056	6,370	9,188	12,206
8 Counties	1,511,028	1,593,555	1,633,394	2,041,743	2,490,926
Annually Compounded Percent Change		1.07%	0.50%	2.26%	2.01%

The appraiser should be careful to explain the meaning of any tables or charts included in a report. Also, he or she should exclude from the report any regional data that fail to relate to the highest and best use and value of the appraised property.

Social attitudes primarily involve a certain quality of lifestyle common to other large urban centers. The demand for improved conditions in transportation and residential and commercial land use, in addition to availability of municipal services, has become prevalent in recent years. An example of response to this demand is the development of satellite communities such as the Woodlands, F.M. 1960-Champions Area, Katy, Kingwood, Sugarland and Clear Lake City.

Houston's political attitude is one which takes a long-term view regarding growth and development of its CMSA. While attempting to attract major employment to the area through active recruiting and tax incentives, the local government realizes the need for improved mass transit as well as other facilities needed to compete on a national basis with other urban centers. Plans for mass transit systems, capable of moving workers from the suburbs to the central business district in large numbers, are being implemented with the assistance of federal grants. The approval of the January, 1988 Metropolitan Transit Authority mobility plan has improved transportation in and around Houston. This plan is funded by an expanded sales tax base as well as funds from other government agencies. A rail system linking the sub-system and transitways to major activity centers, including connections to downtown from the Texas Medical Center, Southwest Freeway, Galleria/Post Oak and Greenway Plaza areas. The plan's scheduled date of completion is 2000. Additional improvements in 1988 and 1989 included major street improvements, bridge and utility work, totalling approximately $1.195 billion.

Culture and recreation are important resources of Houston which enhance its appeal and liveability. Houston is one of only four U.S. cities with permanent companies in the performing arts of theater, opera, ballet and symphony. In addition to the new Wortham Center, other performing centers include Jones Hall, Nina Vance Alley Theater and the Houston Music Hall. Houston additionally offers a number of art galleries and museums.

Recreational and professional sports are popular activities among Houstonians having more than 280 municipal parks with facilities available to them including tennis courts, baseball and softball fields, swimming pools, and numerous trails and parks for both active and passive recreational activities. Over two million people annually visit the 42-acre Houston Zoo. The Astrodome is home to the Houston Astros baseball team and the National Football League's Houston Oilers, while the Summit hosts the Houston Rockets basketball team.

Public education in Houston is under the direction of the Houston Independent School District (HISD). With over 193,000 students and 232 campuses, HISD offers a number of program choices in addition to the regular educational programs stressing basic skills. These include vocational education; foreign language programs; and magnet programs including studies in engineering, health professions, music, and fine arts. HISD has over 20,000 personnel, making it the second largest employer in the city.

Economic Forces

The Houston area's largest single employer (60,000 employees) is the Texas Medical Center (TMC). TMC created the world's largest medical complex and recent expansions and renovations have created hundreds of construction jobs in addition to the permanent jobs which are required to operate and service the new facilities.

Houston is a center for space ventures in both public and private sectors. In the public sector, NASA's Johnson Space Center pumped $820 million into the Houston economy in 1987 and provided approximately 14,000 jobs. A scientific laboratory is projected to be in orbit during the mid-1990s. Approximately 2,000 new jobs for engineers and technical personnel in the Clear Lake area are expected to be created from the $2 billion plus space station project.

In the private sector, various companies based in industries ranging from energy to plastics manufacturing are active in the expanding space industry. Firms which have historically developed governmental rocket boosters are pursuing federal contracts to design and produce rockets for the commercial market. Grumman has recently broken ground on a $50 million civil space headquarters in Houston. A total of 47 major aerospace firms are located in the Houston area at this time.

The Port of Houston ranks third in the nation in total tonnage and second in foreign tonnage. Industrial sites along the 50-mile ship channel provide companies with deep-water access to world markets and a link to 14,000 miles of U.S. waterways. Economically, the Port of Houston generates $3 billion annually and $50 million in local and state tax revenues.

While the Houston economy has been in recovery over the last few years, the Texas banking industry continues to restructure in 1990. Based on a study by a national banking consultant, Sheshunoff & Company, most of the major Texas banks will eventually be owned by out-of-state banks or be recapitalized and owned by new investors. This has been proven the case for five of Houston's largest banks. Sheshunoff anticipates more bank acquisitions as investors gain a better conception of expected loan losses and accurate asset values. Independent banks are expected to profit from the change of ownership of the larger banks and to grow into large regionally owned institutions in the next five to ten years.

Environmental Factors

As the Houston area has grown, flood control has been a growing environmental concern. A number of bond issues have been passed in recent years in order to help finance different flood control problems for growth patterns into the 21st century. While the Houston area is subject to flood problems due to its elevation and soil composition, the problem has been limited, to a large degree, by improvements made by the Harris County Flood Control District.

Summary

The Greater Houston area's future looks promising, with recent economic trends looking more encouraging than any time over the last few years. Despite the recession, which was reflective in nearly all sectors of the economy, there are definite signs of recovery reflected in the Houston economy. Through diversification of both energy-dependent and energy-independent sectors and continued stability of oil prices, Houston's economy should continue to expand.

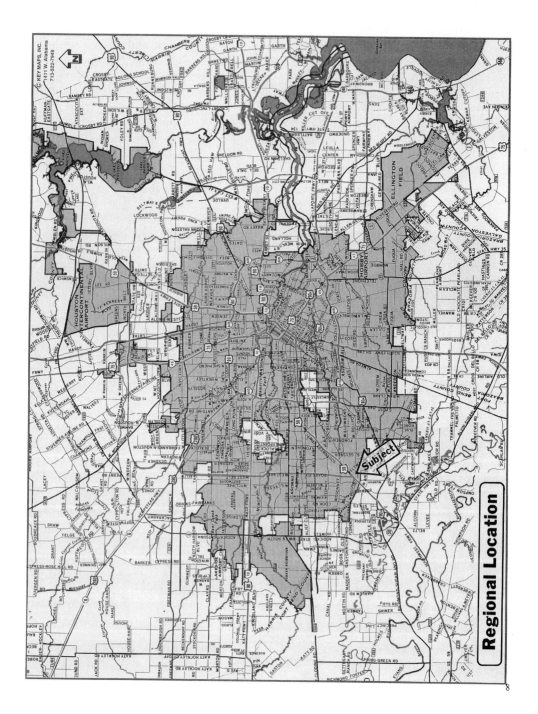

Regional Location

8

484

APARTMENT MARKET OVERVIEW

Harris County Market

A semi-annual survey of the Harris County apartment market is conducted by REVAC. Harris County is divided into 36 different submarket areas in the survey, which includes projects with five or more units. REVAC's Spring 1990 Occupancy and Rental Survey, included 223,383 units of the 399,883 existing units in Harris County. This report distinguishes between owner-paid utility projects and resident-paid utility projects. As the subject property is an individually metered project, the majority of our analysis is based on the resident-paid utility project data.

The Houston apartment market continues to be the most active segment of the Houston commercial real estate marketplace. In fact, Houston leads the country in apartment investment. During an 18-month period from mid-1988 to the end of 1989, more than 25 percent of Houston's entire apartment inventory of 400,000 units changed hands. A reassuring aspect of this market and one that indicates that recovery is well under way is that foreclosures are down dramatically from the previous four years. Sales activity has remained strong, although the actual number of projects sold was down in 1989 from 1988. This decrease occurred because the number of foreclosures decreased and there were fewer projects on the market. Most of the Class A, more desirable projects, had already been sold.

Financing of projects has become more difficult as more lender/owners are requiring all cash as opposed to the very attractive terms they were offering in 1987 and 1988. Buyers who do not have solid financial backing are having problems obtaining financing. The positive news is the increasing numbers of lenders, including local banks, who are beginning to provide funds for refinancing and rehabilitation of older projects.

Building permits.   Another indication that the apartment market has improved can be seen in the dramatic increase in building permits and new project construction. Beginning in July of 1989, the number of building permits for multi-family dwelling units increased significantly. A total of 3,258 units were permitted for the year. As depicted in the following table, building permit activity slowed in the first quarter of 1990.

APARTMENT UNIT BUILDING PERMITS ISSUED IN HARRIS COUNTY (1983 - 1990)

Year	Building permits
1983	14,193
1984	6,569
1985	1,849
1986	266
1987	152
1988	472
1989	3,258
1990 YTD	308

New construction   Until 1989, there had been very little new construction of apartment units for the preceding five years. Since then, Houston/Harris County has experienced a dramatic increase in construction activity with 755 units in three projects starting construction in the six-month period of October 1, 1989 through April 1, 1990. We anticipate an increase in the number of new units on the market this year due to the issuance of 3,258 building permits in 1989 alone. The following depicts new construction in Harris County through Spring 1990.

NEW APARTMENT UNIT CONSTRUCTION HISTORY IN HARRIS COUNTY (1983-1990)

Year	New units	Cumulative units
Prior to 1960	15,710	15,710
1960 - 1969	81,725	97,435
1970 - 1979	189,202	286,637
1980	15,960	302,597
1981	13,747	316,344
1982	26,476	342,820
1983	35,056	377,876
1984	15,762	393,638
1985	2,590	396,228
1986	1,766	397,994
1987	94	398,088
1988	538	398,626
1989	1,207	399,833
1990 YTD	0	399,833
Less Units Removed due to Demolition		9,772
Total Units as of Spring 1990		390,061

Due to the extremely soft market conditions which have been experienced over the past several years, numerous units have been demolished. For this reason, we have adjusted the foregoing cumulative total downward by 9,772 to reflect the number of units which were demolished during this time period.

Occupancy, vacancy, and absorption.   Occupancy improved significantly in most areas of the city causing some dramatic rental increases in the higher quality, better located properties. These increases have made many projects more attractive and saleable to investors.

According to the Spring 1990 REVAC report, the overall physical vacancy for Harris County as of April 1, 1990, was 9.26%, which is below the October 1, 1989 rate of 10.15%. The April 1, 1989 rate was 12.48%. Currently, the overall physical vacancy rate is at its lowest level in over six years. The majority of the submarkets reported increases in occupancy rates during the past year. The following chart depicts a history of physical vacancy of apartment units during the past several years for both owner paid and resident paid (utilities) apartment projects in the Harris County area.

PHYSICAL VACANCY HISTORY FOR HARRIS COUNTY (4/83 - 4/90)

Time period	Vacancy rate
04/83	17.2%
10/83	17.5%
04/84	18.2%
10/84	18.8%
04/85	16.9%
10/85	16.2%
04/86	16.8%
10/86	17.5%
04/87	18.7%
10/87	18.2%
04/88	15.9%
10/88	14.1%
04/89	12.5%
10/89	10.2%
04/90	9.3%

SEMI-ANNUAL VACANCY RATE

Net unit absorption, as defined by REVAC Publications, Inc., is the sum of the net new units absorbed plus the older units absorbed. If the net units absorbed are a plus, that indicates positive growth and demand for new units. However, a negative sign indicates a decrease in demand or negative growth. Harris County reported a positive net unit absorption during the previous 36 months. Of the 36 submarkets, only nine reported negative net unit absorption. The following chart illustrates the history of Harris County net unit absorption.

NET UNIT ABSORPTION HISTORY FOR HARRIS COUNTY (1983 - 1990)

Time period	Total net absorbed	Annualized
Spring 1983	−1,677 Units	
Fall 1983	+6,148 Units	+ 4,471 Units - 1983
Spring 1984	+3,922 Units	
Fall 1984	−2,294 Units	+ 1,628 Units - 1984
Spring 1985	+7,211 Units	
Fall 1985	+3,352 Units	+10,563 Units - 1985
Spring 1986	−2,522 Units	
Fall 1986	−2,705 Units	− 5,227 Units - 1986
Spring 1987	−2,981 Units	
Fall 1987	+2,416 Units	− 565 Units - 1987
Spring 1988	+8,697 Units	
Fall 1988	+7,061 Units	+15,758 Units - 1988
Spring 1989	+7,200 Units	
Fall 1989	+9,129 Units	+16,329 Units - 1989
Spring 1990	+4,843 Units	+ 4,843 Units - 1990

NET ABSORPTION

The positive 15,758 net unit absorption during 1988 was the first positive absorption since 1985. The positive absorption of 16,329 units during 1989 indicates a continuation of the positive absorption trend, and exhibits a strengthening market. This strengthening has continued through the first quarter of 1990.

A comparison of the annual construction, annualized net units absorption, and end of year vacancy rates is shown in the following chart.

ANNUAL CONSTRUCTION, NET ABSORPTION AND VACANCY COMPARISON
FOR HARRIS COUNTY (1983 - 1990)

Year	Annualized unit absorption	End of year vacancy rate	Annual construction
1983	+ 4,471 Units	17.5%	36,056
1984	+ 1,628 Units	18.8%	15,762
1985	+10,563 Units	16.2%	2,590
1986	− 5,227 Units	17.5%	1,766
1987	− 565 Units	18.2%	94
1988	+15,758 Units	14.1%	538
1989	+16,329 Units	10.2%	1,207
1990	4,843 Units	9.3%	0

The foregoing chart indicates that net unit absorption was at a peak during 1989, with the vacancy rate being at one of the lowest levels experienced during the same period of time. Annual construction was at its peak during 1983, when absorption was average and vacancy was high. The most recent figures indicate that the worst is over and that vacancies will most probably continue to decline.

Many apartment projects have been boarded up by the lenders (now owners) throughout Harris County. The purpose of this process is to alleviate the amount of vandalism which often occurs when a property is vacant or not actively managed. Rather than incur the heavy expense of renovation, many project owners are opting to demolish older, non–income-producing apartment properties. Many of the owners demolishing projects today are lenders who have received ownership through foreclosure. Actual demolitions have picked up significantly over the past several months. A total of 9,772 units have been removed via demolition in addition to the non-operating units.

During the past 12 months, REVAC indicates that another 17,802 units have been shut down (non-operating). About 6,837 of the non-operating units are currently being renovated. According to REVAC, the Spring Branch market area has the greatest number of apartment closings of 4,020; the Bellaire-Southwest market area has the second greatest number of closed apartments with 2,348 units.

REVAC notes that the positive net unit absorption may be temporary, or conditional, because as projects are renovated and come back on the market, there will be an increase in supply. Additionally, as non-operating projects are returned to operating status, and if apartment demand does not increase to absorb the surplus, the net unit absorption level could become negative again. There are several submarkets which are experiencing new apartment construction. These areas may experience a drop in net unit absorption as the new units open and come on the market. The areas of Clear Lake and the Inner Loop are the areas which are experiencing the most new construction.

Concessions.   Rental concessions have become less of a consideration during the past few years and are relatively nonexistent. During 1984 and 1985, as an incentive to entice renters into a project, apartment owners offered trips to exotic places, cash, microwave ovens, free rent during some portion of the lease, as well as other promotions. However, those concessions were offered at a time when the quoted rental rates were still high. During 1986 and 1987, owners dramatically dropped rental rates in lieu of offering attractive rental concessions, and began quoting "effective" rental rates. Most recently, however, rental rates have begun to rise.

Rental rates.   As mentioned previously, apartment owners are quoting on an effective rental rate basis. As shown in the following chart, the mean rental rate for individually metered projects had been falling since 1983. However, stability is evident as the mean monthly rental rate has steadily been increasing since 1986 - 1987. The increases of $20.00 and $19.00, during the last reporting periods, resulted in the highest mean monthly rental rates since 1984.

APARTMENT RENTAL RATE HISTORY FOR HARRIS COUNTY 4/84 - 4/90

	Individually metered		Master meter	
Period	Monthly rental	Rental PSF	Monthly rental	Rental PSF
04/84	$348	$.422	$400	$.478
10/84	$344	$.417	$385	$.456
04/85	$339	$.404	$379	$.435
10/85	$319	$.395	$371	$.465
04/86	$318	$.385	$365	$.435
10/86	$318	$.376	$358	$.434
04/87	$306	$.371	$357	$.442
10/87	$305	$.376	$363	$.439
04/88	$305	$.382	$371	$.458
10/88	$313	$.392	$372	$.468
04/89	$326	$.408	$381	$.479
10/89	$343	$.431	$402	$.507
04/90	$363	$.456	$421	$.531

REVAC noted that rental rates lag occupancy rates whether they are rising or falling. This is a "cause and effect" relationship, whereby the owners do not react with rental rate changes until it is reflected in the occupancy figures. Since improvements in occupancy have been noted, rental rates are beginning to rise.

Conclusion.   Foreclosures are expected to continue to decline with sales remaining at the same level as 1989. The properties held by the Resolution Trust Corporation are not anticipated to have a real impact on the market. The few Class A properties remaining should see heavy demand. The lesser quality properties will likely not sell unless the price is very competitive or owner financing is offered.

With approximately 3,000 new units coming on the market, along with over 4,000 rehabilitated units coming back on the market, occupancy could drop in the older, poorly located projects. However, rents will continue to increase in the better projects. Rental rates for new luxury apartments are expected to average $0.85 to $0.90 per square foot.

Lenders will gain more and more confidence in the market and as rents increase, more funds will be available for new as well as existing properties.

A slight change in the buyer profile can be expected. Life insurance companies and other institutional investors will begin looking at the better projects that have proven they can perform and are solid investments with good potential for the future.

Sharpstown - Southwest Market Area

General. REVAC divides Harris County into 36 submarket areas. The subject property is located in the defined REVAC Sharpstown - Southwest market area, which is bound by the Harris County line to the south, Hillcroft to the east, Westpark, Bellaire, and Bissonnet to the north, and Cook and Roark Roads to the west.

The Spring, 1990 occupancy and rental survey for the Sharpstown southwest market area encompasses 57,643 existing apartment units in an area measuring approximately 34 square miles. This market area represents 14.5% of the total Harris County supply of apartment units, and ranks as the largest market area in terms of total number of units.

Construction and building permits. No new apartment units have been constructed in the subject market area since 1988, as has been the situation throughout most of Harris County. The following chart depicts new construction within the Sharpstown - Southwest market, from 1976 through 1990.

NEW CONSTRUCTION HISTORY FOR SHARPSTOWN - SOUTHWEST MARKET AREA

Year	New units	Cumulative units
Prior to 1960	——	0
1960-1969	5,756	5,756
1970-1979	34,881	40,637
1980	3,987	44,624
1981	2,634	47,258
1982	4,552	51,810
1983	4,217	56,027
1984	1,067	57,094
1985	388	57,482
1986	104	57,586
1987	28	57,614
1988	28	57,642
1989	0	57,642
1990	0	57,642

As shown above, the number of new units in this submarket remained relatively steady each year, with the exception of the number of new units added during 1982 and 1983. The majority of new apartment units were added during this period. There are no new apartment projects presently under construction within the market area, and no building permits have been issued. The number of vacant land transactions for multifamily housing has slowed concurrent with the cessation of new apartment construction.

Occupancy.   REVAC's Spring 1990 survey indicated that 4,843 apartment units were absorbed in the entire Houston/Harris County area. A total of 1,741 apartment units were absorbed in the Sharpstown - Southwest market area. The following chart depicts net unit absorption for this market area.

NEW APARTMENT UNIT ABSORPTION HISTORY FOR SHARPSTOWN - SOUTHWEST MARKET AREA 1984 - 1990

Time period	Total net absorption	Annualized
Spring 1984	−13 Units	
Fall 1984	−233 Units	−246 Units - 1984
Spring 1985	+2,957 Units	
Fall 1985	+343 Units	+3,300 Units - 1985
Spring 1986	−184 Units	
Fall 1986	−1,467 Units	−1,651 Units - 1986
Spring 1987	−1,165 Units	
Fall 1987	+780 Units	−385 Units - 1987
Spring 1988	+238 Units	
Fall 1988	+1,180 Units	+1,418 Units - 1988
Spring 1989	+353 Units	
Fall 1989	+1,566 Units	+1,919 Units - 1989
Spring 1990	+1,741 Units	+1,741 Units - 1990 YTD

Vacancy.   According to REVAC, during the period spanning from 1984 to 1988, vacancy rates for resident paid, individually metered projects, had hovered around 18%. Since 1989, vacancy rates have begun to drop, and as shown in the following chart, vacancy rates are currently at the lowest level in over nine years.

% VACANCY RATES - INDIVIDUALLY METERED PROJECTS

Time period	Vacancy level
Spring 1984	23.0%
Fall 1984	23.0%
Spring 1985	17.0%
Fall 1985	15.5%
Spring 1986	15.9%
Fall 1986	18.7%
Spring 1987	20.3%
Fall 1987	18.9%

Spring 1988	17.6%
Fall 1988	16.0%
Spring 1989	15.9%
Fall 1989	13.8%
Spring 1990	11.0%

Absorption. Absorption is an indication of demand. A decrease in demand, coupled with the significant oversupply of units, results in the entire market experiencing external obsolescence. External obsolescence can be measured by decreased rental rates. Current rental rates do not justify the construction of an apartment complex.

As of April 1990, a total of 6,652 vacant apartment units were reported to exist in the Sharpstown - Southwest market area, which is equivalent to a 11.96% physical vacancy rate for all operating units. This is an improvement over the 14.95% vacancy reported in October of 1989. Only one foreclosure has been reported in 1990, down from 27 projects foreclosed in 1989. It is our opinion that the vacancy rate will remain between 10% and 20% for the next several years, before beginning a gradual increase. We do not believe there will be any sharp rises or falls during this recovery process.

Concessions. Fewer concessions are currently being offered and appear to be limited to reduced security deposits or move-in specials of custom paint, wallpaper, and carpet. Most owners have decreased their rental rates and are now quoting effective rental rates.

Rental rates. Rental rates for individually metered projects in the Sharpstown Southwest market area have been rising gradually since Fall 1987. The mean rental rate for Harris County increased for the fifth consecutive reporting period as depicted in the following chart.

MONTHLY RENTAL RATES COMPARISON INDIVIDUALLY METERED PROJECTS

Period	Sharpstown-Southwest	Harris County
Spring 1984	$344	$348
Fall 1984	$330	$344
Spring 1985	$315	$339
Fall 1985	$333	$319
Spring 1986	$298	$318
Fall 1986	$290	$318
Spring 1987	$305	$306
Fall 1987	$287	$305
Spring 1988	$289	$305
Fall 1988	$294	$313
Spring 1989	$309	$326
Fall 1989	$315	$343
Spring 1990	$333	$363

As seen in the foregoing chart, rental rates in the Sharpstown-Southwest market area have always been slightly below the mean rental rate for Harris County as a whole. The difference has become greater than during the early 1980's. Rental rates have increased steadily during the past five reporting periods. It is our opinion that rates will continue to increase during the next several years.

Conclusions.   The physical vacancy rate in the Sharpstown - Southwest area was 11.96% as of April, 1990, slightly greater than the entire overall average for Harris County, which was 9.62%. Occupancy levels for this submarket have shown steady improvement since 1987. In our opinion, the vacancy rate will continue to improve gradually as the population of Houston increases, and job formation improves.

As occupancy levels rise, it appears reasonable that rental rates will continue to increase gradually during the next several years. Rental rates are forecasted to continue an upward trend as demand catches up with supply. As the market continues to firm, rental concessions will most likely become obsolete.

No dramatic new construction of multifamily rental units is anticipated, due to the combined factors of an oversupply of units, as well as the passage of the new tax law, and lack of construction financing. Current rental rates make the construction of a new rental property infeasible. Many apartment facilities in the area are similar in age to the subject property, and are experiencing similar rental rates and occupancy levels.

The subject property is specifically located on the west line of Keegan's Bayou, north of West Bellfort. Several apartment complexes are located in close proximity to the subject property. The majority of land usage in this area consists of retail, multifamily residential, and vacant land. The most comparable apartment projects are located along Keegan's Bayou.

Most of the apartment complexes in the area were constructed about the same time, in the late 1970's, and are individually metered. The projects are in average to good condition. The subject property has been adequately maintained, as have most of the competing projects. As a result of the positive occupancy and rental rate trends, a majority of the apartment managers are addressing major maintenance problems such as plumbing, concrete paving, roofing, HVAC systems, fences, and access gate repairs. The subject is in superior condition as compared to the adjacent complexes; however, it is considered inferior to a number of complexes in the area which have recently been renovated.

We surveyed seven apartment complexes in the area which were considered to be comparable to the subject property. In the final analysis, only five were utilized; however, the others lent support to the analysis. The two comparables were discarded due to recent rehabilitation or extra amenities, such as controlled access gates and fireplaces.

Apartment managers surveyed reported occupancy levels between 75% and approximately 90%. The subject property is currently 92% occupied. Overall, most of the comparable apartment complexes in this area have occupancy levels which are in line with the Sharpstown - Southwest submarket. Complexes which are newer and exhibit superior construction and amenities typically have higher occupancy levels.

Most managers stated that rental rates have increased during the last twelve months. Several managers noted that they had increased their rents several times during the last year. They also noted that occupancies have continued to rise slowly. Given the anticipated economic conditions of the Houston area, it is our opinion that rent levels in this area will continue a gradual increase during the next twenty-four (24) months, as occupancy levels continue to firm. As the population base increases, the excess supply of apartment units will gradually be reduced, and rent levels should return to normal growth levels.

A discussion of marketing techniques, occupancy, and absorption levels for competitive properties should be a part of any income property appraisal assignment.

Subject Property

As was mentioned previously, the Sharpstown - Southwest market area reported a net unit absorption of positive 1,919 units, during 1989. Another 1,741 units were absorbed between October, 1990 and April, 1990. The total five-year net absorption for this area was positive 4,601 units or an average annual absorption of positive 920 units. We projected that the area will continue to absorb the existing inventory of vacant units (6,652) as long as there is no new construction activity.

A 92% stabilized occupancy level for income producing properties is commonly utilized. Since the actual occupancy of the subject property is currently 92%, which is equal to the stabilized occupancy for apartment projects in the area, the subject property has reached stabilization, and therefore, an absorption projection is not necessary. It is our opinion that the occupancy rate will fall slightly as rental rates are increased to feasible levels. Along with the rise in rental rates will most likely come a change in tenant profile. Therefore, it is our opinion that a stabilized occupancy of 92% is reasonable.

The manager stated that occupancy levels for the subject property have gradually increased from 62%, at the beginning of the year, to the current 92% level. This increased occupancy has been steady despite periodic rental rate increases. It is felt that the subject property is in superior condition as compared to neighboring projects of the same age. Major items of deferred maintenance have been, and are continuing to be, corrected. This factor may account for the higher than average occupancy. The following chart summarizes the occupancy history of the subject property.

OCCUPANCY AND RENTAL RATE HISTORY OF THE SUBJECT PROPERTY

Date	Occupancy rate	Avg. $/SF
01/90	62%	$0.36
02/90	66%	$0.36
03/90	63%	$0.36
04/90	71%	$0.37
05/90	72%	$0.38
06/90	81%	$0.40
07/90	89%	$0.40
08/90	92%	$0.42

It is our opinion that the majority of projects in the subject area are in a similar condition as compared to the subject property. In addition, the subject property has standard amenities and an effective age of 12 years. It has been adequately maintained, and can compete well with other apartment complexes in the neighborhood. Therefore, it is our opinion that the subject property will maintain its stabilized occupancy rate, and can continue to increase rental rates.

The projection of market recovery is a function of supply and demand factors, the competitiveness of the specific submarket, and the site-specific characteristics of the property being appraised. A given property in a given submarket may very well exhibit sufficient demand to warrant construction today, while other properties, in other submarkets, may take longer than the macro market to recover.

NEIGHBORHOOD ANALYSIS

A neighborhood may be defined as "a group of complementary land uses".[3]

Neighborhood boundaries are defined because properties within neighborhoods tend to exhibit similar characteristics with regard to land use and overall desirability, and they are affected by similar physical, economic, governmental and social forces.

The subject neighborhood is located in the southwest quadrant of Houston, approximately fifteen miles southwest of the central business district. The neighborhood is bound on the north by Bellaire Boulevard; on the south by West Bellfort; on the east by Wilcrest; and on the west by Hillcroft. The appraised property is located along the west line of Keegan's Ridge, north of West Bellfort and south of Keegan's Bayou. The site is situated south of the Southwest Freeway and Sam Houston Tollway interchange.

The major thoroughfares traversing the subject neighborhood are the Southwest Freeway (U.S. 59), Sam Houston Tollway/West Belt, Wilcrest, South Gessner, Fondren, Hillcroft, Bellaire Boulevard, Beechnut, Bissonnet, and West Bellfort.

[3]*The Dictionary of Real Estate Appraisal*, Page 207.

Access to the subject neighborhood is considered to be very good, as the Southwest Freeway traverses the neighborhood in a southwest/northeast direction, and the Sam Houston Tollway runs north and south near the western perimeter of the neighborhood. The central business district can be accessed directly from the Southwest Freeway; this highway also provides access to Loop 610. The Sam Houston Tollway provides access to I.H. 10 and the Northwest Freeway, and it is now open to Houston Intercontinental Airport. The subject property may be accessed from most any portion of the area from the Southwest Freeway or the Sam Houston Tollway.

Predominant development in the subject neighborhood is primarily commercial along the Southwest Freeway, with some single-family residential adjoining the service roads. Properties along the Tollway are not as densely developed as on the Southwest Freeway. Existing improvements consist of retail, multi-family and office.

Some new construction is taking place along the Southwest Freeway within the subject neighborhood. One of the newest developments is the recently completed Sterling McCall Toyota automobile dealership. A large amount of vacant land is available along West Bellfort, east of the Southwest Freeway/Sam Houston Tollway interchange. However, the majority of the subject neighborhood has been developed and some properties in the area have reached the end of their economic lives. As these properties are razed, new construction will take place in the future.

In the vicinity of the subject property, east of the Southwest Freeway, is some multi-family development and a large amount of vacant land. The area to the west of the freeway is developed with more commercial properties, including a neighborhood shopping center at the intersection of Highway 59 and West Bellfort, and a large number of fast food establishments, along with other small retail properties.

A large portion of the subject neighborhood consists of stable middle-income residential subdivisions which are interspersed between the major thoroughfares. This residential development supports the commercial businesses in the neighborhood.

Property values within the subject neighborhood appear to be stable, as indicated by the data utilized in this analysis. A minimal amount of development is occurring in the subject neighborhood, mostly along southwestern portions of the Southwest Freeway. This area was considered one of the growth areas in Houston until the mid 1980's and, it is showing signs of new growth at the current time.

Summary

In conclusion, the subject is located in an area that is easily accessible and well located relative to major employment centers. The area is supported by a stable, large middle-income residential neighborhood which includes Sharpstown development, which began in the 1960's. The regional Sharpstown Shopping Mall is located within the neighborhood at the intersection of Bellaire and the Southwest

Freeway. Portions of the Southwest Freeway, in the subject neighborhood, are undergoing construction which will widen the freeway from six to eight lanes and add a center HOV lane. The feeder roads will also be widened from two to three lanes on either side. Although traffic is currently somewhat congested due to this construction, the long-term benefits of this expansion project are expected to outweigh the present inconveniences. It appears that the subject area will reflect moderate growth trends in the foreseeable future.

See Chapter 6 for additional discussion of neighborhood analysis.

SITE ANALYSIS

Location

The appraised site is composed of two tracts of land containing 5.5 and 3.733 acres, for a total of 9.233 acres, or 402,189 square feet. This irregularly shaped tract is located along the west line of Keegan's Ridge, north of West Bellfort and south of Keegan's Bayou. The subject tract is located just south of the Southwest Freeway/Sam Houston Tollway interchange.

Adjacent Properties

The Southwest Terrace Apartments are located to the south of the subject site. Ruffino Road dead ends on the north side of the tract, with heavy brush and trees to the east of this northern portion of the site. The western line of the subject tract borders vacant land reportedly owned by the Metropolitan Transit Authority. It is speculated that this tract will be developed with a Park 'N Ride lot or an MTA bus parking lot. Across Keegan's Ridge, to the east of the subject, are more rental apartments.

Shape and Size

The subject site is irregular in shape with 801.42 front feet on Keegan's Ridge, 203.02 front feet on Ruffino Road and 183.46 front feet along an arc located at the intersection of Keegan's Ridge and Ruffino Road. Site plans of the two tracts are located at the end of this section.

Topography and Drainage

The subject tract is basically level and at street grade. No standing water was noted at the time of inspection. Drainage appears to be adequate.

Nuisances and Hazards

Congress passed Public Law 93-234 in 1973 entitled "The Flood Disaster Protection Act of 1973", which prohibits federally insured banks, savings and loans, and other federally insured lending institutions from making, increasing, extending, or renewing any loan on improved property located within a special flood hazard area, as determined by the Federal Insurance Administration, unless there is participation in the Federal Insurance Program. According to the F.I.R.M. Community Panel No. 480296-0150D, dated September 27, 1985, the subject tract lies mostly in Zone C, an area of minimal flood. It appears that the northern portion of the site lies in Zone A4, an area of 100-year flood, and a portion lies in Zone B, an area of 500-year flood. It is recommended that a survey be made by a qualified engineer to determine the exact location of the subject tract within each of the flood zones. A floodplain map follows the surveys at the end of this section.

Soils

We have not reviewed a soils report or toxicity investigation for the subject site. For the purpose of this appraisal, we assume the soil to be free of toxic substances and of adequate load bearing capacities to support any future improvements.

Streets

The west line of the subject has frontage on Keegan's Ridge which is a two-lane, 40-foot-wide, concrete-paved thoroughfare with curbs, gutters and storm sewers. Keegan's Ridge runs north from West Bellfort to Ruffino Road, where it dead ends. The tract also has a small amount of frontage along Ruffino Road which is a two-lane, east/west, 40-foot-wide, concrete-paved right-of-way. Ruffino runs east from Keegan's Ridge, approximately three-quarters of a mile to West Bellfort where it ends.

Utilities

The following utilities are available on the site; the servicing departments are listed below:

Utilities	Servicing department
Electricity	Houston Lighting & Power
Telephone	Southwestern Bell Telephone
Water/Sewer	City of Houston
Natural Gas	Entex

Zoning

The subject property is located within the city limits of Houston and within Harris County, neither of which enforce a zoning ordinance.

Easements

To the best of our knowledge, no adverse easements, encroachments, or restrictions exist.

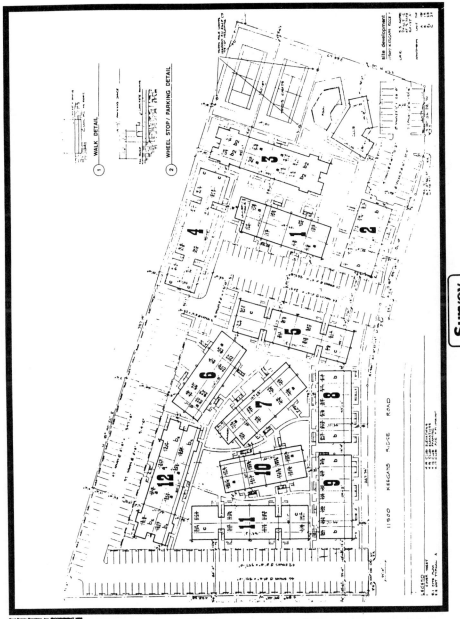

Survey

WALK DETAIL

WHEEL STOP / PARKING DETAIL

Survey

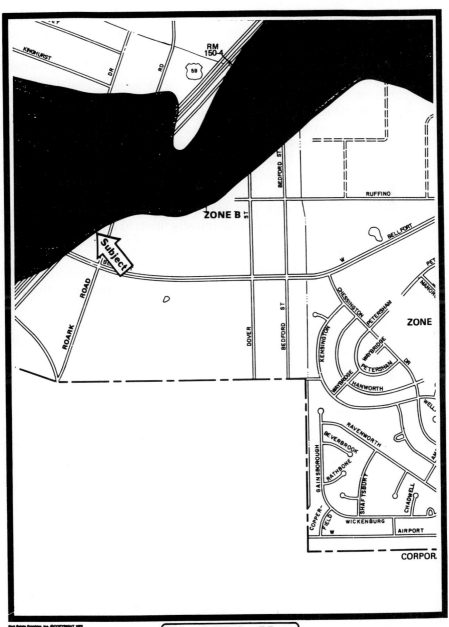

Flood Plain Map

DESCRIPTION OF THE IMPROVEMENTS

The following is a brief discussion of the construction of the subject improvements. A detailed set of the specifications was not provided. The following description of the improvements was obtained from visual inspection of the property. However, inspection of site work, foundation, and structural framing of the subject was not possible on the date of appraisal. Thus, it has been assumed these items have been completed in a normal and workmanlike manner. Please refer to the contingent and limiting conditions section of this report for a more thorough understanding of the conditions upon which the value conclusion contained herein was based.

The subject improvements consist of an existing 318 unit, garden style, multiple family apartment project known as the Keegan's Mill Apartments. The project was constructed in two phases. Phase I was completed in 1977 and consists of 182 units, two laundry rooms, an office/club house and swimming pool situated on a 5.5-acre tract of land. In 1978, the second phase was completed which consists of 136 units and two laundry rooms situated on a 3.733-acre site. The entire complex contains approximately 218,016 square feet of net rentable area in 21 two-story buildings. It is an individually metered project, with residents paying their own electricity. The average unit size is 686 square feet, and the property has a density of 34.44 units per acre.

The apartment buildings are walk up, garden type construction. In addition to the 21 buildings containing the dwelling units, the project includes a 2,586 square foot office/club house and 2,700 square feet in four laundry/boiler/storage rooms, for a total of 223,302 square feet of gross building area. Provided in the addendum of this report are floor plans of each of the units. Gross building area, dimensions and net rentable area of the subject property are based on the building plans contained in the addendum.

> Somewhere near here, the appraiser needs to discuss briefly the history of the property, including such items as dates when additions and alterations to the building(s) occurred. It is recommended that a five-year history of prior sales of the appraised property be fully discussed.

As summarized below, the subject property offers five floor plan options.

UNIT MIX

	Unit type	# Units	% of Project	Rentable sq.ft.	Total sq.ft.	% of project
A	1BR/1BA	160	50.32%	602	96,320	44.18%
B	1BR/1BA	78	24.53%	680	53,040	24.33%
B-2	2BR/2BA/Den	16	5.03%	1,059	16,944	7.77%
C	2BR/1BA	48	15.09%	796	38,208	17.53%
D	2BR/2BA	16	5.03%	844	13,504	6.19%
	Total	318	100.00%	Avg: 686	218,016	100.00%

Parking spaces are unassigned on a "first come - first serve" basis. The total number of parking spaces is 450, which is equivalent to 1.42 spaces per unit. This ratio is considered to be adequate for this type of facility.

An eight-foot wood fence extends along the northern boundary of the site and a six-foot chain-link fence extends along the western and southern boundaries, respectively.

The apartment buildings are generally described as wood frame structures with reinforced concrete slab foundation, single hung windows with aluminum framing, composition shingle pitch roofing, and vertical exterior walls of brick veneer and wood siding. Metal stairways with concrete steps provide access to the upstairs units.

Interior finish consists of painted sheetrock walls and ceilings with some accent wallpaper, hollow core doors, vinyl tile in the kitchen and baths, and carpeting throughout the remainder of the units. The B units, typical of most units in the complex, have some textured walls and wallpaper in the kitchen, a pantry, porcelain sinks and tubs, a cultured marble vanity, breakfast bar, Whirlpool appliances, coat closet, linen closet, large walk-in closet in bedroom with built-in shelves, mini blinds and patio or balcony area. The B2 unit is a mother-in-law plan which has washer/dryer connections and a private patio. The C unit has a sliding glass door with vertical blinds to the balcony or patio off of the living room.

The units have incandescent lighting, porcelain bathtub with shower, and formica-covered counter tops. All electric kitchens are supplied with the following Whirlpool appliances: oven/range, dishwasher, frost-free refrigerator, garbage disposal, and upper hood containing fan and filter. All of the units have smoke detectors and are wired for cable television. All units have individual heating and air conditioning units, with air compressors and coil fans located on the ground.

Based on information provided by the owner and our physical inspection, the improvements have the following construction characteristics.

Structural

Foundation:	Steel reinforced grade level concrete slab.
Framing:	Wood framing. Balconies are steel frame with concrete floors supported with steel.
Exterior Walls:	Brick veneer with wood siding.
Roof:	Composition shingle pitch roof; one building has gable roof.
Gutters/downspouts:	Aluminum gutters and downspouts.
Exterior Doors:	All exterior doors are hollow core wood doors.
Stairs:	Metal stairs with metal pans and concrete pebbled steps.
Exterior Lighting:	Wall-hung porch lamps.

Interior Finish

Ceilings and Walls:	Painted sheetrock walls with some texturing and some wallpaper.
Flooring:	Carpet over pad in all living areas and vinyl tile in kitchen and bathrooms.
Interior Doors:	Hollow core wood doors.
Kitchen Appliances:	Appliances included Whirlpool dishwasher, garbage disposal, oven/range, hood and fan, frost-free refrigerator.
Hot Water:	Three commercial-grade, gas-fired heaters.
Windows:	Tempered single pane glass in aluminum frames.
Heating and Cooling:	Each unit is individually heated and air conditioned by a 1.5-ton system.
Electrical:	Adequate electrical outlets and ceiling mounted light fixtures in each unit. The complex is individually metered. The project appears to conform with local codes.
Plumbing:	Appears to be in conformity with local codes.
Fire Protection:	Smoke alarms

Other Improvements

Landscaping:	Landscaped with mature shrubbery, trees and flowers.
Swimming Pools:	One located near the clubhouse.
Laundry Rooms:	Four on site.
Parking:	Total of approximately 450 concrete paved, open parking spaces. All parking areas are striped. Equivalent to 1.42 spaces per unit.

This outline format is easier for clients and reviewers to determine the physical features of the building(s) than use of a paragraph format. This format begins with the foundation and proceeds through the exterior and interior walls, roof covering, flooring, and plumbing.

Exterior and interior photographs of the improvements follow.

View of typical apartment building located within the complex.

View of playground area.

View of two lighted tennis courts.

View of pool area.

View of typical laundry room facility.

Interior view of clubhouse.

Interior view of the kitchen and dining area in the A unit model.

Interior master bedroom view in a B-2 unit.

ANALYSIS OF IMPROVEMENTS

The subject property is considered to be in average overall condition for a complex of its size and age. The apartment manager informed us that one of the hot water boilers was replaced in 1989 and another is being replaced at this time. She does not expect to replace the third boiler, as it is only a few years old. The manager plans to put a new roof (gable) on one building this year. The roofs over the remaining buildings are in average condition with no major reported problems and only minor patchwork is scheduled. The management plans to install controlled access gates, with two entrances and two exits, this summer. In addition, more sidewalks will be poured on the site. Also planned is the erection of a large billboard sign which will be visible from West Bellfort and somewhat visible from the Southwest Freeway.

We inspected four vacant, unoccupied units in the subject property, and based on our physical inspection, there were few items of deferred maintenance noted, as these were model units.

The manager indicated that four to six units are in need of new carpet and countertops and are currently not rentable, but could be made ready within a short period of time.

The manager informed us that repairs are completed as units are vacated. These repairs consist of painting the interior, replacing wallpaper, replacing some of the flooring with carpeting and vinyl tile. The manager estimated that they need to replace the carpeting in three units at the present time.

In addition to the items of interior deferred maintenance noted, there were exterior deferred maintenance items noted as well. Exterior deferred maintenance included guttering in need of repair, shingle repair, new awnings and tennis screens, patching of concrete driveways, new gable roof on one building and paint touchup of wood siding.

While we were unable to inspect all of the units because of time constraints and the fact that many were occupied, it is reasonable to assume that some deferred maintenance is present, in the form of minor repairs to the occupied units as well. Some of these repairs include painting, cleaning of kitchens and bathrooms, and minor repairs to carpet. We have estimated that the costs associated with this minor repair will be $10,000, and will be sufficient to cure these minor deferred maintenance items.

The swimming pool appeared to be well maintained and in good working order. The parking areas were concrete paved and in average condition, with minor repairs required.

The total deferred maintenance costs were estimated:

ESTIMATED DEFERRED MAINTENANCE ITEMS

Item	Amount
Parking Repairs	$13,300
Minor Repairs	10,000
New Boiler	7,500
Exterior Repairs	6,000
New Gable Roof	6,600
Shingle Repair	1,000
Gutter Repair	3,000
New Awnings & Tennis Screens	2,600
Total:	$50,000

Total deferred maintenance is estimated to be $50,000, or $157 per unit. This estimate is utilized in the cost approach calculations.

The total estimated cost of the planned improvements were estimated as follows:

ESTIMATED PLANNED IMPROVEMENTS

Item	Amount
Install controlled access gates	$50,000
New sidewalks	6,000
Billboard	6,000
Total	$62,000

Total cost of planned improvements is estimated to be $62,000, or $195 per unit. These improvements enhance the value of the property and are not deducted in the cost approach calculations.

Building No. 3 was partially destroyed by fire in June, 1989. The building contains 16 units, eight of which were one-bedroom units that have been completely redone. The remaining eight 2-bedroom/2bath/den units received new carpet and wallpaper. A new roof was installed on that building and the units are currently in leasable condition.

Overall, the complex exhibits a similar degree of physical deterioration as compared to most complexes of similar age. The improvements suffer from external obsolescence, due to the downturn in the Houston economy, and the massive overbuilding which occurred during the early 1980's. A discussion of this external obsolescence is presented in the cost approach. A site plan showing the orientation of the improvements follows.

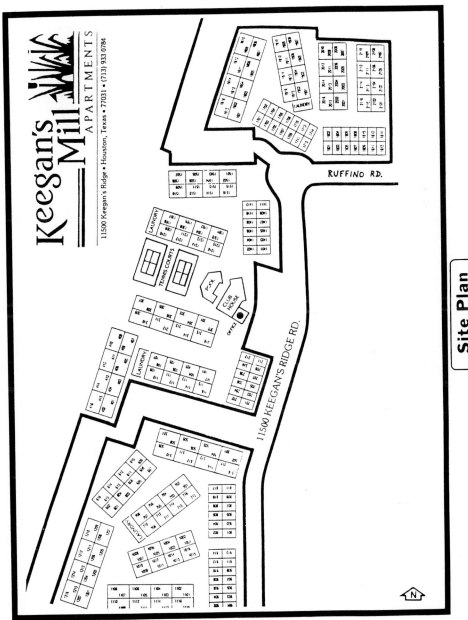

Site Plan

REAL PROPERTY ASSESSMENTS AND TAXES

In 1977, a central appraisal district for each county was created for the purpose of establishing the market value of all real estate within its jurisdiction. Real estate is taxed at 100% of its market value using a rate per $100 of assessed value. Each individual taxing authority establishes an annual tax rate which is used to raise revenue from property within its jurisdiction. Real estate taxes are paid at the end of the calendar year and become delinquent, with penalty, after January 30th of the year following the tax year.

The appraised property is subject to the following taxing agencies with 1989 tax rates as shown:

Authority	Rate
City of Houston	$0.630000
Harris County	$0.560000
Houston Community College	$0.024550
Houston I.S.D.	$0.881893
Total	$2.096443

As mentioned in the legal description, the subject site is divided into two separate tracts. Each tract has its own tax account number, assessed value, and tax assessment. According to the Harris County Tax Records, Tract I contains 5.50 acres and 182 apartment units under account no. 041-056-000-0029. Tract II contains 3.7329 acres and 136 apartment units under account no. 041-056-000-0056. This acreage is the same as the acreage derived from the legal description provided.

The 1988, 1989, and 1990 assessed values of the subject property for the above mentioned jurisdictions were $4,496,600, $2,615,870, and $2,615,870, respectively, and are broken down between land and buildings as follows:

Property	1988		1989 & 1990	
	Total	/Sq.ft.	Total	/Sq.ft.
Land	$1,206,570	$ 3.00	$1,206,570	$3.00
Building	$3,290,030	$15.07	$1,409,300	$6.46
Total	$4,496,600	$18.07	$2,615,870	$9.46

The 1989 taxes have been paid to Harris County and the city of Houston. However, taxes are delinquent to HISD/Houston Community College in the amount of $1,840.42 for Tract I and $1,375.26 for Tract II.

In our opinion, the subject is underassessed and a future reassessment at a much higher value is likely. Real estate taxes on comparable apartment projects indicate that the current taxes for the subject property of $0.26 per square foot fall at the low end of the range. Therefore, we have estimated taxes utilizing the 1988 assessment which we feel is more representative of the value of the subject in today's market. We estimated that the tax rate for 1990 will increase by approximately 4%. Applying the estimated tax rate of 2.1803 to the 1988 assessed value of $4,496,600, results in estimated real estate taxes of $98,039.37, or $0.45 per square foot for 1990.

HIGHEST AND BEST USE

The two distinct types of highest and best use are the highest and best use as if the site were vacant, and the highest and best use as if the site were improved. Both use determinations require consideration of the physical, legal, probable, and financially feasible uses to which the site and the improvements could be put. A comprehensive neighborhood and site analysis is essential in estimating the highest and best use of the site, as if vacant. The improvement analysis contributes to the highest and best use as improved conclusion.

Highest and best use may be defined as:

The reasonably probable and legal use of vacant land or an improved property, which is physically possible, appropriately supported, financially feasible, and that results in the highest value. The four criteria the highest and best use must meet are legal permissibility, physical possibility, financial feasibility, and maximum productivity.

The two distinct types of highest and best use are the highest and best use as if the site were vacant and the highest and best use as if the site were improved. Both use determinations require consideration of the physical, legal, probable, and financially feasible uses to which the site and the improvements could be put. A comprehensive neighborhood and site analysis is essential in estimating the highest and best use of the site as if vacant. The improvement analysis contributes to the highest and best use as improved conclusion.

Highest and best use of a site as though vacant may be defined as:

The use of a property based on the assumption that a parcel of land is vacant or can be made vacant through demolition of any improvements.[4]

Highest and best use of a site as though improved may be defined as:

The use that should be made of a property as it exists.[4]

The subject site will first be analyzed as vacant, and then an analysis of the property as improved will follow. This analysis will pertain to the subject property according to the four essential tests.

Highest and Best Use as Vacant

Physical possibility. Many physical characteristics of a site can affect the use to which it can be put. These characteristics can include size, configuration,

[4]*The Dictionary of Real Estate Appraisal*, Page 149.

location, road frontage, topography, easements, utility availability, flood plain, and surrounding land use patterns.

The subject site is composed of two irregularly shaped tracts consisting of 5.5 acres in Tract I and 3.733 acres in Tract II, for a total of 9.233 acres, or 402,189 square feet. Although irregularly shaped, the large amount of frontage and the configuration allow adequate physical utilization of the site. Each tract has frontage on Keegan's Ridge and some frontage on Ruffino Road.

The topography of the site is basically flat and level, and drainage appears to be adequate. A portion of the site appears to be located in a 100 year flood plain.

Properties located within the immediate area are predominantly multifamily complexes, vacant land, and retail facilities with multifamily development adjacent to the subject.

The subject site has adequate utility capacity and enjoys a relatively good functional size and shape, with a large amount of frontage, and is not affected by any adverse easements or restrictions. However, a portion of the northwestern section of the site lies within a 100 year flood plain. Access to the site is considered to be adequate, as the site may be reached via either direction on Keegan's Ridge from West Bellfort or Ruffino Road. The subject neighborhood is currently in a stable life stage; however, some further fluctuations in property values may occur due to the oversupply of most types of commercial real estate.

After considering all the physical characteristics of the site noted above, plus other data in the site analysis section of this report, physically possible land uses would include a variety of development, but are directed to multifamily development. Physically possible uses would include apartments, office building, retail center, hotel, motel, office/service center, industrial facility, or others. The primary physical deterrents to other types of development are the subject property's location, accessibility, and configuration.

Retail centers are typically developed on tracts with ample frontage along major thoroughfares and at corner locations of major thoroughfares. Within the immediate neighborhood, along West Bellfort, and the Southwest Freeway, there is retail space available. The optimum location for retail usage in the neighborhood is along West Bellfort, the Southwest Freeway, the Sam Houston Tollway, and at other major intersections.

Warehouse development usually occurs on secondary thoroughfares in industrial areas. As the subject site is surrounded by a variety of uses, which include single and multifamily residential, industrial development is not suitable. Office development is also not suitable as there is a vast amount of vacant office space currently available near the subject neighborhood.

Legal permissibility. As mentioned in the zoning section of this report, the subject property is not legally limited by zoning classifications. Therefore, any use not environmentally prohibited would be permitted. Legally permissible uses would include an office building, apartments, retail center, hotel, motel, industrial facility, or others.

Financial feasibility.   In view of present market conditions, financial feasibility is directly proportional to the amount of net income that could be derived from the subject property. Rents had declined over the past few years, but are currently stable, and are beginning to show signs of improvement. After having eliminated all other development from our analysis, the financial feasibility of multifamily development must be tested.

The overall vacancy rate for this submarket is 11%, which is slightly below feasible levels. In addition, current rental rates do not justify new construction, as net income levels would not provide an adequate return of and return on invested capital, in comparison with alternative investments. Based on the area's current supply of vacant units and historical absorption, we have concluded that the area currently includes about a two-year supply of existing vacant units.

We do not believe there will be any sharp rises or falls during this recovery process. Based upon the cost approach, we have concluded that construction of apartments would not be feasible today. Rents are below feasible levels, and a recovery is too far removed to justify construction of a new apartment project in today's market, at today's costs.

Maximum productivity.   After considering the current economic climate and the subject property's location and financial feasibility of certain land uses, more than likely, a present development of the land would produce a negative cash flow for multifamily development.

However, due to the subject property's location and the socioeconomic status of the neighborhood, we are of the opinion that the demand for multifamily apartment units would produce the highest net return over the longest period of time.

Conclusion.   The subject site is not legally limited to any particular usage by zoning or deed restrictions. Although the site is appropriately suited for multifamily housing, it is our opinion this type of improvement is not economically feasible to construct today.

After considering the physical characteristics of the site, the nature of the neighborhood, and feasibility of most all uses, it is our opinion that the current highest and best use for the subject site, as if vacant, would be to remain vacant until the supply and demand for multifamily housing approaches equilibrium, then proceed with development of this type of facility.

In conclusion, the highest and best use of the site, as though vacant, would be to hold as a speculative investment until sufficient demand for multi-family housing is generated by a combination of increased population and a reduction in inventory through demolition.

Highest and Best Use as Improved

The highest and best use of a property as improved pertains to the use that should be made of an improved property in light of its improvements. The use that maximizes an investment property's return on a long-term basis is its highest and best use as improved. Two reasons exist for analyzing the highest and best use of a property as improved. The first is to identify the use of the property that can be expected to produce the highest overall return for each dollar of capital invested. The second reason to estimate the highest and best use of the property is to help identify comparable properties.

The four criteria used in the highest and best use as vacant analysis must also be used in the highest and best use as improved discussion.

Physical possibility.   Based on the subject site's size and configuration, and the improvement's positioning relative to the subject site, it is felt that it would not be physically possible to increase the size of the current improvements. It is our opinion that the site is functionally adequate for its present use. Those complexes had densities of 27 to 33 units per acre. The subject site is developed to a density of 34.44 units per acre (318 units / 9.233 acres = 34.44 units per acre), which is at the high end of the range of most of the comparable complexes surveyed. This is a sufficient density and is within industry standards.

Thus, based on the aforementioned factors, it is our opinion that the improvements represent the largest amount of space that could currently be developed under current site conditions.

Legal permissibility.   Within the scope of a legal analysis, the subject site would be adaptable to any number of uses since it is not limited to any zoning or known deed restrictions. Additionally, as the existing improvements are not environmentally prohibited, the existing improvements are considered to be legally permissible.

Financial feasibility.   Based on the economic conditions for alternative market segments, it was concluded that the subject property's present improvements as an apartment complex are satisfactory to fulfill this test.

Maximum productivity.   As was discussed in the improvement analysis section of this report, the improvements are in average condition, and had a normal amount of physical deterioration expected for a complex this age. However, current market conditions have resulted in many owners undertaking deferred maintenance projects that have been put off for long periods of time. As a result, deferred maintenance projections are low, and expenses are extremely high, compared to previous years.

The occupancy rate of the subject property is currently similar to its market area. Additionally, the comparables analyzed suggest that under competent management, the subject property could produce an adequate return to substantiate its existence. Therefore, it is our opinion that the subject site is functionally adequate for its present use. Overall, it is our opinion that the site is suited for apartment development.

As the subject site is not vacant, but improved with an existing apartment complex, pool, tennis courts, and parking areas, the existing improvements represent the highest and best use of the site unless the existing improvements are judged to be of no contributory value to the subject site. Since our analysis of the subject site indicated that the existing improvements do contribute to the value of the property over and above the value of the site, it is unlikely that they would be removed unless a higher return could be achieved with another use. We can conceive of no other probable, alternative, legal use which would economically justify the removal of the existing improvements.

There are no economically viable alternative uses to which the subject property could be converted. Condominium conversion is not feasible because Texas has never been conducive to successful condominium development. Therefore, conversion to this use is not economically justified. There are no neighborhood trends developing which would adversely affect the value of the property.

Marketability of the subject property at this time is possible only at reduced prices, below replacement costs, due to the current economic conditions previously discussed. However, recent apartment sales have indicated that the market is recovering. Sales prices have risen over the last year to more reasonable levels. However, they are still not above replacement costs.

Conclusion. The complex is compatible with the surrounding land uses, and is currently generating occupancy levels equivalent to the overall submarket. It is our opinion that as rents are increased, the occupancy of the subject property will continue to exceed or be in line with the occupancy level of the micro, Sharpstown - Southwest market. Therefore, it is our opinion that the highest and best use, as improved, is its existing use, with continued operation as an apartment complex, which represents the optimal use of the site at the present time. However, occupancy and rent levels must remain at satisfactory levels to justify continued operation. Otherwise conversion of use or demolition may become a viable alternative.

> After reading the "Highest and Best Use" section in Chapter 3, would you have changed this section of the appraisal report? Explain.

MARKETABILITY

Occupancy rates, rental rates, and sales are on the rise in the Houston apartment market. As previously mentioned, the average occupancy for resident-paid projects in the Sharpstown-Southwest market area is 89% and the average rental rate is $333 per unit or $0.422 per square foot. Each of these figures is above those figures for years past and appear to be steadily increasing. The table below, which compares sales and foreclosures, shows a progressive sales trend and a steady decline in foreclosures since 1988. Note that 1990 figures are for the first quarter only.

APARTMENT SALES AND FORECLOSURES, SHARPSTOWN-SOUTHWEST MARKET
AREA

Year	Sales		Foreclosures	
	Units	# Projects	Units	# Projects
1987	8,044	33	8,522	39
1988	10,104	39	14,313	53
1989	10,232	54	7,820	27
1990	3,017	17	488	1

The location of the subject property is considered to be very good as it is situated south of the Southwest Freeway/Sam Houston Tollway interchange. The Tollway, in this vicinity, is currently under construction; however, when completed it is expected to dramatically increase the traffic flow, accessibility, and exposure of the subject neighborhood.

Considering the location of the subject property and current apartment market conditions in the southwest region of Houston, it is our opinion that a marketing period of approximately one year appears to be reasonable for the subject property.

VALUATION ANALYSIS

There are three approaches in real estate valuation: the cost approach, the sales comparison approach, and the income approach.

 The cost approach involves the estimation of reproduction or replacement cost of the improvements, less accrued depreciation. This value is then added to the estimated value of the land based upon recent comparable land sales. The resulting figure is an indication of the value of the subject property via the cost approach.

 The sales comparison, or market data, approach is based on a comparison between comparable improved sales and the subject property. Adjustments are made for differences between the comparable sales and the subject to arrive at a value indication of the appraised property.

 The income approach involves the estimation of the economic rent of the subject property based on actual rentals of similar properties. An estimate of value is formulated by analyzing and interpreting the subject property's income-producing capabilities. The property's income stream is capitalized into an indication of value.

COST APPROACH

The cost approach to value involves five basic steps. The value of the site as if vacant is first estimated. The replacement cost new of the improvements is then estimated. Replacement cost includes direct costs, indirect costs, and entrepreneurial profit. The third step involves estimating depreciation, which includes physical deterioration, functional obsolescence, and external obsolescence. In the fourth step, the total accrued depreciation is subtracted from replacement cost new of the improvements, resulting in the depreciated value of the improvements. Finally, the depreciated value of all the improvements is added to the estimated site value to arrive at the value of the property as indicated by the cost approach.

Valuation of the Site

In order to estimate the value of the subject site, the direct sales comparison method is used. In this method, normal market sales of similar sites are compared to the subject site with respect to such factors as location, zoning, physical characteristics, financing conditions and date of the sale. These various differences in the comparable site sales are then adjusted, if necessary, to arrive at an indicated value for the subject site.

As might be anticipated in a market which has been depressed for several years, there were few recent sales of multi-family sites disclosed by our investigation. Since 1983-1984, there has been an oversupply of apartment units in this sector. Therefore, we have expanded our market area in order to find more recent sales of multi-family sites. The market area investigated includes southwest Houston. A brief summary of these sales follows:

LAND SALES SUMMARY CHART

No.	Location	Date of sale	Size (Ac)	Price/SF
1	W line of Kirkwood, N of U.S. 59	05/88	2.002	$4.50
2	NWC of Sugar Branch & Center Parkway	03/90	8.740	$3.00
3	NEC Gulfton and Westward	05/90	7.640	$5.60
4	NWC of Minetta and Haviland	04/89	6.960	$3.50
5	NEC Clarewood and Bonhomme	12/89	4.970	$2.87

Complete information with reference to each land transfer may be found in the addendum of this report. A comparable land sales map is located on the following page, followed by an adjustment grid showing the adjustments made to each sale. A discussion of each comparable land sale as it relates to the appraised site follows the chart.

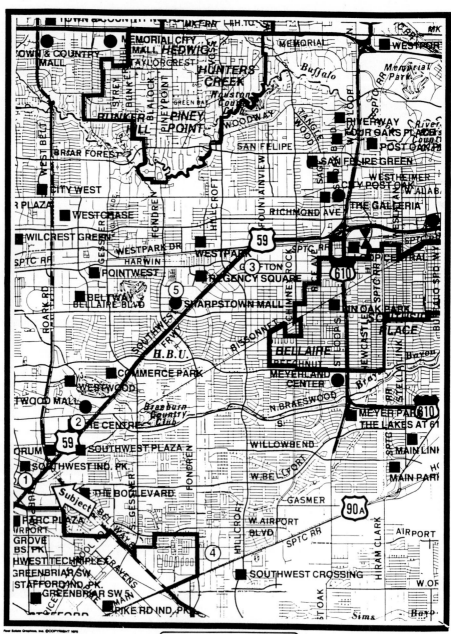

Land Sales Map

ANALYSIS OF COMPARABLE LAND SALES

Date of Appraisal: 01-Aug-90	Annual Value Change:	Size Adjustment Rate:
	1987... -12%	10%
	1988... 0%	
	1989... 0%	
	1990... 0%	

Sale No.	Sale date	Size (Ac)	Price /SF	Location	Adjustments								Indicates
					Cond	Time	Size	Location	Access	Frontage	Other	Total	
1	13-May-88	2.00	$4.50	W/L Kirkwood, 478' N of SW Fwy	$0.00 0%	$0.00 0%	($1.02) -23%	$0.00 0%	$0.00 0%	$0.00 0%	($0.45) -10%	($1.47) -33%	$3.03
2	30-Mar-90	8.74	$3.00	NWC Sugar Branch & Centre Pkwy	($0.60) -20%	$0.00 0%	($0.03) -1%	$0.00 0%	$0.00 0%	$0.00 0%	($0.30) -10%	($0.93) -31%	$2.07
3	23-May-90	7.64	$5.60	NEC Gulfton and Westward	($1.12) -20%	$0.00 0%	($0.15) -3%	($0.56) -10%	$0.00 0%	$0.00 0%	($0.56) -10%	($2.39) -43%	$3.21
4	24-Apr-89	6.96	$3.50	NWC Minetta and Haviland	($0.70) -20%	$0.00 0%	($0.14) -4%	$0.35 10%	$0.18 5%	$0.00 0%	($0.35) -10%	($0.66) -19%	$2.84
5	15-Dec-89	4.97	$2.87	NEC Clarewood & Bonhomme	$0.00 0%	$0.00 0%	($0.27) -9%	$0.00 0%	$0.00 0%	$0.00 0%	($0.29) -10%	($0.55) -19%	$2.32
Subject		9.23 Acres											

> It is helpful to a reader to include the adjusted sales price for each compara-
> ble sale. Some appraisers use an adjustment grid to reveal the individual
> adjustments.

Discussion and adjustment of comparable land sales.   This data sample was utilized to derive a land value estimate for the subject tract as vacant by
making the following adjustments. Refer to the grid chart preceding this analysis
for a summation of all adjustments which were applied.

Financing.   This adjustment seeks to ascertain the cash equivalent sale
price relative to the definition of market value as set forth previously. Cash equivalency analysis considers any variance between the actual contract interest rate
and the conventional interest rate, as well as alternative financing sources required for a relatively low cash down payment. The included sales involved terms
which did not require adjustments for cash equivalency or cases where complete
terms were not available for cash equivalency analysis.

Conditions of Sale.   There are no known unusual circumstances involved
in the sales except for Sale Nos. 2, 3, and 4 which were purchased by Alief I.S.D.,
Houston I.S.D. and the City of Houston, respectively. A negative 20% adjustment
was made to these sales for inflated sales price.

Market Conditions (Date of Sale).   This may be an important consideration since property values tend to fluctuate over time. This fluctuation is dictated
by market activity. In times of economic expansion property values will show an
increase in value over time, whereas, in times of economic contraction, property
values will stabilize or decline. If an extended period of economic contraction
exists, the marketplace will exert a downward pressure on once stable property
values. This downward pressure will exist until there is a general increase in optimism about the future among buyers. Ideally, an adjustment for time is extracted
by comparison of the sale and subsequent resale of the same tract of land, with the
only difference being the time frame involved. The sales utilized in this analysis
ranged in date from May 1988 to May 1990, with no paired sales available. There
have been no measurable changes in the market since the beginning of 1988.
Therefore, no time adjustment was warranted.

Location.   The value of a site is influenced by its accessibility, visibility
and its proximity to areas of development. Generally speaking, the more accessible the property is, the more valuable it would be. Proximity to current development also affects value. In most cases, properties closer to areas of development
and along major thoroughfares are more valuable on a per unit basis than properties further from development areas and on secondary roadways.

Size.   Typically, property values and property size vary inversely. Thus,
larger tracts tend to sell for lower per unit values than do smaller tracts. This is
mainly due to the fact that smaller parcels usually have more intense uses than do
larger parcels. Size, in this instance, is not absolute and there generally exists a
range within which tracts are comparable. In addition, a tract which is too small

for feasible development may suffer a loss in value. The subject site consists of 9.233 acres, while the included sales range from 2.002 acres to 8.74 acres. Separate size adjustments were made to the sales comparables, relative to the subject tract, due to their size difference. The size adjustment was based on a 10% upward or downward adjustment for every doubling or halving in size of the sale property, as shown on the adjustment grid chart.

Physical Characteristics.   The physical characteristics of each comparable sale were considered. These attributes included drainage, topography, shape, amount of frontage, and utility availability. All of the sales had similar topographies, thus no adjustments were deemed necessary. The availability of utilities was not a major consideration for properties in the subject area, therefore, no adjustment was applied to the sales for this factor. The subject tract is irregular in shape and was felt to have slightly inferior utility as compared to some of the comparable sales.

Sale No. 1 sold in May of 1988, for a cash price of $4.50 per square foot. The tract is located along the west line of Kirkwood, approximately 478 feet north of US 59. As this sale occurred after the fall in values, it was not given a time adjustment. The tract is smaller than the subject tract, so a negative size adjustment was warranted. The location is considered similar to the subject. A downward adjustment was made to this sale as it is considered to have superior utility. The adjustments resulted in an adjusted sales price of $3.03 per square foot.

Sale No. 2 closed on March 30, 1990, for a cash price of $3.00 per square foot. This tract contained 8.74 acres of land at the northwest corner of Sugar Branch and Centre Parkway. This location is just east of the West Belt. This is a very recent sale, therefore no time adjustment was warranted. In a normal balanced market we would not have to use the sale involving a representative of the government as the grantee. However, since there are so few recent land transactions, these must be used. Therefore, a negative adjustment was given to the sales price due to the grantee involved. Sale No. 2 is approximately the same size as the subject site, and therefore requires a minimal size adjustment. This site has a slightly inferior location, but is a corner site. Therefore, no location adjustment was necessary. A negative adjustment was made for superior utility. The adjustments resulted in an adjusted sales price of $2.07 per square foot.

Sale No. 3 was closed on May 23, 1990, for a cash price of $5.60 per square foot. No time adjustment was necessary, as this is a very recent sale. This tract contained 7.64 acres of land on the corner of Gulfton and Westward. A negative adjustment was made for condition of sale due to purchase by Houston I.S.D. This corner site has a location slightly superior to the subject in a densely developed area. Therefore, a negative location adjustment was made. An additional downward adjustment was made for superior utility. A negative size adjustment was also necessary. The adjusted sales price was $3.21 per square foot.

Sale No. 4 closed on April 24, 1989, for $3.50 per square foot. This tract contained 6.96 acres of land located at the northwest corner of Minetta and Haviland, and was purchased by the City of Houston. A negative adjustment was given to the sales price due to the grantee involved. For reasons mentioned previously, it was not given a time adjustment. A location adjustment was warranted, because this sale has inferior location characteristics, as compared to the subject site. This tract is smaller than the subject site in size, and therefore required a small downward size adjustment. A negative adjustment was made for superior utility. The resulting adjusted sales price for this sale was $2.84 per square foot.

Sale No. 5 occurred December 15, 1989 and is located on the northeast corner of Clarewood and Bonhomme in Houston, Harris County, Texas. This 4.97 acre tract has 352 feet of frontage on Clarewood and 477 front feet on Bonhomme. The site sold for $2.87 per square foot. This tract is considered similar in location to the subject. This sale is somewhat smaller in size than the subject; a negative adjustment was made for this item. A downward adjustment was made for utility. The resulting adjusted sales price for this comparable was $2.32 per square foot.

Conclusion.   The adjusted sales prices ranged from $2.07 per square foot to $3.21 per square foot. The average adjusted sale price was $2.69 per square foot. Sale No. 2, which indicated $2.07 per square foot, was most comparable to and closest in location to the subject site. Most weight was given to Sale No. 2. After having analyzed the comparable sales and market activity in the area, considering the characteristics of the immediate neighborhood, and taking into account factors that tend to influence value, including adjustments for size, location, flood plain status, utility and other physical characteristics, it is our opinion that the market value of the subject site, is $2.50 per square foot.

It is our opinion that the subject property has a market value of $2.50 per square foot, or:

Value PSF		Area		Indicated site value
$2.50	×	402,189 SF	=	$1,005,473
		Say: $1,000,000		

See Chapters 7 and 8 for an explanation of site analysis and valuation considerations.

Valuation of the Improvements

Having estimated the market value of the subject site, the next step requires estimating the replacement cost of existing improvements. Replacement cost is defined as "The cost of construction, at current prices, of a building having utility equivalent to the building being appraised, but built with modern materials and according to current standards, design, and layout."[5]

The cost analysis which follows is based primarily on data from Marshall & Swift Valuation Service, a nationally recognized cost valuation guide, and has been checked with data compiled from similar projects in this area.

[5]*The Dictionary of Real Estate Appraisal*, Page 254.

Direct costs.   Direct costs consist of building costs (materials and labor) and site improvements. In construction, expenditures for items other than labor and materials include contractor's overhead and profit, administrative costs, professional fees, financing costs, taxes, interim interest, insurance during construction and permanent financing fees. These items are also included in the direct costs. The estimated direct replacement cost new of the appraised improvements include approximately $4,762,558 for construction of the buildings. Other direct costs include concrete paving and walks, exterior lighting, pool, tennis courts, and landscaping. These are estimated to be $276,350. Total direct costs are $5,038,908.

In addition to these direct costs, an entrepreneurial profit allowing compensation for the risks associated with development of the project must be included within the indirect cost estimate. In the case of the subject property an entrepreneurial profit of approximately 12% is estimated to be appropriate in order to attract developers to undertake the construction of this project. This 12% is multiplied by all direct and other indirect costs. The indicated entrepreneurial profit for the subject is $604,669. Total replacement cost new is the sum of other direct costs, indirect costs, and entrepreneurial profit. The total replacement cost new of the subject improvements is estimated to be $5,643,577.

Accrued depreciation must be deducted from this cost estimate. Accrued depreciation is defined as the difference between replacement cost new of the improvements and the present worth of those improvements, both measured as of the date of appraisal. In measuring accrued depreciation, the appraiser is interested in identifying the loss in utility experienced by the subject property in its present condition as compared to the utility it would have as a new improvement. The modified economic age/life method was utilized to estimate accrued depreciation.

The effect of curable items of accrued depreciation is recognized in the modified economic age/life method. The cost to cure all curable items of deferred maintenance and functional obsolescence is first estimated. This sum is then deducted from the replacement cost new of the improvements.

Deferred maintenance reflects physical items in need of immediate repair, which would be based on whether a typical purchaser would consider it necessary once the property was purchased. Upon inspection, several items of deferred maintenance, which were estimated at $50,000, were noted. These items included hot water heater replacement, roof repair, paint and cleanup cost. Curable depreciation, or deferred maintenance, is deducted from replacement cost new before the incurable elements are calculated.

The estimated economic life of comparable apartment projects is approximately 40 years. The physical age of the improvements is 12 years and its estimated effective age is the same, or 12 years. The remaining economic life of the project is estimated to be 28 years. Accrued depreciation is the ratio of the effective age to the total economic life, or 30% of the adjusted replacement cost new. The incurable accrued depreciation is $1,678,073.

Functional obsolescence, as previously defined, arises by use of the property which may represent a use other than the highest and best use. The subject property represents improvements which are the highest and best use of the site. As defined within highest and best use, should the site be vacant today, the estimated highest and best use would probably be to retain the site for future multi-family development. This is attributed to the oversupply of similar type properties in the immediate neighborhood. The appraised property's below market rental rates are caused by the oversupply of multi-family projects in the Houston area. The measure of this loss in value is achieved in the external obsolescence calculations which are outlined in the following paragraphs.

> Clients are better able to understand the analysis and conclusions if brief and clear definitions of specialized terms such as "functional obsolescence" are included.

An analysis of competing apartment projects is included in the marketability/feasibility section of this report. The subject property is currently approximately 92% occupied, which is considered to be a stabilized occupancy level. However, current rents are below the level required to make new construction feasible. Rent levels in the range of $0.45 per square foot are necessary to make new apartment construction feasible. In the current market, this rent is not achievable, and as the cost approach indicates, new construction is not feasible today based on current rent levels. According to our calculations, it appears that the subject should achieve or surpass rents of $0.45 per square foot in approximately two years. Therefore, we have estimated that the subject property will experience external obsolescence for the next two years of operation. The amount of external obsolescence is calculated by taking the difference between the net operating income at current rents and the net operating income at the pro forma rent of $0.45 per square foot for years one and two in the discounted cash flow. The present value of this loss is calculated by discounting the loss at the property discount rate of 13.0%. These calculations follow.

EXTERNAL OBSOLESCENCE CALCULATIONS

Year......		1	2	3
Annual Gross Rental Income		$1,177,286	$1,177,286	$1,177,286
Ancillary Income	$140	44,520	46,746	49,083
Total Gross Income		1,221,806	1,224,032	1,226,369
% Vacancy & Col. Loss		8%	8%	8%
Vacancy & Col. Loss		(97,744)	(97,923)	(98,110)
% Rental Concessions		0%	0%	0%
Rental Concessions		0	0	0
Effective Gross Income		$1,124,062	$1,126,109	$1,128,260
Operating Expenses				
Expenses		616,985	647,835	680,226
Management	5% of EGI	56,203	56,305	56,413

Total Operating Expenses		$673,188	$704,140	$736,639
Economic Net Operating Income		450,873	421,969	391,620
Projected Net Operating Income		335,430	382,706	401,841
External Obsolescence		115,443	39,264	(10,221)
Discounted Obsolescence	13.0%	$102,162	$30,749	
Total External Obsolescence		$132,911		

External obsolescence is estimated to be $132,911. When this figure is added to the calculations for accrued depreciation, the total amount of depreciation for the subject is $1,860,984. Deducting this amount from the estimated replacement cost new indicates a depreciated replacement cost new of $3,782,593. Adding the site value, previously estimated to be $1,000,000, results in an indicated value estimate, according to the cost approach, of $4,782,593, or when rounded, $4,780,000.

The calculations of the cost approach follow.

COST APPROACH CALCULATIONS

Direct costs	Area	Unit cost	Total
Dwelling Units	218,016	$21.12	$4,604,498
Common Facilities	5,268	$21.12	111,260
Balconies	5,000	$9.36	46,800
Other Site Improvements			
Concrete Paving	126,000	$1.25	$157,500
Concrete Walks	28,000	$1.00	28,000
Exterior Lighting	126,000	$0.09	11,340
Swimming Pool	130	$127	16,510
Tennis Courts			43,000
Landscaping			20,000
Total Direct Costs			$5,038,908
Entrepreneurial Profit	12.0%		604,669
Total Replacement Cost New			$5,643,577
Accrued Depreciation			
Incurable	30.0%	(1,678,073)	
Curable		(50,000)	
Functional		0	
External		(132,911)	
Total Accrued Depreciation			(1,860,984)
Depreciated Value of Improvements			$3,782,593
Site Value 9.23 Acres @	$2.50	/SF	1,000,000
Indicated Value			$4,782,593
			(R) $4,780,000

> According to the advantages and disadvantages listed for the depreciated cost approach in Chapter 11, is this valuation approach appropriate for this appraisal assignment?

SALES COMPARISON APPROACH

The sales comparison approach involves comparing similar improved properties that have recently sold to the subject property. The sales comparison approach for an improved property is based upon the principle of substitution, which states that one is not justified in paying more for a property than that amount with which one can go into the open market and purchase a similar property with equal desirability and utility, provided there is no undue delay. The methodology of this approach basically involves extracting sales of similar property with equal desirability and utility from the market place, provided there is no undue delay. Information pertaining to both the economics and the consideration involved is confirmed and this information is utilized to develop various units of comparison. The final step involves applying the extracted units of comparison to the appropriate actual and/or projected physical and economic information for the subject.

Three primary units of comparison have been extracted from the market data. These are the effective gross income multiplier (EGIM), the sales price per square foot of net leasable area (SP/SF), and the sales price per unit (SP/Unit). The sales price per square foot and the sales price per unit are based upon physical characteristics of a property, whereas the effective gross income multiplier reflects economic characteristics. Considering the type of property involved, all three of these units of comparison are considered to be applicable to the subject.

Complete information with reference to each comparable sale follows. Cash equivalency adjustments are required for Sale Nos. 1 and 2. A map showing the location of each sale precedes the sales. Following the sales is a chart listing all sales and summarizing pertinent information concerning these sales, such as the indicated price per square foot, the expense ratio, the effective gross income, and the overall capitalization rates. Each sale is then discussed and analyzed individually.

> Determine if this property was valued on the basis of potential or effective gross income. After reviewing Chapter 9, discuss the relative merits of each of these appraisal methods.

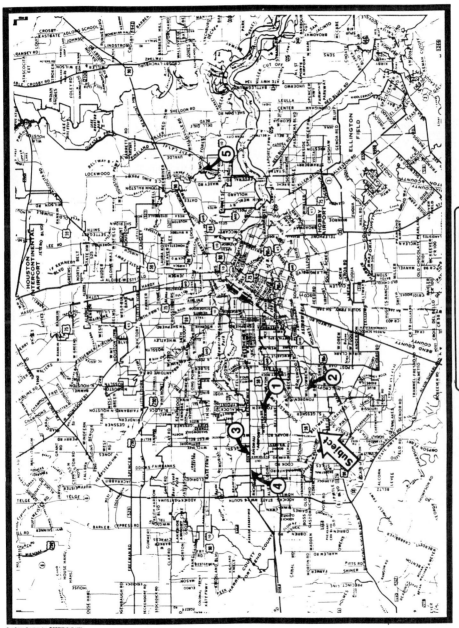

Improved Sales Map

APARTMENT SALE NO. 1

Project:	Spring Meadows Apartments; 3401 Ocee, Houston, TX
Key Map:	490 X
Grantor:	Travelers Insurance Company
Grantee:	M.D. Sass - Restructured Real Estate Fund - I, L.P.
Date of Sale:	December 27, 1989
Recording Data:	FC 165-68-0529
Legal Description:	9.17 Acres, Reserve E, Richmond Square, Beckman Canfield Survey, A-215, Harris County, Texas
Land Area:	9.17 Acres
Rentable Area:	238,800 Square Feet
Number of Units:	304
Average Unit Size:	786 Square Feet
Year Built:	1979
Construction Type:	Wood frame construction, two story, with brick veneer exteriors, pitched composition shingled roofs, garden walk-up complex.

Individually Metered: Yes

Number	Unit type	Area SF
56	1BR/1BA	500 SF
80	1BR/1BA	700 SF
80	1BR/1BA	825 SF
48	2BR/2BA	975 SF
40	2BR/2BA	1,050 SF

Occupancy at Time of Sale: 93%

Sales Price: $4,738,000

Terms: $3,790,400 note to Travelers, 20% cash down, 30 year amortization, at interest rates of 7% in year 1, 7.5% in year 2, 8.5% in year 3, 9.5% in years 4 and 5, call in year 5.

Cash Equivalent Sales Price: $4,500,000

Economic Indicators: PSF

Gross Income:	$1,110,360	$4.65
Vacancy and Collection (8%)	88,829	.37
Effective Gross Income:	1,021,531	4.28
Expenses:	719,500	3.01
Net Operating Income:	$ 302,031	$1.26

Appraisal Indicators:

GIM:	4.05
EGIM:	4.41
Overall Rate:	6.71%
Sales Price PSF:	$18.84
Sales Price Per Unit:	$14,803

CASH EQUIVALENCY CALCULATIONS

Method one

Hypothetical 1st lien

Sale price	$4,738,000
Down payment	$947,600
Initial loan balance	$3,790,400
Hypothetical 1st lien (75% L-T-V 1st lien)	$3,553,500

Hypothetical 2nd lien

Initial balance	$3,790,400
Less 1st lien	$3,554,500
Hypothetical 2nd lien	$236,900

Year	Annual debt service	P.W. cash flow at 9.00%
Year 1	$283,698	$260,274
Year 2	$298,159	$250,955
Year 3	$327,880	$253,184
Year 4	$358,557	$254,011
Year 5	$358,557	$233,037
Total P.W. Cash Flow:		$1,251,460
Balloon: $3,288,184		$2,137,094
Total P.W.: 1st Lien		$3,338,554

Year	Annual debt service	P.W. cash flow at 12.00%
Year 1	$18,913	$16,887
Year 2	$19,877	$15,846
Year 3	$21,859	$15,559
Year 4	$23,904	$15,191
Year 5	$23,904	$13,564
		$77,046
Balloon $219,212 2nd Lien		$124,387
		$201,433

Conclusion:

Total P.W. 1st Lien	$3,388,554
Total P.W. 2nd Lien	$201,433
Down Payment	$947,600
Indicated Cash Equivalent Sale Price	$4,537,588

Method two

Sale price	$4,738,000
Down payment	$947,600
Initial loan balance	$3,790,400

Year	Annual debt service	P.W. cash flow at 9.75%
Year 1	$302,612	$275,728
Year 2	$318,036	$264,039
Year 3	$349,739	$264,564
Year 4	$382,461	$263,614
Year 5	$382,461	$240,195
		$1,308,140
	$3,507,396	$2,202,735
Total P.W.:		$3,510,875

Conclusion:

Total P.W. of Loan	$3,510,875
Down Payment	$947,600
Indicated Cash Equiv. Sale Price	$4,458,475

Reconciliation:

Method One Indicated Cash Equivalent Sale Price:	$4,537,588
Method Two Indicated Cash Equivalent Sale Price:	$4,458,475
Concluded Cash Equivalent Sale Price:	$4,500,000

APARTMENT SALE NO. 2

Project:	Sunset Point Apartments; 6111 Willowbend, Houston, TX
Key Map:	530 Z
Grantor:	Penn Mutual Life Insurance Company (215) 625-5000
Grantee:	Jerome Bergman for B-R Sunset Associates Limited Partnership - (201) 549-0370
Date of Sale:	November 2, 1989
Film Code:	161-63-0909
Legal Description:	4.14 Acres out of Part of Reserve "A," Fondren Southwest Northbrook, Section 1, B.B.B.& C.R.R. Survey, Abstract 180, Houston, Harris County, Texas
Land Area:	4.14 Acres
Rentable Area:	101,160 SF
Number of Units:	140
Average Unit Size:	723 SF
Year Built:	1978
Construction Type:	Wood frame construction, two story, with brick veneer exteriors, combined use of pitched composition shingled roofs and flat built up roofs, garden walk-up complex.

Individually Metered: Yes

Number	Unit type	Area SF
32	1BR/1BA	504 SF
36	1BR/1BA	670 SF
24	2BR/1BA	812 SF
48	2BR/2BA	863 SF

Occupancy at Time of Sale: 100%

Sales Price: $1,800,000

Terms: $360,000 cash down, $1,440,000 note, 30 year amortization, interest only during years 1 through 5, at 7% in Year 1, 7.5% in Year 2, 8% in Year 3, 9% in Year 4, 9.5% in Year 5, and 10% during Years 6 and 7. Call in Year 7.

Cash Equivalent Sales
Price: $1,620,000

Economic Indicators: PSF

Gross Income:	$ 460,000	$4.55
Vacancy and Collection 8%	36,800	0.37
Effective Gross Income (92%):	423,200	4.18
Expenses:	318,500	3.00
Net Operating Income:	$ 119,700	$1.18

Appraisal Indicators:

GIM:	3.52
EGIM:	3.83
Overall Rate:	7.39%
Sales Price PSF:	$16.01
Sales Price Per Unit:	$11,571

CASH EQUIVALENCY CALCULATIONS

Method one

Hypothetical 1st lien

Sale price	$1,800,000
Down payment	$360,000
Initial loan balance	$1,440,000
Hypothetical 1st lien (75% L-T-V 1st lien)	$1,260,000

Hypothetical 2nd lien

Sale price	$1,440,000
Down payment	$1,260,000
Initial balance Less 1st lien	$180,000
Hypothetical 2nd lien	

Year	Annual debt service (1st lien)	P.W. cash flow at 10.00%	Annual debt service (2nd lien)	P.W. cash flow at 12.00%
Year 1	$88,200	$80,182	$12,600	$11,101
Year 2	$94,500	$78,099	$13,500	$10,480
Year 3	$100,800	$75,733	$14,400	$9,849
Year 4	$113,400	$77,454	$16,200	$9,762
Year 5	$119,700	$74,324	$17,100	$9,079
Year 6	$132,689	$74,899	$18,956	$8,867
Year 7	$132,689	$68,090	$18,956	$7,812
Total P.W. Cash Flow:		$528,781		$66,949
Balloon:	$1,192,582	$611,983	$170,369	$70,213
Total P.W.:	1st Lien	$1,140,764	2nd Lien	$137,162

Conclusion:

Total P.W. 1st Lien	$1,140,764
Total P.W. 2nd Lien	$137,162
Down Payment	$360,000
Indicated Cash Equivalent Sale Price	$1,637,926

Method two

Sale price	$1,800,000
Down payment	$360,000
Initial loan balance	$1,440,000

Year	Annual debt service	P.W. cash Flow at 11.05%
Year 1	$100,800	$90,770
Year 2	$108,000	$87,576
Year 3	$115,200	$84,120
Year 4	$129,600	$85,218
Year 5	$136,800	$81,002
Year 6	$151,644	$80,856
Year 7	$151,644	$72,811
		$582,353
	$1,362,951	$654,411
Total P.W.:		$1,236,763

Conclusion:

Total P.W. of Loan	$1,236,763
Down Payment	$360,000
Indicated Cash Equiv. Sale Price	$1,596,763

Reconciliation:

Method One Indicated Cash Equivalent Sale Price:	$1,637,926
Method Two Indicated Cash Equivalent Sale Price:	$1,596,263
Concluded Cash Equivalent Sale Price:	$1,620,000

APARTMENT SALE NO. 3

Project:	Water Song Apartments; 11770 Westheimer, Houston, TX
Key Map:	489 T
Grantor:	California Federal Savings & Loan
Grantee:	Lakewood-Westheimer
Date of Sale:	January 5, 1989
Recording Data:	FC 137-69-2146
Legal Description:	8.78 acres H.K. Lewis Survey, Abstract 42, Harris County, Texas
Land Area:	8.78 Acres
Rentable Area:	203,608 SF
Number of Units:	272
Average Unit Size:	749 SF
Year Built:	1978
Construction Type:	Wood frame construction, two story, with brick veneer exteriors, flat built-up roofs, garden walk-up complex.
Individually Metered:	Yes

Number	Unit type	Area SF
52	1BR/1BA	517 SF
100	1BR/1BA	682 SF
52	1BR/1BA	812 SF
68	2BR/2BA	975 SF

		PSF
Occupancy at Time of Sale:	65%	
Sales Price:	$3,650,000	
Terms:	Cash to the Grantor.	
Cash Equivalent Sales Price:	$3,650,000	
Economic Indicators:		PSF
Gross Income:	$ 855,000	$4.20
Vacancy and Collection 8%	68,400	.34
Effective Gross Income:	786,600	3.86
Expenses:	600,000	2.95
Net Operating Income:	$ 186,600	$ .92
Appraisal Indicators:		
GIM:	4.27	
EGIM:	4.64	
Overall Rate:	5.11%	
Sales Price PSF:	$17.93	
Sales Price Per Unit:	$13,419	

APARTMENT SALE NO. 4

Project:	Ashford on the Green; 2700 South Dairy Ashford, Houston, Texas
Key Map:	488 V
Grantor:	First Nationwide Bank
Grantee:	John M. Area III

Date of Sale:	May 15, 1989	
Recording Data:	FC # 147-62-1182	
Legal Description:	6.48 acres of land being part of the Meadows on Ashford Subdivision, William Hardin Survey, Abstract 24, Harris County, Texas.	
Land Area:	6.48 Acres	
Rentable Area:	166,842 SF	
Number of Units:	178	
Average Unit Size:	937 SF	
Year Built:	1982	
Construction Type:	Two-story garden style apartments with brick and wood siding and swimming pool.	
Individually Metered:		

Number	Unit type	Area SF
36	1BR/1BA	622
8	1BR/1BA	776
28	2BR/1BA	790
66	2BR/2BA	1,103
8	2BR/2BA	1,113
24	3BR/2BA	1,245
8	3BR/2BA	1,142

Occupancy at Time of Sale:	98%
Sales Price:	$3,750,000
Terms:	$750,000 down; $3,000,000 note from grantor at undisclosed terms. Assumed to be at market rates.
Cash Equivalent Sales Price:	$3,750,000

Economic Indicators:

	Actual (98%)	PSF	Stabilized (92%)	PSF
Gross Income:	$ 744,000	$ 4.46	$ 800,842	$ 4.80
Vacancy and Collection (2%):	(14,880)	(0.09)	(64,067)	(0.38)
Effective Gross Income:	729,120	4.37	736,775	4.42
Expenses:	(475,500)	(2.85)	(478,904)	(2.87)
Net Operating Income:	$ 253,620	$ 1.52	$ 257,871	$ 1.55

Operating Expense Ratio: 65%
Units of Comparison:
  GIM: 4.68
  EGIM: 5.09
  Overall Rate: 6.88%
  Sales Price/SF: $ 22.48
  Sales Price/Unit: $21,067

APARTMENT SALE NO. 5

Project:	The Forrester Apartments; 12800 Woodforest, Houston, Texas
Key Map:	456Z
Grantor:	Forrester J.V.
Grantee:	Olympia Investors I, Ltd.
Date of Sale:	April 30, 1990
Recording Data:	FC # 175-67-1802
Legal Description:	10.09 acres of land in Forrester Apartments, Sections 1 and 2, Harris County, Texas
Land Area:	10.09 Acres
Rentable Area:	214,732 SF
Number of Units:	314
Average Unit Size:	684 SF
Year Built:	1981

Construction Type: Two-story garden style apartments with brick and wood siding, pitch roof and swimming pool.

Individually Metered:

Number	Unit type	Area SF
32	Efficiency	414
48	1BR/1BA	539
56	1BR/1BA	632
44	1BR/1BA	676
48	1BR/1BA	689
38	1BR/1BA (studio)	818
48	2BR/2BA	965

Occupancy at Time of Sale: Low 90%

Sales Price: $5,500,000

Terms: Cash to seller

Cash Equivalent Sales Price: $5,500,000

Economic Indicators: Stabilized (92%)

		PSF
Gross Income:	$1,185,321*	$ 5.52
Vacancy and Collection (8%):	(94,826)	(0.44)
Effective Gross Income:	1,090,495	5.08
Expenses:	(644,196)*	(3.00)
Net Operating Income:	$ 446,299	$2.08

Operating Expense Ratio: 59%

Units of Comparison:

GIM:	4.64
EGIM:	5.04
Overall Rate:	8.11%
Sales Price/SF:	$25.61
Sales Price/Unit:	$17,516

* Estimated

SUMMARY OF COMPARABLE IMPROVED SALES

Sale	Date	Sale price	Cash Eq SP	Age	Units	SF NLA	Site (Ac)	EGI	Exp	NOI
1	27-Dec-89	$4,738,000	$4,500,000	1979	304	238,800	9.17	$1,021,531	$719,500	$302,031
2	11-Feb-89	$1,800,000	$1,620,000	1978	140	101,160	4.14	$423,200	$303,500	$119,700
3	05-Jan-89	$3,650,000	$3,650,000	1978	272	203,608	8.78	$786,600	$600,000	$186,600
4	15-May-89	$3,750,000	$3,750,000	1982	178	166,842	6.48	$736,775	$478,904	$257,871
5	30-Apr-90	$5,500,000	$5,500,000	1981	314	214,732	10.09	$1,090,495	$644,196	$446,299
Subject:				1978	318	218,016	9.23	$1,002,542	$667,112	$335,430

UNITS OF COMPARISON

Sale	Expense ratio	NOI/ sq.ft.	Avg. sq ft	Density	$/Unit	$/SF	EGIM	OAR
1	0.70	$1.26	786	33.15	$14,803	$18.84	4.41	6.71%
2	0.72	$1.18	723	33.82	$11,571	$16.01	3.83	7.39%
3	0.76	$0.92	749	30.98	$13,419	$17.93	4.64	5.11%
4	0.65	$1.55	937	27.47	$21,067	$22.48	5.09	6.88%
5	0.59	$2.08	684	31.12	$17,516	$25.61	5.04	8.11%
Subject:	0.67	$1.54	686	34.44				

Analysis of Apartments Sales

As indicated, the comparable sales occurred from January, 1989, through April, 1990. The properties involved ranged in size from 101,160 to 214,732 square feet of net rentable area. The subject contains 218,016 square feet of net rentable area. The properties ranged in age from six to eleven years at time of sale. The subject is 12 years old. The subject has an average unit size of 686 square feet, while the comparables range in unit size from 684 square feet to 937 square feet.

Sale No. 1 transpired in December, 1989 for a cash equivalent sale price of $18.84 per square foot of net rentable area. The Spring Meadows Apartments are located at 3401 Ocee. The apartments contain a net rentable area of 238,800 square feet and contain 304 units. The apartment project was constructed in 1979. Amenities include two pools, laundry facilities and covered parking. The apartments have a brick veneer exterior, concrete slab and beam foundation, composition shingle roof, and patios/balconies. The apartments were approximately 93% occupied at the time of sale. The property had a net operating income of $1.26 per square foot and an expense ratio of 70%. In addition, the effective gross income multiplier was 4.41 and the overall rate was 6.71%.

Sale No. 2 transpired in February, 1989 for a cash equivalent price of $16.01 per square foot of net rentable area. The Sunset Point Apartments are located at 6111 Willowbend. The apartments contain 140 units and a net rentable area of 101,160 square feet with an average unit size of 723 square feet. The apartments were constructed in 1978. Amenities include swimming pool and laundry facilities. The apartments were 100% occupied at the time of sale. They had a net operating income of $1.18 per square foot and an expense ratio of 72%. The effective gross income multiplier was 3.83 and the overall rate was 7.39%.

Sale No. 3 transpired in January, 1989 for a cash equivalent sale price of $17.93 per square foot. The project was 65% occupied at the time of sale, therefore, an upward adjustment was made for rent loss. Water Song Apartments are located at 11770 Westheimer. The apartments were constructed in 1978. They contain 203,608 square feet of net rentable area. Amenities include two swimming pools, spa, and three laundry areas. The apartments were approximately 65% occupied at the time of sale, and were subsequently rehabed after the sale. The property had a net operating income of $0.92 per square foot and an expense ratio of 76%. The economic indicators include an EGIM of 4.64 and an overall rate of 5.11%.

Sale No. 4 transpired in May, 1989 for a cash equivalent sale price of $22.48 per square foot. The Ashford on the Green Apartments are located at 2700 South Dairy Ashford. The apartments, originally built as condominium units in 1982, contain approximately 166,842 net rentable square feet in 178 units. Amenities include a swimming pool. The apartments were 98% occupied at the time of sale. The project had a net operating income per square foot of $1.55 and an expense ratio of 65%. Other economic indicators include an effective gross income multiplier of 5.09 and an overall rate of 6.88%.

Sale No. 5 transpired in April, 1990 for a cash sale price of $25.61 per square foot of net rentable area. The Forrester Apartments are located at 12800 Woodforest. The apartments contain 214,732 square feet of net rentable area in 314 units. The complex was constructed in 1981. Amenities include a swimming pool and laundry facilities. At the time of sale, the project was experiencing occupancy in the 90 percent range. Estimated income and expenses resulted in a net operating income of $2.08 per square foot. Other economic indicators for the project, based on our estimates, are a 5.04 effective gross income multiplier and an overall rate of 8.11%.

The sales were analyzed for various characteristics which were different in relation to the subject property. These characteristics typically include financing, date of sale, location, age/condition, quality of construction and amenities. However, relatively few differences were noted, except for age, financing, and location.

Financing.   This adjustment seeks to ascertain the cash equivalent sale price relative to the definition of market value as set forth previously. Computations related to the cash equivalency adjustment were based on a comparison of actual financing terms to conventional terms consisting of the loan to value ratio and interest rate which might typically be available in the open market. Adjustments were required for Sale Nos. 1 and 2. The calculations for these cash equivalency adjustments are part of the sale information sheets.

Conditions of sale.   None of the included sales had conditions of sale indicated that would require an adjustment.

Market conditions (date of sale).   As indicated in the regional analysis section of this report, the current economic situation of the area is weaker than experienced during the earlier years of this decade. As a result, overall development activity has diminished. The over-supply found in virtually all sectors of the real estate market has combined with persistent soft demand patterns to create a stabilizing effect on the pricing structure within the various types of improved properties. The economy of the area had worsened at a rapid pace between 1985 and 1987, with oil prices dropping by 50%. Additionally, the new tax laws compounded problems associated with the current excessive supply in the real estate industry. However, the sales range in date from January, 1989 to April, 1990, and based upon the fact that economic indicators during this time period were showing virtually no change, no adjustment for time was considered necessary.

Quality/age.   The subject property was considered to be in average condition with average construction quality and is approximately 12 years old. The sales range in age from six to eleven years at the time of sale and are considered to be of average to good quality construction. Sale No. 4 was constructed in 1982 and required a negative age adjustment of 25% for its relative newness at the time of sale. Sale No. 5, constructed in 1981, received a negative age adjustment of 15%.

Occupancy.   The subject has a current occupancy level of 92%, while the sales range in occupancy levels from a low of 65% to a high of 100%. Only Sale No. 3 had an occupancy level significantly lower than the subject. This sale was 65% occupied at the time of sale and a 10% upward adjustment was applied for this factor. The remaining sales required no adjustment.

Project density.   The subject property has a project density of 34.4 units per acre while the included sales had project densities ranging from 27.5 units per acre to 33.8 units per acre with a mean of 31.3 units per acre. The sales did not vary greatly relative to the subject and no adjustments were made for density.

Location.   The location of a property has a direct effect on the property's ability to command a quality income stream. Those properties which possess superior or inferior location attributes were adjusted upward or downward in comparison to the subject property. Sale Nos. 1 and 2 required 5% upward adjustments as they were considered slightly inferior to the subject in location. Although not located on a major thoroughfare, the subject is located near the Southwest Freeway/Beltway 8 interchange, which provides superior access and exposure to traffic. The other sales front on major streets and no adjustment was required.

Average unit size.   Typically, as average unit size increases, the price per unit increases. This was shown to be true in this case as evidenced by the comparable sales. We utilized paired sales, shown in the chart below, to arrive at an adjustment for this item.

	Comparable A	Comparable B
Date of Sale	12/21/89	12/22/89
Location	10881 Richmond	3400 Woodchase
Construction	Brick / Wood	Brick / Wood
Year Built	1980	1976
Price Per Unit	$14,416*	$15,476
Average Unit Size	732 Sq. Ft.	780 Sq. Ft.

* Adjusted for age of complex

These sales were considered similar in location, construction and date of sale. A downward adjustment was made to Comparable A to compensate for newer construction. The average size per unit varied from 732 square feet to 780 square feet for Comparables A and B, respectively. Comparable A had an adjusted sales price per unit of $14,416 and Comparable B sold for $15,476 per unit. The percent difference in average unit size for these two sales is 6.55%, and the percent difference in sale price is 7.35%.

Based upon this analysis, it appears that for every 6.55% difference in average unit size, there is a 7.35% difference in sale price. As Sale Nos. 1 through 4 are larger than the subject in average unit size, we applied a negative adjustment for difference in unit size to these sales. Sale No. 5 has virtually the same size units as the subject and no adjustment was necessary.

Sales Price Per Square Foot

The first unit of comparison extracted from the improved market data is the sales price per square foot. The actual range is from $16.01 to $25.61 per square foot. The indicated adjusted range is from $16.81 to $21.77 per square foot of net rentable area. An analysis of the comparable improved sales on a square foot basis follows.

The mean indicated by the six comparable sales is $18.99 per square foot of net rentable area. All of the comparables sold since January, 1989. Since market conditions for multi-family projects have changed very little over that short period of time, no adjustments were made to any of the sales for market conditions. All five sales were considered comparable to the subject property; however, more weight was given to Sale Nos. 1 through 3, as they required fewer adjustments. The weighted average adjusted price per square foot is $18.78.

The price per square foot of net rentable area can be considered a function of the net operating income each property generates per square foot of net rentable area. Therefore, the net operating income per square foot was analyzed. The subject's net operating income per square foot was estimated to be $1.54 per square foot. This falls closest to Sale Nos. 1 and 4, which have net operating incomes per square foot of $1.26 per square foot and $1.55 per square foot, respectively. These two sales indicate a price per square foot of net rentable area in the range of $19.78 per square foot to $16.86 per square foot. After analyzing the market information available, $18.75 per square foot of net rentable area is suggested which equates to the following initial value indication:

218,016 Sq. Ft. of Net Rentable Area × $18.75/Sq. Ft. = $4,087,800

An adjustment grid follows on p. 546.

Sales Price per Unit

The second unit of comparison extracted from the improved market data is the sales price per unit. The actual range for the price per unit comparison is from $11,571 to $21,067. The indicated adjusted range is from $8,931 to $14,934 per unit. In addition to the adjustment made for age, occupancy and location made in the price per square foot analysis, an adjustment for average unit size was made to arrive at an estimate for sales price per unit. An analysis of the sales on a per unit basis follows.

The average adjusted price per unit is $12,760. However, more weight was placed on Sale Nos. 2, 3, and 5, as they required overall fewer adjustments. The weighted average adjusted price per unit is $12,673. After analyzing the market information available, $12,673, or $12,700 (rounded) per unit is suggested, which equates to the following initial value indication:

318 units × $12,700 per unit = $4,038,600

ANALYSIS OF COMPARABLE APARTMENT SALES (PER SQUARE FOOT BASIS)

Date of Appraisal: 01-Aug-90

Annual Value Change:
1987... -12%
1988... 0%
1989... 0%
1990.. .0%

Sale	Sale date	Location	NRA (SF)	Price per SF	Adjustments							Indicates
					Time	Age	Occupancy	Density	Location	Other	Total	
1	27-Dec-89	Spring Meadows	238,800	$18.84	$0.00 0%	$0.00 0%	$0.00 0%	$0.00 0%	$0.94 5%	$0.00 0%	$0.94 5%	$19.78
2	11-Feb-89	Sunset Point	101,160	$16.01	$0.00 0%	$0.00 0%	$0.00 0%	$0.00 0%	$0.80 5%	$0.00 0%	$0.80 5%	$16.81
3	05-Jan-89	Water Song	203,608	$17.93	$0.00 0%	$0.00 0%	$1.79 10%	$0.00 0%	$0.00 0%	$0.00 0%	$1.79 10%	$19.72
4	15-May-89	Ashford on the Green	166,016	$22.48	$0.00 0%	($5.62) -25%	$0.00 0%	$0.00 0%	$0.00 0%	$0.00 0%	($5.62) -25%	$16.86
5	30-Apr-90	The Forrester	214,732	$25.61	$0.00 0%	($3.84) -15%	$0.00 0%	$0.00 0%	$0.00 0%	$0.00 0%	($3.84) -15%	$21.77

Subject 218,016 SF
Avg: 183,482 SF

Average Adjusted $/SF $18.99
Weighted Average Adjusted $/SF $18.78

ANALYSIS OF COMPARABLE APARTMENT SALES (PER UNIT BASIS)

Date of Appraisal:
01-Aug-90

Annual Value Change:
1987. . . . −12%
1988. . . . 0%
1989. . . . 0%
1990. . . . .0%

Sale	Sale date	Avg. SF	Price per unit	Location	Adjustments							Indicates
					Time	Age	Occup	Density	Location	Unit size	Total	
1	27-Dec-89	786	$14,803	Spring Meadows	$0.00 0%	$0.00 0%	$0.00 0%	$0.00 0%	$1,480 5%	($1,923) −13%	($443) −3%	$14,360
2	11-Feb-89	723	$11,571	Sunset Point	$0.00 0%	$0.00 0%	$0.00 0%	$0.00 0%	$579 5%	($556) −5%	$22 0%	$11,593
3	05-Jan-89	749	$13,419	Water Song	$0.00 0%	$0.00 0%	$1,342 10%	$0.00 0%	$0.00 0%	($1,098) −8%	$244 2%	$13,663
4	15-May-89	937	$21,067	Ashford on the Green	$0.00 0%	($5,267) −25%	$0.00 0%	$0.00 0%	$0.00 0%	($6,869) −33%	($12,136) −58%	$ 8,931
5	30-Apr-90	684	$17,516	The Forrester	$0.00 0%	($2,267) −15%	$0.00 0%	$0.00 0%	$0.00 0%	$46 0%	($2,582) −15%	$14,934

Subject 686 SF
Avg: 768 SF

Average Adjusted $/SF $12,760
Weighted Average Adjusted $/SF $12,673

The initial value estimated by utilizing the price per square foot was $4,087,800. The initial value indicated by utilizing the price per unit was $4,038,600. By placing equal weight on both values, the indicated value by the physical units of comparison, when rounded, is $4,060,000.

Effective Gross Income Multiplier

The third unit of comparison is the effective gross income multiplier. The effective gross income multiplier shows the relationship between the effective gross income attributable to a property and the overall sale price. In this regard, it can be utilized to illustrate a point of tendency for income producing properties, and is generally not adjusted for factors such as size, age, and location. These adjustments are presumably compensated for in the market rent for a property. Therefore, if properties are not truly comparable to the subject, the indicated value for the subject via the effective gross income method might be somewhat distorted. The degree of comparability is typically based upon expense ratios and financing terms.

Sale	EGIM	ER	NOI PSF
1	4.41	.70	$1.26
2	3.83	.72	1.18
3	4.64	.76	0.92
4	5.09	.65	1.55
5	5.04	.65	2.08
Subject		.67	1.67

The effective gross income multipliers extracted ranged from 3.83 to 5.09. The expense ratios formed a tight range from 0.65 to 0.72. The subject had an expense ratio of 0.67. The subject's expense ratio is at the lower end of the range formed by the comparable sales. Gross income multipliers tend to correlate with expense ratios, with higher expense ratios being associated with lower effective gross income multipliers. Sale Nos. 4 and 5 each have expense ratios of 0.65, similar to the subject, with effective gross income multipliers in a range of 5.04 to 5.09. However, these are sales of newer complexes which are felt to be superior. Therefore, an effective gross income multiplier of in the range of 5.04 and 5.09 is considered to be too high.

Also, in our opinion, the subject's expense ratio is slightly lower than Sale Nos. 1 through 3 because rents have increased since the date of sale. The subject is most similar in age and quality of construction to Sale Nos. 1 through 3. Equal weight has been given to Sale Nos. 1 and 2, as they form tight expense ratio and NOI per square foot ranges. We have concluded an effective gross income multiplier of 4.10 for the subject property.

In the income approach section we have estimated the effective gross income for the subject property. In this instance, the stabilized effective gross income for the subject has been estimated at $1,002,542. This figure is utilized in the following calculation along with the previously determined effective gross income multiplier to indicate the total value for the property.

Effective Gross Income × EGIM = Indicated Value
$1,002,542   ×   4.10   = $ 4,110,442
$4,110,000 (rounded)

Correlation

The two value indications provided by the physical and economic units of comparison of the sales comparison approach are as follows:

Physical Units of Comparison:	$4,060,000
Economic Units of Comparison:	$4,110,000

The effective gross income multiplier method puts primary weight on the income producing capabilities of a property and converts the effective gross income into a value indication. A primary requirement of this method is that the expense ratios of the comparable sales are similar to the estimated expense ratio of the subject property. The effective gross income multiplier method is typically considered a reliable approach because it is based on the income-producing ability of a property.

The sales price per square foot and the sales price per unit, or the physical units of comparison, are generally reliable indicators of value. The analysis of the physical units of comparison typically involves making adjustments. The number of variables involved allow for a greater range of interpretation of the indicated sales prices. However, since few adjustments were made, this is considered a reliable approach.

Both value indications are in relatively close alignment and are mutually supportive. Equal weight has been assigned to each indication of value. Based on this criteria, the indicated value of Keegan's Mill Apartments via the sales comparison approach is $4,085,000.

Explain which of the three units of comparison (EGIM, SP/SF, and SP/Unit) provides the most reliable indication of value for the appraised property.

INCOME CAPITALIZATION APPROACH

C

In the income approach, an estimate of value is formulated by analyzing and interpreting the subject property's income-producing abilities. The process of converting income into value is known as capitalization.

The principal assumption of the income approach is that there is a definite relationship between a property's value and the income it can produce. The premise behind the income approach is that it discounts to present worth the future income benefits a property will produce during the remainder of its economic life or during a projected term of ownership for the typical purchaser. In this approach, gross income and various expenses are estimated by market data comparison and the resulting net income is capitalized into value at an appropriate rate which would attract investors to this type of property.

Several methods are available to analyze the income stream. The direct capitalization method is usually given primary consideration as an indicator of value for the income approach analysis. In addition, a six-year discounted cash flow analysis was also utilized.

Analysis of Market Rental Rates

The first step in the income approach is to estimate the market rental rate of the subject property. Based upon an analysis of the subject's current rental schedule, as well as analysis of the rental rates in the subject neighborhood, market rentals for the subject property were estimated.

The quoted monthly rentals for existing apartment complexes considered in this report ranged from $0.332 per square foot to $0.481 per square foot. The rental rates varied depending upon their location, amenities, physical characteristics, and age of project. All of the comparables were individually metered and built during the mid 1970's to early 1980's.

We surveyed seven apartment complexes in the market area which were thought to be comparable to the subject property. However, in the final analysis only five were used. The others were disregarded due to superior condition after rehabilitation.

Our study of the market indicated that there were a number of individually metered projects within the immediate area. Additionally, the majority of the complexes were in average condition, and built during the past 12 years. Therefore, the subject property may compete effectively with complexes in the area.

As was discussed in the apartment market overview section of this report, the target market area has been experiencing rental demand slightly below the city as a whole. It is our opinion that the information in these comparable rentals is indicative of market rental rates in the area. The number of apartment projects that are offering promotions has been greatly reduced in the past year.

Detailed information regarding the comparable rental properties follows. A map showing the location of each rental precedes the rental information.

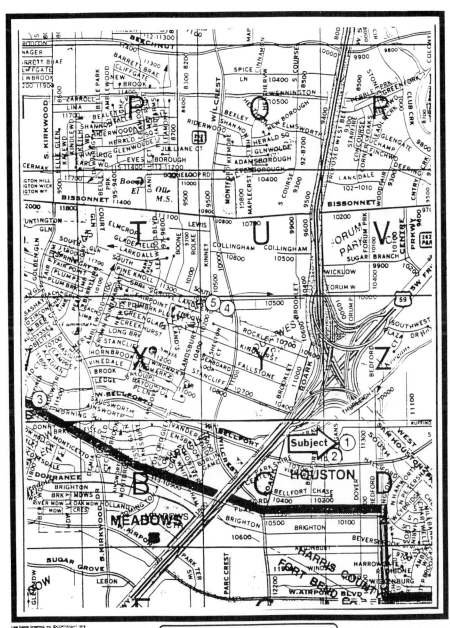

Comparable Rentals

APARTMENT RENT COMPARABLE NO. 1

Project:	Point of the Southwest; 11505 Keegan's Ridge Road, Houston, Texas
Telephone:	(713) 933-1263
Survey Date:	July, 1990
Age:	1976
Number of Units:	250
Rentable Area:	182,725 SF
Average Unit Size:	731 SF
Parking:	Open concrete
Utilities:	Tenant
Stated Occupancy:	87%
Condition:	Average
Construction:	Wood frame construction, two-story buildings, combined use of brick veneer and composition wood siding exteriors.
Amenities:	Complex: three laundry rooms, pool, weight room, tanning bed.
	Units: some washer/dryer connections, mini blinds, cable available.
Quality:	Average
Promotions/Concessions:	Deposit and last month free
Comments:	Drive-by inspection revealed above-average deferred maintenance.

Unit type	Area SF	Monthly rent	Rent per sq.ft.
1BR/1BA	625	$235	$.376
1BR/1BA	700	$245	$.350
2BR/1BA	900	$325	$.361
2BR/2BA	1,100	$395	$.359

APARTMENT RENT COMPARABLE NO. 2

Project:	Southwest Terrace; 10200 West Bellfort, Houston, Texas
Telephone:	(713) 933-9590
Survey Date:	July, 1990
Age:	1977
Number of Units:	250

Rentable Area:	172,544 SF
Average Unit Size:	690 SF
Parking:	Open concrete parking
Utilities:	Tenant
Stated Occupancy:	75%
Condition:	Average to fair
Construction:	Wood frame construction, two-story buildings, combined use of brick veneer and wood siding exteriors, pitched composition shingled roofs.
Amenities:	Complex: pool, jacuzzi, two laundry rooms.
	Units: mini blinds
Quality:	Average
Promotions/Concessions:	Last month free on 7-month lease
Comments:	Drive-by inspection revealed above-average deferred maintenance.

Unit type	Area SF	Monthly rent	Rent PSF
Eff.	504	$205	$.407
1BR/1BA	606	$230	$.308
1BR/1BA	680	$250	$.368
2BR/1BA	796	$320	$.402
2BR/2BA	900	$350	$.389

APARTMENT RENT COMPARABLE NO. 3

Project:	Southwest Village; 11726 W. Bellfort, Houston, Texas
Telephone:	(713) 495-6167
Survey Date:	July, 1990
Age:	1975
Number of Units:	198
Rentable Area:	146,790 SF
Average Unit Size:	741 SF
Parking:	Open concrete parking
Utilities:	Tenant
Stated Occupancy:	88%
Condition:	Average

Construction:		Wood frame construction, two-story buildings, combination brick veneer and wood siding exterior, flat built-up roofing.	
Amenities:		Complex: clubroom, laundry room	
		Unit: outside storage, mini blinds, cable available.	
Quality:		Average	
Promotions/Concessions:		None. Effective rents are being quoted.	

Unit type	Area SF	Monthly rent	Rent PSF
1BR/1BA	505	$235	$.465
1BR/1BA	707	270	.382
2BR/1BA	904	340	.376
2BR/2BA	965	400	.415

APARTMENT RENT COMPARABLE NO. 4

Project:	Winding Trails Apartments; 10300 Wilcrest, Houston, Texas
Telephone:	(713) 933-1200
Survey Date:	July, 1990
Age:	1978
Number of Units:	438
Rentable Area:	369,016 SF
Average Unit Size:	842 SF
Parking:	Open concrete parking
Utilities:	Tenant
Stated Occupancy:	90%
Condition:	Average
Construction:	Wood frame construction, two-story buildings, brick veneer and wood siding exteriors with pitched composition shingled roofs
Amenities:	Complex: two pools, five laundry rooms, clubroom, tennis court
	Units: mini blinds, cable, washer/dryer connections
Quality:	Average
Promotions/Concessions:	$100 off with apartment guide advertisement

Unit type	Area SF	Monthly rent	Rent PSF
1BR/1BA	650	$260	$.400
1BR/1BA	750	290	.387
1BR/1BA	850	300	.353
2BR/1BA	910	345	.379
2BR/2BA	960	375	.391
2BR/2BA	1,056	400	.379

APARTMENT RENT COMPARABLE NO. 5

Project:	Woodstone Apartments; 10250 Lands End, Houston, Texas
Telephone:	(713) 933-1331
Survey Date:	July, 1990
Age:	1983
Number of Units:	144
Rentable Area:	96,528 SF
Average Unit Size:	670 SF
Parking:	Open concrete parking
Utilities:	Tenant
Stated Occupancy:	85%
Condition:	Average to good
Construction:	Wood frame construction, two-story buildings, combined use of brick veneer and composition wood siding exteriors with pitched composition shingled roofs.
Amenities:	Complex: pool, jacuzzi and one laundry room
	Units: microwave, washer/dryer connections, cable available, fireplace and vaulted ceilings in some units
Quality:	Good
Promotions/Concessions:	$100 for first month.

Unit type	Area SF	Monthly rent	Rent PSF
Eff.	468	$250	$.534
1BR/1BA	659	310	.470
1BR/1BA	683	350	.512
1BR/1.5BA	711	360	.506
2BR/2BA	1,033	475	.460

As indicated throughout the report, the Houston market area has experienced a downturn in its economic base during 1986 through 1988; however, it appears to be stabilizing. Coupled with an overbuilding period, occupancy levels for the apartment market throughout the Houston area dropped below breakeven levels; however, the excess apartment units are gradually being absorbed. Development and construction of multi-family projects in the past two to three years have declined, and no new construction is anticipated in the subject neighborhood in the near future, as the area currently appears to be in a recovery period.

A brief analysis of this rental data indicates that property managers and building owners in this immediate area are relatively consistent in their basis or method of rentals. In other words, the majority of the agents and owners negotiate leases on an unfurnished basis, with tenant paying electricity. The majority of the leases in this area are negotiated on a 6- or 12-month term.

The unit type and/or types from each rent comparable that were considered most similar to the three basic unit types for the subject were isolated and examined. This process is summarized in the following tables, each of which is followed by analysis of the data collected.

Rental Survey - Units A & B
One Bedroom/One Bath Units
602 and 680 Square Feet

The following rental rates ranged from $230 to $350 per month, and from $.350 to $.512 per square foot per month.

Rental no.	Complex	Unit size	Effective monthly rent	
			Aggregate	Per sq. ft.
1	Point of the Southwest	625 SF	$235	$.376
		700 SF	$245	$.350
2	Southwest Terrace	606 SF	$230	$.380
		680 SF	$250	$.368
3	Southwest Village	505 SF	$235	$.465
		707 SF	$270	$.382
4	Winding Trails	650 SF	$260	$.400
		750 SF	$290	$.387
		850 SF	$300	$.353
5	Woodstone	659 SF	$310	$.470
		683 SF	$350	$.512

The following table shows the current rent and the estimated market rent for Units A and B of the subject.

Unit	Curr. quoted rent	Size	Est. market rent	Rent PSF
A	$235	602 SF	$245	$.407
B	$250	680 SF	$265	$.390

Rent Comparable 4 was considered most similar to the subject. Rent Comparable 5 is superior to the subject property in terms of amenities and services provided. Rent Comparables 1, 2, and 3 are considered inferior in condition.

It is our opinion that the currently quoted rental rates are slightly below the current market. As of August 1, 1990, the A units had a vacancy of 8% and the B units had a vacancy of 5%. Therefore, considering these low vacancy rates, we increased the quoted rental rates to $245 and $265 for the 602 and 680 square foot units, respectively. It is also our opinion that the estimated effective market rental rates are supported by the competing projects.

Rental Survey - Unit C
Two Bedroom/One Bath Units
796 Square Feet

The following rental rates ranged from $320 to $345 per month, and from $.361 to $.402 per square foot per month.

Rental no.	Complex	Unit size	Effective monthly rent Aggregate	Per sq. ft.
1	Point of the Southwest	900 SF	$325	$.361
2	Southwest Terrace	796 SF	$320	$.402
3	Southwest Village	904 SF	$340	$.376
4	Winding Trails	910 SF	$345	$.379

The following are rents for Plan C of the subject.

Unit	Curr. quoted rent	Size	Est. market rent	Rent PSF
C	$350	796 SF	$350	$.440

Rent Comparables 1 through 4 are inferior to the subject property, in terms of condition, with Rent Comparable 4 being the most similar.

It is our opinion that the currently quoted rental rates are at current market. A 6% vacancy was reported for Unit C as of August 1, 1990. Taking these factors into consideration we have utilized a rental rate of $350 per month for the C units. It is our opinion that the estimated effective market rental rates are supported by the competing projects.

Rental Survey - Units B-2 and D
Two Bedroom/Two Bath & Two Bedroom/Two Bath/Den Units
844 and 1,059 Square Feet

The following rental rates ranged from $350 to $475 per month, and from $.359 to $.460 per square foot per month.

			Effective monthly rent	
Rental no.	Complex	Unit size	Aggregate	Per sq. ft.
1	Point of the Southwest	1,100 SF	$395	$.359
2	Southwest Terrace	900 SF	$350	$.389
3	Southwest Village	965 SF	$400	$.415
4	Winding Trails	960 SF	$375	$.391
		1,056 SF	$400	$.379
5	Woodstone	1,033 SF	$475	$.460

The following are the current rents and estimated market rents for Pans B-2 and D.

Unit	Curr. quoted rent	Size	Est. market rent	Rent PSF
B-2	$450	1,059 SF	$450	$.425
D	$375	844 SF	$375	$.444

Rent Comparable 5 is superior to the subject in amenities and services provided. Rent Comparables 1, 2, and 3 are in inferior condition.

It is our opinion that the currently quoted rental rates are at market for both units. A 31% vacancy rate was recorded for the B-2 unit as of August 1, 1990. However, this is a very popular unit based on its previous rental history and should lease up quickly. The D unit had only a 6% vacancy. Taking these factors into consideration, we estimated the market rental rate at $450 per month for the B-2 unit and $375 per month for the D unit. It is our opinion that the estimated effective market rental rate is supported by the competing projects.

Conclusion. Based on the information presented earlier, we have estimated a pro forma rent schedule for the subject property. In our opinion, the current rents on Units B-2, C, and D are at market levels. We concluded that Units A
and B could command higher rents. However, since leases are already in effect at
current levels, we have not increased rents in the stabilized pro forma, but we incorporated this increase in Year 2 of the discounted cash flow. The following
chart represents the estimated monthly market rents for each of the units in the
subject property utilized in the direct capitalization calculations.

Plan	Type	Area	Monthly rental Per unit	Per SF
A	1BR	602	$235	$0.39
B	1BR	680	$250	$0.37
B2	2BR	1,059	$450	$0.42
C	2BR	796	$350	$0.44
D	2BR	844	$375	$0.44

We have concentrated our rental survey on those apartment complexes
which were the most comparable to the subject property. While there are additional apartment complexes in the general area, they were either considered to be
superior or inferior to the subject property. We have surveyed these complexes to
determine their rental rates, but have not presented them in this report, as they
are not considered to be comparable.

According to the on-site property manager, there are currently no concessions or promotions, and effective rental rates are being quoted for all units. The
foregoing effective rental rates are supported by the market, and will be utilized in
our discounted cash flow model and stabilized income pro forma.

Other income. The subject property also receives other income from
vending machines, laundry facilities, and the forfeiture of security deposits. According to the 1989 operating statement for the subject property, other income
was approximately $140 per unit. This is considered reasonable and is used in our
gross potential income calculations.

Direct Capitalization

In estimating gross potential income, it is necessary to analyze all income to the
subject property. Total gross potential rental income is estimated to be
$1,045,200. In addition to the rental income, projects typically have other
sources of miscellaneous income, such as monies from vending machines, laundry machines, and forfeited deposits. The miscellaneous income is $140 per unit
per year, or $44,520. The estimated gross potential income is $1,089,720.

The next step in direct capitalization is to estimate the vacancy and collection loss. The subject currently has an occupancy of 92% which is considered stable in the current market. For purposes of this appraisal, we have estimated an 8% vacancy and collection loss for the appraised property on a stabilized basis. Based on a rate of 8%, the vacancy and collection loss for the subject is $87,178. Therefore, the stabilized effective gross income is $1,002,542.

Expenses.   In order to arrive at a net operating income for the subject property, the annual expenses incurred in producing this income must be deducted. Operating expenses are annual cash outflows borne by the owner/investor of the income-producing property as a necessary cost of generating the gross income the property is capable of producing. The expense figures are stabilized annual expenses payable by the owner over the income projection period.

In estimating operating expenses, various categories of expenses have been compared in detail to the actual income and market expenses of similar apartment projects. The 1989 operating expenses and the 1990 operating expenses through May were available for the subject property and were utilized in this report. Other expenses were estimated from market data. Copies of the 1989 and 1990 operating statements are contained in the addendum.

Taxes.   Real estate taxes for 1990 were estimated to be $98,107, or $0.45 per square foot. A detailed discussion of real estate taxes may be found in the tax analysis section of the report.

Insurance.   Insurance typically covers fire, extended coverage, and owners's liability. The expense is usually based on age, type of construction, condition, size, and location. The insurance for the subject property is $0.12 per square foot, or $26,162.

Salary Expense.   This item covers salaries and related expenses. Salary expenses were estimated to be $141,710 or $0.65 per square foot.

Utilities.   Utility expense is the cost of electricity for common areas and water supplied to the subject property. The utilities for the subject property were $115,548 or $0.53 per square foot.

Contract services.   This item includes budget for landscaping service, on-site security, pest control, and garbage removal. We projected total charges at $43,603 or $0.20 per square foot.

General and administrative.   General administrative expense includes expenses such as telephone service, office supplies, furniture rental, and miscellaneous expenses. The expense was estimated to be $71,945, or $0.33 per square foot.

Repair and maintenance.   Maintenance expenses may cover interior and exterior repairs such as the roof, foundation, and the structural soundness of the exterior walls. These expenses can vary depending upon the type and quality of construction, age and condition, and size of the improvements. Repair and maintenance for the subject was estimated to be $65,405 or $0.30 per square foot.

Leasing expense.   Leasing expense includes such items as leasing commissions and model furniture rental. This expense is projected to be $32,702, or $0.15 per square foot.

Advertising and promotion.   Advertisement expense is the cost of placing ads, promotions, and referral discounts. Advertisement expense was $21,802, or $0.10 per square foot.

Management.   Management is an expense item which reflects the cost incurred in the day-to-day operation of the property. A management fee of 5% of effective gross income should accurately reflect the location, size, and quality of the subject improvements. This is consistent with amounts currently being charged in competing properties. When applied to the effective gross income, the management expense represents $50,127 per year.

The total projected expenses are approximately 67% of the effective gross income, or $677,112, or $3.06 per square foot. The expenses per square foot of net rentable area and the expense ratio are both considered units of comparison. When operating expenses are deducted from effective gross income, a net operating income of $335,430 is indicated.

Overall rate estimate.   As previously discussed in the sales comparison section, the comparable sales for apartment complexes are located in the general subject area. Although there are some dissimilarities between the subject and the available comparables, it is believed that the overall rates provided represent a reliable basis for estimating the appropriate rate for the subject. The following is a brief summary of the pertinent information regarding the transactions:

Apt. sales	Sale date	OAR
1	12/89	6.71%
2	11/89	7.39%
3	01/89	5.11%
4	05/89	6.88%
5	04/90	8.11%

As indicated, the overall rates range from 5.11% to 8.11%. This is a relatively narrow range of capitalization rates. However, these rates are considered to be on the low end of the scale for apartment properties.

Our research of the apartment sales reported herein and other more recent sales tend to indicate that going-in capitalization rates are increasing due to decreasing upside potential. However, the subject property, in our opinion, is expected to remain at stabilized occupancy while rents are increased, as various improvements are planned for the subject project such as controlled access gates, and the completion of Beltway 8, the Sam Houston Tollway, in the vicinity of the subject and the general upward trend in the Houston apartment market.

We have utilized an overall rate of 8.5%, which is slightly above the range, but is considered appropriate for this type of property because of the tenant profile, the make-up of the neighborhood, the condition of the improvements and the risk involved. The selected capitalization rate is supported by a study provided by *The Appraiser*, published in May, 1990. The study indicates stabilized capitalization rates range from 7% to 9% for apartments. The market data indicate a capitalization rate near the middle of the range of this study.

> After reviewing Chapter 15, discuss the relative merits of using the direct capitalization method.

When the net operating income of $335,430 is capitalized at a rate of 8.5%, the resulting value indication by direct capitalization is $3,946,235. The value indicated by the direct capitalization approach, when rounded, is $3,950,000.

Calculations of the income approach by direct capitalization follow on p. 563.

Discounted Cash Flow Analysis

Two methods of analysis have been considered in order to arrive at an estimate of value by the income approach. The first method, direct capitalization, was outlined earlier. In addition to direct capitalization, a discounted cash flow analysis is included as part of the income approach. The discounted cash flow analysis forecasts net operating income for a typical holding period, estimated to be ten years, and an estimated reversion value of the property at the end of that holding period based on the capitalization of the projected Year 11 income stream. These future benefits are discounted at an appropriate yield rate to indicate the present value of the subject property.

The present value of the income streams and the reversion at the end of the holding period were analyzed by discounted cash flow model with data for the model extracted from the market study and the direct capitalization analysis. This analysis is illustrated at the end of this section. The model is based on the following assumptions.

Discounted cash flow assumptions

1. Year 1 rental rates were based on current actual rental rates. As rents on Units A and B were considered to be below market, the rates which were considered to be at market levels were incorporated in Year 2. In Years 2 through 5, rents are projected to increase by 5% annually. These higher rates

DIRECT CAPITALIZATION CALCULATIONS
RENT SCHEDULE:

Plan	Unit type	Area	No. units	Total area	Monthly Per unit	Monthly Per SF	Gross rent	Annual rent
A	1BR	602	160	96,320	$235	$0.39	$37,600	$ 451,200
B	1BR	680	78	53,040	$250	$0.37	19,500	234,000
B2	2BR	1,059	16	16,944	$450	$0.42	7,200	86,400
C	2BR	796	48	38,208	$350	$0.44	16,800	201,600
D	2BR	844	16	13,504	$375	$0.44	6,000	72,000
Total / Avg:		686	318	218,016	$274	$0.40	$87,100	$1,045,200

Ancillary Income:	$140 /Unit/Year		44,520
Gross Potential Income:			$1,089,720
Less: Vacancy & Collection Loss		8%	87,178
Effective Gross Income:			$1,002,542
Operating Expenses:			
Real Estate Taxes	$0.45 /SF		$98,107
Insurance	$0.12 /SF		26,162
Salary Expense	$0.65 /SF		141,710
Utilities	$0.53 /SF		115,548
Contract Services	$0.20 /SF		43,603
General & Administrative	$0.33 /SF		71,945
Repair & Maintenance	$0.30 /SF		65,405
Leasing Expense	$0.15 /SF		32,702
Advertising & Promotion	$0.10 /SF		21,802
Management	5% of EGI		50,127
Total Operating Expenses:	$3.06 /SF		$667,112
Net Operating Income:			$335,430
Net Operating Income: Capitalized at		8.50%	$3,946,235
Indicated Value:			(R) $3,950,000

reflect the current lower market rental rates and an annual inflation factor of 5%. Rents are projected to increase at a stabilized rate of 4% per year from year 6 until the end of the projection period.

2. Stabilized vacancy and collection loss is considered to be 8%. The subject is currently 92% occupied.

3. Expenses were based on actual and market expenses and are increased at 5% per year for each year of the study period.

4. To estimate reversion, the eleventh year net operating income has been capitalized using a 9.5% terminal capitalization rate. The terminal capitalization rate of 9.5% is 100 basis points greater than the capitalization rate utilized in the direct capitalization section of the report, because of the older age of the property at the end of the holding period. The sales expenses are estimated to be 3%.

5. The resulting cash flows were discounted at 13%.

The net present value of the income stream, plus the value of the reversion, when discounted at 13%, is supportive of the value derived by direct capitalization. Discount rates can be estimated by examining alternative investment opportunities and adjusting the degree of risk. The prime rate at the date of appraisal was 10%. Mortgage funds would be available at interest rates one to two points above prime. Equity investors are generally requiring yields of 15% to 20% on quality real estate investments. Generally, as the degree of security decreases, the required yield rate will increase. There are inherent risk factors in real estate and additional management burdens which are not present in a bond investment. The current rates for corporate bonds (AAA, A, BAA) range from 8.75% to 10.40%. Because bonds are more liquid than real estate, the discount sales on real estate are generally higher than bond yields. The performance of real estate is dependent upon the degree or quality of management, unexpected competition, or economic cycles. Therefore, it entails a greater degree of risk than government-backed bonds on fixed-rate mortgages. Considering these factors and the particular attributes of the subject property concerning competitive pressures within the Houston market, a discount rate higher than the bond rates would be required. A discount rate at the higher end of the range equates to the risk involved with this type of property and the market. Assuming that there is an average degree of risk, capital would be attracted to projects similar in scope to the appraised property at a discount rate of 13% for the property on a "free and clear basis" without a mortgage. A study provided by *The Appraiser*, May, 1990, indicates discount rates for apartments range from 10% to 14%.

The value indicated by the discounted cash flow analysis is $4,000,000, when rounded. Calculations of the discounted cash flow analysis follow.

What is the relation between the capitalization rate and discount rate used in the appraisal of this apartment complex? See Chapters 15 and 17.

DISCOUNTED CASH FLOW ANALYSIS
MONTHLY RENTAL ($/UNIT)

Plan	Area	No. units	Total area	1	2	3	4	5	6	7	8	9	10	11
				Year...										
A	602	160	96,320	$235	$257	$270	$284	$298	$310	$322	$338	$355	$373	$392
B	680	78	53,040	$250	$278	$292	$307	$322	$335	$348	$366	$384	$403	$423
B2	1,059	16	16,944	$450	$473	$496	$521	$547	$569	$592	$621	$652	$685	$719
C	796	48	38,208	$350	$368	$386	$405	$425	$442	$460	$483	$507	$533	$559
D	844	16	13,504	$375	$394	$413	$434	$456	$474	$493	$518	$544	$571	$599
Total		318	218,016											
Annual Gross Rental Income				$1,045,200	$1,132,362	$1,188,980	$1,248,429	$1,310,851	$1,363,285	$1,417,816	$1,488,707	$1,563,142	$1,641,299	$1,723,364
Ancillary Income	$140			44,520	46,746	49,083	51,537	54,114	56,820	59,661	62,644	65,776	69,065	72,518
Total Gross Income				1,089,720	1,179,108	1,238,063	1,299,967	1,364,965	1,420,105	1,477,477	1,551,351	1,628,918	1,710,364	1,795,883
% Vacancy & Col. Loss				8%	8%	8%	8%	8%	8%	8%	8%	8%	8%	8%
Vacancy & Col. Loss				(87,178)	(94,329)	(99,045)	(103,997)	(109,197)	(113,608)	(118,198)	(124,108)	(130,313)	(136,829)	(143,671)
% Rental Concessions				0%	0%	0%	0%	0%	0%	0%	0%	0%	0%	0%
Rental Concessions				0	0	0	0	0	0	0	0	0	0	0
Effective Gross Income				$1,002,542	$1,084,779	$1,139,018	$1,195,969	$1,255,768	$1,306,496	$1,359,279	$1,427,243	$1,498,605	$1,573,535	$1,652,212
Operating Expenses														
Taxes	$0.45 /SF			$98,107	$103,013	$108,163	$113,571	$119,250	$125,212	$131,473	$138,047	$144,949	$152,196	$159,806
Insurance	$0.12 /SF			26,162	27,470	28,844	30,286	31,800	33,390	35,059	36,812	38,653	40,586	42,615
Salary Exp	$0.65 /SF			141,710	148,796	156,236	164,048	172,250	180,862	189,905	199,401	209,371	219,839	230,831
Utilities	$0.53 /SF			115,548	121,326	127,392	133,762	140,450	147,472	154,846	162,588	170,718	179,254	188,216
Contract Serv	$0.20 /SF			43,603	45,783	48,073	50,476	53,000	55,650	58,432	61,354	64,422	67,643	71,025
Gen & Admin	$0.33 /SF			71,945	75,543	79,320	83,286	87,450	91,822	96,414	101,234	106,296	111,611	117,191
Repair & Main	$0.30 /SF			65,405	68,675	72,109	75,714	79,500	83,475	87,649	92,031	96,633	101,464	106,538
Leasing Exp	$0.15 /SF			32,702	34,338	36,054	37,857	39,750	41,737	43,824	46,016	48,316	50,732	53,269
Advertising	$0.10 /SF			21,802	22,892	24,036	25,238	26,500	27,825	29,216	30,677	32,211	33,821	35,513
Management	5% of EGI			50,127	54,239	56,951	59,798	62,788	65,325	67,964	71,362	74,930	78,677	82,611
Total Operating Expenses				$667,112	$702,074	$737,177	$774,036	$812,738	$852,772	$894,783	$939,522	$986,499	$1,035,823	$1,087,615
Net Operating Income				$335,430	$382,706	$401,841	$421,933	$443,030	$453,725	$464,496	$487,720	$512,106	$537,712	$564,597
Reversion Value													$5,765,000	
Total Cash Flows				$335,430	$382,706	$401,841	$421,933	$443,030	$453,725	$464,496	$487,720	$512,106	$6,302,712	
Discounted Cash Flows 13.0%				$296,841	$299,715	$278,496	$258,780	$240,459	$217,932	$197,439	$183,461	$170,472	$1,856,705	
Indicated Value...........				$4,000,000										

Correlation. The two value indications provided by the two methods of the income approach are as follows:

Direct Capitalization	$3,950,000
Discounted Cash Flow	$4,000,000

The direct capitalization method places most emphasis on current market rates and factors. The rates are obtained from the comparable sales by dividing the net operating income by the sale price. The strength of this analysis is its emphasis on market rates.

The discounted cash flow analysis is also a reliable indicator of value. This method provides for return on and return of capital because investors' assumptions are applied. It stimulates these assumptions and converts the future benefits to present value. The assumptions and number of variables allow for a greater range of interpretation, thus weakening the discounted cash flow analysis somewhat. Discounted cash flow analysis more accurately reflects the impact of the lower rental and occupancy rates found in the current market.

Direct capitalization and the discounted cash flow analysis are both considered reliable indicators of value and the values indicated by each method are in close alignment. Each of the methods in this analysis is considered well supported by the market data. The indicated value of Keegan's Mill Apartments via the income approach is estimated to be $3,980,000.

RECONCILIATION AND FINAL VALUE ESTIMATE

> See Chapter 22 for a discussion of the purpose of the valuation conclusion or value reconciliation.

The indicated value of the subject apartments by the three approaches to value is as follows:

Value Indicated by the Cost Approach	$4,780,000
Value Indicated by the Sales Comparison Approach	$4,085,000
Value Indicated by the Income Approach	$3,980,000

The reconciliation process involves weighing the value indications provided by each method in light of its dependability as a reflection of the probable actions of users and investors in the marketplace. All important facts and data concerning the subject property have been investigated and analyzed in detail. All three approaches available in valuing the subject property were utilized in this appraisal.

The income approach is considered the most reliable method due to the income-producing potential of the subject property. The necessary components of the approach such as the gross income, vacancy and credit loss, operating expenses and overall capitalization rate are all based on actual or market figures.

The gross income for the property was established from the actual rental rates of the subject property and market data obtained by analyzing the gross income of similar properties. It is believed that both the vacancy and collection loss and the operating expenses are estimated by reliable and accurate methods. This information is utilized to project gross and net operating incomes for the subject. The overall capitalization and discount rates were derived from market data.

The cost approach utilized current replacement cost figures existing in present-day construction. The methodology of this approach basically involves estimating the contributory value of the subject improvements as well as the value of the land, as if vacant. The cost data were based on the Marshall & Swift calculator cost method and confirmed by similar projects in the area. The estimated values of the improvements and land are combined with the result being the value indication via the cost approach. The value indicated by the cost approach is higher than the values indicated by the other two approaches to value; however, it does support the income and sales comparison approaches. This illustrates that constructing a multi-family project in the Houston area under current market conditions is not feasible.

The sales comparison approach is considered generally reliable. The strength of this approach is that if comparable market data are available, they should accurately reflect the attitudes of the typical buyers and sellers in the marketplace. This method of property valuation reflects both the physical characteristics of a property as well as economic characteristics. The primary units of comparison utilized in this approach include the price per square foot of net rentable building area, the price per dwelling unit, and the effective gross income multiplier. Because of the recent market activity, the sales comparison approach is strengthened.

After careful consideration of the values, previous information and examination of the value indications, it is our opinion that the estimated market value of the fee simple interest in the appraised property, as-is, as of August 1, 1990, was:

FOUR MILLION DOLLARS
($4,000,000)

What, if any, changes would you make in this actual appraisal report after having reviewed Chapter 22?

CERTIFICATE

The undersigned do hereby certify that, to the best of our knowledge, except as otherwise noted in this appraisal report:

The statements of fact contained in this report are true and correct.

The reported analyses, opinions, and conclusions are limited only by the reported assumptions and limiting conditions, and are our personal, unbiased professional analyses, opinions, and conclusions.

We have no present or prospective interest in the property that is the subject of this report, and we have no personal interest or bias with respect to the parties involved.

Our compensation is not contingent on an action or event resulting from the analyses, opinions, or conclusions in, or the use of, this report.

Our analyses, opinions, and conclusions were developed, and this report has been prepared, in conformity with the requirements of the Code of Professional Ethics and the Standards of Professional Practice of the American Institute of Real Estate Appraisers.

The use of this report is subject to the requirements of the American Institute of Real Estate Appraisers relating to review by its duly authorized representatives.

As of the date of this report, I, Gerald Burke Schulz, MAI, have completed the requirements under the continuing education program of the American Institute of Real Estate Appraisers.

We have made a personal inspection of the property that is the subject of this report.

No one provided significant professional assistance to the persons signing this report, except as may be noted elsewhere in this report.

Neither all nor any part of the contents of this report (especially any conclusions as to value, the identity of the appraiser or the firm with which he is connected, or any reference to the American Institute of Real Estate Appraisers or to the MAI or RM designation) shall be disseminated to the public through advertising media, public relations media, news media, sales media or any other public means of communication without the prior written consent and approval of the undersigned.

Julie W. Ashby   _G.B. Schulz_

Houston, Texas

Would you modify the certificate of value? If so, explain how and why (see Chapters 22 and 23).

QUALIFICATIONS OF
GERALD BURKE SCHULZ

Education:

Texas A & M University - B.S. Electrical Engineering

Technical Training:

American Institute of Real Estate Appraisers:

Course 1A-1 - Real Estate Appraisal Principles
Course 1A-2 - Basic Valuation Procedures
Course 1B-1 - Capitalization Theory and Techniques Part I
Course 1B-2 - Capitalization Theory and Techniques Part II
Course 1B-3 - Capitalization Theory and Techniques Part III
Course 2-1 - Case Studies in Real Estate Valuation
Course 2-2 - Valuation Analysis and Report Writing
Course 2-3 - Standards of Professional Practice
Course 6 - Real Estate Investment Analysis

Business Affiliations:

President of Love & Schulz, Real Estate Consultants and Appraisers, Houston, Texas. Owner and operator of a commercial cattle ranch, Atascosa and Live Oak Counties, Texas.

Business Experience:

Nine years of experience in the appraisal of commercial, industrial, special purpose, residential, and farm and ranch properties. Income properties appraised include office buildings, warehouses, hotels, apartments, shopping centers, and distribution and service facilities. Experience includes the appraisal of raw land and commercial, industrial, and residential subdivisions.

Four years' experience with a major construction and home building firm, including the management of the marketing department and supervision of the real estate branch. Five years' experience in the development, merchandising and marketing of electrical and mechanical equipment used in the construction and home building industry.

Trade Area:

The State of Texas and the southern portion of the United States, including the Houston, Galveston, Beaumont, Bryan-College Station, Victoria, San Antonio, and Corpus Christi areas, and the Rio Grande Valley.

Professional Affiliations and Designations:

Member - American Institute of Real Estate Appraisers (MAI), Certificate No. 7604
Licensed Real Estate Broker - State of Texas, License No. 200390
Chairman - Publications Committee, South Texas Chapter No. 29, AIREA
Member - Admissions Committee, South Texas Chapter No. 29, AIREA
Member - Regional Ethics and Counseling Panel, AIREA

> What is the primary purpose of the "Qualifications" section?

QUALIFICATIONS OF
JULIE W. ASHBY

Education:

B.S. in Physiology, Oklahoma State University, 1984
M.S. in Applied Health Science, Oklahoma State University, 1988

American Institute of Real Estate Appraisers Course Work:

Course 1A-2 - Basic Valuation Procedures
Course 1B-A - Capitalization Theory and Techniques, Part A

Spencer School of Real Estate Course Work:

Real Estate Principles and Practices
Real Estate Finance
Real Estate Law

Professional Experience:

Income properties appraised include warehouses, apartments, restaurants, and distribution and service facilities. Experience includes the appraisal of raw land, commercial, and industrial properties.

Trade Area:

South Central and Southeast Texas including Houston.

Professional Affiliations:

Licensed Real Estate Salesman, State of Texas (#404814)
Licensed Real Estate Salesman, State of Florida (#0531909)
MAI Candidate of American Institute of Real Estate Appraisers, Candidate No. M90-0841

CONTINGENT AND LIMITING CONDITIONS
(Unless Otherwise Stated in this Report)

The estimate of value for the property analyzed in the attached report is subject to the following limiting conditions:

The legal description furnished the appraisers is assumed to be correct. No responsibility is assumed for matters legal in character, nor is any opinion rendered as to title. It is assumed that there is full compliance with all applicable federal, state and local environmental regulations and laws unless non-compliance is stated, defined and considered in the appraisal report. All existing liens and encumbrances, if any, have been disregarded, and the property is analyzed as though free and clear and under responsible ownership and competent management.

The boundaries of the land and the dimensions and size thereof as indicated to the appraisers are assumed to be correct, no provision having been made for a special survey of the property. Valuation is reported without regard to questions of encroachments.

All engineering is assumed to be correct. The plot plans and illustrative materials in this report are included only to assist the reader in visualizing the property.

The information contained in this report and identified as having been furnished by others is believed to be reliable, but no responsibility is assumed for its accuracy.

No responsibility is assumed, nor is any guarantee made, as to the structural soundness of the improvements. It is assumed that there are no hidden or unapparent conditions of the property, subsoil, or structures that render it more or less valuable. No responsibility is assumed for such conditions or for arranging for engineering studies that may be required to discover them.

It is assumed that all applicable zoning and use regulations and restrictions have been complied with, unless a non-conformity has been stated, defined and considered in the appraisal report.

It is assumed that all required licenses, certificates of occupancy, consents, or other legislative or administrative authority from any local, state, or national government or private entity or organization have been or can be obtained or renewed for any use on which the value estimated contained in this report is based.

It is assumed that the utilization of the land and improvements is within the boundaries or property lines of the property described and that there is no encroachment or trespass unless noted in the report.

Possession of this report, or a copy thereof, does not carry with it the right of publication, nor may it be used for any other purposes by any but the applicant without the previous written consent of the appraisers.

The appraisers, by reason of this report, are not required to give testimony or attendance in court, or any other hearing with reference to the property in question, unless arrangements therefore have been previously made.

The distribution of the total valuation in this report between the land and the improvements applies only under the existing program of utilization. The separate valuations for land and improvements should not be used in conjunction with any other appraisal and are invalid if so used.

The appraisers have no present or contemplated future interest in the property which is not specifically disclosed in this report. Neither their employment for making this analysis nor the fee to be received therefore are contingent upon the valuation placed on the property.

No attempt was made, unless otherwise noted in the attached report, to detect the presence of various potentially hazardous materials or conditions upon the subject site or within or upon the subject improvements, and the appraisers are not qualified to do so. These hazardous materials or conditions could include, but are not limited to, the existence of toxic waste (within or around the subject site, presently or in the past), UREA formaldehyde foam insulation, ACM's (asbestos containing materials), or communicable diseases from present or former occupants. The existence of any such hazardous materials or conditions could adversely affect the value of the property. Unless otherwise stated in the attached report, the appraisers have no knowledge of the existence of any such materials or conditions. Therefore, no responsibility is assumed for any such conditions, or for any expertise or engineering knowledge required to discover them. The client is urged to retain an expert, if desired. The value estimate is predicated on the assumption that there are no such hazardous conditions or materials present that would cause a loss in value.

Neither all nor any part of the contents of this report (especially any conclusions as to value, the identity or the appraisers or the firm with which they are connected, or any reference to the American Institute of Real Estate Appraisers or to the MAI or RM designation) shall be disseminated to the public through advertising media, public relations media, news media, sales media or any other public means of communication without the prior written consent and approval of the undersigned.

ADDENDUM

Items such as those listed in the Addendum in the Table of Contents in this illustrative appraisal report usually are found here. However, in order to conserve space in this appendix they are only mentioned.

III
Case Studies

CASE STUDY 1: LAND DEVELOPMENT APPROACH TO VALUE

A 100-acre tract of land within city limits is to be subdivided into 280 building sites, averaging 80 feet in width.

There is active demand for homes in the $110,000 to $130,000 price bracket. The average price per home is estimated at $125,000. The ratio of site to property value in like subdivisions is 1 to 5 ($1.00 land to $4.00 building investment).

The proposed subdivision is to be improved with all required city utilities, including 60-foot-wide paved roads fitted with concrete curbs and gutters, water, drainage, and sanitary disposal. Telephone and electric service facilities, including streetlights, are to be supplied through underground cables laid in steel conduit.

Analysis of development plans indicates total development costs per lot are:

Development costs	$ 7,350
Underground electric utility lines	1,200
Engineering	800
Development fee	4,076
Interest, taxes, legal fees	500
Sales commission (10%)	2,100
Total development costs, excluding overhead and advertising	$16,026
First-year average sale price of lots (expected to increase by 7% annually)	$25,000

The following information is also available:

Water and sewage distribution connections are estimated at $400 per lot. The developer is to receive a refund of $200 under city regulations at the time each lot is tapped onto the main and becomes active by customer use.

No extra cost for telephone lines or site connections are chargeable to the developer.

Advertising and field overhead costs are estimated at 3.0 percent of gross sales.

Developers currently expect a 10 percent yield on this type of development. The investment period is scheduled to extend over a 4-year period. Lot sales of 70 per year are considered a reasonable certainty.

Based on market analysis and the information, as stated previously, supplied by informed sources, derive the value of the undeveloped tract of land under alternative options as follows:

1. The development for the entire 280-lot subdivision is to be completed and all utilities to be installed during the first year. What price could an investor afford to pay for this land on the basis of the development program given previously?
2. Suppose that the developer chose to spread out his costs for development, underground electric utility lines, and development fees over 3 years. What effect would this have on the present value of the property? Which development program would you advise him to select?

CASE STUDY 2: APARTMENT HOUSE PROPERTY

Based on the field and property data presented next, estimate the following:

1. Value by depreciated cost approach.
2. Value by sales comparison approach.
3. Value by capitalized income approach.
4. Final estimate of value based on correlation of value findings. Explain your decision in the derivation of the final estimate of value.

Neighborhood: Location

The subject property is located in a desirable residential area zoned R-5 for high-rise apartments. The neighborhood area is 95 percent developed with a variety of apartment structures ranging in height from three to eight stories. Structures vary in age from 2 to 20 years. All are in good physical condition.

The area is well located within walking distance of a good elementary school, within two blocks of neighborhood shopping, and six blocks from a university campus. A bus stop is one-half block to the north at the intersection of North Beach Boulevard and 14th Street. The distance to the central business district is 3 miles and bus transportation is available at 30-minute intervals from 6 a.m. to 7 p.m. and every hour from 7 p.m. to 2 a.m.

The occupants of the area are mostly college students who in groups of two to four share apartments. The reported vacancy ratio averages 6 to 8 percent.

The trend is for continued land use as apartment development. The rental range for unfurnished apartments is $250 to $300 for two-room, kitchen, and bath, and $300 to $400 for three-room, kitchen, and bath apartments. The property is located in the middle of the block on 14th Street between Beach Boulevard to the west and 5th Avenue to the east. The site measures 100 feet on 14th Street to a depth of 150 feet.

Improvement Data

The subject apartment is a nearly new five-story masonry structure. The exterior walls are brick veneer over concrete block. A partial basement contains the manager's apartment, the heating, air-conditioning, and elevator equipment, and adequate storage facilities for tenants. There are 40 two-room and bath apartments and 20 three-room and bath apartments. Each apartment is equipped with an electric range, dishwasher, and refrigerator.

The building measures 80 feet on 14th Street to a depth of 90 feet. The overall building height is 56 feet.

The building roof is built up and topped with crushed granite as protection against heavy rains. The windows are made of aluminum sash and of awning-type manufacture.

The floors are carpeted throughout over concrete subfloors. The basement apartment has vinyl tile over concrete slab. The basement utility area is reinforced concrete.

The interior walls are furred out, insulated, and finished with drywall masonry board. Good-quality paint is used throughout except for the living room walls, which are attractively finished with wallpaper. The interior trim is white spruce.

The two-room apartments contain 500 square feet and the three-room apartments contain 700 square feet. All bathrooms are fully tiled and fitted with pastel-colored fixtures. Each apartment has extra clothes closets off the entrance foyer and a walk-in closet in the master bedroom. The kitchen floors are covered with grease-proof vinyl tile.

The entire structure is centrally heated and air conditioned with a Carrier Climatrol furnace and condenser. Two standard automatic elevators serve the building. Off-street parking is adequate. The remaining economic life is judged to be 50 years. Accrued depreciation is negligible. There is no deferred maintenance. The lobby furniture is valued at $3,000. The land value is well established at $6.00 per square foot.

Assessment and Insurance Data

The subject property is assessed for ad valorem tax purposes at $1,500,000. Taxes are levied at $1.36 per $100 of assessed value by the county and at $0.84 by the city.

Comprehensive and fire insurance is based on 80 percent of building replacement cost new. The insurance rate is 25¢ per $100 per year. Public liability insurance costs $350 per year.

Comparative Sales

	Sale			
	1	2	3	4
Date of sale	Current	6 months ago	Current	2 years ago
Sale price	$2,070,000	$1,065,000	$2,161,000	$2,270,000
Land value	$ 195,000	$ 95,000	$ 210,000	$ 260,000
Number of apartments	67	40	64	80
Number of rooms	158	94	151	197
Effective gross income	$ 300,000	$ 152,140	$ 304,366	$ 334,000
Operating ratio	42%	40%	42%	39%
Remaining economic life	45 years	40 years	50 years	48 years
Effective age	5 years	10 years	None	2 years

Time adjustment: 6 months, none; 1 year, +5%; 2 years, +10%. Apply the straight-line method of asset recapture in adjusting for building age. Except for age, apartment structures are comparable in all respects, including location.

Revenue and Expense Data

Rental income

    30—2-room apartments at $400
    10—2-room apartments at $325
    15—3-room apartments at $530
     5—3-room apartments at $625
     1—Basement at $300

The vacancy and collection loss allowance is 6 percent. Note that no revenue is collected from the superintendent, who occupies the unfurnished basement apartment. The rental amount is considered part of the superintendent's wages.

Operating expenditures

Management 5% of effective gross income	
Payroll-superintendent	$ 6,000
Electricity	2,400
Water and sewage charge	2,800
Heating fuel	2,600
Legal and administrative	1,000
Painting and decorating—every 3 years	
$240 for 2-room apartments	
$320 for 3-room apartments	
Exterior maintenance every 5 years—$8,000	
Supplies	900
Corporate income tax	26,000
Elevator contract	2,000
Amortization	43,500

Repairs and general maintenance	1,400
Interest on mortgages	63,800

Reserve for replacements

Ranges—15-year life, cost each	$ 560
Refrigerators—15-year life, cost each	545
Dishwashers—12-year life, cost each	430
Lobby furniture—10-year life	3,000
Equipment—furnace and pumps—15-year life	20,000

Apply the annuity method of capitalization in deriving value via the income approach to value.

The market indicates availability of mortgage funds up to 75 percent of property value at 10.0 percent interest. Equity funds are obtainable at an 8 percent return. Land investors seek an 8.0 percent return, whereas apartment investors expect 10.5 percent total return.

Cost Data

Analysis of comparable buildings constructed in recent months as well as information obtained from informed investor-builders support a replacement cost new of $50.00 per square foot exclusive of furniture and kitchen equipment (ranges, refrigerators, and dishwashers). Depreciation is considered negligible. The estimated remaining economic life of the subject property is 50 years.

CASE STUDY 3: RETAIL STORE PROPERTY

Based on the field data presented next, analyze the pertinent information and *set up schedules* essential to the derivation of estimates as follows:

1. Value of land.
2. Depreciated cost approach to value.
3. Sales comparison approach to value.
4. Discount rate applicable to subject property.
5. Capitalized income approach to value.
6. Reconciliation and final estimate of value.

In all schedules justify—by explanatory statements—the conclusions reached.

Purpose of Appraisal

To estimate the market value of the subject property for possible sale or long-term lease.

Street Address

925 Broadway, Capital City.

Legal Description

Lot 6, Block 42 Old Survey of Capital City, as shown in Plat Book 6, page 72 in the Circuit Court records, Lee County, Any State.

Highest and Best Use

The subject property conforms to existing zoning regulations, is similar to other nearby properties, generally conforms with adjacent land use activities, and there is sufficient although diminished demand for retail activities. Therefore, its current use constitutes the highest and best use of the site.

National Data

For several years, the national economy continued on a course of expansion. However, over the last several months, the former engine of prosperity appears to have run out of steam. Several economic forces have combined to cause depressed real estate markets in many sections of the country. In the prior 5 years, mortgage funds were readily available for almost any proposed real estate venture— financially justified or not. Consequently, a 10- to 15-year inventory of space, offices in particular, was built. Following this high inventory buildup came an economic recession fueled in part by Congressional fiscal mismanagement and the collapse of the thrift industry.

    Today, and probably for another 3 to 4 years, many regions will continue to have overbuilt real estate markets which in time will adversely affect the return on both businesses occupying real estate and real estate itself.

City Data

The community is best known as a trading center for Lee County, with a population of 120,000 people. The city is bisected by four important U.S. highways and is well located midway between two large commercial cities 110 miles to the northeast and 90 miles to the southwest.

    The community is one of the leading cities in the state. Its diverse economic activities assure continuous population growth and relative freedom from the adverse effects of extreme swings of the business cycle.

Neighborhood Data

The subject property is located in the "hub" of the city and within the old Court House Square. This central business neighborhood encompasses approximately eight blocks bounded by Washington Street on the north, Birch Street on the east, Fort Bliss Avenue on the south, and Maury Street on the west.

    The construction of neighborhood shopping centers on Main Street and on Gulf Boulevard during the past 8 years has diverted business activity from the subject location. The removal of the old county court house and its relocation two blocks northwesterly of the business center has also affected adversely the available purchasing power. As a result, a number of store locations are vacant and for rent and land values on the west and south side of the square have declined from an estimated $2,000 per front foot in 1983, to $1,500 per front foot in 1993, or 2.5 percent a year.

There is every indication that property values on the square are about to stabilize. The city has purchased the old hotel property and announced plans to convert the entire east block of the square into a park and parking lot facility. This form of urban renewal should benefit materially the remaining business properties by eliminating blighted properties and further by attracting shoppers from outlying areas to the central city. The store facilities to the south and east of the city square are expected to benefit substantially from the construction of expanded parking lot facilities.

Properties in this neighborhood of the city can anticipate a stable and gradually improving financial and value position in the years ahead.

Site Data

The subject property is located on the south side of the city square and in the center of the block bounded by Broadway on the north, Magnolia Street on the west, Main Street on the east, and King Avenue on the south.

The lot is above street grade and measures 32 feet east and west and 119 feet north and south. The stair area is jointly owned and used; 1.5 feet of space belong to each of the adjoining properties. The entire stairwell is 3 feet wide. All streets in the area are paved and fitted with sidewalks, curbs, and gutters. All public utilities, including storm and sanitary sewage, gas, telephone, electricity, and city water, are available and connected to the site. Fire and police protection are both adequate and efficient.

Improvement Data

The improvements consist of a two-story structure built of solid brick, painted white with a stuccoed store front facade. Girders are of wood as are the studs of the interior plastered walls. The roof is built up with layers of tar-mopped roofing felt. The upstairs windows are of aluminum sash and of awning-type manufacture. The store windows are of standard sheet glass.

The store area is served by two water closets and two lavatories, all in working condition. There are no water closet facilities in the upstairs storeroom areas. Electric wiring has been replaced in the downstairs store area and in the front one-half of the upstairs area. The rear upstairs storage area has old-fashioned wiring that should be replaced to eliminate a possible fire hazard.

The store finished flooring is carpeting in the customer display area and asphalt tile over concrete slab in the storage and work areas. The upstairs floors are of heart pine over rough pine subflooring.

The building is approximately 80 years old and appears structurally in sound condition. The effective age is 45 years. The store front will have to be modernized in 3 to 5 years. Complete renovation, including ceiling repairs and redecoration, will be required at the termination of the present lease at an estimated cost of $25,000.

The store area is served with a modern gas-fired heat pump of Arkla Servel Sun Valley manufacture that provides all-year heat and air conditioning.

The remaining economic life under normal maintenance is estimated to be 15 years. Accrued depreciation, not including deferred maintenance, is estimated at 1 1/2 precent a year over the effective building age.

Building Cost

Replacement cost new is based on comparative building costs and estimated at $35.00 per square foot for the downstairs area of 2,876 square feet, at $31.00 per square foot for the upstairs area (1,900 square feet), and at $29.50 per square foot for the 263-square-foot "lean-to" structure.

Present Occupancy

The subject property is presently leased for $967 per month payable in advance for the downstairs and upstairs areas. The "lean-to" is rented on a month-to-month basis for $50. Properties in this commercial area are rented for periods of 5 to 7 years with options to renew for a like period. The present lease expires at the end of the current month. Similar properties are experiencing vacancies of 8 percent.

All interior repairs and decorating are the responsibility of the lessee. The lessee pays increases in taxes over those paid at the time of the lease date. The lessor pays for taxes, which currently amount to $1,250 per year, plus a special sewer and water tax of $130 per year. The insurance cost is $363, management fees are 7 percent, and exterior maintenance and repairs average $655. The remaining economic life is 15 years. The heating and air-conditioning system has an estimated life of 15 years.

Market Data

Sale 1: Unimproved site	
Sale price	$67,500
Date of sale	6 months ago
Lot size	40′ × 115′
Location	Corner
Subject location rating	0.95
Sale 2: Unimproved site	
Sale price	$75,000
Date of sale	Current
Lot size	44′ × 110′
Location	Corner
Subject location rating	0.90

Sale 3: Unimproved site
Sale price	$50,000
Date of sale	2 years ago
Lot size	44′ × 110′
Location	Interior
Subject location rating	1.25

Sale 4: Unimproved site
Sale price	$90,000
Date of sale	Current
Lot size	60′ × 100′
Location	Interior
Subject location rating	1.00

Sale 5: Store property
Sale price	$127,500
Date of sale	1 year ago
Effective gross income	$16,000
Estimated operating ratio	35%
Building effective age	50 years
Remaining economic life	15 years
Improvement/property ratio	30%
Building area	7,800 sq ft

Sale 6: Store and loft property
Sale price	$116,000
Date of sale	6 months ago
Effective gross income	$14,145
Estimated operating ratio	32%
Building effective age	55 years
Remaining economic life	10 years
Improvement/property ratio	35%
Building area	7,750 sq ft

Sale 7: Store property
Sale price	$130,000
Date of sale	1 year ago
Effective gross income	$16,455
Estimated operating ratio	38%
Building effective age	45 years
Remaining economic life	20 years
Improvement/property ratio	25%
Building area	7,700 sq ft

Sale 8: Store property
Sale price	$104,000
Date of sale	1 year ago
Effective gross income	$13,350
Estimated operating ratio	35%
Building effective age	40 years

Remaining economic life	20 years
Improvement/property ratio	26%
Building area	5,320 sq ft

Market price adjustments are as follows:

Sale 6 months ago	5% up
Sales 1 year ago	10% up
Sales 2 years ago	15% up

CASE STUDY 4: STORE AND OFFICE BUILDING

Analyze the following field data and information obtained from reliable sources and prepare schedules to support the following:

1. Depreciated cost approach to value.
2. Capitalized income approach to value.
3. Sales comparison approach to value.
4. Reconciliation of value estimates and final value conclusion.

Site Data

The subject store and office building is favorably located south of the county court house at the intersection of Pine and Broad streets. The site fronts on Pine Street for a distance of 110 feet to a depth of 120 feet.

The site is level, above street grade, and is furnished with all city utilities as well as with natural gas, telephone, and cable television services. Parking is provided across the street on a similar site 100 feet by 125 feet which is leased by the subject property owner for a period of 10 years with the option to renew for an additional 5-year lease term at a monthly rental of $1,600.

Improvement Data

The subject property is a four-story steel-reinforced structure faced with natural rock. It was built 5 years ago and is in excellent physical condition. No deferred maintenance was observed.

The structure contains stores and offices on the ground floor, offices on the second, third, and fourth floors, and a fully equipped restaurant on the fourth floor. A single automatic elevator serves the building.

The interior walls are furred out, plastered, and covered with washable wallpaper in the hallways. The interiors of all offices are mahogany paneled. Doors are of stained solid oak and fitted with high-grade solid brass door locks and hinges. Floors are of reinforced concrete and covered with wall-to-wall nylon carpet laid over foam rubber. Ceilings are soundproofed with acoustical tile. Picture window construction admits adequate daylight. The fluorescent lighting is recessed to stimulate daylight. The structure is fully and thermostatically heated. The air-conditioned cooling capacity is 105 tons output. Each office has outside exposure, providing good lighting throughout.

Building Cost Data

The structure contains 34,400 square feet. Replacement cost new is confirmed by local builders and architects at $41.00 per square foot exclusive of carpets, drapes, and restaurant furnishings and equipment. The replacement cost of furnishings and fixtures is as follows:

Carpets and drapes	$75,000
Restaurant furnishings	$76,000

Income and Expense Data

The subject property has a total net rentable area of 26,000 square feet. The ground floor contains 5,500 square feet and rents at $10.50 per square foot. Upstairs offices occupy 19,500 square feet and rent for $9.50 per square foot. The restaurant is leased for a period of 5 years at $2,900 per month. All offices and stores are under lease for periods of 5 to 10 years.

The operating expenses experienced by the subject property appear in line with average office building operating costs as reported by the Research Division of the National Association of Building Owners and Managers. Applicable operating expenditures based on net rentable square-foot area is as follows:

Cleaning	99.0¢
Electric	37.0¢
Heat	10.4¢
Air conditioning	31.6¢
Plumbing	4.8¢
Elevator	26.6¢
General expense	27.0¢
General repairs	16.4¢
Alterations	6.8¢
Decorating	9.4¢
Recapture	45.2¢
Management	25.0¢
Mortgage amortization	64.8¢
Taxes and insurance	164.6¢
Estimated life of restaurant furnishings	10 years
Estimated life of carpets and drapes	20 years

Market Indexes

Comparative sales indicate a unit value for the land at $20 per square foot. Similar buildings have been acquired at six times the annual gross income.

Investment capital is available as follows:

First mortgage two-thirds of value at 12%, 25-year term, monthly installments
Second mortgage one-fifth of value at 13%, 20-year term, 7-year balloon
Equity at 10%

The effective age is 3 years and the remaining economic life is 45 years. The annuity method of capitalization is indicated.

CASE STUDY 1: SUGGESTED SOLUTION

	Year 1	Year 2	Year 3	Year 4
Lot sales				
70 × $25,000	$ 1,750,000			
70 × 26,750		$1,872,500		
70 × 28,623			$2,003,610	
70 × 30,626				$2,143,825
Plus utility refund, 70 × $200	14,000	14,000	14,000	14,000
Total revenue	$ 1,736,000	$1,858,500	$1,989,610	$2,129,825
Less: Development cost				
(280 × $7,350)	$ 2,058,000	—		
Underground electric utility lines				
(280 × $1,200)	336,000	—		
Engineering				
(280 × $800)	224,000	—		
Development fee				
(280 × $4,076)	1,141,280	—		
Interest, taxes, legal fees				
(70 × $500)	35,000	35,000	35,000	35,000
Sales commission				
(10% × $1,750,000, etc.)	175,000	187,250	200,361	214,382
Advertising and field overhead costs				
(3% × $1,750,000, etc.)	52,500	56,175	60,108	64,315
Water and sewer connection fee				
(70 × $400)	28,000	28,000	28,000	28,000
Total expenses	$ 4,049,780	$ 306,425	$ 323,469	$ 341,697
Net sales revenue	$(2,313,780)	$1,552,075	$1,666,141	$1,788,128
Times present worth at 10%	0.909091	0.826446	0.751315	0.683013
	$(2,103,437)	$1,282,706	$1,251,797	$1,221,315
Total present worth of 100-acre tract for prescribed subdivision plan	$1,652,381 or $16,524/acre			

CASE STUDY 1: ALTERNATIVE PLAN SUGGESTED SOLUTION

	Year 1	Year 2	Year 3	Year 4
Total revenue				
(unchanged)	$1,736,000	$1,858,500	$1,989,610	$2,129,825
Less:				
Development cost				
(280 × $7,350)/3	$ 686,000	$ 686,000	$ 686,000	—

Electric utility lines				
(280 × $1,200)/3	112,000	112,000	112,000	—
Development fee				
(280 × $4,076)/3	380,427	380,427	380,427	—
Engineering				
(70 × $800)	56,000	56,000	56,000	56,000
Interest, taxes, legal fees				
(70 × $500)	35,000	35,000	35,000	35,000
Sales commission				
(10% × $1,750,000, etc.)	175,000	187,250	200,361	214,382
Advertising and field overhead costs				
(3% × $1,750,000, etc.)	52,500	56,175	60,108	64,315
Water and sewer connection fee				
(70 × $400)	28,000	28,000	28,000	28,000
Total expenses	$1,524,927	$1,540,852	$1,557,896	$ 397,697
Net sales revenue	$ 211,073	$ 317,648	$ 431,714	$1,732,128
Times present worth at 10%	0.909091	0.826446	0.751315	0.683013
	$ 191,885	$ 262,519	$ 324,353	$1,183,066
Total present worth of 100-acre tract under staged development plan		$1,961,823 or $19,618/acre		

By staging the three categories of development expenses over a 3-year period, the present value of the prospective 100-acre subdivision is increased by 19 percent ($19,618 versus $16,524 an acre). Thus the latter method of development is recommended.

CASE STUDY 2: SUGGESTED SOLUTION

1. Depreciated Cost Approach to Value

Replacement cost new: building area	
80′ × 90′ × 5 stories = 36,000 sq ft	
36,000 sq ft × $50.00	$1,800,000
Add cost of furniture and appliances:	
60 ranges at $560	33,600
Furniture	3,000
60 refrigerators at $545	32,700
60 dishwashers at $430	25,800
Total cost new	$1,895,100
Less accrued depreciation	—
Depreciated replacement cost new	$1,895,100
Add land value by comparison	
15,000 sq ft × $6.00	90,000
Total value—under cost approach	$1,985,100
Rounded to $1,985,000	

2. Sales Comparison Approach to Value

	Sale number			
	1	2	3	4
Sale price	$2,070,000	$1,065,000	$2,161,000	$2,270,000
Time adjustment	None	None	None	1.10
Adjusted price	$2,070,000	1,065,000	2,161,000	2,497,000
Land value	$ 195,000	95,000	210,000	260,000
Building value	$1,875,000	970,000	1,951,000	2,237,000
Age and condition	1.11[a]	1.25	1.00	1.04
Adjusted for age	$2,297,700	1,331,250	2,161,000	2,596,880
Number of apartments	67	40	64	80
Number of rooms	158	94	151	197
Price per apartment	$ 34,294	33,281	33,766	32,461
Price per room	$ 14,542	14,162	14,311	13,182
Effective gross income	$ 300,000	152,100	304,366	334,000
Gross income multiplier	6.9	7.0	7.1	6.8

Market value of subject property
1. 60 apartments at $33,750 per apartment $2,025,000
2. 140 rooms at $14,300[b] per room $2,002,000
3. Effective gross income $293,787 × 6.9 (multiplier) $2,027,130

[a]50 years/45 years = 1.11.

[b]Market indexes based principally on sale 3, because no adjustment for condition and age of building was necessary.

The indicated value via the sales comparison approach is

$2,025,000

3. Income Approach to Value

Gross revenue
30 apartments at $400 × 12	$ 144,000
10 apartments at $325 × 12	39,000
15 apartments at $530 × 12	95,400
5 apartments at $625 × 12	37,500
Total revenue	$ 315,900
Less 7% vacancy and collection losses	22,113
Effective revenue	$ 293,787

Less operating expenses
Management 5%	$14,689	
Real estate taxes		
City	$1,500,000 at 0.0136	20,400
County	$1,500,000 at 0.0084	12,600

Insurance 0.0025 × $1,440,000	3,600	
Liability insurance	350	
Payroll	6,000	
Electricity	2,400	
Water and sewage service	2,800	
Heating fuel	2,600	
Legal, etc.	1,000	
Painting and decorating	5,333	
Exterior repairs	1,600	
Supplies	900	
Elevator contract	2,000	
Repairs and general maintenance	1,400	
Reserves for replacements		
Ranges $33,600 ÷ 15	2,240	
Refrigerators $32,700 ÷ 15	2,180	
Dishwashers $25,800 ÷ 12	2,150	
Lobby furniture $3,000 ÷ 10	300	
Equipment $20,000 ÷ 15	1,333	
Total operating expenses and reserves		$ 85,875
Net operating income		$ 207,912
Interest rate 8.0%		
Income to land		
9.0% × $90,000		8,100
Income residual to building		$ 199,812
Building value		
$119,812 × 9.459140		
($a_{\overline{n}}$ at 10.5%, 50 yr)		$1,890,050
Add land value of		90,000
Total value—income approach		$1,980,050
Rounded to $1,980,000		

4. Reconciliation

Analysis of valuation data discloses the following indications of value:

1. Depreciated cost approach $1,985,100
2. Sales comparison approach   2,025,000
3. Income approach   1,980,000

    The depreciated cost approach provided assistance in arriving at a conclusion of value for the appraised property. This approach is especially appropriate for new or nearly new structures such as the subject property.

    Since only four sales were available for comparison purposes and considerable adjustments were necessary to compensate for the time of sale, building age, and differences in land value, the sales comparison approach in this instance is not wholly reliable as an index of value.

The income approach provides for the subject property a strong indication of its value. Several competitive income properties were available for analysis.

Based on the considerations detailed previously and the practice of expressing value in rounded numbers, it is the appraiser's professional and considered opinion that the apartment property has a value as of the date of this appraisal in the amount of

Two Million Dollars ($2,000,000)

Certified by
John Doe, MAI, SRA
Appraiser

CASE STUDY 3: SUGGESTED SOLUTION

Land Value

		Sale number		
	1	2	3	4
Price	$67,500	$75,000	$50,000	$90,000
Time adjustment	1.00	1.00	1.05	1.00
Price—adjusted	$67,500	75,000	52,500	90,000
Front feet	40	44	44	60
Area (sq ft)	4,600	4,840	4,840	6,000
Price per front foot	$ 1,688	1,705	1,193	1,500
Price per square foot	$ 14.67	15.50	10.85	15.00
Corner location adjustment	0.95	0.90	1.25	1.00
Adjusted price (front feet)	$ 1,604	1,534	1,491	1,500
Adjusted price (sq ft)	$ 13.94	13.95	13.56	15.00

Sale 4 required no adjustment and is judged most comparable. Sale 4 also falls well within the limits of comparable value set by sales 1 to 3.

The indicated value of the subject property—based on market comparison—is

32 front feet at $1,500 = $48,000

Depreciated Cost Approach

Replacement cost new:		
Downstairs	2,876 sq ft at $35.00	$100,600
Upstairs	1,900 sq ft at $31.00	58,900
Lean-to	263 sq ft at $29.50	7,759
Total replacement cost new		$167,319
Deferred maintenance:		
Ceiling repairs and		
redecorating throughout	$25,000	

Wear, tear, and obsolescence
based on effective age of
45 years at 1.5% per
year = (67.5%) ×
($167,319 − $25,000)   96,065

Total accrued depreciation   121,065

Depreciated building cost $ 46,254

Add land value—by comparison
(32 front feet × $1,500)   48,000

Total value via depreciated
cost approach $ 94,254
Rounded to $94,250

Overall Capitalization Rate from Market Data

	\multicolumn{4}{c}{Sale number}			
	5	6	7	8
A. Price	$127,500	$116,000	$130,000	$104,000
B. Effective gross income	$ 15,940	14,700	17,800	13,280
C. Operating expense ratio (%)	35	32	38	35
D. Net operating income	$ 10,361	9,996	11,036	8,632
E. Overall capitalization rate;				
$D \div A$	8.1	8.6	8.5	8.3

Based on market analysis of comparable properties, an overall capitalization rate of 8.5 percent is indicated.

Sales Comparison Approach

	\multicolumn{4}{c}{Sale number}			
	5	6	7	8
Sale price	$127,500	$116,000	$130,000	$104,000
Effective gross income per square foot	$ 2.05	$ 1.83	$ 2.74	$ 2.51
Effective age—adjustment	+0.11	+0.22	0	−0.11
Time adjustment	+0.10	+0.05	+0.10	+0.10
Total adjustments	+0.21	+0.27	+0.10	−0.01
Adjusted sale price	$154,275	$147,320	$143,000	$102,960
Building area (sq ft)	7,800	7,750	7,700	5,320
Property value per square foot	$ 19.78	$ 19.01	$ 18.57	$ 19.35
Gross income multiplier	8.0	8.2	7.9	7.8

A property value of $19.00 per square foot is indicated. The gross multiplier indicated is 8.0. Based on these indices of value and giving more weight to the sale price indicators, the sales comparison approach yields the following value results:

Indicated subject property value	5,039 sq ft at $19.00	$95,741
Effective gross income	$11,224 × 8.0	$89,792
Rounded to $93,000		

Income Approach

Gross income		$12,200
Vacancy and collection loss 8%		976
Effective gross income		$11,224
Operating expenses		
Real estate taxes	$1,250	
Special tax	130	
Insurance	363	
Exterior expenses	655	
Management (7%)	786	
Total operating expense		3,184
Net operating income		$ 8,040
Capitalized at 8.5%		
$8,040 ÷ 0.085		
Value by capitalized income approach		$94,588
Rounded to $94,600		

Value Reconciliation

Value by depreciated cost approach	$94,250
Value by sales comparison approach	93,000
Value by capitalized income approach	94,600

The analysis of comparable sales and income data support a final value estimate for the subject property of $94,000.

CASE STUDY 4: SUGGESTED SOLUTION

1. Depreciated Cost Approach

Replacement cost new:	
Building: 34,400 sq ft at $41.00	$1,410,400
Carpets and drapes	75,000
Restaurant furnishings	76,000
Total replacement cost new	$1,561,400

Less: Accrued depreciation:
  Building—6.7% × $1,410,000
    (3 yr/45 yr)[1] $94,000
  Carpets and drapes—
    $75,000 at 25% (5 yr/20 yr)[1]   18,750
  Restaurant furnishings—
    $76,000 at 50% (5 yr/10 yr)[1]   38,000   150,750
Depreciated replacement cost $1,410,650
Add: Land value—13,200 sq ft at $20   264,000
  Value via cost approach $1,674,650
    Rounded to $1,675,000

2. Capitalized Income Approach

Gross income
  Ground floor—5,500 sq ft at $10.50 $ 57,750
  Upstairs offices—19,500 sq ft at $9.50   185,250
  Restaurant—$2,900/month × 12
    months   34,800
Total gross income $277,800
Less: Vacancy and collection losses
  (negligible)[2]   0
Effective gross income $277,800
Less: Operating expenses
  Cleaning $0.990 per square foot
  Electric   0.370 "   "   "
  Heat   0.104 "   "   "
  Air conditioning   0.316 "   "   "
  Plumbing   0.048 "   "   "
  Elevator   0.266 "   "   "
  General expense   0.270 "   "   "
  General repairs   0.164 "   "   "
  Alterations   0.068 "   "   "
  Decorating   0.094 "   "   "
  Management   0.250 "   "   "
  Taxes and insurance 1.646 "   "   "
    $4.586 per square foot
Total fixed expenses and maintenance
  costs
    26,000 sq ft at $4.586 $ 119,236

[1]Based on straight-line depreciation.

[2]Vacancy and collection losses are assumed to be negligible since the building space is under leases for periods of 5 to 10 years, and in view of the favorable location of the property.

Replacement of carpets and drapes	3,750[3]
Replacement of restaurant furnishings	7,600[4]
Parking lot $1,600/month × 12	19,200
Total operating expenses	$ 149,786
Net operating income	$ 128,014
Less: Income attributable to land	
$264,000 at 7.5%[5]	19,800
Income attributable to building	$ 108,214
Capitalized value of building income over remaining economic life of 45 years at 7.5% interest under the annuity income method =	
$108,214 × 12.8186	$1,387,155
Add: Land value	264,000
Total value	$1,651,155
Rounded to $1,651,000	

3. Sales Comparison Approach

Gross income $277,800 × 6.0 (multiplier)	$1,666,800
Rounded to $1,667,000	

4. Reconciliation

The following value estimates were derived from an analysis of the available valuation data:

Depreciated cost approach	$1,675,000
Capitalized income approach	1,651,000
Sales comparison approach	1,667,000

The depreciated cost approach is useful as a guide to value since the appraised property is relatively new. Secondary reliance, however, must be attributed to this approach since the improvement is not new, and more reliable estimates are provided by the other approaches to value. Thus the depreciated

[3]Based on 20-year life, straight-line depreciation.

[4]Based on 10-year life, straight-line depreciation.

[5]The interest rate is calculated by use of market data as follows:

Value of subject site	$20.00 per square foot
Annual rental of similar site across street ($19,200/12,500 sq ft)	$1.54 per square foot
R_L = $1.54/$20 = 7.7%	

Rounded to 7.5%; also applicable as the building discount rate.

cost approach, yielding an estimate within 1 percent of the final estimate, was used only as a check on the reliability of the final estimate of value.

Market value may be defined as the estimated price that a property will bring in the open market—given sufficient time and assuming knowledgeable buyers and sellers.

The final estimate of value of this property is based primarily on the sales comparison approach since no adjustments were required. The income approach—which yields an estimate that is within about 1 percent of the final estimate—reinforces the reliability of the sales approach.

The subject property in the opinion of the appraiser warrants a value as of the date of this appraisal in the amount of

One Million Six Hundred Seventy Thousand Dollars ($1,670,000)

IV
Suggested Solutions to Chapter Review Exercises

CHAPTER 1

1. Everyone has a scale of preference for given goods or services. This preference, between an individual and the object or service wanted, is influenced continuously and in varying degrees by personal traits and by the cultural, religious, and governmental forces that influence each person as a member of society.

2. It is that price that occurs when the forces of supply and demand are in equilibrium and no artificial or temporary barriers impede either supply or demand.

3. The specific value sought by the appraiser should be clearly stated in the letter of transmittal as well as in the body of the appraisal report, and a definition of value should be fully expressed in order to prevent misinterpretation and error in acting on the basis of a value estimate.

4. The key components of the market value definition used by financial institutions are:
   (a) Buyer and seller are typically motivated.
   (b) Both parties are well informed or well advised, and acting in what they consider their best interests.
   (c) A reasonable time is allowed for exposure in the open market.
   (d) Payment is made in terms of cash in U.S. dollars or in terms of financial arrangements comparable thereto.
   (e) The price represents the normal consideration for the property sold unaffected by special or creative financing or sales concessions granted by anyone associated with the sale.

5. A knowledge of the value characteristics (utility, scarcity, demand, and transferability) is useful in appraising real property and changes in any of these characteristics allows the appraiser to measure value. Any improvement in any of the value characteristics results in the enhanced value of the affected object.

6. The market value concept as currently known has the strengths of being widely accepted and is a normative concept or one that refers to typical behavior, such as usual management, motivations, and expectations of parties in a real estate transaction. On the other hand, the weaknesses of the market value concept include the incorrect presumption that ordinary buyers and sellers are bestowed with the patience, resources, and mental prowess to be fully cognizant of all conditions influencing the present future uses of the property. It depicts what ought to be in an ideal sense rather than the actual conditions that face market participation.

594

CHAPTER 2

1. Contributions to present-day appraisal practices by the early schools of economic thought are:
   (a) Mercantilism—stressed a "natural" value based on competitive forces in place of "just" value; emphasized production rather than distribution of wealth.
   (b) Physiocrats—did not regard value as intrinsic in things; the concepts of price and value were accepted as interchangeable terms.
   (c) Classical economics—argued that the value of any good or service is equal to the quantity of labor which it allows its owner to purchase; stressed a distinction between "value in use" and "value in exchange"; pointed out the difference between "market value" and "market price"; Malthus held that production does not create its own demand; initiated rent theory and began the residual procedure of valuation; "normal" value and market or price were distinguished.
   (d) Austrian school of economics—developed the marginal utility theory of value; began the idea that interest was a measure of time preference for consumption and the present worth theory for discounting future benefits; stressed the importance of demand as a value determinant.
   (e) Historical and institutional school—rejected the "economic man" philosophy.
   (f) Neoclassical and equilibrium school of economics—Marshall emphasized a dynamic value theory.
   (g) Early twentieth-century value theory—Mitchell developed the business cycle theory and showed how one phase of the economy leads to subsequent stages.

2. The most probable selling price is a prediction rather than a measure of the price that a property will likely bring; similarly, the most probable use is market oriented and depicts the use to which the land and building would probably be put instead of representing an idealized value maximization model or abstract set of conditions.

3. Ross's band-of-investment method of developing a risk rate pioneered the use of mortgage terms and equity returns. Yet, it was deficient in its failure to provide for equity or debt recapture.

4. Babcock's criticism of the misuse of the cost approach was based on appraisers substituting it for direct market evidence of value.

5. Ellwood substituted the forecast holding period used by investors in place of the much longer and uncertain remaining economic life of a building, held that property appreciated as well as depreciated, and integrated mortgage financing into his development of capitalization rates.

6. The following represent significant contributions to presently used appraisal procedures:
   (a) Irving Fisher's linking of interest rate to income and present value.
   (b) Frederick Babcock's emphasis that sales in themselves were not indicative of market value and his criticism of appraisers falling back on the depreciated cost approach instead of fully developing the market approach.
   (c) Richard Ratcliff's advocacy of the most probable value concept.
   (d) Thurston Ross's band-of-investment theory, later refined by Edwin Kazdin as a means for developing capitalization rates.
   (e) Leon Ellwood's preparation of financial tables and emphasis of an appraisal methodology that more faithfully reflected the actual practices of real estate investors.

CHAPTER 3

1. Real estate includes land, building improvements, as well as anything permanently affixed to the land or buildings where the reasonable intent—as supported by the method of annexation and the relationship of the parties involved at the time of annexation—causes the article to be classified as a fixture.

2. Police power is the sovereign power of government to restrict the use of real property in order to protect the well-being of its citizens. No compensation is due the affected property owners when this power is invoked. Eminent domain is the right of government to acquire all or part of an owner's land provided that the use is public and just compensation is paid to the property owner.

3. An accurate highest and best use analysis is necessary in real property appraising since it provides the basis for the appraised value. If the highest and best use is inaccurate, so will be the amount of the appraised value.

4. The key terms in the highest and best use concept are:

   succession of uses relates to all the short- and long-term uses that allow a property to realize its highest value; *available uses* are important to this concept since only such uses can cause actual value to be realized; *legal uses* mean those uses actually allowed by private and public land use controls and agreements; *physically permitted uses* refer to all those uses permitted by soil conditions, topography, and site shape; and *sufficient demand* simply means that after all the other conditions are met, in order for the property to achieve its full potential, there must be prospective buyers who are able to acquire the property.

5. The marginal productivity concept is applied to the sales comparison approach by revealing the value added or loss due to the presence or absence of a particular feature. If, for example, 200-foot-deep lots sell for $50,000 and 150-foot-deep sites command a price of $45,000, the 50-foot additional depth beyond 150 feet appears to be worth $5,000. Analysis of such differences in value can be applied to an appraised site.

6. All physical and tangible items that have attributes of, or claims to objects of, value are classified as wealth. Property is a right to control, use, and own wealth. Property as here defined is intangible. The appraiser is concerned with the valuation of (property) rights in and to wealth. The larger the rights, as a general rule, the greater the future benefits and hence the greater the present value.

7. This statement is true. Where legal requirements cause an increase in construction costs without offsetting the benefits resulting from a better housing (and nonhousing) product, land values will tend to be lower. Land is "residual" in character under a highest and best use. Legal impediments that lower income inevitably lower the value of land that is subject to adverse controls. This is especially true where communities are competing with each other for population growth and economic development.

CHAPTER 4

1. Breaking down racial and sex barriers has greatly broadened employment and housing opportunities for racial minorities and women. The results have been to expand real estate markets and to qualify both groups for more expensive housing. Thus housing demand has risen along with values due to these improved employment and housing opportunities.

2. Generally, the sequence of events associated with municipal housing rent control laws has been (a) the quality of housing suffers and the quantity is reduced, (b) the private ownership sector withdraws, and (c) the government (using tax dollars) attempts to provide replacement housing.

3. The average household size in this country has decreased from 4.93 in 1890 to 2.66 in 1987. The effect of these smaller households has been to stimulate the demand for housing.

4. The rate of savings influences a nation's well-being. If this rate is too low, then insufficient capital is available to maintain modern industry, causing that nation to be noncompetitive in a worldwide economy, with a resulting rising level of unemployment. An unusually high rate of savings could prove harmful to the economy by reducing the level of consumption.

5. By venturing into investments with which savings and loans had little experience, losses mounted sharply and many thrifts failed nationwide.

6. In recent years there has been a leveling off in the rate of home ownership in this country. Such a "steady-state" condition is neither unusual nor unexpected since many people today prefer the more mobile and less burdensome life-style that is provided by apartment living. It can be conjectured that home ownership causes a greater sense of social responsibility and interest in society and the well-being of neighborhoods and communities. A shift toward apartment residency has fostered the growth of the ministorage industry. Any abatement in home ownership would probably retard suburban nonresidential growth, which traditionally provides residential supporting services.

7. No, zoning regulations cannot prevent value decline. Zoning regulations, however, must be complemented by demand, appropriate access, and transportation as well as suitable site conditions.

CHAPTER 5

1. As a rule the downward swing of the real estate cycle precedes the downward swing of business activity caused by business recession, and lags long beyond the period of general business recovery.

2. Earlier causes of urbanization—such as government, commerce, culture, religion, courts, and mutual protection—can be applied to present regional analysis. An understanding of the motivation for earlier people agglomerating aids us in analyzing contemporary regions since many of these basic motivations persist today.

3. The names and basic features of each of the urban growth theories follow:
   (a) *Concentric ring growth theory* by Ernest Burgess divided a city into a series of fixed rings extending from the center (central business district) outward through the successive zones of transition, low-income housing, middle-to-high-income housing, to the commuter's zone.
   (b) *Axial growth theory* by Richard Hurd depicted city growth along transportation routes, with the resulting land use patterns resembling the spokes of a star.
   (c) *Sector growth theory* by Homer Hoyt focused on residential neighborhoods. He found that high-grade residential areas progressed along lines of travel toward flood-free areas, open country, and toward the homes of community leaders.

(d) *Multiple-nuclei growth theory* by Chauncey Harris and Edward Ullman revealed discrete forms of land use activity with certain similar activities grouped together because they benefited from close proximity and certain activities located away from other dissimilar activities, such as homes and factories.

4. There are different interpretations of this question by each student. Nevertheless, a person analyzing a region would benefit from a knowledge of the different land uses in different parts of a region, the natural and fabricated forces that shape urban growth, and a more informed view of metropolitan growth and decline that these static growth models can cause.

5. Economic base analysis assists in the understanding of regional economy by showing how a region "earns its living." It breaks a community down into the export and service industries, and then strives to forecast any change in employment for these two components of the local economy.

6. The main purposes of regional economic and population analysis are to determine demographic trends, diversity and strength of employment opportunities, proposed directions and nature of future growth, and the comparative supply and demand for real estate.

7. In addition to the 10 economic measures listed in the chapter, other possibilities are rental levels and vacancy levels for different categories of realty, changes in mortgage terms and interest rates, average number of days required to sell a home, developed but unsold residential sites, capital improvement budgets for each local jurisdiction, and changes in vehicular traffic on specified roads.

CHAPTER 6

1. The two major misconceptions in neighborhood analysis in the past have been to approach it from (a) an idealized notion of what a neighborhood should be rather than what it actually is, and (b) a misguided belief that the introduction of racial minorities automatically caused property values to decline.

2. Linkages are defined as external economies or centripetal forces. Linkages are the periodic interaction between people or establishments that hold them together. Examples of linkages are where machine work is subcontracted by one business for other nearby businesses or where close proximity to legal or advertising services makes a particular location attractive for a small business unable to afford such specialized in-house staff.

3. A neighborhood's popularity and property values in it rise and fall in a cyclical manner. The appraiser must know which phase of its life cycle a neighborhood is in when an appraisal is made of a property in the neighborhood so that he or she can accurately estimate the effect of neighborhood age and obsolescence on the amenities of ownership or income from its use over the remaining economic life of the subject property.

4. Neighborhoods can be delineated in the following ways: physical boundaries, legal and governmental factors, and price levels of residences.

5. The answer to this question is based on each person's experiences.

6. Ten residential neighborhood characteristics that should be investigated by the appraiser include nature of terrain, drainage facilities, proximity to schools, stores, and recreational facilities, freedom from hazards and adverse influences, income and education of residents, age grouping and size of families, extent of development, percentage of homes that are owner occupied, and zoning and deed restrictions.

7. The earlier practice of "redlining" was intended to indicate neighborhoods that had septic system failures. Later it was used by mortgage lenders to avoid making loans in high-risk neighborhoods. By failing to infuse mortgage capital into these neighborhoods, owners lacked funds to sell and repair their homes, which accelerated the decline of the neighborhood and in turn the value of properties in such urban areas.

8. Traffic analysis is important in all types of neighborhoods. Neighborhood traffic conditions play a crucial role in the success of retail districts and, especially, shopping centers. These centers are largely dependent on a sizeable unimpeded flow of vehicular traffic. For industrial neighborhoods it is important that there be adequate access to markets, sources of materials, subcontractors, and a skilled work force; adequate circulation and parking for trucks are also needed. Residential neighborhoods are enhanced when public transit is readily available at reasonable costs.

CHAPTER 7

1. Ten square chains (10×66 ft $\times 66$ ft) equals 1 acre.
2. A square acre has 43,560 square feet, 208.71 feet on each side (solve for the square root of 43,560 sq ft).
3. Three major concerns in conducting a site analysis are:
   (a) Determining the highest and best use.
   (b) Measuring the marginal productivity of the site.
   (c) Determining the optimum size and depth of the site.
4. One advantage of the monument method of site description is that it is based on a physical survey of the property, using physical landmarks. A disadvantage of this method is that the physical landmarks or monuments may be moved or disappear over time.
5. A knowledge of soil conditions is important to a proper site analysis because such conditions affect the potential use and value of a site. For example, a contaminated site may be unusable for its intended purpose, but appraisers should not give unqualified opinions on possible environmental hazards.
6. The inherent weakness of depth tables is that they are inflexible and may bear little relationship to local site value patterns.
7. The Corps of Engineers considers hydrology, vegetation, and soil in determining if an area in question is wetland.

CHAPTER 8

1. Five purposes for separate site appraisals include:
   (a) Local real estate tax assessments.
   (b) Separation of land and improvements for federal taxes.
   (c) To ascertain a property's highest and best use.
   (d) Insurance.
   (e) Site leases.
2. The stated consideration (price) may be inaccurate in a deed for any of the following four reasons:
   (a) The buyer may want to give the appearance of having paid a higher price than was actually paid.

(b) The seller may try to save money by paying a lower transfer fee or tax than is justified by the actual sale price.

(c) In some states, only the cash portion of transactions need be considered; whereas in others, state revenue stamps represent the full consideration of the sale.

(d) In the case of property exchanges, the interested parties may understate or overstate the transaction price for tax or other purposes which prove mutually advantageous.

3. An appraiser should thoroughly understand the conditions that existed when a property sold in order to measure accurately the current value of the appraised property. For example, a site may have sold as an unfinished parcel, lacking its present zoning and curbs and gutters. Also it may have sold in a "buyers' market" whereas at the date of appraisal the market had reversed to become a "sellers' market."

4. The four basic categories of adjustments made for comparable sales are date of sale, conditions of sale, location, and physical features. These adjustments may be in some combination of percentage, dollar, plus or minus, or by multiplication. The appraiser should never adjust for features not considered by market participants.

5. The sales comparison approach is preferable over the land residual method whenever there is a sufficient number of recent sales of similar properties. It is an easily understood method that is based on actual transactions. On the other hand, the land residual method provides a useful method for judging the highest and best use of a site. Further, it has its place when there is a dearth of comparable land sales and the value of the improvements can be accurately judged.

6. The subdivision developmental method is an acceptable alternative to the sales comparison method when the tract of land is capable (physically and economically) of being subdivided. Accompanying its use should be an accurate highest and best use analysis, an accurate accounting of all the expenditures necessary to produce the forecast income, accurate depiction of the income each year of the marketing period, and careful selection and use of the discount rate.

7. (a) No, the buildings have identical values. The extra cost of blasting rock is a charge ascribable to land. (b) After blasting, yes—before blasting, no. The value of lot B before blasting was only $5,000. (c) The blasting expenditure is a land development cost chargeable to land to bring it up to its highest and best use.

CHAPTER 9

1. See Chapter 16 for the calculator keystroke sequence or use Table 9.1.

Installment to amortize 1 for 11%, 25 yr $\dfrac{0.009801}{0.011010} = 0.890191$
Installment to amortize 1 for 12%, 20 yr

Cash equivalent = ($200,000)(0.80)(0.890191) $142,431
+ Down payment (0.20 × $200,000)   40,000
                                                                    $182,431

2. A comparatively small net adjustment may not represent the most comparable sale because of several offsetting positive and negative adjustments. For example, a net adjustment of $500 could result from five positive adjustments of $25,000 and six negative adjustments equal to $24,500.

3. Adjustments should be made for the time and conditions of sale prior to considering differences in the physical and locational features in order to reveal the price that the sale property would have brought in the current market.

4. (a) Paired data set analysis involves the selection of two or more comparable sales and isolating one value attribute in a sale not found in the other sales in order to judge that attribute's effect on value. (b) This process works providing the sales selected are sufficiently similar and individual value-influencing factors actually can be identified.

5. A problem that can occur when applying a market-derived GIM to an appraised property's effective gross income is that some property owners simply will not furnish the needed effective gross income information. Also, there is the potential problem of the appraiser obtaining a GIM based on potential gross income and applying it to the effective gross income of the appraised property.

6. The advantages of the GIM as a means of estimating market value are:
   (a) It is readily understood by clients.
   (b) It is based exclusively on market events.
   The disadvantages of the GIM appraisal technique include:
   (a) Its being based on a property's gross income which might be similar to an appraised property's gross income, but the net operating income of the comparable property may differ sharply from that of the appraised property.
   (b) It fails to account for the remaining economic life of either the sale or subject property.
   (c) Adjustments in the gross income or sale price tend to distort the GIM since property features already have been considered and "adjusted" by the buyer and seller.

CHAPTER 10

1. The higher the rise of a roof, the more lasting the roof shingle coverage, because of lessened wear and tear from rain, hail, snow, or strong winds. A rise that is too slight permits rain and wind to drive under the shingles, weakening the shingle fastenings and the undercover roof seal.

2. The "R value" measures the insulating quality of the material. The higher the R value, the better the insulation.

3. Elevations show the exterior sides of a building as it appears after all structural work has been completed. As a rule, each building side is viewed by an elevation and, for identification, marked as north, south, east, and west or by structural designation as front, rear, left, and right side elevation.

4. Six attributes of good floor planning include:
   (a) Orientation of rooms to capture prevailing breezes, sunshine, and beauty of area views surrounding the property.
   (b) Proper placing of picture windows and large window areas to assure adequate light and ventilation for all rooms.
   (c) Provision for entrance hall or foyer (with guest closet space) to shield living room from direct view and drafts.
   (d) Grouping of bed and bedroom areas to assure maximum of privacy. A separate entrance to the bedroom wing or access without a view from or crossing of living room area is considered a must.
   (e) Proper functional layout of kitchen area to conserve steps in housekeeping.
   (f) Location of kitchen near entrance and side doors to minimize traffic flow.

5. Written specifications supplement the plans, elevations, and related drawings and sketches. In fact, written instructions are deemed of greater importance than graphic illustrations, and where these two are in conflict, it is the written word that is guiding and

legally binding. Specifications historically have served as a contract document between builder and owner and are intended to avoid disputes or misunderstandings concerning details of construction. They permit accurate estimating of required labor, quality of materials, and costing of contractors' and subcontractors' services in accordance with plan requirements. Specifications also safeguard against expensive omissions when construction costs are estimated and minimize construction delays due to misunderstanding of building plans.

6. Five matters of structural design that affect revenue, maintenance, management, and, possibly, the remaining economic life of the building are:
   (a) Good lighting and adequate, concealed telephone and electric wiring to serve anticipated maximum service loads.
   (b) Sufficiency of central heating under individual unit or zone controls.
   (c) Capacity and readiness to supply air conditioning where competitively necessary.
   (d) High ratio of net rentable area as a percentage of total building square-foot area.
   (e) Necessary off-street parking.

7. (a) 146 square feet. (b) 18 square feet. (c) 260 square feet. (d) 1,208 square feet.

CHAPTER 11

1. Estimation of a site's highest and best use establishes a "yardstick" against which accrued depreciation of the improvements is measured. That is, accrued depreciation is the difference between cost new and market value. Market value in turn is a function of a site's highest and best use.

2. (a) The most important advantage of the depreciated cost approach is that it can be used to estimate the financial feasibility of a proposed property. That is, if the value indicated by the sales and income approaches exceeds the current reproduction cost, the property is feasible. The major disadvantage of the depreciated cost approach is that it requires great diligence in maintaining current cost data as well as in carefully recognizing differences in cost due to different building sizes and quality of materials. (Other answers may be selected by the reader.)
   (b) *Advantage.* Any time the value of a property exceeds its reproduction cost, the developer is justified in proceeding with the venture, assuming that a sufficient profit margin is realized.
   Disadvantage. Often, and especially for old properties, it is often much too time consuming and expensive for an appraiser to use the depreciated cost approach. Additionally, the accrued depreciation estimate for such properties may be so large as to have questionable merit.

3. Accrued depreciation may be defined as the difference between the current cost new of a building(s) and its current market value.

4. The principal difference between direct and indirect construction costs is that direct costs include labor and materials, whereas indirect costs are all other costs, including such charges as property management fees and professional service fees. Indirect costs are as important as direct costs, but are more easily overlooked by appraisers.

5. The comparative advantages of the replacement cost method are that it is based on modern materials, methods, and technology which are comparatively easy to obtain. Functional obsolescence is already excluded from this cost. On the other hand, the reproduction cost offers the advantage of showing the current cost of recreating the appraised building exactly as it was built and of the original materials. The latter costs

may more readily be visualized and computed since the appraiser is attempting to find the present cost of an actual building with all of its physical features available for inspection.

6. **(a)** Quantity survey method

   Advantage. It is the most comprehensive and detailed method and is preferred by architects for its accuracy in determining the cost of residences.

   Disadvantage. It is too time consuming for most appraisal assignments and is best used by trained cost estimators.

   (b) Unit-in-place (segregated) construction method

   Advantage. It generally represents how most residential and small commercial property builders prepare their cost bids; it is fairly well understood by clients.

   Disadvantage. It is unreliable unless the appraiser inspects the building and judiciously compares the nature and quality of the building to the benchmark building in a construction cost manual or to figures provided by local contractors.

   (c) Comparative unit method

   Advantage. This method provides speedy cost estimates by the appraiser and is sufficiently accurate for standardized and relatively new buildings.

   Disadvantage. Generally, no two buildings are exactly alike in kind and quality of construction; and unless adjustments are made to reflect these differences, the margin of possible error may prove too great to make the estimate reliable as a guide to building costs.

   (d) Cost indexing method

   Advantage. Relatively simple to use and is based on the actual construction cost of an appraised building.

   Disadvantage. The accuracy of the original construction cost may not be verifiable and national or regional indexes may be inapplicable.

CHAPTER 12

1. Accrued depreciation is similar to amortization in that both measure loss in value. However, these two concepts differ in that accrued depreciation measures actual or estimated loss in value, as expressed by the difference between the current cost new and the market value of the building(s), whereas amortization provides for future recapture of an asset via reserve provisions. Amortization is also known as "book depreciation" and is an accounting rather than an economic concept.

2. The causes of accrued depreciation for each of the three forms of accrued depreciation are:

   (a) *Physical deterioration.* Caused by (1) wear and tear through use, (2) action of the elements such as termites, and (3) structural impairment through neglect, fire, water, explosion, and vandalism.

   (b) *Functional obsolescence.* Caused by (1) faulty design, (2) inadequacy of structural facilities, (3) superadequacy of structural facilities, and (4) outmoded equipment.

   (c) *External obsolescence.* Caused by (1) neighborhood hazards and nuisances, (2) change in zoning and highest and best land use classification, (3) over- or underimprovement of land, and (4) decreasing demand.

   A prospective owner or tenant would probably account for each of these deficiencies by paying a lower price or rental for such adversely affected property.

604

3. Economic life is more important than physical life for investment purposes because at the end of a building's productive or economic life the investor probably will need to raze or rehabilitate the building even though the structure may be structurally adequate and capable of surviving for many more years.

4. Building value = replacement cost minus accrued depreciation.

Replacement cost =	$120,000
− Accrued depreciation	
($120,000)[15/(15 + 45)]	30,000
Depreciated building cost	$ 90,000
+ Lot value	15,000
Total property value	$105,000

5. The principal criteria used to determine if a building suffers from curable or incurable physical deterioration are (a) the necessity to cure defects to provide for efficient (economical) operation and (b) the cost to cure relative to the value added or the increase in net operating income for the property as a whole.

6. Functional obsolescence-curable is defined as modernization and improvements which are essential and economically justified and which would be found in a new and comparable building. Five examples of this form of obsolescence are modernization of bathroom and kitchen, upgrading insulation, modernizing the heating system, adding needed closets, and replacing outdated fixtures.

7. The steps involved in estimating market value via the engineering breakdown method are:
(a) Estimate physical deterioration-curable.
(b) Estimate physical deterioration-incurable by breaking the structure into its major parts and via the age-life method and estimating the deterioration per structural part.
(c) Estimate functional obsolescence-curable.
(d) Estimate functional obsolescence-incurable.
(e) Estimate external obsolescence—as related to improvements.
The total of these deductions is the total accrued depreciation. Care must be taken to avoid duplicating depreciation charges.

8.

Current reproduction cost	$135,000
Present value of dwelling	
($125,000 − $28,000)	97,000
Depreciated cost of dwelling	$ 38,000
Annual rate of depreciation	
($38,000/$135,000) ÷ 14 years	2%

9. Office building:

Sale price $175,000 at 125% of cost
Cost = $175,000 ÷ 1.25 = $140,000
Gain = $175,000 − $140,000 = $35,000

Apartment building:

Sale price: $175,000 at 75% of cost
Cost = $175,000 ÷ 0.75 = $233,333

$$\text{Loss} = \$233,333 - \$175,000 = \$58,333$$
$$\text{Net loss} = \$58,333 - \$35,000 = \$23,333$$

CHAPTER 13

1. Market rent is defined as the amount of rent the appraised property probably would command at the date of appraisal. Contract rent is the rental income earned by the property as a result of contractual commitments which bind owners and tenants for a stipulated future time. These two rents are equal when the contract rent matches the prevailing rent for similar properties.

2. At that future time when an improved property's building income is surpassed by the land earnings, it is likely that the site has become too valuable to be encumbered by the existing improvements. At this time, the building has reached the end of its economic life and will need to be renovated or demolished.

3. The following five items should be considered by an appraiser in estimating the amount of market rent for rental property: (1) building size, (2) quality of construction, (3) neighborhood, (4) location and site characteristics, and (5) amount and quality of furnishings and fixtures.

4. The appraiser must account for unusually high vacancy levels during the "rent-up" period even though vacancies may stabilize at lower levels later because to use the unrealized higher occupancy (lower vacancy) level overstates the income and in turn the present value of the appraised property.

5. Unless the appraiser accurately accounts for the actual leased area for comparable rental properties, the income applied to the appraised property probably will either be under- or overstated.

6. For short-term leases, the lessor generally pays all operating costs, whereas the lessee tends to bear these expenses under long-term leases.

7. The accuracy of an appraisal report can be improved by the appraiser understanding such future payment provisions in leases as how much space and under what terms the space is being leased. The demised premises are measured differently, the netness of leases varies, and a variety of future payment provisions exists. The appraiser must know more than simply the square-foot rental per month or year for the comparable and appraised properties.

8. Yes—assuming all other things remain equal—the passage of time has affected the value of this property. The building is 10 years older and thus nearer the end of its economic life. Value is based on the present worth of future rights to income, and these inevitably are reduced as the structure ages, even though annual income does not diminish.

9. To the extent that past managerial practices influence future income favorably or unfavorably, value is affected. Past managerial practices are of interest to an appraiser because exceptional management over past years may reduce future operating costs and produce a flow of income in excess of that which ordinarily can be anticipated under "typical" operations. Conversely, poor management over past years may cause excessive operational outlays in future years in order to bring the property up to the income performance expected under "typical" management and operation.

10. Past and present income serve as benchmarks for forecasting the anticipated future flow of income. Value should always be based on future rights to income and not solely on established past or present income.

CHAPTER 14

1. The following three items in an owner's income-expense statement should be disallowed for appraisal purposes: (1) mortgage debt service, (2) capital improvements shown as operating expenses, and (3) building depreciation.

2. Fixed expenses are those expenses that must be paid regardless of the occupancy level. Variable expenses tend to vary with the occupancy level and include the property management fee, repairs, and utility charges.

3. An argument for including replacement reserves in the operating expenses is that unless these future expenses are recognized on an annualized basis, the net operating income will be overstated for the appraised property. Conversely, if expense data compiled for comparable properties omit this charge, but appraisers include it for the subject property, its appraised value will in turn be distorted.

4. Answers to this problem will vary. Assume the following for purposes of illustration:

Net operating income, excluding real estate taxes	$72,000
Market derived capitalization rate	10%
Tax rate (as related to market value)	2%

   Market value = $72,000 ÷ 0.12
   = $600,000

5. An inaccurate operating expense ratio can distort the estimated net operating income for an appraised property in the following three ways:
   (a) Different building designs can cause different expense ratios.
   (b) Buildings of different ages or in different locations can experience different income levels but the same square-foot expenses.
   (c) The netness of leases can alter the share of expenses paid by the lessor and in turn affect the operating expense ratio.

6. Replacement reserves can be set up in the following three ways:
   (a) Identify the short-lived items that must be replaced during the remaining economic life of the building; determine how many times the item will need to be replaced; estimate its cost; determine the total cost; and finally, determine the annualized average replacement cost.
   (b) Estimate the replacement cost of the short-lived item for its initial replacement. Multiply this cost by the appropriate sinking fund factor, using the number of years the replacement item is expected to last.
   (c) Forecast replacement reserves over the expected holding period for the investment. The annual dollar requirements for these replacement costs are then computed by multiplying the replacement costs by a sinking fund factor for the remaining period.
   Each student should express his or her own reasons for choosing one of the foregoing methods.

7. Property B has the greater value because of its favorable operating ratio compared with property A. The income from B is less risky than the income from property A; hence income from B will be capitalized at a lower rate. A 20 percent drop in revenue wipes out the net operating income for A but lowers the net operating income for B by only $8,000, or 40 percent.

8. Gross revenue ($300 × 12 × 40) $144,000
    Collection and vacancy losses 10%[a]   14,400
    Effective gross revenue $129,600

Operating Expenses	As reported	As adjusted	
Taxes on land and building	$14,400	$14,400	
Power and light	1,200	1,200	
Depreciation provision[b]	9,600		
Repairs	4,800	4,800	
Renovating and painting	7,200	7,200	
Janitor expense	1,200	1,200	
Extermination	360	360	
Replacements:			
40 ranges[c]			
(8-year life)	18,000	2,250	
40 refrigerators[c]			
(12-year life)	36,000	3,000	
New roof[d]	6,600	330	
Legal fees	720	720	
Corporation tax[e]	1,800		
Income tax[e]	2,100		
Mortgage interest[f]	7,200		
Mortgage amortization[f]	6,000		
Management fees	7,200	6,270	
Water	2,700	2,700	
Fire insurance			
(3-year policy)	3,600	1,200	
Paving assessment	2,400		
Promotion and advertising	1,500	1,500	
Adjusted operating expenses			$47,130
Net operating income			$82,470

9. In practice depreciation is estimated as a "rate" per annum and this rate of amortization or rate of future depreciation is added to the prevailing risk rate to form a capitalization rate. In this case depreciation as an amount must not be deducted as an operating expense. To do so would penalize the property twice and lower the value accordingly—and erroneously.

[a]It is good business practice to provide for collection and vacancy losses.

[b]In appraising, the depreciation provision should not be treated as an operating expense. The capitalization process already provides for a return of the building's capital value. It is customary to capitalize over the life of the building, or an even shorter period. Depreciation thus is automatically accounted for through amortization in the capitalization process.

[c]Since the equipment has 8- and 12-year service lives, the expenses per annum should only include the proportionate share of such expenses, in this case as follows:

    Ranges $18,000 ÷ 8 = $2,250 per annum
    Refrigerators $36,000 ÷ 12 = $3,000 per annum

[d]Expenditure for a new roof based on 20-year life.

[e]Corporation taxes and income taxes are not operating expenses but rather income expenses. Personal or corporate taxes are not considered in the appraising of real property.

[f]Mortgage payments or amortization are not considered unless the problem calls for valuation of the equity.

10. (a)

Net operating income after taxes		$ 1,600,000
Taxes as billed		615,000
Net operating income		$ 2,215,000
Land rate of capitalization:		
Discount rate	0.09	
Tax rate	0.03	
Total rate	0.12	
Land income: $I = V \times R$		
$\$5,000,000 \times 0.12$		600,000
Income residual to building		$ 1,615,000
Building value:		
Interest rate	0.090	
Recapture rate	0.025	
Tax rate	0.030	
Total capitalization rate	0.145	
Value: $V = I/R$		
$\$1,615,000 \div 0.145$		$11,137,931
Property value:		
Building (rounded)		$11,140,000
Land		5,000,000
Total		$16,140,000

(b) Property taxes:

   $\$16,140,000 \times 0.03$ $ 484,200

(c) Net income after taxes:

   $\$2,215,000 - \$484,200 = \$1,730,800$

CHAPTER 15

1. An amortization rate provides for the periodic recapture of an investment at a designated interest rate and is part of a mortgage rate. A mortgage rate consists of both an amortization rate and an interest rate.

2. A capitalization rate generally is applied to an appraised property's net operating income, whereas a factor such as a gross income multiplier is applied to either the potential gross income or the effective gross income of a property. Income is divided by a capitalization rate and multiplied by a factor to derive value.

3. Beginning with $V = I/R$, it can be changed as follows to find R and I: $R = I/V$ and $I = R \times V$.

4. The basic difference between an equity dividend and an equity yield rate is that the former considers the relationship of cash flow to the investor's equity investment; the latter rate is based on this relationship plus any forecast future change in value that might occur upon sale of the property.

5. $R_M = 0.1406$; $R_E = 0.07$; $R_o = ?$ (Either use a financial calculator or the Annual Constants table in Appendix V.)

$$0.75 \times 0.1406 = 0.1055$$
$$0.25 \times 0.07 = 0.0175$$
$$R_o = 0.1230$$

The previously computed capitalization rate is applied to the NOI even though the equity dividend rate is based on before-tax cash flow. This may prove to be an interesting topic for class discussion.

6. $V_M = \$36,800/0.1406$
$\qquad = \$261,735$
$V_o = \$261,735/0.75$
$\qquad = \$348,981$
$R_o = \$46,000/\$348,981$
$\qquad = 0.1318$

7.

Potential gross income	$25,000
less vacancy and collection losses (6%)	1,500
Effective gross income	$23,500
less operating expenses (40% EGI)	9,400
Net operating income	$14,100

$R_o = \$14,100/\$117,500$
$\qquad = 0.1200$

8. $R_o = Y_o - \Delta a$
$\qquad = 0.11 - (-0.20/10)$
$\qquad = 0.11 + 0.02$
$\qquad = 0.13$

9. $R_o = \$77,000/\$550,000$
$\qquad = 0.1400$
$R_L = \$12,000/\$100,000$
$\qquad = 0.1200$

$\qquad 1.00 \times 0.14 = 0.1400$
$\qquad \underline{-0.15 \times 0.12 = 0.0180}$
$\qquad 0.85 \quad R_B \qquad 0.1220$

$R_B = 0.1220/0.85$
$\qquad = 0.1435$

10. All other things remaining equal, a decline in income because of the imposition of added taxes lowers the value of the affected property.
   (a) The value of the land prior to the imposition of the tax was
$$V = I/R \text{ or } \$2,000 \div 0.10 = \$20,000$$
   (b) The value of the land after the tax levy is
$$V = I/R \text{ or } \$1,800 \div 0.10 = \$18,000$$
   (c) The value reduction at 8% $= V = I/R = \$200 \div 0.08 = \$2,500$.

11. **(a)** An *overall capitalization rate* is derived by dividing the net operating income by the total value (land and improvements) of a property. **(b)** A *fractional rate* is a ratio computed by dividing the income attributable to a fraction of the property by the value of the part. Thus mortgage rates, equity rates, land rates, and building rates are fractional rates.

12. Property A $\quad 0.25 \times 6\% = 1.5\%$
$\qquad\qquad\qquad 0.75 \times 8\% = \underline{6.0}$
$\qquad\qquad\qquad$ Total $\quad = 7.5\%$

Property B $0.50 \times 6\% = 3.0\%$
$0.50 \times 9\% = \underline{4.5}$

Total $= 7.5\%$

Property C $0.75 \times 7\% = 5.25\%$
$0.25 \times 9\% = \underline{2.25}$

Total $= 7.5\%$

13. The overall capitalization rate (R_o) is equal to the property yield rate (Y_o) when no future change in value is expected. R_o usually accounts only for current income and value, whereas Y_o includes the current relationship in addition to all future changes in income and value.

CHAPTER 16

1. The compound amount of 1 for 10%, 22 years = 8.140275:

Future worth of 1 per period $(S_n) = (S^{n-1})/i$

$$= \frac{8.140275 - 1}{0.10}$$

$$= \frac{7.140275}{0.10}$$

$$= 71.402750$$

Sinking fund factor $= (1/S_n)$ $\quad = \dfrac{1}{71.402750}$

$$= 0.014005$$

2. To make the calculations, it first is necessary to find either the compound amount of 1 or the present worth of 1 factors.

3. Use the 10 percent sinking fund factor for 12 years:

$$0.046763 \times \$10,000 = \$467.63$$

4. Use the 10 percent compound amount of 1 factor for 16 years:

$$4.594973 \times \$5,000 = \$22,975$$

Note: This problem assumes annual installments.

5. First find the R_M for 25 years and then the R_M for 17 years (25 − 8). R_M (25 years) = 0.110168; R_M (17 years) = 0.124664:

Mortgage balance $= (0.110168/0.124664)(\$75,000)$
$= \$66,279$

Equity buildup $= \$75,000 - \$66,279$
$= \$8,721$

Thus the client will not accumulate via amortization the desired $10,000.

6. If Table 16.1 is used, it must be extended to 65 years by multiplying some combination of factors equal to 65 years.

Present worth $= (0.008519)(0.239392)(\$600,000)$
$= \$1,224$

7. The present worth of income receivable at the beginning of the period requires that the EOY factor be adjusted to a BOY factor as follows:

PW $= (7.606080)(1.10)(\$4,000)$
$= \$33,467$

8. Years 1–3   2.486852 × $10,000 $24,869
       4–6 (4.355261 − 2.486852) × $12,000   22,421
       7–9 (5.759024 − 4.355251) × $13,500   18,951

   Total present worth $66,241

9. Original investment of $3,000 at 9 percent compound interest
    over 10 years should grow to $3,000 × 2.367364 $7,102

   Annuity of $100 at 9 percent compound interest
    over 10 years should grow to $100 × 15.192930   1,519

   Total investment at end of tenth year $8,621

10. (a) The present value of an annuity is the total discounted present worth of each annuity payment. (b) The present value of an annuity of $1.00 at 10 percent interest over a period of 3 years is $2.49. [See the present worth of annuity (present value of 1 per period) table in this chapter.]

11. (a) $500 × 7.606080 (PW of annuity at 10 percent) $3,803
    (b) $500 × 9.999270 (PW of annuity at 10 percent) $5,000
    (c) $500 × 10 or $500 ÷ 0.10 $5,000

12. The 10 percent sinking fund table shows a rate per dollar of 0.017460. Multiplying this by $1,000 gives the answer of $17.46. If $17.46 is placed in a sinking fund annually at 10 percent compound interest over a period of 20 years, the fund will accumulate to $1,000 over this period of time.

13. The table of amortization for a $10,000 mortgage over 8 years at 10 percent interest per annum is

Year	Month	Periodic payment	0.8333 percent interest	Amortization	Remaining value
0	0	—	—	—	$10,000.00
0	1	$151.74	$83.33	$68.41	9,931.59
0	2	151.74	82.76	68.98	9,862.61

14.

	Year 1	Year 2	Years 3–40
Net operating income	$47,500.00	$60,000.00	$70,000.00
Building life—40 years			
Property rate—10%			
Present value factor at 10%	0.0909091	0.826446	8.043514
Present value of property returns	$ 4,318	$ 49,587	$ 563,046

Property value = $4,318 + $49,587 + $563,046 = $616,951

CHAPTER 17

1. A capitalization rate may be converted into a perpetuity factor by finding its reciprocal. For example, if the annual capitalization rate is 8% the perpetuity factor is 1 divided by 0.08, or 12.50.

2. $V = I/R$; $R = 0.10$ (interest) + 0.020952 (sinking fund factor)
         = 0.120952
  $V = \$10,000/0.120952$
    = \$82,677

3. $V = I/R$ or $V = I \times R$
    = \$10,000/0.110168   = \$10,000 \times 9.077040
    = \$90,770   = \$90,770

4. The annuity method of capitalization is similar to the sinking fund method except that no fund is established in which the annual amortization provisions are to accumulate. Instead, the periodic payments for amortization of investment capital are made available to the property user or owner for immediate reinvestment in other property. The rates of earning for both the property as a whole and for portions of the investment returned each year through amortization provision—and which are available for reinvestment—are considered as being the same.

5. $V = I \times R$
    = \$10,000 \times 9.077040
    = \$90,770

6. Both NPV and IRR are discounted cash flow techniques where future income is discounted to produce a present value. NPV is based on a specified discount rate, and if the discounted inflows and outflows produce a positive value, the proposition under study is judged to be feasible. IRR goes a step further to indicate the exact yield rate for the investment.

7. (a) \$350,000 (\$200,000 land plus \$150,000 cost of remodeling)

  (b)

\$200,000 at 9%	\$18,000
\$150,000 at 11.5% (9% + 2.5%)	17,250
Taxes	14,500
Total net rental	\$49,750

  (c)

\$200,000 at 9%	\$18,000
\$250,000 at 13% (9% + 4%)	32,500
Taxes	14,500
Total net rental	\$65,000

  (d) As shown in part (c), the prudent buyer wants a return on the investment at the going rate, plus amortization requirements to recapture the value of the investment over the estimated remaining life of the improvements, plus property taxes due.

CHAPTER 18

1. The relative merits of each of the three physical residual techniques are:
  (a) *Land residual technique.* Applies when the appraised buildings are new and their values are known or can be estimated with reasonable accuracy.
  (b) *Building residual technique.* Useful when the site value can readily be estimated by the comparable sales approach and the building is old and substantially depreciated.
  (c) *Property residual technique.* Applicable when it is difficult to allocate total property income between the site and building(s), or when the building is old or there is a lack of comparable site sales.

2. NOI $ 25,000
   Less income to building (I_B)
     ($150,000)(0.10 + 0.05)   22,500

   Income available to land (I_L) $ 2,500
   Land value ($2,500/0.10) $ 25,000
   + Building value   150,000
   Property value $175,000

3. Value of income stream
    (7.606080 × $50,000) $ 380,304
   + Value of reversion
    (0.239392 × $300,000)   71,818

   Present worth of property $ 452,122

4. Use linear change equation $R = Y - \Delta\ 1/n$
   NOI $ 75,000
   − Building income ($100,000)(0.10 − 0.10/10)   9,000

   = Land income $ 66,000
     Capitalized at land rate (0.10 − 0.80/10)
   = Land value $3,300,000
   + Building value   100,000
   = Property value $3,400,000

5. NOI $ 90,000
   − Land income
     ($200,000)(0.10 − 0.025)   15,000

   = Building income $ 75,000
     Capitalized at building rate (0.10 − 0.0029)
   = Building value (rounded) $ 772,400
   + Land value   200,000
   = Property value $ 972,400

$$CR_L = \frac{\Delta I \times Y}{\Delta I + Y} = \frac{(0.30/9)(0.10)}{0.30/9 + 0.10} = \frac{(0.0333)(0.10)}{0.0333 + 0.10} = 0.0250$$

$$CR_B = \frac{(0.03/9)(0.10)}{0.03/9 + 0.10} = \frac{0.0003}{0.1033} = 0.0029$$

6. NOI $ 50,000
   Capitalized by R_o, using $R_o - \Delta a$
    0.10 − ($2,500/$50,000) = 0.05
   Property value ($50,000 ÷ 0.05) $1,000,000

7. (a) Whenever land value is known with accuracy, the appraiser should use the building
    residual method of capitalization.

  (b) Net operating income $12,000
     Less income to land $20,000 × 0.08 $1,600
     Less income to furnishings
      $11,000 × 0.20   2,200   −3,800

    Net income residual to building $ 8,200
    Building value = $8,200 ÷ 0.12 = $68,333

8. Total value $150,000
    Land value   −25,000

Building value $125,000
Total income $14,000
Land income $25,000 × 0.06   −1,500

Building income $12,500
(a) Building rate $12,500 ÷ $125,000 = 0.10 or 10%
(b) Building rate   0.10
    Recapture rate (straight line)   −0.05

Interest rate   0.05 or 5%
(c) Building rate—Inwood factor
        (factor = value ÷ income) 10.0000
        solve by interpolation
        7.5% Inwood factor   10.194
        8.0% Inwood factor   9.818

    0.5% differential factor   0.376
    7.5% Inwood factor   10.194
    X% Inwood factor   10.000

        X differential   0.194

$$\frac{X}{0.5} = \frac{0.194}{0.376}$$

$0.376X = 0.5 \times 0.194$

$X = \frac{0.097}{0.376}$ hence $X = 0.258$

Interest rate that corresponds with Inwood factor of 10.00 = 7.5% + 0.258% = 7.758%

CHAPTER 19

1. It is desirable to calculate the value of the unencumbered fee interest prior to estimating the value of the leased fee or the leasehold interests so that the entire unencumbered value can serve as a benchmark against which the reasonableness of the value of the parts can be judged.

2. Under the terms of a lease, a landlord is entitled to:
    (a) Receive the contract rent agreed on under terms of the lease for the duration of the lease period.
    (b) Repossession of the property upon termination of the lease.

3. Present value of market rent
        $14,000 × 6.144567 $ 86,024
    Present worth of excess rent
        $1,000 × 5.426243   5,426

                                                                                        $ 91,450
    Reversionary property value
        $100,000 × 0.385543 $ 38,554

    Total value of leased fee $130,004

4. Year 1 $1,000 × 0.909091 $ 909
     2   1,200 × 0.826446   992
   3–5   1,500 (3.790787 − 1.735537)   3,083
 6–10   2,200 (6.144567 − 3.790787)   5,178
(beginning of period premise)
PW of income stream $ 10,162
                                          × _1.10_
                                          $ 11,178

+ Reversionary value of property
  ($200,000 × 0.385543)   _77,109_

Total present value of property $ 88,287

5. (a)   Economic rent $10,000
    − Contract rent   _8,000_

        Leasehold income $ 2,000
        Value of leasehold estate
          ($2,000 × 3.790787) $ 7,582
(b)   Leasehold value $ 7,582
    + Leased fee value   _90,293_

        Total property value $97,875

6. (a) A sandwich leasehold occurs when a leasehold interest is subleased to a third party; the original lessee becomes a sublandlord and both legally and economically is sandwiched between the fee owner and the subtenant.

(b) (1) Leased fee interest at 10%, 7 years:
        $2,000 × 4.868419 $ 9,737
    + PW of land reversion
        $100,000 × 0.513158   _51,316_

        Total PW of leased fee $61,053
  (2) Sandwich leasehold:
        Subtenant annual rental $ 3,000
        Market annual rental   _2,000_

        Sandwich leasehold rental $ 1,000
        Discounted at 12%, 7 years   × 4.563757

        PW of sandwich leasehold $ 4,564
  (3) Sublessee's interest:
        PW of property $70,000
    − Value of leased fee $ 61,053
    − Value of sandwich leasehold   _4,564_   _65,617_

        Value of sublessee's interest $ 4,383

7. An annuity of $600 invested at compound interest of 7 percent over 5 years will grow to $600 × 5.75 or $3,450. This amount represents the full value of the leasehold to date.

8. (a) The lessor's interest:
    $10,000 (for 5 years) × 4.2124 $ 42,124
    $12,000 (for next 35 years) × 10.8339
      (15.0463 − 4.2124)   130,007
    Land reversion = $240,000 × 0.0972   _23,328_

      Total lessor's interest $195,459

(b) The lessee's interest:

1. Land income $240,000 × 0.06	$14,400	
Less contract rent for 5 years	10,000	
Net to lessee	$ 4,400	
2. Land income next 35 years	$14,400	
Less contract rent	12,000	
Net to lessee	$ 2,400	
Value: $4,400 × 4.2124		$ 18,535
$2,400 × 10.8339		
(15.0463 − 4.2124)		26,001
Total value in land		$ 44,536
Value of building as appraised		160,000
Total value, lessee		$204,536

Summary:

Lessor's interest	$195,459
Lessee's interest	204,536
Total	$399,995
Rounded	$400,000

9. (a) Mrs. A's interest:

Income of $3,000 × 9.644159 (35-year present value factor)	$ 28,932
Land reversion $75,000 × 0.035584	2,669
Total	$ 31,601

(b) Mr. B's interest at 10% for 35 years:

Income of $8,000 − $3,000 = $5,000 × 9.644159 = $48,221

(c) Mr. C's interest at 10%:

Income of $12,000 − $8,000 = $4,000 × 9.644159 = $38,577

In practice the interests of B and C would be discounted at higher rates—perhaps 12 and 14 percent, respectively.

CHAPTER 20

1. The equity yield rate differs from the equity dividend rate by accounting for future value changes in addition to the "cash-on-cash" return recognized by the equity dividend rate.

2. The steps in computing equity dividend rate are:
1   Compute potential gross income
2 − vacancy and collection losses
3 = effective gross income
4 = operating expenses
5 = net operating income
6 − annual mortgage debt service
7 = cash flow (before taxes)

Equity dividend rate = cash flow (step 7) divided by owner's equity.

3. NOI $50,000
  − Mortgage debt service
    ($200,000 × 0.75)(0.110168)   16,525

  Annual cash flow $ 33,475
  PW of 1/period for 10 years × 6.144567

  PW of equity position $ 205,689
  Sale price of property $ 300,000
  − Mortgage balance in 10 years
    ($150,000)(0.110168/0.131474*)   125,692

  Equity value 10 years hence $ 174,308
  Reversionary value factor   × 0.385543

  Present value of equity reversion $ 67,203
  + Mortgage value at date of appraisal   150,000

  Total value of property $ 422,892
  *R_M for remaining loan term of 15 years.

4. Loan balance after 6 years
    ($190,000)(0.008775/0.009173*) $ 181,756
  Thus equity buildup
    ($190,000 − $181,756) $ 8,244
  *R_M for remainder of loan term of 24 years, see Appendix V.

5. Interest paid during fifteenth year:

  Annual mortgage payment
    ($190,000 × 0.008775 × 12) $ 20,007

  Find loan balance at beginning and end of year 15.

  Loan balance at beginning of year 15
    0.008775/0.010459* 0.838990
  *R_M for remaining loan term of 16 years.

  Less loan balance at end of year 15
    0.008775/0.010746* 0.816583
  *R_M for remaining loan term of 15 years.

  Loan amortization in year 15 0.022407
  × Original loan × $ 190,000

  Equity accumulation $ 4,257
  Annual loan payment $ 20,007
  − Equity accumulation 4,257

  = Interest paid in year 15 $ 15,750

6. Property A equity yield = 11.85%
  Property B equity yield = 8.90%

7. R = $Y - MC^* +$ dep. or − app. $1/S_n$
    = 0.14 = (0.80)(0.039224) − 0.10 × 0.151284
    = 0.14 − 0.031379 − 0.015128
    = 0.093493

  PW = $48,000/0.093493
    = $513,408

$^*C = Y + (P \times 1/S_n) - R_M$
$= 0.14 + (1 - 0.110168/0.117460)(0.151284) - 0.110168$
$= 0.14 + (0.062081)(0.151284) - 0.110168$
$= 0.14 + 0.009392 - 0.110168$
$= 0.039224$

8. (a) *Equity income* is the income left after deduction for periodic costs (interest and amortization) of borrowed mortgage funds. (b) *Trading on the equity* is the practice of borrowing funds at a rate less than that earned by the property as a whole. Trading on the equity increases the rate of earnings on the equity capital.

9. $I = V \times R = \$10,000 \times 0.011366 = \$113.66$

10. Property income	$ 60,000
Mortgage—debt service payments	37,920
Equity—cash flow	$ 22,080

(a) Present worth of cash
flow—10 years at 10%
$\quad$ $22,080 \times 6.144567$ $\qquad\qquad$ $135,672
Present worth of cash
reversion on date of
sale: $500,000 − $263,400

(b) Add present worth of
reversionary equity
$\quad$ $236,600 \times 0.385543$ (10%) $\qquad\qquad$ 91,219

(c) Total present worth of equity $\qquad\qquad$ $226,891
(d) Add present value of mortgage $\qquad\qquad$ 300,000

(e) Purchase price to yield 10%
rate of equity return $\qquad\qquad$ $526,891
$\qquad$ Rounded to $527,000

11. Solution:

Purchase price		$400,000
Mortgage loan		280,000
Cash-equity investment		120,000
Selling price $400,000 \times 0.925$		$370,000
Mortgage balance—15 years remaining—$2,702.06 monthly payment $\times$ 93.057439* (180-month factor at 10%)		251,447

*See the calculator keystroke sequence in Chapter 16 or table.

(a) Reversion to equity		$118,553
$\quad$ Revenue	$45,000	
$\quad$ Debt service	32,425	
(b) Cash flow	$12,575	

Trial interest yield rate of 10%:
Present worth of $12,575 for 5 years
$\quad$ $12,575 \times 3.790787$ $\qquad\qquad$ $ 47,669
Present worth of reversion of
$\quad$ $118,553 \times 0.620921$ $\qquad\qquad$ 73,612

Total present value of equity at 10% $\qquad\qquad$ $121,281

Trial interest yield rate of 11%:
Present worth of $12,575 for 5 years
$12,575 × 3.69587* $ 46,476
*See the calculator keystroke sequence in Chapter 16 or table.
Present worth of reversion of
$118,553 × 0.593451   70,355

Total present value of equity at 11% $116,831

Interpolation for accurate yield rate:
1. Equity value at 10% $121,281
    Equity value at 11%   116,831

    Differences for 1% $ 4,450
2. Equity value at 10%   121,281
    Equity value at X%   120,000

    Difference $ 1,281

$$\frac{\$1,281}{\$4,450} = 0.29\% + 10\% = 10.29\%$$

12. $$P = \frac{R_M - I}{R_{MP} - I} = \frac{0.110168 - 0.10}{0.131474 - 0.10} = \frac{0.010168}{0.031474} = 0.323060 \times \$100,000 = \$32,306$$

This is a variation of the method used in this chapter. R_M represents the annual mortgage rate for 25 years and R_{MP} is the rate for 15 years.

CHAPTER 21

1. Public bodies have been given the power of eminent domain since the strength of private ownership is derived from the strength and power of a sovereign government formed to enforce and protect such rights as are vested in the individual under constitutional guardianship. It is fundamental, therefore, that rights essential to the maintenance and welfare of society must be paramount to those claimed by individuals in the pursuit of their separate interests.

2. The following six legal requirements generally must be followed by government to protect private rights when the power of eminent domain is used:
    (a) Authority and necessity of taking.
    (b) Indication of public use for which land is condemned.
    (c) Survey of land and description.
    (d) Complaint and summons of owners.
    (e) Identification of interest to be acquired.
    (f) Necessary parties defendant.
    (g) Legal testimony before proper tribunal.
    (h) Petition that property be condemned.

3. Just compensation is defined as payment for the value of the property physically taken and to offset a loss in value, if any, to the remaining parcel on account of severance of a part from the unity of the whole property. Excluded are losses incurred by the exercise of the police power of the government.

4. The conventional definition of market value generally prohibits consideration of eminent-domain-related real estate conveyances because the "willing buyer–willing seller" concept is seldom fulfilled. In fact, the seller generally is unwilling to sell his or her property to the condemnor.

5. Economic unity is established by the following court-proved rules:
   (a) *Contiguity of location.* The affected property must be a continuous, unbroken tract.
   (b) *Unity of ownership.* The condemned property must be under the same ownership.
   (c) *Unity of use as evidenced by economic unity (utility) rather than physical unity.* This means that the entire property must be placed to the same type of use so that if, for example, agricultural land is acquired its damages do not carry over to the remaining commercial land.
6. The before-and-after rule for appraising land for eminent domain projects involves estimating the value of the whole property before the taking and again after the taking. The difference in value is judged to be the just compensation due the property owner.
7. Consequential damages relate to just compensation for a property owner in that in practice they denote damage suffered by owners as a result of proposed public improvements where no real property is physically taken.

CHAPTER 22

1. (a) The appraisal process is defined as an orderly plan of action used to produce a professional appraisal report.
   (b) An understanding of this process benefits the appraiser by aiding him or her to reach a sound conclusion or estimate of value.
2. Appraisers ordinarily make the following four assumptions regarding appraisals:
   (a) That the title is held in fee simple and that no legal claims, easements, restrictions, or other rights affect the title or use of the property except those stated to the appraiser by the applicant.
   (b) That the title and his or her valuation are subject to corrections which an accurate survey of the property may reveal.
   (c) That the sale of property will be on a cash or cash-equivalent basis.
   (d) That no responsibility is taken by the appraiser for matters legal in nature.
3. An appraiser should define the appraised value in his or her report in order to avoid serious misunderstanding and possibly disciplinary action either under the code of ethics to which professional appraisers, as members of their respective appraisal societies, subscribe or as enforced by state licensing bodies.
4. The reconciliation process allows the appraiser to correlate each of the approaches to value to produce a final value conclusion. Care must be taken in weighing the results on the basis of accuracy and completeness of data and in the light of market conditions that prevail on the date of the appraisal.
5. Steps in the "Analyses and Conclusions" section of an appraisal are:
   (a) Explanation of the appraisal process and the methods used to reach the value conclusions.
   (b) Separate analysis via the depreciated cost, market sales comparison, and capitalized income approaches.
   (c) Reconciliation of the values indicated by each of the approaches used.
   (d) Inclusion of a statement of limiting conditions, certificate of value, and a statement of the appraiser's professional qualifications.
6. Characteristics of a well-written appraisal report include: being logical and orderly; being clear, direct, yet comprehensive; being readable; avoiding use of the first person; and using appropriate words, summaries, and illustrations.

7. Professional appraisers generally discourage use of the letter report because it does not include the steps leading to the appraiser's value conclusion and it is often unusable for loan or sale purposes.

8. Certification is where the appraiser warrants his or her findings and disclaims any personal interest in the property that could influence his or her value findings. Limiting conditions is where the appraiser sets forth the areas—in the fields of surveying, engineering, or law—in which he or she disclaims liability.

9. The purpose of the appraisal is used to state the task involved and the rationale for the appraisal.

10. The employer or appraiser signing the report is as responsible as the individual preparing the appraisal for the content and conclusions of the appraisal. Using a conditional label next to the signature of the employer or supervisor or signing a form report on the line over the words "review appraiser" does not exempt that individual from adherence to these standards.

11. **(a)** The appraiser stated that the fuel oil storage tank behind the dwelling was not nearly the size of the one next to the garage.
    (b) Regardless of the extent of flooding, the comparable sale site should be used in this appraisal report.
    (c) Most similar properties sell for about $100 per square foot.
    (d) There are few comparable land sales surrounded by paved roads.

CHAPTER 23

1. Education is important to professionals so that they keep abreast of modern developments in theory and practice. This education may be obtained in a formal setting or informally through experience, intensive reading, attendance at seminars, workshops, and through related organizational and professional activities.

2. The real estate appraiser is responsible to the public by estimating value objectively and independently of the client's cause or the compensation paid for services rendered. The appraiser should charge a fee that relates to the quantity and character of the service; commissions should always be avoided. As a rule, competitive bidding should be avoided unless it recognizes differences in appraisers' experience, skill, integrity, and education.

3. An appraiser should never speak disparagingly of another appraiser because it leaves bitter feelings. One cannot rise above competition by trying to pull others down. Such success comes from hard work, preparation, and maintenance of high professional standards.

4. A confidential relationship should be maintained between the appraiser and his or her clients because to do otherwise may undermine the client's interests and may have serious repercussions for practitioners as well as for the person and the profession.

5. The Real Estate Appraisal Foundation is responsible for funding and making appointments to its two boards. The Real Estate Appraisal Standards Board develops and promulgates uniform standards, whereas the Qualifications Board develops education, experience, and examination criteria to be used in the licensing and certification of appraisers in the various states.

6. In appraising proposed improvements, an appraiser must consider (a) plans, specifications, or other related documents; (b) evidence indicating the probable completion time

of the proposed improvements; and (c) evidence supporting development costs, anticipated earnings, occupancy projections, and anticipated competition at date of completion.

7. Standard 3 requires that an appraiser in reviewing an appraisal and reporting the results must form an opinion as to the adequacy and appropriateness of the report being reviewed and must clearly state the nature of the review process followed and observe specific guidelines.

8. Standards 4 and 5 differ from Standards 1 and 2 in that the analyst must identify clearly the client's objectives, identify alternative courses of action and the optimum course to achieve the client's objectives, define and delineate the market area, and analyze current and potential changes in supply and its effect on demand.

V
Financial Tables

PRESENT WORTH OF AN ANNUITY OF $1 TABLE FOR SELECTED INTEREST RATES BASED ON STRAIGHT-LINE THEORY OF DEPRECIATION UNDER THE DIRECT-RING METHOD OF CAPITALIZATION[a]

Period	10%	Period	10%
1	0.90909	26	7.22230
2	1.66667	27	7.29714
3	2.30771	28	7.36844
4	2.85714	29	7.43594
5	3.33333	30	7.50019
6	3.74995	31	7.56098
7	4.11765	32	7.61905
8	4.44444	33	7.69231
9	4.73687	34	7.72732
10	5.00000	35	7.77780
11	5.23809	36	7.82607
12	5.45464	37	7.87234
13	5.65227	38	7.92823
14	5.83328	39	7.95919
15	5.99999	40	8.00000
16	6.15385	41	8.03923
17	6.29644	42	8.07696
18	6.42855	43	8.11326
19	6.55308	44	8.14817
20	6.66667	45	8.18197
21	6.77415	46	8.21429
22	6.87500	47	8.24565
23	6.96966	48	8.27588
24	7.05882	49	8.30510
25	7.14286	50	8.33333

[a]What $1 payable periodically for the remaining economic life of an investment and with annual interest paid on the entire investment is worth today.
Formula:

$$\text{Ring factor} = \frac{1}{\text{str.-line rate}} \text{ or } \frac{1}{\text{int. rate} + \text{depre. rate}}$$

Example: Factor for 20 years is

$$\frac{1}{0.10 + 1/20} = \frac{1}{0.10 + 0.05} = \frac{1}{0.15} = 6.6667$$

AMORTIZATION SCHEDULE FOR A $50,000 INVESTMENT PROVIDING FOR
ANNUAL AMORTIZATION AND INTEREST AT 10 PERCENT OVER A
30-YEAR PERIOD[a]

| Year | Annual payment | Interest on investment at 10% | Amortization | | Remaining investment |
			Annual	Cumulative	
1	$5,303.96	$5,000.00	$ 303.96	$ 303.96	$49,696.04
2	5,303.96	4,969.60	334.36	638.32	49,361.68
3	5,303.96	4,936.17	367.79	1,006.11	48,993.89
4	5,303.96	4,899.39	404.57	1,410.68	48,589.32
5	5,303.96	4,858.93	445.03	1,855.71	48,144.29
6	5,303.96	4,814.43	489.53	2,345.24	47,654.76
7	5,303.96	4,765.48	538.48	2,883.72	47,116.28
8	5,303.96	4,711.63	592.33	3,476.05	46,523.95
9	5,303.96	4,652.40	651.56	4,127.61	45,872.39
10	5,303.96	4,587.24	716.72	4,844.33	45,155.67
11	5,303.96	4,515.57	788.39	5,632.72	44,367.28
12	5,303.96	4,436.73	867.23	6,499.95	43,500.05
13	5,303.96	4,350.01	953.95	7,453.90	42,546.10
14	5,303.96	4,254.61	1,049.35	8,503.25	41,496.75
15	5,303.96	4,149.68	1,154.28	9,657.53	40,342.47
16	5,303.96	4,034.25	1,269.71	10,927.24	39,072.76
17	5,303.96	3,907.28	1,396.68	12,323.92	37,676.08
18	5,303.96	3,767.61	1,536.35	13,860.27	36,139.73
19	5,303.96	3,613.97	1,689.99	15,550.26	34,449.74
20	5,303.96	3,444.97	1,858.99	17,409.25	32,590.75
21	5,303.96	3,259.08	2,044.88	19,454.13	30,545.87
22	5,303.96	3,054.59	2,249.37	21,703.50	28,296.50
23[b]	5,303.96	2,829.65	2,474.31	24,177.81	25,822.19
24	5,303.96	2,582.22	2,721.74	26,899.55	23,100.45
25	5,303.96	2,310.05	2,993.91	29,893.46	20,106.54
26	5,303.96	2,010.65	3,293.31	33,186.77	16,813.23
27	5,303.96	1,681.32	3,622.64	36,809.41	13,190.59
28	5,303.96	1,319.06	3,984.90	40,794.31	9,205.69
29	5,303.96	920.57	4,383.39	45,177.70	4,822.30
30	5,303.96	482.23	4,821.73	50,000.00	0.00

[a]Assumes end-of-year payments.

[b]After the loan is approximately 75% expired, the original principal has been only 50% amortized.

ANNUAL CONSTANTS FOR MONTHLY MORTGAGE PAYMENTS (R_M)

Nominal annual interest rates ($i\%$)	Loan terms			
	15 years	20 years	25 years	30 years
6	0.101263	0.085972	0.077316	0.071946
7	0.107859	0.093036	0.084814	0.079836
8	0.114678	0.100373	0.092618	0.088052
9	0.121712	0.107967	0.100704	0.096555
10	0.128953	0.115803	0.109044	0.105309
11	0.136392	0.123863	0.117614	0.114279
12	0.144020	0.132130	0.126387	0.123434
13	0.151829	0.140589	0.135340	0.132744
14	0.159809	0.149222	0.144451	0.142185
15	0.167950	0.158015	0.153700	0.151733
16	0.176244	0.166951	0.163067	0.161371
17	0.184680	0.176016	0.172536	0.171081
18	0.193250	0.185197	0.182092	0.180850
19	0.201945	0.194482	0.191722	0.190667
20	0.210756	0.203859	0.201414	0.200522

FUTURE AND PRESENT VALUE USING 9 PERCENT ANNUAL INSTALLMENTS

Years	1 Compound amount of 1 $S^n = (1+i)^n$	2 Future worth of 1 per period $S_n = \frac{S^n - 1}{i}$	3 Sinking fund factor $1/S_n = \frac{i}{S^n - 1}$	4 Present value of 1 $V^n = \frac{1}{S^n}$	5 Present value of 1 per period $a_n = \frac{1 - V^n}{i}$	6 Installment to amortize 1 $1/a_n = \frac{i}{1 - V^n}$
1	1.090000	1.000000	1.000000	0.917431	0.917431	1.090000
2	1.188100	2.090000	0.478469	0.841680	1.759111	0.568469
3	1.295029	3.278100	0.305055	0.772183	2.531295	0.395055
4	1.411582	4.573129	0.218669	0.708425	3.239720	0.308669
5	1.538624	5.984711	0.167092	0.649931	3.889651	0.257092
6	1.667100	7.523335	0.132920	0.596267	4.485919	0.222920
7	1.828039	9.200435	0.108691	0.547034	5.032953	0.198691
8	1.992563	11.028474	0.090674	0.501866	5.534819	0.180674
9	2.171893	13.021036	0.076799	0.460428	5.995247	0.166799
10	2.367364	15.192930	0.065820	0.422411	6.417658	0.155820
11	2.580426	17.560293	0.056947	0.387533	6.805191	0.146947
12	2.812665	20.140720	0.049651	0.355535	7.160725	0.139651
13	3.065805	22.953385	0.043567	0.326179	7.486904	0.133567
14	3.341727	26.019189	0.038433	0.299246	7.786150	0.128433
15	3.642482	29.360916	0.034059	0.274538	8.060688	0.124059
16	3.970306	33.003399	0.030300	0.251870	8.312558	0.120300

17	4.327633	36.973705	0.027046	0.231073	8.543631	0.117046
18	4.717120	41.301338	0.024212	0.211994	8.755625	0.114212
19	5.141661	46.018458	0.021730	0.194490	8.950115	0.111730
20	5.604411	51.160120	0.019546	0.178431	9.128546	0.109546
21	6.108808	56.764530	0.017617	0.163698	9.292244	0.107617
22	6.658600	62.873338	0.015905	0.150182	9.442425	0.105905
23	7.257874	69.531939	0.014382	0.137781	9.580207	0.104382
24	7.911083	76.789813	0.013023	0.126405	9.706612	0.103023
25	8.623081	84.700896	0.011806	0.115968	9.822580	0.101806
26	9.399158	93.323977	0.010715	0.106393	9.928972	0.100715
27	10.245082	102.723135	0.009735	0.097608	10.026580	0.099735
28	11.167140	112.968217	0.008852	0.089548	10.116128	0.098852
29	12.172182	124.135356	0.008056	0.082155	10.198283	0.098056
30	13.267678	136.307539	0.007336	0.075371	10.273654	0.097336
31	14.461770	149.575217	0.006686	0.069148	10.342802	0.096686
32	15.763329	164.036987	0.006096	0.063438	10.406240	0.096096
33	17.182028	179.800315	0.005562	0.058200	10.464441	0.095562
34	18.728411	196.982344	0.005077	0.053395	10.517835	0.095077
35	20.413968	215.710755	0.004636	0.048986	10.566821	0.094636
36	22.251225	236.124723	0.004235	0.044941	10.611763	0.094235
37	24.253835	258.375948	0.003870	0.041231	10.652993	0.093870
38	26.436680	282.629783	0.003538	0.037826	10.690820	0.093538
39	28.815982	309.066463	0.003236	0.034703	10.725523	0.093236
40	31.409420	337.882445	0.002960	0.031838	10.757360	0.092960

FUTURE AND PRESENT VALUE USING 10 PERCENT MONTHLY INSTALLMENTS

	1 Compound amount of 1 $S^n = (1+i)^n$	2 Future worth of 1 per period $S_{\overline{n}|} = \dfrac{S^n - 1}{i}$	3 Sinking fund factor $1/S_{\overline{n}|} = \dfrac{i}{S^n - 1}$	4 Present value of 1 $V^n = \dfrac{1}{S^n}$	5 Present value of 1 per period $a_{\overline{n}|} = \dfrac{1 - V^n}{i}$	6 Installment to amortize 1 $1/a_{\overline{n}|} = \dfrac{i}{1 - V^n}$
Months						
1	1.008333	1.000000	1.000000	0.991735	0.991735	1.008333
2	1.016736	2.008333	0.497925	0.983539	1.975274	0.506258
3	1.025208	3.025069	0.330570	0.975410	2.950685	0.338904
4	1.033752	4.050278	0.246896	0.967349	3.918035	0.255229
5	1.042366	5.084030	0.196694	0.959355	4.877390	0.205027
6	1.051053	6.126397	0.163228	0.951426	5.828817	0.171561
7	1.059812	7.177450	0.139325	0.943563	6.772380	0.147658
8	1.068643	8.237262	0.121399	0.935765	7.708146	0.129732
9	1.077549	9.305906	0.107458	0.928031	8.636177	0.115791
10	1.086528	10.383456	0.096307	0.920362	9.556540	0.104640
11	1.095583	11.469984	0.087184	0.912755	10.469295	0.095517
Years						
1	1.104713	12.565568	0.079582	0.905212	11.374508	0.087915
2	1.220390	26.446915	0.037811	0.819409	21.670854	0.046144
3	1.348181	41.781821	0.023933	0.741739	30.991235	0.032267
4	1.489354	58.722491	0.017029	0.671432	39.428160	0.025362
5	1.645308	77.437072	0.012913	0.607788	47.065369	0.021247
6	1.817594	98.111313	0.010192	0.550177	53.978665	0.018525
7	2.007920	120.950418	0.008267	0.498027	60.236667	0.016601
8	2.218175	146.181075	0.006840	0.450820	65.901488	0.015174
9	2.450447	174.053712	0.005745	0.408088	71.029355	0.014078
10	2.707041	204.844978	0.004881	0.369406	75.671163	0.013215

11	2.990504	238.860492	0.004186	0.334391	79.872985	0.012519
12	3.303648	276.437875	0.003617	0.302695	83.676528	0.011950
13	3.649584	317.950100	0.003145	0.274003	87.119542	0.011478
14	4.031743	363.809198	0.002748	0.248031	90.236200	0.011082
15	4.453919	414.470344	0.002412	0.224521	93.057438	0.010746
16	4.920303	470.436373	0.002125	0.203239	95.611258	0.010459
17	5.435523	532.262776	0.001878	0.183974	97.923008	0.010212
18	6.004693	600.563212	0.001665	0.166536	100.015632	0.009998
19	6.633463	676.015596	0.001479	0.150750	101.909902	0.009812
20	7.328073	759.368830	0.001316	0.136461	103.624619	0.009650
21	8.095418	851.450237	0.001174	0.123526	105.176801	0.009507
22	8.943114	953.173772	0.001049	0.111817	106.581857	0.009382
23	9.879575	1065.549089	0.000938	0.101218	107.853729	0.009271
24	10.914096	1189.691570	0.000840	0.091624	109.005045	0.009173
25	12.056944	1326.833392	0.000753	0.082939	110.047230	0.009087
26	13.319464	1478.335753	0.000676	0.075078	110.990629	0.009009
27	14.714186	1645.702391	0.000607	0.067961	111.844605	0.008940
28	16.254954	1830.594505	0.000546	0.061519	112.617636	0.008879
29	17.957060	2034.847238	0.000491	0.055688	113.317391	0.008824
30	19.837399	2260.487900	0.000442	0.050409	113.950820	0.008775
31	21.914633	2509.756088	0.000398	0.045631	114.524207	0.008731
32	24.209382	2785.125915	0.000359	0.041306	115.043244	0.008692
33	26.744421	3089.330559	0.000323	0.037390	115.513083	0.008657
34	29.544911	3425.389403	0.000291	0.033846	115.938387	0.008625
35	32.638649	3796.638004	0.000263	0.030638	116.323378	0.008596
36	36.056343	4206.761180	0.000237	0.027734	116.671875	0.008571
37	39.831913	4659.829611	0.000214	0.025105	116.987341	0.008547
38	44.002835	5160.340233	0.000193	0.022725	117.272903	0.008527
39	48.610506	5713.260852	0.000175	0.020571	117.531398	0.008508
40	53.700662	6324.079483	0.000158	0.018621	117.765390	0.008491

FUTURE AND PRESENT VALUE USING 11 PERCENT ANNUAL INSTALLMENTS

Years	1 Compound amount of 1 $S^n = (1+i)^n$	2 Future worth of 1 per period $S_n = \dfrac{S^n - 1}{i}$	3 Sinking fund factor $1/S_n = \dfrac{i}{S^n - 1}$	4 Present value of 1 $V^n = \dfrac{1}{S^n}$	5 Present value of 1 per period $a_n = \dfrac{1 - V^n}{i}$	6 Installment to amortize 1 $1/a_n = \dfrac{i}{1 - V^n}$
1	1.110000	1.000000	1.000000	0.900901	0.900901	1.110000
2	1.232100	2.110000	0.473934	0.811622	1.712523	0.583934
3	1.367631	3.342100	0.299213	0.731191	2.443715	0.409213
4	1.518070	4.709731	0.212326	0.658731	3.102446	0.322326
5	1.685058	6.227801	0.160570	0.593451	3.695897	0.270570
6	1.870415	7.912860	0.126377	0.534641	4.230538	0.236377
7	2.076160	9.783274	0.102215	0.481658	4.712196	0.212215
8	2.304538	11.859434	0.084321	0.433926	5.146123	0.194321
9	2.558037	14.163972	0.070602	0.390925	5.537048	0.180602
10	2.839421	16.722009	0.059801	0.352184	5.889232	0.169801
11	3.151757	19.561430	0.051121	0.317283	6.206515	0.161121
12	3.498451	22.713187	0.044027	0.285841	6.492356	0.154027
13	3.883280	26.211638	0.038151	0.257514	6.749870	0.148151
14	4.310441	30.094918	0.033228	0.231995	6.981865	0.143228
15	4.784589	34.405359	0.029065	0.209004	7.190870	0.139065
16	5.310894	39.189948	0.025517	0.188292	7.379162	0.135517

17	5.895093	44.500843	0.022471	0.169633	7.548794	0.132471
18	6.543553	50.395936	0.019843	0.152822	7.701617	0.129843
19	7.263344	56.939488	0.017563	0.137678	7.839294	0.127563
20	8.062312	64.202832	0.015576	0.124034	7.963328	0.125576
21	8.949166	72.265144	0.013838	0.111742	8.075070	0.123838
22	9.933574	81.214310	0.012313	0.100669	8.175739	0.122313
23	11.026267	91.147884	0.010971	0.090693	8.266432	0.120971
24	12.239157	102.174151	0.009787	0.081705	8.348137	0.119787
25	13.585464	114.413307	0.008740	0.073608	8.421745	0.118740
26	15.079865	127.998771	0.007813	0.066314	8.488058	0.117813
27	16.738650	143.078636	0.006989	0.059742	8.547800	0.116989
28	18.579901	159.817286	0.006257	0.053822	8.601622	0.116257
29	20.623691	178.397187	0.005605	0.048488	8.650110	0.115605
30	22.892297	199.020878	0.005025	0.043683	8.693793	0.115025
31	25.410449	221.913175	0.004506	0.039354	8.733146	0.114506
32	28.205599	247.323624	0.004043	0.035454	8.768600	0.114043
33	31.308214	275.529222	0.003629	0.031940	8.800541	0.113629
34	34.752118	306.837437	0.003259	0.028775	8.829316	0.113259
35	38.574851	341.589555	0.002927	0.025924	8.855240	0.112927
36	42.818085	380.164406	0.002630	0.023355	8.878594	0.112630
37	47.528074	422.982490	0.002364	0.021040	8.899635	0.112364
38	52.756162	470.510564	0.002125	0.018955	8.918590	0.112125
39	58.559340	523.266726	0.001911	0.017077	8.935666	0.111911
40	65.000867	581.826066	0.001719	0.015384	8.951051	0.111719

VI
Land Measurement Table

Acreage

Acres	Square feet	1 acre equals rectangle:	
		Width	Length
1	43,560		
2	87,120	16.5	2,640.0
3	130,680	33.0	1,320.0
4	174,240	50.0	871.2
5	217,800	66.0	660.0
6	261,360	75.0	580.8
7	304,920	100.0	435.6
8	348,480	132.0	330.0
9	392,040	150.0	290.4
10	435,600	208.71	208.71

Linear measure

12 inches (in.)	make 1 foot	(ft)
3 feet	make 1 yard	(yd)
5½ yards or 16½ feet	make 1 rod	(rd)
40 rods	make 1 furlong	(fur)
8 furlongs, 320 rods, or 5,280 feet	make 1 statute mile	(mi)

Square measure[a]

144 square inches (sq. in.)	make 1 square foot	(sq ft)
9 square feet	make 1 square yard	(sq yd)
30¼ square yards	make 1 square rod	(sq rd)
160 square rods or 43,560 square feet	make 1 acre	(A)
640 acres	make 1 square mile	(sq mi)

Surveyor's linear measure

7.92 inches (in.)	make 1 link	(l)
25 links	make 1 rod	(rd)
4 rods or 66 feet	make 1 chain	(ch)
80 chains	make 1 mile	(mi)

Surveyor's square measure

625 square links (sq l)	make 1 pole	(P)
16 poles	make 1 square chain	(sq ch)
10 square chains	make 1 acre	(A)
640 acres	make 1 square mile	(sq mi)
36 square miles (6 mi square)	make 1 township	(Tp)

Metric conversions

$$1 \text{ meter} = \begin{cases} 39.37 \text{ inches} \\ 3.28083 \text{ feet} \\ 1.0936 \text{ yards} \end{cases}$$

1 centimeter = 0.3937 inch

$$1 \text{ millimeter} = \begin{cases} 0.03937 \text{ inch, or} \\ \text{approximately} \\ 1/25 \text{ in.} \end{cases}$$

1 kilometer = 0.062137 mile

1 foot = 0.3048 meter

$$1 \text{ inch} = \begin{cases} 2.54 \text{ centimeters} \\ 25.4 \text{ millimeters} \end{cases}$$

1 yard = 0.9144 meter

1 rod = 5.029 meters

1 mile = 1.6093 kilometers

[a]1 acre in square form equals 208.71 feet on each side.

VII
Valuation Symbols and Equations

SYMBOLS

a	Annualizer
app	Appreciation, expressed as a percentage of initial value or income
ATCF	After-tax cash flow (post–income taxes)
BOP	Beginning of period, converted for EOP by multiplying EOP factor by $(1 + i)$
BTCF	Before-tax cash flow
C	Mortgage coefficient
CF	Cash flow, generally considered the same as BTCF
CR	Compound rate
DCR	Debt coverage ratio
Δ	Change, especially total change in value or income over a specified period
dep	Depreciation, expressed as a percentage of initial value or income
DS	Debt service, the dollar amount required to repay a mortgage, usually expressed on an annual basis
EGI	Effective gross income, sometimes called collectible rent
EGIM	Effective gross income multiplier
EOP	End of period
F	Reciprocal of capitalization rate; a factor
f	Mortgage rate, same as R_M
GI	Gross income, also called potential or forecast gross income
GIM	Gross income multiplier
I	Income
i	Effective interest rate; nominal annual interest rate divided by number of installments per year
I_B	Building income
I_E	Equity income
I_o	Property income
IRR	Internal rate of return
M	Loan-to-value ratio (L/V)
n	Projection or holding period, sometimes called number of compounding periods
NIR	Net income ratio

NOI   Net operating income
NPV   Net present value
OE   Operating expenses
OER   Operating expense ratio
$1/x$ Reciprocal; 1 divided by a quantity
P Percentage of loan amortized for projection period
PW   Present worth, or present value
R_B Building capitalization rate
R_E Equity dividend rate
R_L Land capitalization rate
R_M Mortgage rate, including principal amortization and effective interest rate; sometimes called annual mortgage constant rate
R_o Overall capitalization rate
Σ Sum of
V Value
V_B Value of building
V_E Value of equity
V_L Value of land (site)
V_M Value of mortgage
V_o Value of entire property
Y_E Equity yield rate
Y_o Property yield rate

Present and Future Functions of 1

Present

V_n	Present worth of 1, the reversion factor	$1/S^n$
$a_{\overline{n}\rvert}$	Present worth of 1 per period, sometimes called Inwood factor	$\dfrac{1 - V^n}{i}$
$1/a_{\overline{n}\rvert}$	Installment to amortize	$\dfrac{i}{1 - V^n}$

Future

S^n	Compound amount of 1	$(1 + i)^n$
$S_{\overline{n}\rvert}$	Future worth of 1 per period	$\dfrac{S^n - 1}{i}$
$1/S_{\overline{n}\rvert}$	Sinking fund factor, sometimes called amortization rate	$\dfrac{i}{S^n - 1}$
MB	Mortgage balance, sometimes called balloon	

EQUATIONS

$a = 1/S_{\overline{n}\rvert}$ for level income stream and changing value; $a = 1/n$ for straight-line income and value change; a = annual compound rate for exponential change in income and value

$$C = Y + (P \times 1/S_{\overline{m}|}) - R_M$$

$$\text{DCR} = \text{NOI/DS}$$

$$\Delta I = \frac{R \times D}{R + D} \quad \text{where } R \text{ is the interest rate and } D \text{ is the recapture rate}$$

$>$ = greater than

$$I = V/R$$

$$\text{IRR} = \text{CF}_o + \frac{\text{CF}_1}{1 + \text{IRR}} + \frac{\text{CF}_2}{(1 + \text{IRR})^2} + \frac{\text{CF}_3}{(1 + \text{IRR})^3} + \cdots + \frac{\text{CF}_3}{(1 + \text{IRR})^n} = 0$$

$<$ = less than

$$\text{MB} = \frac{a_{\overline{m}|} \text{ for full loan term}}{a_{\overline{m}|} \text{ for remaining loan term}}$$

$$\text{NIR} = 1 - \text{OE/EGI}$$

$$\text{NPV} = \text{CF}_o = \frac{\text{CF}_1}{1 + i} = \frac{\text{CF}_2}{(1 + i)^2} + \frac{\text{CF}_3}{(1 + i)^3} + \cdots + \frac{\text{CF}_n}{(1 + i)^n}$$

$$\text{OER} = \text{OE/EGI}$$

$$P = \frac{R_M - I}{R_{MP} - I} \quad \text{where } P \text{ is the percentage of the loan paid off in the projection period, } R_M \text{ is the mortgage rate for the full loan term, } I \text{ is the nominal annual interest rate, and } R_{MP} \text{ is the mortgage rate for the projection period}$$

$$P = \frac{1/S_{\overline{m}|}}{1/S_{\overline{MP}|}}$$

$$R = I/V$$

$$R = Y - MC + \text{dep. } 1/S_{\overline{m}|}$$

$$R = Y - MC - \text{app. } 1/S_{\overline{m}|}$$

$R = Y$ when there is no forecast change in value

$R > Y$ when the property is expected to depreciate

$R < Y$ when the property is expected to appreciate

$$R_B = \frac{(I_o) - (V_L \times R_L)}{V_B} \quad \text{a similar procedure is used to compute } R_L \text{ and } R_E$$

$$R_M = 1/S_{\overline{m}|} + i$$

$$R_o = Y_o - \Delta a$$

$$R_o = (M)(R_M)(\text{DCR})$$

$$R_o = 1 - \text{OER/EGIM}$$

$$V = \text{GI} \times \text{GIM}$$

$$V = I/R$$

$$Y_o = R_o + \Delta a$$

Index

Accounting methods, 28
Accrued depreciation
  breakdown (or observed condition) method of, 242-248
  economic age—life method of, 241-242
  market extracted, 248-250
  meaning of, 236-237, 463
  merits of use of, 250
  and operating expense analysis, 276
  theory, 238-239
  versus amortization, 237-238
Actual income, 255-256
Adjoining properties, 142
Adjustments. *See* Comparable sales adjustments
Advance payment lease, 383-384
Aerial photography, 125-126
After-tax income, 32
Age cycles, 98-100
Age-group analysis, 89
Air conditioning, 199-200
American Institute of Real Estate Appraisers, 36
American Society of Farm Managers and Rural Appraisers, 36
Amortization rate, 298, 463
Annuity
  capitalization method, 345-349
  definition of, 315, 463
  ordinary, 318
Annuity due, 318
Anticipation of future benefits, 54, 463
Appraisal
  demonstration report, 442-443
  forms, 110-112
  letter (abbreviated) report, 444
  letter of opinion, 444
  methods. *See* Land appraisal methods

Appraisal (*Contd.*)
  narrative report, 443
  organizations, 35-36
  process, 430-435, 463
  report, 435-440, 471-572
  report writing, 440-442
  short-form reporting, 444-446
  standards, 35, 207, 435-440, 450-460
Appraisal Institute, 36
Appraisal Institute of Canada, 36
Appraisal of Real Estate, The, 27
Appraised value, 8, 469
Appraisers, 193, 208
Aquinas, St. Thomas, 17-18
Architecture, 104
Assessed value, 8, 469
Atkinson, Harry Grant, 29
Austrian School of Economics, 22-23
Average income, 255-256
Axial growth theory, 82

Babcock, Frederick, 27-29, 35, 258
Balance, 55-56, 463
Band of investment, 29
Band-of-investment rate selection method, 299-301, 463
Barter value, 10, 18, 21
Bastiat, Frédérick, 21
Bearings, 120
Before-and-after land valuation, 417-418
Beginning of a period (BOP), 331
Benchmark properties, 255
Böhm-Bawerk, Eugene, 23
Boeckh Building Valuation Manual, 231
Book value, 8, 469
Breakdown (or observed) depreciation method, 242-243
Building
  capitalization rate, 297, 463
  codes, 194, 207
  components, 194-200
  inspection, 208-209
  measurements, 204
  plans, 200-202
  residual valuation technique, 358, 364-368
Building Experience and Exchange Report, 278
Building Officials and Code Administration International, Inc. (BOCA), 194
Built-ins, 199
Bundle of rights, 42-43, 412, 463
Burgess, Ernest W., 80
Business cycles, 25, 71-72

Cabinetwork, 199
Capacity, 47-49, 463
Capital expenditures, 287
Capitalization, 10, 36, 463
  amortization rate, 298
  annuity method of, 345-349
  band-of-investment rate selection method, 299-301
  building capitalization rate, 297
  composite capitalization rate, 299, 464
  deriving rates of, 293-295
  direct, 297
  and discounted cash flow, 349-353
  equity dividend rate, 299
  equity yield rate, 299
  Hoskold factor table of, 341-349
  income in perpetuity, 340-341
  interest rate, 296, 463
  Inwood factor table of, 341-349, 467
  land capitalization rate, 298
  market extracted building and land capitalization rates, 302-303
  market extracted overall capitalization rate, 301-302
  mortgage rate, 298-299, 463
  mortgage terms rate selection method, 301
  of nonperpetuity income, 341-349
  overall capitalization rate, 297
    via simplified mortage-equity analysis, 306-307
    with constant income and value change, 306
    with level income of changing value, 304-305
    with straight-line change in income and value, 305-306
  physical residual techniques of, 357-376
  property yield rate, 299
  rate, 296, 297
  Ring factor table of, 341-349
  sinking fund method of, 344-345
  straight-line method of, 342-344
Capital value, 8, 469
Carey, Henry, 21
Cash equivalency, 5, 168-172, 463, 467
Cash-on-cash, 394, 464
Cash value, 8, 469
Chamberlain, Edward, 24
Checks, 121
Cities, 80-86, 91-93
City planning, 92-93
Civil Rights Act of 1968, 106
Closets, 199
Commercial cost services, 231-233
Commercial property, 184-186
Community centers, 112
Community growth, 89-91

Comparable sales adjustments, 149-155, 167-184
Comparative advantage, 80, 464
Comparative unit estimating, 219, 220, 223, 225
Composite capitalization rate, 299, 464
Compound interest
    converting end-of-period to beginning-of-period payments, 331-332
    compound amount of 1 table, 314-315, 464
    Ellwood tables, 335
    and extending table functions, 330
    future worth of 1 per period table, 315-319
    Hoskold factor table, 334
    and importance of logarithmic functions, 328-329
    installment to amortize 1 table, 325-328
    intermediate period values, 329-330
    interpolating intermediate values, 330-331
    Inwood (coefficient) table, 334
    and mortgage problems, 333
    present worth of 1 per period table, 323-325
    present worth of 1 table, 321-323
    sinking fund factor table, 320-321
    valuing deferred payments, 332-333
Computers, 34-35, 231-233. *See also* Microcomputers
Concentric ring theory, 80-81
Condemnation
    appraising
        and consequential damage, 421
        and due process of law, 413-414
        eminent domain and, 413
        and excess condemnation, 421-422
        just compensation and, 414
        and legal meaning of value, 415
        and measures of value, 415-418
        and severance damage, 418-420
        and treatment of benefits, 420-421
    bundle of rights and, 412-413
    excess, 421-422
    inverse, 421
    trials, 422-427
Condominiums, 127-128
Conduct. *See* Professionalism
Conformity, 54-55, 56, 464
Consequential damages, 464
Consistent use, 51, 464
Consumer Price Index, 268
Contract for deed, 148, 464
Contract rent, 50, 256-257, 464
Contractual limitations, 141-142
Contribution. *See* Marginal productivity
Convenience centers, 112
Corner lot, 139-140

Cost. *See also* Depreciated cost
  definition of, 464
  direct, 214, 464
  estimating
    and use of commercial cost services, 231-233
    comparative unit method of, 219, 220, 223, 225
    cost indexing method of, 230
    the new house, 227-230
    quantity survey method of, 217
    the standard or base house, 223, 226
    unit-in-place construction method of, 217-218, 222, 223
  indirect, 214
  replacement, 215-216
  reproduction, 215-216
  versus value, 213-214
Courses, 123
Curable functional obsolescence, 246
Curable physical deterioration, 243, 245

Deed
  restrictions, 141-142, 464
  revenue stamps and, 147
Demand, 6-7, 23, 464
Demographics, 67-68. *See also* Age-group analysis
Depreciated cost, 28-29, 36
  advantages and disadvantages, 212-213
  cost estimating, 217-233
  measuring accrued depreciation, 236-250
  steps in, 211-212
Depreciated value, 8, 469
Depreciation. *See* Accrued depreciation
Der Isolierte Staat (The Isolated State), 22
Deterioration, 238-239, 243-246
Direct capitalization, 297
Direct costs, 214, 464
Discounted cash flow (DCF)
  and internal rate of return (IRR), 351-353
  use of, 349-351
Discounting, 10. *See also* Compound interest
Distances, 124
Division of labor, 19
Doors, 198
Due process, 413-414
Dynamic value, 24

Easements, 141, 464
Economic(s)
  age-life depreciation method, 241-242

Economic(s) (*Contd.*)
   forces affecting value, 68-72, 74
   life, 239-241, 464
   measures of community growth, 89-91, 464
   of neighborhoods, 106-110
   theory, 17-39
   value, 8, 469
Education, 450-451
Effective age, 464
Effective gross income, 270, 464
Effective Gross Income Multiplier (EGIM), 186
Efficiency, 49-50, 465
Electrical installations, 199
Elevations, 202
Ellwood, Leon W., 31-32, 406
Ellwood Tables for Real Estate Appraising, 335, 393, 406-408
Eminent domain, 18, 43-44, 413, 465
Encroachments, 141-142
End of a period (EOP), 331
Environment
   flood hazard, 131, 134
   health hazards, 105
   hydrology, 135
   site contaminiation, 135
   soil surveys, 131, 133
   topographical analysis, 130-132
   wetlands, 132, 135
Equal-unit-value land valuation, 418
Equilibrium School of Economics, 24
Equity, 276
   dividend rate, 299, 394, 465
   yield rate, 299, 394, 465
   yields, 34
Escalator clause, 465
Escheat, 44, 465
Excess condemnation, 421-422, 465
Excess rent, 257, 465
Exchange value, 8, 469
Expert witness, 422
Exterior walls, 194, 196
External obsolescence, 239, 465
Extrinsic value, 5-6, 469

Face value, 8, 469
Fair value, 8, 469
Federal Home Loan Mortgage Corporation (Fannie Mae), 110
Federal Housing Administration (FHA), 63, 207
Federal Reserve System, 295

Fee determinable, 43
Fee simple, 42, 43, 465
Fee simple interest, 465
Fee upon conditions, 43
Fisher, Irving, 27
Fixed charges, 277, 465
Fixed-rental lease, 380-381
Fixtures, 42, 142, 465
Flat rental, 267, 465
Flat roof, 197
Flood hazard, 131, 134
Floor construction, 196
Floor planning, 201-202, 204-208
Footings, 194
Foundation
  plan, 201
  walls, 194
Functional obsolescence, 239, 465
Future worth of 1 per period table, 315-319

Gable, 197
Gambrel roof, 197
Gentrification, 99-100
George, Henry, 22, 62
Gettel, Ronald E., 34, 301
Gibbons, James E., 32
Graded rent clause, 267-268
Gross income multiplier (GIM), 30, 31, 186-189, 275
Gross income multiplier of overall capitalization rate, 303-304
Gross National Product (GNP), 68
Ground lease, 378-379
Growth
  population, 64-66
  urban, 80-86

Harris, Chauncey D., 85
Heating systems, 199-200
Hiag, Robert M., 87
Highest and best use, 27, 44-51, 119, 465
Hip roof, 197
Home Owners Loan Corporation Act, 62
Hoskold factor tables, 334, 341-349
Housing demand, 66-67
Hoyt, Homer, 82, 87
Hurd, Richard M., 82
Hydrology, 135

Improved value, 8, 469
Improvements
  public, 420-421
  site, 142-143
  street, 105, 136
  subsurface, 142-143
Imputation, 23
Income/Expense Analysis—Conventional Apartments, 278
Income
  actual versus average, 255-256
  adjustments, 270-271
  after-tax, 32
  bracketing, 89
  capitalization of, 339-355
  collectible, 270
  effective gross, 270-271
  estimating quantity of flow of, 257-259
  and importance of typical management, 257
  lease analysis, 263-270
  and market versus contract rents, 256-257
  as a measure of value, 254-255
  net operating, 255, 467
  nonperpetuity, 341-349
  in perpetuity, 340-341
  potential, 270
  quality and duration of, 259-262
  rental schedule construction and, 263
  stability, 106
  statements, 270
  stream, 254-255
Incurable external obsolescence, 247-248
Incurable functional obsolescence, 246-247
Incurable physical deterioration, 245-246
Index clause, 268, 466
Indirect costs, 214, 466
Industrial districts, 114-115
Industrial properties, 184-186
Inflation, 295
Inspection. *See* Building inspection
Installment to amortize 1 table, 325-328, 466
Institute of Real Estate Management, 278
Insulation, 200
Insurable value, 8, 469
Insurance, 145
Integrity, 450-451
Intellect, 450-451
Interest, 23, 466
Interior walls, 196-197
Internal rate of return (IRR), 351-353, 466
International Building Owners and Managers Association (BOMA), 278

Intrinsic value, 5-6, 18, 469
Inverse condemnation, 421
Investment value, 8, 469
Inwood (coefficient) table, 334, 341-349, 467

Judgment, 450-451
Just compensation, 414, 466
Justified price, 29
Just value, 18

Kazdin, S. Edwin, 29-30
Keynes, John Maynard, 24, 25-26
Kinnard, William, 33
Kniskern, Philip W., 29

Laissez faire, 20
Land
  alloidal ownership of, 40, 61-62
  appraisal methods
    land/property value ratio approach, 159-161
    land residual earnings approach, 155-157
    land value extraction, 162
    sales comparison approach, 146-155, 165-192
    subdivision development approach, 157-159
  capitalization rate, 298, 466
  definition of, 118, 466
  residual character of, 359
  residual return. *See* Rent
  residual valuation technique, 358, 360-364, 466
Landmarks. *See* Surveys, monument method
Law of diminishing returns, 47, 48
Leasehold
  estate, 466
  value, 8, 469
Leases, 141, 466
  advance payment of, 383-384
  analysis of, 263-270
  and component interest valuation, 379-380
  escalator clause, 268
  and fixed-rental, 380-381
  flat rental, 267
  graded rent clause, 267-268
  gross, 267
  ground, 378-379
  index clause, 268
  long-term, 377-378
  and netness of lease, 266-267

Leases (*Contd.*)
  percentage clause, 268-269
  sale and lease-back, 269-270
  sandwich, 379, 387-389
  short-term, 377-378
  step-up ground, 381-383
  and valuation of leaseholds, 384-386
Leverage, 393-396
Life estate, 43
Linkages, 98, 466
Liquidation value, 8, 469
Loan balance. *See* Mortgage(s)
Location, 22
Lusht, Kenneth M., 34

Malthus, Thomas, 19, 20
Management, 257
Mansard roof, 197
Marginal productivity, 53, 119, 466
Marginal utility, 23
Market
  conditions, 5
  extracted building and land capitalization rates, 302-303
  extracted depreciation, 248-250
  extracted overall capitalization rate, 301-302
  merger, 23
  price, 5, 20, 23, 30
  rent, 50, 256-257, 466
  sales comparison, 36
  value, 9-13, 20, 396, 415, 466
  value adjustments. *See* Comparable sales adjustments
Marshall, Alfred, 24
Marshall Valuation Service, 226, 231
Marx, Karl, 21
May, Arthur A., 30
Medici, Giuseppe, 30
Menger, Karl, 23
Mercantilism, 18
Metes and bounds, 120, 123-124
Microcomputers, 34-35
Miles, W. Porcher, 33
Mill, John Stuart, 21, 22
Mitchell, Wesley Clair, 25
Modified internal rate of return (MIRR), 352-353, 466
Mortgage(s)
  and amortization payments, 276
  ascertaining loan balances of, 404-405
  as contractual limitations, 141
  interest on, 276, 295

Mortgage(s) (*Contd.*)
  loan approval, 109
  loan value, 8, 469
  and mortgage-equity appraising, 393-411
  rate, 298-299, 466
  terms rate selection method, 301
Most probable use, 33, 467
Multiple Listing Service (MLS), 148-149
Multiple-nuclei growth theory, 85-86
Multiple regression, 183-184

National Association of Real Estate Boards Appraisal Division Committee on
      Standards of Practice, 36
National Fair Housing Act, 106
National Trust for Historic Preservation, 63
Natural value. *See* Market value
Neighborhood(s)
  age cycle of, 98-100
  analysis form reports, 110-112
  boundaries, 102
  characteristics, 100
  definition of, 97-98, 467
  economic characteristics of, 106-110
  and industrial districts, 114-115
  linkages, 98
  location of, 102-105
  and office districts, 113-114
  retail districts in, 112-113
  social values of, 105-106
Net operating income, 255, 467
Net present value (NPV), 350-351, 467
New house estimating, 227-230
New Zealand Institute of Surveyors, 36
Normal value, 22
Nuisance value, 8, 469

Objective value, 3, 18
Obsolescence, 239, 246-248
Odd-shaped lot, 138
Office districts, 113-114
Operating expense ratio (OER), 301
Operating expense(s)
  and capital expenditures, 287
  classification of, 277-280
  income deductions versus, 276
  ratios, 285-287
  and reserves for replacements, 283-285

Operating expense(s) (*Contd.*)
  statements of, 280-283
  and taxes, 276-277
Ordinary annuity, 318
Organization of Petroleum Exporting Countries (OPEC), 60
Overall capitalization rates, 297, 304-307, 467
Overimprovement, 56
Owner occupancy, 107
Ownership limitations, 43-44

Paired data set analysis, 180-181
Parcel, 118, 467
Partitions, 196-197
PCBs (polychlorinated biphenyls), 135
Percentage adjustments, 467. *See also* Sales comparisons
Perpetuity, 340-341
Physical life, 239-241, 467
Physiocrats, 18-19
Piers, 194
Pigou, A.C., 24
Plan reading, 200-202
Plottage, 140
Plumbing, 199
Police power, 43, 467
Politics, 61-64, 73
Population growth, 64-65, 72-73, 88-89
Potential Gross Income Multiplier (PGIM), 186
Potential value, 8, 469
Preindustrial cities, 79
Present value, 23
Present worth of 1 per period table, 323-325
Present worth of 1 table, 321-323, 467
Prevailing financing equivalency. See Cash equivalency
Price, 467
Primary city, 91, 467
Principles of Economics, 24
Principles of Political Economy and Taxation, 20, 22
Probable price, 11-13, 467
Professionalism, 450-460
Progress and Poverty—The Remedy, 22, 62
Property
  appraising versus equity appraising, 396-404
  and bundle of rights, 42-43
  legal concept of, 41-42
  ownership limitations, 43-44
  residual valuation technique, 358, 368-374
  taxation and assessments, 108
  turnover, 107

Property (*Contd.*)
  valuation
    anticipation of future benefits, 54
    balance, 55-56
    conformity, 54-55
    consistent use, 51
    economic forces influencing, 68-72
    highest and best use, 44-51
    marginal productivity, 53
    political forces affecting, 61-64
    social forces influencing, 64-68
    state or regional forces affecting, 72-74
    substitution, 52
    supply and demand, 53
  wealth versus, 41
  yield rate, 299, 467
Public transportation, 104-105
Public utilities, 136
Pyramid roof, 197

Quantity survey estimating, 217
Quesnay, Francois, 18-19

Racial discrimination, 97, 106
Ranges, 122
Ratcliff, Richard U., 31
Rate-selection methods, 299-301
Rates of return, 295-299
Real estate, 40-41, 42, 57, 77-78, 467
Real property, 40, 468
Real value, 8, 469
Reconciliation, 434, 468
Redlining, 106
Regional analysis, 86-88
Regional centers, 112-113
Regression analysis, 146, 181-184
Regulation, 35, 145
Remaining economic life, 239-241, 468
Rent, 20
  contract, 50, 256-257
  control, 63
  deficiency, 257, 468
  excess, 257
  market, 50, 256-257
  schedules, 263
Rental value, 8, 469
Replacement costs, 30, 215-216, 468

Replacement value, 8, 470
Reproduction costs, 20, 215-216, 468
Reserves for replacement, 278, 283-285, 468
Residential Cost Handbook, 231
Retail districts, 112-113
Revenue stamps, 147-148
Ricardo, David, 19, 20-21, 80
Ring factor tables, 341-349
Robertson, Dennis H., 24
Robinson, Joan, 24
Roof construction, 197-198
Ross, Thurston H., 29
Royal Institution of Chartered Surveyors, 36
R value, 468

Sale and lease-back, 269-270, 468
Sales comparison(s)
  for commercial and industrial properties, 184-186
  description of, 146-155
  and detailed property analysis adjustment techniques, 174-177
  and gross income multipliers, 186-189
  market comparison adjustments and, 173-174
  and overall property rating adjustment techniques, 177-178
  and use of percentage adjustments, 179-181
  regressions analysis and, 181-184
  time and transfer terms adjustments, 167-172
  and verification of sales, 166
Sales value, 8, 470
Salvage value, 8, 470
Sandwich lease, 379, 387-389, 468
Savings and loans, 61
Scarcity, 6, 468
Schmutz, George L., 30
Secondary city, 91, 468
Sectional views, 202
Sections, 121-122
Sector growth theory, 82-84
Segregated cost estimation method, 217
Selling price, most probable, 31
Severance damage, 418-420, 468
Sewer systems, 136
Simple linear regression, 181-183, 468
Single-tax doctrine, 22, 62
Sinking fund amortization, 298, 468
Sinking fund capitalization, 344-345, 468
Site
  analysis
    adjoining structures and, 142-143

Site (*Contd.*)
    aerial photography and, 125-126
    and condominium subdivisions, 127-128
    contractual limitations and, 141-143
    identification, 119-120
    metes and bounds survey method, 123-124
    monument survey method, 124-125
    principles, 119
    and public utilities, 136
    purpose, 119
    rectangular survey system, 121-123
    shape, size, depth, and corner location and, 136-140
    and site identification, 119-130
    street address identification, 129-130
    and street improvements, 136
    subdivision method, 126-127
    and terrain and soil characteristics, 130-135
    zoning and, 141-143
  contamination, 135
  definition of, 118, 468
  identification
    aerial photography, 125-126
    condominium subdivisions, 127-128
    metes and bounds, 120, 123-124
    monument method, 124
    rectangular survey method, 121
    street addresses, 128-130
    subdivision method, 126-127
  improvements, 142-143
  methods. *See* Land appraisal methods
Situs qualities, 130
Smith, Adam, 19-20
Social values, 105-106
Society of Real Estate Appraisers, 36
Society of Residential Appraisers, 36
Soil
  percolation testing, 103-104, 468
  quality, 103
  surveys, 131, 133
Specifications, 202, 204
Speculative value, 9, 470
Square-foot method of land valuation, 418
Stable value, 9, 470
Standard (base) house estimate, 223, 226
Standard Industrial Classifications (SIC), 87-88
Standards, 35, 207, 435-440, 450-460
State transfer tax, 148
Static value, 24
Straight line capitalization, 342-344

Straight line depreciation, 298
Streets
  improvements, 105, 136
  patterns of, 104
  in site identification 128-130
Subcontractor's cost estimation method, 217
Subdivisions, 126
Substitution, 52, 468
Summa Theologica, 17
Supply and demand
  and concept of objective value, 3, 18
  principle of, 53, 468
Supply-side economics, 26
Surveys
  metes and bounds, 120, 123-124
  monument method, 124
  rectangular, 121

Tableau economique, 19
Tax certiorari, 277
Taxes, 396
  grantor's tax, 148
  local assessments, 145
  and operating expense analysis, 276-277
  as an ownership limitation, 44
  regulations, 145
  and tax advantages, 269
Tenancy, 107
Terms of sale, 5
Terrain, 103, 130-131
Theory. *See* Economic theory; Valuation theory
Tiers, 122
Title II—Real Estate Appraisal Reform Amendments, 35
Titles, 141-142
Title VIII, Civil Rights Act of 1968, 106
Topographical analysis, 130-132
Townships, 121
Tract, 118, 468
Trading on equity, 276, 393-396
Transferability, 7, 469
Transportation, public, 104-105
Trials, 423-427
Tribal communities, 78-79
Typical management, 257

Ullman, Edward L., 85
Underconsumption, 20, 25, 70
Underimprovement, 56

Unearned increment, 22, 62
Unemployment, 70
Uniform Residential Report Form, 209, 445-447
Uniform Standards of Professional Appraisal Practice, 435, 444, 457-460
Unit-in-place estimating, 217-218, 222, 223
Unitized use. *See* Consistent use
Urbanization, 78-86
Urban renewal, 63
Use value, 9, 470
Utilities. *See* Public utilities
Utility, 6, 253, 469

Valuation
  before-and-after method, 417-418
  equal-unit-value method of, 417-418
  physical residual techniques of, 357-376
  theory, 27-35
Valuation for Real Estate Decisions, 33
Valuation of Real Estate, The, 258
Value
  appraised, 8, 469
  assessed, 8, 469
  barter, 10, 18, 21
  book, 8, 469
  capital, 8, 469
  cash, 8, 469
  characteristics of, 6-7
  in condemnation appraising, 415
  creation of, 5-6
  depreciated, 8, 469
  dynamic, 8
  economic, 8, 469
  equal-unit, 417-418
  exchange, 8, 469
  extrinsic, 5-6, 469
  face, 8, 469
  fair, 8, 469
  improved, 8, 469
  individual versus market, 1-3
  insurable, 8, 469
  intrinsic, 5-6, 18, 469
  investment, 8, 469
  just, 18
  leasehold, 8, 469
  liquidation, 8, 469
  market, 9-13, 20, 396, 415
  market conditions affecting, 3-5
  measures of, 415-418
  mortgage loan, 8, 469

Value (*Contd.*)
  normal, 22
  nuisance, 8, 469
  objective, 3, 18
  potential, 8, 469
  present, 8
  real, 8, 469
  reconciliation, 434-435
  rental, 8, 469
  replacement, 8, 470
  sales, 8, 470
  salvage, 8, 470
  speculative, 8, 470
  stable, 9, 469
  static, 24
  terms of sale affecting, 5
  theory, 17-39
  types of, 7-8
  use, 9, 470
  versus cost, 213-214
  warranted, 9, 470
Value in exchange, 20
Value in use, 13, 20, 470
Variable expenses, 278, 470
Verification of sales, 166
Veterans Administration, 63
Villages, 79
von Thünen, Johann Heinrich, 22
von Weiser, Freidrich, 23

Warranted value, 9, 470
Wealth, 470
Wealth of Nations The, 19
Wendt, Paul, 30
Wetlands, 132, 135, 470
Windows, 198-199
Wisconsin Colloquium on Appraisal Research, 32-33

Zerbst, Robert H., 34
Zoning, 56, 109, 141-143